MCSE Guide to
Microsoft® Windows® XP Professional, Second Edition, Enhanced

James Michael Stewart
Brian McCann
Angel Melendez

THOMSON

COURSE TECHNOLOGY

Australia • Canada • Mexico • Singapore • Spain • United Kingdom • United States

THOMSON

COURSE TECHNOLOGY

MCSE Guide to Microsoft® Windows® XP Professional, Second Edition, Enhanced

is published by Course Technology

Senior Editor:
William Pitkin III

Product Manager:
Nick Lombardi

Developmental Editor:
Jill Batistick

Production Editor:
Kristen Guevara

Manufacturing Coordinator:
Trevor Kallop
Melissa Hulse

Technical Edit/Quality Assurance:
Marianne Snow
Christian Kunciw

Marketing Manager:
Guy Baskaran

Associate Product Managers:
Mirella Misiaszek
David Rivera
Sarah Santoro

Editorial Assistant:
Jenny Smith

Cover Design:
Steve Deschene

Text Designer:
GEX Publishing Services

Compositor:
GEX Publishing Services

Disclaimer
Course Technology reserves the right to revise this publication and make changes from time to time in its content without notice.

ISBN-13: 978-0-619-21751-8
ISBN-10: 0-619-21751-0

Contents

TABLE OF
Contents

CHAPTER FOUR
Managing Windows XP File Systems and Storage   131

Introduction

Welcome to *MCSE Guide to Microsoft Windows XP Professional, Second Edition, Enhanced*. This book offers you real-world examples, interactive activities, and hundreds of hands-on activities that reinforce key concepts and help you prepare for a career in Microsoft network administration. This book also features troubleshooting tips for solutions to common problems that you will encounter in the realm of Windows XP Professional administration.

This book offers in-depth study of all the functions and features of installing, configuring, and maintaining Windows XP Professional as a client operating system. Throughout the book, we provide detailed Activities that let you experience firsthand the processes involved in Windows XP Professional configuration and management. We then provide pointed Review Questions to reinforce the concepts introduced in each chapter and to help you prepare for the Microsoft certification exam. Finally, to put a real-world slant on the concepts introduced in each chapter, we provide Case Projects to prepare you for situations that must be managed in a live networking environment.

Intended Audience

MCSE Guide to Microsoft Windows XP Professional, Second Edition, Enhanced is intended for people who are getting started in computer networking as well as experienced network administrators who are new to Windows XP Professional. To best understand the material in this book, you should have a background in basic computer concepts and have worked with applications in the Windows environment.

New to This Edition

- A new, full-color interior design brings the material to life and full-color screenshots provide a more detailed look at the Microsoft Windows XP interface.

- Appendix B provides detailed lab setup instructions to assist instructors in preparing labs for class.

- Appendix C features expanded and more comprehensive chapter summaries to assist students in reviewing the material covered in each chapter.

- Two new Practice Exams are provided. One is located in the back of the textbook and perforated so that it can be handed in as a homework assignment or test. The second is posted on *www.course.com* in the password protected Instructor's Resource section, along with the Solutions to both exams. The questions on these Practice Exams are modeled after the types of questions students will see on the actual MCSE 70-270 certification exam. In addition to helping students review what they have learned, they have the added benefit of preparing them for the certification exam.

- Our CoursePrep ExamGuide content is now included in PDF format on the CD that accompanies this textbook. This content features key information, bulleted memorization points, and review questions for every exam objective in an easy-to-follow two-page-spread layout. This is an excellent resource for self-study before taking the 70-270 certification exam.

Chapter Descriptions

There are 15 chapters in this book, as follows:

Chapter 1, "Introduction to Windows XP Professional," introduces the latest Windows operating systems family—including Windows XP Professional and Windows Server. NET—and describes the major features of the Windows environment. In addition, it explores the architecture of Windows XP Professional and related operating systems. Finally, it defines the minimal system requirements for Windows XP Professional and introduces the two major networking models under which Windows XP can be used.

In **Chapter 2**, "Installing Windows XP Professional," we discuss how to decide whether to perform an upgrade or a fresh installation of Windows XP Professional. We also explore how to boot using multiple operating systems. In addition, we examine installation options such as unattended installations; whether to install using Windows XP setup disks, CD-ROM, or across the network; finally, we describe the various setup and advanced installation options.

Chapter 3, "Using the System Utilities," examines the tools used to manage Windows XP Professional, namely, the Microsoft Management Console (MMC), Administrative Tools, Task Scheduler, and Control Panel applets. These tools are used to install and configure new hardware, create hardware profiles for changing system configurations, and configure PC cards and multiple displays.

In **Chapter 4**, "Managing Windows XP File Systems and Storage," we explore the differences between basic and dynamic storage and discuss the drive configurations supported by Windows XP. This chapter also introduces file systems supported by Windows XP Professional: FAT, FAT32, and NTFS. In addition, we describe permissions, sharing, and other security issues related to file systems. From an administrative standpoint, we also discuss drive, volume, and partition maintenance and administration under Windows XP Professional.

We introduce you to the concepts involved in working with users, groups, profiles, and policies in **Chapter 5**, "Users, Groups, Profiles, and Policies." This discussion includes setting up, naming, and managing local users and groups and default user and group accounts. From there, we examine the Windows XP Professional logon authentication process. This chapter concludes with in-depth coverage of the creation and management of user accounts, profiles, and local security policies.

Chapter 6, "Windows XP Security and Access Controls," teaches you about the Windows XP security model and the key role of logon authentication. We show you how to customize the logon process, discuss domain security concepts, and provide additional instructions for setting up the local computer policy. This chapter also shows you how to enable and use auditing. We conclude this discussion on security with details on encrypting NTFS files, folders, or drives using the encrypting file system (EFS).

We cover the world of networking Windows XP in **Chapter 7**, "Windows XP Network Protocols." Here, you'll explore the protocols supported by Windows 2000. In addition, we detail the intricacies of configuring and managing TCP/IP, and of configuring and managing NetWare access using the NWLink protocol and the Client Service for NetWare (CSNW).

We examine remote access to Windows 2000 Professional in **Chapter 8**, "Internetworking with Remote Access." You'll learn how to use remote access under Windows XP, configure various RAS connection types, work with telephony services and connections, manage RAS security, and troubleshoot RAS connection problems.

In **Chapter 9**, "Printing and Faxing," we discuss Windows XP print terminology and architecture, and examine the special features of the Windows XP print system. We provide hands-on instruction for creating and managing printers and printer permissions, and explain how to take advantage of XP's built-in fax and fax sharing support. This chapter concludes with a discussion on troubleshooting printing and faxing problems.

Chapter 10, "Performance Tuning," gives you the information you need to understand the performance and monitoring tools found in Windows XP. You'll learn how to create a Counter log for historical analysis, configure Alert events to warn of performance problems, and establish a baseline of normal system operation against which to measure Windows XP Professional performance. Finally, we discuss how to detect and eliminate bottlenecks to keep your system running as efficiently as possible.

In **Chapter 11**, "Windows XP Professional Application Support," we discuss how to deploy DOS, Win16, OS/2, and POSIX applications. Finally, we explore how to fine-tune the application environment for DOS and Win16.

Chapter 12, "Working with the Windows XP Registry," discusses the function and structure of the Registry, which is the underlying database that stores system configuration information in Windows XP. This chapter describes the purpose of each of the five Registry keys, how to use the Registry editing tools, defines the fault-tolerant mechanisms for the Registry, and provides information on how to back up and restore the Registry.

In **Chapter 13**, "Booting Windows XP," we explain the steps that Windows XP Professional goes through during the boot process. This discussion includes the operation of the key Windows XP startup files, the boot options offered via the Advanced Options Menu, and how to troubleshoot system restoration by using Safe Mode. In addition, we explore how to edit the Boot.ini file to manipulate the boot process, and how multi-boot configurations are created and how they function.

We introduce you to disaster protection and recovery concepts in **Chapter 14**, "Windows XP Professional Fault Tolerance." Here, you'll learn how to back up data and settings on Windows XP Professional and recover a Windows XP Professional client's applications and data. In addition, we introduce IntelliMirror technology and describe its key features, as well as remote operating system installation, and how it can be used with IntelliMirror to recover a PC remotely. Finally, we show you how to use the Recovery Console and the Safe Mode options for recovering or repairing damaged Windows XP Professional installations.

This book concludes with **Chapter 15**, "Troubleshooting Windows XP." Here, we examine how to collect documentation about your systems to aid in troubleshooting and preventing problems, and review common sense approaches to troubleshooting. In addition, we discuss how to troubleshoot general problems with Windows XP and use some of the troubleshooting tools found in Windows XP Professional.

Features and Approach

MCSE Guide to Microsoft Windows XP Professional, Second Edition, Enhanced differs from other networking books in its unique hands-on approach and its orientation to real-world situations and problem solving. To help you comprehend how Microsoft Windows XP Professional concepts and techniques are applied in real-world organizations, this book incorporates the following features:

- **Chapter Objectives**—Each chapter begins with a detailed list of the concepts to be mastered. This list gives you a quick reference to the chapter's contents and is a useful study aid.

- **Activities**—Activities are incorporated throughout the text, giving you practice in setting up, managing, and troubleshooting a network system. The Activities give you a strong foundation for carrying out network administration tasks in the real world. Because of the book's progressive nature, completing the Activities in each chapter is essential before moving on to the end-of-chapter materials and subsequent chapters.

- **Chapter Summaries**—Each chapter's text is followed by a summary of the concepts introduced in that chapter. These summaries provide a helpful way to recap and revisit the ideas covered in each chapter.

- **Key Terms**—All of the terms within the chapter that were introduced with boldfaced text are gathered together in the Key Terms list at the end of the chapter. This provides you with a method of checking your understanding of all the terms introduced.

- **Review Questions**—The end-of-chapter assessment begins with a set of Review Questions that reinforce the ideas introduced in each chapter. Answering these questions will ensure that you have mastered the important concepts.

- **Case Projects**—Finally, each chapter closes with a section that proposes certain situations. You are asked to evaluate the situations and decide upon the course of action to be taken to remedy the problems described. This valuable tool will help you sharpen your decision-making and troubleshooting skills, which are important aspects of network administration.

- **Tear-Out Practice Exam**—A 50 question tear-out exam is included in the back of the text. The questions are modeled after the actual MCSE certification exam and the exam is on perforated pages so students can hand it in as an assignment or an exam. The answers to the Practice Exam are included as part of the Instructor Resources.

- **On the CD-ROM**—The CD-ROM includes CoursePrep® test preparation software, which provides sample MCSE exam questions mirroring the look and feel of the MCSE exams. The CD also contains a complete CoursePrep ExamGuide workbook in PDF format. It devotes an entire two-page spread for every exam objective, featuring bulleted memorization points and review questions for self-study before exam day.

Text and Graphic Conventions

Additional information and exercises have been added to this book to help you better understand what's being discussed in the chapter. Icons throughout the text alert you to these additional materials. The icons used in this book are described below.

Tips offer extra information on resources, how to attack problems, and time-saving shortcuts.

Notes present additional helpful material related to the subject being discussed.

The Caution icon identifies important information about potential mistakes or hazards.

Each Activity in this book is preceded by the hands-on icon.

Case Project icons mark the end-of-chapter case projects, which are scenario-based assignments that ask you to independently apply what you have learned in the chapter.

Instructor's Resources

The following supplemental materials are available when this book is used in a classroom setting. All of the supplements available with this book are provided to the instructor on a single CD-ROM.

Electronic Instructor's Manual. The Instructor's Manual that accompanies this textbook includes additional instructional material to assist in class preparation, including suggestions for classroom activities, discussion topics, and additional projects.

Solutions are provided for the end-of-chapter material, including Review Questions, and where applicable, Hands-On Activities and Case Projects. Solutions to the Practice Exams are also included.

ExamView®. This textbook is accompanied by ExamView, a powerful testing software package that allows instructors to create and administer printed, computer (LAN-based), and Internet exams. ExamView includes hundreds of questions that correspond to the topics covered in this text, enabling students to generate detailed study guides that include page references for further review. The computer-based and Internet testing components allow students to take exams at their computers and also save the instructor time by grading each exam automatically.

Practice Exam. A second 50 question Practice Exam is included as part of the Instructor Resources. Like the tear-out Practice Exam in the text, the questions are modeled after the actual MCSE certification exam. The answers to this exam are also included as part of the Instructor Resources.

PowerPoint presentations. This book comes with Microsoft PowerPoint slides for each chapter. These are included as a teaching aid for classroom presentation, to make available to students on the network for chapter review, or to be printed for classroom distribution.

Instructors, please feel at liberty to add your own slides for additional topics you introduce to the class.

Figure files. All of the figures and tables in the book are reproduced on the Instructor's Resource CD, in bitmap format. Similar to the PowerPoint presentations, these are included as a teaching aid for classroom presentation, to make available to students for review, or to be printed for classroom distribution.

Minimum Lab Requirements

Hardware:

All hardware should be listed on Microsoft's Hardware Compatibility List for Windows XP.

Component	Requirement
CPU	233-MHz Pentium or higher microprocessor (P5 or equivalent compatible clone) or a Compaq Alpha processor with the latest firmware version installed (except for DECpc 150 AXP, DEC 2000-500, Multia, and AXPpci 33 processors)
Memory	128 MB of RAM for Intel (256 MB or more recommended; 4 GB maximum)
Disk Space	2 GB hard disk with a minim of 1.5 GB of free space
Monitor	SVGA or higher resolution monitor
Keyboard	Keyboard
Pointing Device	Microsoft Mouse or compatible pointing device
Drives	A CD-ROM drive (12X or faster recommended) or network access, for networked installation; a high-density 3.5 inch disk drive
Networking	Internet connectivity recommended. Network connectivity not required.
Cards	A Windows XP-compatible network adapter card and related cable

Software:

- Microsoft Windows XP Professional for each computer

- The latest service packs (if available)

Set Up Instructions:

To successfully complete the Activities, you need a computer system meeting or exceeding the minimal system requirements for Windows XP Professional. Confirming those requirements and installing Windows XP Professional (along with available service packs) is covered in Chapters 1 and 2.

ACKNOWLEDGMENTS

Thanks to Ed Tittel and LANWrights, Inc. for handing over the revision of this book completely into my hands. Working with you guys has always been a pleasure and I look forward to numerous future co-endeavors—or at least mutually beneficial coup d'état. Thanks to the wonderful staff at Course Technology, including Jill Batistick, Nick Lombardi, and Will Pitkin, for putting up with me during this process. Thanks also to reviewers George Rausch, Scott Spitzberg, and Vy Nguyen, whose insightful comments were of invaluable assistance in creating this text. To my parents, Dave and Sue, thanks for your love and consistent support. To my sister Sharon and nephew Wesley, its great having family like you to spend time with. To Mark, congratulations on rug rat number two. To Herbert and Quin, when everything else is going great, you keep me grounded by puking on the carpet—thanks. And finally, as always, to Elvis—you must have transcended and become a god because you are everywhere.

ABOUT THE AUTHOR

James Michael Stewart is a security professional who has been developing security- and certification-related content and courseware for over nine years. Michael is the author of a wide range of technical books on the subjects of Microsoft operating systems, networking, Internet, security, and certification. Michael's previous works focusing on Windows XP include the following: *Microsoft Windows XP Power Pack*; *Course Prep Study Guide: Exam #70-270, Installing, Configuring, and Administering Microsoft Windows XP Professional*; *Using Windows XP Professional*, and *Using Windows XP Home*. Michael also teaches a Windows security course at COMDEX and Networld+Interop, which includes a significant amount of Windows XP material. Michael holds the following certifications: CISSP, TICSA, CIW SA, Security+, CTT+, MCT, CCNA, MCSE+Security Windows 2000, MCSE NT & W2K, MCP+I, and iNet+.

1

INTRODUCTION TO WINDOWS XP PROFESSIONAL

After reading this chapter and completing the exercises, you will be able to:

- ◆ Describe the Windows Networking family of products
- ◆ Describe the major features of the Windows XP environment
- ◆ Understand the Windows XP intelligent user interface
- ◆ Define the minimum system requirements for Windows XP Professional
- ◆ Understand the two major networking models under which Windows XP can be used
- ◆ Understand the architecture of Windows XP

The pace of technological advances in the computing world is faster than ever before. Consumers can now purchase computer systems with power and capabilities that were mere fantasies just a few years ago, and do so at a lower cost. Microsoft has endeavored to remain competitive among these new powerful systems by continuing to improve its operating system (OS) products. One of the latest offers in the Microsoft OS product line is Windows XP, a client OS designed to take advantage of new hardware and the Internet to produce unsurpassed performance for network activities and application execution.

The major sections in this chapter introduce you to the Microsoft networking family of products, help you decide between Windows XP Professional and Windows XP Home Edition, review the major features of Windows XP, inform you of the minimum system requirements for Windows XP, explore the two primary networking models supported by Windows XP, and provide an overview of the system architecture of Windows XP.

THE MICROSOFT NETWORKING FAMILY

The Microsoft networking family is a collection of **operating systems (OS)**. OSs work directly with hardware to provide the environment for other software to operate. Each OS can participate in a network as either a **server** or **client**. A server is a computer that hosts resources for use by other systems on the network. A client is a computer that accesses resources on a network hosted by servers. Clients are typically the systems on a worker's desk.

The collection of Microsoft networking operating systems consists of a wide range of products offered over a period spanning more than ten years, including: Windows XP, Windows Server 2003, Windows 2000, and Windows ME; older family members include Windows NT, Windows 98, Windows 98 Second Edition (SE), Windows 95, and Windows for Workgroups.

Windows XP

The Windows XP product family builds upon the best features of Windows 2000 and Windows 98/SE/ME, and includes advanced Internet, security, and connectivity technologies. The result is a network and desktop operating system that offers unsurpassed functionality, security, resource management, and versatility.

Windows XP currently consists of five products: Windows XP 64-Bit Edition, Windows XP Media Center Edition, Windows XP Tablet PC Edition, Windows XP Home Edition, and Windows XP Professional.

Windows XP 64-Bit Edition

Windows XP 64-Bit Edition is a specialized version of Windows XP Professional designed for the 64-bit Itanium 2 processor from Intel. This version was released in the spring of 2003. While offering substantially improved performance over the more common 32-bit processors, 64-bit hardware is fairly expensive. Thus, the deployment of Windows XP 64-Bit Edition is limited until the hardware becomes more reasonably priced. Windows XP 64-Bit Edition is not on the 70-270 certification exam and therefore is not discussed further in this book. For more information on this version of Windows, visit *www.microsoft.com/windowsxp/64bit/default.asp*.

Windows XP Media Center Edition

Windows XP Media Center Edition is a version of Windows XP designed specifically for computers that serve as multimedia operation centers. This version is tuned to maximize your experiences with video, audio, images, television, and CD/DVD playback. Windows XP Media Center Edition is not on the 70-270 certification exam and therefore is not discussed further in this book. For more information on this version of Windows, visit *www.microsoft.com/windowsxp/mediacenter/default.asp*.

Windows XP Tablet PC Edition

Windows XP Tablet PC Edition is a version of Windows XP designed specifically for use on a Tablet PC. The primary features of this version are improved speech and pen capabilities. Tablet PCs allow you to write on the screen using a penlike stylus just as you would a pad of paper. The OS is able to interpret your writing into editable text. Windows XP Tablet PC Edition is not on the 70-270 certification exam and therefore is not discussed further in this book. For more information on this version of Windows, visit *www.microsoft.com/windowsxp/tabletpc/default.asp.*

Windows XP Home Edition

The Home Edition version of Windows XP is designed for standalone home use. It is basically the same OS as Windows XP Professional, but does not support several of the business-level features, including Encrypting File System (EFS), domain client capability, offline files, Internet Protocol Security (IPSec), Automated System Recovery (ASR), Remote Desktop, and Internet Information Server (IIS). A **domain** is a collection of networked systems that are managed and secured by one or more server systems called domain controllers. For a complete list of "missing" features, see either the *Microsoft Windows XP Professional Resource Kit* or the *Windows XP Comparison Guide* Web page at *www.microsoft.com/windowsxp/home/howtobuy/choosing2.asp.*

Windows XP Professional

Windows XP Professional can be used as a standalone system or can be a workgroup or domain network client. Designed for speed and reliability, Windows XP Professional brings a solid computing environment to desktop and mobile computers. Windows XP Professional is the ideal client operating system for connecting to and interacting with a Windows 2000 Server or Windows Server 2003 domain. The majority of this book focuses on the Professional version of Windows XP.

Windows Server 2003

The Windows XP family originally included the server product that is now called Windows Server 2003. Both XP and 2003 were part of the project named "Whistler." However, Microsoft decided to develop the server products of Whistler much further than the client products. As a result, the primary client products (Windows XP Professional and Windows XP Home Edition) were released in October of 2001. The Windows Server 2003 product line diverged from Windows XP and became its own unique product line. The Windows Server 2003 products were released in the spring of 2003.

The Windows Server 2003 product line has gone through numerous name changes during its development. As the product moved toward a final release, its name changed from Whistler to XP Server, then 2002 Server, then .NET Server, and finally Windows Server 2003. The Windows Server 2003 product line includes several distinct versions: Standard Edition, Enterprise Edition, Datacenter Edition, Web Edition, and Small Business Server.

Other Client Operating Systems

The Microsoft Windows product line includes several client operating systems in addition to Windows XP Professional. These client OSs are (in chronological order) Windows 2000 Professional, Windows NT 4.0 Workstation, Windows ME, Windows SE, Windows 98, Windows 95, and Windows for Workgroups.

Note that any Microsoft Windows client operating system can be used on a Microsoft network. However, the older platforms typically support fewer network capabilities than the new platforms. Therefore, only Windows XP Professional, 2000, and NT clients can actually become domain members. All other client operating systems can access domain shared resources but are not true domain members nor are they protected by the security and management infrastructure of Active Directory. See the Domain Model section later in this chapter and in Chapter 4 "Managing Windows XP File Systems and Storage," for more information.

For more information on earlier Windows operating systems, see *www.microsoft.com/ windows/*. To see a general comparison of capabilities and features of Windows XP Professional with several older versions of Windows, visit *www.microsoft.com/windowsxp/pro/ evaluation/whyupgrade/featurecomp.asp*.

CHOOSING BETWEEN WINDOWS XP PROFESSIONAL AND WINDOWS XP HOME EDITION

One of the biggest decisions computer owners face is what operating system to use. When you purchase a new computer system, you are often stuck with whatever OS is bundled with the system you purchase. If you already own a computer, you can choose to upgrade or replace your existing OS with something new. Microsoft is not the only OS vendor, but Microsoft Windows products are the most widely deployed. For the most part, your bundled OS choices on new computers are limited to Windows XP Professional and Windows XP Home Edition.

Choosing between the two OSs begins with answering the following questions:

- Do you need to connect to a large Microsoft network? If you need to connect to a large Microsoft network, then you need to select Windows XP Professional. A large Microsoft network is typically a domain network based on Windows NT, Windows 2000 Server, or Windows Server 2003. Windows XP Home Edition does not include domain connection capabilities.

- Do you need to remotely access your computer? If you need to connect to your computer remotely and access both your data and applications, then you need Remote Desktop. This is a feature that is found in Windows XP Professional, but not in Windows XP Home Edition.

- Do you need to protect sensitive files? If you need to protect sensitive files stored on your system, you need the Encrypting File System (EFS). EFS is a feature of Windows XP Professional, but not of Windows XP Home Edition.

- Do you need a wide range of fault tolerance and recovery options? If you need the ability to restore damaged files, recover from failures, and even restore the system to a previous state, you need Windows XP Professional. The capabilities to protect your system against loss are not as robust in Windows XP Home Edition.

- Are you a power user? If you want to use a two-CPU computer, want to deploy IIS, want to use multiple languages, or a host of other "power user" activities, Windows XP Professional is better suited for you than Windows XP Home Edition.

- Are you pursuing certification? If you need a system to act as a lab for you to study for various Microsoft certification exams, especially 70-270, then you need Windows XP Professional.

- What is your budget? If you answered no to all of the previous questions, then you can probably get by with Windows XP Home Edition. However, if you can afford the additional expense, we recommend getting Windows XP Professional. If you spend a reasonable amount of time on your computer each week, you will soon find yourself desiring the additional capabilities of Windows XP Professional over that of Windows XP Home Edition.

It is a very common occurrence for a computer user to find themselves needing the capabilities and features of Windows XP Professional while working from a Windows XP Home Edition system. Most consumer PC retailers sell new computer systems with Windows XP Home Edition preinstalled. While some PC vendors offer the option to upgrade to Windows XP Professional for a fee, it is not always an obvious or apparent offer. Thus, some new PC buyers find themselves with a great new computer system that is limited by the preinstalled operating system, namely Windows XP Home Edition.

No matter how you arrived in the situation, if you are running Windows XP Home Edition and need Windows XP Professional, you can upgrade. The upgrade process is fairly straightforward and painless, given a few caveats. First, you need to purchase Windows XP Professional. Second, you need to verify that your computer system meets the minimum system requirements of Windows XP Professional. (See the Windows XP Professional Web site at *www.microsoft.com/windowsxp/default.asp*, or the Windows XP Professional packaging, or the Windows XP Professional Hardware Requirements section later in this chapter for more information. Third, ensure that your hardware and software is compatible using the Upgrade Advisor (see Chapter 2 "Installing Windows XP Professional" for more information). Fourth, back up any important data before starting the upgrade process. This can be accomplished with floppies, burning CDs, moving files to other workgroup members, tape backup, or using the Files and Settings Transfer Wizard (see Chapter 5 "Users, Groups, Profiles, and Policies" for more information). Fifth, perform an antivirus scan on your system.

Once you've handled each of these items, you can proceed with the actual upgrade installation process. The upgrade installation process is basically inserting the CD into the drive, selecting the upgrade to install, and following the self-explanatory prompts.

For more details on the upgrade process, see Chapter 2 or visit the Windows XP Professional Upgrade Center Web site at *www.microsoft.com/windowsxp/pro/howtobuy/upgrading/default.asp*.

THE WINDOWS XP ENVIRONMENT

The Windows XP operating environment is a hybrid of Windows 2000 and Windows ME. The combination of the Windows 2000 core reliability and security with the Windows ME **Plug and Play** capability and connectivity has produced an operating system that is rich in function and features. Plug and Play is the capability of a system to automatically detect the presence of new hardware and install the appropriate device driver. The following sections highlight many of the characteristics of the Windows XP environment.

Multiple Processors

Windows XP Professional supports true **multiprocessing**; support for up to two CPUs is included in every standard version of Windows XP Professional. Multiprocessing is the capability of supporting multiple CPUs. Windows XP Home can support only a single CPU.

On multiple-CPU systems, as many processes or threads as there are CPUs can execute simultaneously; that is, if you are running Windows XP Professional on a system that has two CPUs, then two threads or processes can run at the same time. This means that multiple applications can execute simultaneously, each on a different processor. The system administrators can adjust the priority levels and affinity for processors and processes to make sure that preferred applications get a bigger slice of the available execution time.

Multitasking

One of the great features of Windows XP is **multitasking**. Multitasking is a mode of CPU operation in which a computer processes more than one task at a time. Windows XP supports two types of multitasking—preemptive and cooperative.

Preemptive multitasking is a processor-scheduling regime in which the OS maintains strict control over how long any execution thread (a single task within a multithreaded application, or an entire single-threaded application) may take possession of the CPU. This scheduling regime is called preemptive because the operating system can decide at any time to swap out the currently executing thread if a higher-priority thread makes a bid for execution; the termination of the lower-priority thread is called preemption. Windows XP supports multiple threads and allows duties to be spread among processors. Most native

Windows XP applications are written to take advantage of threads, but older applications may not be as well equipped.

Cooperative multitasking describes a processor-scheduling regime wherein individual applications take control over the CPU for as long as they like (because this means that applications must be well behaved, this approach is sometimes called "good guy" scheduling). Unfortunately, this type of multitasking can lead to stalled or hung systems, should any application fail to release its control over the CPU.

Windows 3.x is one of the most familiar examples of this type of environment; it runs on top of **MS-DOS**, a single-threaded operating system. Windows 3.x is a 16-bit environment that employs cooperative multitasking. In contrast, native 32-bit Windows XP applications have no such limitations. The default for Windows XP is that all 16-bit Windows applications run within a single virtual machine, which is granted only preemptive CPU access. This guarantees that other processes active on a Windows XP machine will not be stymied by an ill-behaved Windows 3.x application.

Multithreading

Multithreading refers to a code design in which individual tasks within a single process space can operate more or less independently as separate, lightweight execution modules called **threads**. Threads are called lightweight execution modules because switching among or between threads within the context of a single process involves very little overhead, and is therefore extremely quick. A thread is the minimal unit of code in an application or system that can be scheduled for execution.

Within a process, all threads share the same memory and system resources. A **process**, on the other hand, is a collection of one or more threads that share a common application or system activity focus. Processes are called heavyweight execution modules because switching among them involves a great deal of overhead, including copying large amounts of data from RAM to disk for outbound processes; then, that process must be repeated to copy large amounts of data from disk to RAM for inbound processes. Under Windows XP, it normally takes more than 100 times longer to switch among processes than it does to switch among threads.

Multithreading allows an operating system to execute multiple threads from a single application concurrently. A CPU can technically only execute a single thread at a time. However, the capabilities of a CPU are divided into time cycles or time slices, each measured in nanoseconds. Multiple threads can all be active, but only one is executing at any given instance. However, the process of switching between each active thread is so fast, we perceive the system to be running many programs at the same time even on a single CPU system. If the computer on which such threads run includes multiple CPUs, threads can even execute simultaneously, each on a different CPU. Even on single-CPU computers, threaded implementations speed up applications and create an environment in which multiple tasks can be active between the foreground (what's showing on the screen) and the background (what's not on screen). Windows XP is extremely adept and efficient at multithreading.

File Systems

Windows XP supports three file systems that can be used to format volumes and partitions on hard drives:

- *FAT (file allocation table)*—The file system originally used by DOS (actually, the Windows XP implementation is an extension of Virtual FAT [VFAT], which includes support for long filenames, 2 GB files, and 4 GB volumes). Windows XP FAT is also known as FAT16. Any Windows OS since DOS can access FAT-formatted volumes.

- *FAT32*—An enhancement of the FAT16 file system developed for Windows 95 OSR2, and included in Windows 98. Windows XP includes support for FAT32 primarily to gain the 4 GB file and 32 GB volume size improvement over FAT16. FAT32 volumes created by Windows 95 OSR2 or Windows 98 can be mounted under Windows XP. Only Windows 98 OS2 and later can access FAT32 volumes.

- *New Technology File System (NTFS)*—A high-performance, secure, and object-oriented file system first introduced in Windows NT. This is the preferred file system for Windows XP. Windows XP Professional supports NTFS v.5. This is the same version of NTFS supported in Windows 2000 and Windows Server 2003. Only Windows NT (SP4), Windows 2000, Windows XP, and Windows Server 2003 can access NTFS volumes.

 Versions of Windows NT up through 3.51 (that is, not including NT 4.0 or Windows 2000) supported HPFS (High Performance File System), which was originally present in OS/2 and LAN Manager. Windows XP does not support HPFS.

Active Directory

Active Directory is the control and administration mechanism of Windows XP that is supported by Windows 2000 Server and Windows Server 2003 to create, sustain, and administer a domain or group of related domains. Active Directory combines the various aspects of a network—users, groups, hosts, clients, security settings, resources, network links, and transactions—into a manageable hierarchical structure. Active Directory simplifies network administration by combining several previously distinct activities, including security, user account management, and resource access, into a single interface.

Windows XP Professional does not include support utilities for installing or managing Active Directory. However, by joining a domain, Windows XP Professional interacts with the Active Directory for all resource- and security-related communications. Using Windows XP Professional in an Active Directory domain network is discussed in Chapter 5.

Security

Windows XP incorporates a variety of security features with a common aim: to enable efficient, reliable control of access to all resources and assets on a network. Windows XP security features begin with a protected mandatory logon system, and include memory protection, system auditing over all events and activities, precise controls on file and directory access, and all types of network access limitations.

Numerous third-party companies offer security enhancements or extensions to Windows XP that cover everything from biometric authentication add-ons (allowing fingerprints or retinal scans to be used in controlling system access) to firewalls and proxy servers that isolate Windows XP-based networks from the Internet or other publicly accessible networks.

One of the more popular features of the Windows XP security system is the inclusion of the Kerberos v5 authentication protocol. Kerberos is used to authenticate clients and servers to the network (that is, to ensure that they are both valid members of a domain) before communication between them is permitted.

Compatibility

Windows XP supports a wide range of applications through application subsystems that emulate the native environment of each application type. In other words, a virtual machine is created for each application, which is fooled into seeing itself as the sole inhabitant of a computer system that matches its execution needs. Windows XP supports the following application types:

- DOS 16-bit
- Native 32-bit (**Win32**)
- Windows 3.1 and Windows for Workgroups 16-bit (**Win16**)

 Windows XP Professional supports most Windows 95/98/2000-based programs, in particular Windows 32-bit business programs. It also supports most MS-DOS-based programs. The primary exceptions are MS-DOS applications that access hardware directly.

Storage

Windows XP Professional supports huge amounts of hard disk and memory space:

- *RAM*—4 GB (gigabytes)
- *Hard disk space*—2 TB (terabytes) for NTFS volumes, 32 GB for FAT32 volumes, and 4 GB for FAT16 volumes

Connectivity

The Windows XP core OS supports a wide variety of networking protocols:

- *NWLink*—Microsoft's 32-bit implementation of Novell's NetWare native protocol stack, IPX/SPX (Internetwork Packet Exchange/Sequenced Packet Exchange)
- *Transmission Control Protocol/Internet Protocol (TCP/IP)*—The set of protocols used on the Internet. This protocol suite has been embraced by Microsoft as a vital technology.

Windows XP is compatible with many existing network types and environments and has native support for the following:

- TCP/IP-based intranets and the Internet
- Integrated remote access networks
- Macintosh networks
- Microsoft networks (MS-DOS, Windows for Workgroups, and LAN Manager)
- Enhanced NetWare connectivity
- Wireless network connectivity

System Recovery

Windows XP boasts the broadest system recovery mechanisms of any Windows OS to date. In addition to traditional backup capabilities and the automated self-protecting mechanisms of NTFS and the Registry, Windows XP includes System Restore, Automated System Recovery (ASR), Recovery Console, device driver rollback, and numerous alternative boot options.

Remote Capabilities

Windows XP builds on the networking capabilities of the Windows product line by introducing more options for remote connectivity. Two such features are Remote Desktop and Remote Assistance. Remote Desktop allows you to access your office computer's user environment from a remote system as you would through a Terminal Services connection. Remote Assistance is used to invite a remote user to view or control your desktop, often to help you perform some work or configuration task. Remote Assistance also enables users to chat and transfer files.

Help and Support Services

Windows XP boasts the most comprehensive Help system ever included in a Windows OS. The Help and Support Center offers several means to access information, including many step-by-step guides, topical and index organizations, and online help for new items.

INTELLIGENT USER INTERFACE

Windows XP has a new desktop layout and look compared to previous versions of Windows. Microsoft has labeled layout and look as the "user experience." The user experience is simply the task-based visual design of the operating system. The new user experience is fresh and easy to use, but not so different that you can't make use of existing Windows know-how. Over the course of writing this book, we were first a bit frustrated by the new layout and organization, but within a week we found that we preferred the XP user experience over those of Windows 2000 or Windows ME. It seems more straightforward, more intelligent, and focused on getting things done.

Windows XP comes with a new default color scheme based on greens and blues, though the color scheme can be fully customized. If you prefer the boxy gray interface of Windows 2000, you can always switch over to the Windows Classic visual style. Additionally, Windows XP includes new 3-D graphical elements and smoothing of edges and corners. The new look and feel is known as a visual styling, and is nothing more than a "skin" for the entire OS.

One of the most obvious changes to the interface is the Start menu. It appears too bulky at first due to its double-column format (see Figure 1-1). The left column of icons includes a quick line to a Web browser and e-mail client. Under these you can "pin" your own selection of icons (we've pinned Windows Explorer). Pinning is accomplished by right-clicking an item anywhere in the Start menu and clicking on the Pin to Start menu command in the shortcut menu.

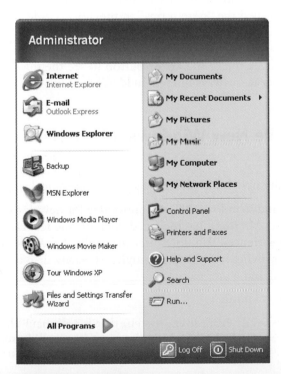

Figure 1-1   The Windows XP Start menu

Below the pinned items is a list of the most recently accessed applications. By default, only the last six are displayed; this can be extended up to 30. At the bottom of the column is the All Programs item, which contains the rest of the Start menu subfolders and icons that were located within the Programs section of the Windows 2000 Start menu. The right column of the Windows XP Start menu includes quick links to My Documents, My Recent Documents, My Pictures, My Music, My Computer, My Network Places, Control Panel, Printers and Faxes, Help and Support, Search, and the Run command.

> As you explore the new Windows XP interface, you are bound to find many subtle changes and added features that make using the computer easier. Depending on the hardware and drivers installed on your computer as well as vendor configuration, your Start menu may differ from this description.

Another interesting feature is the improved taskbar. Within Windows XP, active application buttons on the taskbar are grouped by type. For example, if you have more than five or six applications running, two or three of which are Windows Explorer-type applications, they are cascaded into a single taskbar button. This multiapplication taskbar button acts like a pull-down list, enabling you to select the individual application with a single click.

Windows XP also offers a quick launch icon bar. It is disabled by default, but when enabled, it appears just to the right of the Start button. It's a great place to store often-accessed applications for quick one-click launching.

Windows XP also has improved system tray icon management (note that Microsoft has altered this terminology—what was called the "system tray" in previous Windows versions is referred to as the Notification Area in Windows XP Professional). Instead of allowing icons to string out beside the clock taking up taskbar space, the inactive or rarely accessed icons are hidden. If you ever need access, just click the round arrow button to see them all. You can also configure each icon as to whether it is always hidden, hidden when inactive, or always displayed.

Activity 1-1: Introducing the New Windows XP Interface

Time Required: 5 minutes

Objective: Become familiar with the new look of Windows XP Professional.

Description: Just as Windows 95 and Windows NT 4.0 introduced a new look for the Microsoft Windows operating systems, Microsoft has modified the look and feel for its latest desktop client. At first glance, an experienced Windows user may balk at the layout of the Start menu and icons. However, after giving it a try, most people, especially first-time users, will find Windows XP to be efficient and easier to use.

To explore the desktop and Start menu:

1. To boot and log on to a Windows XP Professional system that is a domain client or configured for Classic logon, press **Ctrl+Alt+Delete**, then provide a valid username and password.

2. Notice the lack of icons on the desktop.

3. Double-click the **Recycle Bin**. This reveals all items that have been deleted but are still recoverable.

4. Select **File**, **Close**.

5. Click the **Start** button on the taskbar.

6. Notice the items that appear in the Start menu by default: Internet, E-mail, My Documents, My Recent Documents, My Pictures, My Music, My Computer, My Network Places, Control Panel, Printers and Faxes, Help and Support, Search, Run, Log Off, and Turn Off Computer.

NOTE
Depending on the hardware and drivers installed on your computer as well as vendor configuration, your Start menu may differ from this description. For example, instead of Turn Off Computer, you may see Shut Down.

7. Click **Turn Off Computer**. This reveals a dialog box where you can choose to log off, stand by, hibernate, turn off the computer, restart the computer, or cancel.

8. Click **Cancel**.

9. Select **Start**, **Run**. This reveals the Run dialog box, where you can enter a filename, or browse to a path and filename to launch.

10. Click **Cancel**.

11. Select **Start**, **Help and Support** to open the Help and Support Center interface. Explore this interface.

12. Close the Help system by clicking the **Close** button in the upper-right corner of the dialog box.

13. Select **Start**, **Search**. This opens a menu with many selections, each of which is an interface used to locate different types of objects, files, people, etc.

14. Select **File**, **Close**.

15. Select **Start**, **My Recent Documents**. This opens a menu that lists the most recently accessed documents or files.

16. Select **Start**, **All Programs**. This opens the first of several levels of menus in which all of the applications, tools, and utilities of the system are organized for easy access. Explore this multilevel menu.

17. Select **Start**, **My Documents**. This reveals the default storage location for your personal documents, faxes, and pictures.

18. Select **File**, **Close**.

19. Select **Start**, **My Computer**. This reveals a list of all drives present on the system, plus a link to Control Panel.

20. Select **File**, **Close**.

For a hands-on tour of the new features of Windows XP's user interface, take the Windows XP tour offered to you during your first logon. If you have already skipped the tour or you want to review the tour again, you can find it in the Accessories subfolder of your Start menu: Start, All Programs, Accessories, Tour Windows XP.

OVERVIEW OF NEW FEATURES

Windows XP includes a broad range of new features or improvements that add capabilities to the Windows product line. Although most of these are not covered on the certification exams, you'll probably discover they are welcome additions to the previous versions of Windows.

IntelliMirror

Although IntelliMirror is not new, it has been fully integrated into Windows XP. IntelliMirror was first developed for Windows 2000. It offers a fault-tolerant system to protect system and data files from loss. It backs up user data, maintains user system configuration, automates application installation, and can even be used to deploy new clients. IntelliMirror is discussed in greater detail in Chapter 14, "Windows XP Professional Fault Tolerance."

Windows Messenger Service

Windows XP now includes integrated video, voice, and text conferencing as part of the Windows Messenger Service. Windows Messenger makes online collaboration easier than in previous versions. Using Windows Messenger, you can trade contact lists, exchange files, share applications, and write on a multiuser whiteboard. These capabilities can be used over an office LAN or the Internet.

Windows Media Player 8

Windows XP sports Windows Media Player 8. This version of this Microsoft multimedia tool can be used to play CDs and DVDs, view recorded movies, play live or recorded music or local music files, search and organize digital media, copy music to portable devices, and even burn your own CDs.

Windows Movie Maker

Windows Movie Maker is a new application within the Windows environment. It enables you to transform your own camcorder recordings into amateur home movies. This multifaceted application can combine video or audio from external analog and digital recording devices with downloaded content to produce a custom presentation. Just think, you can produce your own home movies if you can cut and paste, drag and drop, and point and click.

Windows XP has broader support for digital images than any previous version of Windows. This includes specialized media folders that operate like thumbnail depositories or slide shows right in Windows Explorer. Windows XP offers image manipulation and editing capabilities and quick access to online photo printing. You can submit your images to a print shop and have them shipped to you.

Autoplay

Autoplay is not a feature new to Windows, but Windows XP has taken Autoplay to a whole new level. Instead of automatically playing an audio CD or launching an application when a CD is inserted, you can configure what the system does based on the type of CD (i.e., audio, video, images, documents, software, data, etc.). You can play the CD, open a slide show, print, and more.

Desktop

Although the desktop still looks basically the same, it has also been enhanced to allow the user to customize its functionality. In addition, the Start menu, Startup folder, and taskbar can all be customized for individual needs. Any customization performed by a user is automatically stored in their user profile. Thus customization changes are persistent across logons. If the Windows XP system is a domain client, roaming profiles can be used so the user sees the same desktop no matter what Windows XP system they logon to.

ACTIVITY

Activity 1-2: Setting Up the Desktop

Time Required: 10 minutes

Objective: Customize the desktop to your preferences.

Description: Every person is unique in the way they work and how they like to have things appear. These preferences can be seen by how a person organizes their desk. There are some people who like to keep their files in piles on their desks, whereas others like to use file cabinets and desk organizers to keep their desktops neat and tidy. These preferences can be applied to the Windows desktop, as well.

To customize the desktop:

1. Right-click a blank area of the desktop.
2. Select **New**, **Shortcut** from the menu.
3. Click **Browse** in the window that appears.
4. Locate and select **Notepad.exe** in the main Windows XP directory (the default is WINDOWS). Click OK.

5. Click **Next**.

6. Click **Finish**. A shortcut to Notepad now appears on the desktop.

7. Right-click a blank area of the desktop.

8. Select **Arrange Icons By**, and then click **Auto Arrange**.

9. Notice that the icons on the desktop have repositioned themselves in a uniform pattern.

10. **Right-click** a blank area of the desktop.

11. Select **Properties**.

12. On the **Desktop** tab, take note of the current selection, and then select an item from the list of background images.

13. Click **OK**.

14. To restore the desktop to its original settings, repeat Steps 10 through 13 using the original setting. Delete the shortcut you created by selecting it and pressing the **Delete** key, and then confirm the deletion by clicking the **Yes** button.

WINDOWS XP PROFESSIONAL HARDWARE REQUIREMENTS

Windows XP Professional requires a minimum configuration of hardware to function. It is important that your system comply with these minimum requirements. Microsoft also publishes recommended system requirements that list the hardware necessary to maximize the performance of the operating system. Compliance with the minimum hardware requirements only guarantees functionality; optimum performance requires exceeding these requirements.

Here are the Microsoft-defined minimum requirements:

- 233 MHz CPU or higher microprocessor
- 64 MB of RAM (128 MB or more recommended; 4 GB maximum)
- 1.5 GB of free space
- VGA (800 x 600) or higher resolution monitor
- Keyboard
- Microsoft Mouse or compatible pointing device (optional)

The recommended system requirements are:

- P2 300 MHz CPU or higher microprocessor
- 128 MB of RAM (4 GB maximum)
- 2 GB of free space

- SVGA (800 x 600) or higher resolution monitor
- 12x or faster CD-ROM drive

If you are installing from a CD-ROM drive, you need:

- A CD-ROM or DVD drive
- High-density 3.5-inch disk drive, unless you configured your PC to boot from the CD-ROM drive and can start the setup program from a CD, or if you have an existing OS that can access the CD-ROM drive

If you are installing over a network, you need:

- Windows XP-compatible network interface card (NIC) and related cable
- Access to the network share that contains the set-up files

Hardware Compatibility List

When it comes to configuring a Windows XP machine, the Microsoft **Hardware Compatibility List (HCL)** is an essential piece of documentation. The HCL contains all known Windows XP-compatible hardware devices. The HCL also points to each device's driver, which may be native (included as part of the Windows XP installation program), on a subdirectory of the Windows XP CD, or available only from the device's vendor. Because Windows XP works properly only if a system's hardware is Windows XP-compatible, it is always a good idea to use the HCL as your primary reference when evaluating a prospective Windows XP system or when selecting components for such a system.

Finding the HCL

Finding the HCL is not always easy. The easiest place to look is on your Windows XP CD-ROM in the Support folder, where it exists as a text and a Help file. However, the HCL is not a static document; Microsoft's Quality Labs are constantly updating this file. The version of the HCL on the Windows XP CD-ROM will quickly become outdated, because many new drivers and devices are introduced on a regular basis.

 It's a good idea to consult the most current version of the HCL, especially when you are working with brand-new hardware. The most recent version of the HCL is available for online viewing through the Help and Support Center's Find compatible hardware and software for Windows XP link or on the Microsoft Web site at *www.microsoft.com/hcl/default.asp*. On the other hand, if you have access to a copy of the TechNet CD, a new copy of the HCL is published on TechNet each time it changes.

Why the HCL Is So Important

Windows XP controls hardware directly; it does not require access to a PC's BIOS (basic input/output system), as is the case with Windows 95/98 and earlier versions of DOS and

Windows. Although this gives Windows XP a much finer degree of control over hardware, it also means that Windows XP works only with devices with drivers written specifically for it. This is especially true for SCSI adapters, video cards, and network interface cards.

CAUTION Don't be misled into thinking that because a device works with previous versions of Windows, it will work as well (or at all) with Windows XP. There's no substitute for systematically checking every hardware device on a system against the HCL. Windows XP does support most hardware supported by Windows 2000 and Windows ME, but there may be exceptions.

In addition, it is important to note that Microsoft's technical support policy is that any hardware that is not on the HCL is not supported for Windows XP. If you ask Microsoft for support on a system that contains elements not listed in the HCL, they may blame all problems on the incompatible hardware and not provide any technical support at all. Instead, they may refer you back to the non-HCL device's manufacturer.

Fortunately, Windows XP automatically investigates your hardware and determines whether the minimum requirements are met and whether any known incompatibilities or possible device conflicts are present in the system. So, if you check out the major components manually on the HCL, you can probably get away with letting the installation routine check the rest of the system. If you *really* want to be sure, you can employ the Windows XP Hardware Compatibility Tool to detect your hardware and declare it compatible or not. This tool can be ordered online at: *www.microsoft.com/whdc/hwtest/default.mspx*. Additionally, you can run the WINNT32 command with the /checkupgradeonly parameter to run the Upgrade Advisor. See Chapter 2 for more information.

Preparing a Computer to Meet Upgrade Requirements

To upgrade a computer from a previous operating system to Windows XP, you must first verify that the components of that computer (CPU, memory, storage space, video, keyboard, mouse, etc.) match or exceed the minimum system requirements defined by Microsoft.

Activity 1-3: Verifying Windows XP Professional Hardware Compatibility

ACTIVITY

Time Required: 1 hour

Objective: Check hardware compatibility.

Description: Before installing Windows XP Professional, the user should verify that all hardware that is installed in the computer is on the Hardware Compatibility List (HCL). Any hardware that is not on the list could prevent a successful installation of the operating system and should be removed prior to the installation being initiated.

To verify hardware components are on the HCL:

1. Open the computer case.

2. Make a list of all present components, including model and manufacturer.

3. For each of the hardware requirements of Windows XP, verify that the component in your computer meets or exceeds the requirements.

4. For each additional component found in the computer, verify that it is listed on the HCL. The HCL can be found online at: *www.microsoft.com/whdc/hcl/ search.mspx*. Use this Web site to quickly search for your products to confirm compliance with Windows XP.

5. Remove any non-HCL-compliant devices and replace them with HCL-compliant devices.

NETWORKING MODELS

There are two networking models to which a Windows XP Professional computer can belong: a **workgroup** or a domain.

Workgroup Model

Microsoft's **workgroup model** for networking distributes resources, administration, and security throughout a network. Each computer in a workgroup may be a server, a client, or both. All computers in a workgroup are equal in stature and responsibility and are therefore called peers. That's why a workgroup model network is also known as a **peer-to-peer** network.

In a workgroup, each computer also maintains its own unique set of resources, accounts, and security information. Workgroups are quite useful for groups of less than 10 computers and may be used with groups as large as 25 to 50 machines (with increasing administration difficulty). Table 1–1 lists the advantages and disadvantages of workgroup networking.

Table 1-1   Advantages and disadvantages of workgroup networks

Advantages	Disadvantages
Easy-to-share resources	No centralized control of resources
Resources are distributed across all machines	No centralized account management
Little administrative overhead	No centralized administration
Simple to design	No centralized security management
Easy to implement	Inefficient for more than 20 workstations
Convenient for small groups in close proximity	Security must be configured manually
Less expensive, does not require a central server	Increased training to operate as both client and server

Domain Model

By dedicating one or more servers to the job of controlling a domain, the **domain model** adds a layer of complexity to networking. But the domain model also centralizes all shared resources and creates a single point of administrative and security control. In a domain, it is recommended that any member act exclusively either as a client or as a server. In a domain environment, servers control and manage resources, whereas clients are user computers that can request access to the resources controlled by servers.

Centralized organization makes the domain model simpler to manage from an administrative and security standpoint, because any changes made to the domain accounts database automatically proliferate across the entire network. According to Microsoft, domains are useful for groups of 10 or more computers. Microsoft estimates that the maximum practical size of a single domain is somewhere around 25,000 computers, but also describes other multidomain models that it claims have no upper limit on size. In real-world application, 3000 computers is believed to represent a reasonable upper boundary on the number of machines in a single domain.

No matter how many computers it contains, any Windows domain requires at least one **domain controller (DC)**. The domain controller maintains the domain's Active Directory, which stores all information and relationships about users, groups, policies, computers, and resources. (*Note*: Active Directory is a feature of Windows 2000 Server and Windows Server 2003 domains. Windows NT domains are not Active Directory domains.)

More than one domain controller can exist in a domain; in fact, it is recommended that you deploy a domain controller for every 300 to 400 clients. Unlike domain controllers in a Windows NT 4.0 network, all Windows 2000 Server and Windows Server 2003 domain controllers are peers. All other servers and clients on a domain-based network interact with a domain controller to handle resource requests. Table 1-2 summarizes the advantages and disadvantages of the domain model.

Table 1-2   Advantages and disadvantages of domain networks

Advantages	Disadvantages
Centralized resource sharing	Significant administrative effort and overhead
Centralized resource controls	Complicated designs; requires advanced planning
Centralized account management	Requires one or more powerful, expensive servers
Centralized security management	Absolute security is hard to achieve
Efficient performance for a virtually unlimited number of workstations	Expense for domain controllers increases and access decreases with network size
Users need to be trained only to use clients	Some understanding of domain networks remains necessary
Not restricted to close proximity	Larger scope requires more user documentation and training

Windows XP Architecture

The Windows XP internal organization and architecture deeply influence its capabilities and behavior. The following sections explain the two Windows XP major operating modes and the memory architecture in detail.

The Meaning of Modular

Windows XP is a modular operating system. In other words, Windows XP is not built as a single large program; instead, it is composed of numerous small software elements, or modules, that cooperate to provide the system's networking and computing capabilities. Each unique function, code segment, and system control resides in a distinct module, so that no two modules share any code. This method of construction allows Windows XP to be easily amended, expanded, or patched as needed. Furthermore, the Windows XP components communicate with one another through well-defined interfaces. Therefore, even if a module's internals change (or a new version replaces an old one), as long as the interface is not altered, other components need not be aware of any such changes (except perhaps to take advantage of new functionality that was previously unavailable).

All Windows XP processes operate in one of two modes: **user mode** or **kernel mode**. A **mode** represents a certain level of system and hardware access, and is distinguished by its programming, the kinds of services and functions it is permitted to request, and the controls that are applied to its requests for system resources. Each mode contains only those specific components and capabilities that might be needed to perform the set of operations that is legal within that mode.

The use of modes in Windows XP is very similar to their use in UNIX and VMS, and contributes to the modularity and built-in security mechanisms of Windows XP.

User Mode

All user interaction with a Windows XP system occurs through one user mode process. User mode is an isolated portion of the system environment in which user applications execute. User mode permits only mediated access to Windows XP system resources. In other words, any user mode requests for objects or services must pass through the Executive Services components in the kernel mode to obtain access. In addition to supporting native 32-bit Windows **application programming interfaces (APIs)**, a variety of user mode subsystems enable Windows XP to emulate Win16 and DOS environments.

Windows XP supports three core environment subsystems: Win32, Win16, and DOS. The Win32 subsystem supports Windows XP, Windows 2000, Windows NT, and Windows 9x 32-bit applications directly. Through the emulation of virtual DOS machines (VDMs) and Windows 3.x (WOWEXEC), Windows XP supports both DOS and Windows 16-bit applications.

Each subsystem is built around an API that enables suitable Win16 or DOS applications to run by emulating their native operating systems. However, even though other subsystems may be involved in some applications, the Win32 subsystem controls the Windows XP user interface and mediates all input/output requests for all other subsystems. In that sense, it is the core interface subsystem for applications in user mode.

 Windows XP is an object-oriented operating system; in user mode, any request for a system resource ultimately becomes a request for a particular object. An **object** is a collection of attributes with associated data values, plus a set of related services that can be performed on that object. Files, folders, printers, and processes are examples of objects. Because objects may be shared or referenced by one or more processes, they have an existence independent of any particular process in the Windows XP environment. Objects are identified by type (which defines what attributes and services they support) and by instance (which defines a particular entity of a certain type—for example, there may be many objects of type "file," but only one object can have a particular unique combination of directory specification and filename). Windows XP can control access to individual objects, and it can even control which users or groups are permitted to perform particular services related to such objects.

As part of the Windows XP user mode, the security subsystem is solely responsible for the logon process. The security subsystem works directly with key elements in the kernel mode to verify the username and password for any logon attempt, and permits only valid combinations to obtain access to a system.

Here are the steps for logging into Windows XP:

1. During a logon attempt, the security subsystem creates an authentication package that contains the username and password provided in the Windows XP Security logon window.

2. This authentication package is then turned over to the kernel mode, where a module called the security reference monitor (SRM)—the portion of the security subsystem that verifies usernames and passwords against the security accounts database—examines the package and compares its contents to a security accounts database.

3. If the logon request is invalid, an incorrect logon message is returned to the user mode. For valid requests, the SRM constructs an access token, which contains a summary of the logged-on user's security access rights. The token is then returned to the security subsystem used to launch the shell process in user mode.

 To gain access to the Windows XP logon interface (as a domain client or as a workgroup/standalone system in class logon mode), the user must enter a special key combination called the Windows XP attention sequence: Ctrl+Alt+Delete are pressed simultaneously. The attention sequence calls the Windows XP logon process; because this key sequence cannot be faked remotely, it guarantees that this process (which also resides in a protected memory area) is not subject to manipulation by would-be crackers.

Kernel Mode

The kernel mode, which is a highly privileged processing mode, refers to the inner workings, or **kernel**, of Windows XP. All components in kernel mode take execution priority over user mode subsystems and processes. In fact, some key elements within the kernel mode remain resident in memory at all times, and cannot be swapped to disk by the Virtual Memory Manager. This is the part of the operating system that handles process priority and scheduling; it's what provides the ability to preempt executing processes and schedule new processes, which is at the heart of any preemptive multitasking operating system such as Windows XP.

The kernel insulates hardware and core system services from direct access by user applications. That's why user applications must request any accesses to hardware or low-level resources from the kernel mode. If the request is permitted to proceed—and this mediated approach always gives Windows XP a chance to check any request against the access permitted by the access token associated with the requester—the kernel handles the request and returns any related results to the requesting user mode process. This mediated approach also helps maintain reliable control over the entire computer and protects the system from ill-behaved applications. At a finer level of detail, the kernel mode may be divided into three primary subsystems—the Executive Services, the kernel, and the hardware abstraction layer (HAL)—each of which is discussed in the following subsections.

Executive Services

The **Executive Services** are the interfaces that permit kernel and user mode subsystems to communicate. All processes in Windows XP consist of one or more threads coordinated and scheduled by the kernel. Executive Services use the kernel to communicate with each other concerning the processes they share. The kernel runs in privileged mode along with the HAL and the other Executive Services. This means that the kernel is allowed direct access to all system resources. It cannot be paged to disk, meaning that it must run in real memory. A misbehaving kernel process can stall or crash the operating system—a primary reason why direct access to this level of system operation is not available to user mode applications.

The Windows XP Executive Services consist of these modules:

- I/O Manager
- Security Reference Monitor (SRM)
- Internal Procedure Call (IPC) Manager
- Virtual Memory Manager (VMM)
- Process Manager
- Plug and Play Manager
- Power Manager
- Windows Manager

- File Systems Manager
- Object Manager

The I/O Manager handles all operating system input and output, including receiving requests for I/O services from applications, determining what driver is needed, and requesting that driver for the application. The I/O Manager is composed of the following components:

- *Cache Manager*—Handles disk caching for all file systems. This service works with the Virtual Memory Manager to maintain performance. It also works with the file system drivers to maintain file integrity.

- *Network drivers*—Actually a subarchitecture in and of itself, network drivers are the software components that enable communication on the network.

- *Device drivers*—32-bit and multiprocessor-compatible minidrivers that enable communication with devices.

The Security Reference Monitor (SRM) compares the access rights of a user (as encoded in an access token) with the access control list (ACL) associated with an individual object. If the user has sufficient rights to honor an access request after the access token and ACL are reconciled, the requested access is granted. Whenever a user launches a process, that process runs within the user's security context and inherits a copy of the user's security token. This means that under most circumstances, any process launched by a Windows XP user cannot obtain broader access rights than those associated with the account that launched it.

The Internal Procedure Call (IPC) Manager controls application communication with server processes such as the Win32 subsystem—the set of application services provided by the 32-bit version of Microsoft Windows. This makes applications behave as if **dynamic link library (DLL)** calls were handled directly, and helps to explain the outstanding ability of Windows XP to emulate 16-bit DOS and Windows runtime environments.

The **Virtual Memory Manager (VMM)** keeps track of the addressable memory space in the Windows XP environment. This includes both physical RAM and one or more paging files on disk, which are called **virtual memory** when used in concert.

The Process Manager primarily tracks two kernel-dispatched objects: processes and threads. It is responsible for creating and tracking processes and threads and then for deleting them (and cleaning up) after they're no longer needed.

The Plug and Play Manager handles the loading, unloading, and configuration of device drivers for Plug and Play hardware. This manager allows the hot-swapping of devices and on-the-fly reconfiguration. Additionally, if a non-Plug and Play device uses a Plug and Play-supporting device driver, it can be controlled through this manager.

The Power Manager is used to monitor and control the use of power. Typically, the services offered by the Power Manager are employed on notebook computers running on batteries or in other environments in which power is an issue. Some of the power-saving features offered include hard drive and CD-ROM drive power-down, video/monitor shutdown, and peripheral disconnection.

The Windows Manager introduces a method of network-based centralized control to Windows XP. It can be used to distribute software, manage systems remotely, and provide a programming interface for third-party management software.

The File System Manager is responsible for maintaining access and control over the file systems of the Windows XP environment. The File System Manager controls file I/O transfers for all the file systems.

The Object Manager maintains object naming and security functions for all system objects; it allocates system objects, monitors their use, and removes them when they are no longer needed. The Object Manager maintains the following system objects:

- Directory objects
- ObjectType objects
- Link objects
- Event objects
- Process and thread objects
- Port objects
- File objects

Activity 1-4: Monitoring Windows XP Activity

Time Required: 10 minutes

Objective: Use Task Manager to view active applications, processes, and performance.

Description: Windows NT kernel operating systems (Windows NT, Windows 2000) have always had a version of Task Manager that allows the user to view active applications and their state (active or not responding). Along with viewing which applications are active, the user can view the active processes and a basic chart to indicate processor/ memory use on the computer. Windows XP has expanded this useful tool to include added details on the Performance tab.

To explore Task Manager:

1. Right-click a blank area of the taskbar. Select **Task Manager** from the shortcut menu.

2. Look at the Applications tab of Task Manager. This lists all applications currently active in user mode.

3. Click the **Processes** tab of Task Manager. This lists all processes currently active. It also lists details about each process, such as its process ID, its CPU usage percentage per second, and its total CPU execution time.

4. Click the **Performance** tab of Task Manager. This tab shows graphs detailing the current and historical use of the CPU and memory. This tab also lists details about memory consumption, threads, and handles.

5. Click the **View** menu, and then click **Show Kernel Times**. This alters the graphs so activities of the kernel mode are shown in red, and activities of the user mode are shown in green. Spend several minutes observing this interface. You will see that the graphs change periodically to reflect the changes in the activities of each mode.

6. To close this view, select **File**, **Exit Task Manager** from the menu.

The Hardware Abstraction Layer

The goal of the **hardware abstraction layer (HAL)** is to isolate any hardware-dependent code in order to prevent direct access to hardware. This is the only module written entirely in low-level, hardware-dependent code. It is the HAL that helps to make Windows XP scalable across multiple processors. The HAL is built during the initial installation of the operating system. If there is a significant change to the core elements of the computer (i.e., CPU, motherboard, memory type, etc.), the HAL must be rebuilt or properly upgraded. This may require reinstallation of the OS (such as an upgrade install) or a specialized driver replacement activity (such as in the case of switching from single to multiple CPUs).

Memory Architecture

The memory architecture of Windows XP helps make this operating system robust, reliable, and powerful. As noted earlier, Windows XP Professional can manage as much as 4 GB of RAM.

Windows XP uses a flat (non-multidimensional) 32-bit memory model. It is based on a virtual memory, **demand paging** method that is a flat, linear address space of up to 4 GB allocated to each 32-bit application. Demand paging is the memory characteristic where an application can request (i.e., demand) a specific item from memory. If that item is currently stored in the paging file, the Virtual Memory Manager pages it into physical RAM. Non-32-bit Windows applications, such as Win16 and MS-DOS, are managed similarly, except that all subsystem components, including the actual application, run within a single 4 GB address space.

 The unit of memory that the VMM manipulates is called a **page**, and is 4 KB in size. Pages are stored to and retrieved from disk-based files called page files or paging files. These files are also used for memory reindexing and mapping to avoid allocating memory between unused contiguous space or to prevent fragmentation of physical memory.

1

CHAPTER SUMMARY

- This chapter introduced you to the features and architecture of Windows XP. There are two versions: Windows XP Professional and Windows XP Home Edition. Windows XP offers a distinct operating environment that boasts portability, multitasking, multithreading, multiple file systems (FAT, FAT32, NTFS), Active Directory, robust security, multiple clients, multiple processors, wide application support, large RAM and storage capacity, and a wide range of network connectivity options. Windows XP is an inherently networkable operating system with built-in connectivity solutions for NetWare and TCP/IP, allowing easy implementation on multivendor networks.

- Windows XP has specific minimum hardware requirements; the Hardware Compatibility List (HCL) lists all devices known to be compatible with Windows XP.

- Windows XP can participate in either of two networking models—workgroup or domain.

- Windows XP is based on a modular programming technique. Its main processing mechanism is divided into two modes. User mode hosts all user processes and accesses resources through the Executive Services. The kernel mode hosts all system processes and mediates all resource access. The separation of modes provides for a more stable and secure computing environment. User mode supports the application subsystems that enable Windows XP to execute DOS, WIN16, and WIN32 software. Kernel mode's Executive Services manage all operations, including I/O, security, IPC, memory, processes, Plug and Play support, power, distributed control, file systems, objects, and graphical devices.

- The Windows XP virtual memory model combines the use of both physical RAM and paging files into a demand paging mechanism to maximize memory use and efficiency. Windows XP is easy to use, offers new storage capabilities, provides improved Internet access, and maintains strict security.

KEY TERMS

Active Directory — A centralized resource and security management, administration, and control mechanism used to support and maintain a Windows 2000 Server or Windows Server 2003 domain. The Active Directory is hosted by domain controllers.

application programming interfaces (APIs) — A set of software routines referenced by an application to access underlying application services.

client — A computer used to access network resources.

cooperative multitasking — A computing environment in which the individual application maintains control over the duration that its threads use operating time on the CPU.

demand paging — The act of requesting free pages of memory from RAM for an active application.

domain — A centralized enterprise model used in Microsoft networks.

domain controller (DC) — A computer that maintains the domain's Active Directory, which stores all information and relationships about users, groups, policies, computers, and resources.

domain model — The networking setup in which there is centralized administrative and security control. One or more servers are dedicated to the task of controlling the domain by providing access and authentication for shared domain resources to member computers.

dynamic link library (DLL) — A Microsoft Windows executable code module that is loaded on demand. Each DLL performs a unique function or small set of functions requested by applications.

Executive Services — The collection of kernel mode components designed for operating system management.

FAT (file allocation table) — The file system used in versions of MS-DOS. Supported in Windows XP in its VFAT form, which adds long filenames and 4 GB file and volume sizes.

FAT32 — The 32-bit enhanced version of FAT introduced by Windows 95 OSR2 that expands the file and volume size of FAT to 32 GB. FAT32 is supported by Windows XP.

hardware abstraction layer (HAL) — One of the few components of the Windows XP architecture that is written in hardware-dependent code. It is designed to protect hardware resources.

Hardware Compatibility List (HCL) — Microsoft's updated list of supported hardware for Windows XP.

kernel — The core of the Microsoft Windows XP operating system. It is designed to facilitate all activity within the Executive Services.

kernel mode — The level where objects can be manipulated only by threads directly from an application subsystem.

mode — A programming and operational separation of components, functions, and services.

MS-DOS — One of the most popular character-based operating systems for personal computers. Many DOS concepts are still in use by modern operating systems.

multiprocessing — The ability to distribute threads among multiple CPUs on the same system.

multitasking — The ability to run more than one program at the same time.

multithreading — The ability of an operating system and hardware to execute multiple pieces of code (or threads) from a single application simultaneously.

New Technology File System (NTFS) — The high-performance file system supported by Windows XP that offers file-level security, encryption, compression, auditing, and more. Supports volumes up to 16 exabytes theoretically, but Microsoft recommends volumes not exceed 2 terabytes.

NWLink — Microsoft's implementation of Novell's IPX/SPX protocol, used for Microsoft Networking or for facilitating connectivity with Novell Networks.

object — A collection of data and/or abilities of a service that can be shared and used by one or more processes.

operating system (OS) — The software designed to work directly with hardware to provide a computing environment within which production and entertainment software can execute, and which creates a user interface.

1

page — An individual unit of memory that the Virtual Memory Manager manipulates (moves from RAM to paging file and vice versa).

peer-to-peer — A type of networking in which each computer can be a client to other computers and act as a server as well.

Plug and Play — The ability of Windows XP to recognize hardware, automatically install drivers, and perform configuration changes on the fly.

preemptive multitasking — A computing environment in which the operating system maintains control over the duration of operating time any thread (a single process of an application) is granted on the CPU.

process — A collection of one or more threads.

server — The networked computer that responds to client requests for network resources.

Transmission Control Protocol/Internet Protocol (TCP/IP) — A suite of protocols evolved from the Department of Defense's ARPANet. It is used for connectivity in LANs as well as the Internet.

thread — The most basic unit of programming code that can be scheduled for execution.

user mode — The area in which private user applications and their respective subsystems lie.

virtual memory — A Windows XP kernel service that stores memory pages that are not currently in use by the system in a paging file. This frees up memory for other uses. Virtual memory also hides the swapping of memory from applications and higher-level services.

Virtual Memory Manager (VMM) — The part of the operating system that handles process priority and scheduling, providing the ability to preempt executing processes and schedule new processes.

Win16 — The subsystem in Windows XP that allows for the support of 16-bit Windows applications.

Win32 — The main 32-bit subsystem used by Win32 applications and other application subsystems.

workgroup — A networking scheme in which resources, administration, and security are distributed throughout the network.

workgroup model — The networking setup in which users are managed jointly through the use of workgroups to which users are assigned.

REVIEW QUESTIONS

1. Which of the following application environments does Windows XP support as long as kernel mode/user mode restrictions are maintained?

   a. PICK

   b. SunOS

   c. OS/2

   d. X-Windows

   e. MS-DOS

2. Windows XP supports a maximum of of memory and a maximum of of disk space.

3. Which of the following are kernel mode components in Windows XP? (Choose all that apply.)

   a. virtual DOS machines

   b. Security Reference Monitor

   c. hardware abstraction layer

   d. Win16 subsystem

4. Windows XP supports only cooperative multitasking. True or False?

5. Windows XP supports the HPFS file system. True or False?

6. Windows XP has inherent support for facilitating connectivity to which of the following? (Choose all that apply.)

   a. Novell NetWare

   b. Solaris printers

   c. Linux

   d. TCP/IP networks

7. Memory pages are stored in units of:

   a. 2 KB

   b. 4 KB

   c. 16 KB

   d. 64 KB

8. Windows XP Professional is the client product that came out of the Whistler development project. What is the server product that came out of this development project?

   a. Windows XP Server

   b. Windows Advanced Server

   c. Windows 2000 Server

   d. Windows Server 2003

9. If you want users to share resources, but have no concern for local security on the system, which operating system would be your best choice?

   a. Windows 98

   b. Windows NT Workstation

   c. Windows XP Professional

   d. Windows 2000 Server

10. Which of these configuration specifications supports the installation of Windows XP Professional?

   a. Intel 233 MHz Pentium, 128 MB of RAM, 2 GB disk space

   b. Compaq Alpha, 48 MB of RAM, 2 GB disk space

   c. Intel 486DX/66, 16 MB of RAM, 800 MB disk space

   d. Intel 133 MHz Pentium, 24 MB of RAM, 2 GB disk space

11. A dual-boot computer hosts both Windows 98 and Windows XP Professional. You need to download an 8 GB data file that will be used by both operating systems. What file system should you use to format the host volume?

   a. FAT

   b. FAT32

   c. NTFS

   d. HPFS

12. You are setting up a computer for the purpose of sharing files. Each user must have specific levels of access based on their identity. You also want the security system to employ encryption authentication to verify the identity of both the server and client before a data transfer can occur. Which operating system would be the most effective solution?

   a. Windows 98

   b. Windows XP Professional

   c. Windows NT Workstation

   d. Windows XP Home Edition

13. The two networking models supported in Windows XP are _____ and _____ .

14. The three file systems supported in Windows XP are _____ , _____ , and _____ .

15. When a user presses the Ctrl+Alt+Delete key combination in Windows XP after booting, what happens?

   a. The computer reboots.

   b. The logon screen appears.

   c. A "blue screen of death" occurs.

   d. A command prompt appears.

16. Windows XP runs on top of DOS. True or False?

17. Which of the following are required to install Windows XP on Intel-based computers?

    a. a SCSI CD-ROM drive

    b. a tape backup device

    c. a network interface card

    d. none of the above

18. Which of the following new features of Windows XP are system recovery mechanisms?

    a. ASR

    b. Autoplay

    c. System Restore

    d. device driver rollback

19. Administrators desiring a centralized model of resource management should consider the _____ network model.

    a. workgroup

    b. domain

    c. peer-to-peer

    d. multitasking

20. All direct access to hardware is mediated by which component?

    a. kernel

    b. Win32 subsystem

    c. hardware abstraction layer

    d. Executive Services

21. Windows XP Professional natively supports up to how many processors?

    a. 1

    b. 2

    c. 4

    d. 32

22. Which of the following is a disadvantage of workgroup networking?

    a. Resources are distributed across all machines.

    b. no centralized security management

    c. supports unlimited workstations

    d. requires one or more powerful, expensive servers

23. Which of the following is an advantage of domain networking?

    a. Perfect security can be maintained.

    b. simple to design

    c. centralized resource controls

    d. supports 10 to 20 workstations

24. When a DOS application that is used to manipulate files on a hard drive is launched on a Windows XP Professional system, in what mode does the process execute?

    a. user

    b. kernel

    c. protected

    d. IPC

25. Windows XP can:

    a. burn CDs.

    b. submit images for online printing.

    c. videoconference over the Internet.

    d. create home movies.

CASE PROJECTS

CASE PROJECTS

Case Project 1-1

You are planning a network in which users need to have a centralized location, where discretionary access control is a necessity. This will be an environment in which consistency is a must.

Required result:

❑ All users must be able to access the server from any computer within the network through a single logon.

Optional desired results:

❑ Users must also be required to logon before accessing anything on their local machine.

❑ Users will all have the exact same desktop GUI.

Proposed solution:

❑ Install Windows 2000 Server as the server platform. Establish a Windows domain. On half of the users' desktops install Windows 98, and on the other half install Windows XP Professional. Have all computers configured as part of the Windows domain.

Which results does the proposed solution produce? Why?

    a. The proposed solution produces the required result and produces both of the optional desired results.

    b. The proposed solution produces the required result but only one of the optional desired results.

    c. The proposed solution produces the required result but neither of the optional desired results.

    d. The proposed solution does not produce the required result.

CASE PROJECTS

Case Project 1-2

You have been instructed to evaluate the status of the network environment at Site A. Your goal is to evaluate the current network and determine, first of all, whether upgrading is necessary. If so, the next step is to determine which operating system will be the migration choice: Windows XP Professional or Windows 98. Finally, determine what steps are necessary before the migration can proceed.

Site A has 220 computers currently running Windows 3.1. They are running all 16-bit applications from the DOS and Windows environments. They plan on migrating to Microsoft Office 2000. Each computer has the following hardware configuration:

❐ Intel 486 DX4/100

❐ 8 MB of RAM

❐ 540 MB hard drive

❐ NIC (network interface card)

❐ VGA monitor

Users will not be allowed to share files at the desktop. They will not roam from computer to computer, so all of their files can be stored locally on their own computers.

Which migration path makes the most sense? Why?

    a. no migration

    b. Windows XP Professional

    c. Windows 98

If migration to Windows XP Professional is necessary, what must be done to establish optimum but cost-effective performance?

2

INSTALLING WINDOWS XP PROFESSIONAL

After reading this chapter and completing the exercises, you will be able to:

- ◆ Determine if an upgrade is possible
- ◆ Boot multiple operating systems
- ◆ Plan an installation or upgrade
- ◆ Understand the types of installations available
- ◆ Work with important setup and advanced installation options
- ◆ Work with WINNT and WINNT32
- ◆ Understand partitioning, volume licensing, and activating Windows XP
- ◆ Set up Windows XP Professional and upgrade to multiple processors
- ◆ Remove Windows XP Professional

A number of issues must be considered when installing any operating system (OS), and Windows XP Professional is no exception. This chapter details the various steps that must be taken to get Windows XP up and running. You start off by examining the issue of upgrading versus installing, then proceed into a discussion of multiboot systems. From there, the text illustrates the planning process that should precede an actual installation. The chapter discusses the various methods of manual and automated installation, drive partitioning, licensing, and activation. A complete install walk-through is followed by upgrading to multiple CPUs and removing Windows XP from a system.

UPGRADING VERSUS INSTALLING

When installing Windows XP Professional, you have a choice between upgrading an existing installation or performing a completely clean installation. This chapter focuses mainly on clean installations. However, it provides more than sufficient information about the upgrade process. The following subsections help you decide which option is right for you.

Upgrading

Upgrading is an option when you have a version of Windows already installed and want to preserve some settings and other information from the previous installation, including password files, desktop settings, and general configuration.

Windows XP Professional can be installed as an **upgrade** over an existing installation of the following operating systems:

- Windows 95 OSR2, Windows 98, Windows 98 SE, and Windows ME
- Windows NT 4.0 Workstation (with Service Pack 6 or later)
- Windows 2000 Professional (with any service packs)
- Windows XP Home Edition
- Windows 95. However, because Microsoft no longer supports Windows 95, it is effectively off their radar. The upgrade won't retain as much information as an upgrade from Windows 98, but it is possible.

NOTE Windows XP Home Edition can be used to upgrade only Windows 98, Windows 98 SE, or Windows ME. An upgrade install cannot be performed from any Server version of Windows.

Typically, you'd select an upgrade installation when you want to retain your existing desktop, system settings, and network configuration. The process of upgrading to Windows XP Professional from Windows 2000 Professional is fairly straightforward, having been designed to retain as many of the existing configuration and software settings as possible. The only items that are not retained are system utilities or drivers specific to the existing OS that are updated or removed for Windows XP. To upgrade, execute **WINNT32** from the \I386 folder on the CD, and then select the upgrade option from the pull-down list box (see Figure 2-1). WINNT32 is the setup installation utility that initiates and manages the installation (or upgrade) of Windows XP. This utility is discussed in a later section in this chapter.

When performing an upgrade install from Windows 95, Windows 98, Windows 98 SE, or Windows ME to Windows XP Professional, you need to assess and test your backups. Compressed backups created from these legacy versions of Windows using the native Windows backup utility are not compatible with the backup utility of Windows XP

Figure 2-1   Choosing the Upgrade option from the Windows Setup Wizard

Professional. Only backups created without compression under Windows 95, Windows 98, Windows 98 SE, or Windows ME can be used by Windows XP Professional. If you find yourself in the situation where you've already performed the upgrade to Windows XP Professional before discovering that your backups used compression, there is a workaround. Simply restore the files to another system such as Windows 95, Windows 98, Windows 98 SE, or Windows ME, then move them over to your Windows XP Professional system.

Often when upgrading from a previous version of Windows to Windows XP Professional, you want to retain as many of the previous system settings and personal data files as possible. Windows XP Professional includes several tools to help make this process as painless as possible. These include the Files and Settings Transfer Wizard and the User State Migration tools. These tools must be used before the upgrade installation process is started. Please see Chapter 5 "Users, Groups, Profiles, and Policies" for a discussion of these tools.

When upgrading from any version of Windows to Windows XP Professional, it is important to ensure that Windows XP compatible device drivers are installed. While most drivers are automatically upgraded when the installation is performed, this is not always the case, especially for devices that are obscure or that are using nonstandard drivers. Nonstandard drivers can be any version of a driver not found on the original driver distribution disks for the device or on the installation CD of the version of Windows being upgraded. If you discover some interfaces or commands unavailable after an upgrade to Windows XP, check the device drivers for Windows XP compatibility. This problem is most often experienced with video drivers. If the driver is not fully compatible with Windows XP, the Display applet may not function properly.

Clean Installation

In contrast to an upgrade, a **clean installation** installs a completely new version of Windows XP Professional without regard to any existing files or settings. To migrate from any other OS not included in the bulleted list in the previous section requires a full or clean installation. This means that Windows NT Server, Windows 2000 Server, and Windows 3.1 are "upgraded" only by a clean installation that overwrites them instead of retaining data.

If you are having problems with your existing OS and the environmental settings are not that important, a clean installation is a better option. A clean or complete installation can be performed onto a system with a blank hard drive, over an existing OS, or in such a way as to create a multiboot system. A **multiboot system** is a computer that hosts two or more operating systems that can be booted by selecting one from a boot menu or boot manager each time the computer is powered up.

WINDOWS XP UPGRADE ADVISOR

The Windows XP Upgrade Advisor is a utility that inspects your computer to determine whether or not the hardware and software are compatible with Windows XP. The Upgrade Advisor can only be used on a system with an existing Windows OS. The Upgrade Advisor can be obtained from the Microsoft Web site at *www.microsoft.com/windowsxp/pro/howtobuy/upgrading/advisor.asp*. It is a large download of over 50 MB. It is recommended to use the Upgrade Advisor while your system is still connected to the Internet. This allows the tool to employ the latest information about hardware and software compatibility. Once downloaded, execute the Upgrade Advisor. Follow the simple wizardlike prompts to initiate a system scan. Once the scan is completed, a report is displayed listing any problems. This report can be saved to a file for future reference. If incompatibilities are discovered, you must either find an updated driver, software version, or replace the item in your system before installing Windows XP.

BOOTING MULTIPLE OPERATING SYSTEMS

It is possible to install more than one OS on the same computer, allowing you to choose the OS to be used at boot time. Unless you deliberately overwrite, or **format**, the **partition** or volume (a space set aside on a disk and assigned a drive letter that can occupy all or part of the disk) where another OS is located, installing Windows XP Professional does not affect OSs already residing on the computer. In most cases, a dual-boot or multiboot system is created by installing each application into its own partition or volume or onto its own hard drive. For the best results when creating a multiboot system, you should install the OSs in chronological order of their original release dates from oldest to newest. If you fail to install OSs in chronological order, the boot partition's files will not be properly updated, and therefore you will be unable to boot to all (if any) of the installed OSs.

Windows XP can be dual-booted with any Microsoft OS and even OS/2. You can create a **dual-boot system** with Windows XP and other operating systems, such as Linux. However, these operating systems require third-party boot and partition managers, such as Partition Magic from PowerQuest (*www.powerquest.com*) or System Commander from V Communications (*www.v-com.com*).

In most cases (when third-party multiboot software is not used), you want to install Windows XP on a system with an existing OS rather than installing Windows XP before another OS. This enables the Windows XP Setup routine to configure the boot loader properly. The **boot loader** is the software that shows all currently available operating systems and permits the user to choose which one should be booted through a menu. At boot time, you can choose the OS you want to run, as shown in Figure 2-2.

```
Please select the operating system to start:

  Microsoft Windows XP Professional
  Microsoft Windows 2000 Professional

Use the up and down arrow keys to move the highlight to your choice.
Press ENTER to choose.
Seconds until highlighted choice will be started automatically: 30




For troubleshooting and advanced startup options for Windows, press F8.
```

Figure 2-2   The Windows XP Professional boot menu

The BOOT.INI file is a text file that creates the Windows XP boot loader's menu. The BOOT.INI file is located on drive C: or the first hard drive partition on the disk. It is flagged as hidden and read-only so you must change the attributes before you can see or edit this file. To remove an OS from the boot loader or edit its entry in the boot loader menu, you have to edit the BOOT.INI file manually. If you plan on making changes, it is always a good idea to create a backup of the original in case you cause an error. Additionally, the Startup options in Control Panel can also be used to modify these parameters in Windows NT, 2000, and 2003, as discussed in Chapter 3 "Using The System Utilities."

If you plan to use more than one OS, it's important to consider which **file system** to use and whether data must be accessible to more than one OS on the same machine. Windows XP can be installed on a FAT (File Allocation Table), FAT32, or an NTFS (New Technology File System) partition. Note that FAT, FAT32, and NTFS are covered in Chapter 1, "Introduction to Windows XP Professional," and Chapter 4, "Managing Windows XP File Systems and Storage." Only NTFS supports the majority of the Windows XP file security features, and a partition formatted with NTFS is invisible to other operating systems that don't support NTFS. If you want to share data between operating systems on the same computer, you need to create a FAT or FAT32 volume.

PLANNING THE INSTALLATION

If you plan on creating a dual-boot or multiboot system with Windows NT Workstation 4.0 and Windows XP Professional, you must create the system in a specific order. First, install Windows NT Workstation 4.0 into its own partition, volume, or hard drive. Second, install Service Pack 4 or greater. This adds NTFS v.5.0 support to Windows NT Workstation 4.0. Third, install Windows XP Professional into its own partition, volume, or hard drive.

Careful planning is essential for the smooth installation of any OS. The importance of checking hardware against the HCL was discussed in Chapter 1, but that's only the beginning. It's also important to consider the following:

- The type of installation you want to perform, such as attended or unattended

- The partition on which the OS files will be stored and how that partition is to be formatted

- Your computer must meet Microsoft's minimum hardware requirements before you attempt an installation. Otherwise, you'll be unable to install the OS properly and will waste a significant amount of time. (See Chapter 1 for a review of the hardware requirements.) The Setup routine performs a system check during installation. If your system fails to meet the minimum requirements, Setup is terminated automatically.

- Windows XP Professional can be installed onto a multiprocessor system that hosts two CPUs. The installation routine automatically configures the system to use multiple CPUs if they are present on the system. However, if you install Windows XP Professional with a single CPU and later add a second CPU, you must reinstall Windows XP or perform an upgrade installation. This is necessary to update the hardware-specific Hardware Abstraction Layer (HAL) (motherboard, CPU, and so on) for multiprocessor support.

You can perform an upgrade installation if your system meets all of the following conditions:

- The current OS is supported as a platform that Windows XP Professional can upgrade (see information earlier in this chapter).

- You want to replace your current OS with Windows XP, retaining as much configuration and setting information as possible.

- You are prepared to handle possible problems or incompatibilities caused by hardware and software under Windows XP that might not be present under the current OS.

You can perform a clean or full installation if at least one of the following is true:

- Your system has a freshly formatted hard drive, or a new blank hard drive has just been installed.

- You want to install Windows XP over your existing OS, but that OS is not on the list of operating systems that support upgrading to Windows XP.

- You want to replace your existing OS with Windows XP.

- You want to create a dual-boot or multiboot configuration with the existing operating system(s) and Windows XP.

TYPES OF ATTENDED INSTALLATIONS

For attended (manual) installations (unattended installations are covered in a later section), you have a choice between a network installation or a CD installation. Use the method that grants the fastest access to the distribution files, meets your current OS and network capabilities, and complies with your organization's deployment policies. If you have a local CD-ROM drive, this is usually faster than pulling the files from a network share. Furthermore, the installation proceeds faster if you can boot from the CD rather than starting from an existing OS, or even using the boot floppies.

Microsoft has created many options to launch the Setup procedure to ensure that at least one method is available to any computer system. Alternatively, you can copy the contents of the Windows XP Professional CD to a local drive with sufficient space and perform the installation from a local folder, as opposed to a CD or a network share.

Installing over the Network

Performing a network installation simply means launching the Setup routine from a network share instead of a local device. To install Windows XP Professional over the network, you must have an existing OS (or a boot floppy) with network connectivity and access privileges to the Windows XP Professional distribution files through a network share (whether that share is a shared CD-ROM drive on a server or a copy of the files on a server's hard drive). The subdirectory that contains the installation files is the \I386 folder on the Windows XP CD. Set the general access permissions (i.e., the Everyone or the Domain Users group) on this share to read-only. The install is initiated by executing the WINNT or WINNT32 command (see the WINNT and WINNT32 section later in this chapter). Some systems allow this command to be executed through My Network Places or Network Neighborhood; other systems support the use of a UNC name (\\servername\I386\WINNT32), and still other systems require that you map a drive to the network share first.

From DOS (and operating systems installed over DOS), drive letters are mapped using the command-line syntax of net use *x*: *servername**directory* (where *x* is the drive letter to which you want to map the shared network directory, *servername* is the name of the server on which the files are stored, and *directory* is the name of the installation directory). On Windows 95, 98, and NT, drive letters are mapped using the Tools, Map Network Drive command in Windows Explorer.

Activity 2-1: Network Installation Setup

Time Required: 15 minutes

Objective: Prepare a Windows 2000 Server or Windows Server 2003 as a network installation point for Windows XP Professional.

Description: When installing any operating system from a CD to a number of workstations, the CD can become a bottleneck and a single point of failure. Using a single CD, only one computer can be set up at a time. If the CD becomes damaged or lost, you have to wait for a replacement before you can continue to install Windows XP. To reduce the amount of time wasted waiting for one install to complete before moving on to the next, it is often a better idea to copy the installation files onto a server that is accessible to all workstations and install from that single point on the network.

To make the Windows XP Professional installation files available for network installations from a Windows 2000 Server computer:

1. Using an Administrator account, log on to the Windows 2000 Server or Windows Server 2003 computer that will be sharing the files.

2. Insert the Windows XP Professional installation CD into the CD-ROM drive on the server. The autorun mechanism opens the CD splash screen and prompts you whether to upgrade. Click **Exit** to close the splash screen.

3. Launch Windows Explorer.

4. Select the CD-ROM drive icon in the left pane.

5. Locate the \I386 directory in the right pane, and drag and drop it to the C: drive icon in the left pane (or another hard drive with at least 500 MB of free space). The entire directory will be copied to your hard drive.

6. Once the copy process is complete, select the **I386 folder** on the hard drive and right-click it. Select **Sharing** from the shortcut menu.

On Windows 2000/2003, the shortcut menu item is Sharing, while on Windows XP, the shortcut menu item is Sharing and Security.

7. Click the **Share this folder** option button. Provide a share name, such as **WXPPro** (see Figure 2–3).

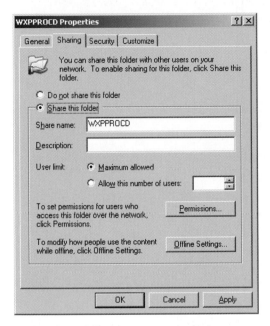

Figure 2-3   Creating a network share

8. Click **Permissions**, and then click **Add**. If not already present as a defined permission, locate and select the **Everyone** group, click **Add**, and then click **OK**.

9. While the Everyone group is highlighted in the Permissions dialog box, verify that the Allow Read access permission has been granted to the Everyone group (see Figure 2-4). If it hasn't been granted, click the **Allow Read** check box. Click **OK** to close the Permissions dialog box. Click **OK** to close the Properties dialog box.

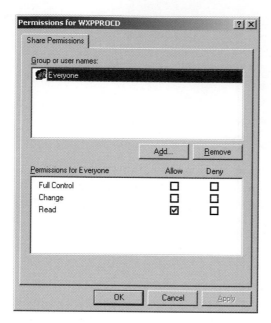

Figure 2-4   The Share Permissions tab of the Permissions for Windows XP Professional dialog box

CD-ROM Installation Launched from Setup Boot Floppies

Another common installation method is using the **setup boot disks** (or **floppies**) to initiate the installation from a local CD-ROM drive. This is the preferred method if you must install storage drivers manually, when your system will not boot from the CD, when an existing OS is not present, or when network access is not available. To initiate this process, place the Windows XP Professional CD into an HCL-compliant CD-ROM drive, place the first of the setup boot floppies in the floppy drive, and then reboot the system. You are prompted to insert each floppy in turn.

If the setup boot floppies aren't available, you can create new ones. The utility to create the boot floppies can be downloaded from the Microsoft downloads area located at the following URL: *www.microsoft.com/downloads*. Search for the tool using the keywords "xp setup disks". Once downloaded, launch this utility, follow the prompts, and insert the preformatted blank floppies when instructed to do so.

Using a Bootable CD

The Windows XP Professional CD is self-booting. Thus, if your computer hardware supports this feature, you can bypass the setup floppies by allowing the computer to boot from the CD. This method is faster than the floppy method, and is the most common installation method for individual installations. This method can be used regardless of the presence of an OS on the system or network access.

If your system supports bootable CDs, it is often a good idea to eject all bootable CDs before rebooting your system. This is especially true if your system automatically boots from bootable CDs instead of prompting you to press a key to boot from the CD upon the initial POST (Power On Self Test). In most cases, it is a good idea to disable bootable CDs through your computer system's CMOS after you've installed Windows XP.

CD-ROM Launch from Existing OS

The Setup process can be launched from an existing OS or from a boot floppy that contains CD-ROM drivers. Launching Setup requires the execution of the WINNT (DOS or Windows 3.x) or WINNT32 (Windows 95, 98, NT, 2000, XP, 2003) file from the \I386 directory.

Important Setup Option Differences

Launching Setup using the various methods mentioned in the previous section results in one of two setup initializations. To make discussion of these two setup initializations a little easier, the two are called the text mode setup method and the GUI setup method.

Text Mode Setup

The text mode setup method is used when you initialize the setup from any method other than launching Setup from a preexisting Windows OS. When Setup is initiated through an existing Windows OS, many of the settings prompts displayed during the text-only portion of Setup are skipped because the settings have already been defined.

GUI Setup Method

The GUI setup method employs an initialization Setup Wizard to preselect or predefine several setup options (i.e., those options for which you are prompted during the text-only portion of Setup). The first option is whether to perform an upgrade installation or a clean installation (see Figure 2-1). An upgrade installation retains as much of the existing system information as possible. A clean installation completely ignores all existing settings. If you perform an upgrade installation, the wizard prompts you to read and agree to the license agreement, then it copies the required files to the hard drive before rebooting the system. Once rebooted, Setup runs through the text-only portion without prompts, then proceeds to the GUI portion.

If you elect to perform a clean installation, the wizard prompts you to read and agree to the license agreement and provide the product key, then prompts you to change setup options. The Setup Options page of the Windows Setup Wizard offers an Advanced Options button, an Accessibility Options button, and a primary language selection pull-down list box. The primary language selection is used to set the base language and region for the system. Accessibility Options are used to enable the magnifier and narrator options for use during Setup.

Advanced Options are used to set the following:

- Source path (default is *cdrom_drive*:\I386)

- Systemroot name (i.e., where Windows XP will be installed; the default is \WINDOWS)

- Whether to copy all files from the CD before rebooting

- Whether to allow manual selection of destination partition during Setup

Mark the check box that allows you to select the destination partition manually during Setup. Otherwise, Setup automatically selects the first partition on the first drive in the system. This location is not always the best choice, especially if you are creating a multiboot system or your first hard drive has insufficient space.

Then, Setup prompts you to decide whether you want to upgrade the drive (i.e., format the destination partition) with NTFS. Next, Setup asks whether you want to download updated setup files from the Microsoft Web site to use for the installation (a.k.a. Dynamic Update). If you have Internet access, this can save you time later. Finally, Setup copies required files to your hard drive, then reboots the system. Once rebooted, Setup starts the text-only portion and continues in much the same manner as the text mode setup method. However, the prompts that have been predefined are skipped.

Dynamic Update is a new feature added to the installation process in Windows XP that enables Setup to download updates and patches for Windows XP before installation actually begins. Thus, after installation is completed, the resulting system is fully up-to-date with all downloadable updates. Dynamic Update downloads the same components offered by the Windows Update tool. If you elect not to allow Dynamic Update during the installation, you can use Windows Update to install the available patches afterward.

ADVANCED CUSTOMIZED INSTALLATION OPTIONS

As the number of clients that need Windows XP installed increases, attended installations become less appealing. Windows XP supports both unattended and customized installation options, both of which are used often in enterprise network deployments. Both options require significant system and setup script preparation and preconfiguration, most of which are automation options. This means the installation of Windows XP can be configured to require little or no human interaction. If you are deploying hundreds or thousands of clients, using one or more unattended installation techniques can greatly reduce the time required to complete the task.

Unattended installations proceed in much the same manner as an attended installation, except that an **answer file** is used to provide the responses to all the setup prompts. In addition, an answer file can be used to install additional applications after the OS installation is complete.

Custom installations are modified versions of Windows XP designed to fit a specific hardware or software configuration. Custom installations can also employ an answer file to provide system-specific answers to the customized installation.

The following sections discuss the various means by which an installation can be automated and customized. However, regardless of the level of automation and customization, planning and managing an enterprise deployment of Windows XP is a complex undertaking.

Automated Installations

Windows XP offers an automated installation option through the use of an answer file, a process known as **unattended installation**. This installation method is often preferred in multiple installations because you don't have to respond to installation prompts, but instead you provide a script containing the appropriate answers. Although it can take a little time and practice to set up an unattended installation, it can save time if you must install Windows XP on several machines. Windows XP further simplifies multiple duplicate installations with the **uniqueness database file (UDF)**. The UDF works in conjunction with the answer file, allowing you to override some settings in the answer file to further streamline the unattended installation process. Rather than creating a new answer file for every change to the installation, you can just specify a separate UDF. Most information is covered in the answer file, but if a setting exists in both the specified UDF and in the answer file, the UDF takes precedence.

Unattended Installations

To initiate an unattended installation, execute WINNT with the /U and /S options, or WINNT32 with the /UNATTEND and /S options. This instructs Setup to perform an unattended installation using the files stored in the location you specify with the /S switch. To further customize the installation, you can use a UDF in combination with an answer file (the file that provides answers to installation prompts for unattended installations; the default sample is called UNATTEND.TXT) by specifying /UDF on the setup command line.

 If you are planning to perform a clean installation on a computer that does not have an operating system installed, and you want to install from a CD in unattended mode, the answer file must be available on a floppy disk and named WINNT.SIF. This file has the same sections and entries as UNATTEND.TXT.

The \I386 directory on the Windows XP Professional CD contains a file called UNATTEND.TXT that is used for configuring unattended installations on that type of platform (it's the answer file under discussion). If you must install several copies of Windows

XP Professional that vary slightly (for example, the username differs), you can use a UDF to supplement the answer file and override its parameters as needed.

The UNATTEND.TXT file included with Windows XP Professional contains default settings for a typical installation, as follows:

```
; Microsoft Windows XP Personal, Professional, Server,
Advanced Server and Datacenter

;(c) 1994 - 2000 Microsoft Corporation. All rights
reserved.
; Sample Unattended Setup Answer File
; This file contains information about how to automate the
installation
; or upgrade of Windows Codename Whistler so the
; Setup program runs without requiring user input.
;
[Unattended]
Unattendmode = FullUnattended
OemPreinstall = NO
TargetPath = *
Filesystem = LeaveAlone

  [UserData]
FullName = "Your User Name"
OrgName = "Your Organization Name"
ComputerName = *
ProductKey= "JJWKH-7M9R8-26VM4-FX8CC-GDPD8"

[GuiUnattended]
; Sets the Timezone to the Pacific Northwest
; Sets the Admin Password to NULL
; Turn AutoLogon ON and login once
TimeZone = "004"
AdminPassword = *
AutoLogon = Yes
AutoLogonCount = 1
[LicenseFilePrintData]
; For Server installs
AutoMode = "PerServer"
AutoUsers = "5"

[GuiRunOnce]
; List the programs that you want to launch when the
machine is logged into for the first time

[Display]
BitsPerPel = 8
XResolution = 800
YResolution = 600
```

```
VRefresh = 70

[Networking]
[Identification]
JoinWorkgroup = Workgroup
```

This file can be modified either manually or with the **Setup Manager Wizard**. The Setup Manager Wizard is a tool used to create UNATTEND.TXT files. Complete details on how to edit this file and all of the possible syntax combinations are contained in the Microsoft Windows XP Professional Resource Kit, which includes the wizard for creating or editing your own fully customized UNATTEND.TXT files.

The Setup Manager Wizard is made available through the Windows Support Tools Setup Wizard (see Activity 2-2) or it can be found in the DEPLOY.CAB file within the \Support\Tools directory on the distribution CD. If you are working from Windows XP, you can access the contents of the .cab file just like any other compressed folder. Double-clicking on the SETUPMGR.EXE file from within the .cab file initiates an extraction process; once extracted to the location of your choice, the file can be executed from its new location. Once launched, the Setup Manager Wizard can be used to create a variety of installation scripts, including the following:

- Duplicate current system's configuration, edit an existing UNATTEND.TXT file, or create a new file from scratch.

- Create uninstall scripts, SYSPREP installation scripts, or RIS installation scripts.

- Create scripts for Windows XP Home Edition, Windows XP Professional, Windows Server 2003, Enterprise Server, or DataCenter Server.

- Fully automated (no user interaction), read-only (user can view settings on each page but no changes can be made), GUI (text portion is automated), provide defaults (recommended settings are defined, but user can change during setup), or hide some configuration setup pages.

Answer Files and UDFs

You can create a UDF in a text editor such as EDIT or Notepad. It should look something like the following:

```
[UniqueIDs]
    UserID1 = Userdata,GuiUnattended,Network
    UserID2 = Userdata,GuiUnattended,Network

 [UserID1:UserData]
 FullName = "Hans Delbruck"
 ComputerName = "Monster"

 [UserID1:GuiUnattended]
 TimeZone = " (GMT+01:00) Prague, Warsaw, Budapest"
```

```
[UserID1:Network]
JoinDomain = "LabTechs"

[UserID2:UserData]
FullName = "Francis N. Stein"
ComputerName = "Doctor"

[UserID2:GuiUnattended]
TimeZone = "(GMT-06:00) Central Time (US & Canada)"

[UserID2:Network]
JoinDomain = "MadScientists"
```

When you've finished the UDF, save it as a text file and store it on disk. It's often helpful to name UDFs for the people using them, because such files are likely to be customized for individuals.

Activity 2-2: Windows XP Support Tools

Time Required: 20 minutes

Objective: Install the Windows XP support tools.

Description: Microsoft has championed the use of "wizards" to simplify the life of end users and support staff alike. In Windows XP Professional, a number of support tools have been made available to the administrator. These support tools have been simplified by putting them into the form of wizards to shorten the learning curve for these features.

To install the Windows XP support tools:

1. Log on to your Windows XP Professional computer with Administrator privileges.

2. Insert the Windows XP Professional CD into the CD-ROM drive. When the splash screen appears, click **Exit** to close it. If any other windows appear, close them as well.

3. Open the Run dialog box by clicking **Start**, and then **Run**.

4. Click **Browse**.

5. Locate the CD-ROM drive, find the \SUPPORT\TOOLS directory, select **SETUP.EXE**, and then click **Open**.

6. Click **OK** to execute the installation.

7. The Windows Support Tools Setup Wizard appears. Click **Next**.

8. Click the **I Agree** option button. Click **Next** to accept the End User License Agreement.

9. Provide your name and organization name (if applicable). Click **Next**.

10. Select the **Typical installation method** (it's the default). Click **Next**. The Complete option installs every available tool and is more suited for administrators. The default installation path is \Program Files\Support Tools.

11. Click **Install Now** to start the installation.

12. When the copying is complete, click **Finish**.

Activity 2-3: Unattended Installation Preparation

Time Required: 20 minutes

Objective: Create an answer file for an unattended installation of Windows XP using the Setup Manager Wizard.

Description: As much as they would like to, network administrators and IT support staff cannot be in more than one place at one time. To allow workstations to be set up without a support person being present, an administrator can create an answer file for the installation(s). The answer file provides the installation process all of the necessary answers that the administrator would normally be entering during the installation. In this way, it is almost as if the administrator can be in many places at one time.

In this activity, you use the Setup Manager Wizard from the Microsoft Windows XP Professional Resource Kit included on the Windows XP Professional distribution CD.

To create an answer file for an unattended installation:

1. Log on to your Windows XP Professional computer with Administrator privileges.

2. Insert the Windows XP Professional CD into the CD-ROM drive. When the splash screen appears, click **Exit** to close it. If any other windows appear, close them as well.

3. Launch Windows Explorer.

4. Open the \SUPPORT\TOOLS folder on the Windows XP distribution CD.

5. Double-click the **DEPLOY.CAB** file.

6. Double-click **SETUPMGR.EXE**.

7. The Select a Destination dialog box appears (see Figure 2-5). Expand **My Computer** and select drive **C**.

Figure 2-5   The Select a Destination dialog box

8. Click **Make New Folder** and name it **setupmgr**.

9. Click **Extract**.

10. Using Windows Explorer, open the \setupmgr folder you just created.

11. Double-click **setupmgr** to launch the Windows Setup Manager Wizard.

12. When the Windows Setup Manager Wizard launches, click **Next**.

13. Select **Create a new answer file** (the default; see Figure 2-6). Click **Next**.

Figure 2-6   The first screen of the Windows Setup Manager Wizard

14. Select **Windows Unattended Installation** answer file. Click **Next**.

15. Select **Windows XP Professional**. Click **Next**.

16. Select **Fully automated** (see Figure 2-7). Click **Next**.

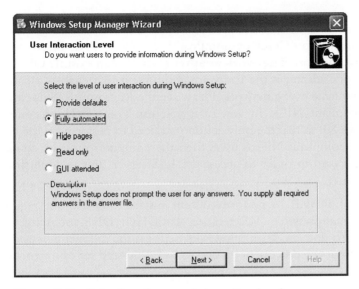

Figure 2-7   Selecting the user interaction level

17. Select **No, this answer file will be used to install from a CD**. Click **Next**.

18. Mark the check box to accept the license agreement. Click **Next**.

19. Provide a name and organization for the answer file. Click **Next**.

20. Proceed through the remainder of the settings screens by providing the requested information or selections and clicking **Next**.

21. Once you reach the Additional Commands page, click **Finish**.

22. Provide the path and filename for the answer file or accept the default filename and location. Click **OK**.

23. The answer file is saved. To create a new file, select **New** from the File menu.

24. To edit an existing answer file, select **File**, **Open**.

25. To close the wizard, select **File**, **Exit**.

Using Remote Installation Service (RIS)

The Remote Installation Service (RIS) is a Windows Server-based service that allows operating systems to be automatically installed onto target systems (e.g., clients) over the network with nothing more in the target system than a NIC and possibly a boot floppy. RIS in Windows XP has been expanded from its limited functionality under Windows 2000. When used from a Windows Server 2003, RIS can install any version of Windows XP and Windows 2003 remotely, along with Windows 2000 Professional, Server, and Advanced Server. (Windows 2000 DataCenter Server cannot be installed remotely with Windows Server 2003 RIS.)

RIS is used to push installations over a network to a client. RIS can install Windows XP on clients that have a Dynamic Host Configuration Protocol (DHCP) PXE-based remote boot ROM, an RIS boot disk-supported **network adapter (NIC)**, or an existing OS. A network interface card or network adapter is the hardware component that enables a computer to connect to and communicate over a network. Please see the Microsoft RIS documentation for a list of PXE-compliant NICs. In any case, you can completely preconfigure the installation of Windows XP so that the only action you need to perform on the client is to power it on. If a PXE-compliant NIC is used, then the computer must be configured to boot from the network card in order to access the RIS server (this is done through the computer's CMOS).

RIS takes advantage of DHCP to perform system installations without requiring the installer to visit the destination system. RIS requires that DHCP, DNS, and Active Directory be present and active on a domain. To employ RIS, perform the following steps (*Note:* This is a high-level overview of the process, not a detailed step-by-step set of instructions):

1. Verify that all systems comply with hardware requirements.

2. Install a Windows 2000 Server or Windows Server 2003 as a standalone/member server. Install Remote Installation Services as an optional component during the installation or after initial installation is complete.

3. If DNS is not already present in the domain, install it.

4. Promote the Windows Server to a domain controller.

5. If DHCP is not already present on the domain, install it.

6. Initiate the configuration procedure for RIS by launching RISETUP.EXE from the Run command. Using the Wizard, configure RIS for your requirements and network design.

7. Authorize RIS with Active Directory through the DHCP Manager.

8. Use the Directory Management snap-in to further configure RIS and define remote installation parameters.

RIS can be used to install just the basic OS or it can be used for the deployment of systems that have all necessary applications installed and all critical settings configured. When RIS is used to deploy fully configured systems, a prototype system is created with all of the needed applications installed and all necessary configuration settings made (this requires the use of the RIPrep tool).

One of the key factors in a successful RIS deployment is to properly install applications. One common mistake is to install applications so that only the local administrator has access. In order to avoid this problem, once the prototype system has been fully installed, the user profile for the local administrator should be copied into the default user profile. Then the Everyone group should be granted Allow Full Control permissions. Thus, when normal users log on for the first time, they receive a copy of the default profile with all of the correct Start menu items and Registry settings for the installed applications.

Using RIS to deploy clients does greatly simplify the installment process, especially when dozens or hundreds of target clients are involved. However, upwards of 1 GB or more of data are transferred to each client. This amount of network traffic can cause a significant reduction in the network performance for all other systems on the network. In order to keep this effect to a minimum, many large organizations designate a single segment as the new client deployment segment. This segment consists of the RIS server and little else. This segment is also isolated from the rest of the network so the traffic occurring here does not degrade the available bandwidth elsewhere. New clients are connected to this segment for the RIS installation process. Once installation is completed, the client is moved to its appointed position out on the production network.

When new target clients are in a different subnet than the RIS and DHCP servers, it is important to properly configure the network's routers to forward DHCP requests from the clients to the DHCP server. Simply having the router configured to forward BOOTP packets is not sufficient, it must be configured to forward the various DHCP packets (e.g., DISCOVER, OFFER, REQUEST, and ACK).

As you can see, employing RIS is not a simple task. For additional details on RIS, see the Microsoft Windows .NET Server or the Windows XP Professional Resource Kit.

Using Windows Installer Service (WIS)

Microsoft has added the Windows Installer Service (WIS) to Windows XP to simplify the deployment of multiple applications onto new clients. WIS combines the setup procedures for multiple applications into a single administrative action. WIS also centralizes application installations and simplifies the daunting task of maintaining updated software throughout a network. For more information on the Windows Installer Service, see the Microsoft Windows .NET Server or Windows XP Professional Resource Kit.

Using Systems Management Server (SMS)

Windows XP can also be installed remotely using Systems Management Server (SMS). However, SMS can only be used to upgrade clients to Windows XP; it does not support clean installations. SMS offers a wide range of controls, including automated application installation and configuration settings control. In most cases, SMS should only be considered if it is already in use on the network; the complexity of SMS outweighs its benefits in remote client upgrade installations.

Using Remote Installation Preparation (RIPrep)

Remote Installation Preparation (RIPrep) is a utility used to create RIS distributable images of a fully configured prototype computer. RIPrep must be used in conjunction with RIS. The basic process for using RIPrep is: first install the base OS onto the target prototype system using RIS; next install all applications and fully customize the prototype system; and finally, use RIPrep to create a new system image of the fully configured prototype. Once the image is created, it is available for installation on RIS target clients. Any target system that receives the fully configured prototype RIS image must have the same HAL but not necessarily the exact same hardware as the original prototyped system.

Using SYSPREP

SYSPREP is a system duplication tool used to duplicate an entire hard drive (a process often called imaging, cloning, or ghosting). This tool is useful when installing Windows XP onto multiple similar systems. However, each system must have at least closely matching, if not almost identical, core hardware configurations. Basically, you install Windows XP onto a single computer, add all applications, and make all configuration changes. This system is the master that is duplicated to the other systems. SYSPREP cannot be used to upgrade a system; it can only be used to perform a full-image installation onto an empty partition or to overwrite an existing OS.

The three files used by SYSPREP are: SYSPREP.EXE, SETUPCL.EXE, and SYSPREP. INF. These files must be in a folder named SYSPREP on the same drive as the main Windows folder or on a floppy. Once the SYSPREP process is completed, the SYSPREP folder is automatically deleted from the hard drive.

The SYSPREP image, if smaller than about 650 MB, can be distributed on a CD as an alternative to network distribution. A CD-based SYSPREP image does not require network connectivity to complete an installation. Plus, if the client supports bootable CDs, then no OS need be present on the client.

SYSPREP enables Windows XP and installed applications to be deployed quickly on multiple computers that have the exact same hardware components. SYSPREP must be used with a third-party disk-imaging product because it only prepares a system for duplication, it does not perform the duplication. Basically, SYSPREP removes the configurable settings of a system that are defined in a typical UNATTEND.TXT file and prepares the system to redetect all Plug and Play devices the next time the system is booted. After the source computer or any duplicated computer is rebooted, a new SID is created automatically. A mini-setup wizard prompts you for local system-specific data, such as computer name, product ID, and username (the mini-wizard can be managed through scripts to fully automate the process), and forces a full redetection of Plug and Play hardware.

To use SYSPREP, you can perform the following general steps:

1. Install Windows XP Professional.

2. Install any additional applications, services, or drivers.

3. Customize and configure the applications and services.

4. Run SYSPREP to prepare the system for duplication. After SYSPREP completes this task, it shuts down the system.

5. Use a disk imaging or duplication product to duplicate the disk.

6. The next time the original system or any duplicated drive is booted, the Windows XP Professional installation redetects Plug and Play devices and prompts you for any information it wasn't able to obtain.

TIP

SYSPREP can be used with a SYSPREP.INF file, which contains the same information and uses the same structure and syntax as the UNATTEND.TXT file created by the Setup Manager. When a customized SYSPREP.INF file is provided for the target system, the installation process does not prompt for setup information. The SYSPREP.INF file can be provided on a floppy or placed in a folder on the system drive (i.e., C:\) named \SYSPREP.

SYSPREP can be used with these command-line parameters (each parameter must be preceded by a dash or hyphen when used):

- *audit*—Reboots the system without generating new SIDs or executing any item in the [OEMRunOnce] section of the WINBOM.INI file. It is used only after the system is already in -factory mode.

- *quiet*—Disables display of confirmation dialog boxes

- *nosidgen*—Prevents the regeneration of the security ID on reboot, and should only be used when you are not cloning the current system or deploying domain controllers

- *pnp*—Forces a full refresh of Plug and Play on next reboot, and should only be used on systems with legacy and non-Plug and Play devices; Plug and Play devices do not need a forced refresh.

- *reboot*—Reboots the system after SYSPREP is finished (default action of SYSPREP is to shut down without rebooting); often used with -factory or to test or audit a system after preparation

- *noreboot*—Shuts down the system but does not reboot after SYSPREP is finished. This option should only be used for testing; do not use this parameter when performing system duplications. This option forces changes to several Registry keys (SID, OemDuplicatorString, etc.), which makes the system unsuitable for duplication. Without this parameter, SYSPREP automatically shuts down without a reboot.

- *clean*—Removes all entries from the critical devices database that is referenced by the [SysprepMassStorage] section of the SYSPREP.INF file.

- *forceshutdown*—Forces a shutdown of the system after SYSPREP is finished. This parameter should be used on systems with an ACPI BIOS that will not shut down properly using the default SYSPREP processes.

- *factory*—Places the OS into factory mode where custom preinstallations of software, updated drivers, changes to the file system, edits to the Registry, etc., can be made. After customization is complete, use the -reseal parameter. See the Microsoft Windows XP OEM Preinstall Kit (OPK) Web site at *www.microsoft.com/oem/* for details.

- *reseal*—Prepares the OS for deployment on customer systems. It is used after the -factory parameter has been used and a system customized.

- *mini*—Configures the system to use a mini-setup wizard instead of Windows Welcome upon next reboot. This parameter only has an effect on Windows XP Professional, not Windows XP Home Edition.

- *activated*—Does not reset the grace period for Windows product activation. This parameter should be used only if XP was activated before duplication.

WINNT AND WINNT32

Earlier in this chapter, there were a number of references to WINNT, WINNT32, and some of the switches that can be used with them. You might be wondering, however, what the difference is between them, why you'd use each one, and what the complete set of switches is for each command. The function of these two command-line tools has changed since their use in Windows 2000 and Windows NT. In Windows XP, they each have a unique and specific purpose. It is in this section that you get the details.

WINNT

WINNT, the 16-bit setup tool, is designed to be launched from DOS and operating systems that rely upon DOS (such as Windows 3.x and Windows for Workgroups 3.x). WINNT is designed for standard and automated installations with few additional options. The command-line syntax for the WINNT command is as follows (this material is taken from the online Help information obtained from the "winnt /?" command):

```
WINNT [/s[:sourcepath]] [/t[:tempdrive]]
[/u[:answer_file]]
[/udf:id[,UDF_file]] [/r:folder] [/rx:folder]
[/e:command] [/a]
```

- /s[:sourcepath]—Specifies the source location of the Windows XP files. The location must be a full path of the form x:\[path] or \\server\share[\path]. The default is the current folder.

- /t[:tempdrive]—Directs Setup to place temporary files on the specified drive and to install Windows XP on that drive. If you do not specify a location, Setup attempts to locate a drive for you.

- /u[:answer_file]—Performs an unattended setup using an answer file (requires /s). The answer file provides answers to some or all of the prompts to which you normally respond during Setup.

- /udf:id[,UDF_file]—Indicates an identifier (id) that Setup uses to specify how a uniqueness database file (UDF) modifies an answer file (see /u). The /udf parameter overrides values in the answer file, and the identifier determines which values in the UDF file are used. If no UDF_file is specified, Setup prompts you to insert a disk that contains the $Unique$.udb file.

- /r[:folder]—Specifies an optional folder to be installed. The folder remains after Setup finishes

- /rx[:folder]—Specifies an optional folder to be copied. The folder is deleted after Setup finishes

- /e—Specifies a command to be run at the end of the GUI-mode portion of Setup

- /a—Enables accessibility options

WINNT32

WINNT32, the 32-bit setup tool, is designed to be launched from 32-bit operating systems (such as all versions of Windows 95, 98, NT, 2000, ME, XP, and 2003). WINNT32 is designed for standard and automated installations and offers several options for source and destination locations as well as debug logging. The command-line syntax for the WINNT32 command is as follows (this material is taken from the online Help information obtained from the "winnt32 /?" command):

```
winnt32 [/checkupgradeonly] [/cmd:command_line]
[/cmdcons] [/copydir:i386\folder_name]
[/copysource:folder_name] [/debug[level]:[filename]]
[/dudisable][/duprepare:pathname] [/dushare:pathname]
[/m:folder_name][/makelocalsource] [/noreboot]
[/s:sourcepath] [/syspart:drive_letter]
[/tempdrive:drive_letter] [/udf:id [,UDB_file]]
[/unattend[num]:[answer_file]]
```

- /checkupgradeonly—Checks your computer for upgrade compatibility with Windows XP. If you use this option with /unattend, no user input is required. Otherwise, the results are displayed on the screen, and you can save them under the filename you specify. The default filename is UPGRADE.TXT in the systemroot folder.

- /cmd:command_line—Instructs Setup to carry out a specific command before the final phase of setup. This would occur after your computer has restarted and after Setup has collected the necessary configuration information but before the setup is complete.

- /cmdcons—Installs the Recovery Console as a startup option on a functioning computer. The Recovery Console is a command-line interface from which you can perform tasks, such as starting and stopping services and accessing the local drive (including drives formatted with NTFS). You can use the /cmdcons option only after normal setup is finished.

- /copydir:i386*folder_name*—Creates an additional folder within the folder in which the Windows XP files are installed. *Folder_name* refers to a folder that you have created to hold modifications just for your site. For example, you could create a folder called Private_drivers within the I386 source folder for your installation and place driver files in the folder. Then you could type /copydir:i386\Private_ drivers to have Setup copy that folder to your newly installed computer, making the new folder location systemroot\Private_drivers. You can use /copydir to create as many additional folders as you want.

- /copysource:*folder_name*—Creates a temporary additional folder within the folder in which the Windows XP files are installed. *Folder_name* refers to a folder that you have created to hold modifications just for your site. For example, you could create a folder called Private_drivers within the source folder for your installation and place driver files in the folder. Then you could type/copysource:Private_drivers to have Setup copy that folder to your newly installed computer and use its files during setup, making the temporary folder location systemroot\Private_drivers. You can use /copysource to create as many additional folders as you want. Unlike the folders /copydir creates, /copysource folders are deleted after Setup is completed.

- /debug[level]:[*filename*]—Creates a debug log at the level specified, for example, /debug4:Debug.log. The default log file is C:\systemroot\Winnt32.log, and the default debug level is 2. The log levels are as follows: 0 represents severe errors, 1 represents errors, 2 represents warnings, 3 represents information, and 4 represents detailed information for debugging. Each level includes the levels below it.

- /dudisable—Prevents Dynamic Update from running. Without Dynamic Update, Setup runs only with the original setup files. This option disables Dynamic Update even if you use an answer file and specify Dynamic Update options in that file.

- /duprepare:*pathname*—Carries out preparations on an installation share so that it can be used with Dynamic Update files that you downloaded from the Windows Update Web site. This share can then be used for installing Windows XP for multiple clients.

- /dushare:*pathname*—Specifies a share on which you previously downloaded Dynamic Update files (updated files for use with Setup) from the Windows Update Web site, and on which you previously ran /duprepare:*pathname*. When run on a client, this parameter specifies that the client installation makes use of the updated files on the share specified in pathname.

- /m:*folder_name*—Specifies that Setup copies replacement files from an alternate location. Instructs Setup to look in the alternate location first, and if files are present, to use them instead of the files from the default location.

- /makelocalsource—Instructs Setup to copy all installation source files to your local hard disk. Use /makelocalsource when installing from a CD to provide installation files when the CD is not available later in the installation.

- /noreboot—Instructs Setup not to restart the computer after the file copy phase of setup is completed so that you can execute another command.

- /s:sourcepath—Specifies the source location of the Windows XP files. To copy files from multiple servers simultaneously, type the /s:sourcepath option multiple times (to a maximum of eight). If you type the option multiple times, the first server specified must be available or setup fails.

- /syspart:*drive_letter*—Specifies that you can copy setup startup files to a hard disk, mark the disk as active, and then install the disk in another computer. When you start that computer, it automatically starts with the next phase of Setup. You must always use the /tempdrive parameter with the /syspart parameter. You can start WINNT32 with the /syspart option on a computer running Windows NT 4.0, Windows 2000, Windows XP, or Windows 2003. The computer cannot be running Windows 95, Windows 98, or Windows ME.

- /tempdrive:*drive_letter*—Directs Setup to place temporary files on the specified partition. For a new installation, Windows XP is also installed on the specified partition. For an upgrade, the /tempdrive option affects the placement of temporary files only; the OS is upgraded in the partition from which you run WINNT32.

- /udf:id [,UDB_file]—Indicates an identifier (id) that Setup uses to specify how a uniqueness database (UDB) file modifies an answer file (see the /unattend entry). The UDB overrides values in the answer file, and the identifier determines which values in the UDB file are used. For example, /udf:RAS_user, Our_company.udb overrides settings specified for the RAS_user identifier in the Our_company.udb file. If no UDB_file is specified, Setup prompts the user to insert a floppy disk that contains the $Unique$.udb file.

- /unattend—Upgrades your previous version of Windows 98, Windows ME, Windows NT 4.0, or Windows 2000 in unattended setup mode. All user settings are taken from the previous installation, so no user intervention is required during setup.

- /unattend[num]:[answer_file]—Performs a fresh installation in unattended setup mode. The specified answer_file provides Setup with your custom specifications. Num is the number of seconds Setup waits after it finishes copying the files before it restarts your computer. You can use num on any computer running Windows

98, Windows ME, Windows NT, Windows 2000, Windows XP, or Windows 2003. Using the /unattend command-line option to automate Setup affirms that you have read and accepted the Microsoft License Agreement for Windows XP. Before using this command-line option to install Windows XP on behalf of an organization other than your own, you must confirm that the end user (whether an individual or an entity) has received, read, and accepted the terms of the Microsoft License Agreement for Windows XP. OEMs might not specify this key on machines being sold to end users.

The WINNT and WINNT32 syntax information was taken directly from the Help information obtained by using the /? parameter for each of these commands at the command prompt.

PARTITIONING THE HARD DISK

You might want to partition your hard disk before installing Windows XP Professional, for reasons such as the following:

- Some people wish to create a partition for Windows XP itself and another partition for their data files.

- When creating a multiboot system, you need separate partitions for each OS.

- Many people create a DOS boot partition that's accessible when booting from a floppy so they can run diagnostic software and utilities that run only on DOS. They can still store data in a more secure NTFS partition that is inaccessible unless the system is booted to Windows XP.

Although it's possible to install Windows XP on a FAT or FAT32 partition, neither version of FAT provides the advanced security features of NTFS, so you must determine which file system (or which combination of file systems) is most appropriate for your needs. Chapter 4 "Managing Windows XP File Systems and Storage" discusses the criteria for choosing a file system and details the capabilities and implications of choosing file systems supported by Windows XP. For now, suffice it to say that FAT/FAT32 partitions provide no security; if you require the assignment of rights to system resources, NTFS is the file system to use. There are other deciding factors as well, as covered in detail in Chapter 4. Partition selection is covered in more detail under the Text-only Portion of Setup section of this chapter.

Right now, it's important to know that the **active partition** is the partition that houses the Windows XP boot files. This is very important: if the computer doesn't know where to look for the boot files, it can't start. You can use the DOS **FDISK** utility to partition the hard disk before installation, or you can use the partitioning interface encountered during Setup.

The DOS FDISK utility can be used to create and delete partitions. However, it has limited capabilities with NTFS. FDISK can see and delete only primary NTFS partitions. FDISK cannot see or delete NTFS-formatted logical drives in an extended partition. The tool DELPART can be used to delete any type of partition from a hard drive, including NTFS.

TIP

The active partition from which the computer initially boots is termed the system partition. The system partition hosts the boot menu files. The partition where the main Windows XP OS files reside is termed the boot partition. These terms can seem backward, but they are the official Microsoft terms. The system and boot partition can be the same partition.

ACTIVITY

Activity 2-4: Disk Partitioning

Time Required: 10 minutes

Objective: Remove and create partitions using the FDISK command.

Description: Even in the "dark ages" before Windows, there was a need to change the partition configuration of disk drives. The DOS method of performing this task was and still is the FDISK utility. This is a text-based utility that allows the user to delete, create, set active, and display partitions and their information. Unlike utilities such as Partition Magic, however, all data on the partition/disk is destroyed. Please remember to back up data whenever you use FDISK or any other utility to modify a partition—just to be on the safe side.

To use the FDISK utility to divide the hard disk into two partitions:

CAUTION

Back up any data currently on the disk before repartitioning it! FDISK (or any partitioning utility) permanently destroys any data currently on the hard disk.

1. Boot the computer to DOS by selecting it from the boot menu (if it is listed) or by using a DOS boot disk provided by your instructor.

2. Move to the directory containing the FDISK utility. (To find it, type **DIR FDISK.* /s** to search all subdirectories on the current disk.)

3. Type **FDISK** and press **Enter** to start the utility. When FDISK starts, you see a menu of the following four options:

   - Create DOS partition or Logical DOS Drive
   - Set active partition
   - Delete partition or Logical DOS Drive
   - Display partition information

NOTE

If your computer has more than one hard disk, you'll see a fifth option, Change current fixed drive. Additionally, you may get a prompt that states "Your computer has a disk larger than 512MB. Do you wish to enable large disk support?" Select Yes and continue with the following steps.

TIP

You may see a prompt that states "Should NTFS partitions on all drives be treated as Large (Y/N)." If you do see the prompt, press Y on your keyboard and continue with the following steps.

4. Type **4** and then press **Enter** to view the partitions currently on the hard disk. In this example, it is assumed that you see a single primary DOS partition. After reviewing the information, press **Esc** to return to the main menu. If no primary partitions are present, skip to Step 9.

5. Once at the main menu screen, type **3** and press **Enter** to delete the primary partition. When asked which partition to delete, type **1** and press **Enter**.

6. When prompted, type the volume label (if any) for the partition you're deleting. The label is listed at the top of the screen with other volume information. If there is no volume label, just press **Enter**. (Note: If you have more than one partition, you may be prompted for the partiton number before being prompted for the label.)

7. Type **Y** and press **Enter** to confirm the deletion of the selected partition.

8. Press **Esc** to return to the main menu.

9. From the main menu, type **1** and press **Enter** to choose to create a DOS partition. Then, type **1** and press **Enter** to create a Primary DOS partition.

10. Type **N** and press **Enter** when asked whether you want to use the maximum available space. When prompted, type in the size (in megabytes) or percentage of disk space of the partition you want to create and press **Enter**. For installing Windows XP, a drive size of 2 GB or more is recommended. Press **Esc** to return to the main menu.

11. From the main menu, type **2** and press **Enter** to set the active partition. When prompted, type **1** to choose the partition you just created.

12. Press **Esc** to return to the main menu, then **Esc** again to exit FDISK.

13. Press **Esc** to reboot the computer. You need to install an OS (such as Windows XP) to format the partition.

NOTE

It's unnecessary to partition the remaining space on the drive now; you can do that while installing Windows XP.

VOLUME LICENSING

In order for your installation of Windows XP Professional to be valid and legal you must have a user license. If you purchase a Windows XP Professional product package from a brick-and-mortar or an online retail store, you receive an original installation CD along with a special 25-digit product key. If you need to install Windows XP Professional on more than a handful of systems, then purchasing a volume license makes more sense financially. When you purchase a volume license, you obtain a special volume license version of the Windows XP Professional installation CD along with a list of your special volume license product keys. The consumer product key does not work with a volume license installation CD, and a volume license product key does not work with a consumer installation CD. Attempting to do so results in an error stating "Invalid product key," and you are unable to complete the installation.

Microsoft offers several levels or types of volume licensing. For example, you can purchase as few as five licenses in volume or as many as 100,000 or more. For complete details on volume licensing and how to purchase them, please visit the Windows XP Professional Volume Licensing Discounts for Organizations Web site at *www.microsoft.com/windowsxp/ pro/howtobuy/pricingvolume.asp*.

ACTIVATING WINDOWS XP

Microsoft has begun a serious campaign against software piracy. As it becomes easier and easier to trade applications anonymously over the Internet, Microsoft wants to curb the number of pirated copies of its operating systems. One of the latest innovations in this area is **product activation**, a mechanism by which a product has a finite initial functional lifetime. For Windows XP, this period is 30 days, after which the product must be activated to continue functioning. The process of activation is a type of registration in which the product, its product key, and the hardware signature of your computer are correlated and enrolled in a Microsoft database. Microsoft assures their product users that the process of activation is completely anonymous, yet specific enough to prevent the same product key from being reused on a different computer.

Activation has both benefits and drawbacks. One benefit is that it ensures that you've purchased a fully licensed and valid product and did not inadvertently obtain a pirated copy. Unfortunately, the drawbacks of activation are many. First and foremost, if you make a significant change to your hardware, your activation can be invalidated. What constitutes a significant change has not been defined fully by Microsoft. It definitely means changing motherboards, but can also include changing a drive controller, video controller, or adding additional CPUs. In any case, you can reactivate, but you have to contact Microsoft directly by phone. A second drawback is that activation must be completed even if you don't have Internet access. Activation is quick and painless if you have Internet access. If not, you need to activate your product by phone. Microsoft has set up dedicated activation numbers and has included complete information on phone activation in the README.TXT file on the distribution CD and through the Activate Windows Wizard.

After the initial installation, you have 30 days to activate your product before it no longer fully functions. Afterward, Windows XP functions only enough to allow you to complete a product activation. Windows XP reminds you every few days about activation through a pop-up window.

Activation can be completed during or after setup. You are prompted to activate during setup as long as you don't join a domain, or activation can be automated if you use an unattended setup mechanism. After setup, activation can be initiated manually through the Start menu. The Activate Windows command appears at the top of the All Programs section of the Start menu (before activation only) and in the All Programs, Accessories, System Tools subsection.

The Activate Windows Wizard offers three options: activate Windows over the Internet, activate Windows over the telephone with a customer service representative, or to skip activation now but remind you every few days.

The Internet option is usually completed in seconds. To complete an Internet-based activation simply select Yes, let's activate Windows over the Internet now, click Next, select whether to Register (select No), click Next, then click Finish. That's it.

To activate Windows XP over the phone, select the second option of Yes, I want to telephone a customer service representative to activate Windows, then click Next. A how-to page is displayed detailing the four steps necessary to complete activation:

1. Select your location (i.e., the country from which you are calling). This causes the correct toll-free and toll-charged telephone numbers for you to appear.

2. Call one of the numbers displayed to speak with a customer service representative. Follow any instructions given to you by the Microsoft activation customer service representative.

3. Sometime during the call, you are asked to provide the installation ID. This 50-digit number is displayed in Step 3.

4. The Microsoft activation customer service representative then reads back to you a confirmation ID in 6-digit blocks. As you are given these digits, type them into the text fields provided (labeled A through G). Once the entire confirmation ID has been entered, click Next. At this point Windows XP is activated and is now ready for use. Clicking Finish closes the Activation Wizard dialog box and returns you to the desktop.

The Microsoft activation customer service representative might ask you to change your product key through the Change Product Key button. This button should be used only if specifically instructed to do so.

Activation is considered mandatory. That is, it's mandatory if you want to use Windows XP for longer than 30 days. When you perform the activation process, you are also prompted to register with Microsoft. Registration is optional; it is simply the mechanism by which Microsoft obtains demographic information about its product users and signs them up to receive Microsoft advertisement and promotional mailings. You are only prompted to Register when using the Internet activation process.

If you want or need more information about Activation, please visit the Windows XP Product Activation Web page at *www.microsoft.com/windowsxp/pro/evaluation/overviews/activation.asp*. On this page there is a link to a video that clearly explains and demonstrates the various means to activate Windows XP.

WINDOWS XP PROFESSIONAL SETUP: STEP-BY-STEP FROM FLOPPIES OR FROM A BOOTABLE CD

Installing Windows XP Professional is not difficult. You should be able to perform a typical installation without a hitch. In this section, you walk through a clean installation using the six setup boot floppies and a local CD-ROM drive, based on the following assumptions:

- Your computer's hardware is HCL-compliant and all required device drivers are found on the distribution CD.

- Your computer has no preexisting operating systems installed.

- You have the six setup floppies. If you don't already have the setup floppies, follow the instructions in the section Creating Setup Boot Floppies located earlier in this chapter.

- You will select the default or typical settings for this installation.

- You will be using a specific IP address. You must know the IP address, subnet mask, and default gateway. If you don't know these yet, you can use 172.16.1.1 for the IP address and 255.255.0.0 for the subnet mask as working placeholders.

- You will be a member of an existing domain. You'll need to know the name of this domain and the authentication information for an Administrator account. If a domain is not available, you can choose to join a workgroup and give it any name you want.

- The connecting network offers Internet access to clients. This means you need to know your default gateway (that's the IP address of the router or proxy system acting as the gateway to the Internet). You might also need the IP addresses of one or two DNS (Domain Name System) servers from the Internet. Your network administrator or your Internet service provider (ISP) should be able to provide this information. See Chapter 8, "Internetworking with Remote Access," for more details on Internet connectivity. If you are using DHCP, information such as the subnet mask and DNS server(s) is provided automatically.

If your computer system supports bootable CDs, then you can launch the installation process straight from the CD-ROM drive. To launch the installation straight from the installation CD, configure your computer to boot from the CD, place the CD into the CD-ROM drive, turn the power on to your system, and if prompted indicate to boot from the CD. (*Note:* Some systems require you to press the spacebar to boot from the CD, while others automatically boot from the CD if a bootable CD is discovered in the CD-ROM drive.) Once the system starts to boot from the CD, it inspects your system then it displays the license agreement. If you start at Step 7 in Activity 2-5, you can complete the installation following the rest of the steps from that activity.

The Windows XP installation procedure is fairly self-regulating and self-healing. In most cases, if you hit a snag, starting over or just rebooting often resolves the issue. However, in those instances when you can't seem to get the installation to work properly, you should see Chapter 15, "Troubleshooting Windows XP," and review the Troubleshooting Installation Problems section.

Now that these preparation details are out of the way, you can get started.

Activity 2-5: Manual Install of Windows XP

ACTIVITY

Time Required: 1 hour, 45 minutes (depending on your computer hardware)

Objective: Install Windows XP without using any of the automated features (unattend file, RIS, imaging, etc.)

Description: Manually installing Windows XP Professional is similar to previous versions of Windows NT kernel operating systems (NT, 2000). Booting from floppies or a CD to initiate the install, the user then responds to questions starting with prompts being presented in a text-based screen. Once a cursory version of Windows is installed, the install process switches over to a GUI-based screen to complete the install. The only real difference in the Window XP install process is that at the end of the installation, the user is prompted to activate their Windows XP installation. This is Microsoft's latest attempt at reducing the number of pirated installs of its operating systems.

To manually install Windows XP Professional:

1. Insert the first setup boot floppy disk into the floppy drive or CD into the CD-ROM drive.

2. Turn on the computer. If your system supports bootable CDs, you may be prompted to press any key to boot from CD [watch for it since it may appear and disappear quickly right after the POST (power on self-test) sequence] and then proceed to Step 4.

3. After data is copied from the first disk, you are prompted to insert Disk #2. Remove Disk #1, insert Disk #2, then press **Enter**. Repeat this for Disks #3, #4, #5, and #6.

4. After Disk #6, or after the boot process from the CD is complete, the Windows XP Professional setup routine prompts you whether to setup, repair, or quit:

   Press **Enter** to continue with the installation.

5. Setup prompts you to insert the Windows XP Professional CD into your local CD-ROM drive. Do so, and then press **Enter** to continue.

6. Setup then inspects your hard drives. This should take only a few seconds.

If your computer employs new hardware, especially drive controllers, such as brand new SCSI or IDE controller technology, the Windows XP installation CD may not include drivers for the new hardware. During this phase of the text-mode setup, the status line at the bottom of the screen displays a prompt to press F6 if you need to install any OEM drivers. The setup process only pauses for a few seconds, so be ready for this. Once you press F6, you are prompted to insert a floppy with the OEM driver. Once the driver is loaded, the setup process continues. Don't forget to remove the floppy before the reboot at Step 12.

7. Next, you are presented with the license agreement. Using the Page Down key, scroll through this document. Once you've read it, press **F8** to continue with the installation.

8. Next, Setup searches for preexisting operating systems on your computer. If any are found, you are prompted whether to perform a repair or to continue with a clean installation. Because it is assumed you are installing onto a new system, press **Esc** to continue with a clean installation.

9. Next, you are prompted for the destination drive and partition where Windows XP Professional is to be installed. Using the arrow keys, you can select either a preexisting partition or an area of unpartitioned space. Because it is assumed you are installing onto a new computer, there should be only unpartitioned space. Select the unpartitioned space on the first (or only) hard drive, then press **Enter**.

If you do not want to make the largest partition possible, then you can create a partition manually using the C command (in this context, C stands for Change the partition size). First select an unpartitioned space, then press C. You are prompted for the size of the partition to create. Once created, the newly created partition can be selected from the original drive and partition list. If you need to delete an existing partition, you can do so by selecting it and pressing D. You need to confirm this process, so be sure to read the next screen and follow its instructions. Once the partition has been deleted, the list of drives and partitions is updated. Be careful when using this interface, because changes are made immediately to the drive's configuration.

10. Next, Setup prompts for the type of file system to use when formatting the selected destination partition. The file system currently in use is the default selection. We recommend sticking with the default (format with NTFS) and pressing **Enter**.

The list of options includes only versions of FAT and NTFS. NTFS is the recommended file system for Windows XP and supports volumes (i.e., partitions) up to 2 terabytes. Partitions up to 4 GB can be supported by the FAT file system. If a partition larger than 2 GB is used (even though its maximum volume size is 4 GB) and FAT is selected, setup automatically formats the partition with FAT32. FAT32 has the same features as FAT but can support volumes up to 32 GB (i.e., its maximum file size is still 4 GB).

You also have the option of selecting a quick format versus the normal format. Quick format only erases the directory structure. If the destination partition was preformatted, you can choose the quick option. However, if you are using a new hard drive, just created a new partition, or are overwriting an existing partition, use the normal option.

11. Setup formats your selected partition. This can take considerable time for larger partitions. Once the formatting is complete, Setup reinspects the hard drive(s), builds a file list, then starts copying files from the CD. This process can take even longer than the formatting. Fortunately, both the formatting and the copying processes display a progress bar. Eventually, the copy process is complete. Remove Disk #6 from the floppy drive and press **Enter**. (*Note*: If you are performing an installation using just the bootable installation CD, there is no need to remove any floppies since there are none present.)

12. After 15 seconds, Setup reboots automatically and takes you into the GUI (graphical user interface) portion of the Windows XP Professional setup process. If your system has a bootable CD, eject the CD before rebooting (if your system always boots from a bootable CD if present) or do not press the spacebar when your system prompts you to do so (if your system always prompts for confirmation to boot from a bootable CD). If Setup needs it again before installation is complete, it prompts for it.

13. Eventually the Regional and Language Options page of the Setup Wizard appears. If you need to alter the defaults of English/United States for standards and formats, or text input languages, use the Customize and Details buttons. Otherwise, click **Next** to continue.

While working through the GUI portion of the setup, be very careful when clicking the Next button. Often the system takes several seconds or even a minute to alter the display even after you've clicked the Next button. You should click the Next button only *once* and wait until the system responds, or wait at least five minutes, before clicking again. Otherwise, you might inadvertently skip a page of the Wizard, and in some cases, you are unable to use the Back button. If you suspect that you have skipped a Wizard page and are unable to reach it with the Back button, you can cycle the power on your computer to restart the GUI portion of setup.

14. Next, you are prompted for your name and an organization name. Type these in the appropriate fields. You can leave the Organization field blank if you are an individual. Click **Next** to continue.

2

15. Next, you are prompted for the Windows product key. This key can be found in the documentation you received when you purchased your copy of Windows XP. Carefully type it, and click **Next** to continue.

16. Next, you are prompted for a computer name and the password for the Administrator user account. Provide these in the appropriate fields. Click **Next**.

17. If a modem is present in your computer and is properly detected by Setup, you are prompted for your area code. Provide this. Click **Next**.

18. Setup prompts you to set and confirm the time, date, and time zone. Set these. Click **Next**.

19. Setup loads drivers for the networking components it has detected. You are prompted to either accept these default settings or change them. If you are using DHCP clients and servers, accepting the typical settings is sufficient. If you need to specify an IP address, you must select the custom settings. It is assumed you are using an assigned IP address, so select **Custom settings**. Click **Next**.

20. Setup displays the name of the detected NIC near the top of the dialog box. The following network components are listed in a center field: Client for Microsoft Networks, File and Printer Sharing for Microsoft Networks, QoS Packet Scheduler, and Internet Protocol (TCP/IP). (Others can be listed by default as well.) You need to make changes only to the protocol, so select **Internet Protocol (TCP/IP)** and click **Properties**. This opens the Internet Protocol (TCP/IP) Properties dialog box. Select the **Use the following IP address** option button, and then fill in the fields for IP address (either the one you are assigned or the placeholder 172.16.1.1), subnet mask (either the one you are assigned or the placeholder 255.255.0.0), and default gateway (either the one you are assigned or leave this blank). Fill in any of the applicable optional settings, and click **OK** when finished. Then click **Next** to complete the Custom settings for Networking.

21. Next, you are prompted for the name of the workgroup or domain of which this system will be a member. Select the **Workgroup** or **Computer Domain Name** option button, then provide the appropriate name in the text field (if a workgroup or domain on the network is detected, that name is used by default). Click **Next** to continue.

22. If you selected to join a domain, you are prompted for the name and password of an Administrator account in that domain. This is used to create a computer account in the domain for your new Windows XP Professional system. Provide these details, then click **OK**.

23. Setup installs and configures the remainder of the system components. This can take nearly 30 minutes. If the installation routine encounters any problems, a dialog box appears offering you the opportunity to view the SETUPERR.LOG file of these errors. Click **Yes** to view it now, or click **No**.

24. Eventually, Setup needs to reboot again. This can occur automatically, or you might be prompted to confirm the reboot.

25. After the reboot, you must perform a few final configuration steps. After the components of Windows XP have been installed, you are prompted to configure the regional and personal settings. These include your time zone and screen resolution. If you joined a workgroup, skip to Step 32.

26. If you joined a domain, the Network Identification Wizard appears. Click **Next**.

27. The User Account page of the Network Identification Wizard can be used to create an administrative-level user account. In most cases, this is not recommended; it's better to create administrative accounts after the installation is complete. Select the **Do not add a user at this time** option button. Click **Next**.

28. Click **Finish**.

29. The Welcome to Windows logon prompt is displayed. Press **Ctrl+Alt+Delete**.

30. The Log On to Windows dialog box appears. Provide the password for the Administrator account (the administrator username is already provided by default), or provide both the username and password of a domain user account. Click **OK** (or press **Enter**).

31. After several minutes of processing and establishing user profile defaults, the desktop is displayed. You've successfully logged on and completed the installation of Windows XP Professional. At this point, Windows XP is fully installed; however, you still need to activate Windows XP (see the Activating Windows XP section earlier in this chapter).

32. Joining a workgroup results in a slightly different end-of-installation process. The Welcome to Microsoft Windows XP screen appears. An animated Wizard audibly welcomes you to Windows XP. Once the audio is complete, click **Next**. (*Note:* The audio welcome plays even if you do not have sound capabilities; you must wait until the introduction is complete and the Next button turns green before proceeding.)

33. The system is checked automatically for Internet connectivity. No matter what is found, you are prompted to indicate whether the system gains Internet access through a local network or through a dial-up connection. Assuming you have Internet connectivity through your network, click the appropriate option button. Click **Next**.

34. The Ready to activate Windows dialog box appears. Select the **Yes, activate Windows over the Internet now** option button unless you have a specific reason not to do so. You can always activate Windows XP later from the Start menu or taskbar (see the Activating Windows XP section earlier in this chapter). Click **Next**.

35. The Ready to register with Microsoft screen appears. Registration is optional. Click the **No, I don't want to register now, let's just activate Windows** option button. Click **Next**.

36. The Who will use this computer? screen is displayed. Type at least one user name in the fields provided. Click **Next**.

37. The Thank You! page appears. Click **Finish**. The Windows XP Welcome screen appears; If you entered more than one user in the "Who will use this computer?" screen, you must choose the appropriate username, and supply a password, if prompted. If you did not enter more than one user, the desktop will appear.

Once Windows XP Professional has been installed, you need to apply service packs and other updates. These updates are necessary to provide the best security available and to correct problems and bugs with the OS. The process of installing service packs and updates can be accomplished through several means. You can predownload the necessary service packs and updates and configure the installation process to include them automatically, you can slipstream a service pack into a copy of the installation files off of the CD, you can configure the OS to download updates automatically, or you can visit the Windows Update Web page and control downloads manually. These options are discussed in Chapter 14 "Windows XP Professional Fault Tolerance," under the section Automatic Updates and Windows Update and in Chapter 15 "Troubleshooting Windows XP" under the section Applying Service Packs and Hot Fixes.

UPGRADING TO MULTIPLE PROCESSORS

It is becoming a common practice to purchase computer hardware that is capable of supporting multiple CPUs while only initially installing a single CPU onto the motherboard. Once Windows XP Professional is installed, you need to update the HAL before installing a second CPU into the system. If you fail to properly update the HAL, a STOP error indicating a HAL mismatch occurs upon attempted reboot.

The process of updating the HAL is not difficult. The complete step-by-step details on performing this operation are found on the Use Device Manager to Switch from Uniprocessor to Multiprocessor Support Web page at *www.microsoft.com/windows2000/techenthusiast/tricks/administration/uniprocessor.asp*. These instructions are written for Windows 2000, but they are exactly the same for Windows XP. For the details on which HAL option to select, see the Microsoft Knowledge Base article 309283 "HAL Options After Windows XP or Windows Server 2003 Setup" at *http://suport.microsoft.com/default. aspx?scid=kb;en-us;309283*.

REMOVING WINDOWS XP PROFESSIONAL

Unlike most other Windows operating systems, Windows XP offers an uninstall or rollback capability; however, it is supported only when an upgrade is performed over Windows 95/98/OSR2/SE/ME. When an upgrade installation is performed over one of these versions of Windows 9x, Setup automatically creates backup files, which consume about 300 MB of drive space in addition to the 650 MB needed by Windows XP itself.

This rollback feature not only allows you to uninstall Windows XP and return to your previous OS, it also protects you during the upgrade installation. If the installation fails, Setup automatically restores the system to its preinstallation attempt state. If you do not use this rollback capability after 60 days, you are prompted whether to retain the rollback data or delete it to free up the drive space.

To employ the rollback, you need only use the Add or Remove Programs applet. Just select the Windows XP item from the list and click the Change/Remove button. Follow the simple wizard to confirm the removal, and after the rollback is complete, the system reboots to your previous OS.

If you did not upgrade from Windows 9x, there is no simple uninstall or rollback capability available to you in Windows XP. In fact, you have to be quite determined to remove Windows XP. Windows XP can be removed from a system in one of two ways. One option is to destroy the partition(s) where Windows XP has made its mark (i.e., the boot and system partitions), then repartition, format, and install some other OS. The other option is available only if you installed Windows XP onto a FAT (not FAT32) partition. In this case, just delete all of the Windows XP files and rebuild the MBR (typically with the MS-DOS command FDISK /MBR). It is also a good idea to have a DOS or Windows boot disk that contains sys.com for reapplying the system files after using the /MBR switch.

The easiest method of removing Windows XP is to destroy the installation and start fresh with another OS. Because this process most likely destroys data, especially if it is on the boot or system partitions, the first step should be to back up all data that you consider important.

Activity 2-6: Removing Windows XP

Time Required: 15 minutes

Objective: Remove Windows XP and prepare the computer for another operating system.

Description: Although Microsoft operating systems seem to be the most commonly installed OSs on PCs, and Windows XP Professional is the latest desktop OS offered by Microsoft, there are still times when a computer must be prepared for a different operating system to be installed on it. The setup process of Windows XP provides a method for completely removing all traces of Windows XP from the computer.

WARNING! If you perform this activity, the Windows XP operating system is removed from your computer. You will be required to install an OS before you will be able to use the computer.

To remove Windows XP:

1. Boot the computer using the setup boot floppies or a bootable CD, as if you were installing Windows XP.

2. Continue through the same setup steps as described earlier in this chapter in Activity 2-5.

3. Once you reach the step that prompts you for the destination drive and partition, use this interface to delete all partitions (or at least all NTFS partitions). Use the arrow

keys to select each partition, press **D** to delete, then **L** to confirm. Once all partitions are deleted, press **F3** to exit. You have to confirm the termination of Setup by pressing **F3** again.

4. At this point, your computer's hard drive is not partitioned. Use a DOS disk or a Windows 95/98/NT installation boot disk to start the installation process for another OS.

TIP

In addition to Setup's built-in capabilities for deleting partitions, you could also employ another Microsoft tool, DELPART (as mentioned earlier in this chapter).

CHAPTER SUMMARY

❑ In this chapter, you learned how to install and uninstall Windows XP Professional and became acquainted with all the tools and information necessary to do so.

❑ You learned how to choose hardware for a successful installation, how to install Windows XP both locally and across the network, how to use the switches that come with WINNT and WINNT32, and how to run Setup. You also learned about answer files and performing an unattended network installation.

❑ The Remote Installation Service (RIS) was discussed, and you learned the basic steps to install this service.

❑ Imaging (or ghosting) a Windows workstation is a handy skill to have when installing the OS on multiple workstations.

❑ The FDISK DOS utility can be used to partition hard drives.

❑ Windows XP, unlike earlier versions of the Windows OS, needs to be activated on each computer, or the license expires thirty days after installation.

❑ There are differences between upgrading and installing Windows XP, and these differences mean that the information you must provide during setup may be different.

KEY TERMS

active partition — The partition the computer uses to boot.

activating Windows — A new Microsoft requirement to prevent software piracy by registering installations of Windows XP with the signature of its supporting hardware.

answer file — A text file, also called a response file, that contains a set of instructions for installing Windows XP.

boot loader — The software that shows all operating systems currently available and, through a menu, permits the user to choose which one should be booted.

BOOT.INI — The text file that creates the Windows XP boot loader's menu.

clean installation — The installation method in which an OS is installed without regard for preexisting operating systems. In other words, all settings and configurations are set to the OS defaults.

DOS prompt — The common name for the command-line window available from DOS and Windows.

dual-boot system — A computer that is configured to use two operating systems.

FDISK — A DOS utility used to partition a hard disk. The DOS FDISK tool can see and manipulate only primary NTFS partitions; it cannot even view logical drives in an extended partition formatted with NTFS.

file system — The method used to arrange, read, and write files on disk. Windows XP supports the NTFS, FAT, and FAT32 file systems.

format — The process of rewriting the track and sector information on a disk; it removes all data previously on the disk.

hardware abstraction layer (HAL) — One of the few components of the Windows XP architecture that is written in hardware-dependent code. It is designed to protect hardware resources.

multiboot system — A computer that hosts two or more operating systems that can be booted by selecting one from a boot menu or boot manager during each bootup.

network adapter — Another name for network card; the piece of hardware that enables communication between the computer and the network.

new installation — See clean installation.

partition — A space set aside on a disk and assigned a drive letter. A partition can take up all or part of the space on a disk.

product activation — A mechanism by which a product fails if not registered within a specified time period. To be activated, a product must be registered with a correlated product key and hardware signature.

setup boot disks (or floppies) — The disks used by Windows XP to initiate the installation process on computer systems that do not have an existing OS, do not have a CD-ROM that supports bootable CDs, or do not have network access to a Windows XP distribution file share. These disks can be created by running the MAKEBOOT file from the BOOTDISK directory on the distribution CD.

Setup Manager — The Windows XP tool that provides you with a GUI for creating an answer file.

SYSPREP — The Windows XP utility used to clone a system.

unattended installation — A Windows XP installation that uses a script and does not require user interaction.

uniqueness database file (UDF) — A text file that contains a partial set of instructions for installing Windows XP; used to supplement an answer file, when only minor changes are needed that don't require a new answer file.

upgrade — The installation method in which data and configuration settings from the previous operating systems remain intact. The level or amount of retained data varies based on the existing operating system's type.

WINNT — The 16-bit Windows XP installation program.

WINNT32 — The 32-bit Windows XP installation program.

REVIEW QUESTIONS

1. Windows XP can be installed onto a computer system in a multiboot configuration with what other operating systems without requiring special third-party software? (Choose all that apply.)

   a. DOS

   b. OS/2

   c. Linux

   d. Windows 95

   e. Windows 2000

2. Microsoft supports only problems caused by hardware not on the Hardware Compatibility List. True or False?

3. Which of the following operating systems can be upgraded to Windows XP Professional? (Choose all that apply.)

   a. Windows 3.x

   b. Windows for Workgroups 3.x

   c. Windows XP Home Edition

   d. Windows 98

   e. Windows NT 4.0 Workstation

   f. Windows 2000 Server

   g. Windows 2000 Professional

4. Data stored on a partition formatted with FAT32 are accessible only from Windows XP. True or False?

5. Which of the following is the correct location for the x86 installation files on the installation CD?

   a. the root directory of the CD

   b. \SUPPORT\I386

   c. \INSTALL\I86

   d. none of the above

6. When sharing an installation folder across the network, you should assign it the _____ permission.

7. Which of the following situations allow a floppyless installation? (Choose all that apply.)

   a. The network is not yet functioning.

   b. The hard disk for the computer on which Windows XP is being installed is not yet formatted.

   c. No CD drivers are present for the existing OS.

   d. Windows 95 is already installed on the computer.

8. Windows XP can be installed with only the distribution CD if the computer's hardware is properly configured. True or False?

9. How are setup floppy disks created?

    a. WINNT32 /OX

    b. MAKEBOOT

    c. WINNT32 /B

    d. Download the creation utility from the Microsoft Web site.

10. The DOS utility used to create and delete partitions on a hard disk is called
    _____ .

11. Windows XP must be installed on an NTFS partition. True or False?

12. Which of the following statements is true? (Choose all that apply.)

    a. The entries in a uniqueness database file override those in an answer file, when the two are used together.

    b. An answer file is used to script text-mode setup, whereas a UDF scripts GUI-mode setup.

    c. If you have several installations to complete that differ only in the username, then you can use an answer file to customize the settings in the UDF.

    d. Answer files can be created using the Setup Manager Resource Kit tool.

13. The maximum volume size for FAT32 partitions is 2 terabytes. True or False?

14. What file system can be used on an installation destination directory for Windows XP Professional if the partition is 4 GB in size?

    a. FAT

    b. FAT32

    c. NTFS

    d. HPFS

15. When removing Windows XP, all NTFS partitions can be deleted with just FDISK. True or False?

16. Which of the following commands is used to prevent the regeneration of the security ID on reboot of a Windows XP installation?

    a. SYSPREP –noreboot

    b. SYSPREP –audit

    c. SYSPREP –factory

    d. SYSPREP –nosidgen

17. Running _____ disables display of confirmation dialog boxes when using SYSPREP.

2

18. To map a network drive from a DOS computer, which command do you use?

    a. NET START

    b. NET LOGON

    c. NET USE

    d. NET CONNECT

19. The _____ WINNT32 switch is used to prevent Dynamic Update from running.

20. At what point in the installation do you have the option of converting the file system to NTFS?

    a. after selecting the installation partition

    b. after the EULA has been agreed to

    c. at the end of the GUI-mode portion of installation

    d. You must convert the partition after setup has been completed.

21. The UNATTEND.TXT file included as a sample on the Windows XP Professional CD can be used as is to perform an upgrade of Windows NT Workstation. True or False?

22. Unattended or automated installation scripts can be created to perform which of the following functions? (Choose all that apply.)

    a. Duplicate an existing system's configuration.

    b. Create a read-only installation where viewers can step through the installation but not make any configuration changes.

    c. Automate only the GUI portion of Setup.

    d. Provide custom defaults but allow installer to change settings.

    e. Duplicate the settings of a Windows NT Workstation system.

23. No matter from which OS you launch a network installation of Windows XP, what is the one action you must perform?

    a. Install TCP/IP.

    b. Map a network drive to the Windows XP share.

    c. Preformat a 4 GB partition with FAT32.

    d. Use SYS C: to repair the MBR.

24. You're preparing for a network installation of Windows XP. Which of the following is not required to accomplish this? (Choose all that apply.)

    a. Copy the \SUPPORT directory from the installation CD to the server supplying the installation files.

    b. Share the installation directory with Read permissions.

    c. Boot the destination client computer onto the network.

    d. Run WINNT32 /N on the network server.

25. You want to change the menu description for Windows XP in the boot loader's menu. What file do you edit to make the change?

    a. DOSNET.INF

    b. UNATTEND.TXT

    c. BOOT.INI

    d. WINNT.INI

CASE PROJECTS

Case Project 2-1

You're in charge of organizing the installation of Windows XP Professional on a number of networked computers that currently host only DOS. Some of these computers have applications in common, but not all of them, and you need to set usernames and computer names for each installation. You've got a lot to take care of, so you'd like the installation to go as quickly as possible. Which of the following should you use? Choose all that apply, and justify your choice(s).

    a. SYSPREP.INF

    b. a uniqueness database file

    c. SYSPREP

    d. WINNT32

Case Project 2-2

Describe the five types of answer files that can be created by the Setup Manager Wizard from the Microsoft Windows XP Professional Resource Kit. Also, describe a scenario for each type of answer file that explains why that type is best suited for the situation.

Case Project 2-3

From a newly installed Windows XP Professional system with Internet access, launch the Windows Update item from the Start menu. Upgrade the system with the latest service packs and patches. Describe the process and what results you obtained.

3

USING THE SYSTEM UTILITIES

After reading this chapter and completing the exercises, you will be able to:

- ◆ Understand and use the Control Panel applets
- ◆ Describe the versatility of the Microsoft Management Console
- ◆ Understand Administrative Tools
- ◆ Describe PCMCIA and PC Cards

Windows XP includes a wide range of system utilities in Control Panel and in Administrative Tools. A thorough knowledge of these utilities can help you manage, tune, and improve your system. Some of the more advanced tools are actually Microsoft Management Console (MMC) snap-in tools and utilities. MMC snap-ins are powerful administration and management utilities that you'll soon find indispensable. Windows XP also has reliable support for PC Cards (PCMCIA) which are commonly used for NIC, modem, and wireless interface adapters.

CONTROL PANEL OVERVIEW

As with previous Microsoft operating systems, **Control Panel** is one of the most important centralized locations for management utilities under Windows XP. The Windows XP Control Panel will seem familiar, so you shouldn't get lost. However, you'll find several new **applets** and a whole new view. An applet is another word for a small application or utility that is designed for a limited range of function or capability.

By default, Control Panel appears in Category view (see Figure 3-1), which groups common functions of the Control Panel applets into interfaces called categories. By launching a category and answering the appropriate questions, you are taken to the appropriate applet's dialog box to perform most of the common activities related to system configuration (see Figure 3-2). The categories are simply an alternative navigational method to the same configuration interfaces in the Classic view of Control Panel. From within a category wizard, you can jump to the specific applet related to the desired function by clicking it in the list at the bottom of the screen. Those more comfortable with a Windows NT-style interface can switch to what Microsoft calls the Classic view. Switching between Classic view and Category view is simple—just click the Switch to command located in the left column of Control Panel.

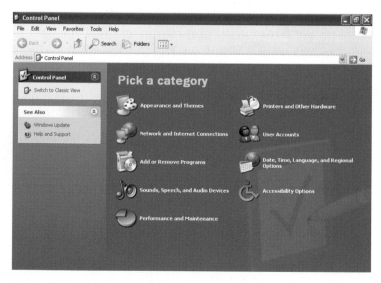

Figure 3-1   Control Panel in Category view

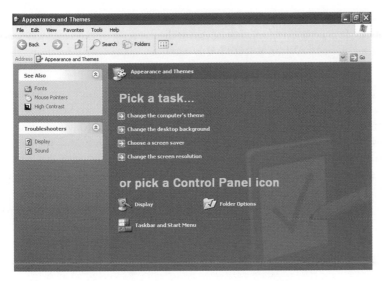

Figure 3-2 The Appearance and Themes Wizard

The Category view offers nine groupings for various common configuration changes. Table 3-1 lists the categories and their related applets. Take a little time to explore the category wizards on your own. You'll probably find them self-explanatory; no further guidance on their use may be needed.

Table 3-1 Categories in Control Panel

Categories	Related applets
Accessibility Options	Accessibility Options
Add or Remove Programs	Add or Remove Programs
Appearance and Themes	Display, Folder Options, Taskbar, and Start menu
Date, Time, Language, and Regional Options	Date and Time, Regional, and Language Options
Network and Internet Connections	Internet Options, Network Connections
Performance and Maintenance	Administrative Tools, Power Options, Scheduled Tasks, System
Printers and Other Hardware	Game Controllers, Keyboard, Mouse, Phone and Modem Options, Printers and Faxes, Scanners and Cameras
Sounds, Speech, and Audio Devices	Speech, Sounds, and Audio Devices
User Accounts	User Accounts

While in Category view, you can click any of the nine primary categories. Once a category is selected, the Control Panel window displays two sections titled "Pick a task" and "or pick a Control Panel icon." Under the first heading are several commonly performed tasks, such as "Choose the screen resolution" or "Add a printer." Clicking any of these tasks launches a wizard that guides you through the completion of the selected task. If you need to perform an activity within this category that is not listed as a task, select the appropriate Control Panel icons to open the control applet itself. The only category that does not display a list of tasks and icons is the Add or Remove Programs category. When selected, this category takes you directly to the Add or Remove Programs applet.

If you are a newcomer to Windows, you'll find Category view a simpler way to navigate the Windows XP configuration interface. If you are a Windows veteran, you might find the categories too restrictive. In the details column to the left of the category area, you can click the Switch to Classic View option to get to the display of the individual applet icons (see Figure 3-3). Control Panel hosts the applets and utilities used to install and configure **devices** and software (particularly **services**). There are several common or basic applets that always appear in Control Panel, but other applets can be added depending on the services, components, or applications installed with Windows XP. The common Control Panel applets are discussed in the following sections.

Figure 3-3   The Control Panel applet icons in Classic View

Accessibility Options

The Accessibility Options applet is where special interface features can be enabled and tuned for the visual-, audio-, or movement-impaired user. There are five tabs in this applet. The Keyboard tab is used to configure:

- *StickyKeys*—Enables the use of Ctrl, Shift, or Alt by pressing once instead of requiring holding.

- *FilterKeys*—Enables the ability to ignore quick or repeated keystrokes.

- *ToggleKeys*—Plays a tone when Caps Lock, Scroll Lock, or Num Lock is active.

The Accessibility Options applet's Sound tab is used to configure SoundSentry and ShowSounds. SoundSentry displays visual clues, such as a title bar, window, or the desktop when the system plays a sound. ShowSounds is used to force the display of captions when sounds or speech are played.

3

The Display tab sets the display to a high-contrast color scheme to improve reading. The options include black on white, white on black, or any defined color scheme (through the Display applet's Appearance tab). The default Use High Contrast setting is High Contrast Black (large). This tab is also used to set the cursor blink rate and cursor width.

The Mouse tab is used to enable numeric pad control of the mouse cursor, called MouseKeys. When enabled, the arrows on the numeric keypad control the direction of mouse cursor movement. The Settings button opens a window for additional configuration settings, including speed and acceleration of the pointer, configuring the MouseKeys shortcut, and whether or not to use MouseKeys when NumLock is on or off.

The General tab is used to set the following controls:

- Disable or turn off accessibility options after the system is idle a specified length of time
- Display warning when enabling accessibility options
- Play a sound when turning a feature on or off
- Enable support for serial-connected key devices
- Apply all settings to logon desktop and/or to new users

To configure Accessibility Options, enable or disable each offered feature on the various tabs and fine-tune these features by selecting the optional settings that offer the most help interacting with the system. Troubleshooting Accessibility Options is handled in the same manner as the initial configuration. Walk through the tabs and the configuration settings of each feature to make sure the desired settings are selected. If the Accessibility Option involves a device such as a special keyboard, mouse, or other item, always check the driver for that device and contact the vendor for additional troubleshooting tips. It is possible for a problem to exist with the I/O device and not with the native Accessibility Options of Windows XP.

In addition to the Accessibility Options in Control Panel are the set of tools found in the Accessibility folder of the Start Menu (All Programs, Accessories, Accessibility). These include the Accessibility Wizard, Magnifier, Narrator, the On-Screen Keyboard, and the Utility Manager.

The Accessibility Wizard is a typical Windows XP configuration wizard that quickly configures your system for special access needs. This wizard prompts you for information about your accessibility needs such as text size, color, display configuration, sound, and pointer configurations. The Magnifier is used to zoom in on items displayed on the monitor like a portable magnifying glass. The Narrator can be used to read aloud text from any window or document. The On-Screen Keyboard can be used to enter text using just a pointing device. The Utility Manager is used to start these three Accessibility tools automatically when a user logs in, locks the workstation, or launches the Utility Manager itself. These tools are very self-explanatory. If you'd like to learn more about them, just launch them.

Add Hardware

Installing hardware under Windows XP is fairly straightforward. Upon starting, the system polls the entire computer for new devices. If any are found, Windows XP attempts to identify them. This is successful for most **Plug and Play (PnP)** devices and some non-Plug and Play devices. Windows XP installs **drivers** automatically or prompts you for an alternative source path for drivers. If new hardware is not detected, the Add Hardware Wizard can be used to install vendor-supplied drivers manually. The Add Hardware applet is actually an informative, easy-to-use Wizard and is used to add a new device or troubleshoot a device that is not functioning properly.

Windows veterans may recall that this applet was called Add or Remove Hardware in Windows 2000. Its name and functions have changed in Windows XP. Removing or disabling a hardware device is now the sole domain of Device Manager. It is part of the System applet, but is also accessible from the properties of the Hardware tab in My Computer, and on the Hardware tab through Device Manager in the System applet.

When adding new hardware, you should always begin by installing the device physically. You should then boot the computer and wait a few moments to see if Windows XP detects it. If not, look for a vendor-provided installation utility. Only after PnP fails and you confirm that there is no vendor-supplied installation utility should you use the Add Hardware applet to install the device drivers for the new device. The Wizard itself is easy to follow without additional instructions.

Use the Add Hardware Wizard to install DVD players, CD players, tape devices, scanners, modems, network interface cards, multimedia devices, video devices, smart card readers, cameras, IrDA (Infrared Data Association) devices, wireless devices, Universal Serial Bus (USB) devices, and any other handheld or desktop device or peripheral. Always check with the vendor for the latest device drivers.

Once a device is installed, it can be configured and managed through Device Manager. This tool is accessed from the Start menu (Start, Control Panel, Administrative Tools, Computer Management). Use Device Manager to alter device settings, update drivers, add or remove a device within a hardware profile, and verify device functionality. See the Device Manager section later in this chapter for more information on configuring and managing devices with Device Manager. Troubleshooting any device is a matter of verifying that the proper driver is installed and that the correct settings for the device are made. This information can be verified through Device Manager. Furthermore, Device Manager can be used to update, replace, or remove drivers for installed devices. This is accomplished using the Uninstall or Update buttons on the Drivers tab of a device's Properties dialog box accessed through Device Manager.

As for troubleshooting, this wizard really only offers one option—reinstalling the device driver. If you want to explore other troubleshooting options, look to Device Manager.

Add or Remove Programs

Add or Remove Programs is actually three tools in one. The first tool, Change or Remove Programs, can be used to change or remove installed applications (see Figure 3-4). In this mode, it displays installed applications, their drive space usage, and how often the application is actually used. This mode also allows you to change or remove the application, but only if the application's setup routine offers a partial or optional setup method. Applications appear only if they comply with the Windows application programming interface (API) for installation and properly register themselves during installation. If you suspect an application does not meet these requirements, you might want to initiate the installation from the Add New Programs tool.

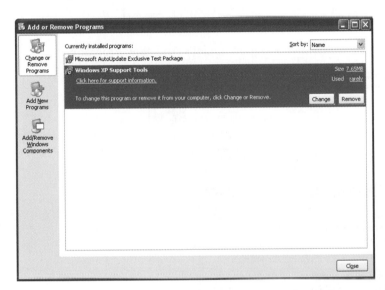

Figure 3-4   The Add and Remove Program applet's Change and Remove Programs

The second tool, Add New Programs (see Figure 3-5), is used to install new applications from a vendor-supplied distribution floppy or CD, from the Microsoft Update site, or over a network through IntelliMirror and Windows Installer. The third tool is the Add/Remove Windows Components Wizard (see Figure 3-6). This tool is used to install or remove native components of Windows, such as the Faxing service, the Indexing service, or Internet Information Server.

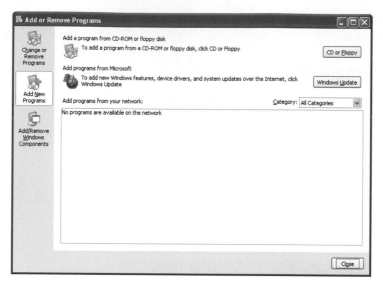

Figure 3-5   The Add and Remove Program applet's Add New Programs

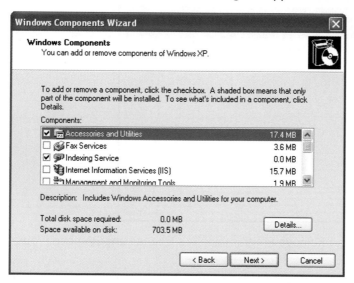

Figure 3-6   The Add and Remove Program applet's Add/Remove Windows Components

Activity 3-1: Add/Remove Applications

Time Required: 10 minutes

Objective: Review the Windows components that can be added or removed using the Add/Remove Programs Wizard.

Description: It never seems like you are able to set up a computer with applications and just leave it. New applications and components are always being released, and as much as you would like to leave everything installed, it makes sense to remove these applications and components when they are no longer being used. Most applications are written with their own uninstall component to make the administrator's job easier. However, to remove a Windows component, it must be done from the Add/Remove Programs applet in Control Panel.

 This activity assumes Control Panel is in Classic view.

To add a Windows component:

1. Open Control Panel by clicking **Start**, **Control Panel**.
2. Double-click **Add or Remove Programs**.
3. Select **Add/Remove Windows Components**.
4. The Windows Components Wizard displays the list of available components.
5. Select each item (do not click the check box) and notice if the Details button becomes highlighted.
6. If the item has Details available, click the **Details** button to view the additional options. Click **Cancel** to return to the list of available components.
7. Continue checking each of the items that has Details, and take note of the disk space requirement for each.
8. Click **Cancel** to return to the **Add or Remove Programs** applet.
9. Close the **Add or Remove Programs** applet by clicking **Close**.

Administrative Tools

The Administrative Tools applet in Control Panel is actually a folder pointing to the same place as the Administrative Tools item in the Start menu (which, by default, is not displayed on Windows XP Professional). The contents of Administrative Tools are briefly discussed later in this chapter and in relevant chapters later in this book.

Date and Time

The Date and Time applet is used to set the calendar date, clock time, and time zone for the system. On the Date & Time tab, you can set the month from a pull-down list, the year with scroll buttons, and select the day from the displayed month calendar. Time is adjusted by highlighting the hour, minute, second, AM/PM, and either using the scroll buttons or typing a new value. When you set the time, the clock is set directly in the system's BIOS. The Time

Zone tab displays a world map and a pull-down list to select time zones. Time zone information is stored internally as either a negative or a positive offset to Greenwich Mean Time (GMT). The Time Zone tab also supports automatic updates for daylight savings time and normal time, in those areas where such seasonal time changes occur.

Activity 3-2: Setting the Time

Time Required: 10 minutes

Objective: Configure the date, time, and time zone for your computer.

Description: The little clock in the corner of your computer screen is not the only use for the time and date settings in your computer. Most applications, and all Microsoft applications, use the clock to automatically enter the date/time into documents using the chosen format. In addition, this information is saved with the file and can be used for document version tracking. If files are created on workstations and then moved onto a server and each workstation has the date/time/time zone set incorrectly, it would be very difficult to perform document version tracking. In this activity, you will configure the date, time, and time zone for your computer.

This activity assumes Control Panel is in Classic view.

To set the calendar date, clock time, and time zone for the system:

1. Click **Start**, **Control Panel**.

2. Double-click **Date and Time**.

3. Use the pull-down list to select the correct month.

4. Use the scroll buttons to select the correct year.

5. Select the current date from the displayed month calendar.

6. Click the hours in the time field below the analog clock. Use the up and down arrow buttons to adjust the hour to the current time.

7. Select the minutes in the time field. Use the up and down arrow buttons to adjust the minutes to the current time.

8. Select the seconds in the time field. Use the up and down arrow buttons to adjust the seconds to the current time.

9. Select the AM/PM designation in the time field. Use the up and down arrow buttons to adjust the designation to the current time.

10. Select the **Time Zone** tab.

11. Use the pull-down list to select the time zone for your area.

12. Click **OK** to close the **Date and Time** applet.

On nondomain member Windows XP systems, a third tab appears within this applet. The Internet Time tab allows you to define a time server on the Internet for synchronizing the local clock. This tab appears only on standalone or workgroup systems, because domain members are automatically synchronized with their domain controllers.

Display

The Display applet is used to choose from a wide range of interface changes and preference settings. The Display applet can also be accessed by right-clicking over an empty area of the desktop and selecting the Properties command from the shortcut menu. There are five tabs in this applet.

The Themes tab is used to select the overall visual styling of the user interface. The new colorful 3-D interface is called Windows XP. The gray-based stylings of Windows XP are called Windows Classic. Other interface schemes can be downloaded, or you can create your own by modifying the other four tabs of the Display applet and saving your settings.

The Desktop tab is used to select the wallpaper graphic and center, tile, or stretch the image. You can also customize the desktop by clicking the Customize Desktop button and selecting the General tab. You can select desktop icons to display (My Documents, My Computer, My Network Places, and Internet Explorer), change desktop icons, enable the Desktop Cleanup Wizard (see Chapter 14, "Windows XP Professional Fault Tolerance") to execute every 60 days, and define Web elements to display on the desktop.

The Screen Saver tab is used to set the screen saver, define the wait period before launching the screen saver, and to set the energy-saving features of the monitor (this links to the Power Options applet, through which all power features are configured).

The Appearance tab is used to set the window and button scheme, color scheme, and font size. Various display Effects (such as ClearType) and Advanced settings (such as individual display element color changes) can also be configured. ClearType is a new method of displaying fonts on LCD displays to produce a more readable text.

The Settings tab is used to set the screen resolution and color quality. There are also buttons to aid in troubleshooting and accessing advanced settings. The Troubleshoot button launches the Help and Support Center's Video Display Troubleshooter. This is a type of wizard that asks questions about your problem and offers solutions to resolve the issue. The Advanced button opens a properties dialog box for the combined settings of your video card and monitor. This dialog box may have numerous tabs depending on your hardware and the installed drivers. This dialog box has five tabs by default.

The General tab is used to set the DPI; by default this is set to 96 DPI. On this tab you can also select how to manage display change settings. The options are to restart the system before applying display changes, apply the changes without restarting, and ask before applying the new settings.

The Adapter tab lists details about the video card itself, such as chip type, DAC type, memory size, adapter string, and BIOS information. From this tab, you can access the video card's properties dialog box (the same one accessible through Device Manager) and a list of all the modes supported by the card. A mode is a combination of screen resolution, color depth, and screen refresh rate. See the Device Manager section later in this chapter for details on using device specific Properties dialog boxes for configuration changes and troubleshooting.

The Monitor tab is used to set the screen refresh rate. This tab also is used to access the monitor's properties dialog box (the same one accessible through Device Manager).

The Troubleshoot tab is used to set hardware acceleration of the video card and whether to enable write caching. If you are having display problems (e.g., corrupted images, shadowed cursors, rendering problems, failures of DirectX applications, or system crashes), adjusting the level of hardware acceleration downward may help correct the problem.

The Color Management tab is used to install color profiles. Color profiles are used to fine-tune how the video card and monitor display colors. If you are an image or video professional, color clarity and trueness are important. A color profile can be built to adjust and tune the display of colors for your specific video card and monitor combination. Predefined color profiles are usually included with your video card's driver set. Please contact the vendors of your video card or monitor for additional color profiles.

Depending on your hardware, you may have one or more additional tabs in this video card and monitor combo Properties dialog box. Often these additional tabs include device-specific information and configuration settings.

Windows XP supports Dualview, which is the capability to use multiple display devices. Configured from the Display applet's Settings tab, Dualview allows a notebook to display the desktop on both the local LCD panel and an external monitor. On some notebooks it also allows you to expand your desktop over the second external display. Dualview also allows multiple monitors to be used simultaneously on desktop systems. If multiple monitors are installed on the system, you can manage them from this applet.

On most notebooks and on some desktop systems, you may have a single video card with two or more video ports. If you have a multiport video card, the Settings tab of the Display applet indicates this by prefacing the name of the video card with "(Multiple Monitors)." If you know your hardware supports Dualview but the Settings tab of the Display applet does not list two monitors or does not say "(Multiple Monitors)," upgrade your video drivers.

To add additional monitors to your configuration, power down the system and install the additional video cards and connect the monitors. Boot the system and install any necessary video drivers. Open the Display applet and select the Settings tab. Select each new monitor in turn and mark the Extend my Windows desktop onto this monitor check box. Each time you make this setting on another monitor, you are stretching your desktop across an additional monitor.

Once you have multiple monitors installed, you need to select a primary display. The primary display is the monitor the system uses to display the booting process and the logon prompt. It is also the screen where the Start menu, taskbar, and newly started program windows appear by default. No matter how many monitors you have configured, the Start menu and Taskbar only appear on the primary monitor.

To set the primary monitor, go to the Settings tab of the Display applet, click the monitor icon you wish to become your primary display, then mark the check box labeled Use this device as the primary monitor. If the selected monitor is already the primary, this check box is not available.

Once the primary monitor is set, you can arrange the orientation of your monitors and the size/shape of your desktop. To arrange your monitors and therefore the shape and size of your desktop, right-click over one of the monitors and select Identify. A large number appears over each monitor. Now, click and drag the monitors around into the shape you desire. Note the arrangement of the monitor icons does not have to be exactly the same as the physical arrangements of your monitors.

Activity 3-3: To Add Additional Monitors to Your Configuration

Time Required: 10 minutes

Objective: Add monitors to your configuration.

Description: At times, you will need to add additional monitors to your configuration. In this activity, you will add additional video cards and monitors. Using multiple monitors allows you to spread your desktop over multiple screens. Multiple monitors greatly expands your workspace.

To add the monitors:

1. Turn off the computer and install additional Peripheral Component Interconnect (PCI) or Accelerated Graphic Port (AGP) video cards.

2. Connect the monitors into each PCI or AGP video card that you installed.

3. Turn on the computer and install any necessary video drivers.

4. Right-click an empty area of the desktop, and click **Properties**.

5. Click the **Settings** tab.

6. Select each new monitor in turn and select the **Extend my Windows desktop onto this monitor** check box. Then click **OK**.

You must use PCI or AGP video cards when configuring multiple displays. With Windows XP Professional and the right hardware, you can connect up to 10 individual monitors to a single computer.

Folder Options

The Folder Options applet accesses the same configuration interface as the Tools, Folder Options command from Windows Explorer and My Computer. The four tabs of this applet are used to set the functional and visual parameters of the folders on the system. The General tab is used to enable/disable the display of common tasks in folders, to open a folder in a new or current window, and to choose whether a single- or double-click opens an item. The View tab is used to set advanced settings, such as show hidden files, hide file extensions, and use simple file sharing. The File Types tab is used to define or associate file extensions with applications. The Offline Files tab is used to enable offline network browsing by caching resources locally. See Chapter 4, "Managing Windows XP File Systems and Storage," for more details on this applet and its uses.

Fonts

The Fonts applet lists all currently installed fonts used by the Windows XP system; additional fonts can be added and unused fonts can be removed. Double-clicking a font reveals a sample window displaying details about the font and several sized examples of it (see Figure 3-7).

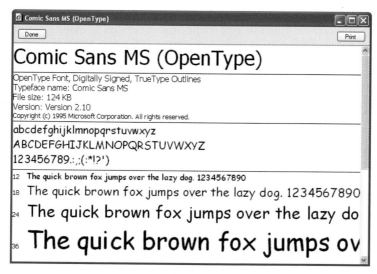

Figure 3-7   A Font sample display window

Game Controllers

The Game Controllers applet is used to install and configure the operation of joysticks and other specialized gaming controls that can be attached to sound cards or serial ports. This interface offers access to device-specific properties and troubleshooting aid.

Internet Options

The Internet Options applet is used to define settings for Internet Explorer and general Internet access. This applet is discussed in Chapter 8, "Internetworking with Remote Access."

Keyboard and Mouse

The Keyboard applet is used to modify keyboard functions. Settings include the Repeat delay, Repeat rate, and Cursor blink rate. The Mouse applet is used to modify mouse settings, including switching functions of left and right buttons, double-click speed, the graphics used for pointers, how the pointer moves (speed and acceleration) and appears (mouse trails or no mouse trails), wheel scrolling, and snapping to objects.

Network Connections

The Network Connections applet is used to manage all network connections of a Windows XP system. This includes local area network links as well as RAS and WAN links. This applet is discussed in Chapter 7 and Chapter 8.

Activity 3-4: Configuring Windows XP for Standalone Use

Time Required: 15 minutes

Objective: Configure Windows XP to run as a standalone computer.

Description: Not all instances of Windows XP are installed in a network. There are many people who want to use Windows XP at home because of its many attributes—stability, versatility, ease of use, and so on. Although it has been built to be an integral part of any Microsoft network, it is also capable of operating on its own. In this activity, you will configure your computer to be a standalone Windows XP workstation.

This activity assumes Control Panel is in Classic view.

To configure Windows XP Professional for standalone home use:

1. Click **Start**, **Control Panel**.
2. Double-click **System**.
3. Select the **Computer Name** tab.
4. Click the **Network ID** button.
5. The Network Identification Wizard starts. Click **Next**.

6. Select **This computer is for home use and is not part of a business network**. Click **Next**.

7. Click **Finish**.

8. You will be prompted to restart the system for the changes to take effect. Click **OK**.

Phone and Modem Options

The Phone and Modem Options applet is used to define dialing locations, install and configure modems, and configure Remote Access Service (RAS) and Telephony API (TAPI) related drivers and services. This applet is covered in detail in Chapter 8.

Power Options

The Power Options applet is used to set the system's power-saving and battery management features. Windows XP supports both Advanced Configuration and Power Interface (ACPI) and Advanced Power Management (APM) standards for power management. These standards extend battery life by powering down unused devices to reduce the power drain caused by the system. You'll find one or both of these power management technologies on most notebooks and many desktop systems.

Advanced Power Management (APM) was originally included with Windows 95. APM placed power management responsibility onto the operating system and the computer's hardware BIOS. However, wake-on device activation was not possible. With the development of ACPI, a more comprehensive power management solution was available. ACPI can power down individual devices or system components and repower them when needed by the OS, applications, or external entities. ACPI can also control the system using soft power switches. This is the ability for the system to be put into a suspended state or awaken from that state with the click of the mouse or a press of a button (on the keyboard or computer case). ACPI is what makes PC cards (previously known as PCMCIA cards) able to be hot-swapped and notebooks to be hot-docked.

If ACPI support is not enabled on your computer hardware when you first install Windows XP, you must reinstall (or at least perform an upgrade install) Windows XP immediately after enabling ACPI support through the computer's BIOS. The HAL must be rebuilt to include ACPI support. Otherwise, your system will experience STOP errors during start and will not complete the start process.

The Power Options applet has different tabs depending on the composition of the computer hardware and BIOS-enabled power management features. For example, the Alarm tab used to set a notebook battery warning alarm is not present on desktop systems. The Power Options applet can be accessed through Control Panel or by double-clicking the battery or AC plug icon in the Notification Area.

Some of the tabs typically found in the Power Options dialog box are: Power Schemes, Alarm, Power Meter, Advanced, Hibernate, and UPS.

The Power Schemes tab (see Figure 3-8) is used to select a power scheme profile. There are several predefined power schemes for common types and uses of computers. These include Home/Office Desk, Portable/Laptop, Presentation, Always On, Minimal Power Management, and Max Battery. Each of these schemes is designed with either power or use in mind. You can employ a predefined scheme or create your own. The two primary settings are Turn off monitor and Turn off hard drives after a specified length of time in minutes or hours or never. You can also define whether the system will enter standby mode or hibernation mode (only if supported and enabled; see later in this section for standby and hibernation details). You also have the ability to define different power scheme settings for when the system is running off of AC power and battery power on systems with batteries.

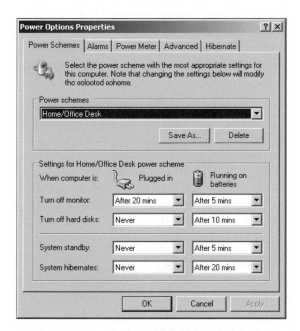

Figure 3-8 The Power Options applet, Power Schemes tab

The Alarms and Power Meter tabs appear only if you are working on a system with an internal battery, such as a notebook. The Alarms tab is used to set a low battery and/or critical battery alarm. The alarms are set as a percentage of total charge remaining. A common setting is to trigger the low battery alarm at 10% and the critical battery alarm at 3%. When either alarm is triggered, there are several alarm notifications or events that can take place. Clicking the Alarm Action button for either alarm type allows you to select and configure the actions for each alarm independently. The alarm action options are to play an alert sound, display a warning message, initiate a standby, hibernate, or shutdown operation, whether to force standby or shutdown even if a program stops responding, and whether to run a program or script. The Power Meter tab displays the power status of the AC plug and the batteries. Double-clicking the battery icon displays additional information about the battery.

The Advanced tab displays various power management controls depending on your computer hardware and whether ACPI is enabled. The controls on this tab can include whether to display the power icon in the notification tray at all times and whether to prompt for a password when resuming from standby. By default, the power icon appears only when the system is running on batteries. You can also control the actions of the system when the power button, sleep button, or lid close sensor are used. When you close your notebook computer, the OS can do nothing or put the system into standby or hibernate mode. When you press the power or sleep buttons, the OS can do nothing, ask you what to do, place the system into standby or hibernate mode, or initiate a shutdown.

The Hibernate tab is used simply to enable the hibernate function of the system. If hibernation is supported by your hardware, then this tab is available to you. This tab also displays the amount of hard drive space required on your boot partition (i.e., the partition where your main Windows folder resides). The size of the hibernation file is slightly larger than the total size of your virtual memory (i.e., your physical RAM plus the size of your paging file[s]).

There are two interesting and useful modes or states that Windows XP supports: standby and hibernate. Standby is the mode where the system goes into a lower power consumption mode. In this state the computer is still operating and all open applications are still open. The state of the computer, all open applications, and all unsaved data are stored in memory. The system can quickly return from standby mode to a fully operational mode in just a few seconds. However, if there is a power loss, all unsaved data is lost and the system performs a normal boot the next time the power button is used. Standby should be used when you want to put the system into low-power consumption mode for a short period of time and you desire to return to work as quickly as possible.

Hibernation mode is where the state of the system is saved to a temporary data file on the hard drive and the computer is fully powered off. All data is retained even if your system experiences a complete power failure because the system state is saved to the hard drive. Restoring from hibernation takes longer than restoring from standby but less time than a normal boot. Once the system is restored from hibernation, you are returned to the desktop with all of your previously active applications. Hibernation should be used when you want to save power or are unsure of the amount of power you have remaining and you want to return to your existing workspace.

If your system is capable of going into both standby and hibernation mode, you may see only one of these options displayed in some dialog boxes. For example, the Turn Off Computer dialog box has only three buttons. The left button is used for both standby and hibernation. Standby is displayed by default. To access the hibernation action, press and hold the Shift key.

The UPS tab is used to configure how the computer interacts with an uninterruptible power supply device. A UPS protects your computer from various power fluctuations as well as provides you a window of time to safely power down your system (manually or automatically) when a complete power failure occurs. After you've selected your specific UPS device (via the Select button), you can configure how your system reacts to various power conditions detected by the UPS. UPS configuration includes setting notification alarms, program or script execution, and shutdown or hibernation initiation. Please consult the documentation from your UPS vendor on how to properly configure UPS support.

Activity 3-5: Configuring Power Options

Time Required: 10 minutes

Objective: Learn how to configure power options.

Description: In this activity, you will learn how to create a new power scheme. The power scheme determines how the power-intensive components (e.g., hard drives and monitors) of your system operate. By customizing a power scheme, you can tune your power saving options to your needs.

To create a new power scheme:

This activity assumes Control Panel is in Classic view.

1. Click **Start**, click **Control Panel**.
2. Click **Power Options**.
3. On the Power Schemes tab, select **Portable/Laptop**.
4. In the Turn off monitor list box, select **After 20 mins**.
5. In the Turn off hard disk list box, select **After 20 mins**.
6. Click **Save As**, and then in the Save Scheme text box, type **PowerScheme**. You have just created a new power scheme.
7. Click **OK**.

Printers and Faxes

The Printers and Faxes applet is used to install, share, and configure many types of output devices. This applet is used not just for physical print devices, but also for specialized printers, such as film printers, slide printers, and faxes. Once a printer is in use, this applet also grants access to the print queue for management purposes. This applet is covered in detail in Chapter 9, "Printing and Faxing."

Regional and Language Options

The Regional Options tab of the Regional and Language Options applet (see Figure 3-9) is used to define location-specific uses or requirements for numbers, currency, time, dates, and more. You can select a predefined regional scheme based on language or country, then define or customize specifics.

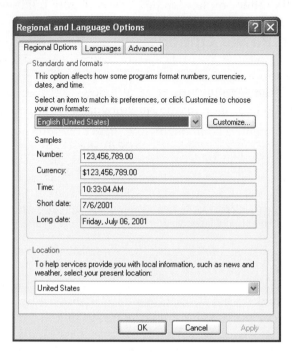

Figure 3-9   The Regional and Language Options applet, Regional Options tab

You use the Languages tab to configure the default input language to use for text entry, as well as keyboard settings. Through the Details button, you can configure the default input language, the installed languages, and whether to use the language bar. The language bar is an always–on–top, pull–down selector that enables quick switching between one input language and another. You can also define hot key sequences to switch between language options. On the Languages tab, you can select to install the files necessary to support complex script and right-to-left languages (such as Thai) or the files necessary to support East Asian languages (such as Japanese).

The Advanced tab allows you to configure language support for non–Unicode programs and select Code page conversion tables (i.e. programming language interpreters); you can also apply these settings to the current user account and the default user profile.

To enable and configure multiple language support, you must decide whether you want only the ability to read and write documents in multiple languages or if you need multiple input locales. An **input locale** is a combination language and keyboard layout used to define how data is entered into the computer. To enable multiple languages for documents, click the Details button on the Languages tab of the Regional and Language Options dialog box. This opens the Text Services and Input Languages dialog box where you can add other

3

languages to your system. You can also click the Key Settings button to define shortcut key sequences that can be used to switch between languages. Once multiple languages are defined, you can also switch between them using the locale indicator, which appears in the icon tray of the taskbar.

Windows XP Professional is available in a multilanguage edition called the Windows XP Multilingual User Interface Pack. This is a six CD collection which includes the base English version of Windows XP Professional and 33 add-on packs of localized resources for other languages. Users first install the English version of Windows XP, then using the MUISetup tool, the user can install one or more of the Multilingual User Interface Packs. The Multilingual User Interface Pack is used to create customized language editions of Windows XP. The standard Windows XP Professional version is able to add language support, but is not fully capable of supporting other languages on the same level as a fully localized version. A localized version of Windows XP Professional is simply a version created for a specific country, region, locale, and language. The United States local version is the standard English version. Microsoft ships 24 localized versions of Windows XP (i.e., English plus 23 other languages).

The first version of Windows to have a Multilingual User Interface Pack version was Windows 2000 Professional. If an upgrade installation is performed on a Multilingual version of Windows 2000 Professional to Windows XP Professional, you must use Windows XP Professional's Multilingual User Interface Pack to reinstall any additional language user interfaces. Otherwise, languages other than English supported by Windows 2000 Professional are lost or discarded during the upgrade process. Each regional version of Windows XP Professional only has the user interface installation files for that specific language.

Scanners and Cameras

The Scanners and Cameras applet is used to install drivers and configure digital cameras and optical scanners. Once installed, these devices can be used with graphics and imaging software to create digital images of real-life or printed materials.

Scanners and cameras generally fall under the category of multimedia. Most digital cameras, scanners, and other imaging devices are Plug and Play devices and Windows XP Professional installs them automatically when you connect them to your computer. If your imaging device is not installed automatically when you connect it, or if it does not support Plug and Play, use the Scanners and Cameras applet to install drivers and configure digital cameras and optical scanners.

 NOTE Hardware such as cameras and scanners consumes system resources. If you have a docked laptop computer that uses multimedia hardware, you should consider using a different hardware profile that disables the multimedia devices when the computer is not docked. This saves system resources and possibly even battery power.

Scheduled Tasks

The **Scheduled Tasks** applet is used to automate starting and running various tasks. Tasks can be scheduled to run at a specific time, repeat on intervals, when the system starts, at logon, or when idle. Tasks can be run within the security context of a specific user account. The Add Scheduled Task Wizard, which appears in the Scheduled Tasks folder, walks you step by step through the scheduling process, making scheduling as convenient as possible. Once a task is defined, you can edit its scheduled properties by right-clicking the item and selecting Properties from the shortcut menu.

Scheduled tasks can be moved from system to system. This allows you to define administrative actions or batch files on a single computer, then place them on client systems from a central location.

To troubleshoot the scheduled tasks, you must verify the settings of each defined task. The most common cause of a task not running when expected is an incorrect time or date setting. You should also check the path for the tool, script, or program to be launched, as well as any advanced settings that deal with idle time and repeat executions. You should always double-check your work to eliminate programming errors when scheduling tasks.

Activity 3-6: Scheduling Tasks

Time Required: 15 minutes

Objective: Use Scheduled Tasks to automatically start an application (Calc.exe) at a specified time.

Description: There are times when an administrator or a user would like to have an application start automatically without the requirement of a person sitting in front of the keyboard (or access the computer remotely). One such task may be to back up files to a mass storage device (such as a tape, Zip drive, another hard drive, and so on) during nonworking hours. This activity is going to step through scheduling Calc.exe, the calculator application in Windows, to run at a certain time.

This activity assumes Control Panel is in Classic view.

To create an automated task:

1. Click **Start**, **Control Panel**.
2. Double-click **Scheduled Tasks**.
3. Double-click **Add Scheduled Task** to run the Scheduled Tasks Wizard.
4. Click **Next**.
5. Select **Calculator** from the list.

6. Click **Next**.

7. Select **One time only**.

8. Click **Next**.

9. Set the time to 3 minutes from the present.

10. Click **Next**.

11. Enter the administrator username and password (the password must be entered twice). Click **Next**.

12. Click **Finish**.

13. Wait the remainder of the three minutes to see the calculator application start automatically.

14. Close the calculator application.

Sounds and Audio Devices

The Sounds and Audio Devices applet is used to customize the sound scheme (system events that cause sounds), to set the master volume, configure speakers, set audio device preferences, and configure or troubleshoot multimedia devices.

Activity 3-7: Custom Sound

Time Required: 15 minutes

Objective: Customize the sounds for different events on the computer.

Description: Most people are aware of the sounds that your computer makes when it is started, shut down, a mistake is made, and so on. Some people prefer to hear something different than what Microsoft has selected or even provided. There are many other sounds available that an individual may prefer to hear when shutting down their computer. A user may even use a sound that he or she has recorded themselves. By using the Sound Scheme applet in Control Panel, it is possible to create different schemes for whatever mood you may be in.

This activity assumes Control Panel is in Classic view.

To create a custom sound scheme:

1. Click **Start**, **Control Panel**.

2. Double-click **Sounds and Audio Devices**.

3. Select the **Sounds** tab.

4. Use the Sound scheme pull-down list to select **Windows Default**.

5. If prompted to save the previous scheme, click **No**.

6. Select **Asterisk** from the list of Program events.

7. Use the Sounds pull-down list to select **(None)**.

8. Select **Exit Windows** from the list of Program events.

9. Use the Sounds pull-down list to select **Windows XP Logoff Sound**. (If you have extension display enabled, the .wav extension is included in the sound file's name.)

10. Click the **Save As** button.

11. Give the sound scheme a name, such as **Windows Example 1**. Click **OK**.

12. Click **OK** to close the Sounds and Audio Devices applet.

13. Save any work that may be open, and select **Start**, **Turn Off Computer**, then click the **Restart** button. Notice the sound that plays as Windows shuts down.

Speech

Windows XP includes a text-to-speech capability that reads document text. The voice is not perfect, but it is understandable. This applet configures the text-to-speech functions for applications written to Microsoft's Speech API (SAPI). Such applications offer an additional Language toolbar, from which you can enable text-to-speech conversion and initiate the reading of the entire document or selected areas of text. This applet controls only SAPI-enabled applications and is distinct from the Narrator Accessibility Accessory (for more information, read the "Text to Speech" overview available from the Microsoft Help and Support Center for Windows XP).

System

The System applet is used to configure or control many system-level and core operational functions of Windows XP. This is probably the most important Control Panel applet. Familiarity with this applet is essential for the Microsoft 70-270 exam and for maintaining a functional, efficient, and operational system. The System applet has seven tabs.

The General tab displays the operating system version, service pack level, registered user name, and basic computer information, such as CPU type, speed, and amount of physical RAM.

The Computer Name tab (see Figure 3-10) is used to join a domain/workgroup and change the computer name. This tab is also accessed from the Network Connections window by selecting the Network Identification item on the Advanced menu. The Network ID button starts the Network Identification Wizard. The Change button is used to quickly change the name of the system or for altering membership in a domain or workgroup. See Chapters 7 and 8 for details on using the controls from the Computer Name tab.

Figure 3-10 The System applet, Computer Name tab

The Hardware tab is used to access the Add Hardware Wizard (see earlier section), enable and disable driver signing requirements, access Device Manager, and define **hardware profiles**. All of these items are covered in sections later in this chapter.

The Advanced tab is used to access controls for performance settings (set optimization for visual effects, processor scheduling, memory usage, and **virtual memory**; see Chapter 10, "Performance Tuning"), user profiles (see Chapter 5, "Users, Groups, Profiles, and Policies"), startup and recovery, environmental variables, and error reporting. These last three items are covered in sections later in this chapter.

The System Restore tab controls the amount of disk space to use for system restoration (see Chapter 14).

The Automatic Updates tab manages how Windows Update downloadable packages are handled (see Chapter 14).

The Remote tab enables, disables, and configures Remote Assistance and Remote Desktop (see Chapter 7).

The following sections discuss additional configuration options available in this applet.

Driver Signing

Driver signing is used to identify drivers that have passed the Microsoft Windows Hardware Quality Labs evaluation and tests. The configuration of driver signing through the System applet warns users when a nonsigned driver is being installed. Clicking the Driver Signing button on the Hardware tab of the System applet reveals the Driver Signing Options dialog box, which presents the following three options:

- *Ignore*—Install the software anyway and don't ask for my approval.
- *Warn*—Prompt me each time to choose an action.
- *Block*—Never install unsigned driver software.

Configuring driver signing involves nothing more than selecting one of these three options. If you are an administrator or power user, you are offered an additional option with the Make this action the system default check box. Checking this box standardizes the driver signing settings for all users. Otherwise, these settings only apply to the current user account. The only method of troubleshooting driver signing is to return to this dialog box and ensure the desired option is selected.

The heart of the driver signing restriction mechanism is the File Signature Verification tool. This tool is used automatically by the system to verify whether software is signed at the time of installation. But you can take advantage of this tool for other purposes. This tool can be started from the Help and Support Center, the SIGVERIF.EXE file can be executed from the Start, Run command or a command prompt, or selecting the File Signature Verification Utility selection from the Tools menu of the System Information utility (Start, All Programs, Accessories, System Tools, System Information). Clicking Start on this tool starts a system-wide check for any unsigned system files. To test the signing of any other file, click the Advanced button, then set the tool to search for only system files, any file (*.*), or specific file types (such *.dll or *.exe) for unsigned files. You can also search within the default main \WINDOWS folder or any folder on the system with or without including their subfolders. The results of a File Signature Verification scan are recorded to a log file—SIGVERIF. TXT—by default.

When installing drivers for backup devices, any user with the ability to install new hardware can install the necessary device drivers. However, only users that are members of the Backup Operators group are able to access and use an installed backup device.

Device Manager

Once a device is installed, you can verify that it is working properly by using Device Manager (see Figure 3-11). You can access this tool by clicking the Device Manager button on the Hardware tab of the System applet. Device Manager lists all installed and known devices and indicates their status. (*Note:* You can also reach Device Manager through the Computer Management administration tool by selecting Device Manager from the System Tools console tree.) A yellow exclamation point or a stop sign over a device's icon indicates problems or conflicts.

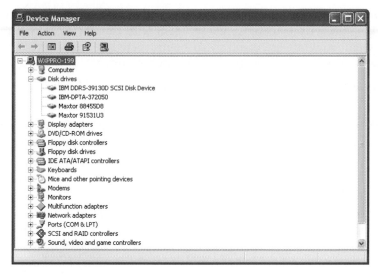

Figure 3-11   Device Manager

Activity 3-8: Managing Devices

Time Required: 5 minutes

Objective: Verify that there are no problems with the CD-ROM drive using Device Manager.

Description: When you suspect there is a problem with a device, the best method to ensure that nothing is wrong or to troubleshoot an actual problem is to use Device Manager. In Device Manager, both graphical and text-based information are provided that alert the user to issues whenever there is a problem. There is also a troubleshooting button that provides a wizard for stepping through the basic steps to find the problem and resolve it.

This activity assumes Control Panel is in Classic view.

To monitor and manage a device via Device Manager:

1. Click **Start**, **Control Panel**, **Administrative Tools**.
2. Double-click **Computer Management**.
3. In the System Tools section in Computer Management, select **Device Manager**.
4. Double-click the **DVD/CD-ROM drives** item to expand its contents.
5. Select one of the items that appear.
6. Select **Action**, **Properties**.

7. Notice the Device status message. If all is well, the message should state that the device is working properly. If there were a problem with this device, information about the problem would be listed and you'd be instructed to click the **Troubleshoot** button to access the troubleshooting wizard.

8. Select the **Properties** tab. This is where you configure specific hardware device settings.

9. Select the **Driver** tab. This is where you can obtain information about the current driver as well as details on updating, replacing, or removing the current driver.

10. Click **OK**.

11. Close the Computer Management tool.

By double-clicking a device, you open that device's Properties dialog box. By default, the General tab (see Figure 3-12) is displayed first. On this tab, you can access the type, manufacturer, and location settings; view the device's status; and enable or disable the device in the current hardware profile. Additionally, you can click the Troubleshoot button to access troubleshooting recommendations from the Windows XP Help and Support Center.

Figure 3-12   A device's Properties dialog box, General tab

The Driver tab (see Figure 3-13) enables you to change driver settings or install or upgrade device-related drivers. This tab displays information about the installed driver for this device and offers four buttons: Driver Details, Update Driver, Roll Back Driver, and Uninstall.

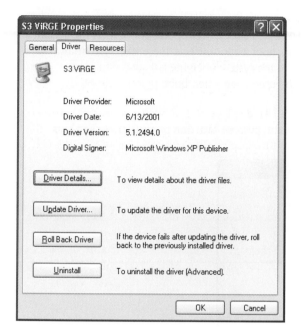

Figure 3-13 A device's Properties dialog box, Driver tab

The functions of the buttons are as follows:

- Clicking the Driver Details button displays a windows listing all of the files that compose the device driver for this device.

- Clicking the Update Driver button initiates the Hardware Update Wizard. This wizard is used to update or replace the current device drivers. You can allow the wizard to work automatically ("Install the software automatically (Recommended)"), and it will search all local drives, including floppies and CDs. You can also take a more manual approach ("Install from a list or specific location (Advanced)") by pointing the wizard to just removable media and/or a specific drive or folder ("Search for the best driver in these locations"). If you already know the exact location of the new driver, you can point the wizard at it directly ("Don't search, I will choose the driver to install").

- Clicking the Roll Back Driver button uninstalls the current driver and uses the previously installed driver. In order to use this capability, you must have had a previously installed driver to return to. This is a great feature to use if you install a new or updated driver only to discover problems.

- Clicking Uninstall removes the driver from the system. If you fail to remove the uninstalled hardware before the next reboot, the system will most likely detect it and automatically reinstall the drivers.

The Roll Back Driver option is often preferable to the Last Known Good Configuration boot option. The Roll Back Driver option only affects the specific device driver while the LKGC boot option affects the entire system and will eliminate any changes made to the system since the last successful reboot. The Roll Back Driver option can be used even when booting into Safe Mode.

The Resources tab (See Figure 3-14) displays the device's resource settings and shows whether there are other devices in the system that have conflicting settings.

Figure 3-14   A device's Properties dialog box, Resources tab

The tabs that appear in a device's Properties page vary depending on the type of device. For example, disk drives contain a tab for volume information; other devices have a tab for device-specific properties or resources.

If a new device is not a Plug and Play device, there is a good possibility that its current settings will conflict with existing hardware. If you want to add a device that isn't Plug and Play, it's always a good idea to find out what hardware resources are available. You can use this information either to preset the device (if jumpers and dip switches are present) or to configure the device once it is installed and its driver loaded. The four main areas of hardware resource conflict are:

- **IRQ**—The interrupt request level that is used to halt CPU operation in favor of the device. Windows XP supports 16 interrupts, namely IRQ 0 to 15.

3

- *I/O port*—The section of memory used by the hardware to communicate with the operating system. When an IRQ is used, the system checks the I/O port memory area for additional information about what function is needed by the device. The I/O port is represented by a hexadecimal number.

- *DMA (Direct Memory Access)*—A channel used by a hardware device to access memory directly, i.e., bypassing the CPU. Windows XP supports eight DMA channels, numbered 0 to 7.

- *Memory*—The area of physical memory hosted by the motherboard that is used by a device to perform its operations. These memory areas are reserved and cannot be used by any other device or process on the system.

You can check the current state of these resources through Device Manager by selecting Resources by type or Resources by connection from the View menu. Using the data presented, you can configure new hardware so that it does not conflict with any existing devices or drivers. Once a driver is installed, you might be able to alter its resource requirements through the device's Properties dialog box's Resource tab. To access this configuration area, complete the following activity:

Activity 3-9: Hardware Resource Configuration

Time Required: 5 minutes

Objective: Use Device Manager to verify and configure the resources for hardware.

Description: Unlike Windows NT, Windows XP is capable of automatically installing hardware devices through Plug and Play. As long as the device is capable of being installed through PnP, Windows XP should be capable of installing it. However, there can be times when a non-PnP device may conflict with another device or where the resources are not assigned correctly. In those cases, the administrator must manually modify the configuration of one or more devices. The simplest method of doing this is through Device Manager.

In this activity, it is assumed that Control Panel is in Classic view.

To access the hardware resource configuration area:

1. Click **Start**, **Control Panel**, then double-click **System**.
2. Select the **Hardware** tab.
3. Click the **Device Manager** button.
4. Locate the device (click the plus sign to expand the lists) in the list and select it.
5. Right-click the device, and select **Properties** from the shortcut menu.
6. Click the **Resources** tab.

7. Uncheck the **Use automatic settings** check box, and then click **Change Setting** to manually configure the device's configuration.

Hardware Profiles

A hardware profile is similar to a user profile (see Chapter 5) in that it is a collection of custom settings specific to a particular situation. Just as user profiles are specific to the user account used to log onto the system, hardware profiles are specific to the conglomeration of hardware currently composing the computer (including both internal and external devices and network connections). A hardware profile is most often used on portable computers for which hardware configurations change often. Typically, a hardware profile is used to enable or disable network support, modem, external monitors, and docking stations. Hardware profiles can also be employed whenever there is a hardware change between bootups, such as with removable media, PC Cards, disconnected peripherals, and so forth. You can even use hardware profiles to disable devices to help maximize battery life on portable systems.

In most cases, hardware profiles are not strictly required on Plug and Play–compatible systems, but most users find them more convenient than installing and removing drivers each time the system boots with a new hardware configuration. Basically, a hardware profile is a list of all installed devices with selections as to which devices are not enabled for a particular profile. For example, on a notebook computer that is away from the office, a hardware profile could be used to disable networking hardware.

On a system with multiple hardware profiles, the system attempts to select the hardware profile that matches the discovered hardware (Windows XP performs a hardware system check during initial bootup). If an exact match is not found, you are prompted as to which hardware profile to use. Furthermore, you can select one profile as the default profile. When the system fails to locate a profile that matches existing hardware and the defined timeout period expires, the default hardware profile is used. (This is a configurable option.)

Hardware profiles are created through the Hardware Profiles dialog box. To access this dialog box, click the Hardware Profiles button on the Hardware tab of the System applet. Initially, there is only one hardware profile present, the current configuration, with all known devices installed and enabled (assuming you've taken time to troubleshoot any conflicts).

Activity 3-10: Multiple Hardware Configurations

Time Required: 20 minutes

Objective: Use hardware profiles to set up different hardware configurations for a workstation.

Description: A number of Windows operating systems automatically detect when hardware is added or removed from a computer and attempt to install or remove the device and its drivers. In some instances, you may have a computer on which the hardware configuration changes on a regular basis and you want to avoid adding and removing drivers. A docked laptop is one such example. The laptop may be plugged into a docking station, but you also take it with you to meetings where it is still plugged into the network, but not into a docking station.

In this activity, it is assumed that Control Panel is in Classic view.

To create a new hardware profile:

1. Open Hardware Profiles by selecting **Start**, **Control Panel**, then double-click **System**. Select the **Hardware** tab, and then click the **Hardware Profiles** button.

2. Select an existing hardware profile.

3. Click the **Copy** button.

4. Provide a name for the new profile, then click **OK**.

5. Reboot the computer.

6. While restarting, select the new hardware profile when prompted.

7. Click **Start**, **Control Panel**, **System**. Select the **Hardware** tab, and then click the **Device Manager** button.

8. For each device you want to remove from this hardware profile, open its Properties (right-click the device and select **Properties** from the shortcut menu). Items that may be removed from a hardware profile include a mouse, modems, or scanners.

9. On the General tab of each device's Properties (refer to Figure 3-12), change the Device usage pull-down list to **Do not use this device in the current hardware profile (disable)**.

10. For each device you want to restore to this hardware profile, open its Properties (right-click the device and select **Properties** from the shortcut menu).

11. On the General tab of each device's Properties, change the Device usage pull-down list to **Use this device (enable)**.

12. When you've made all the desired changes, close Device Manager.

Activity 3-11: The Mobile Computer

Time Required: 20 minutes

Objective: Create a hardware profile that does not use a NIC.

Description: People who use a laptop computer at the office usually take that same computer home to do work. When at home, there probably won't be a network to connect the computer to, so resources that are used for the NIC could be freed up for potential use by other devices. When the no-NIC hardware profile is chosen during bootup, Windows XP is started as if there was never a NIC installed in the computer.

 This activity assumes Control Panel is in Classic view.

To create a hardware profile for a mobile computer:

1. Click **Start**, **Control Panel**.

2. Double-click **System**.

3. Select the **Hardware** tab.

4. Click the **Hardware Profiles** button.

5. Select an existing hardware profile.

6. Click **Copy**, provide a new name, such as **Mobile Profile – no NIC**, then click **OK**.

7. Click **OK** to close the Hardware Profiles dialog box.

8. Click **OK** to close the System Properties dialog box.

9. Restart the system.

10. When prompted, select the new hardware profile using the arrow keys and press **Enter**.

11. Log onto the system (**Ctrl+Alt+Delete**), providing your username and password if applicable.

12. Click **Start**, **Control Panel**, then double-click **System**. Select the **Hardware** tab, and then click the **Device Manager** button.

13. Click the plus sign to expand the **Network adapters** item.

14. Select the listed NIC.

15. Right-click the NIC, and select **Properties** from the shortcut menu.

16. Change the **Device Usage** pull-down menu to read **Do not use this device in the current hardware profile (disable)**.

17. Click **OK**.

18. Close Device Manager.

19. Now, your system has a normal hardware profile and a profile that has the NIC disabled for use when not connected to the network. Each time you reboot, you can select the appropriate hardware profile.

Once you have defined two or more hardware profiles, you need to make a couple of setting changes to the Hardware Profiles dialog box. First, select which profile should be the default by using the up and down arrows to move the most often used profile to the top of the list. Second, select whether to wait indefinitely for a hardware profile selection or to use the default if no selection is made after a specified time period. This setting applies only when the system cannot automatically determine which profile to use based on discovered hardware.

If there are two or more hardware profiles which have very similar device collections, the system may not be able to automatically detect which hardware profile to use. For example, if you have a docked hardware profile and an undocked hardware profile, the system may not be able to detect the differences in hardware when docked and undocked. In this situation, you are prompted as to which hardware profile to use every time you start your system. To eliminate this problem, you either need to further customize the specifics of the hardware profiles to make automatic detection more accurate, delete hardware profiles that are not used, or set a default hardware profile and a short selection delay.

If Windows XP Professional identifies your computer as a portable unit, the "This is a portable computer" check box is selected. If Windows XP Professional determines that your portable computer is docked, it automatically selects that option.

Startup and Recovery

The Startup and Recovery Options dialog box (see Figure 3-15) allows you to define system startup parameters and specify how STOP errors are handled. You access this dialog box by clicking the Settings button under the Startup and Recovery heading on the Advanced tab of the System applet. Startup controls are found in the region of this window labeled System startup. The startup controls are used to set the default operating system, the selection timer for the boot menu, and the selection timer for the recovery options. The startup controls can be set here with the offered parameters or you can edit the BOOT.INI file directly by clicking the Edit button. The default setting for both timers is 30 seconds. This can be reduced to 5 or 10 seconds to speed system startup.

The options in the area labeled System failure in this window are a bit more esoteric. They provide special controls to deal with an outright Windows XP system crash. When the whole system halts due to a STOP error, the contents of the computer's virtual memory can be dumped to a .dmp file (which resides in the *%systemroot%*\minidump or \windows\minidump folder, by default). Although this dump file is of little use to most users and can usually be discarded, the information it contains can be invaluable when debugging system or application problems.

You have the options of disabling the dump file by selecting "(none)" or selecting from three different sizes of memory dumps: Small memory dump (64 KB), Kernel memory dump, or Complete memory dump. By default, the dump file is placed in the root of the boot drive (i.e., the partition or volume where the main Windows folder resides) and given the name MEMORY.DMP. You can change the placement and name of the dump file by editing the

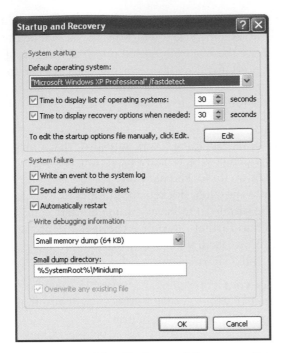

Figure 3-15   The Startup and Recovery dialog box

pathname field. If you select one of the two larger dump file sizes, you can also elect whether or not to overwrite any existing dump file. There are also options for writing an event to the system log, sending administrative alerts, and restarting the system automatically.

Environmental Variables

The Environment Variables dialog box is accessed by clicking the Environment Variables button on the Advanced tab of the System applet. The bottom pane of the tab controls settings for systemwide environment variables; the top pane controls local user environment variables. Only a local user who is currently logged on can set variables on this tab. These variables are used to control how Windows XP operates, particularly how older 16-bit Windows or DOS programs behave within Virtual DOS Machines (VDMs), within which they must run in the Windows XP environment.

Error Reporting

Microsoft has provided Windows XP the ability to report errors regarding the OS and installed applications. Whenever a system or application error occurs and Internet access is available, an anonymous error report is sent to Microsoft. Error reporting is enabled by default. You can select to report OS and/or program errors. You can even select which programs to report. You reach this tool by clicking the Error Reporting button on the Advanced tab of the System applet.

This feature has no immediate benefits or drawbacks for you, but it can help Microsoft develop fixes and patches for Windows XP and possibly improve its future OS products.

Taskbar and Start Menu

The Taskbar and Start Menu applet is the same properties dialog box accessed by right-clicking the Start button and selecting the Properties command from the shortcut menu. The Taskbar tab controls taskbar appearance (lock, auto-hide, keep on top, group similar, and show quick launch) and Notification Area settings (show clock and hide inactive Notification Area icons). The Customize button allows you to define whether specific system tray icons disappear when inactive, remain hidden, or are always displayed. The Start Menu tab is used to select either the Windows XP new stylized Start menu or the Classic Start menu (from Windows 2000). The Customize button for each of these options is used to configure additional settings, such as large or small icons, number of recently accessed programs to display, Internet and e-mail shortcuts, and display of Start menu items, such as link, menu, or hidden.

User Accounts

The User Accounts applet is used to create and manage local user accounts, passwords, and .NET passports, to access the Local Users and Groups tool (part of Computer Management from Administrative Tools), and to specify whether Ctrl+Alt+Delete is required to log on. This tool is discussed in Chapter 5.

MICROSOFT MANAGEMENT CONSOLE OVERVIEW

The **Microsoft Management Console (MMC)** is a graphical interface shell. The MMC provides a structured environment for consoles, snap-ins, and extensions that offer controls over services and objects. A **console** is like a document window; one or more consoles can be loaded into the MMC. Each console can host one or more snap-ins. A **snap-in** is a component that adds control mechanisms to the MMC console for a specific service or object. Each snap-in can support one or more extensions (i.e., specialized tools). Each snap-in (and any of its related extensions) is designed to manipulate a specific service or type of object in the Windows XP local, remote, domain, or Active Directory environment. For example, the Users and Groups snap-in is used to manage local users and groups. The MMC does not provide any management capabilities itself; it merely provides the interface mechanism and environment for system and object controls.

The MMC architecture was created to simplify administration of the Windows networking environment. Versions of the MMC are included with IIS 4.0 and other products deployed on Windows 98 and Windows NT. However, MMC was not fully realized until the final release of Windows 2000 and has been included as a core element of Windows XP.

The most beneficial feature of the MMC is its flexibility. The MMC provides a general-purpose framework that Microsoft has used to consolidate systems management facilities of all kinds, and that third parties often use to incorporate snap-ins for managing their tools as well. It provides a consistent interface for all management tools, thereby enhancing usability and shortening the learning curve when new snap-ins are added. Additionally, multiple snap-ins can be combined in a custom administration layout to suit each administrator's particular needs or responsibilities. No other management tool offers such a wide range of customization.

MMC settings and layout options can be stored as an .msc file, allowing your custom configurations of snap-ins and extensions to be reused later on the same computer or transferred to other systems. The .msc file contains all of the windows currently open in the MMC. These files can be moved from system to system with ease. In addition, you can assign, grant, or restrict access to the .msc files (and the controls they offer) through system policies based on user, group, or computer. Thus, you can selectively and securely assign administrative tasks to nonadministrative users.

The MMC Console

The MMC console itself is a fairly straightforward interface. To open the MMC without a snap-in, just execute MMC from the Start, Run command. There are really only two parts to the main MMC console: the main menu bar and the console window display area. The main menu bar contains the Console, Window, and Help drop-down menus and a movable mini-icon bar with one-click shortcuts to common activities (New, Open, Save, and New Windows). The console display area functions just like any other Windows application that supports multiple document windows.

Consoles have three important parts (see Figure 3-16): console menu bar, console tree, and details pane. The console menu bar contains the Action and View menus, the contents of which change based on the snap-ins and extensions present and active in the console. The console menu bar also contains a mini-icon toolbar of one-click shortcuts to common functions found in the Action and View menus. The console tree is the left pane or division of the console display area, where the loaded snap-ins and extensions are listed, along with context selections (such as computers, domains, users, divisions, and so on). The details pane is the right pane or division of the console display area, where the details associated with the active item from the console tree are displayed.

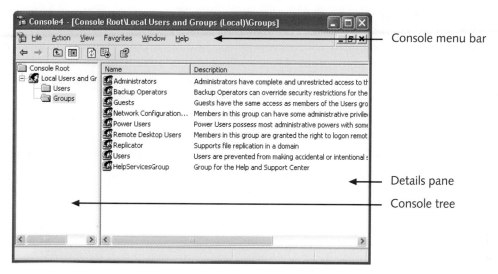

Figure 3-16   The parts of the Microsoft Management Console

Snap-Ins

Snap-ins are the components added into a console that actually perform the actions on services or objects. There are two types of snap-ins: standalone snap-ins and extension snap-ins. Standalone snap-ins are typically referred to simply as snap-ins. They provide the main functions for system administration and control; Windows XP Professional is equipped with a set of snap-ins. The extension snap-ins add functionality to a standalone snap-in. A single extension can be used on any snap-in with similar service/object context. Multiple extensions can be present for a single snap-in. For example, the Computer Management snap-in can be extended by the Event Viewer and Device Manager extensions.

Once you've added and configured a console's snap-ins (see later this chapter), you can save the console to an .msc file in one of four formats. The first and default format is **Author Mode,** which allows users to add and remove snap-ins, create new windows, view the entire console tree, and save new versions of the console. The other three formats are all **User Mode**. Intended for end users, these formats prevent adding or removing snap-ins or resaving the console file. The three types of User Mode formats are: Full Access; Delegated Access, Multiple Windows; and Delegated Access, Single Window. Full Access allows users to create new windows and view the entire console tree. The Delegated Access formats prevent users from viewing portions of the console tree. The Multiple Windows version allows users to create new windows but not close existing windows, whereas the Single Window allows viewing of only one window. The format of the .msc file is changed through the Console, Options command.

Using the MMC

Windows XP is equipped with several preconfigured consoles designed to offer administrative control over your system. These tools are found mainly in Administrative Tools (see the following section), a folder within Control Panel, though it also can appear on the Start menu if configured through the Taskbar and Start Menu applet.

All of the snap-ins for creating the Administrative Tools can also be used to create your own custom consoles. In addition to these predefined consoles, installing other services or applications can add other predefined consoles for custom or unique console controls.

Some snap-ins can serve as standalone snap-ins or as extensions to another snap-in. For example, Device Manager and Event Viewer can be configured to stand alone or as extensions of Computer Management. Once you've added one or more snap-ins (i.e., they appear in the list on the Add or Remove Snap-In dialog box), you can add or modify extensions by selecting the Extensions tab.

Activity 3-12: Microsoft Management Console

Time Required: 10 minutes

Objective: Create an MMC for managing the local computer.

Description: The MMC is an interface for administering most things on the computer, domain, tree, forest, and so on. It is fully customizable, in that the administrator can add as many or few items to the MMC as he or she wants. In addition, multiple MMC files can be created with each having a different focus. One could be created for managing hardware, another for software, and yet another for user accounts. In this activity, you will set up a console for managing the local computer.

To create an MMC for system management:

1. Click **Start**, **Run**, type **mmc.exe**, and then click OK.
2. Select **File**, **Add/Remove Snap-in**.
3. Click **Add**.
4. Locate and select **Computer Management** from the **Add Standalone Snap-in** dialog box.
5. Click **Add**.
6. Select **Local computer** (if necessary).
7. Click **Finish**.
8. Click **Close**.
9. Select the **Extensions** tab.
10. Ensure the **Add all extensions** check box is selected.

11. Click **OK** to return to the MMC. Notice the Computer Management snap-in is listed in the console tree.

12. Maximize the console root window by double-clicking its title bar.

13. Select **File**, **Save As**.

14. Change to the directory where you want to store the console file.

15. Give the console file a name, such as **COMPMGT.MSC**. Click **Save**.

16. Select **File**, **Exit**.

ADMINISTRATIVE TOOLS

The Administrative Tools are a collection of system configuration utilities that Microsoft deemed powerful and dangerous enough to separate from the Control Panel applets. You must have administrative privileges to use the seven Administrative Tools on Windows XP Professional: Component Services, Data Sources (ODBC), Event Viewer, Local Security Policy, Performance, Services, and Computer Management.

Component Services is a tool used mainly by application developers. However, this tool can also be used by system administrators who need to custom configure a system for a specific application. This tool is used to administer COM and COM+ applications. If you want to explore the uses of this tool, consult the online Help material and the Microsoft Windows .NET Server Resource Kit.

Data Sources (ODBC) is a tool used to configure the OS to interact with various database management systems, such as SQL Server or FoxPro. This tool is often used in applications designed for enterprise-wide or Web-based deployments; if your application can already access data from an SQL server, proper configuration of the ODBC Source Administrator will let it access data from a FoxPro database as well. To explore the uses of this tool, consult the online Help material and the Microsoft Windows .NET Server Resource Kit.

The Event Viewer is used to view system messages regarding the failure or success of various key occurrences within the Windows XP environment. Details of system errors, security issues, and application activities are recorded in the logs viewed through the Event Viewer. This tool is discussed in Chapter 10, "Performance Tuning."

Local Security Policy is used to configure local security settings for a system. It is similar to, but more specific than, a group policy for a domain, site, or OU. This tool is discussed in Chapter 6, "Windows XP Security and Access Controls."

The Performance item is used to access System Monitor and the Performance Logs and Alerts tool. This is discussed in Chapter 10, "Performance Tuning."

Services is used for stopping and starting services and configuring the startup parameters for services (such as whether to start when the system starts, whether to employ a user account security context to start the service, and so on). There is an activity for using this tool in Chapter 15, "Troubleshooting Windows XP."

Computer Management (see Figure 3-17) is an MMC console that serves as a common troubleshooting and administration interface for several tools. The Computer Management console is divided into three sections: System Tools, Storage, and Services and Applications.

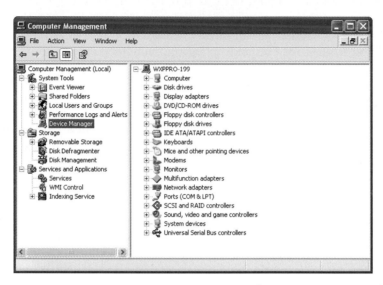

Figure 3-17   Computer Management, with Device Manager selected

The System Tools section contains five tools:

- ■ *Event Viewer*—Described earlier in this chapter. This tool is discussed in Chapter 10 and Chapter 15.

- ■ *Shared Folders*—Used to view the shared folders on the local system. This interface shows hidden shares, current sessions, and open files. This tool also allows you to view and alter the share configuration settings of user limit, caching, and permissions. From the Shares subfolder, you can create new shares. From the Sessions subfolder, you can disconnect all sessions or just one specific session (i.e., force out any users connecting to the system). From the Open Files subfolder, you can disconnect all open files or one specific open file (i.e., stop users from accessing currently open files from this system).

- ■ *Local Users and Groups*—Used to create and manage local user accounts and groups. Details on use, examples, and activities for this tool are found in Chapter 5.

- ■ *Performance Logs and Alerts*—Used to access the Performance monitoring tool of Windows XP. The use of this tool in troubleshooting is rather tedious and complex (see Chapter 10 for examples and activities involving this tool).

- *Device Manager*—Used to view and alter current hardware configurations of all existing devices. See the description of Device Manager earlier in this chapter.

The Storage section of Computer Management has three tools for storage device administration. Details on use, examples, and activities for these tools are found in Chapter 4.

- *Removable Storage*—Used to manage removable media, such as floppy disks, tapes, and Zip drives.

- *Disk Defragmenter*—Used to improve the layout of stored data on drives by reassembling fragmented files and aggregating unused space.

- *Disk Management*—Used to view and alter the partitioning and volume configuration of hard drives.

The Services and Applications section contains management controls for various installed and active services and applications. The actual contents of this section depend on what is installed on your system. Some of the common controls on a Windows XP Professional system include:

- *Indexing Service*—Used to define the corpus (collection of documents indexed for searching) for Indexing Service. For information on using this tool, consult the Microsoft Windows .NET Server Resource Kit.

- *WMI Control*—Used to configure Windows Management Instrumentation (WMI).

- *Services*—See the description of Services earlier in this chapter. This tool is discussed in Chapter 15.

PCMCIA or PC Cards

As a fully Plug and Play-compatible operating system, Windows XP includes support for **PCMCIA** (Personal Computer Memory Card Interface Specification) or **PC Cards**. These are credit card-sized devices that plug into a slit port found on most notebooks and some desktop computers. The plug-in operation is very similar to inserting a cartridge into a game. Most computers that support PC Cards have two slots, allowing up to two additional devices to be added to the system. PC Cards can be just about any device, including memory expansions, SCSI cards, NICs, modems, or proprietary peripheral interfaces.

Card services are installed automatically when Windows XP is installed onto a HAL-supported notebook or portable computer (or a desktop computer with a PC Card slot device). Once installed, most of the tasks and processes required to manage and enable PC Card support are handled automatically by Windows XP. Unlike Windows NT and Windows 95/98, Windows XP does not have a PC Card (or PCMCIA) applet. Your only real control is through the Unplug or Eject Hardware icon in the Notification Area. Double-click this icon to instruct the system to stop using and release control of the PC Card device so it can be removed. In most cases, it is a good idea to use this tool to stop the driver of a particular device before unplugging it from the system. This helps prevent system errors and data loss by allowing the system to finish using the device, clear all related buffers, and disable the drivers and dependent services. Once a new card is reinserted, the system detects and enables it automatically.

There are three types of PCMCIA card standards:

1. Type I
   a. Cards can be up to 3.3 mm thick
   b. Typically used to add memory to a laptop
2. Type II
   a. Cards can be up to 5 mm thick
   b. Typically used to add a network card or modem to a computer
3. Type III
   a. Cards can be up to 10.5 mm thick
   b. Usually used to connect a portable hard drive

CHAPTER SUMMARY

- In this chapter, you learned about the various applets and tools found in Control Panel and Administrative Tools.
- The Accessibility Options applet is used to configure special interface enhancements for the visual-, audio-, or movement-impaired user.
- The Add Hardware applet is used to install and troubleshoot devices.
- The Add or Remove Programs applet is used to change or remove applications, install new applications, or change installed Windows components.
- The Administrative Tools applet is used to access the administrative tools.
- The Date and Time applet is used to set calendar date, clock time, and time zone.
- The Display applet is used to configure and manage your screen resolution. This tool is also used to configure multiple screens.
- The Regional and Language Options applet is used to set location-specific language items.
- The Power Options applet is used manage the power conservation options, such as ACPI, and shut down options, such as Standby and Hibernation.
- The Scheduled Tasks applet is used to automate tasks.
- The Sounds and Audio Devices applet is used to configure audio schemes.
- The System applet is used to configure and manage numerous aspects of a system. This includes hardware profiles, driver signing, device configuration, driver rollback, and startup and recovery options.

3

❑ This chapter also discussed the Microsoft Management Console and the Administrative Tools.

❑ Computer Management is a collective interface for several tools used for system management and troubleshooting.

❑ This chapter also discussed the processes of installing hardware, using hardware profiles, and dealing with PC Cards.

KEY TERMS

applet — A tool or utility found in Control Panel that typically has a single focused purpose or function.

Author Mode — The condition of a console that allows users to add and remove snap-ins, create new windows, view the entire console tree, and save new versions of the console.

console — The collection of snap-ins and extensions saved as an .msc file loaded into the MMC that offers administrative controls.

Control Panel — The collection of tools and utilities (called applets) within Windows, where most system- and hardware-level installation and configuration take place.

device — A physical component, either internal or external to the computer, that is used to perform a specific function. Devices include hard drives, video cards, network interface cards, printers, and so on.

DMA (Direct Memory Access) — A channel used by a hardware device to access memory directly, bypassing the CPU. Windows XP supports eight DMA channels, numbered 0 to 7.

driver — A software element that is used by an operating system to control a device. Drivers are usually device specific.

hardware profile — A collection of custom device settings used on computers with changing physical components.

input locale — A combined language and keyboard layout used to define how data is entered into a computer.

I/O port — The section of memory used by the hardware to communicate with the operating system. When an IRQ is used, the system checks the I/O port memory area for additional information about what function is needed by the device. The I/O port is represented by a hexadecimal number.

IRQ — The interrupt request level that is used to halt CPU operation in favor of the device. Windows supports 16 interrupts, namely IRQ 0 to 15.

Microsoft Management Console (MMC) — The standardized interface into which consoles, snap-ins, and extensions are loaded to perform administrative tasks.

PC Cards — The modern name of the PCMCIA technology. PC Cards are credit card-sized devices typically used to expand the functionality of notebook or portable computers.

PCMCIA — The older name for the technology now called PC Cards. PCMCIA stands for Personal Computer Memory Card International Association.

Plug and Play (PnP) — A technology that allows an operating system to inspect and identify a device, install the correct driver, and enable the device, all without user interaction. Plug and Play simplifies the adding and removing of hardware and can often offer on-the-fly reconfiguration of devices without rebooting.

Scheduled Tasks — The component of Windows XP used to automate the execution of programs and batch files based on time and system conditions.

service — A software element used by the operating system to perform a function. Services include offering resources over the network, accessing resources over the network, print spooling, and so on.

snap-in — A component that adds control mechanisms to a console for a specific service or object, thereby extending the functionality of that console (as with snap-ins for the MMC).

User Mode — The condition of a console that prevents adding or removing snap-ins or resaving the console file.

virtual memory — The combination of physical RAM and page file space used by the operating system to enlarge usable memory for processes.

REVIEW QUESTIONS

1. Which of the following tools is the primary interface through which most Windows XP administration tasks are performed?

   a. Display Applet

   b. Computer Management

   c. Scheduled Tasks

   d. My Computer

2. The MMC offers native administration controls without snap-ins. True or False?

3. In the context of the MMC, what are extensions used for? (Choose all that apply.)

   a. to alter the display of the MMC

   b. to restrict controls based on user accounts

   c. to add additional functionality to standalone snap-ins

   d. to allow remote administration of services and objects

4. The MMC can be used to manipulate services and objects on local and remote systems. True or False?

5. Which .msc mode allows users to create new windows but prevents them from viewing some parts of the console tree? (Choose all that apply.)

   a. Author Mode

   b. User Mode: Full Access

   c. User Mode: Delegated Access, Multiple Windows

   d. User Mode: Delegated Access, Single Window

6. Which of the following are tools found in the Administrative Tools section of Control Panel? (Choose all that apply.)

    a. Computer Management

    b. My Computer

    c. Event Viewer

    d. Utility Manager

7. What is the best tool in Windows XP for automating a recurring task?

    a. AT

    b. CRON

    c. Scheduled Tasks

    d. Event Viewer

8. Which of the following can trigger the start of an automated event? (Choose all that apply.)

    a. user logon

    b. system idle

    c. exact time

    d. system startup

9. Automated tasks can be halted when the system switches to battery power. True or False?

10. Which applet is used to configure ToggleKeys and SoundSentry?

    a. Sound and Multimedia

    b. Keyboard

    c. Accessibility Options

    d. System

11. If you want to use the numeric keypad to control the mouse insertion point movement, what applet must you open to configure this option?

    a. Sound and Multimedia

    b. Keyboard

    c. Accessibility Options

    d. System

12. The Add Hardware applet can be used to perform which of the following actions? (Choose all that apply.)

    a. Troubleshoot an existing device.

    b. Disable a PC Card driver before it is removed.

    c. Configure multiple display layout.

    d. Install and uninstall drivers for new hardware already present in a Windows XP system.

13. Plug and Play devices, although automatically detected by the operating system during bootup, always require the user to employ the Add Hardware applet to install the device driver. True or False?

14. What applet should you use to add Windows components distributed on the Windows XP Professional CD?

    a. System

    b. Add or Remove Programs

    c. Date and Time

    d. Regional Settings

15. The Date/Time applet changes the time only as it is seen by Windows XP; the system's BIOS settings must still be changed through DOS. True or False?

16. What applet is used to switch the functions of the mouse buttons?

    a. Accessibility Options

    b. Regional Settings

    c. Mouse

    d. System

17. Home/Office Desk, Presentation, and Portable/Laptop are examples of predefined _____ .

    a. hardware profiles

    b. user profiles

    c. Power Options settings

    d. system profiles

18. Troubleshooting help for an audio card can be accessed through which applet? (Choose all that apply.)

    a. Device Manager

    b. System

    c. Sounds and Audio Devices

    d. Accessibility Options

19. What applet can be used to change domain or workgroup membership?

    a. System

    b. Add Hardware

    c. Accessibility Options

    d. Workgroup Settings

20. Once you install Windows XP, you must reinstall the entire operating system to rename the computer. True or False?

21. When a STOP error occurs, what can the system do? (Choose all that apply.)

    a. Write an event to the system log.

    b. Send an administrative alert.

    c. Write a memory dump file.

    d. Restart the system.

22. What tool is used to ensure that a newly installed device is functioning properly?

    a. System

    b. Add Hardware

    c. Device Manager

    d. Administrative Tools

23. Which of the following system resources may often find themselves in contention for non–Plug and Play devices? (Choose all that apply.)

    a. paging file space

    b. I/O Port

    c. priority CPU cycles

    d. IRQ

24. What convention or mechanism is used on Windows XP to manage changing hardware configurations smoothly across restarts?

    a. Plug and Play

    b. user profiles

    c. manually installing and removing drivers

    d. hardware profiles

25. A hardware profile can be chosen automatically by the system during bootup. True or False?

Case Projects

Case Project 3-1

1. You need to delegate administrative tasks to nonadministrative users, but you are concerned about granting too much power to users. What can you do?

2. You want to participate in the SETI@home project (*http://setiathome.ssl.berkeley. edu/*). However, the utility consumes most of the CPU cycles when it is active. How can you participate in this project but still be able to get other work done on your computer?

3. You have a notebook computer with a docking station. The docking station hosts a 21" monitor, a DVD drive, a tape backup, and a color printer. What is the best method to enable your notebook computer to use the devices on the docking station while avoiding problems when not connected to the docking station?

MANAGING WINDOWS XP FILE SYSTEMS AND STORAGE

After reading this chapter and completing the exercises, you will be able to:

♦ Understand basic and dynamic storage

♦ Understand the drive configurations supported by Windows XP

♦ Understand the FAT, FAT32, and NTFS file systems

♦ Understand Windows XP drive, volume, and partition maintenance and administration

♦ Understand how to manage folder-level properties

♦ Understand permissions, sharing, and other issues related to file systems

The Windows XP file storage subsystem offers a versatile disk management system. Windows XP supports both basic and dynamic storage, large disk volumes, fault-tolerant drive configurations, and secure access controls. The complexity and versatility of Windows XP storage capabilities make this a reliable platform for home and office use. This chapter discusses the decisions you need to make and actions you need to take to deploy Windows XP to provide the most effective and efficient storage solution for your needs.

FILE STORAGE BASICS

Windows XP supports two types of storage: basic and dynamic. **Basic storage** is the storage method with which most Microsoft PC users are familiar. It centers on partitioning a physical disk. Partitioning is a method for dividing a hard drive into logical divisions that can each host a different file system and are uniquely assigned a drive letter. **Dynamic storage** is a new method supported only by Windows XP and Windows 2000. Dynamic storage is not based on partitions but on **volumes**. In function, volumes are no different than partitions. However, Microsoft's dynamic storage mechanism uses a different process to perform the drive division activity. The dynamic storage technology allows for more flexibility in drive configurations, allows for drive changes with fewer calls to restart the machine, and offers better support for system recovery.

From a user's perspective, the only difference between basic and dynamic storage is the additional ability to create expanded volumes and fault-tolerant configurations on dynamic drives. An expanded volume is a division of a hard drive that can be increased in size even while it contains data.

Basic Storage

Basic storage is the traditional, industry-standard method of dividing a hard drive into partitions. A partition is a logical division of the physical space on a hard drive. Each partition can be formatted with a different file system. Partitions must be formatted before they can be used by an operating system.

Activity 4-1: Creating a Disk Partition

Time Required: 20 minutes

Objective: Use Disk Management to create a new partition.

Description: The minimum disk space recommended for Windows XP is 2 GB. It is often recommended that the initial partition on the computer be set up to cover the minimum recommendations but *not* use the entire hard disk. Once Windows XP is installed, Disk Management can be used to format and configure the unallocated disk space as required. In this activity, you use the unallocated space on the basic disk to set up a new primary partition.

To create a partition on a basic drive:

This activity requires that a basic drive with unallocated space be present in the system. Additionally, the drive must have either only three primary partitions or only two primary partitions if an extended partition is present. This project also assumes the Control Panel is in Classic view.

1. Open Control Panel (**Start, Control Panel, Switch to Classic View**, if necessary).

2. Double-click **Administrative Tools**.

3. Double-click **Computer Management**.

4. Expand the **Storage** console node if necessary (click the plus sign to the left of the node).

5. Select **Disk Management**.

6. Right-click an unallocated area of a basic drive, and then click **New Partition**.

7. The New Partition Wizard opens. Click **Next**.

8. Select **Primary partition**. Click **Next**.

9. Select the amount of space to use in this partition. **Accept the default of the maximum space available**. Click **Next**.

10. Assign a drive letter. Accept the default. Click **Next**.

11. Select the file system to format this partition. Accept the default of NTFS. Click **Next**.

12. The wizard displays a list of the actions to be performed in creating this partition. Click **Finish**. The system creates the partition, formats the drive, and assigns the drive letter. The display of the drive is updated to reflect the new partition.

There are two types of partitions: primary and extended. A **primary partition** is a division of a hard drive that can be marked active and therefore used to boot the computer. An **extended partition** is a division of a hard drive that can be subdivided into additional divisions or drives called logical drives. Also, extended partitions cannot be marked active, and therefore cannot be used to boot the computer.

A single hard drive can host up to four primary partitions, or it can host up to three primary partitions and a single extended partition. An extended partition can be further divided into logical drives. Only primary partitions and logical drives can be formatted with a file system. Thus, a single hard drive can appear as one or more accessible or usable drives (that is, after the partition is properly formatted).

A primary partition can be marked **active**. This informs the computer's BIOS to start from a specific primary partition which contains the starting information for an operating system. Only primary partitions can be active and only a single partition can be active at any time. The active partition does not have to be the first partition on the drive.

ACTIVITY

Activity 4-2: Activating a Partition

Time Required: 10 minutes

Objective: Use Disk Management to make a different partition active.

Description: To be able to start from a partition, the partition must be primary and it must be active. Only one partition may be active at any one time. In this activity, you make the partition that was created in the previous activity the active partition.

This Activity should be performed with great care. Marking the wrong partition as active results in a system that will not be able to start. If you make a mistake and change the active partition, you can restore it using a DOS start disk and the FDISK tool to re-mark the correct partition as active.

To mark a partition active on a basic drive:

This activity requires that Activity 4-1 be completed first.

1. Take note of which partition is currently marked active: Healthy (Active). If the system partition is marked active, then the designer will show Healthy (System).

2. Right-click the partition created in Activity 4-1, and then click **Mark Partition as Active**. The Disk Management drive display shows the partition as active: Healthy (Active). (If your system partition is the active partition, you may see a warning prompt about changing this. Click Yes to continue. However, be sure to return the system partition to active status after completing this activity.)

3. Right-click the partition that was marked active at the beginning of this activity, and then click **Mark Partition as Active**. The Disk Management drive display shows the partition created in Activity 4-1 as active: Healthy (Active).

In basic storage, volumes or volume sets are two to 32 partitions combined into a single logical structure formatted with a single file system. Volume sets can be extended simply by adding another partition. But volume sets can be reduced in size only by breaking the set and creating a new set. The act of breaking the set destroys (or at least makes inaccessible) all data stored on the volume. A volume set can span multiple partitions on one or more physical drives. A volume set is represented in the operating system by a single **drive letter**. A volume set provides no fault tolerance. If a single drive or partition in a volume set fails, all data in the set is destroyed.

The dynamic storage method uses a slightly different definition for the term "volume," so be careful to review the context when it is discussed.

Typically, you want to create partitions or volumes as large as the operating system and file system allow. Under Windows XP, those sizes are as follows:

- *FAT*—4 GB
- *FAT32*—32 GB
- *NTFS*—4 TB

Each formatted partition or volume set is assigned a drive letter. Letters A and B are typically reserved for floppy drives, but letters C through Z can be used for formatted partitions and volumes hosted on the hard drive. Thus, only 24 formatted partitions can be accessed from Windows XP. This limitation does not impose a serious restriction in most situations.

The basic storage type supports a wide range of disk configurations, from single, formatted partitions (often called drives or logical drives) to fully fault-tolerant **Redundant Array of Independent Disks (RAID-5)** configurations. RAID configurations combine two or more hard drives into a single accessible volume that provides for higher performance or the ability to restore data in the event of a drive failure. The main difference between basic storage and dynamic storage is that basic storage disk structures require a system restart when changed.

Windows XP supports this traditional method of storage for backward compatibility. In other words, Windows XP can take control of drive configurations (see the Drive Configurations section later in this chapter) from previous operating systems (Windows 2000, NT, 95, 98, ME, and DOS). However, the drive structures must conform to the current restrictions of the file systems they host and the hosted file system must be supported by Windows XP (FAT, FAT32, or NTFS). However, Windows XP does not support creation of basic storage drive structures beyond single, formatted partitions. It can manage only existing structures.

Windows XP can be installed only onto basic storage partitions. There are two partitions associated with Windows XP: system partition and boot partition. Take careful note of their descriptions, because many people get them confused. The **system partition** is the active partition where the boot files (required to display the boot menu and initiate the starting of Windows XP) are stored. The **boot partition** hosts the main Windows XP system files and is the initial default location for the paging file (these are generally the \WINDOWS and \WINNT directories). The boot partition can be the same partition as the system partition, or it can be any other partition (or logical drive in an extended partition) on any drive hosted by the computer.

Note that the drive letters of the system partition and boot partition cannot be changed. In addition, once Windows XP is installed, the boot partition drive can be transformed into a dynamic storage device, but the system partition host must remain a basic storage device.

 Neither the system partition nor the boot partition can be a member of a volume set or stripe set; however, they both can be the source of the original partition or drive in a disk mirror and disk-duplexing configuration.

Dynamic Storage

Dynamic storage is a type of storage technique (Microsoft documentation labels it as a new standard) introduced in Windows 2000 that does not use partitions. Instead, this method views an entire physical hard drive as a single entity. Microsoft's dynamic storage mechanism uses a different process to perform the drive division activity than does the legacy partitioning technology. The dynamic storage technology allows for more flexibility in drive configurations, allows for drive changes with fewer restarts, and offers better support for system recovery.

When an entire physical drive is viewed as a single entity, it can be divided into one or more volumes. This storage method offers drive structures from **simple volumes** (entire hard drives as a single formatted entity) to fully fault-tolerant RAID-5 configurations.

 The main difference between dynamic storage and basic storage is that dynamic storage structures can be expanded on the fly without restarting Windows XP.

Only Windows 2000 Server, Windows 2000 Professional, Windows Server 2003, and Windows XP Professional systems can access data on dynamic storage volumes; most other operating systems, including Windows 95, 98, ME, XP Home Edition, and NT on a multiboot system cannot access dynamic volumes.

Unlike basic storage drives, dynamic storage drives belong to the OS on which they were created. A dynamic storage drive created by Windows XP Professional must be imported into Windows 2000 Server, Windows 2000 Professional, or Windows Server 2003 on a multiboot system for these other OSs to access the contents of the dynamic drive. However, this process changes its ownership. In addition, the drive must be reimported into Windows XP Professional to return it to its original owner. This process is known as importing a foreign disk.

Any hard drive, with or without partitions, can be transformed into dynamic storage hosts through a selection wizard. This wizard is started when the **Disk Management** tool is accessed (Start, Control Panel, Switch to Classic View, Administrative Tools, Computer Management, Storage, Disk Management) and a physical hard drive is present with no predefined partitions. This wizard appears only the first time Disk Management is accessed after booting, after adding a new drive, or deleting all partitions on a drive. You are prompted whether to enable dynamic storage on the new or blank local drives.

Existing drives with partitions can be upgraded to dynamic storage by using the Convert to Dynamic Disk command. Converting a drive does not cause data loss or any change in the existing partition structure (other than converting them into volumes). Plus, existing drive configurations (mirror, duplex, stripe, and spanned volumes) can be upgraded to a dynamic volume. This command appears in the shortcut menu when you right-click a drive header—not a volume—in Disk Management. The drive(s) must have at least 1 MB of unallocated space, and you must restart for the changes to take effect.

Once a drive is converted to host dynamic storage, it is labeled as such in Disk Management (see Figure 4-1).

Once you have a dynamic storage host, the next step is to create a volume. A volume is a portion of one or more hard disks that is combined into a single logical structure, formatted with a single file system, and accessed through a single drive letter (also called a **mount point**).

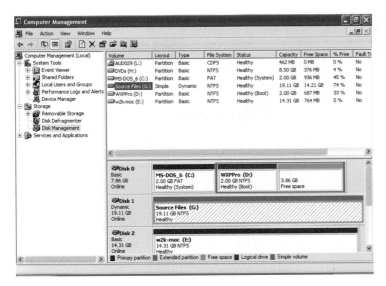

Figure 4-1   A dynamic volume seen through the Disk Management portion of Computer Management

Activity 4-3: Creating a New Volume

Time Required: 15 minutes

Objective: Use the Disk Management tool to create a new volume and format it with a file system.

Description: When adding new hard drives into a system, you must create formatted volumes in order to store data on the drives. In this activity, you accomplish this process by using the Disk Management tool. (You will need an unallocated dynamic storage device to complete this activity.)

1. Open Control Panel (**Start**, **Control Panel**).

2. Double-click **Administrative Tools**.

3. Double-click **Computer Management**.

4. Expand the **Storage** console node if necessary (click the plus sign to the left of the node).

5. Select **Disk Management**.

6. From within Disk Management, right-click an unallocated dynamic storage device, and then click **New Volume**. This starts the New Volume Wizard. Click **Next**.

7. You are prompted as to what type of volume to create. Click **Simple**. Click **Next**. (See the Drive Configurations section later in this chapter.)

8. Select the available dynamic storage devices and how much of each device to use in the volume being created (see Figure 4-2). Click **Next**.

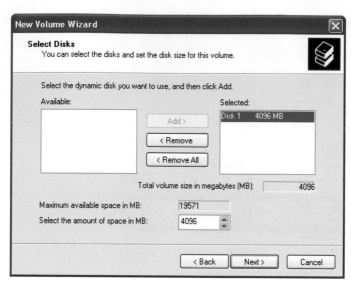

Figure 4-2   Select Disks dialog box of the New Volume Wizard

9. Next, you are prompted to select a drive letter, a mount point, or to not assign a drive letter at all (see Figure 4-3). Select the option that suits your purposes. Click **Next**. (See the Drive Letters and Mount Points section later in this chapter.)

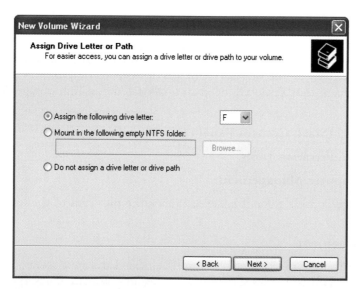

Figure 4-3   Assign Drive letter or Path dialog box of the New Volume Wizard

10. Select whether to format the volume and with which file system (see Figure 4-4). Click **Next**.

11. Click **Finish** to implement volume creation.

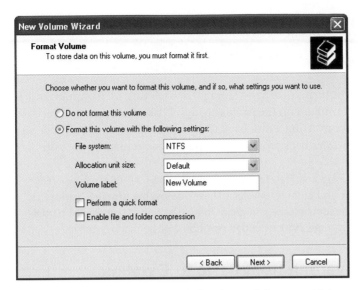

Figure 4-4 Format Volume dialog box of the New Volume Wizard

Table 4-1 compares the functions and capabilities of basic and dynamic storage devices.

Table 4-1 Functions and capabilities of basic and dynamic disks

Tasks	Basic disk	Dynamic disk
Create and delete primary and extended partitions	X	
Create and delete logical drives within an extended partition	X	
Format and label a partition and mark it as active	X	
Delete a volume set	X	
Break a mirror from a mirror set	X	
Repair a mirror set	X	
Repair a stripe set with parity	X	
Upgrade a basic disk to a dynamic disk	X	
Create and delete simple, spanned, striped, mirrored, and RAID-5 volumes		X
Extend a volume across one or more disks		X
Add a mirror to, or remove a mirror from, a mirrored volume		X
Repair a mirrored volume		X
Repair a RAID-5 volume		X
Check information about disks, such as capacity, available free space, and current status	X	X
View volume and partition properties such as size	X	X
Make and change drive-letter assignments for hard disk volumes or partitions and CD-ROM devices	X	X
Create volume mount points	X	X
Set or verify disk sharing and access arrangements for a volume or partition	X	X

This table was reproduced from the *Microsoft Windows XP Professional Resource Kit* from Microsoft Press.

Dynamic drives can be returned to basic storage by deleting all volumes and issuing the Convert to Basic Disk command on the drive through Disk Management. Because you must delete the volumes first, converting a disk back to basic storage destroys all data on that drive. Therefore, you should always back up all your data before returning to basic storage.

The inclusion of Plug and Play technology in Windows XP brings support for removable media and storage devices. These **removable storage devices** or storage media can contain only a single primary partition. They cannot participate in dynamic storage, host extended partitions, or be marked active.

Activity 4-4: Converting from Basic to Dynamic

Time Required: 5 minutes

Objective: Use Disk Management to convert a basic disk to a dynamic disk.

Description: In this activity, you convert a basic partition to a dynamic partition.

To convert a basic drive to a dynamic drive:

This activity requires that a second hard drive (a basic drive) be present on the system. Removable disks cannot be converted. Please ensure that the disk selected is an internal drive.

1. Select a basic disk in Disk Management. If necessary, open Computer Management.

2. Right-click the basic disk, and then click **Convert to Dynamic Disk**.

3. A list of all hard drives present on the system is displayed. The disk you selected is already checked. Do not change the status of the check boxes on this list. Click **OK**. Disk Management displays the drive as Dynamic.

4. Click the **Convert** button in the Disks to Convert dialog box and confirm the conversion by clicking **Yes** to any warning messages that may appear.

Activity 4-5: Creating a New Volume on a Dynamic Disk

Time Required: 10 minutes

Objective: Create a volume on a dynamic disk.

4

Description: New volumes can be created on basic or dynamic disks. There is no difference in the process between the two types of disks. In this activity, a new volume is to be created on the dynamic disk that was created in a previous activity.

To create a volume on a dynamic drive:

1. Right-click the unallocated space on a dynamic drive, and then click **New Volume**. This starts the New Volume Wizard.

2. Click **Next**.

3. Select the volume type to create. In this case, click **Simple**. Click **Next**.

4. For a simple volume, you need only unallocated space from a single drive. Make sure the drive is listed in the Selected dynamic disk field.

5. In the Select the amount of space in MB field, enter an amount of about half of the maximum available space. Click **Next**.

6. Assign a drive letter. Accept the defaults. Click **Next**.

7. Select the file system to format the new volume. Accept the default of NTFS. Click **Next**.

8. The Wizard displays a list of actions to be performed in creating the new volume. Click **Finish**.

Activity 4-6: Extending a Volume

Time Required: 10 minutes

Objective: Use Disk Management to extend a volume.

Description: When a disk is running low on disk space, most people assume that they need a bigger drive. In most cases, another drive may be one option that is overlooked. In this activity, the user is to extend a volume so that the partition uses space from two different disk drives.

To extend a volume:

This activity requires that Activity 4-5 be completed first.

1. Right-click the volume created in Activity 4-5, and then click **Extend Volume**.

2. The Extend Volume Wizard opens. Click **Next**.

3. Make sure the drive with unallocated space is listed in the Selected dynamic disk field.

4. Change the size of the remaining unallocated space to add to the existing volume to 80 percent of that available (if there is 200 MB remaining, change the number to 180). Click **Next**.

5. The Wizard displays a list of actions to perform in extending the volume. Click **Finish**. Disk Management displays the extension with the same drive letter as the original volume.

Activity 4-7: Reverting from Dynamic to Basic

Time Required: 5 minutes

Objective: Use Disk Management to convert a dynamic disk back to a basic disk

Description: Previously, a basic disk had been converted to dynamic. In a similar manner, a dynamic disk can be converted to basic. This activity has the user perform that task.

To revert a dynamic drive to a basic drive:

This activity requires that Activity 4-4 be completed. As in the previous activity, the disk you select should be internal.

1. If there are any volumes on the drive, they must be removed before converting back to basic. Use Activity 4-12 to delete any volumes from the drive.

2. Right-click the drive used in Activity 4-4, and then click **Convert to Basic Disk**. Disk Management displays the drive as Basic.

DRIVE CONFIGURATIONS

Windows XP is able to import and maintain multidrive configurations from previous OSs which remain as basic storage. Windows XP can create new single partitions on basic storage drives. However, to create new multidrive configurations, Windows XP requires that only dynamic storage devices be used. There are five drive configurations, or structures, used by Microsoft operating systems, but only the following three are supported by Windows XP:

- *Simple volume*—All or part of a single drive. Does not provide any fault tolerance. NTFS volumes can be extended; FAT and FAT32 volumes cannot be extended.

- *Spanned volume*—A volume configuration of two or more parts (up to 32) of one or more drives, or a volume configuration of two or more entire drives. Elements of the spanned volume do not have to be equal in size. Data is written to the first drive in the volume until it is full, and then it continues with the next drive. This is also called an extended volume. Spanned volumes don't provide any fault tolerance. If one partition or volume in the set fails, all data is lost. Spanned volumes cannot be part of a striped volume or a **mirrored volume**. A mirrored

4

volume is a volume which has an exact real-time backup or duplicate of itself on another hard drive. NTFS spanned volumes can be extended; FAT and FAT32 spanned volumes cannot. The system volume and boot volume cannot be extended. Volume sets can be reduced in size only by breaking the set and creating a new set. The act of breaking the set destroys all data stored on the volume.

- **Striped volume**—Two or more volumes (up to 32) of one or more drives or two or more entire drives (up to 32). Data is written to all drives in equal amounts (in 64 KB units) to spread the workload and improve performance. Each part or drive must be roughly equal in size. Striped volumes do not provide any fault tolerance: If one partition or drive in the set fails, all data is lost. Striped volumes cannot be mirrored or extended. Boot and system partitions cannot be part of a striped volume. This can also be called a stripe set or a striped set. This type of drive configuration is also known as RAID 0 (Redundant Array of Independent Disks). Windows XP Professional can only create RAID 0 stripe sets, but it can import any preexisting RAID drive configuration.

NOTE   No matter what disk configuration is used, always protect your data by using a regularly scheduled backup system.

Just as single or standalone dynamic drives from other Windows OSs can be imported into Windows XP Professional, so can preexisting multivolume or multidrive structures. This process is simple and straightforward when the drive structures are based on dynamic drives from Windows 2000 Server, Windows 2000 Professional, Windows XP Professional, or Windows Server 2003. However, if the drive structure is originally from Windows NT, the drive structure will appear in Disk Management and each drive from the set is assigned a drive letter. These drives will be labeled as Failed and are inaccessible.

Fortunately, Microsoft has created a tool to help you save the data from inaccessible drive structures. The tool is called FTONLINE. It is part of the Windows Support tools found in the \Support\Tools folder on the Windows XP Professional installation CD. You need to extract the FTONLINE tool from the SUPPORT.CAB file before it can be used.

The basic use of this tool is to execute the command "ftonline x" from a command prompt where x is the drive letter of the first disk from the failed drive structure. FTONLINE temporarily mounts the failed drive structure to the drive letter. If the mount succeeds, an Online success message is displayed. For the rest of your current logon session, you can access the data stored on this legacy drive structure. Microsoft recommends that you immediately create a backup copy of the data stored on this structure, destroy the partitions, re-create the drive structure using dynamic storage, then restore the data from backup. FTONLINE is designed as a short-term recovery tool, not as a permanent means to access legacy drive structures.

If multivolume drive configurations are used on a system, take care to move all of the drives hosting volumes from the configuration to the new system. Otherwise, you will be unable to access or back up the data even when using FTONLINE.

FILE SYSTEMS

Windows XP supports the File Allocation Table (**FAT**, also called **FAT16**) and **FAT32** file systems, and the **New Technology File System (NTFS)**. Windows XP retains FAT for backward compatibility with other operating systems. This allows easy upgrade from another operating system to Windows XP and enables multiboot systems to **share** data drives (when basic storage is used). FAT32 is used to support larger volumes and offer multiboot shared drives with Windows 98, ME, and Windows 95 OSR2. NTFS is the preferred file system to use with Windows XP.

FAT and FAT32 are both collectively referred to as FAT in most Microsoft documentation. The separate terms are used only when the distinctions between FAT and FAT32 are important.

FAT, FAT32, and NTFS all support **long filenames (LFNs)** with lengths up to 256 characters. Also, FAT and FAT32 store 8.3 equivalents of LFNs for compatibility with DOS-based utilities that do not recognize LFNs. It is very important to use LFN-supporting utilities when performing any disk or file operation involving LFNs.

FAT and FAT32

FAT was originally developed for DOS. It has experienced several revisions and upgrades as support for FAT was included in newer operating systems. FAT under Windows XP maintains backward compatibility with previous operating systems while supporting newer features or capabilities. In addition, on Windows XP, FAT is most often used to format floppies and other removable media.

Here are the important features of FAT (under Windows XP):

- Supports volumes up to 4 GB in size
- Most efficient on volumes smaller than 256 MB
- Root directory can contain only 512 entries
- No file-level compression
- No file-level security
- Maximum file size is 4 GB

FAT32 is simply an enhanced version of FAT originally released with Windows 95 OSR2. FAT32's main feature change is its volume size. Windows XP can support and access FAT32 volumes up to 2 TB in size, but only volumes up to 32 GB can be created. FAT32 volumes have a minimum size of 512 MB. FAT32 volumes support a maximum file size of 4 GB.

A FAT volume is divided into clusters. A **cluster** is a group of one or more **sectors** divided into a single nondivisible unit. A sector is the smallest division (512 bytes) of a drive's surface. Due to the limitations of the file system, only a certain number of clusters can be addressed. For FAT16, the maximum number of clusters is 65,536. For FAT32, the maximum number of clusters is 268,435,456 (see Table 4-2).

Table 4-2 FAT16 and FAT32 cluster sizes

Drive size	FAT16 cluster size	FAT32 cluster size
260 to 511 MB	8 KB	Not supported
512 to 1023 MB	16 KB	4 KB
1024 MB to 2 GB	32 KB	4 KB
2 to 4 GB	64 KB	4 KB
4 to 8 GB	Not supported	4 KB
8 to 16 GB	Not supported	8 KB
16 to 32 GB	Not supported	16 KB
>32 GB	Not supported	32 KB

Before the release of Windows 95, the maximum allowable FAT volume size was 2 GB. But with the use of 64 KB clusters, this was extended to 4 GB. However, 64 KB clusters caused problems with some older drive utilities. Thus, Windows XP always warns you when you attempt to format a 2 GB to 4 GB partition with FAT16.

NTFS

NTFS offers, among other things, significantly larger volume support, file by file compression, and file by file security. Windows XP NTFS volumes can be accessed by Windows NT 4.0 with Service Pack 4 applied as well as Windows 2000 and Windows Server 2003 systems. However, Windows NT 4.0 is unable to access files that are using features not present with NTFS when Windows NT 4.0 was released (such as encryption through EFS).

NTFS is the preferred file system of Windows XP. Here are the important features of NTFS under Windows XP:

- Support for volumes up to 2 TB in size
- Most efficient on volumes larger than 10 MB
- Root directory can contain unlimited entries
- File-level compression
- File-level security

- File-level encryption (see Chapter 6, "Windows XP Security and Access Controls")

- **Disk quotas**, which are a means to limit drive space consumption by users

- POSIX support (POSIX subsystem support is not included in Windows XP Professional)

- File size is limited only by the size of the volume.

- NTFS cannot be used to format floppies or most other removable media.

The version of NTFS included with Windows XP (NTFS v5) is different from that of Windows NT out of the box (NTFS v4). In fact, you must have Service Pack 4 installed on Windows NT to access Windows XP NTFS volumes. Microsoft does not recommend a multiboot system with pre-SP4 Windows NT and Windows XP for this reason. If you are planning a dual-boot system with Windows NT 4.0 and Windows XP Professional, you need to install Windows NT 4.0 first, then apply SP4 or greater before installing Windows XP Professional into a separate volume.

FAT and FAT32 volumes on a system can be migrated to the NTFS format without losing data. However, to return to FAT, the volume must be deleted, re-created, and formatted, and the data must be copied back onto the new volume.

NTFS manages clusters more efficiently than FAT32, as shown in Table 4-3.

Table 4-3   NTFS default cluster sizes

Volume size	Sectors per cluster	Cluster size
512 MB or less	1	512 bytes
513 to 1024 MB	2	1 KB
1025 to 2048 MB	4	2 KB
2049 to 4096 MB	8	4 KB
4097 to 8192 MB	16	8 KB
8193 to 16,384 MB	32	16 KB
16,385 to 32,768 MB	64	32 KB
> 32,768 MB	128	64 KB

NOTE   File-level compression cannot be used on volumes with a cluster size greater than 4 KB.

Converting File Systems

When you first format a drive in Windows XP, you have the option of selecting FAT, FAT32, or NTFS. If, at a later date, you decide you need to change the format, you have only two options: reformat with the new file system or convert from FAT/FAT32 to NTFS. A backup should precede either process to ensure that you do not lose data.

The first option of reformatting is easy; simply employ one of the disk tools, such as Disk Management, and format the volume with a new file system. Remember that all data stored on the drive will be lost, so without a backup, you will not be able to recover from a format. The second option employs the CONVERT.EXE command-line tool. This tool can be used to convert FAT or FAT32 volumes to NTFS. It has two command-line parameters: /fs:ntfs and /v. The first specifies the conversion that should result in the NTFS file system.

The second option turns on verbose mode so all messages regarding the conversion are displayed. When started, CONVERT attempts to convert the drive immediately. If the drive is locked (i.e., a process has an open file from the volume to be converted), the conversion will occur the next time the system is booted up.

To convert an NTFS volume to FAT or FAT32, you must back up your data, reformat the volume, then restore your data.

Activity 4-8: Converting to NTFS

Time Required: 20 minutes

Objective: Use the CONVERT command to convert a FAT partition to NTFS.

Description: When upgrading from Windows 98 to Windows XP, you may leave the partition as FAT. This is sometimes done so that if you decide not to use Windows XP, you can uninstall it. The process is quite simple, but a backup of the files on the partition should always be done before converting. In this activity, you convert a partition (not the system partition) from FAT to NTFS.

To convert a FAT partition to NTFS:

This activity requires that a FAT volume exists on your Windows XP system. This volume will be converted to NTFS. Proceed only if the conversion of this volume will not compromise your system. If you have a multiboot system with operating systems that require a FAT partition, this activity may render those other OSs inaccessible.

1. Select **Start**, **All Programs**, **Accessories**, **Command Prompt**.

2. Change drives to the FAT partition, such as typing **g:**. Then press **Enter**. Here *g* represents the drive letter of the partition you wish to convert.

3. Type **convert *g:* /fs:ntfs /v**, where *g:* is the drive letter of the FAT volume to convert; press **Enter**.

4. Look in Windows Explorer to see the volume label of the partition, then type the current label for the drive to be converted.

5. Press **Enter** after you have typed the volume label.

6. You may be prompted whether to complete the conversion at the next restart; if so press **Y**. Restart your system. The drive is converted as part of the startup process.

7. If you are not prompted about restarting, the conversion takes place immediately. Once complete, a Conversion complete message is displayed.

If you use the CONVERT command to initiate a conversion to NTFS, and decide before you restart that you don't want to convert the volume, you can cancel the process. To cancel a CONVERT action, do the following:

1. Edit the Registry.

2. Using REGEDT32, locate the BootExecute value entry in the HKEY_LOCAL_MACHINE\SYSTEM\CurrentControlSet\Control\SessionManager key.

3. Change the content of that value entry from "autocheck autoconv \DosDevices\x: /FS:NTFS" (where x is the drive letter of the volume) to "autocheck autochk *". You can also elect to delete the string rather than replace it. Either of these actions prevent the NTFS conversion.

File Compression

File-level compression is the ability to compress data on the basis of single files, folders, or entire volumes. File compression offers the benefit of being able to store more data in the same space, but at the cost of some performance. Performance suffers because every time the compressed data is read or written to, the system must perform either a compression or a decompression activity. This extra work slows down file access activities.

The amount of compression achieved depends on the data stored in the object (that is, text can often be compressed significantly, whereas executables cannot). Windows XP Professional manages the compression through the NTFS file system drive. Each time a compressed file is read, it must be decompressed while it is being read. Likewise, when saving a compressed file, copying a file into a compressed folder, or creating a new file in a compressed folder, the data to be stored must be compressed in memory before it is written to the drive.

Configuring and managing file compression involves enabling or disabling the file compression attribute on one or more files or folders. File compression appears as just another attribute of NTFS file/folder objects on the Advanced Attributes dialog box, as seen in Figure 4-5. And, just like all other attributes, file compression can be set on a file-by-file basis or by setting the attribute on a container. When the Compress contents to save disk space check box is selected, the object(s) are compressed. When this check box is cleared, the object(s) are expanded back to their original size. Troubleshooting compression usually involves either recompressing or removing compression from files or restoring files from backup to replace those that were damaged during the compression process.

You must have Full Control over an object to compress or encrypt it. If you have Take Ownership permissions over an object, you can obtain Full Control permissions over that object by taking ownership.

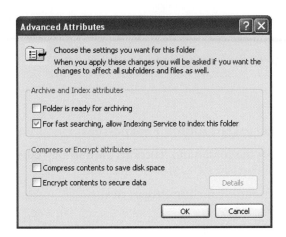

Figure 4-5   The Advanced Attributes dialog box

A file or folder can be compressed or encrypted (using EFS), not both. Compression and encryption are mutually exclusive attributes on NTFS volumes. For information on EFS, please see Chapter 6.

NOTE

Activity 4-9: Compressing and Decompressing a Folder

ACTIVITY

Time Required: 30 minutes

Objective: Use Windows Explorer to compress and decompress a folder and its contents.

Description: In an effort to increase the amount of free space on a disk drive, you can compress the contents of a file, folder, or partition. As long as the file format is NTFS, the contents can be compressed. It is a good rule of thumb to compress only static data and never compress system or boot files and folders. In this activity, you compress and decompress a folder and its contents.

To compress and decompress a folder:

This activity requires that Windows XP be installed and an NTFS partition be present.

NOTE

1. Close all programs, and then open **Windows Explorer** by clicking **Start**, **All Programs**, **Accessories**, **Windows Explorer**. (*Note*: Only files and folders that are not currently open or selected can be compressed.)

2. Locate and select any folder on your hard drive, such as C:\Program Files.

3. Right-click the folder, and then click **Properties**.

4. On the General tab, take note of the Size and Size on disk values. Click the **Advanced** button.

5. Check the **Compress contents to save disk space** check box.

6. Click **OK**.

7. Click **OK**.

8. Click the **Apply changes to this folder, subfolders and files** option button.

9. Click **OK**. The system compresses the folder and its contents (this may take several minutes).

10. Right-click the same folder again, and then click **Properties**.

11. On the General tab, take note of the Size and Size on disk values. The Size on disk value should be smaller than the original value.

12. On the General tab, click the **Advanced** button.

13. Uncheck the **Compress contents to save disk space** check box.

14. Click **OK**.

15. Click **OK**.

16. Click the **Apply changes to this folder, subfolders and files** option button.

17. Click **OK**. The system decompresses the folder and its contents; this may take several minutes.

DISK MANAGEMENT ACTIONS

In addition to creating volumes and transforming devices into dynamic storage, the Disk Management tool offers several other useful features. The All Tasks submenu of the Action menu is context-based, depending on the type of object selected. The All Tasks submenu is the same menu that pops up when you right-click a drive, partition, or volume object. Here are the commands that appear in this menu:

- *Change Drive Letter and Paths*—Changes the drive letter of basic disks and dynamic disks or the mount point of dynamic disks

- *Convert to Basic Disk*—Transforms a dynamic disk into a basic disk; requires that all volumes be deleted

- *Convert to Dynamic Disk*—Transforms a basic storage device into a dynamic storage device

- *Delete Partition*(or *Delete Logical Drive*)—Destroys a partition and returns the space to unallocated status

- *Explore*—Opens the selected volume or partition in a Windows Explorer window

- *Extend Volume*—Adds additional unallocated space to an existing volume

- *Format*—Formats a volume or partition with a file system

- *Import Foreign Disks*—Imports a dynamic disk when moved from one computer to another. Windows XP Professional can import dynamic disks from Windows 2000 Server, Windows 2000 Professional, Windows XP Professional, and Windows Server 2003. This command can be used to import single dynamic drives or multidrive structures hosted on dynamic disks.

- *Mark Partition as Active*—Marks a primary partition active

- *New Logical Drive*—Creates a new logical drive within an extended partition

- *New Partition*—Creates a partition on a basic disk

- *New Volume*—Starts a wizard to create a new simple, spanned, or striped volume

- *Open*—Opens the selected volume or partition into a new window

- *Properties*—Opens the Properties dialog box for the selected object

- *Reactivate Disk*—Brings dynamic disks back online after being powered down, disconnected, or corrupted

- *Reactivate Volume*—Recovers volumes from a failed status

- *Remove Disk*—Deactivates a removable drive

The Action menu itself has two other non-context-sensitive commands:

- *Help*—Opens the Help utility

- *Refresh*—Updates drive letters, file system, volume, and removable media information, and determines which previously unreadable volumes are now readable

- *Rescan Disks*—Updates hardware information by rescanning all attached storage devices (including removable media) for changes in configuration. This command is useful if you've added or removed a drive and the display has not been updated to accommodate the change.

The following series of activities will help you become familiar with some of these commands.

Activity 4-10: Changing Drive Letters

Time Required: 5 minutes

Objective: Change the letter assigned to a drive using the right-click menu.

Description: Letters are assigned to drives to provide a way to relate to them. These letters can be used to reference the drives in scripts or by applications. In this activity, you change the drive letter of a partition that does *not* contain the boot or system files.

To change a drive letter on a volume or partition:

1. From within Disk Management, right-click a partition or volume. Be sure not to select the boot or system partition. Click **Change Drive Letter and Paths** on the shortcut menu.

2. Select the current drive letter, then click **Change**.

3. Click the **Assign the following drive letter** option button.

4. Click the list box arrow to select a different letter for this drive.

5. Click **OK**.

6. You are warned about changing drive letters. Click **Yes**. The Disk Management display reflects the drive letter change.

Activity 4-11: Deleting a Partition

Time Required: 5 minutes

Objective: Delete a partition.

Description: When configuring a computer, partition configurations sometimes need to be changed. This often involves the deletion of one or more partitions. In this activity, you delete a partition created in Activity 4-1.

To delete a partition from a basic drive:

This activity requires that Activity 4-1 be completed.

1. Find the partition created in Activity 4-1.

2. Right-click the partition, and then click **Delete Partition**.

3. To confirm the deletion, click **Yes**.

Activity 4-12: Deleting a Volume

Time Required: 10 minutes

Objective: Use Disk Management to delete a volume.

Description: Reconfiguring drives and partitions sometimes includes the removal of volumes. In this activity, the volume that was created in Activity 4-5 is deleted.

To delete a volume:

This activity requires that Activity 4-5 be completed.

1. Right-click the volume created in Activity 4-5, and click **Delete Volume**.

2. To confirm the deletion, click **Yes**. Disk Management displays the drive that is not hosting volumes and consists only of unallocated space.

Disk Management can be used to manipulate storage devices on remote computers. Simply select the "Computer Management (Local)" item in the console tree and issue the "Connect to another computer" command from the Action menu. This opens a list of all known networked systems. Once you've selected another system, you can perform the same disk management functions as if you were sitting at that machine.

The Properties Dialog Boxes

The Properties dialog boxes of drives, volumes, and partitions offer additional details and configuration settings.

The Properties Dialog Box for Drives

A drive's (not volume or partition) Properties dialog box (see Figure 4-6) has four tabs: General, Policies, Volumes, and Driver. This Properties dialog box is the same one accessible from the Device Manager. The General tab displays details about the drive's model, device type, manufacturer, location in drive chain, and status. At the bottom of this tab, you can access the Troubleshooter by clicking the Troubleshoot button and set whether this device is enabled or disabled in the current hardware profile.

The dialog box that you see may be slightly different than the one shown in Figure 4-6. For example, if the computer you are using has SCSI hard drives, there will be an additional "SCSI Properties" tab in the dialog box.

The Policies tab is used to configure the write caching and safe removal settings for the device. There are two option buttons: Optimize for quick removal and Optimize for performance. Fixed hard drives are set automatically to Optimize for performance and allow only the Enable write caching on the disk check box to be controlled (it is marked by default). Removable drives can be configured with either of the two option buttons. However, the latter setting requires the use of the Safely Remove Hardware icon in the taskbar to avoid losing data, whereas the former allows for instant device removal.

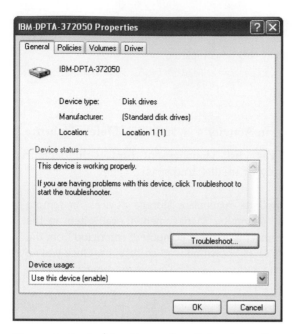

Figure 4-6   A drive Properties dialog box, General tab

The Volumes tab (see Figure 4-7) displays additional details about the device and its hosted volumes, including the following:

- *Disk*—The ordinal number of the disk, such as Disk 0, Disk 1, etc.

- *Type*—The storage type: Basic, Dynamic, or Removable

- *Status*—The status of the device: Online, Offline, Foreign, Unknown

- *Partition Style*—The partitioning scheme used on the drive; options are MBR (Master Boot Record) on x86 systems, GPT (GUID Partition Table) on Itanium systems, or Not Applicable for unknown or uninitialized devices

- *Capacity*—The maximum storage capacity of the drive

- *Unallocated space*—The amount of space not used in a partition or volume

- *Reserved space*—The amount of space reserved for use by the operating system

- *Volumes*—The volumes and capacity of each volume or partition on the drive

The Driver tab displays details about the device driver used by the drive. From this tab, you can find details about how the driver can be accessed, update the driver or roll back to the previous driver, or uninstall the device driver (that is, remove the device from the system).

Figure 4-7   A drive Properties dialog box, Volumes tab

The Properties Dialog Box for Partitions or Volumes

You can right-click a partition or volume to access the Properties dialog box. However, an NTFS-formatted partition or volume in a domain has two additional tabs that are not present on FAT/FAT32-formatted partitions or volumes. The tabs of the Properties dialog box are: General, Tools, Hardware, Sharing, Security, and Quota (the latter two are NTFS only).

The General tab (see Figure 4-8) of a partition or volume Properties dialog box displays the following:

- *Label*—The customizable name of the volume or partition; FAT drives can be labeled with up to 11 characters, whereas the labels in NTFS can contain 32 characters.
- *Type*—The type of disk: local, network connection, floppy disk drive, CD-ROM drive, RAM disk, removable drive, or mounted disk
- *File System*—The file system used on the disk: CDFS (for CDs), FAT, FAT32, NTFS, and UDF (Universal Disk Format common on DVD and compact discs)
- *Used Space*—The amount of space used by stored files
- *Free Space*—The amount of space still available in the partition
- *Capacity*—The total amount of space in the partition

- *Graph*—A graphical pie chart representation of used and free space

- *Disk Cleanup*—A button to access the Disk Cleanup tool (see the Disk Cleanup section later in this chapter)

- *Compress drive to save disk space*—By default, files in the root of a drive are compressed automatically; the entire drive is compressed only when this option is selected.

- *Allow Indexing Service to index this disk for fast file searching*—Indexes the disk

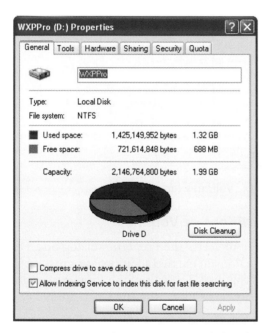

Figure 4-8   A volume Properties dialog box, General tab

The Tools tab (see Figure 4-9) offers access to the following:

- *Error-checking*—Accesses the Check Disk tool to find and repair errors on a drive

- *Defragmentation*—Accesses the **Defragmentation** tool to reduce file fragmentation

- *Backup*—Accesses the NT Backup utility to back up files (see Chapter 14, "Windows XP Professional Fault Tolerance")

The Hardware tab (see Figure 4-10) lists all physical storage devices and their type. This dialog box accesses the same Troubleshooting and Properties (for drivers) utilities that the Device Manager accesses.

Figure 4-9 A volume Properties dialog box, Tools tab

Figure 4-10 A volume Properties dialog box, Hardware tab

The Sharing tab (see Figure 4–11) is used to share partitions with the network. The Security tab (see Figure 4–12) is used to set the NTFS access permissions on the volume or partition as a whole. Individual users or groups can be defined with unique permissions of Allow or Deny for each of the listed object-specific actions.

Figure 4-11   A volume Properties dialog box, Sharing tab

Figure 4-12   A volume Properties dialog box, Security tab

The Quota tab (see Figure 4-13) is used to define disk-use limitations on NTFS volumes and partitions. The quota is defined on a general basis and can be fine-tuned for each individual user. The options include the following:

- *Enable quota management*—Turns on the quota system

- *Deny disk space to users exceeding quota limit*—Prevents users from gaining more space when in violation of the quota

- *Do not limit disk usage*—Disables systemwide quota level

- *Limit disk space to*—Sets maximum amount of drive space that can be accessed by a single user

- *Set warning level to*—Sets a threshold that, when exceeded, warns users about nearing their quota limit

- *Log event when a user exceeds their quota limit*—Adds an item to the Event Viewer

- *Log event when a user exceeds their warning level*—Adds an item to the Event Viewer

- *Quota Entries*—Opens a dialog box where individual quota settings for each user can be fine-tuned

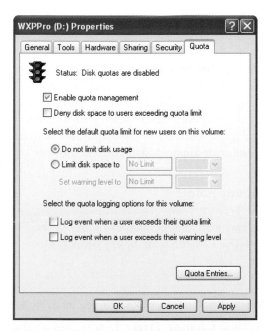

Figure 4-13   A volume Properties dialog box, Quota tab

Drive Letters and Mount Points

Windows XP uses drive letters to grant applications and user interface utilities access to file system resources. Drive letters A and B are typically used for floppy disks, but in the absence of floppy drives, these letters can be employed as mappings for network shares. Drive letters C through Z are used for local hard drives or mappings for network shares. Even without floppies, the first hard drive is always labeled with C. The drive letters assigned to the system and boot partitions or volumes cannot be changed, but all other drive letters can be changed. In Disk Management, the Change Drive Letter and Paths command is used to alter a drive letter, apply a mount point path, or remove a drive letter. This command is accessed by selecting a volume or partition, and then right-clicking to open the shortcut menu.

A mount point is an alternative to drive letters. A mount point connects a FAT/FAT32 or NTFS volume or partition to an empty directory on an NTFS volume or partition. This allows more than 24 (or 26) volumes to be present on a single machine. The empty directory becomes the gateway to the linked volume. Just to make this clear, a mount point must be hosted on a NTFS-formatted volume or partition. The mount point is the gateway or doorway pointing to the root of another volume or partition. Mount points give you more storage space through a preexisting drive letter. Mount points can be used on system and boot partitions while most multidrive configurations cannot.

Activity 4-13: Creating a New Mounted Volume

Time Required: 15 minutes

Objective: Create a mount point on an NTFS folder using Disk Management. Create a new map point to Partition B.

Description: In the past, mapping drives in Microsoft networks has always been restricted to the letters of the alphabet. In most cases, this was not a problem, but it still limited some people. In this activity, you map an empty folder (NTFS) to a volume instead of the traditional alphabet letter. In this activity, a mounted volume point is created on Partition A to point to Partition B. This may be useful if the space on one partition is becoming full, and rather than expanding the volume (no unallocated space), you create a mounted volume for storing data on a different drive.

To create a mounted volume or mount point:

This activity requires that at least two partitions be present on the system. Partition A must be formatted with NTFS. Partition B can be any partition other than the boot or system partitions.

1. From within Disk Management, locate Partition A. Take note of its drive letter.

2. Right-click **Partition B**, and then click **Change Drive Letter and Paths**.

3. Click **Add**.

4. Make sure the **Mount in the following empty NTFS folder** option is selected.

5. Click **Browse**.

6. Locate Partition A by using its drive letter (see Step 1). Select the drive letter.

7. Click **New Folder**.

8. Type a name for the new folder, such as **MapPartB**, then press **Enter**.

9. Make sure the newly created folder is highlighted. Click **OK**.

10. The path to the new folder is now listed in the text field under the Mount in the following empty NTFS folder option. Click **OK**.

11. Open **Windows Explorer (Start, All Programs, Accessories, Windows Explorer)**.

12. Expand **My Computer**.

13. Expand **Partition A**.

14. Notice the mounted volume appears as a drive icon with the name of the folder you created. Select the **mount point**. Notice that the contents of Partition B are displayed in the right pane.

15. Close **Windows Explorer (File, Close)**.

It is possible to create an infinite-regression mount point by mapping a volume to an empty directory that it hosts. Although this is valid, it can cause system overflows when disk utilities attempt to follow the infinite path.

Activity 4-14: Deleting a Mounted Volume

Time Required: 5 minutes

Objective: Delete the mounted volume that was created in the last activity.

Description: A mounted volume may be deemed unnecessary. Rather than cause confusion, it is best to remove the mounted volume. In this activity, you remove a mounted volume.

To delete a mounted volume or mount point:

This activity requires that Activity 4-13 be completed.

1. Right-click **Partition B** from Activity 4-13, then select **Change Drive Letter and Paths** from the shortcut menu.

2. Select the mounted volume mapping (i.e., the listed mount point).

3. Click **Remove**.

4. You are asked to confirm the deletion. Click **Yes**.

Disk Cleanup

Disk Cleanup is a tool used to free up space on hard drives by removing deleted, orphaned, temporary, or downloaded files. The utility can be started from the General tab of the Properties dialog box from any drive or through Start, All Programs, Accessories, System Tools, Disk Cleanup. When started from a drive's properties, it automatically scans that drive for space that can be freed. When started from the Start menu, the utility prompts you to select the drive to scan for cleaning. The scanning process can take several minutes, especially on large drives that have an excessively large amount of files.

When scanning is complete, the Disk Cleanup for (*drive:*) dialog box is displayed (see Figure 4-14). The Disk Cleanup tab lists the file types that can be removed and how much space they currently consume. The View Files button can be used to see the selected file type's details through the My Computer window. Selecting the check box beside a listed file type causes those files to be deleted (not placed in the Recycle Bin) when OK is clicked.

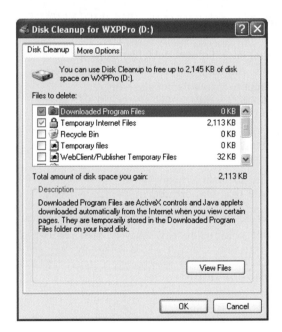

Figure 4-14   Disk Cleanup dialog box

The More Options tab offers access to the Add/Remove Windows Components utility, the Change or Remove Programs utility, and the System Restore utility. The first two of these are the same utilities that can be accessed through the Add/Remove Programs applet in Control Panel. The System Restore item deletes all but the most recent restore point. See Chapter 14 for more information on System Restore.

Check Disk

Check Disk (Error-checking) is an inspection utility used to examine disk integrity and locate both logical and physical errors on a hard drive. In some cases, logical errors can be corrected. Physical errors are marked and avoided in all future drive accesses by the operating system. Logical errors are bad pointers in the directory structure of a file system, whether FAT, FAT32, or NTFS. Often these errors can be corrected. However, in those cases where correction is not possible, Check Disk saves the data of orphaned fragments to text files in the root directory of the drive using incremental filenames of FILE0001, FILE0002, and so on.

Error-checking—called ScanDisk Check Disk in earlier versions of Windows—is accessed by clicking the Check Now button on the Tools tab of a drive's Properties dialog box. Once started, it prompts you to automatically fix file system errors or to Scan for and attempt recovery of bad sectors. Check Disk usually requires restarting the system to scan NTFS volumes.

The system uses Check Disk when it detects an improper system shutdown or errors in the directory structure of a drive. This usually occurs during the start and execution processes, and results are displayed on a blue screen (the one where the operating system name, version, build, number of processors, and memory size is detailed).

 The Error-checking tool that ships with Windows XP is specifically designed to manage the file systems supported by Windows XP. Do not use Check Disk or ScanDisk from any other operating system to attempt repairs on Windows XP hard drives.

Defragmentation

As files are written, altered, deleted, rewritten, and so on, the storage device develops gaps between used and unused space. As gaps are used to store files instead of contiguous free space, fragmentation occurs. **Fragmentation** is the division of a file into two or more parts, where each part is stored in a different location on the hard drive. As the level of fragmentation on a drive increases, the longer it takes for read and write operations to occur. Defragmentation is the process of reorganizing files so they are stored contiguously and no gaps are left between files.

The Windows XP defragmentation utility is designed for FAT, FAT32, and NTFS volumes. Thus, it can reduce or eliminate fragmentation on your hard drives. The defragmentation utility is accessed either from the Tools tab of a drive's Properties dialog box or through Start, All Programs, Accessories, System Tools, Disk Defragmenter.

The Disk Defragmenter (see Figure 4-15) lists all drives in the system. By selecting a drive, you can select one of the following options: Analyze the drive for fragmentation or Defragment the drive. Both processes display a graphical representation of the file storage condition of the drive. Once either process is complete, you can view a report that details the findings of the procedure.

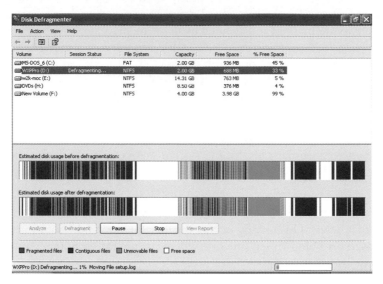

Figure 4-15   Disk Defragmenter

 The Disk Defragmenter does not offer a built-in scheduling feature; nor can it be executed from a command line. You must manually defragment or deploy a third-party utility that automates scheduled defragmentation.

NOTE

FSUTIL

FSUTIL (file system utility) is a powerful command-line utility that can perform a wide range of functions. This tool can be only used by administrators, and even then it should be used with caution. The syntax and parameters of FSUTIL are fairly complex, so take the time to fully review and understand each command before you execute it. For this reason, an exhaustive list of the syntax and parameters of this tool is not included in this text; instead, you are encouraged to use the Help and Support Center to access the online documentation by searching on FSUTIL.

The basic commands and actions of FSUTIL are as follows (*Note:* These are the top-level commands; all of them have numerous additional parameters not listed here):

- *behavior*—Defines whether 8.3 character filenames are generated, whether extended characters are accepted in 8.3 filenames on NTFS, how to update the last access time stamp on NTFS volumes, how often quota events are written to the system log, and how much drive space is reserved for the MFT zone

- *dirty*—Queries, sets, and clears the dirty bit for a volume, which causes autochk to scan the volume for errors when the system is next started

- *file*—Finds files by security IDs, sets the 8.3 name of a file, sets the file's valid data length, and so on

- *fsinfo*—Displays information about drives, drive types, volumes, NTFS attributes, and file system statistics

- *hardlink*—Creates a hard link for a file. All files have at least one hard link. A single file on NTFS can have multiple hard links. Each hard link can be used to access the file. Only after all hard links are deleted is the file actually deleted.

- *objectid*—Manages object IDs

- *quota*—Manages quota settings

- *reparsepoint*—Queries or deletes reparse points. A reparse point is a file system identifier used by volume mount points and directory junction points.

- *sparse*—Manages sparse files. A sparse file is any file with one or more regions of unallocated data within it. Applications view the allocated regions as all zeros, even though no disk space is used within that area to represent the zeros.

- *usn*—Manages the USN (update sequence number) change journal, which maintains a persistent log of all file system changes made to a volume

- *volume*—Dismounts or queries volumes for the amount of free space

FOLDER OPTIONS

The Folder Options applet accesses the same configuration interface as the Tools, Folder Options command from Windows Explorer and My Computer. The four tabs of this applet are used to set the functional and visual parameters of the folders on the system.

The General tab is used to enable or disable the display of common tasks in folders, to open a folder in a new or current window, and to choose whether a single or double click opens an item.

The View tab is used to set advanced settings for how files and folders appear and behave in Windows Explorer and My Computer windows. The settings on this tab include:

- Automatically search for network folders and printers—enabled by default

- Display file size information in folder tips—enabled by default

- Display simple folder view in Explorer's Folders list—enabled by default

- Display the contents of system folders—disabled by default

- Display the full path in the address bar—enabled by default

- Display the full path in the title bar—disabled by default

- Do not cache thumbnails—disabled by default
- Hidden files and folders—set to Do not show hidden files and folders by default
- Hide extensions for known file types—enabled by default
- Hide protected operating system files—enabled by default
- Launch folder windows in separate process—disabled by default
- Managing pairs of Web pages and folders—set to Show and manage the pair as a single file by default
- Remember each folder's view settings—enabled by default
- Restore previous folder windows at logon—disabled by default
- Show Control Panel in My Computer—disabled by default
- Show encrypted and compressed NTFS files in color—enabled by default
- Show pop-up description for folder and desktop items—enabled by default
- Use simple file sharing—enabled by default

The File Types tab is used to define or associate file extensions with applications. The settings on this tab are usually configured automatically by the OS and installed software. If you need to customize file and application association, please see the Microsoft Windows XP Professional Resource Kit for detailed guides.

The Offline Files tab is used to enable offline network browsing by caching resources locally. This topic is discussed later in this chapter.

FILE SYSTEM OBJECT LEVEL PROPERTIES

In addition to the drive and volume/partition-level controls for storage devices, there are folder- and object-level controls. These controls are accessed through the Properties dialog boxes of either a folder or an object. Plus, there are minor differences depending on whether the file system is FAT/FAT32 or NTFS. But there are no differences in these dialog boxes between basic or dynamic disks.

The following sections detail the differences in Properties dialog boxes for each of the object types. The Sharing, Security, and Customize tabs of these dialog boxes are discussed in a later section in this chapter.

NTFS Folder Object

An NTFS folder object's Properties dialog box has three tabs: General (see Figure 4-16), Sharing, and Security. The General tab offers the following information:

- *Name*   The customizable name of the object

- *Type*—Lists object type (File Folder)

- *Location*—The path of the object

- *Size*—The size in bytes of the object, including its contents

- *Size on disk*—The actual amount of drive space used to store the object

- *Contains*—Lists the number of files and folders it contains

- *Created*—Lists the creation time and date of the object

- *Attributes: Read-only*—A check box used to prevent writing to, changing, or deleting from the object

- *Attributes: Hidden*—A check box used to hide the object from view

- *Advanced button (see Figure 4-16): Folder is ready for archiving*—A check box that indicates whether this folder and, optionally, its contents are ready to be backed up. See Figure 4-17.

- *Advanced button: For fast searching, allow Indexing Service to index this folder*—A check box that, when selected, preindexes the folder, and, optionally, its contents for faster searching

- *Advanced button: Compress contents to save disk space*—A check box used to compress the folder, and, optionally, its contents

- *Advanced button: Encrypt contents to secure data*—A check box used to encrypt the folder, and, optionally, its contents

Figure 4-16   A NTFS folder object's Properties dialog box, General tab

NOTE Once the Properties dialog box for the object is closed, all changes to the settings through the Advanced button require confirmation by clicking the OK button.

Figure 4-17 Advanced Attributes dialog box

FAT/FAT32 Folder Object

A FAT/FAT32 folder object's Properties dialog box has three tabs: General (see Figure 4-18), Sharing, and Customize. The General tab offers the following information:

- *Name*—The customizable name of the object
- *Type*—Lists object type, (File Folder)
- *Location*—The path of the object
- *Size*—The size in bytes of the object, including its contents
- *Size on disk*—The actual amount of drive space used to store the object
- *Contains*—Lists the number of files and folders the folder object contains
- *Created*—Lists the creation time and date of the object
- *Attributes: Read-only*—A check box used to prevent writing to, changing, or deleting from the object
- *Attributes: Hidden*—A check box used to hide the object from view
- *Attributes: Archive*—A check box that indicates whether this object should be included in the next backup operation

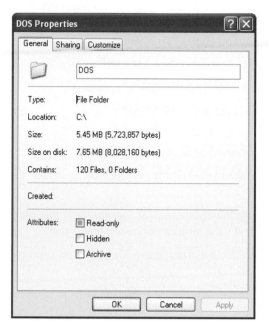

Figure 4-18 A FAT/FAT32 folder object's Properties dialog box, General tab

NTFS File Object

An NTFS file object's Properties dialog box has three common tabs: General (see Figure 4-19), Security, and Summary. If the NTFS file object is a Windows application, its Properties dialog box has two additional tabs: Version and Compatibility. If the NTFS file object is a DOS application, its Properties dialog box has five additional tabs: Program, Font, Memory, Screen, and Misc. These five additional tabs are used to configure the applications in a DOS environment.

The General tab offers the following information:

- *Name*—The customizable name of the object
- *Type of file*—Names the file type or defines it as a *blank* file where *blank* is the file's extension; if the type is shortcut, all properties in the dialog box are for the shortcut, not the original item.
- *Description (application files only)*—Names the utility or application
- *Opens with (nonapplication files only)*—Lists the application used to open the file
- *Change (nonapplication files only)*—A button for altering the application used to open the file
- *Location*—The path of the object
- *Size*—The size in bytes of the object

- *Size on disk*—The actual amount of drive space used to store the object
- *Created*—Lists the creation time and date of the object
- *Modified*—Lists the last time and date of a change to the object
- *Accessed*—Lists the last time and date this object was accessed
- *Attributes: Read-only*—A check box used to prevent writing to, changing, or deleting from the object
- *Attributes: Hidden*—A check box used to hide the object from view
- *Advanced button: File is ready for archiving*—A check box that indicates that this file is ready to be backed up
- *Advanced button: For fast searching, allow Indexing Service to index this file*—A check box that when selected preindexes the object for faster searching
- *Advanced button: Compress contents to save disk space*—A check box used to compress the object
- *Advanced button: Encrypt contents to secure data*—A check box used to encrypt the object

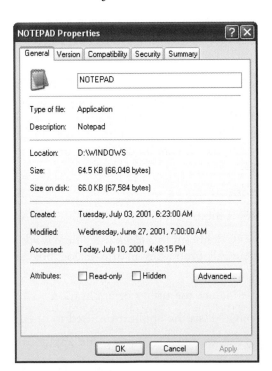

Figure 4-19   An NTFS file object's Properties dialog box, General tab

The Summary tab is used to define description and origin details for the object. These details include Title, Subject, Category, Keywords, Comments, Source, Author, and Revision Number. This information can be used to refine searches.

FAT/FAT32 File Object

A FAT/FAT32 file object's Properties dialog box has a single common tab: General (see Figure 4-20). If the FAT/FAT32 file object is a Windows application, its Properties dialog box has an additional tab: Compatibility. The Compatibility tab is used to configure the application's compatibility with Windows XP, especially if it is a Windows 95, 98, NT 4, or 2000 application. If the FAT/FAT32 file object is a DLL file or driver file, its Properties dialog box has an additional tab: Version. The Version tab lists the version information for the file. If the FAT/FAT32 file object is a DOS application, its Properties dialog box has five additional tabs: Program, Font, Memory, Screen, and Misc. These five additional tabs are used to configure the application's DOS-run environment. See Chapter 11 "Windows XP Professional Application Support" for complete details about these application-specific tabs.

The General tab offers the following information:

- *Name*—The customizable name of the object

- *Type of file*—Names the file type or defines it as a *blank* file where *blank* is the file's extension; if the type is shortcut, all properties in the dialog box are for the shortcut, not the original item.

- *Description (application files only)*—Names the utility or application

- *Opens with (nonapplication files only)*—Lists the application used to open the file

- *Change (nonapplication files only)*—A button for altering the application used to open the file

- *Location*—The path of the object

- *Size*—The size in bytes of the object

- *Size on disk*—The actual amount of drive space used to store the object

- *Created*—Lists the creation time and date of the object

- *Modified*—Lists the last time and date of a change to the object

- *Accessed*—Lists the last time and date this object was accessed

- *Attributes: Read-only*—A check box used to prevent writing to, changing, or deleting the object

- *Attributes: Hidden*—A check box used to hide the object from view

- *Attributes: Archive*—A check box that indicates that this object should be included in the next backup operation

Figure 4-20   A FAT/FAT32 file object's Properties dialog box, General tab

NTFS-Mounted Volume Object

An NTFS-mounted volume object's Properties dialog box has four tabs: General (see Figure 4-21), Sharing, Security, and Customize. The General tab offers the following information:

- *Name*—The customizable name of the object
- *Properties*—A button used to access the mounted volume's Properties dialog box; this is the same dialog box as is seen through Disk Management
- *Type*—Lists object type (Mounted Volume)
- *Location*—The path of the object
- *Target*—Names the mapped volume
- *Created*—Lists the creation time and date of the object
- *Attributes: Read-only*—A check box used to prevent writing to, changing, or deleting the object
- *Attributes: Hidden*—A check box used to hide the object from view
- *Advanced button: Folder is ready for archiving*—A check box that indicates that this folder and optionally its contents are ready to be backed up
- *Advanced button: For fast searching, allow Indexing Service to index this folder*—A check box that when selected preindexes the folder, and optionally its contents, for faster searching

- *Advanced button: Compress contents to save disk space*—A check box used to compress the folder and optionally its contents

- *Advanced button: Encrypt contents to secure data*—A check box used to encrypt the folder and optionally its contents

Figure 4-21 A NTFS-mounted volume object's Properties dialog box, General tab

FAT/FAT32-Mounted Volume Object

Recall that a mounted volume is one that has been mapped to a folder on another volume. A FAT/FAT32-mounted volume object's Properties dialog box has three tabs: General, Sharing, and Customize. The General tab offers the following information:

- *Name*—The customizable name of the object

- *Properties*—A button used to access the mounted volume's Properties dialog box; this is the same dialog box that would be seen through Disk Management.

- *Type*—Lists object type (Mounted Volume)

- *Location*—The path of the object

- *Target*—Names the mapped volume

- *Created*—Lists the creation time and date of the object

- *Attributes: Read-only*—A check box used to prevent writing to, changing, or deleting the object

- *Attributes: Hidden*—A check box used to hide the object from view
- *Attributes: Archive*—A check box that indicates that this object should be included in the next backup operation

Managing NTFS Permissions

NTFS is the only file system supported by Windows XP that offers file-level security. NTFS security determines what can be done to a file system object and who can perform those actions. There are different permissions for folders and files.

NTFS File and Folder Permissions

NTFS file and folder permissions are nearly identical. The dialog boxes and control interfaces for files and folders are the same. The only differences are: (1) files do not offer child inheritance options (because files are child objects, they do not have child objects themselves), and (2) some obvious permissions apply only to folders or only to files. In some cases, the same permission name has a different meaning for files and folders. In other cases, similar permissions have different names, but both names are listed in both dialog box contexts.

The NTFS permissions are as follows:

- *Read*—Allows users to view and access the contents of the folder or the file
- *Write (folders)*—Allows users to create new folders and files within the folder
- *Write (files)*—Allows users to overwrite the file and change attributes
- *List Folder Contents (folders only)*—Allows users to see the names of the contents of the folder
- *Read & Execute (folders)*—Allows users to reach files and folders through folders in which they do not have access permission; also, allows users to view and access the contents of the folder
- *Read & Execute (files)*—Allows users to run applications and to view and access the file
- *Modify (folders)*—Allows users to delete the folder and its contents; also, allows users to create new folders and files within the folder and to view and access the contents of the folder
- *Modify (files)*—Allows users to delete the file, to overwrite the file and change attributes, to run applications, and to view and access the file
- *Full Control (folders)*—Grants users complete and unrestricted access to all functions of the folder and its contents

- *Full Control (files)*—Grants users complete and unrestricted access to all functions of the file

These NTFS permissions are configured on the Security tab of the object's Properties dialog box (see Figure 4-22). This tab offers the following controls (to view the Security tab, you need to disable "Use simple file sharing"):

- *Group or user names*—Lists the users and groups for which permissions are assigned for this object

- *Add button*—Used to add users and groups to the Name list

- *Remove button*—Used to remove users and groups from the Name list

- *Permissions*—The level of access to be granted or denied to the selected group or user

- *Allow*—A column of check boxes used to grant permission to a user or group

- *Deny*—A column of check boxes used to restrict permission to a user or group

- *Advanced button*—Accesses detailed permissions, auditing, ownership settings, and effective permissions. **Auditing** is used to record information in a log file about occurrences on the computer system, such as file and object access.

Figure 4-22   The Security tab of an NTFS object's Properties dialog box

To change permissions for a user or group, select that user or group in the Name list. If the user or group is not present, use the Add button to include that user or group in the list. Once a user or group is selected, the Permissions field displays the current settings for that specific selection. Selecting or deselecting the Allow or Deny check boxes for each permission level defines the custom permissions for the selected user or group. To remove a user or group, select it in the Name list and click the Remove button. When a user or group is not listed on the Security tab for an object, that user or group has no effective permissions to that object. In other words, the user or group is prevented from accessing the object.

Clicking the Advanced button reveals a four-tabbed dialog box where more detailed access control settings can be defined. The Permissions tab (see Figure 4-23) of the Access Control Settings dialog box is used to define detailed permissions on a per user or group basis. Similar to the previous dialog box, users and groups are included in the list through the Add button and deleted with the Remove button. This dialog box also offers two more check boxes. The first check box has the same inheritable permissions as was seen in the previous dialog box. The second check box appears on folder dialog boxes only and offers the Reset permissions on all child objects, and enable propagation of inheritable permissions option. This control resets child object inheritance settings.

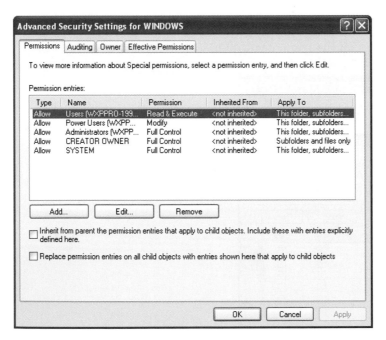

Figure 4-23 The Advanced Security Settings Properties dialog box for an NTFS object, Permission tab

To edit the permissions of a user or group, select them from the list and click Edit. The Permission Entry dialog box (see Figure 4-24) is displayed showing all of the object-specific permissions and the familiar Allow and Deny check boxes. The detailed NTFS object permissions are:

- Full Control
- Traverse Folder / Execute File
- List Folder / Read Data
- Read Attributes
- Read Extended Attributes
- Create Files / Write Data
- Create Folders / Append Data
- Write Attributes
- Write Extended Attributes
- Delete Subfolders and Files
- Delete
- Read Permissions
- Change Permissions
- Take Ownership

Figure 4-24   The Permission Entry dialog box

The Permission Entry dialog box allows you to:

- Change the user or group to which these settings apply (only on objects that do not inherit their permissions).

- Set the application of these permissions to (folders only): this folder only; this folder, subfolder, and files; this folder and subfolders; this folder and files; subfolders and files only; subfolders only; or files only.

- Clear all Allow and Deny check boxes.

- Apply these permissions to objects and/or containers within this container only (folders only).

The Auditing tab on the Access Control Settings dialog box is used to define events that result in an audit detail being written to the Event Viewer's Security log. This tab looks and functions the same as the Permissions tab. Two check boxes regarding inheritance appear at the bottom, but they apply to audit settings instead of permissions. Users and groups are included or deleted with the Add and Remove buttons. Selected users and groups are edited through the View/Edit button. This button reveals a similar dialog box with all of the detailed permissions. Selecting Allow or Deny on this dialog box indicates that when a user or group performs this action, an audit detail is written to the Event Viewer Security log. See Chapter 5, "Users, Groups, Profiles, and Policies" and Chapter 6 for more information on auditing.

The Owner tab lists the current owner of this object. To change ownership, select a new owner from the list of possible owners in the center field; this lists your user account and group memberships (which have Take Ownership permissions on this object). It also offers a check box to replace the ownership on all child elements with the settings on this object (folders only).

The Effective Permissions tab is used to view the actual permissions of a group or user for the current object based on all relevant permissions. Relevant permissions include all explicitly defined permissions directly on the object as well as all inherited permissions. Use the Select button to select the user or group to calculate the effective permissions.

Rules for Working with NTFS Permissions

Keep these rules in mind when working with NTFS permissions:

- NTFS object permissions *always* apply, no matter if the accessing user is local or remote (i.e., over a network through a share).

- NTFS object permissions are cumulative—all user-specific permissions are added to all group-specific memberships (assuming the user account is a member of that group), the resultant accumulation of permissions (i.e., the most permissive) is the access level enjoyed by the user.

- NTFS file permissions override any contradictory settings on the parent or container folder.

- Deny overrides all other specific Allows. Be sure not to configure conflicting permissions. Deny overrides any other specific permission assigned to the user account or inherited permissions from group memberships.

- When disabling inheritance for an NTFS object, select to either Copy the parent object's permissions to the current object or Remove permissions assigned from the parent and retain only object-specific settings. In both cases, Copy and Remove, all subsequent changes to the parent do not affect the child object.

Inheritance of Permissions

Copying and moving NTFS objects is an important subject due to the inheritance of permissions. When a new object is created, it always assumes the permissions (and other settings and attributes) of its parent or container. Keeping this in mind can help you understand what happens when an NTFS object is copied or moved.

There are four different situations in which inheritance comes into play:

- *Moving an object within the same volume or partition*—Moving an object within the same volume or partition is actually just a minor change in the location pointer for the object. Thus, its new location is not caused by creating a new file, but just changing its location address. Such objects retain their original settings.

- *Copying an object within the same volume or partition*—Involves creating a new object; the new object inherits the settings of its immediate parent container (i.e., folder).

- *Moving an object from one volume or partition to another*—Involves creating a new object. First, the system copies the file to the new destination, then it deletes the original. Creating a new object in this manner causes that new object to inherit the settings of its new parent or container.

- *Copying an object from one volume or partition to another*—Involves creating a new object. The new object inherits the settings of its immediate parent container (i.e., folder).

When moving or copying an object from an NTFS volume to a FAT volume, all NTFS settings are lost and the object inherits the FAT attributes and settings of its new container. When moving or copying an object from a FAT volume to an NTFS volume, the object inherits the NTFS settings and permissions of its new container.

TROUBLESHOOTING ACCESS AND PERMISSION PROBLEMS

In most access problems, either the resource object has the wrong settings or the user account has the wrong settings. A resource object can have incorrect permissions settings due to inheritance, lack of inheritance, moving/copying, or simple human error. A user account can have the incorrect permissions due to improper group membership, improper permission settings on a valid group, or human error.

To resolve permission or access problems, follow this procedure:

1. Determine what valid access the user should have.

2. Inspect the resource object's permissions based on groups and the specific user and what actions are set to Allow or Deny.

3. Inspect the share's permissions based on groups and the specific user and what actions are set to Allow or Deny.

4. Inspect the user's group memberships (see Chapter 5 for details on working with groups).

5. Attempt to access other resources with the user account from the same computer and a different computer.

6. Attempt to access the problematic resource with the Administrator account from the same computer and a different computer.

These steps should point you directly to the problem and how to resolve it. Taking the time to make the effort systematic prevents you from overlooking small details or the glaringly obvious.

In general, you want to use the following guidelines to design your permission levels and to avoid common problems:

- Grant permission only as needed.

- Rely upon NTFS to restrict access.

- Grant Full Control only when necessary, even on shares.

- Change permissions on a folder level, allow changes to affect all child elements (at least to files, if not subfolders).

- Use multiple folders and subfolders to separate files into groups for different permission levels.

- Stay away from the Deny setting unless absolutely necessary.

Optimizing access to files and folders is simply a process of double verification. The first verification required is to ensure that both the share-object-level permissions and the direct-object-level permissions grant and restrict exactly the activities you want for each user and group. The second verification required is to ensure that group memberships do not grant too much access through accumulation or prevent access due to a specific Deny when access is necessary. Both of these verification processes must be performed manually.

SIMPLE FILE SHARING

Simple file sharing is used when quick and easy file sharing is needed from a Windows XP Professional system. It is commonly used in situations such as home networks where granular control over access is not important.

This feature is effective only when Windows XP is a member of a workgroup. When enabled, as it is by default, all shared folders are accessible by everyone on the network. Folders and drives are shared by dragging and dropping them into the Shared Documents folder. This folder appears within Windows Explorer. Note that no individual user or group access restrictions can be defined. This feature also disables the Sharing tab on a folder/drive object's Properties dialog box.

When simple file sharing is disabled, shared folders can be restricted by user and group permissions. The control for Simple File Sharing is located within Folder Options, on the View tab, at the bottom of the list of Advanced Settings.

NOTE

If Windows XP Professional is a member of a domain, this setting has no effect on sharing or setting share permissions.

MANAGING SHARED FOLDERS

The Sharing tab (see Figure 4-25), found on both FAT/FAT32 and NTFS folder Properties dialog boxes, is used to enable remote access to the folder. This tab offers the following controls:

- *Do not share this folder*—Disables sharing for this folder

- *Share this folder*—Enable sharing for this folder

- *Share name*—The name displayed in browse lists and used in UNC names to access this share

- *Comment*—A comment or description of the share

- *User limit*—Used to allow the maximum possible (as determined by system speed and resources) or to limit to a specified number of simultaneous users

- *Permissions*—This button opens the Share Permissions dialog box (see Figure 4-26), where users and groups are granted or denied Full Control, Change, or Read permissions for this folder through the share.

- *Caching*—This button opens the Caching settings dialog box, where you can enable or disable caching of resources from the current folder and set caching to automatic for documents or programs, or to manual for documents. This feature is used in conjunction with the Offline Files settings of Folder Options to cache network resources for use while not connected to the network.

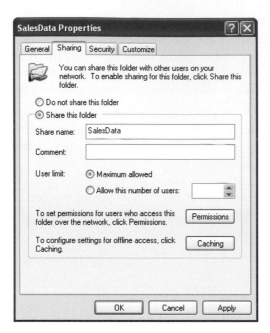

Figure 4-25 A folder object's Properties dialog box, Sharing tab

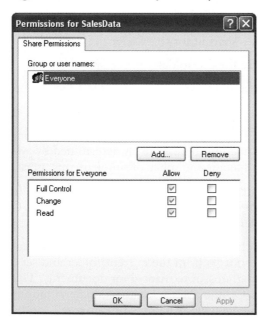

Figure 4-26 The Share Permissions tab of the Permissions for SalesData dialog box

The three Share Permission levels are:

- *Read*—Allows users to access, execute, and open resources through the share
- *Change*—Allows users to create new objects, change and delete existing objects, and to access, execute, and open resources through the share
- *Full Control*—Allows users to perform all actions on resources through the share

Keep in mind these issues when working with shares:

- The three permission levels on a share are the only way to impose security on shared FAT volumes.
- Shares are folders, not individual files.
- Share permissions only apply to the network access point; NTFS permissions must be used to grant or restrict access to objects in the shared folder.
- The default permission for a new share is Full Control for the Everyone group.
- Multiple share permission levels caused by group memberships are cumulative.
- Deny always overrides any other specifics allowed. Be sure not to configure conflicting permissions. Deny overrides any other specific permission assigned to the user account or any permissions inherited from group memberships.
- The most restrictive permissions of cumulative share or cumulative NTFS apply.
- Share permissions only restrict access for network users, not local users.
- A moved folder is no longer shared.
- A copied folder is not shared, but the original folder retains its shared status.

NOTE

Shared folders are easy to recognize because their folder icon now has a blue-sleeved hand supporting the folder.

Accessing shares is done either through Windows Explorer, My Network Places, or by mapping a share to a drive letter. The My Network Places can be used to access resources on the network. This tool offers several network resource access methods:

- *Add Network Place*—A wizard for mapping a share to the My Network Places interface; it does not assign a drive letter to the mapped share.
- *View Network Connections*—Open the Network Connections applet.
- *Computers Near Me*—Lists all computers in your domain or workgroup; each of these can be accessed to reveal shared resources.
- *Entire Network*—Lists all domains or workgroups seen on the network. Each of these can be accessed to see members of those domains or workgroups. Each of these members can be accessed to reveal shared resources.

Accessing shared resources on a Microsoft network is handled through several mechanisms. First, you can map a drive using the Map Network Drive command from Windows Explorer, My Computer, or My Network Places. Second, you can access shared resources through the My Network Places tool. Third, most Open and Save dialog boxes offer a link to My Network Places allowing you to open or save files to remote paths.

Activity 4-15: Creating a Share

Time Required: 10 minutes

Objective: Create a share using Windows Explorer for a specific group.

Description: Sharing files on a workstation can be useful to reduce the amount of repeated data that often exists in a network. In this activity, you create a share for a specific group of users.

To optimize folder access:

This activity requires that Windows XP be installed and that an NTFS partition is present. The XP client must either be a domain member or it must have Simple File Sharing disabled.

1. Start **Windows Explorer** (**Start**, **All Programs**, **Accessories**, **Windows Explorer**).

2. In the left pane, select a drive formatted with NTFS within My Computer.

3. In the right pane, select a folder.

4. Select **File**, **Properties**.

5. Click the **Security** tab.

6. Click the **Add** button.

7. Click the **Advanced** button.

8. Click the **Find Now** button.

9. Locate and select the **Authenticated Users** group.

10. Click **OK**.

11. Click **OK**.

12. Click the **Authenticated Users** group that now appears in the list of names on the Security tab for the NTFS object. Take note of the granted permissions.

13. Select the **Sharing** tab.

14. Select the **Share this folder** option button.

15. Click the **Permissions** button.

16. Click the **Add** button.

17. Click the **Advanced** button.

18. Click the **Find Now** button.

19. Locate and select the **Authenticated Users** group.

20. Click **OK**.

21. Click **OK**.

22. Set the Share permissions for the Authenticated Users group as close to the NTFS file-level permissions as possible.

23. Click **OK**.

24. Click **OK.**

25. In Windows Explorer, select **File**, **Close**.

Activity 4-16: Creating and Removing a Share

Time Required: 10 minutes

Objective: Use Windows Explorer to create and then remove a share.

Description: Whether a Windows XP computer is operating in a domain or a workgroup, there are times when it is useful to be able to allow others access to files on your computer. Shares can be created on just about any folder as long as the user has the right to do so. In this activity, you create a share and assign a specific group access to the share. Once it has been verified that the share exists, you will remove the share.

To share a folder and remove a share:

This activity requires that Windows XP be installed and that an NTFS partition is present. The XP client must either be a domain member or it must have Simple File Sharing disabled.

1. Start **Windows Explorer** (**Start, All Programs, Accessories, Windows Explorer**).

2. In the left pane, select a drive formatted with NTFS within My Computer.

3. In the right pane, select a folder.

4. Select **File**, **Sharing and Security**.

5. Click the **Share this folder** option button.

6. Click the **Permissions** button.

7. Click the **Add** button.

8. Click the **Advanced** button.

9. Click the **Find Now** button.

10. Locate and select the **Authenticated Users** group.

11. Click **OK**.

12. Click **OK**.

13. Click **OK**.

14. Click **OK**.

15. Notice the folder now has a shared hand on its icon.

16. With the folder still selected, select **File**, **Sharing and Security**.

17. Select the **Do not share this folder** option button.

18. Click **OK**.

19. Notice the shared hand on the folder icon disappears.

Activity 4-17: Mapping a Network Drive

Time Required: 10 minutes

Objective: Use Windows Explorer to map a drive to a network share.

Description: It is often useful or necessary to access files that are located somewhere on the network. These files are normally located centrally on a file server, or sometimes on a coworker's computer. A logon script normally performs the drive mappings that are required in an ongoing situation. For temporary access, a user may manually map a drive. In this activity, you create a temporary drive mapping to a share on the network.

To map a network drive:

 This activity requires that the Windows XP Professional be a client on a network with at least one shared folder available for mapping.

1. Start **Windows Explorer** (**Start**, **All Programs**, **Accessories**, **Windows Explorer**).

2. Select **Tools**, **Map Network Drive**.

3. Click the **Browse** button.

4. Using the browse list, locate and select a shared folder from the network.

5. Click **OK**.

6. Select a drive letter using the pull-down list next to **Drive**.

7. Deselect the **Reconnect at logon** check box.

8. Click **Finish**.

WORKING WITH MEDIA FOLDERS AND THE CUSTOMIZE TAB

Media folders are the My Documents, My Music, and My Pictures folders. These specialized folders are the default storage locations for documents, music files, and images respectively. These three top-level media folders cannot be altered; however, any folders you add beneath them can be fully customized through the Customize tab of the folder's Properties dialog box.

The Customize tab (see Figure 4-27) is used to define the type or kind of folder the mount point represents by selecting a folder template, defining a folder picture, and customizing a folder icon. The folder types are:

- Documents (for any file type)
- Pictures (best for many files)
- Photo Album (best for fewer files)
- Music (best for audio files and playlists)
- Music Artist (best for works by one artist)
- Music Album (best for tracks from one album)
- Videos

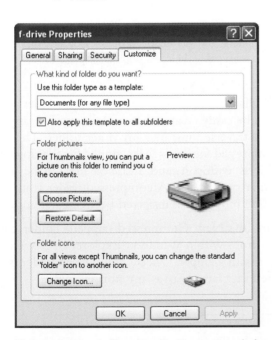

Figure 4-27   A file object's Properties dialog box, Customize tab

Selecting a folder template sets the special features for the mount folder and possibly for all subfolders. Those features include task links in the Quick Tasks menu, viewing and playing options for graphics and audio files, and thumbnails. For example, a Music Album folder can have a thumbnail of the album cover as its folder image. In fact, if you use Windows Media Player to copy an audio CD into a folder, a thumbnail of the album cover is automatically added to the folder icon by Windows XP.

When viewing a media folder, be sure to deselect the Folders button on the toolbar in order to view the Quick Tasks list for the media type. From Quick Tasks, you can view images as slide shows, order prints of images online, and shop for new images and music online.

ZIPPING FILES AND COMPRESSED FOLDERS

Zipped files have become the preferred method of moving large or multiple files around over the Internet. Zipped files are compressed files that house one or more files, and possibly a directory structure, into a single .zip file, such as documents.zip. Zipping files not only makes them smaller, it creates a single filename for transfer and helps ensure delivery (by combining multiple files into a single container and reducing the overall size of the transported files).

Zipping started with the PKZIP command-line tool. Many GUI utilities have been developed to simplify the zipping and extraction processes by adding drag-and-drop capabilities. WinZip is arguably the most popular of these tools.

Windows XP has zipping capabilities built right into the file system. Zipped files are treated as compressed folders. As such, they can be easily created, files and directories can be added or removed, and they can be viewed or traversed just like any other folder. The only real difference between zipped files and compressed folders is that a zipped file is a single file that contains multiple compressed file objects within it, and a zipped file can be moved or transferred between systems as any other type of file. A compressed folder is just a folder with compressed contents that cannot be moved or transferred between systems easily.

A new zipped file can be created using the New, Compressed (zipped) Folder command from the File menu or shortcut menu from within Windows Explorer or My Computer. Zipped folders have an icon of a folder with a zipper. Once a compressed folder is created, you can manipulate its contents in the exact same way as any normal folder.

BURNING CDs

Windows XP includes support for writing files to a blank recordable CD. This feature does require a compatible CD-R or CD-RW drive (to verify this, check the Windows XP Hardware Compatibility List).

ACTIVITY

Activity 4-18: Copying Files to a CD

Time Required: 20 minutes (depending on the amount of data selected)

Objective: Use Windows XP's built-in CD-burning software to copy files from the disk drive to a CD.

Description: As technology has advanced, the media used to store, back up, and transfer data have changed. Floppy disks were once the main medium used by the average user. Then came Zip and Jaz drives. Now, the CD has become the medium of choice for many users. The price of a CD has come down dramatically, and most people are purchasing computers with CD drives that are capable of burning CDs as well. In this activity, you write or "burn" data onto a CD.

To write files to a CD:

1. Insert a blank recordable CD into the CD-R or CD-RW drive.

2. Copy desired files and folders to the CD-recording drive through Windows Explorer or My Computer.

3. Once all files are copied to the CD recording drive, double-click the **CD-recording drive**, then a dialog box opens that displays the temporary holding area where files and folders are stored before actually being written to the CD.

4. Verify that the files and folders, in the layout you desire, are present. Then issue the **Write these files to CD** command from the CD Writing Tasks area. This starts the CD Writing Wizard. Follow its instructions.

5. Once the writing process is finished, you have the option of creating another CD with the same contents.

The CD-burning capabilities of Windows XP also include the ability to duplicate CDs, record audio CDs from other audio CDs or music files (through Windows Media Player), and erase CD-RWs. For more details on using the CD-burning capabilities of Windows XP, consult the Help and Support Center.

USING OFFLINE FILES

One of the biggest problems with mobile computers is granting users access to important files and documents whether they are connected to the office LAN or the Internet, or disconnected from all network mediums. Additionally, this problem is compounded by the hassles of managing file versions between the remote system and the office LAN or the Internet. To resolve this issue, Microsoft has developed a scheme known as Offline Files. Offline Files is a multipart solution that involves file designation, data transfer, and follow-up synchronization.

From a mobile system, you can enable offline access for files and folders on a case-by-case basis. Simply use My Network Places or Windows Explorer to view a list of shared folders or individual files. Right-click an item you want to access while offline, then select Make Available Offline from the shortcut menu. The selected items are transferred to a local storage namespace. Here is the real kicker for this tool: the files and folders made available offline are still accessed in the same manner as if they were not stored locally. Unlike the Briefcase from Windows NT, which made a copy of the file and required you to access the copy through the briefcase container, Offline Files does not change your access methods and maintains the duplicate offline version of the files, and all redirections completely unseen by the user. Offline File's method is much more elegant and logical than the previous schemes. When you are not connected to the network, the browse lists of My Network Neighborhood and Windows Explorer list only those resources cached locally. When a file or folder is marked for offline access, its icon is altered to display a double-rotating-arrow overlay. See Figure 4-28.

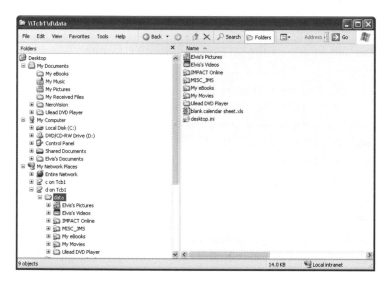

Figure 4-28   Windows Explorer displaying folders marked for offline access

The first time a file is marked for offline availability, Windows XP starts a wizard that introduces the user to the feature and helps with basic configuration. All of the settings offered through the wizard can be accessed at any time through the Offline Folders tab (see Figure 4-29) of the Folder Options command found in the Tools menu of Windows Explorer. The controls on this tab are:

- Enable Offline Files
- Synchronize all offline files when logging on
- Synchronize all offline files before logging off
- Display a reminder every *XX* minutes
- Create an offline files shortcut on the desktop

- Encrypt Offline Files to secure data

- Slider to set the disk space for storing temporary offline files—this sets the amount of drive space that can be used to store automatically cached offline files. Disk space is automatically reserved for any file manually configured using the Make available offline option.

- Delete Files—Removes all cached files

- View Files—Shows a list of all cached files

- Advanced—Determines how your system responds when it is disconnected from the network (i.e., goes offline). The options are to Notify me and begin working offline and Never allow my computer to go offline. You can also define how your system responds when a specific system from the network goes offline.

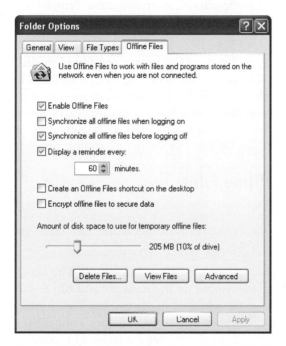

Figure 4-29   Offline Files tab of Folder Options

When the mobile system is reconnected to the network, Windows XP automatically synchronizes the offline files with their LAN-based originals. To alter the default, access the Synchronize Files command in the Tools menu of Windows Explorer. This interface lists all offline folders and their last updated status. To disable synchronization, deselect the check box beside a file or folder. To configure more advanced options, click the Setup button. Through this interface, you can define whether objects are synchronized automatically upon logon or logoff, only when idle, or at scheduled times.

It is only possible to locally cache network files if they are accessible to you through a network share. However, not all files accessible through a network share are cacheable. The creator of the share can disable caching by clearing the Allow caching of files in this shared folder check box in the Caching Settings dialog box. Also in this dialog box, administrators can select whether to allow caching only if manually configured (i.e., end users select the Make available offline option) or whether to automatically force caching of documents and/or programs.

Furthermore, Windows XP automatically prevents caching of all files matching the following type strings: *.slm; *.mdb; *.ldb; *.mdw; *.mde; *.pst; and *.db?. These files types are excluded by default because they are usually open and locked for single user local access, and attempting to access them while offline may corrupt of the data. These defaults can be overridden by defining your own exception list using the Files not cached setting in a group policy object (located in Computer Configuration, Administrative Templates, Network, Offline Files).

By default, files locally cached through Offline Files are cached in the Client Side Cache folder located at %systemroot%\csc. A tool named Cachemov.exe found in the Microsoft Windows XP Professional Resource Kit can be used to move cached files and change the default location of the Client Side Cache (\csc) folder. Cachemov creates a new hidden \csc folder at the root of the selected drive, and then it transfers any existing cache files to the new folder. A user must have at least Modify permissions at the root of the new drive hosting the moved \csc folder in order to support the Offline File's synchronization process.

Activity 4-19: Accessing Offline Files

Time Required: 20 minutes

Objective: Make files located on the network available while not connected to the network.

Description: Data integrity is a major concern to most businesses. The most common method of protecting data is to have all files stored on the network and run regular backups on the network servers. This is great if the network is always "up" or if you are always connected to the network. However, for times when you are not connected or cannot connect to the network, Offline Files makes network files available. This activity steps you through enabling and disabling Offline Files.

To create and disable Offline Files:

This activity requires that Windows XP Professional be a client in a Microsoft Windows network and that some online resources are available through a share.

1. Open **Windows Explorer** (**Start**, **All Programs**, **Accessories**, **Windows Explorer**).

2. Expand the My Network Places area of Windows Explorer.

3. Locate and select a share on any accessible network host.

4. Right-click the selected share and select **Make Available Offline** from the shortcut menu. This starts the Offline Files Wizard.

5. Click **Next**.

6. Verify that the Automatically synchronize the Offline Files when I log on and log off my computer check box is selected. Click **Next**.

7. Verify that the Enable reminders check box is selected and the Create a shortcut to the Offline Files folder on my desktop check box is not selected. Click **Finish**.

8. Select **Yes, make this folder and all its subfolders available offline**, then click **OK**. (This option does not appear if the selected folder does not have subfolders.) After the synchronization process, all files that are stored as Offline Files have a small, double-arrow image added to their icon to identify them.

9. To disable Offline File support, select an enabled folder, right-click, and select **Make Available Offline**. This removes the check mark beside this command and removes the files from local cached storage. Click **Yes, I no longer want this folder and subfolders available online**.

FOLDER REDIRECTION

Folder Redirection is the mechanism of altering the physical storage location of commonly used folders to a network server while retaining the original local access methods. You use Folder Redirection in situations such as when the local hard drive has insufficient space or when data should be accessible from multiple clients on the network.

Folder Redirection can be configured through two different mechanisms. First, local users can alter the location of the My Documents folder through the My Document's Properties dialog box. The Target tab lists the default location as *drive letter*:\Documents and Settings*username*\My Documents. This can be altered by using the Move button to define any other local or network location.

The second means of Folder Redirection occurs through group policy. Within a domain, site, or organizational unit group policy object under User Configuration, such folders as Windows Settings, Folder Redirection, My Documents, Application Data, Desktop, and Start menu can be redirected to a share on a network server. When a user saves a document to the My Documents folder, it is automatically saved both on the local machine and on the network share, if the user is on the network. If the user is not on the network, the document is saved to the user's hard drive. Then, when the user joins the network again, the local version of the document automatically synchronizes with the network version. If the network version of the document had also been modified in that time, the user is prompted as to whether he wants to overwrite his local version or the network version of the document or whether he wants to save both copies of the document.

When either of these redirection methods is used, the redirected items are still accessed in the exact same manner as before by each user. The redirection is handled behind the scenes, completely invisible to the end user.

REMOVABLE MEDIA

Removable media include any storage device—whether read-only, write-once, or rewritable—that is installed onto a Windows XP system. This includes tape devices, DVD and CD-ROM drives, optical drives, Zip and Jaz drives, Bernoulli devices, and so on. If there is a device that has media that can be removed while the power is on (hot-swapped), then it is a removable media device. A removable media device is installed in the same manner as any other device using either Plug and Play at start or the Add Hardware applet.

Once installed, removable media can be configured through Device Manager. You can also manage the media themselves (i.e., tape, disks, CD, DVD, etc.) through the Removable Storage tool found in the Computer Management tool in the Administrative Tools of Control Panel. This tool lists all media that are present on the system and grants you the ability to create custom sets of media for backup or archival purposes. The Computer Management tool can be used to define the media type for each device, set permissions for the media device, and rename the media. It is recommended that you explore the Removable Storage section of the Computer Management tool, especially if you are working with swappable media.

THE MICROSOFT DISTRIBUTED FILE SYSTEM

The Microsoft **Distributed File System (DFS)** is a Windows 2000 or Windows .NET Server-hosted service used to manipulate and manage shared resources. DFS combines shared resources from various locations throughout a network into a single hierarchical system. This allows DFS to be a single access or reference point for a logical tree structure without regard to the physical location of the resources. From a client's perspective, accessing DFS resources is the same as any other network share. This brief discussion of DFS is included here because it is mentioned on the 70-270 exam.

DFS functions by first creating a DFS root on a server system. This root looks and acts much like a share. When shared resources from other systems are mapped under the DFS root, they are called DFS child nodes. The DFS child nodes appear as subfolders underneath the DFS root.

The benefits of DFS include:

- All network resources are organized in a single tree structure.

- User navigation of resources is simplified because the host computer name is not required.

- Powered administration is simplified. If a server that hosts resources fails, the path to a new alternate location can be defined without affecting the path employed by users to gain access.

- Access permissions are preserved.

- The DFS root is accessed in the same way as a normal share.

- Once inside the DFS root, all other resource accesses are simplified and do not require knowing the name of the host systems.

For more information on DFS, see Windows 2000 and Windows .NET Server documentation and resource kits.

CHAPTER SUMMARY

- In this chapter, you learned about basic and dynamic storage. Volume and partitions can be formatted with FAT, FAT32, or NTFS. Preexisting basic storage drive configurations can be managed by Windows XP, but only dynamic devices can be used to create new multipart drive configurations. Basic storage devices can be converted to dynamic devices without damaging the data, but to reverse the process requires that all volumes be deleted before converting them back to basic storage. The Disk Management snap-in is used to perform all drive, partition, and volume-related functions. Windows XP Professional supports simple volumes, spanned volumes, and striped volumes.

- The FAT and FAT32 file systems are retained by Windows XP for backward compatibility with other operating systems on the same multiboot system. FAT does not offer any form of file-level security. NTFS is the recommended file system to use under Windows XP, because it offers file-level security, encryption, and disk quotas.

- Mount points are a new mapping method in Windows XP. This method allows volumes or partitions to be mapped to empty directories on NTFS volumes or partitions. There are several disk-related utilities: Disk Cleanup, Check Disk, and Disk Defragmenter.

- All file system objects within Windows XP have unique properties and controls. In addition, all NTFS objects offer security, encryption, compression, and auditing. NTFS permissions are used to control access to resources. Shares are used to grant access to local resources from across a network.

- Windows XP includes support for simple file sharing, zipped files, CD burning, folder redirection, management of removable media, and support for DFS.

KEY TERMS

active — The status of a primary partition that indicates to the computer's BIOS that it hosts the necessary files to boot an operating system.

auditing — The recording of the occurrence of a defined event or action.

basic storage — The drive division method that employs partitions.

boot partition — The partition that hosts the main Windows XP system files and is the initial default location for the paging file. The boot partition can be the same partition as the system partition or it can be any other partition (or logical drive in an extended partition) on any drive hosted by the computer.

cluster — A group of one or more sectors in a single nondivisible unit.

defragmentation — The process of reorganizing files so that they are stored contiguously and no gaps are left between files.

Disk Management — The MMC snap-in used to manage drives.

disk quota — A feature in Windows that allows you to limit the amount of disk space that can be consumed by a user.

Distributed File System (DFS) — Combines shared resources from various locations throughout a network into a single hierarchical system.

drive letter — One of two methods of accessing formatted volumes under Windows XP. A drive letter can be assigned to a partition or volume or a drive configuration of multiple components.

dynamic storage — The drive division method that employs volumes. It is a new standard supported only by Windows XP and Windows 2000.

extended partition — A type of partition on a basic disk that can be divided into logical drives. Only a single extended partition can exist on a physical disk. When present, only three primary partitions can exist.

FAT (FAT16) — The 16-bit File Allocation Table file system originally introduced with DOS. As supported under Windows XP, it can be used to format partitions or volumes up to 4 GB.

FAT32 — The 32-bit FAT file system. As supported under Windows XP, it can be used to format partitions or volumes up to 32 GB.

fragmentation — The division of a file into two or more parts, where each part is stored in a different location on the hard drive. As the level of fragmentation on a drive increases, the longer it takes for read and write operations to occur.

long file names (LFN) — Filenames up to 256 characters in length, supported by all file systems under Windows XP.

mirrored volume — A drive configuration of a single volume duplicated onto another volume on a different hard drive. Provides fault tolerance. Mirrored volumes are not available on Windows XP.

mount point — A new drive-access technique that maps a volume or partition to an empty directory on an NTFS volume or partition.

New Technology File System (NTFS) — The preferred file system of Windows XP. Supports file-level security, encryption, compression, auditing, and more. Supports volumes up to 2 TB.

primary partition — A type of partition on a basic disk that can be marked active. Up to four primary partitions can exist on a physical disk.

Redundant Array of Independent Disks (RAID-5) — A drive configuration of three or more parts (up to 32) of one or more drives or three or more entire drives (up to 32). Data is written to all drives in equal amounts to spread the workload, and parity information is added to the written data to allow for drive failure recovery. Provides fault tolerance. If one partition or drive fails in the set, the other members can re-create the missing data on the fly. Once the failed member is replaced or repaired, the data on that drive can be rebuilt and restored. This is also known as disk striping with parity. RAID-5 volumes are not available on Windows XP.

removable storage device — Any type of floppy, cartridge, or drive that can be either removed while a system is powered down or as a hot-swappable device.

sector — The smallest division (512 bytes) of a drive's surface.

share — A resource that can be accessed over the network.

simple volume — A drive configuration of all or part of a single drive. Does not provide any fault tolerance. NTFS volumes can be extended; FAT and FAT32 volumes cannot be extended.

spanned volume — A drive configuration of two or more parts (up to 32) of one or more drives or two or more entire drives. The elements of the spanned volume do not have to be equal in size. Data is written to the first drive in the volume until it is full, then it continues with the next drive. It is also called an extended volume. Does not provide any fault tolerance. If one partition or drive in the set fails, all data is lost. Spanned volumes cannot be part of a striped volume or a mirrored volume. NTFS spanned volumes can be extended; FAT and FAT32 spanned volumes cannot be extended. The system partition/volume and boot partition/volume cannot be extended. Volume sets can be reduced in size only by breaking the set and creating a new set. The act of breaking the set destroys all data stored on the volume. Spanned volumes are not available on Windows XP.

striped volume — A drive configuration of two or more parts (up to 32) of one or more drives or two or more entire drives (up to 32). Data is written to all drives in equal amounts (in 64 KB units) to spread the workload and improve performance. Each part or drive must be roughly equal in size. Does not provide any fault tolerance. If one partition or drive in the set fails, all data is lost. Striped volumes cannot be mirrored or extended. Striped volumes are not available on Windows XP.

system partition — The partition that is the active partition where the boot files required to display the boot menu and initiate the booting of Windows XP are stored.

volume — With basic storage, it is a collection of two to 32 partitions into a single logical structure. With dynamic storage, it is any division of a physical drive or collection of divisions into a drive configuration.

REVIEW QUESTIONS

1. Which storage method employs primary and extended partitions?
   a. logical drives
   b. basic
   c. dynamic
   d. spanned volumes

2. When logical drives are present on a basic storage device, how many primary partitions can exist?
   a. 1
   b. 2
   c. 3
   d. 4

3. Which of the following statements are true about a volume set? (Choose all that apply.)
   a. It combines two or more volumes into a single, logical storage area.
   b. It provides fault tolerance.
   c. If one element of the set fails, all data in the set is lost.
   d. It can be assigned a single drive letter.

4. A 4 GB partition or volume can be formatted with what file system? (Choose all that apply.)
   a. FAT
   b. FAT32
   c. HPFS
   d. NTFS

5. What mechanism(s) of Windows XP allow you to access more than 24 or 26 volumes locally on a single system? (Choose all that apply.)
   a. shares
   b. drive letters
   c. DFS
   d. mounted volumes

6. Under Windows XP Professional, it is possible to create new RAID-5 volumes on dynamic and basic drives. True or False?

7. Which partition hosts the main Windows XP system files and is the initial default location for the paging file?

    a. system partition

    b. boot partition

    c. logical partition

    d. dynamic partition

8. The drive configurations supported by Windows XP Professional provide fault tolerance. True or False?

9. What is the best file system for a 250 MB volume on a Windows XP Professional system?

    a. FAT

    b. FAT32

    c. NTFS

    d. HPFS

10. NTFS volumes created under Windows XP cannot be accessed by any other operating system. True or False?

11. Which of the following are true for NTFS under Windows XP? (Choose all that apply.)

    a. supports volumes up to 2 TB in size

    b. supports file-level compression, encryption, auditing, and security

    c. supports disk quotas

    d. supports POSIX file system support

    e. most efficient on volumes smaller than 512 MB

12. Drives can be converted to and from dynamic storage without damaging the hosted data. True or False?

13. The Properties dialog box for a partition or volume gives you quick access to which drive tools? (Select all correct answers)

    a. Check Disk

    b. Defragmentation

    c. Disk Cleanup

    d. Device Manager

    e. Backup

    f. Event Viewer

14. A volume or partition can be attached to a mount point on any other volume or partition. True or False?

15. Quotas can be defined in what manner(s)? (Choose all that apply.)
    a. by user
    b. by drive
    c. by group
    d. by volume or partition

16. Disk Cleanup is used to free space on a hard drive by removing orphaned files, cleaning out the Recycle bin, and shrinking the page file. True or False?

17. The built-in defragmentation utility can be scheduled to automatically reorganize local hard drives. True or False?

18. Which of the following are properties of NTFS file or folder objects but not of FAT file or folder objects? (Choose all that apply.)
    a. Attributes: Read-only
    b. Compress contents to save disk space.
    c. Attributes: Archive
    d. Encrypt contents to secure data.

19. What methods can be used to prevent a user from gaining access to an NTFS resource? (Choose all that apply.)
    a. Do not include the user account (or its groups) in the list of permissions.
    b. Set the user account's permissions to Deny.
    c. Set the user account's permissions to No Access.
    d. Place the user account in the Guests group.

20. NTFS object permissions are used only when a user is local. True or False?

21. Which of the following are true? (Choose all that apply.)
    a. Child objects can inherit the permissions of their parent containers.
    b. Copying files always retains the original settings.
    c. File-level permissions always override contradictory settings on the parent container.
    d. Deny overrides all other specific Allows.

22. Files moved from an NTFS volume to a FAT volume and then to another NTFS volume reassume their original settings. True or False?

23. Which of the following statements is true about shares? (Choose all that apply.)
    a. offers only three levels of permissions
    b. can be cached on client systems
    c. can restrict simultaneous users

4

d. can be individual files or folders

e. overrides NTFS permissions

f. The most restrictive permissions of cumulative share and cumulative NTFS apply.

24. To grant varying levels of access within a share, use NTFS permissions and group files into subfolders. True or False?

25. Which of the following statements is true about the Microsoft Distributed File System? (Choose all that apply.)

a. All network resources are organized in a single tree structure.

b. Access permissions are preserved.

c. A DFS root can be hosted by Windows XP Professional.

d. Once inside the DFS root, all other resource accesses are simplified and do not require knowing the name of the host systems.

CASE PROJECTS

CASE PROJECTS

Case Project 4-1

You must test new media software that plays large multimedia presentations (often 3 MB or larger). The software is being developed for Windows 98, Windows NT, and Windows XP. Can you configure a multiboot system with all three of these operating systems in such a way that a single drive can host at least six media presentations that can be accessed from all three operating systems? If so, how? If not, what other solution(s) can be used?

CASE PROJECTS

Case Project 4-2

The security requirements of your organization state that log files of system access must be retained for at least six months on live accessible drives. In the past, these log files consumed at least 6 GB of drive space per month. However, they are growing larger and at an accelerated rate. Because you don't know exactly how much drive space you'll need over the next six months to a year, what options do you have under Windows XP to comply with the organization's security requirements?

USERS, GROUPS, PROFILES, AND POLICIES

After reading this chapter and completing the exercises, you will be able to:

- Understand Windows XP Professional user accounts
- Understand the different types of logons
- Understand how to log on to Windows XP
- Understand naming conventions
- Create and manage local user accounts
- Planning groups and system groups
- Work with Windows XP as a domain client
- Create user profiles
- Work with group policies
- Troubleshoot cached credentials
- Understand the Files and Settings Transfer Wizard and the User State Migration Tool (USMT)

Many computers are used by more than one person, especially in business or educational environments. Each person is identified to the computer, and ultimately the network, through a unique user account. Typically, a **user account** contains details about the user, including the user's preferred configuration or environmental settings. To establish a system that maintains details about each user, Windows XP uses named access accounts that are protected with password security. These topics are discussed in detail in this chapter.

In this chapter, you are introduced to the types of user accounts employed on Windows XP Professional systems (i.e., local and domain). The types of logons are explored, as well as user groups, user profiles, and group policies.

WINDOWS XP PROFESSIONAL USER ACCOUNTS

Windows XP Professional is designed for use as a network client for a Windows NT, Windows 2000, or Windows Server 2003-based domain network, as a member of a workgroup, or as a standalone operating system. The next sections discuss the issues of local and domain user accounts and how Windows XP supports multiple user accounts.

Types of Windows XP Professional User Accounts

With a Windows XP Professional system, you can create, configure, and manage only **local user accounts**. A local user account exists on a single computer and cannot be used in any manner with domain resources or to gain domain access of any kind. A local user account has no meaning in a domain or any type of network; it is used for local system access. If you are a member of a workgroup, you must have a local user account on each system in order to gain access to resources on another workgroup member's computer. When Windows XP Professional is used as a standalone system or as a member of a workgroup, then it uses local user accounts and **local groups**.

A user account is employed to uniquely identify a user to the system, using a named user account and a password. Tied to this user account are numerous details about the user, security settings, and preferences. A Windows XP Professional local user account stores details about:

- *Security*—Passwords protect user accounts so only authorized individuals can gain access.

- *Preferences*—A user's environmental settings and configuration preferences can be stored as a **profile**, so no matter where a user connects to the network, the preferred desktop and resources are available.

A **domain user account** exists in a domain or in any trusting domain by virtue of being created on a domain controller. A domain user account exists throughout a domain; it can be used on any computer that is a member of that domain. A domain user account is used to gain access to domain resources and can also be used to grant access to local resources. When Windows XP Professional is a domain client, it can assign access permissions to local resources using domain users and groups, but it is unable to create domain users or groups. Nor is it able to alter the membership of domain groups. Domain user accounts as well as using Windows XP Professional as a domain client are discussed later in this chapter.

On a Windows XP Professional system—whether acting as a client in a domain network, a peer-to-peer workgroup, or even as a standalone desktop system—user accounts are used to govern or control access.

How Accounts Interact with a Windows XP Professional System

Users, by way of their user accounts, interact with a computer system. How each user interacts with the system depends on how the Windows XP Professional system is set up. It can be set up in one of the following ways:

- *Standalone system, automatic logon*—All users access local resources through a common user account that automatically logs into the system when it starts.

- *Standalone system*—Each user logs into the system with a unique user account to gain access to local resources.

- *Workgroup member*—Each user logs into the system with a local user account. (When shared resources are accessed on a remote system, a password or credentials for a user account on that remote system must be supplied.)

- *Domain network client*—Each user logs into the system with a unique domain user account to gain access to domain and local resources.

In addition to these items, a Windows XP Professional system maintains a wide range of security settings and preferences that affect a user account. These include **password** policy, **account lockout policy**, **audit policy**, user rights assignment, **security options**, public key policies, IP security policies, and more. Many of these topics are discussed throughout this chapter.

Supporting More Than One User

Operating systems such as Windows XP that can support more than one user are called **multiple-user systems**. Maintaining separate and distinct user accounts for each person is the common feature of all multiple-user systems. Windows XP implements its multiple-user system through the following:

- *Groups*—**Groups** are named collections of users. Each member of a group takes on the access privileges or restrictions defined for that group. Through the use of groups, Administrators can manage many users at one time because a group's settings can be defined once and apply to all members of that group. When the group settings are changed or modified, those changes automatically affect every member of that group. Thus, changing each user's account is not necessary.

    To provide the highest degree of control over resources, Windows XP uses two types of groups: local and global. Local groups exist only on the computer where they are created. Global groups exist throughout a domain. Windows XP Professional can create and manage local groups, but not global groups. Windows XP Professional can add only existing global groups to its local groups to grant access to resources. This distinction is very important, as you'll soon see. Local groups can have members who are users and/or global groups.

- *Resources*—On a network or within a standalone system, resources are defined as any useful service or object, including printers, shared directories, and software applications. A resource can be accessible by everyone across the network or be limited to one person on a single machine, and at any level in between. The range of control over resources within Windows XP is astounding. Details on how to manage resources and how to control who has and who doesn't have access are presented later in this chapter.

- *Policies*—A policy is a set of configuration options that define aspects of Windows XP security. Security policies are used to define password restrictions, account lockouts, user rights, and event auditing. System policies are defined for a user, computer, or a group to restrict the computing environment. Details on both types of policies are discussed later in this chapter.

- *Profiles*—A profile is a stored snapshot of the environmental settings of a user's desktop, Start menu, and other user-specific details. Profiles can exist on a single computer or be configured to follow a user around a network no matter what workstation is used. **User profiles** are discussed in detail later in this chapter.

Now that you've had a brief overview of the multiple-user system of Windows XP, next you learn about these topics in more detail.

TYPES OF LOGON

Windows XP uses **logon authentication** for two purposes: first, to maintain security and privacy within a network; and second, to track computer usage by user account. Each Windows XP user can have a unique user account that identifies that user and contains or references all the system preferences for, access privileges of, and private information about that one user. Thus, Windows XP can provide security and privacy for all users through the mandatory requirement of logon authentication.

Windows XP supports two types of logon: Windows Welcome and classic. The following sections discuss each in turn.

Windows Welcome Logon Method

The Windows Welcome logon is a completely new logon method to the Windows product line. Windows Welcome is designed for use on standalone or workgroup member systems. As the system starts, a list of user accounts with icons appears. To log on, you point and click a username; if a password is defined for the account, you are prompted to enter it before access is granted. If no password is defined for the account, access is granted immediately. Windows Welcome can be used only on standalone or workgroup Windows XP systems; it is not available for use when Windows XP Professional is used as a domain client.

Another feature of Windows Welcome logon is Fast User Switching, which allows Windows XP Professional to switch users without logging off. Fast User Switching is accomplished by clicking Start, Log Off, then clicking Switch User. This returns you to the Windows Welcome logon screen, where you can select another user account.

Notice that the user account from which you just switched now has a listing under the account name on the Welcome logon screen indicating how many programs are still active. The account that is not in use has programs that are still active and running.

Once you finish with the second user account, you can switch to any other account or log off. Logging back onto the system with the user account previously in use restores that desktop environment and all active programs. Fast User Switching can only be used when Windows Welcome logon is used; therefore, it is not an option for Windows XP Professional systems serving as a domain client.

Classic Logon Method

The classic logon method is to press Ctrl+Alt+Delete to access the WinLogon security dialog box. However, the Ctrl+Alt+Delete key sequence can be disabled, so the WinLogon security dialog box appears when the system starts or upon user logout.

 If the system is a domain member, classic logon is the only logon method allowed.

NOTE

When you press Ctrl+Alt+Delete at the default splash screen, the Logon Information dialog box appears. Here, users enter the logon information—username, password, and domain (if a domain client)—then click OK to have the security system validate their information and grant access to the computer. Once users have completed their work, they can log off the computer to make it available for the next user. There is no user switching available when classic logon is used.

The logon mode is set to classic logon automatically when the Windows XP system becomes a domain member. On a standalone or workgroup member Windows XP system, the logon method is set through the User Accounts applet. Just click the Change the way users log on or off command, then on the Select logon and logoff page, click Use the Welcome screen or Use classic logon. When the Welcome screen option is selected, you can also enable the Fast User Switching option.

LOGGING ON TO WINDOWS XP

When Windows XP Professional is installed, it automatically creates two default user accounts: Administrator and Guest. The following sections discuss each in turn.

Administrator

The **Administrator account** is the most powerful user account possible within the Windows XP environment. This account has unlimited access and unrestricted privileges to every aspect of Windows XP. The Administrator account has unrestricted ability to manage all security settings, other users, groups, the operating system environment, printers, shares, and storage devices. Due to these far-reaching privileges, the Administrator account must be protected from misuse. Defining a complicated password for this account is highly recommended. You should also rename this account, thereby increasing the difficulty for hackers attempting to discover a valid username and password.

The Administrator account has the following characteristics:

- It cannot be deleted.
- It cannot be **locked out**.
- It can be **disabled**.
- It can have a blank password (however, this is not recommended).
- It can be renamed (which is recommended).
- It cannot be removed from the Administrators local group.

Account lockout occurs when a user account has been employed unsuccessfully to log into a system repeatedly. The Account Lockout Policy in the Local Security Policy or a Group Policy defines how many login failures can occur before an account is locked out. Once an account is locked out, it is restricted from being used to log into a system or network. Lockout can be configured to last a specific period of time or indefinitely. If the latter, an administrator must manually remove the lockout restriction on a user account to allow it to be used again. Disabling an account is similar in result to a lockout. However, disabling an account is performed manually only by an administrator.

Guest

The **Guest account** is one of the least privileged user accounts in Windows XP. This account has limited access to resources and computer activities. Even so, you should set a new password for the Guest account, and it should be used only by authorized one-time users or users with low-security access. Any configuration changes made to the desktop or Start menu are not recorded in the Guest's user profile. If you do allow this account to be used, you should rename it.

The Guest account is a member of the Everyone group. By default the permissions on new objects and shares are set to default to Everyone - Full Control. This means that a Guest can access any file and folder accessible to the Everyone group on the system if the default permissions were not changed. Therefore it is recommended to leave the Guest account disabled.

The Guest account has the following characteristics:

- It cannot be deleted.
- It can be locked out.
- It can be disabled (it is disabled by default).

- It can have a blank password (it is blank by default).
- It can be renamed (which is recommended).
- It can be removed from the Guests local group.

NAMING CONVENTIONS

Before creating and managing user accounts, you need to understand naming conventions. A **naming convention** is simply a predetermined process for creating names on a network or standalone system. A naming convention should incorporate a scheme for user accounts, computers, directories, network shares, printers, and servers. These names should be descriptive enough so that anyone can figure out to which type of object the name corresponds. For example, you should name computers and resources by department or by use, to simplify user access.

This stipulation of always using a naming convention seems pointless for small networks, but it is rare for small networks to remain small. Most networks grow at an alarming rate. If you begin naming network objects at random, you'll soon forget which resource corresponds to which name. Even with the excellent management tools of Windows XP, you can quickly lose track of important resources if you don't establish a standard way of naming network resources.

The naming convention your organization settles on ultimately doesn't matter, as long as it can always provide you with a useful name for each new network object. To give you an idea of a naming scheme, here are two common rules:

- Usernames are constructed from the first and last name of the user, plus a code identifying his or her job title or department (for example, BobScottAccounting).
- Group names are constructed from resource types, department names, location names, project names, and combinations of all four (for example, Accounting01, AustinUsers, BigProject01, etc.).

No matter what naming convention is deployed, it needs to address the following four elements:

- It must be consistent across all objects.
- It must be easy to use and understand.
- New names should be easily constructed by mimicking the composition of existing names.
- An object's name should clearly identify that object's type.

MANAGING LOCAL USER ACCOUNTS

Before you create new local user accounts, you must decide on the type of user account. On a Windows XP Professional system, there are local user accounts that are just local representations of domain/network user accounts and there are local user accounts created from scratch locally.

The User Accounts applet is used to create a local user account out of an existing domain account. To create a local representation of an existing domain/network user account, use the Add button on the User Accounts applet.

Local Users and Groups is accessed through the Advanced button on the Advanced tab of the User Accounts applet. The Local Users and Groups snap-in is used to create local user accounts from scratch.

User Accounts Applet

The User Accounts applet (see Figure 5-1) is used to perform several functions on local user accounts. This applet can be opened only if you are logged on to the Windows XP Professional system with the Administrator account, logged with a user account that is a member of the Administrators group, or by providing the username, password, and domain when attempting to start the applet. (This last method is known as Secondary Logon.)

Figure 5-1   User Accounts applet, Users tab

The User Accounts applet has two tabs, Users and Advanced. The Users tab displays all active (i.e., nondisabled) user accounts that can be employed to gain local access. This list details the username, the domain, and the group memberships of the user account. The term "domain" in this instance refers to the logical environment where the user account originated. All user accounts created on the Windows XP Professional system have the local computer name listed as its domain (as in WXPPRO-199 in Figure 5-1). All user accounts from a domain (such as those created by Windows NT, Windows 2000, or Windows Server 2003) or other networking environment have the name of that domain listed as its domain.

NOTE This section on managing user accounts focuses on local user account management while the computer is a domain member. The User Accounts applet functions differently when the system is a standalone system or a workgroup member. In those cases, the User Accounts applet becomes a task wizard where user maintenance is performed through easy-to-follow task selections.

Creating a local representation of an existing domain/network user account grants a network user the ability to access resources hosted by the Windows XP Professional system, regardless of whether it is a member of the domain/network. These important user accounts cannot be used to log onto a Windows XP Professional system; they can be used only to access resources over the network hosted on a Windows XP Professional system (i.e., the domain user is authenticated by the domain controller and the local representation of that account is used to gain access to the resources on the client). Plus, the use of local representations allows the Administrator or user of a Windows XP Professional system to create a local security configuration of users and groups that does not rely upon the group memberships of the domain/network. However, it is still possible to add domain users and domain groups to local groups.

Clicking the Add button reveals the Add New User Wizard (see Figure 5-2). If you know the name of the user account and the domain of which it is a member, you can type this information manually. You can also click the Browse button to access the Select User dialog box where you can perform an LDAP query to locate a user. Clicking Next prompts you for the access level to grant the imported user (see Figure 5-3). The selections are:

- *Standard user*—Grants the imported user membership into the local Power Users group

- *Restricted user*—Grants the imported user membership into the local Users group

- *Other*—Grants the imported user membership into the existing local group selected from the pull-down list

Once you click Finish on the wizard, the imported user is added to the list of local users for this computer. To remove an existing user, just select it from the list and click Remove. You are prompted to confirm the user account deletion.

The Properties button on the Users tab of the User Accounts applet is used to access basic properties for the selected user account. A locally created user account's Properties dialog box has two tabs, General and Group Membership. The General tab is used to change the

Figure 5-2 Add New User Wizard, user name and domain page

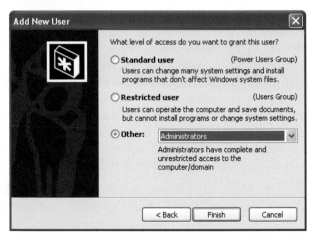

Figure 5-3 Add New User Wizard, level of access page

username, full name, and description. The Group Membership tab allows you to change a user's group membership. An **imported user account**'s properties have only a Group Membership tab; they do not have a General tab. An imported user account can only be a member of a single group. A locally created group can be a member of more than one group, but the Group Membership tab of the Properties dialog box for the user account allows only a single group to be selected. To add a user account to multiple groups requires the use of Local Users and Groups.

Activity 5-1: Importing Accounts

Time Required: 10 minutes

Objective: Add an account from a different domain to your account database.

Description: An Administrator creates accounts in his or her domain for the people that he or she supports. In some instances, such as when companies merge, a person from another domain may need rights or permissions on your domain. In that case, rather than creating a new account in the domain, you can add their account from their domain to your account database. In this activity, you import an account from another domain to your account database.

To import a user account:

This activity requires that a domain be accessible over a network connection.

1. Open Control Panel (**Start**, **Control Panel**).
2. Double-click **User Accounts**.
3. Click **Add**.
4. In the Add New User Wizard, click **Browse**.
5. Select a user account from the list. Click **OK**.
6. Click **Next**.
7. Click **Standard User** when prompted about the level of access to grant this user, and then click **Finish**.
8. Notice the imported user appears in the list of users on the User Accounts applet.

Activity 5-2: Change Group Membership for an Imported Account

Time Required: 10 minutes

Objective: In User Accounts, change the group membership of an imported account.

Description: As with any account, sometimes group membership must be changed for an account to provide a different set of rights and/or permissions. In this activity, you change the group membership for the account that was imported in the previous activity.

To change group membership of an imported user:

This activity requires that Activity 5-1 be completed.

1. In the User Accounts applet, click the imported user created in Activity 5-1.
2. Click **Properties**.

3. On the Group Membership tab, click the **Other** option button.

4. From the pull-down list, click **Power Users**.

5. Click **OK**.

Activity 5-3: Delete an Imported Account

Time Required: 5 minutes

Objective: Delete an imported account using User Accounts.

Description: There are times when an account is imported to provide user access to resources for a temporary period of time. Once the user no longer requires access, that person's account can be removed from the local account database. This does not delete their account from their originating domain. In this activity, you remove the account that had been imported in the first activity.

To delete a user account:

    This activity requires that Activity 5-1 be completed.

1. In the User Accounts applet, click the imported user created in Activity 5-1.

2. Click **Remove**.

3. When asked to confirm, click **Yes**.

The password for locally created users can be changed using the Reset Password button at the bottom of the User Accounts applet (be sure to select the user account first). You are prompted only for the new password and a confirmation of the new password.

Imported user accounts appear in this applet regardless of whether the Windows XP Professional system is logged into the domain from which the accounts are imported. The only requirement is that the applet be able to communicate with the domain through a network connection. If the Windows XP Professional system is physically disconnected from the network media or the domain is not available, the imported user accounts won't be listed. Once the domain of origin returns, the user accounts reappear.

The Advanced tab of the User Accounts applet grants you access to password and passport management, advanced user management, and secure logon settings. Manage Passwords is used to add, remove, or edit logon credentials for various networks and Web sites. The Passport Wizard is used to define your Microsoft Passport account for use in messaging, Microsoft personalized Web pages, and using Passport-restricted Web sites. Advanced user management is discussed in detail in the next section. The Secure logon setting is just a single check box that determines whether the Ctrl+Alt+Delete key sequence is required before the logon dialog box is displayed for the classic logon method.

Local Users and Groups

The Local Users and Groups tool (see Figure 5-4) is accessed by pressing the Advanced button on the Advanced tab of the User Accounts applet or through Computer Management in Administrative Tools. This tool is used to create and manage local users; imported users do not appear in this interface. The console tree hosts only two nodes: Users and Groups. The Users node contains all local user accounts. The Groups node contains all local group accounts.

5

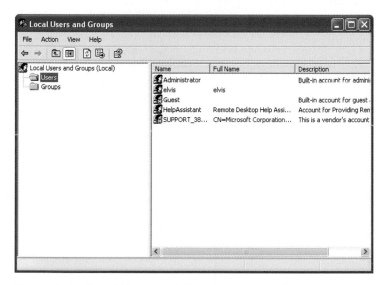

Figure 5-4 Local Users and Groups, Users node

Users Node

Selecting the Users node displays all existing local user accounts. Initially, the Administrator and Guest accounts (as seen in Figure 5-4) are displayed. The HelpAssistant and Support accounts are used to enable Remote Assistance and online Help and Support Services, respectively. The details pane lists the name of the user account, the full name of the user, and the description of the account. By selecting a user account and right-clicking, you can access the account's properties. The Properties dialog box for a local user account has three tabs: General, Member Of, and Profile.

NOTE

All of the right-click shortcut menu commands described in this chapter also appear in the Action drop-down menu when the appropriate object is selected.

The General tab (see Figure 5-5) of a user account's Properties dialog box offers the following:

- *Name of user account*—Not customizable through this dialog box
- *Full Name*—Customizable full name of the person using the account
- *Description*—Customizable text field to describe the purpose or use of the account
- *User must change password at next logon*—A check box used to force a user to change their password the next time they log onto the system
- *User cannot change password*—A check box that prevents the user from altering his or her current password
- *Password never expires*—A check box that exempts this user from the account policy that defines the maximum lifetime of a password
- *Account is disabled*—A check box used to turn off an account. This prevents the account from being used, but it retains the account for security auditing purposes.
- *Account is locked out*—A check box used by the lockout policy when an account meets the lockout parameters

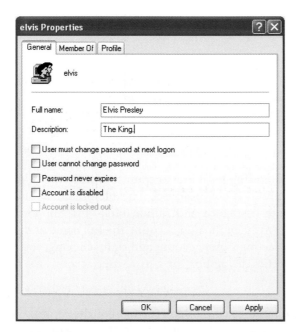

Figure 5-5   A user account's Properties dialog box, General tab

The Member Of tab (see Figure 5-6) lists the groups of which this user account is currently a member. To add group memberships, click the Add button. This opens the Select Groups dialog box. In this dialog box you can type in the name of an existing local group, thus making this user account a member of that group. Or, you can click the Advanced button, which opens a dialog box that searches for groups and displays a list from which to select. To remove a group membership, select it on the Member Of tab and click Remove.

Figure 5-6 A user account's Properties dialog box, Member Of tab

The Profile tab (see Figure 5-7) is used to define the user profile path, logon script, and home folder. Because this is a Windows XP Professional local user, most of the paths used on this tab should be local (i.e., residing on the local computer). Profiles are discussed in detail later in this chapter. The profile path defines the alternate location where a user's profile is to be stored. By default, user profiles are stored in \Documents and Settings*<username>*, where *<username>* is the name of the user to whom the profile belongs or applies. The logon script is the local path to a logon script that can map drive letters, start applications, or perform other command-line operations each time the system starts. The home folder is the default location for the storage of user-created documents and files. By default, the home folder is the \Documents and Settings*<username>*\My Documents folder, but this setting can be used to define an alternate location with either a path statement or with a mapped drive letter to a network share (such as K and \\mainserver\users\steve).

Figure 5-7   A user account's Properties dialog box, Profile tab

When you right-click a username in the details pane, you can choose Properties (the result of which has already been discussed) or these other options:

- *Set Password*—Provides a new password and confirmation; the original password is not required.

- *Delete*—Completely removes a user account from the system, which, once deleted, is not recoverable. Re-creating a new account, even with the same name and configuration, is seen as a different account by the system because its SID (security identifier) has changed.

- *Rename*—Changes the name of the user account

- *Help*—Accesses context-sensitive help

All other controls on a Windows XP Professional system are defined through the **Local Security Policy tool** (discussed later in this chapter). Microsoft Windows NT, 2000, and Server 2003 user management tools offer several other configuration options depending on the resources and services available on a domain level. Consult Windows NT, Windows 2000, or Windows Server 2003 documentation for details on managing domain users.

Activity 5-4: Creating a Local Account

Time Required: 10 minutes

Objective: Create a new local user account using User Accounts.

Description: A good security policy for any company is to make sure each person has his or her own account. That way, specific permissions and rights can be maintained for each person, and the Event log can track the activity of each account. In this activity, you create an account for a new user.

To create a new local user account:

1. Click the **Advanced** tab on the User Accounts applet.

2. Click the **Advanced** button.

3. Click the **Users** node in the console tree of Local Users and Groups.

4. Select **Action**, then click **New User**.

5. In the New User dialog box, enter a username (such as **BobTemp**), full name (such as **Bob Smith**), and description (such as **A temporary account for Bob**).

6. Provide a password and confirm that password.

7. Deselect the User must change password at next logon check box.

8. Click **Create**.

9. Click **Close**.

10. The BobTemp user account is now listed in the details pane.

Groups Node

Selecting the Groups node in the Local Users and Groups applet displays all existing local groups, which are named collections of users. All members of a group share the privileges or restrictions of that group. Groups are used to give a specific level of access to multiple users through a single management action. Once a group has access to a resource, users can be added to or removed from that group as needed. The group concept is key to managing large numbers of users and their access to any number of resources. In fact, if you use the group concept effectively, there should be little need to assign access rights to an individual user.

A local user can be a member of multiple groups. Different groups can be assigned different levels of access to the same resources. In such cases, the most permissive of all granted access levels is used, except when access is specifically denied by one or more groups.

Activity 5-5: Change Group Membership for a Local Account

Time Required: 10 minutes

Objective: Change the group membership of a local account using User Accounts.

Description: As with imported accounts, local accounts need group memberships changed on occasion. In this activity, you add the newest account to the Power Users group and remove the same account from the Users group.

To change group membership for a local user account:

 This activity requires that Activity 5-4 be completed.

1. Click the **BobTemp** user account created in Activity 5-4.
2. Select **Action**, and click **Properties**.
3. Click the **Member Of** tab.
4. Click the **Add** button.
5. Click the **Advanced** button.
6. Click **Find Now**.
7. Select the **Power Users** group.
8. Click **OK**.
9. Click **OK**.
10. Select the **Users** group.
11. Click **Remove**.
12. Click **OK** to close the Properties dialog box.

PLANNING GROUPS AND SYSTEM GROUPS

As you plan your network security (covered in detail in Chapter 6, "Windows XP Security and Access Controls"), user base, and resource allocation, plan how you will manage each of these groups. Think about how groups can be paired with resources to provide a wide range of administrative control. Once your resources are in place and all the required groups have been created, most of your administrative tasks involve adding users to or removing them from these groups.

Working with Groups You've Made

To create and manage groups that can be used both within the domain and in trusting domains, you must have a Windows NT, 2000, or Server 2003 in a client/server environment. If a Windows XP Professional system is part of a domain, its user tools can add global groups to local groups as members.

On a domain scale, a complete system of links from resources to users can be established. Each resource has one or more local groups assigned to it. Each user is assigned to one or more global groups (Figure 5-8). Global user groups are assigned to local resource groups. Each local group can be assigned different levels or types of access to the resource. By placing a global group in a local group, you assign all members of that global group the privileges of the local group, i.e., access to a resource. In other words, domain users are members of global groups that are members of local groups that are assigned access permissions to resources. On a standalone or workgroup system, local users are members of local groups that are assigned access permissions to resources.

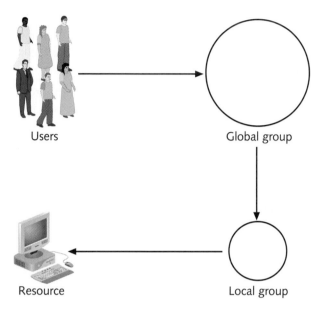

Users   Global group

Resource   Local group

Figure 5-8   Assigning users access to resource using groups

You should plan your group management scheme long before you begin implementation. Planning such a scheme involves applying a naming scheme, dividing users into meaningful groups, and understanding the various levels of access your resources offer. For the group method to be effective, you need to manage all access to resources through groups. Never succumb to the temptation to assign access privileges directly to a user account.

Defining group members is often the most time-consuming process of group management. A group should be formed around a common job position, need of resource, or even geographic location. Some existing groupings you can transform into Windows XP groups are:

- Organizational functioning units, workgroups, or departments
- Authorized users of network programs and applications
- Events, projects, or special assignments
- Authorized users of network resources
- Location or geography
- Individual function or job description

As stated previously, local groups exist only on the computer where they are created. On each computer, all local groups must have a unique name. You can duplicate the names of local groups on different computers, but they are still separate, distinct groups. Using the same name twice on any network, even if the architecture allows it, is not recommended. It can cause confusion as changes are made to the architecture later.

Working with Default Groups

Windows XP Professional has a variety of default groups. When the Groups node is selected in the Local Users and Groups applet, these default groups (as seen in Figure 5-9) are displayed. The default groups are:

- *Administrators*—Members of this group have full access to the computer. The Local Administrator is always a member; additionally, if the system is a member of a domain, the Domain Admins group is a member.

- *Backup Operators*—Members of this group can back up and restore all files and folders on a system. It has no default members.

- *Guests*—Members can operate the computer and save files, but cannot install programs or alter system settings. The default member is the Guest account.

- *Network Configuration Operators*—Members can configure network components. It has no default members.

- *Power Users*—Members can modify the computer, create user accounts, share resources, and install programs, but cannot access files that belong to other users. It has no default members.

- *Remote Desktop Users*—Members can log on remotely. It has no default members.

- *Replicator*—This group is used by special user accounts to facilitate directory replication between systems and domains. It has no default members.

- *Users*—Members can operate the computer and save files, but cannot install programs, modify user accounts, share resources, or alter system settings. Default members are the Authenticated Users group (a nonconfigurable default group) and the Domain Users group if connected to a domain. By default, Windows XP adds all new local user accounts to this group.

- *HelpServicesGroup*—A special group used by the Help and Support Center. The default account for this group is from Microsoft and is meant for support if the user wishes to have Microsoft provide remote support to their desktop. The account name uses the format of SUPPORT_12345678.

The Properties dialog box for a user group allows you to change its description and alter its membership. You can add members to a group from the list of local user accounts or from the list of domain user accounts. Imported user accounts are not listed in this dialog box. Groups can also be deleted or renamed by right-clicking and selecting the command from the shortcut menu.

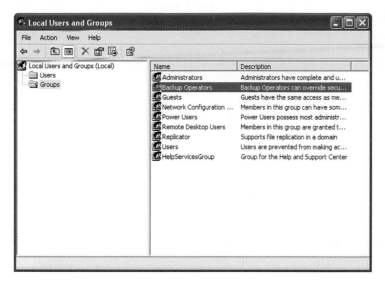

Figure 5-9   Local Users and Groups, Groups node

New groups are created using the New Group command that appears in the shortcut menu when you right-click over a blank area of the details pane. When creating a new group, you must provide the group name, a description of the group, and add members.

Activity 5-6: Create a Local Group

Time Required: 10 minutes

Objective: Create a local group using User Accounts.

Description: As business requirements dictate, new groups may be required to group individuals together because of their common tasks. In this activity, you create a new group for the Sales Department.

To create a local group:

This activity requires that Activity 5-4 be completed.

1. Click the **Groups** node in the console tree.

2. Select **Action**, then click **New Group**.

3. In the New Group dialog box, provide a group name (such as **SalesGrp**) and description (such as **Members of the Sales Department**).

4. Click **Add**.

5. Click **Advanced**.

6. Click **Find Now**.

7. Select the **BobTemp** user.

8. Click **OK**.

9. Click **OK**.

10. Click **Create**.

11. Click **Close**.

Activity 5-7: Delete a Local Group

Time Required: 5 minutes

Objective: Remove a group using User Accounts.

Description: As a company's direction changes, so do group membership requirements. In the event that a company shifts its focus from sales to research, the requirement for a Sales Department may disappear. In this activity, you remove the group that was created in the previous activity.

To delete a group:

This activity requires that Activity 5-6 be completed.

1. Click the **SalesGrp** created in Activity 5-6.

2. Select **Action**, and click **Delete**.

3. When prompted to confirm, click **Yes**.

4. Close the Local Users and Groups tool.

5. Close the User Accounts applet by clicking **OK**.

Working with System Groups and Other Important Groups

Windows XP Professional has several built-in system-controlled groups. System-controlled groups are preexisting groups that you cannot manage but that appear in dialog boxes when assigned group membership or access permissions. These groups are used by the system to control or place restrictions on specific groups of users based on their activities. These groups include: Anonymous Logon, Batch, Creator, Creator Owner, Dialup, Everyone, Interactive, Local Service, Network, Network Service, Remote Interactive Logon, Service, System, and Terminal Server User.

WINDOWS **XP** AS A DOMAIN CLIENT

Windows XP Professional can serve as a client to an Active Directory domain. Domain-based networking is different from workgroup or peer-to-peer networking in one primary sense: there is centralized control of user accounts and overall security.

Windows 2000 Server and Windows Server 2003 are two Microsoft operating systems that can be used as domain controllers to create an Active Directory-based domain network.

When operating in a domain network, a user account can be used to log into any client anywhere on the network. User accounts are part of the domain as a whole rather than restricted to individual systems (as is the case with workgroup networking). Once a user account is created in a domain network, that account can be used anywhere throughout the domain. This allows for much easier management and control of user access to shared resources. Furthermore, domain servers (which may or may not be domain controllers as well) host most of the resources shared with the network. This keeps resources centrally located and makes management of access easier than a workgroup network.

Adding a System as a Domain Client

There are two ways to add a Windows XP Professional system as a client in a domain network:

- The first method of joining a domain requires an Administrator to create a computer account in the domain for the Windows XP Professional system. This is done through the Active Directory Users and Computers utility on a domain controller (such as a Windows 2000 Server or Windows Server 2003). The computer account is simply a computer membership in the domain that has the same name as the computer that is joining the domain. Once a computer account is present in the domain, a user needs only to configure his or her client to connect to that account to join the domain.

- The second method of joining a domain requires the knowledge of a domain Administrator's username and password. In this process, a computer account in the domain is generated from the client. This action requires administrative-level privileges in the domain to accomplish.

Activity 5-8: Joining a Domain: Method 1

Time Required: 20 minutes

Objective: Add a Windows XP Professional system to a domain by creating a computer account on a domain controller.

Description: In order for a Windows XP Professional system to join a domain, it must have a computer account in that domain. This account can be created by an administrator on a domain controller first, then a user can connect to the computer's domain account in order to complete the domain joining process.

To join a domain:

1. Log into a domain controller as a domain Administrator.

2. Click **Start**, **All Programs**, **Administrative Tools**, **Active Directory Users and Computers**.

3. Click the **Computers** folder beneath your domain name in the left panel of the Active Directory Users and Computers window.

4. In the right panel, right-click and select **New**, **Computer** from the shortcut menu.

5. The New Object - Computer dialog box appears. In the Computer name field, type the exact name of the client computer that is joining the domain.

6. Click **Next**.

7. When the Managed page appears, click **Next**.

8. Click **Finish**.

9. Note that the computer account you just created now appears in the right pane of the Active Directory Users and Computers window.

10. Log onto the Windows XP Professional client system using a local account that has computer administration privileges.

11. Click **Start**.

12. Right-click **My Computer** and click **Properties** from the shortcut menu.

13. The System Properties dialog box appears. Click the **Computer Name** tab.

14. On the Computer Name tab, click **Change**.

15. The Computer Name Changes dialog box appears. Click the **Domain** option button.

16. Type the exact name of the domain you wish to join.

17. Click **OK**.

18. Another Computer Name Changes dialog box appears. This one prompts you for the username and password of a domain Administrator. Type these credentials and then click **OK**.

19. A computer account for the client is created in the domain and your client is connected to that computer account. Once this process is complete, a message appears welcoming you to the domain. Click **OK**.

20. Another dialog box appears that states you must restart the computer for the changes to take effect. Click **OK**.

21. Click **OK** to close the System Properties dialog box.

22. The System Settings Change dialog box appears, prompting you to restart the system. Click **Yes** to restart.

23. Once the system restarts, log onto the client using an account from the domain. At this point, the Windows XP Professional client has become a domain client.

Activity 5-9: Joining a Domain: Method 2

Time Required: 20 minutes

Objective: Add a Windows XP Professional system to a domain by knowing a domain Administrator's username and password.

Description: For a Windows XP Professional system to join a domain, it must have a computer account in that domain. This account can be created from the client itself, but you must have knowledge of a domain Administrator's username and password.

To join a domain:

1. Log onto the Windows XP Professional client system using a local account that has computer administration privileges.

2. Click **Start**.

3. Right-click **My Computer** and click **Properties** from the shortcut menu.

4. The System Properties dialog box appears. Click the **Computer Name** tab.

5. On the Computer Name tab, click **Change**.

6. The Computer Name Changes dialog box appears. Click the **Domain** option button.

7. Type the exact name of the domain you wish to join.

8. Click **OK**.

9. Another Computer Name Changes dialog box appears. This one prompts you for the username and password of a domain Administrator. Type these credentials and then click **OK**.

10. A computer account for the client is created in the domain and your client is connected to that computer account. Once this process is complete, a message appears welcoming you to the domain. Click **OK**.

11. Another dialog box appears that states you must restart the computer for the changes to take effect. Click **OK**.

12. Click **OK** to close the System Properties dialog box.

13. The System Settings Change dialog box appears, prompting you to restart the system. Click **Yes** to restart.

14. Once the system restarts, log onto the client using an account from the domain. At this point, the Windows XP Professional client has become a domain client.

Activity 5-10: Leaving a Domain

Time Required: 15 minutes

Objective: Remove a client from a domain.

Description: If you must remove a client from a domain, you must simply join a workgroup. This action returns the system back into a peer-to-peer networking system. This action does not remove the computer account from the Active Directory domain.

To leave a domain:

1. Log onto the Windows XP Professional client system using a local account that has computer administration privileges.

2. Click **Start**.

3. Right-click **My Computer** and click **Properties** from the shortcut menu.

4. The System Properties dialog box appears. Click the **Computer Name** tab.

5. On the Computer Name tab, click **Change**.

6. The Computer Name Changes dialog box appears. Click the **Workgroup** option button.

7. Type the exact name of the workgroup you wish to join. Common default workgroup names include **mshome** and **workgroup**.

8. Click **OK**.

9. You may be prompted to enter the username and password of a local Administrator account. This only occurs if your local user account does not have the user right to change client network memberships.

10. A message appears welcoming you to the workgroup. Click **OK**.

11. Another dialog box appears that states you must restart the computer for the changes to take effect. Click **OK**.

12. Click **OK** to close the System Properties dialog box.

13. The System Settings Change dialog box appears, prompting you to restart the system. Click **Yes** to restart.

14. Once the system restarts, log onto the client using a local account. At this point, the Windows XP Professional client has become a workgroup client.

Controlling a Domain Client

Once Windows XP Professional is a domain client, it is subject to the control of the domain. The domain enforces its control over clients using group policy objects (GPOs). GPOs are really nothing more than Registry templates that are forced onto a system each time it starts or each time a user logs on. GPOs are used to control security settings, system features, software capabilities, and much more. From a client's perspective there is nothing you can do to violate the restrictions imposed on a domain client by GPOs. A GPO is simply a domain-level version of the local security policy. Local security policies are discussed later in this chapter.

Access to Systems and Resources by a Domain Client

Only members of a domain can access systems and resources within that domain. Even if a Windows XP Professional system is configured to be in the same subnet as the domain controller and other domain members, the nonmember system is unable to access anything within the domain. However, domain members can access resources from workgroups if they know correct logon credentials for the resource host in a workgroup.

As a member of a domain, domain resources are accessed through My Network Places. My Network Places can be found in the Start menu, in Windows Explorer, and sometimes even within My Computer (depending on customized configurations). My Network Places gives you the ability to view the names of domain members and examine the contents of their shared resources.

Group Types Assigned By a Domain Client

As a member of a domain, a Windows XP Professional system can still create local users and manage group membership of local users. One significant change in this capability is that as a domain member there are nine group types that can be assigned to local users rather than just three (Administrators, Users, Guests). The nine groups supported by a Windows XP Professional domain client are:

- *Administrators*—Have full control over the local computer
- *Backup Operators*—Can back up and restore files off the local computer. The Backup Operator can back up any file on the local computer regardless of permissions assigned to those files.
- *Guests*—Have same level of access as a User, but are restricted from viewing system logs, and a Guest's profile is not saved
- *HelpServicesGroup*—Used exclusively for diagnostic troubleshooting. Often these types of accounts are employed by members of the Microsoft Help and Support Center in order to access your system remotely.
- *Network Configuration Operators*—Have limited local system access, but can configure network settings
- *Power Users*—Have less access than Administrators, but more than Users. Power Users are can change system time, create local user accounts, install applications, and even create and manage shares.

5

- *Remote Desktop Users*—Have the ability to log on remotely
- *Replicator*—Can replicate files across a domain
- *Users*—Have the rights of normal, standard users with limited system access, but have complete control over any files they own

Active Directory Domain Containers

Another important aspect of domain membership is the use of Active Directory domain containers. A container is just a logically named grouping of Active Directory members (i.e., user accounts and computer accounts). There are three types of Active Directory containers: domains, organizational units (OU), and sites:

- Domains and OUs are used as logical containers, and sites are used as physical containers. Every domain can contain one or more OUs. Each OU can contain one or more OUs are well; thus, OUs can be nested. Think of a domain as a five-story office building (see Figure 5-10). It contains people and computers. An OU can be a floor. Within a floor OU there are rooms. Within some room OUs there are cubicles. Within some cubicle OUs there are filing cabinets with drawers. Within some filing cabinet drawer OUs there are manila folders.

  A network can be a single domain. Within this domain are logical divisions or groupings of computers and users into OUs. Further segmentation can occur by grouping users and computers into subcategories within existing OUs. Computers and users can be a member of only a single OU. But if they are a member of a lower-level OU, then any security or operational controls enforced on higher-level OUs or the domain are applied to them as well. For instance, in the office building example, if all computers are required to use only 17-inch monitors, then all of the computers must have 17-inch monitors. But if a single room OU requires that those monitors be flat screens, then only those computers within that room must meet that requirement. It is common for companies to deploy a network with a domain and OUs to roughly match the department divisions existing in their organization. For example, there may be several top-level OUs such as a Sales OU, Marketing OU, Research OU, and Human Resources OU. Then there may be sub-OUs to the sales OU such as New Sales, Existing Customer Sales, and International Sales. Then maybe there can be further divisions to the International Sales OU such as Germany Sales or Company STR Sales.

- A site could be the assignment of floors four and five to company ABC and the assignment of floors one, two, and three to company XYZ. While they are still part of the same building, the two companies have little communication between each other, but there is significant communication between floors within each company.

  A site is used to help improve how traffic flows across large networks. Computers that are all connected by high-speed communication links are collected into a single site. Different sites are separated by slower, unreliable, or more costly communication links. For example, a company with two offices in different cities might create a single domain across their entire organization but create a unique site at each location. Active Directory replication traffic (the traffic used to support and maintain the domain network) would be restricted over the site-to-site links in order to maintain greater efficiency, security, and prevent excessive bandwidth consumption costs.

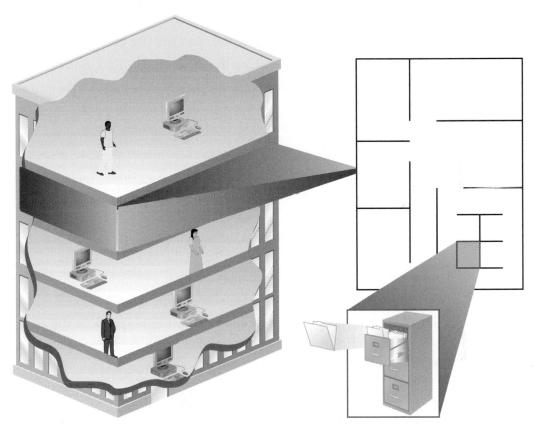

Figure 5-10   A representation of domains and OUs

USER PROFILES

A user profile is a collection of desktop and environmental configurations on a Windows XP system for a specific user or group of users. By default, each Windows XP computer maintains a profile for each user who has logged on to the computer, except for Guest accounts. Each user profile contains information about a particular user's Windows XP configuration. Much of this information is about settings the user can configure, such as color scheme, screen savers, and mouse and keyboard layout.

The material stored in a user profile includes:

- *Application Data*—A directory containing user-specific data, such as for Internet Explorer or Outlook

- *Cookies*—A directory containing cookies accepted by the user through their browser

- *Desktop*—A directory containing the icons displayed on the user's desktop

- *Favorites*—A directory containing the user's list of URLs from Internet Explorer

- *Local Settings*—A directory containing user-specific history information and temporary files

- *My Documents*—A directory containing user-created data

- *NetHood*—A directory containing user-specific network mappings

- *PrintHood*—A directory containing user-specific printer mappings

- *My Recent Documents*—A directory containing user-specific links to recently accessed resources

- *Send To*—A directory containing user-specific links used in the Sent To command of the right-click pop-up menu of files and folders

- *Start Menu*—A directory containing the user-specific Start menu layout

- *Templates*—A directory containing user-specific templates

- *Ntuser.dat*—A file containing Registry information specific to the user. (*Note*: This file cannot be edited directly with Registry editing tools.)

- *Ntuser.dat.log*—A transaction log file that ensures the profile can be re-created in the event of a failure

- *Ntuser.ini*—A file containing profile-related settings, such as which directories should not be uploaded to a roaming profile

Optionally, an Administrator can force users to load a so-called **mandatory profile**. Users can adjust this profile while they're logged on, but all changes are lost as soon as they log off—that is, the settings assigned by the mandatory profile are restored the next time that user logs on. A mandatory profile is created by manually renaming the Ntuser.dat file to Ntuser.man. This technique provides a way for an Administrator to control the look and feel of shared accounts, or to restrict non-Power Users from exercising too much influence over their desktops. In order to alter or edit the mandatory profile, you must either temporarily rename the profile's Registry file back to Ntuser.dat or edit the Registry directly. By temporarily renaming the Registry file, you can log on with a user account employing that profile, make your desired changes, log out, and then return the name back to Ntuser.man. To edit the mandatory profile directly through the Registry, edit the contents of the HKEY_USERS\.DEFAULT key.

User profiles arc managed through the System applet. On the Advanced tab, clicking the Settings button under the User Profiles heading opens the User Profiles dialog box (see Figure 5-11). This dialog box lists all profiles for users who have logged into the Windows XP Professional system. It displays the name of the user account, along with defining its domain of origin, the disk space consumed by the profile, the profile type, its status, and when it was last changed. Profiles can be of two types: local or roaming.

Figure 5-11   User Profiles dialog box

Anytime a user logs onto the system and that user account does not already have a user profile, one is created for him or her. This is done by duplicating the contents of the Default User profile. The All Users profile contains common elements that appear in every user's environment, such as common Start menu items.

Local Profiles

A local profile is a set of specifications and preferences for an individual user, stored on a local machine. Windows XP provides each user with a folder containing their profile settings. Individual profiles are stored in the \Documents and Settings directory. A different location for the Profiles directory can be specified through the Local Users and Groups tool.

Local profiles are established by default for each user who logs onto a particular machine, and reside in the *%username%* subdirectory beneath the \Documents and Settings directory. There are only two ways to create a user profile. The first method is to log on as a user and arrange the information as needed. Upon logout, this information becomes that user's local profile, which can then be transformed into a roaming profile. The second method is to assign a mandatory profile to that user from an existing definition. Even this must be set up by example, rather than through explicit controls.

Roaming Profiles

Windows XP Professional local users (including imported users) have only local profiles. It is not possible to transform a local user's local profile to a roaming profile. However, a domain user account that logs onto a Windows XP Professional system has a local profile created the first time he or she logs on (assuming that the user does not already have a roaming profile on the network). This local profile for the domain user can be transformed into a roaming profile.

A roaming profile resides on a network server to make it broadly accessible. A user whose profile is designated as roaming is able to log onto any Windows XP system on the network, and his or her profile is automatically downloaded to that system. This process avoids having to store a local profile on each workstation that a user uses. The disadvantage to using this kind of profile is that if a user's roaming profile is large, logging on to the network can take a long time because that information must be copied across the network each time that user logs on. In addition, any changes made to the user's profile are uploaded across the network when the user logs off.

The default path designation for a roaming profile is *computername**username* (*computername* is typically a network server, but not necessarily a domain controller). To create a roaming profile, it is necessary to use the Copy to button that appears in the User Profile tab of the System applet on a machine where a local profile for the user already exists. The destination for that copy operation must match the path that defines where the roaming profile resides (as manually defined in the user account); this is the mechanism that tells the startup module where to find a user's roaming profile. Once a local profile is present on a client, such as a Windows XP Professional system, you must use the System applet on that system to copy the profile to a network file server. Then, you must access the Active Directory Users and Computers tool on a domain controller to alter the profile path for the domain user account. You can create a roaming user profile for a local user by modifying the profile path for that user account through the Local Users and Groups tool.

Application of Group Policies

Windows XP has combined several security and access controls into a centralized policy. This centralized policy is called the group policy. There is a local security policy (i.e., a local group policy) for the local system and within a domain. Group policies (GPOs) can be defined for the domain, sites, and organizational units (OUs). All of these group policy types can be managed from a Windows 2000 or Server 2003 system, but only the local computer group policy can be managed from a Windows XP Professional system.

Group policies are applied in the following manner:

1. Any existing legacy Windows NT 4.0 Ntconfig.pol file is applied.

2. Any unique local group policy is applied (read "local group-policy" instead of "local-group policy").

3. Any site group policies are applied.

4. Any domain group policies are applied.

5. Any organizational units (OU) group policies are applied.

One simple way to remember this order is LSDOU (local, site, domain, organizational unit). As long as you can remember that any legacy Windows NT 4.0 Ntconfig.pol files are applied first, then LSDOU can help you keep track of the order of the remainder. Do keep in mind that multiple GPOs can be applied at each Active Directory domain container level. Within each of these containers, there is a manually defined priority order of application. In the list of applicable GPOs, the bottom GPO is applied first and the top GPO is applied last. This means the top GPO has priority and overwrites any settings made by previously applied GPOs. This is a general principle of GPO application; the last GPO to be applied takes precedence over all previously applied GPOs. The cumulative result of this priority application of group policy is known as the effective policy. On Windows XP Professional systems, the effective policy is either all of these group policies properly combined when logged on with a domain user account or only the local group policy (the local group policy applies whether or not a user is logged on). A great tool for extracting this information quickly is Gpresult. Gpresult is a command line tool that displays the applied and effective policy changes to a local system. See Figure 5-12.

Group policies are applied upon startup and each time a user logs on. Group policies are refreshed every 90 minutes on Windows XP Professional if there are any changes and every 16 hours if there aren't.

The Local Security Policy tool is used to edit the local group policy on a Windows XP Professional system. This tool is accessed from the Administrative Tools applet in Control Panel. The local group policy consists of several subpolicies, including password, account lockout, audit, user rights, security options, public key, and IP security.

In the details section of the Local Security Policy tool, notice that each specific policy item is listed with both its local setting and its effective setting. Local settings apply when no one is logged on or when someone is logged on with a local user account. Effective settings apply when someone is logged on with a domain user account. For all policy items, only the local default setting is listed because the effective setting varies based on network configuration.

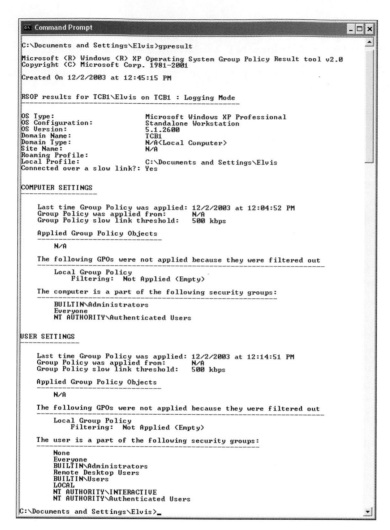

```
Command Prompt                                                    _ □ ×

C:\Documents and Settings\Elvis>gpresult

Microsoft (R) Windows (R) XP Operating System Group Policy Result tool v2.0
Copyright (C) Microsoft Corp. 1981-2001

Created On 12/2/2003 at 12:45:15 PM

RSOP results for TCB1\Elvis on TCB1 : Logging Mode

OS Type:                    Microsoft Windows XP Professional
OS Configuration:           Standalone Workstation
OS Version:                 5.1.2600
Domain Name:                TCB1
Domain Type:                N/A(Local Computer)
Site Name:                  N/A
Roaming Profile:
Local Profile:              C:\Documents and Settings\Elvis
Connected over a slow link?: Yes

COMPUTER SETTINGS

     Last time Group Policy was applied: 12/2/2003 at 12:04:52 PM
     Group Policy was applied from:      N/A
     Group Policy slow link threshold:   500 kbps

     Applied Group Policy Objects
     ---------------------------------
          N/A

     The following GPOs were not applied because they were filtered out
     ----------------------------------------------------------------------
          Local Group Policy
               Filtering:  Not Applied (Empty)

     The computer is a part of the following security groups:
     ----------------------------------------------------------------------
          BUILTIN\Administrators
          Everyone
          NT AUTHORITY\Authenticated Users

USER SETTINGS
------------
     Last time Group Policy was applied: 12/2/2003 at 12:14:51 PM
     Group Policy was applied from:      N/A
     Group Policy slow link threshold:   500 kbps

     Applied Group Policy Objects
     ---------------------------------
          N/A

     The following GPOs were not applied because they were filtered out
     ----------------------------------------------------------------------
          Local Group Policy
               Filtering:  Not Applied (Empty)

     The user is a part of the following security groups:
     ----------------------------------------------------------------------
          None
          Everyone
          BUILTIN\Administrators
          Remote Desktop Users
          BUILTIN\Users
          LOCAL
          NT AUTHORITY\INTERACTIVE
          NT AUTHORITY\Authenticated Users

C:\Documents and Settings\Elvis>_
```

Figure 5-12   An example output of Gpresult

Activity 5-11: Local Security Policy

Time Required: 20 minutes

Objective: Set the local security policy using the Administrative Tools.

Description: No two companies are the same. Because they are all different, it is important that each company sets their local security policy to meet their needs. In this activity, you view and set the local security policy for Windows XP.

To change the local security policy:

1. Open Control Panel (**Start**, **Control Panel**).

2. Double-click **Administrative Tools**.

3. Double-click **Local Security Policy**.

4. Expand the **Account Policies** node.

5. Click the **Password Policy** node.

6. Click **Enforce password history**.

7. Select **Action**, and click **Properties**.

8. In the Settings dialog box, set the value to **5**. Click **OK**.

9. Click **Maximum password age**.

10. Select **Action**, and click **Properties**.

11. In the Settings dialog box, set the value to **60**. Click **OK**.

12. Click **Minimum password age**.

13. Select **Action**, and click **Properties**.

14. In the Settings dialog box, set the value to **2**. Click **OK**.

15. Click **Minimum password length**.

16. Select **Action**, and click **Properties**.

17. In the Settings dialog box, set the value to **6**. Click **OK**.

18. Click the **Account Lockout Policy** node.

19. Click **Account lockout threshold**.

20. Select **Action**, and click **Properties**.

21. In the Settings dialog box, set the value to **3**. Click **OK**.

22. Click **Account lockout duration**.

23. Select **Action**, and click **Properties**.

24. In the Settings dialog box, set the value to **30**. Click **OK**.

25. Click **Reset account lockout counter after**.

26. Select **Action**, and click **Properties**.

27. In the Setting dialogs box, set the value to **15**. Click **OK**.

28. Expand the **Local Policies** node (click the plus sign beside the node).

29. Click the **Audit Policy** node.

30. Click **Audit logon events**.

31. Select **Action**, and click **Properties**.

32. In the Settings dialog box, click **Failure**. Click **OK**.

33. Click **Audit system events**.

34. Select **Action**, and click **Properties**.

35. In the Settings dialog box, select **Success** and **Failure**. Click **OK**.

36. Exit the Local Security Policy tool by selecting **File**, **Exit**.

Password Policy

The password policy (see Figure 5-13) defines the restrictions on passwords. This policy is used to enforce strong passwords for a more secure environment. The items in this policy are:

- *Enforce password history: 0 passwords*—Maintaining a password history prevents reuse of old passwords; a setting of 5 or greater for this item is recommended.

- *Maximum password age: 42 days*—Defines when a password expires and must be replaced; a setting of 30, 45, or 60 days is recommended.

- *Minimum password age: 0 days*—Defines the least amount of time that can pass between password changes; a setting of 1, 3, or 5 days is recommended.

- *Minimum password length: 0 characters*—Sets the number of characters that must be present in a password; a setting of 6 or more is recommended.

- *Password must meet complexity requirements: Disabled*—Determines whether passwords must comply with installed password filters. See the Windows XP Professional Resource Kit or the Microsoft Windows Server 2003 Resource Kit for details.

- *Store password using reversible encryption for all users in the domain: Disabled*—Determines whether CHAP (Challenge Handshake Authentication Protocol) is used to encrypt passwords; leave this disabled unless required by a client.

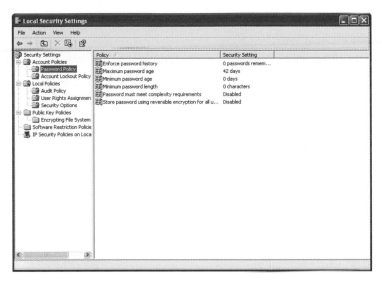

Figure 5-13 Local Security Settings, Password Policy selected

Account Lockout Policy

The account lockout policy defines the conditions that result when a user account is locked out. Lockout is used to prevent brute force attacks against user accounts. The items in this policy are:

- *Account lockout threshold: 0 Invalid logon attempts*—Defines the number of failed logons that must occur before an account is locked out; a setting of 3 to 5 is recommended.

- *Account lockout duration: Not Applicable (defaults to 30 minutes once Account lockout threshold is defined)*—Defines the length of time an account remains locked out; a value of 0 causes locked-out accounts to require administrative action to unlock, a setting of 30 minutes to 2 hours is recommended.

- *Reset account lockout counter after: Not Applicable (defaults to 30 minutes once Account lockout threshold is defined)*—Defines the length of time that must expire before the failed logon attempts for a user account is reset; a setting of 15 minutes is recommended.

Audit Policy

The audit policy defines the events that are recorded in the Security log of the Event Viewer. Auditing is used to track resource usage. Each item in this list can be set to audit the Success and/or Failure of the event. The items in this policy are as follows:

- *Audit account logon events: No auditing*—Audits authentication of a user account on this system when it is used to log on or off another system

- *Audit account management: No auditing*—This item audits the changes to user accounts and group memberships.

- *Audit directory service access: No auditing*—Audits access to Active Directory objects

- *Audit logon events: No auditing*—Audits user account logons, logoffs, and establishment of network connections

- *Audit object access: No auditing*—Audits resource access

- *Audit policy change: No auditing*—Audits changes to the security policy

- *Audit privilege use: No auditing*—Audits use of special rights or privileges

- *Audit process tracking: No auditing*—Audits the activity of processes

- *Audit system events: No auditing*—Audits system-level activities

For more details about auditing, see Chapter 6.

User Rights Assignment

The **user rights assignment** defines which groups or users can perform the specific privileged action. The items in this policy are:

- *Access this computer from the network*—Everyone, Users, Power Users, Backup Operators, Administrators

- *Act as part of the operating system*—None

- *Add workstation to domain*—None

- *Adjust memory quotas for a process*—Local Service, Network Service, Administrators

- *Allow logon through Terminal Services*—Administrators, Remote Desktop Users

- *Back up files and directories*—Backup Operators, Administrators

- *Bypass traverse checking*—Everyone, Users, Power Users, Backup Operators, Administrators

- *Change the system time*—Power Users, Administrators

- *Create a pagefile*—Administrators

- *Create a token object*—None

- *Create permanent shared objects*—None

- *Debug programs*—Administrators

- *Deny access to this computer from the network*—SUPPORT

5

- *Deny logon as a batch job*—None

- *Deny logon as a service*—None

- *Deny logon locally*—Guest, SUPPORT

- *Deny logon through Terminal Services*—None

- *Enable computer and user accounts to be trusted for delegation*—None

- *Force shutdown from a remote system*—Administrators

- *Generate security audits*—Local Services, Network Service

- *Increase scheduling priority*—Administrators

- *Load and unload device drivers*—Administrators

- *Lock pages in memory*—None

- *Logon as a batch job*—None

- *Logon as a service*—Network Service

- *Logon locally*—Guest account, Users, Power Users, Backup Operators, Administrators

- *Manage auditing and security log*—Administrators

- *Modify firmware environment values*—Administrators

- *Perform volume maintenance tasks*—Administrators

- *Profile single process*—Power Users, Administrators

- *Profile system performance*—Administrators

- *Remove computer from docking station*—Users, Power Users, Administrators

- *Replace a process level token*—Local Service, Network Service

- *Restore files and directories*—Backup Operators, Administrators

- *Shut down the system*—Users, Power Users, Backup Operators, Administrators

- *Synchronize directory service data*—None

- *Take ownership of files or other objects*—Administrators

User rights are enabled as defined in the previous list by default. You can alter this configuration through the User Rights Assignment section of the Local Security Policy or Group Policy. Troubleshooting user rights is a process of test, reconfigure, and retest. If you suspect an action cannot be performed that should be possible, test, reset the associated user right, logon again as that user, and retry the action. Be sure to double-check any file or object permissions associated with the action because it can be blocked by lack of access rather than a user right.

For more details on these user rights, consult the Microsoft Windows XP Professional Resource Kit.

Activity 5-12: User Rights

Time Required: 15 minutes

Objective: Change the User Rights Assignment using Administrative Tools.

Description: Windows XP is created with a generic set of User Rights Assignment that meets the basic settings that most companies require. However, there are always individual settings that may need to be changed. In this activity, you change the User Rights Assignment to allow the Power Users group to add workstations to the domain.

To change user rights:

1. Open Control Panel (**Start**, **Control Panel**).
2. Double-click **Administrative Tools**.
3. Double-click **Local Security Policy**.
4. Expand the **Local Policies** node.
5. Click **User Rights Assignment**.
6. Double-click **Add workstations to domain**.
7. Click **Add User or Group**.
8. Click **Advanced**.
9. Click **Find Now**.
10. Locate and select **Power Users**.
11. Click **OK**.
12. Click **OK**.
13. Click **OK**.
14. Close the Local Security Settings dialog box.

Security Options

Security options defines and controls various security features, functions, and controls of the Windows XP environment. The items in this policy are:

- *Accounts*—Administrator account status: Enabled
- *Accounts*—Guest account status: Disabled
- *Accounts*—Limit local account use of blank passwords to console logon only: Enabled
- *Accounts*—Rename administrator account: Administrator
- *Accounts*—Rename guest account: Guest
- *Audit*—Audit the access of global system objects: Disabled

5

- *Audit*—Audit the use of Backup and Restore privilege: Disabled
- *Audit*—Shut down system immediately if unable to log security audits: Disabled
- *Devices*—Allow undock without having to logon: Enabled
- *Devices*—Allowed to format and eject removable media: Administrators
- *Devices*—Prevent users from installing printer drivers: Disabled
- *Devices*—Restrict CD-ROM access to locally logged-on user only: Disabled
- *Devices*—Restrict floppy access to locally logged-on user only: Disabled
- *Devices*—Unsigned driver installation behavior: Warn but allow installation
- *Domain controller*—Allow server operators to schedule tasks: Not defined
- *Domain controller*—LDAP server signing requirements: Not defined
- *Domain controller*—Refuse machine account password changes: Not defined
- *Domain member*—Digitally encrypt or sign secure channel data (always): Enabled
- *Domain member*—Digitally encrypt secure channel data (when possible): Enabled
- *Domain member*—Digitally sign secure channel data (when possible): Enabled
- *Domain member*—Disable machine account password changes: Disabled
- *Domain member*—Maximum machine account password age: 30 days
- *Domain member*—Require strong (Windows 2000 or later) session key: Disabled
- *Interactive logon*—Do not display last username: Disabled
- *Interactive logon*—Do not require CTRL+ALT+DEL: Not defined
- *Interactive logon*—Message text for users attempting to logon: blank
- *Interactive logon*—Message title for users attempting to logon: Not defined
- *Interactive logon*—Number of previous logons to cache (in case domain controller is not available): 10 logons
- *Interactive logon*—Prompt user to change password before expiration: 14 days
- *Interactive logon*—Require Domain Controller authentication to unlock workstation: Disabled
- *Interactive logon*—Smart card removal behavior: No Action
- *Microsoft network client*—Digitally sign communications (always): Disabled
- *Microsoft network client*—Digitally sign communications (if server agrees): Enabled
- *Microsoft network client*—Send unencrypted password to third-party SMB servers: Disabled
- *Microsoft network server*—Amount of idle time required before suspending session: 15 minutes

- *Microsoft network server*—Digitally sign communications (always): Disabled

- *Microsoft network server*—Digitally sign communications (if client agrees): Disabled

- *Microsoft network server*—Disconnect clients when logon hours expire: Enabled

- *Network access*—Allow anonymous SID/Name translation: Disabled

- *Network access*—Do not allow anonymous enumeration of SAM accounts: Enabled

- *Network access*—Do not allow anonymous enumeration of SAM accounts and shares: Disabled

- *Network access*—Do not allow storage of credentials or .NET Passports for network authentication: Disabled

- *Network access*—Let Everyone permissions apply to anonymous users: Disabled

- *Network access*—Named Pipes that can be accessed anonymously: COMNAP, COMNODE, SQL/QUERY, SPOOLSS, LLSRPC, EPMAPPER, LOCATOR, TrkWks, TrkSvr

- *Network access*—Remotely accessible registry paths: System\CurrentControlSet\Control\ProductOptions, System\CurrentControlSet\Control\Print\Printers, System\CurrentControlSet\Control\Server Applications, System\CurrentControlSet\Services\Eventlog, Software\Microsoft\OLAP Server, Software\Microsoft\Windows NT\Current Version, System\CurrentControlSet\Control\ContentIndex, System\CurrentControlSet\Control\Terminal Server, System\CurrentControlSet\Control\Terminal Server\UserConfig, System\CurrentControlSet\Control\Terminal Server\DefaultUserConfig

- *Network access*—Shares that can be accessed anonymously: COMCFG, DFS$

- *Network access*—Sharing and security model for local accounts: Guest only—local users authenticate as Guest

- *Network security*—Do not share LAN Manager hash value on next password change: Disabled

- *Network security*—Force logoff when logon hours expire: Disabled

- *Network security*—LAN Manager authentication level: Send LM & NTLM responses

- *Network security*—LDAP client signing requirements: Negotiate signing

- *Network security*—Minimum session security for NTLM SSP-based (including secure RPC) clients: No minimum

- *Network security*—Minimum session security for NTLM SSP-based (including secure RPC) servers: No minimum

- *Recovery console*—Allow automatic administrative logon: Disabled

- *Recovery console*—Allow floppy copy and access to all drives and all folders: Disabled

- *Shutdown*—Allow system to be shut down without having to logon: Enabled

- *Shutdown*—Clear virtual memory pagefile: Disabled

- *System cryptography*—Use FIPS-compliant algorithms for encryption, hashing, and signing: Disabled

- *System objects*—Default owner for objects created by members of Administrators group: Object creator

- *System objects*—Require case insensitivity for non-Windows subsystems: Enabled

- *System objects*—Strengthen default permissions of internal system objects (for example, Symbolic Links): Enabled

For more details on these security options, consult the Microsoft Windows XP Professional Resource Kit.

GROUP POLICIES

A group policy or GPO is a domain-level version of the local security policy. A domain-level GPO contains two primary divisions. The first division is Computer Configuration (see Figure 5-14). A GPO can contain just configuration settings for a computer or just settings specific to a user (or a group of users). You should notice that the domain-level GPOs have more elements and components than the Local Security Policy. All the items found in the Local Security Policy are found in the Computer Configuration portion of a domain-level GPO under the Security Settings section.

The second division is User Configuration (see Figure 5-15). The User Configuration section of a domain GPO has significantly fewer control categories. This is because most security and functionality controls are managed on a computer basis rather than on a user basis. Editing and working with the Local Security Policy and domain-level GPOs is discussed in Chapter 6.

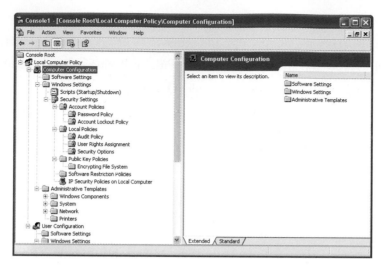

Figure 5-14   Group Policy Object: Computer Configuration

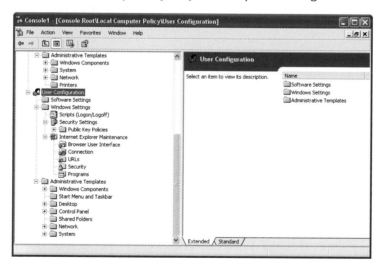

Figure 5-15   Group Policy Object: User Configuration

TROUBLESHOOTING CACHED CREDENTIALS

Windows XP Professional automatically caches a user's credentials in the Registry when a domain logon or .NET Passport logon is performed. Caching of credentials is used to enable a single sign-on requirement. This process allows a user access to shared resources from the network without having to reauthenticate each time. By default, Windows XP caches credentials for the last 10 users who logged on.

Caching of credentials can be disabled through two means from the Windows XP Professional client:

- One method is to enable the group policy setting of Interactive logon: Number of previous logons to cache (in case domain controller is not available). This setting is located within Computer Configuration, Windows Settings, Security Settings, Local Policies, Security Options.

- The second method is to set the cachedlogonscount Registry value within the HKEY_LOCAL_MACHINE\SOFTWARE\Microsoft\Windows NT\CurrentVersion\WinLogon key to 0. It is set to 10 by default. Troubleshooting credential caching typically involves disabling the feature and restarting the system to clear out the previously cached information. Not caching credentials is a more secure configuration.

In addition to caching logon credentials, Windows XP also retains usernames and passwords for resources. These cached resource access credentials are managed through the Stored User Names and Passwords utility. This utility is accessed through the User Accounts applet. If you are a domain member, select the Advanced tab and click Manage Passwords. If you are not a domain member, click the account name and click Manage my network passwords from the Related Tasks lists. From this simple window, you can add, remove, or edit stored credentials. If either of the changes to disable caching of credentials is implemented, Windows XP also disables Stored User Names and Passwords from retaining resource access logon credentials.

Note the following troubleshooting tips:

- If you discover that you are being authenticated as the wrong user account or with the wrong access level, you should remove the stored account information for that server or domain. The next time you attempt to access the resource, you should be prompted for your credentials.

- If you are unable to access resources to which you previously had access, this may indicate that your account has expired or your password must be changed. To remedy this type of situation, edit your account credentials to reflect the updated account information.

- If you find that you can obtain access to a resource to which you should not have access, you should delete the necessary stored credentials to remove this unauthorized access. You should even consider disabling the storage of credentials by enabling the security option within the appropriate group policy.

FILES AND SETTINGS TRANSFER WIZARD

The Files and Settings Transfer Wizard is used to move your data files and personal desktop settings from another computer to your new Windows XP Professional system. You must have some sort of network connection between the two systems; this can be a standard LAN connection, a direct cable connection, or a dial-up connection. Using this wizard, you can transfer files from Windows 95, 98, SE, Me, NT, 2000, or XP systems. To start this wizard, select Start, All Programs, Accessories, System Tools.

To use the wizard, you must be able to execute it on both the new and old systems. If you have the Windows XP Professional CD on hand, you can start the wizard from the \Support\Tools folder (it's called FASTWiz.exe). If you don't have the CD, you can create a wizard disk from which you can run the wizard on the old system. The process involved in using the Files and Settings Transfer Wizard is used in Activity 5-13.

The transfer process can take considerable time. The default settings are to grab nearly every file that is not native to the Windows OS or installed applications. This means every document, sound, movie, image, or other file type is included in the default file selection. There is an option to custom select the files to transfer; therefore, if you have a significant number of files, you may want to use this option to reduce the time and space consumed by the transfer process.

Activity 5-13: Transfer Files and Settings

Time Required: 30 minutes

Objective: Copy files and settings from one operating system onto a Windows XP computer.

Description: It's surprising, but some people are hesitant to accept getting a new computer. For many, it has taken them a long time to get their computer configured just the way they like it. With a new computer, they have to start over. In this activity, the new Windows XP Files and Settings Transfer Wizard is used to prepare a Windows XP machine to be the same as that of a previously configured computer.

To transfer files and settings using the Files and Settings Transfer Wizard:

This activity requires a blank, preformatted floppy disk, a Windows XP Professional system (this will be labeled as the new system in this project), and another system of Windows 9x, NT, 2000, or XP (this will be labeled as the old system in this project). There must be a network communication link between the two systems; this should be established before starting this project.

1. On the new Windows XP Professional system, open the Files and Settings Transfer Wizard (**Start**, **All Programs**, **Accessories**, **System Tools**, **Files and Settings Transfer Wizard**). The Welcome screen of the Wizard appears.

2. Click **Next**.

3. Click **New computer**. Click **Next**.

4. Click **I want to create a Wizard Disk in the following drive**. Click **Next**.

5. Place a blank formatted floppy into the drive and click **OK**.

6. Once the Wizard Disk creation is complete, you see instructions that advise you to take the floppy to the other system, and execute **FASTWiz** before continuing with the wizard on the new system.

7. Go to the old system, logon with the user account from which you want to transfer files and settings. Insert the floppy into the drive and select **Start**, **Run**. Enter **a:\fastwiz** and press **Enter** to execute it.

8. The Welcome to the Files and Settings Transfer Wizard screen appears. Click **Next**.

9. Click **Old computer** on the Which computer is this? page and click **Next**.

10. Select one of the methods to transfer files. This lab assumes you are using a network drive, so select the **Other** option button. Define the path to the folder or drive, using the Browse button if necessary.

11. Click **Next**.

12. On the What do you want to transfer? page, select **Settings only**.

13. Click **Next**.

14. You may see a window that indicates that you need to install specific programs on the new system in order for the transfer process to be fully successful. These programs include applications that are on your old system (such as WinZip, WinAmp, RealAudio, QuickTime Player, Quicken, etc.). Install these programs on the new system before proceeding. Click **Next**.

15. The transfer wizard begins the collection process and stores the data for transfer in the selected path as defined in Step 10. When it is complete, click **Finish**.

16. Go back to the new system.

17. Click **Next**.

18. Click the **Other** option button, then provide the path to the folder or drive used in Step 10, using the Browse button if necessary.

19. Click **Next**.

20. Your files are integrated into the new system. When completed, click **Finish**.

21. You are prompted to log off for the imported changes to take effect. Click **Yes**.

22. Log back on. You should notice that your desktop and user environment now include items and configuration settings from your old system.

User State Migration Tool (USMT)

The Files and Settings Transfer Wizard is an excellent tool for home users and even small businesses. However, it is not versatile enough for use in an enterprise environment. A more robust solution for retaining and moving user configurations and data files is the User State Migration Tool (USMT). USMT supports migration to user data from Windows 9*x*,

Windows NT Workstation 4.0, and Windows 2000 Professional to a Windows XP Professional system. USMT is able to transfer the same files and settings that the Files and Settings Transfer Wizard can, but it is also fully configurable and scriptable. The two command-line utilities that make up USMT are ScanState and LoadState. These two tools read instructions and control parameters from INF files. There are seven default INF files that Administrators can fully customize for their environment.

The command-line syntax for the USMT commands are:

scanstate [/c] [/i:inffile] [/l:logfile] [/v:verboselevel] [/f] [/u] [/x] *<intermediate store>*

loadstate [/i:inffile] [/l:logfile] [/v:verboselevel] [/f] [/u] [/x] *<intermediate store>*

where:

- c—Continue past errors
- i—INF file; multiple INF files are supported.
- l—Log file
- v—Verbosity level from 1-7, with 7 being the most verbose
- f—Transfer the files specified (The default is to perform this action. This switch is primarily for troubleshooting.)
- u—Transfer the user settings (The default is to perform this action. This switch is primarily for troubleshooting.)
- x—Don't transfer user settings or files. Primarily for troubleshooting
- *intermediate store*—The server location to which the settings are transferred.

The ScanState utility is used to create a backup of the user data, then LoadState is used to copy the data onto a new target system.

CHAPTER SUMMARY

- In this chapter, you learned about local users and groups. Windows XP Professional can employ three types of users: locally created users, imported users, and domain users.

- A user account stores preference settings for each individual who uses a computer. Each user can have his own profile that retains all of his preferred desktop settings.

- Users are collected into groups to simplify management and grant access or privileges. Users and groups are managed through the User Accounts applet and the Local Users and Groups utility. Some groups allow you to customize their membership; others are system-controlled groups with memberships that cannot be customized.

- Windows XP Professional has two built-in users, Administrator and Guest, and several built-in groups.

❑ User profiles can be local or roaming. User profiles store a wide variety of personalized or custom data about a user's environment. A user profile can be mandatory just by changing NTUSER.DAT to NTUSER.MAN.

❑ The Local Security Policy tool is used to manage passwords, account lockout parameters, audits, user rights, security options, and more. These controls aid in enforcing security and controlling who is able to perform specific actions on the system.

❑ Group policies are domain-level versions of the local security policy.

❑ The Files and Settings Transfer Wizard can be used to move data files and personal desktop settings from one system to another. The User State Migration Tool is used for enterprise migrations.

5

KEY TERMS

account lockout policy — Defines the conditions that result in a user account being locked out.

Administrator account — The most powerful account possible within the Windows XP environment.

audit policy — Defines the events that are recorded in the Security log of the Event Viewer.

disabled — The state of a user account, which is retained on the system but cannot be used to logon.

domain user account — A user account that can be used throughout a domain.

global group — A group that exists throughout a domain. A global group can be created only on a Windows Server system.

groups — A named collections of users.

Guest account — One of the least privileged user accounts in Windows XP.

imported user account — A local account created by duplicating the name and password of an existing domain account. An imported account can be used only when the Windows XP Professional system is able to communicate with the domain of the original account.

local groups — A group that exists only on the computer where it was created. A local group can have users and global groups as members.

Local Security Policy tool — The centralized control mechanism that governs passwords, account lockout parameters, audits, user rights, security options, public keys, and IP security.

local user account — A user account that exists on a single computer.

locked out — The state of a user account that is disabled due to logon attempts that have repeatedly failed.

logon authentication — The requirement to provide a name and password to gain access to the computer.

mandatory profile — A user profile that does not retain changes once the user logs out. Mandatory profiles are used to maintain a common desktop environment for users.

multiple-user system — An operating system that maintains separate and distinct user accounts for each person.

naming convention — A standardized regular method of creating names for objects, users, computers, groups, etc.

password policy — Defines the restrictions on passwords.

profile — *See* user profile.

security options — Defines and controls various security features, functions, and controls of the Windows XP environment.

user account — A named security element used by a computer system to identify individuals and to record activity, control access, and retain settings.

user profile — A collection of user-specific settings that retain the state of the desktop, Start menu, color scheme, and other environmental aspects across logons.

uer rights assignment — Defines which groups or users can perform the specific privileged action.

Review Questions

1. Windows XP Professional is able to create and manage what types of user accounts?
   a. local
   b. domain
   c. imported
   d. global

2. What types of user accounts can be used on a Windows XP Professional system?
   a. local
   b. domain
   c. imported
   d. global

3. When not connected to a network, what types of user accounts can be employed on a Windows XP Professional system?
   a. local
   b. domain
   c. imported
   d. global

4. A Windows XP Professional system is an operating system that can allow more than one user account to log onto a single system simultaneously. True or False?

5. Which of the following are true of groups?
   a. Several default groups are built into Windows XP.
   b. Groups are named collections of users.

c. The system groups can be deleted through the Local Users and Groups tool.

d. Groups are used to simplify the assignment of permissions.

6. Why does Windows XP require logon authentication?

a. to prevent the spread of viruses

b. to track computer usage by user account

c. to maintain security

d. to promote a naming scheme

7. Which of the following are true for both the Administrator account and the Guest account?

a. cannot be deleted

b. can be locked out

c. cannot be disabled

d. can be renamed

8. When logged on under the Guest account, a user has the same access as other members of what group?

a. Authenticated Users

b. Users

c. Power Users

d. Everyone

9. Imported user accounts can be managed through what applet?

a. User Manager for Domains

b. User Accounts

c. Local Users and Groups

d. Active Directory Users and Computers

10. Which of the following are true of imported users?

a. can only be a member of a single group

b. You can change their password.

c. exist only when their domain of origin is present online

d. are used to grant domain users access to the local resources

11. When creating a new user through the User Accounts applet, the Restricted user selection makes the new user a member of what group?

a. Guests

b. Power Users

c. Users

d. Backup Operators

12. To configure more than one group membership for a local user account requires the use of the User Accounts applet. True or False?

13. When the control item under Secure logon on the Advanced tab of the Users and Password applet is selected, not only is Ctrl+Alt+Delete not required, but the last user account to successfully logon is automatically reused to log onto the system. True or False?

14. You create several new user accounts. You tell everyone they need to logon and change their password to something other than the dummy password you entered to create the account. In the past, you discovered that most users forgot to change the password. What option must you configure to force them to make the change?

    a. User cannot change password

    b. User must change password at next logon

    c. Password never expires

    d. Account is disabled

15. On a Windows XP Professional client, what types of profiles can be used?

    a. Local

    b. Roaming

    c. Mandatory

    d. Dynamic

16. User profiles are stored by default in a subdirectory named after the user account in what default directory on a Windows XP Professional system?

    a. \Winnt\Profiles

    b. \Users

    c. \Profiles

    d. \Documents and Settings

17. The user account Properties dialog box from the Local Users and Groups tool can be used to change the password. True or False?

18. The user tools of Windows XP Professional can create and manage both local and global groups. True or False?

19. Local groups can have global groups as members. True or False?

20. Which of the following groups are not configurable?

    a. Administrators

    b. Interactive

    c. Backup Operators

    d. Creator Owner

    e. Authenticated Users

21. What makes a profile mandatory?

    a. setting a check box through the user account's Properties dialog box

    b. storing it locally

    c. renaming a file with the extension .man

    d. by not connecting to a network

22. The effective policy is the result of applying all network- or domain-hosted security policies, then finally applying the local security policy. True or False?

23. The local security policy is a collection of what individual policies?

    a. password

    b. account lockout

    c. audit

    d. user rights

    e. computer settings

    f. security options

    g. public key

    h. IP security

24. To prevent malicious users from breaking into your computer system by repeatedly trying to guess a password, what built-in security tool can you use?

    a. password policy

    b. IP security

    c. lockout

    d. encryption

25. What control element in Windows XP is used to assign specific privileged actions to users and groups?

    a. auditing

    b. user rights

    c. profiles

    d. security options

CASE PROJECTS

Case Project 5-1

Your notebook computer is attached to a docking station whenever you are in the office. Although your Windows XP Professional notebook does not become a member of the domain when docked, it does have the ability to communicate with the domain. Your docking station hosts a color slide printer. How can you grant printer access to domain users when your notebook is docked?

Case Project 5-2

You are concerned about file security. Recently, a staff member was reprimanded because he restored files to a FAT partition instead of an NTFS partition. The user account is a member of the Backup Administrators group and the Power Users group. Because FAT does not have file-level security, the settings on the files allowed everyone on the network to view the confidential files. How can you change the local security policy to prevent this from occurring in the future?

6

WINDOWS XP SECURITY AND ACCESS CONTROLS

> **After reading this chapter and completing the exercises, you will be able to:**
>
> ♦ Describe the Windows XP security model, and the key role of logon authentication
>
> ♦ Work with access control and customize the logon process
>
> ♦ Disable the default username
>
> ♦ Discuss domain security concepts
>
> ♦ Understand the local computer policy
>
> ♦ Enable and use auditing
>
> ♦ Encrypt NTFS files, folders, or drives using the Encrypting File System (EFS)
>
> ♦ Understand and implement Internet security

Windows XP, like Windows 2000, has been constructed to give a wide range of control over access to its resources. In fact, Windows XP is designed to check access permissions for every request before granting access to resources. In this chapter, you explore the details of the Windows XP security model, its logon process, and the ways in which the operating system associates security information with all objects under its control. In addition, Windows XP efficiently subjects any user's or program's request for system resources to close scrutiny before allowing access to the requested resources. Many of the security issues contained in this chapter discuss how to improve security by manipulating system settings and configuration. Usually these configuration changes are made to the local security policy or Active Directory group policy.

THE WINDOWS XP SECURITY MODEL

Windows XP Professional can establish local security when used as a standalone system or in a workgroup, or participate in **domain security** (either managed by a Windows Server 2003, Windows 2000 Server, Windows NT Server, or some other NOS). Before a user can access any Windows XP resource, he or she must log onto the system by supplying a valid user ID and **password**. A user who successfully logs on receives an **access token**. The access token includes information about the user's identity, any permissions specifically associated with the user's account name, and a complete list of all the groups to which the user belongs. A string of bits represents the token, which is attached to every **process** that the user initializes until that user logs off. In other words, each time a user runs a program, enters a system command, or accesses a resource, a copy of that user's access token accompanies the request.

Each time a user attempts to access a resource, the user's access token is compared with a list of permissions associated with the resource. This list is called an **access control list (ACL)**. The access control list is one of the more important attributes associated with any Windows XP resource. Whenever an object is requested, the ACL and the access token are carefully compared, and a request for the object is granted only when a match is found. Windows XP uses permission settings of Allow and Deny. An Allow setting enables a service for a user or group, whereas a Deny setting disables it. If neither Allow nor Deny is defined for a specific service for a user or group, it defaults to Deny.

If the system finds a match between the access token and the ACL, the request can proceed. If a requested resource is specifically denied in the ACL, or access to a service is not permitted, the request is denied. A match between the access token and the ACL is like finding a key that fits a particular lock. That is, the access token is like a ring of keys that you try in a lock one at a time until a match is found or until there are no more keys to try. Matches between an access token and the ACL can be a function of permissions associated with the individual user's account or permissions that derive from the user's membership in some particular local or global group. Whatever the source of the permissions, the user's request is allowed to proceed unhindered if a match is found.

Windows domain security is centered on Active Directory, the centralized database of security, configuration, and communication information maintained by domain controllers in a Windows network. Active Directory supports everything from authentication of domain users' accounts to accessing shared resources. Windows XP Professional, as a standalone system or as a member of a Windows NT 4.0 domain, does not use Active Directory, relying instead on the Registry and internal security systems to control user access. Note that if a Windows XP Professional system is used in a Windows NT 4.0 domain, it must be authenticated by a domain controller. However, Windows XP Professional participates in Active Directory when it is used as a client in a Windows 2000 Server or Windows Server 2003 domain network. All of the information about the domain and all of the resources shared by the network are managed by Active Directory. Windows XP Professional uses Active Directory to gain access to the domain network.

Logon Authentication

Windows XP logon is mandatory to gain access to the system and to applications and resources. As mentioned in Chapter 5, "Users, Groups, Profiles, and Policies," there are two types of logons available on Windows XP: classic and Windows Welcome. When the Windows XP system is a member of a domain, only the classic method can be used. But, when it is a standalone system or a member of a workgroup, either classic or Windows Welcome can be used.

The logon process typically has two components: identification and authentication. **Identification** requires that a user supply a valid account name (and in a domain environment, the name of the domain to which that **user account** belongs). **Authentication** means that a user must use some method to verify his or her identity. By default in Windows XP, possession of the proper password for an account constitutes authentication, although Windows XP also supports third-party authentication add-ins, including biometric systems that check fingerprints or perform retinal scans and smart card systems that require physical possession of a unique electronic keycard to prove a user's identity. If an account does not have a password assigned to it, the authentication process is skipped.

TIP

Most typical Windows XP systems rely solely on passwords for authentication, so using passwords that are hard to guess is an important aspect of good system security. Good passwords generally include both uppercase and lowercase letters, as well as numbers, for example, Ag00dPA55w0Rd. By creating passwords such as this, it becomes impossible for programs that attempt system break-ins to gain access through using dictionary lists to search for valid passwords. It is important, however, to make passwords easy to remember so users don't write them down, thus creating an additional security risk.

When a user successfully logs onto a Windows XP machine, the security subsystem within the Executive Services layer creates an access token for that user. The access token includes all security information pertaining to that user, including the user's **security ID (SID)** and SIDs for each of the groups to which the user belongs and the associated rights and privileges. Indirectly, through the user rights policy, this collection of SIDs informs the system of the user's rights. An access token includes the following components:

- The unique SID for the account

- A list of groups to which the user belongs

- A list of rights and privileges associated with the specific user's account

Access to the system is allowed only after the user receives the access token. Each access token is created for one-time use during the logon process. Once constructed, the access token is attached to the user's **shell** process, which defines the environment inside which the user executes programs or spawns other processes. (The default shell process for Windows XP is Windows Explorer. It defines the desktop, Start menu, taskbar, and other elements of the default user interface. Alternate shells can be employed from third parties, or even the

6

Windows NT 3.51 Program Manager can be used.) As far as Windows XP is concerned, a process is a computer program designed for some specific function. The term "process" is synonymous with program. All activities within the user mode and kernel mode are performed by a process. Each process is launched using the access token of its parent (i.e., the process that caused it to be launched). When a user launches a process manually, he or she does so through the shell process, usually Windows Explorer, and it is the access token of the shell process that is inherited by the new process.

Resources as Objects

In Windows XP, access to individual resources is controlled at the **object** level. Each object hosts its own access control list that defines which users and groups have access permissions and exactly what type of access they are granted (read, write, print, delete, add, list, etc.). Everything within the Windows XP environment is an object; this includes files, folders, processes, user accounts, printers, computers, etc. Requests for resources, therefore, translate into requests for objects. An individual object is identified by its type, which defines its permitted range of contents and the kinds of operations (called services) that may be performed upon it. Any individual object is an instance of its type and consists of data and a list of services that can be used to create, manipulate, control, and share the data it contains.

Windows XP is able to control access not only at the object level, but also to control which services defined for the object's type a particular security token is allowed to perform or request. All objects are logically subdivided into three parts: a type identifier, a list of services or functions, and a list of named attributes that may or may not have associated data items, called values.

When defining an object, its type describes the kind of entity it is. For example, an object's type may be file, directory, printer, or network share. An object's services define how the object can be manipulated; for example, possible services for a directory object are read, write, and delete. An object's attributes are its named characteristics, such as the file's name and size, whether it is read-only or hidden, and data created for an object whose type is file. The value for these attributes is their content, such as the actual name of the file, selected, not selected, 142,302 bytes, and 10/3/03 04:23:34 PM.

Remember, access or permission to use an object is determined on the basis of the entire object and also for each of the services defined for that object. For example, a user can have access to read a file, such as an e-mail program's executable (.exe) file, but not to edit or delete it. Thus, the user can have permission to access the object in general, but there may be more specific controls about what services they can request in connection with that access.

Activity 6-1: NTFS Permissions

Time Required: 15 minutes

Objective: Set permissions for a group on a file or folder on an NTFS partition.

Description: Encrypting files or folders stops a person from accessing another person's data completely. In some instances, files may need to be shared, but only one person will have permission to modify or delete them. To meet those needs, setting permissions is a better method of controlling access to files. In this activity, you set permissions for a specific group on a file or folder.

To set permissions on a file or folder:

This activity requires that Windows XP be installed and that an NTFS partition be present. In addition, the computer must be a member of a domain.

6

1. Open Windows Explorer by clicking **Start**, **All Programs**, **Accessories**, **Windows Explorer**.

2. In the left pane, select a drive formatted with NTFS within My Computer.

3. In the right pane, select a file or folder.

4. From the File menu, click **Properties**.

5. Click the **Security** tab.

6. Click **Add**.

7. Click the **Advanced** button.

8. Click the **Find Now** button.

9. Select the **Authenticated Users** group.

10. Click **OK**.

11. Click **OK**.

12. Click the **Authenticated Users** group, which now appears in the list of names on the Security tab for the NTFS object.

13. Click the **Modify** check box in the Allow column.

14. Click the **Everyone** group. Notice how the defined permissions for these two groups differ.

15. Click **OK**.

Windows XP automatically grants the Everyone group Full Control to the object whenever a new object or share is created. Thus, you must implement restrictions on new objects and new shares. In other words, Windows XP allows everyone to access new objects by default.

ACCESS CONTROL

The classic Windows XP logon process is initiated through the attention sequence (the Ctrl+Alt+Delete keystroke combination, known to many DOS users as the "three-finger salute"). This attention sequence initiates a hardware interrupt that cannot be "faked" by a program and brings up a logon procedure dialog box that is stored in a protected area of memory, thus securing the system from attack through an unauthorized logon.

This combination of characteristics for the logon authentication procedure is the key to the entire Windows XP security scheme, because all other security features are based on the level of authority granted a user who has successfully logged on. The Windows XP security structure requires a user to log on to a computer with a valid username and password. Without this step, nothing more can be accomplished in the Windows XP environment.

The Windows XP logon procedure provides security through the use of the following:

- *Mandatory logon*—To access the computer, the user must first log on.

- *Restricted user mode*—Until a successful logon takes place, all user-mode privileges are suspended. Among other things, this means that the user cannot launch applications, access resources, or perform any action or operation on the system.

- *Physical logon*—The structure of the logon sequence ensures that the logon occurs from the local keyboard, rather than from some other internal or external source. This is because the attention sequence initiates a hardware interrupt that accepts input only from the local keyboard.

- *User profiles*—Windows XP allows each user who logs on to a particular machine to save user preferences and environment settings, called a user profile. Each user can have a set of specific preferences restored at logon or can be supplied with a mandatory or default set, depending on how the system is configured. A user profile that is configured to follow a user throughout a network is called a roaming profile. (Profiles are covered in detail in Chapter 5.)

CUSTOMIZING THE LOGON PROCESS

A system administrator can alter the default logon process appearance and function using Winlogon. The **Winlogon** process produces the logon dialog box, where username, password, and domain are selected. Winlogon also controls automated logon, warning text, the display of the Shut Down button, and the display of the last user to log onto the system. Winlogon operates in the user-mode portion of the Windows XP system architecture and communicates with the security reference monitor and SAM (Security Accounts Manager) database in the kernel's Executive Services to authenticate users and start their environment shell with an attached user-specific access token. The Winlogon process can be customized to display some or all of the following characteristics:

- Retain or disable the last logon name entered
- Add a logon security warning

- Change the default shell
- Enable/Disable the Winlogon Shut Down button
- Enable automated logon

 NOTE Most of these characteristics can be altered through the Local Security Policy snap-in. All of these characteristics can be controlled through the Registry through the HKEY_LOCAL_MACHINE\SOFTWARE\Microsoft\Windows NT\ CurrentVersion\Winlogon\ key (see Figure 6-1). However, Microsoft recommends using the Local Security Policy console to alter these items instead of the Registry when possible.

6

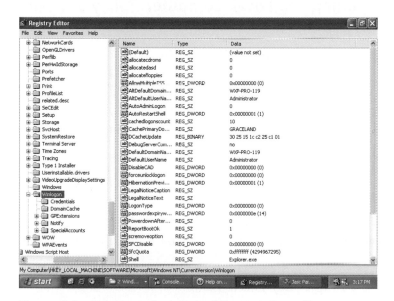

Figure 6-1   Winlogon key viewed through Regedit

Possible configuration changes for the Windows XP logon process are detailed in the following sections.

DISABLING THE DEFAULT USERNAME

By default, the logon window displays the name of the last user to logon. If the same user consistently logs on to a single machine, displaying the logon name is convenient; however, for shared or public-access machines, this provides a key piece of information that someone could use to break into your system. It is possible to change the default by altering the value of its associated Registry key (DontDisplayLastUserName) or Local Security Policy value. Another common form of attack is a dictionary attack, which involves supplying the contents of a dictionary, one word at a time, as a logon password. Avoiding such systematic break-in attempts is why it's a good idea to limit the number of failed logon attempts through the lockout policy.

Disabling this option presents a blank username field at the logon prompt. Note that the related value and its corresponding assignment do not occur in the Registry by default. The value is named DontDisplayLastUserName, and it is of type String, where a value assignment of 1 disables the name display and a value of 0 (zero) enables it. This control appears by default in the Local Computer Policy utility. As noted, it is recommended that you use the local computer policy snap-in to manage this feature rather than edit the Registry.

Activity 6-2: Opening the Local Computer Policy Snap-in

Time Required: 10 minutes

Objective: Add the Local Computer Policy snap-in to the Microsoft Management Console.

Description: The Microsoft Management Console (MMC) is a completely customizable tool for administering your Windows XP computer. Objects may be added to or removed from the MMC depending on what the user wants to manage. In this activity, you add the local computer policy snap-in to the MMC.

To open the Local Computer Policy snap-in:

1. Click **Start**, **Run**, and then type **mmc**.
2. Click **OK**. This opens the Microsoft Management Console.
3. Select **Add/Remove Snap-in** from the File menu.
4. Click the **Add** button.
5. Locate and select **Group Policy** Object Editor.
6. Click **Add**.
7. On the Select Group Policy Object dialog box, notice that Local Computer is listed by default. Click **Finish**.
8. Click **Close** on the Add Standalone Snap-in dialog box.
9. Click **OK** on the Add/Remove Snap-in dialog box.
10. The Local Computer Policy node should now appear in the MMC.

Activity 6-3: Suppressing the Last Username

Time Required: 10 minutes

Objective: Use the Local Computer Policy utility to suppress the display of the last username in the logon screen.

Description: There are usually two pieces of information required to log onto a domain or computer: the username and its associated password. By default, Microsoft operating systems keep the password box blank, but does display the name of the last user to log on at that computer. To increase security, the administrator can set up workstations (and servers) so that the username box is also blank. In this activity, the local computer policy is configured to disable the display of the last username.

To disable the display of the last username on the logon screen:

NOTE

This activity requires that you first complete Activity 6-2.

6

1. In the Local Computer Policy console, click the **plus sign** beside Local Computer Policy to expand its contents.
2. Locate the **Computer Configuration** node. Click its **plus sign** to expand its contents.
3. Locate the **Windows Settings** node. Click its **plus sign** to expand its contents.
4. Locate the **Security Settings** node. Click its **plus sign** to expand its contents.
5. Locate the **Local Policies** node. Click its **plus sign** to expand its contents.
6. Locate and click the **Security Options** node.
7. In the Details pane, locate and click **Interactive logon: Do not display last user name**.
8. Select the **Action** menu, then click **Properties**. The Local Security Policy Setting dialog box for the selected control is displayed.
9. Click the **Enabled** option button.
10. Click **OK**.
11. Log off and log back on. Notice that the last logged on username no longer appears.

Adding a Security Warning Message

Depending on your organization's security policy, you might be legally obligated to add a warning message that appears before the logon prompt appears. Federal law states that if you want to be able to prosecute individuals for unauthorized entry to or use of a system, you must warn all users that usage is monitored, unauthorized access is forbidden, and that unauthorized users might be liable for prosecution.

Two Registry or local security policy values are involved in this effort:

- *LegalNoticeCaption*—Puts a label on the title bar of the legal notice window that appears during logon. This field works best with 30 or fewer characters of text.

- *LegalNoticeText*—Contains text information that provides the details of the warning to be issued to system users. This field may be up to 65,535 characters long, but most warning messages do not exceed 1000 characters in length.

After this feature has been activated and configured, a warning message appears each time a user enters the Windows XP attention sequence. This message requires the user's acknowledgment by clicking OK before the logon window appears.

Activity 6-4: Legal Warning Messages

Time Required: 15 minutes

Objective: Using the Local Computer Policy utility, add a legal warning message to the computer.

Description: No matter what type of security is in place, people will always find a way around it. To provide a legal means of acting against someone that purposely tries to gain unauthorized access to a computer, a legal message can be added that appears before the person logs on. In this activity, you create a legal warning message that states that only authorized users may log onto the computer.

To display a legal warning message at logon:

This activity requires that you first complete Activity 6-2 and assumes the classic logon.

1. In the Local Computer Policy console, locate and select the following subnode: **Computer Configuration**, **Windows Settings**, **Security Settings**, **Local Policies**, **Security Options**.

2. Locate and click **Interactive logon: Message title for users attempting to log on**.

3. Select the **Action** menu, then click **Properties**.

4. Type **Warning!** in the field. Click **OK**.

5. Select **Interactive logon: Message text for users attempting to log on**.

6. Select the **Action** menu, then click **Properties**.

7. In the field, type a warning message similar to the following: **Authorized Users Only! The information on this computer and network is the property of [*organization name here*]. You must have legitimate access to an assigned account on this computer to access any information. Your activities may be monitored. Any unauthorized access will be punished to the full extent of the law.**

8. Click **OK**. Close the console. If prompted to save the console, click **No**.

9. Log off, then log back on to see the appearance of the warning message between pressing Ctrl+Alt+Delete and the appearance of the Winlogon dialog box.

Changing the Shell

The default shell (the application called by Winlogon after a successful logon) is Windows Explorer. You can change the shell to a custom or third-party application depending on the needs or security policy of your organization.

Activity 6-5: Choose a Different Shell

6

Time Required: 20 minutes

Objective: Change the default shell of Windows XP using the Registry Editor.

Description: The Explorer.exe screen is what you see when you log onto a Windows XP computer. Although this can be changed to almost any executable, it may not be very practical to do so. By editing the Registry in this activity, the user changes the default shell to the default shell that was used for Windows NT 3.51.

To change the default shell:

Changing the shell results in a new user interface. The Program Manager does not offer a Start menu, taskbar, Task Manager, and many other interface controls to which you are accustomed with Windows XP. Perform this activity with caution.

1. Click **Start**, **Run**, and then type **regedit**.

2. Click **OK**.

3. Locate and select the key: **HKEY_LOCAL_MACHINE**\SOFTWARE\Microsoft\ Windows NT**CurrentVersion\Winlogon**.

4. Locate and select the **Shell** value.

5. Select **Modify** from the Edit menu.

6. Change the value data from explorer.exe to **progman.exe**.

7. Click **OK**.

8. Click **Exit** on the File menu.

9. The system is now configured to use the Windows NT 3.51 Program Manager as the shell. To return the shell to Windows Explorer, either reopen the Registry editor now and change the Shell value back to its original setting (EXPLORER.EXE), or, if you have already logged in with Program Manager as the shell, use the Run command from the File menu of the Program Manager to open Regedit and make the change.

If you change from the Windows Explorer shell to the Program Manager shell, your system loses its on-screen taskbar and you can no longer use the Start menu to run programs from your desktop. This is why most organizations use the default shell.

Disabling the Shut Down Button

By default, the Windows XP logon window includes a Shut Down button. However, in an environment in which users have access to the keyboard and mouse on a Windows XP machine, this option has the potential for unwanted system shutdowns, regardless of whether the system is a Windows XP Professional or server machine. Fortunately, this option can be disabled. It should be noted, however, that if the user still has access to the physical power switch on the computer, disabling this option might cause more headaches than it solves. A system that has been shut down or restarted through the operating system has a much higher chance of coming back up successfully than one that was just powered off. Note that by default, this button is enabled for Windows XP Professional machines, but disabled for Windows server machines.

The value named Shut Down WithoutLogon is the one you need to edit in either the Registry or the Local Security Policy console. It's enabled (set to the value 1) by default. To disable this button, change its value assignment to 0 (zero); to reenable it, reset its value to 1. When the button is disabled, it still appears in the Winlogon window, but it's dimmed and unusable.

For laptops or other advanced computers with automatic-shutdown capabilities, an additional button labeled Shut Down and Power Off appears. Similar machines might also support a sleep mode, in which all processing is suspended and all power turned off, except for the computer's RAM. In that case, Sleep also shows up as a shutdown option. This particular setting permits users to eliminate most of a computer's power consumption, yet activity can be resumed at the push of a single button or movement of the mouse. If the machine warrants such settings, users can find related Registry values in their Winlogon key settings that help them control how these functions are handled.

Be aware that leaving the Shut Down button enabled means that anyone with access to the keyboard can enter the Windows attention sequence and shut down the local machine.

Automating Logons

Some special- or limited-use Windows XP machines (for example, airport kiosks or hotel information stations) may need to always be available and always logged into a low-security account for access to some dedicated application. Although the logon process cannot be bypassed, the values for username and password can be coded into the Registry to automate logons. This normally is of interest only when installing machines for public use, such as for information centers, kiosks, museum guides, or other situations in which a computer is used to provide information to the public. In such cases, it's important to have computer and user policies to prevent Windows XP-savvy users from attempting to break out of the public application and exploring other, less public aspects of the system (or worse, of the network to which it may be attached).

To set up an automated logon, the following Registry value entries must be defined and set within the HKEY_LOCAL_MACHINE\SOFTWARE\Microsoft\Windows NT\ CurrentVersion\Winlogon key:

- *DefaultDomainName*—Defines the name of the domain to log onto (needed only when logging onto a networked machine that's part of a domain)

- *DefaultUserName*—Defines the default logon account name

- *DefaultPassword*—Defines the password associated with the default account name. This value is not present by default. When the automatic logon feature is disabled, delete this value, because it stores the password in plaintext.

- *AutoAdminLogon*—Instructs the machine to log itself on immediately after the system starts up. A value of 1 automatically logs on using the credentials from the other three values in this list. A value of 0 (zero) disables the automatic logon feature.

CAUTION

Automated logons create a situation in which the computer automatically makes itself available to users without requiring an account name or a password. It is essential, therefore, that this capability be exercised *only* when security is not a concern (if a machine hosts only a single application and is not connected to the network) or if access to the equipment is otherwise controlled.

Automatic Account Lockout

Automatic account lockout disables a user account if a predetermined number of failed logon attempts occur within a specified time limit. This feature is intended to prevent intrusion by unauthorized users attempting to gain access by guessing a password or launching a dictionary attack. The default setting in Windows XP is to allow an unlimited number of failed access attempts to a user account without locking out that account. However, this is not recommended when there is even a remote chance unauthorized people can gain physical access to logon consoles. The Windows XP account lockout feature was discussed in Chapter 5.

DOMAIN SECURITY CONCEPTS AND SYSTEMS

A **domain** is a collection of computers with centrally managed security and activities. A domain offers increased security, centralized control, and broader access to resources than any other computer system configuration. Security policies are domain-wide controls that specify password requirements, account lockout settings, auditing, user rights, security options, and more.

Domain Security Overview

Domain security is the control of user accounts, group memberships, and resource access for all members of a network instead of only a single computer. All the information about user accounts, group memberships, group policies, and access controls for resources are contained in the Active Directory, a database maintained by one or more domain controllers. A **domain controller** is a Windows 2000 Server or Windows Server 2003 system with the Active Directory support services installed and configured.

Kerberos and Authentication Services

Authentication takes place in a Windows domain network under two conditions: interactive logon and network authentication. Interactive logon occurs when you press the attention sequence, then enter your username and password. If you log onto a local system, such as a standalone Windows XP Professional system, all authentication is performed by the local security subsystem. If you are logging onto a domain, the local security subsystem communicates with a domain controller using **Kerberos version 5**—an authentication encryption protocol—to protect your logon credentials.

A **network authentication** occurs when you attempt to connect to or access resources from some other member of the domain network. Network authentication is used to prove that you are a valid member of the domain, your user account is properly authenticated, and that you have access permissions to perform the requested action. The communications that occur during network authentication are protected by one of several methods, including:

- Kerberos version 5

- Secure Socket Layer/Transport Layer Security (SSL/TLS)

- NTLM (NT LAN Manager) authentication for compatibility with Windows NT 4.0

NOTE The authentication protection method is determined by either the communication mechanism (such as IIS or standard network connection) or the settings in the local security policy. Only one of these options is used, but both can be "active" at one time. This ensures that the server can actively respond as the client requests or uses one or the other. The server responds with the same authentication scheme requested by the client.

Kerberos Version 5 Authentication

Windows XP uses Kerberos version 5 as the primary protocol for authentication security. The system uses this protocol to verify the identity of both the client (user) and server (network service or application) upon each resource access. This is known as mutual authentication. It protects the server from unauthorized clients and prevents the user from accessing the wrong or spoofed servers. (A spoofed server is one that is programmed to appear to be a particular server when it is another; this is most common on the Internet when an attacker is trying to gain access to credit card information.)

The Kerberos version 5 authentication system was designed to allow two parties to exchange private information across an open network, such as the Internet. Kerberos version 5 assigns a unique key, called a ticket, to each user that logs on to the network. This unique ticket is then embedded in messages to identify the sender of the message to the message's recipient. The Kerberos process is completely invisible to the user.

Secure Socket Layer/Transport Layer Security

Secure Socket Layer/Transport Layer Security (SSL/TLS) is an authentication scheme often used by Web-based applications and is supported on Windows XP through IIS (Internet Information Server). SSL functions by issuing an identity **certificate** to both the client and server. A third-party Certificate Authority that both the client and server have chosen to trust, such as VeriSign (*www.verisign.com*), issues these certificates. When a resource request is made, the client sends its certificate to the server. The server verifies the validity of the client certificate, and then sends its own certificate to the client, along with an encryption key. The client verifies the validity of the server certificate, and then uses the encryption key to initiate a communication session with the server. This encrypted communication link is used for all future communications during this session. Once the session is terminated, the link must be rebuilt by starting over with the client sending its certificate to the server.

NTLM

NTLM (NT LAN Manager) authentication is the mechanism used by Windows NT 4.0. Windows XP supports this authentication method solely for backward compatibility with Windows NT Servers and Windows NT Workstation clients. NTLM functions by using a static encryption level (40-bit or 128-bit) to encrypt traffic between a client and server. NTLM is significantly less secure than Kerberos version 5.

LOCAL COMPUTER POLICY

Another security control built into Windows XP is the **local computer policy**. This policy is a combination of controls that in Windows NT existed only in the Registry, through system policies, or as Control Panel applet controls. Sometimes the local computer policy is called a software policy or an environmental policy, or even a Windows XP policy.

No matter what name is actually used, the local computer policy is simply the local system's group policy (see Chapter 5). The effective policy is the result of the combination of all group policies applicable to the system.

In a Windows XP domain network environment, the local computer policy is controlled on a domain basis on a Windows domain controller. This control is based on site, domain, and organizational unit group policies. On a Windows XP Professional system, you can manually launch the MMC and add in the Global Policy snap-in to manage or change the local computer policy. You cannot manage domain policies from a Windows XP Professional machine.

There is also a Local Group Policy tool (called the Local Security Policy tool) accessed from Administrative Tools in Control Panel. However, this tool is limited to only the Computer Configuration, Windows Settings, and Security Settings subsection of the full GPO. The remainder of this chapter takes the perspective of working from the MMC snap-in instead of the Administrative Tools utility.

The contents of the local computer policy are determined during installation, based on system configuration, existing devices, and selected options and components. Custom policies can be created through the use of .adm files (administrative templates), such as those used by the Windows NT 4.0 System Policy Editor. Such files from Windows NT 4.0 can be used with Windows XP with some caveats. When you open and edit the local group policy, you are working with the System.adm file. The .adm files used by the Group Policy editor reside in the \inf subfolder of the main Windows XP directory. Third-party software vendors can use custom .adm files to add additional environmental controls based on their software or services. To learn about creating custom .adm files, see the *Microsoft Windows XP Professional Resource Kit* and the *Microsoft Windows Server 2003 Resource Kit*.

The Local Computer Policy snap-in is divided into two sections (see Figure 6-2): Computer Configuration and User Configuration. The Computer Configuration section contains controls that focus on the computer, such as hardware and software settings. The User Configuration section contains controls that focus on the user and the user environment, such as permissions and desktop settings.

Because the Local Computer Policy console contains over 300 individual controls, you should take the time to peruse the entire collection level by level.

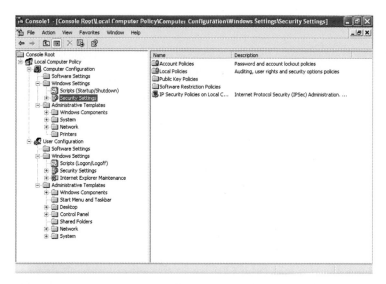

Figure 6-2   Computer Configuration and User Configuration

Computer Configuration

The Computer Configuration section of the Local Computer Policy console contains three subnodes or folders, as follows:

- Software Settings is empty by default; most third-party add-in application settings appear in this node.

- The Windows Settings folder contains two items: Scripts and Security Settings. The Scripts item allows you to define one or more scripts to be automatically executed at system startup or shutdown. The Security Settings node contains settings for Account Policies, Local Policies (Audit, User Rights, and Security Options), Public Key Policies, Software Restriction Policies, and IP Security Policies. Account policies and local policies were discussed in Chapter 5; public key policies and IP Security policies are discussed in the upcoming sections.

- The Administrative Templates folder contains a multilevel collection of computer-related controls. This is covered in detail later in this chapter.

Public Key Policies

There are three purposes for using the **public key policies** control features: to offer additional controls over the Encrypting File System (EFS), to enable the issuing of certificates, and to allow you to establish trust in a certificate authority. Some discussion of certificates and trusting certificate authorities is included in Chapter 8, "Internetworking with Remote Access." Consult the *Microsoft Windows XP Professional Resource Kit* or the *Microsoft Windows Server 2003 Resource Kit* for complete details on public key policies.

Activity 6-6: Encrypting Files and Folders

Time Required: 20 minutes

Objective: Encrypt an NTFS folder to secure its contents.

Description: In this activity, you see how encrypting a folder on the workstation protects the contents from across the network, and also from anyone that may logon locally.

To encrypt a folder with EFS:

The folder must be on an NTFS file system to complete this exercise, and you will need access to at least two different user accounts to complete this exercise. This exercise uses classic logon.

1. Click **Start**, **All Programs**, **Accessories**, **Windows Explorer**.
2. Expand My Computer and select the **C** drive in the left column. (If drive C is not formatted with NTFS, select some other drive that is formatted with NTFS.)
3. Select **File**, **New**, and then click **Folder** on the submenu.
4. Type a name for the folder (such as **EFStemp**), and then press **Enter**.
5. Right-click the new folder, and then click **Properties** on the menu.
6. On the General tab, click the **Advanced** button.
7. Click to place a check mark in the **Encrypt contents to secure data** check box.
8. Click **OK**.
9. Click **OK**.
10. Log off.
11. Logon to the system with a different user account by pressing **Ctrl+Alt+Delete**, and then providing a different username and password.
12. Click **Start**, **All Programs**, **Accessories**, **Windows Explorer**.
13. Locate and try to access the **EFStemp** folder. Notice that you cannot gain access.
14. Log off.
15. Logon with the user account you used to encrypt the folder. Press **Ctrl+Alt+Delete**, and then provide the first username and password you used in this activity.
16. Locate and try to access the **EFStemp** folder. Notice that you cannot gain access.
17. Right-click the **EFStemp** folder, and then click **Properties** on the menu.
18. On the General tab, click the **Advanced** button.
19. Deselect (uncheck) the **Encrypt contents to secure data** check box.

20. Click **OK**.

21. Click **OK**.

IP Security Policies

IP Security (IPSec) is a security measure added to TCP/IP to protect communications between two systems using that protocol. IPSec negotiates a secure encrypted communications link between a client and server through public and private encryption key management. IPSec can be used over a RAS or WAN link (through L2TP) or within a LAN. In either case, IPSec creates a secured point-to-point link between two systems. IPSec offers protection against a wide range of security problems, including: eavesdropping, data modification, identity spoofing, password attacks, denial-of-service attacks, man-in-the-middle attacks, compromised security key attacks, sniffer attacks, and Application-layer attacks.

IPSec is configured and enabled on each system through the Option tab of the Advanced TCP/IP Settings dialog box. IPSec is enabled by default, but it is not configured. To configure IPSec, you must select one of the IPSec policies defined for your system or network. These policies are defined through the Group Policy node.

IPSec can be used in one of two modes: transport or tunneling. In transport mode, an IPSec link can be established between any two systems on the network. In tunneling mode, an IPSec link can be established only between two specific systems. In other words, transport mode allows connections between any two systems on a network that are configured to use IPSec, whereas tunneling mode can be used only between two distinct partners. IPSec tunneling mode is often used to establish secure pathways between systems that often communicate critical or sensitive data, such as routers, gateways, or domain controllers.

The IP Security policies govern how a system communicates through TCP/IP, based on your defined security needs. Windows XP includes three predefined IPSec policies; however, you can create and manage your own custom IPSec policies. None of the predefined IPSec polices are enabled or assigned by default. For information on creating custom IPSec policies, consult the *Microsoft Windows XP Professional Resource Kit* or the *Microsoft Windows Server 2003 Resource Kit*.

The three predefined IPSec policies are as follows:

- The Client (Respond Only) policy is for systems that do not require secure communications at all times. This policy initiates a secure communications link only when another system requests it. This policy does not initiate secure communications by default.

- The Server (Request Security) policy is for systems that need to use secure communications most of the time. This policy always requests that communications be secured, but allows unsecured communications to occur if IPSec is not available on the other system.

- The Secure Server (Require Security) policy is for systems that require secure communications at all times. This policy allows communications only if the remote system offers IPSec. Each of these policies can be modified through their Properties dialog box. However, Microsoft recommends creating new policies instead of modifying the default policies.

For an IPSec link to be established—whether as a VPN L2TP link over the Internet or simply a secured connection between two systems on the same LAN—a common authentication method must be defined and available on both systems acting as the end points of the secure pipeline. Multiple authentication methods can be defined on a single system, but without a common method or rule, communication does not take place.

IPSec supports three types of authentication methods:

- Kerberos version 5 is the default and preferred method of authentication and can be used by any client within the domain to establish a secured IPSec link.

- Public key certificate authentication can be used when systems not running Kerberos must be linked or when the systems are not members of the same domain. Public key certificate authentication is often used when linking across the Internet and over remote access links. Windows XP and Windows 2000 both support X.509 version 3 certificates. This type of authentication requires at least one commonly trusted certificate authority (CA) between the two connecting systems. Without a commonly trusted CA, the link is not established.

- The use of a preshared key is supported by Windows XP IPSec, but it is seen as the least secure authentication option. It simply requires that each system use a common predetermined key (a key is a string of characters, like a password). This preshared key is used to protect the initial authentication of a IPSec link. Preshared key authentication can be used by nearly any computer system that supports IPSec, thus not limiting connections to systems supporting Kerberos version 5, Windows 2000/XP, or supporting a common public key certificate type or CA.

Administrative Templates

Administrative templates offer controls on a wide range of environmental functions and features. The administrative templates are Registry-based group policy information. In other words, administrative templates are used to overwrite the Registry of a client or server system to force compliance with the group policy. The Administrative Templates folder in the Computer Configuration node of the Local Computer Policy snap-in contains folders and subfolders with specific control items focused on a single aspect of the computer or environmental function. The controls available through the Administrative Templates folder include the following:

- Controlling security and software updates for Internet Explorer
- Controlling access and use of the Task Scheduler and Windows Installer
- Controlling logon security features and operations

- Controlling disk quotas
- Managing how group policies are processed
- Managing system file protection
- Managing offline access of network resources
- Controlling printer use and function

User Configuration

The User Configuration portion of the Local Computer Policy console is structured in much the same way as the Computer Configuration portion. The User Configuration folder is also divided into three subfolders, as follows:

- Software Settings is empty by default. Any user-specific Microsoft or third-party software settings appear in this folder.

- The Windows Settings folder contains three items: Internet Explorer Maintenance, Scripts (Logon/Logoff), and Security Settings. The Internet Explorer section is used to control user-specific activities of IE, such as browser interface appearance, connection methods, links, and security zones. The Scripts item allows you to define one or more scripts to automatically execute at user logon or logoff. Security Settings is initially empty, but can become a container for user-specific (rather than computer-specific) security controls.

- The Administrative Templates folder contains a multilevel collection of user-specific, functional, and environmental Registry-based controls. These controls are for the local computer only; if the computer is a member of a domain, some of these controls may be overwritten by a group, a computer, or by an organizational unit policy from the domain.

The items contained in the User Configuration's Administrative Templates section include the following:

- Internet Explorer configuration, interface, features, and functions controls
- Windows Explorer management (interface, available commands, and features)
- MMC management
- Task Scheduler and Windows Installer controls
- Start menu and taskbar features management
- Desktop environment management
- Control Panel applet management
- Offline network access control
- Network connection management

6

■ Logon and logoff script management

■ Group policy application

For more information on any control in the Local Computer Policy snap-in, open the control's Properties dialog box (right-click and select Properties) and view the Explain tab (see Figure 6-3).

TIP

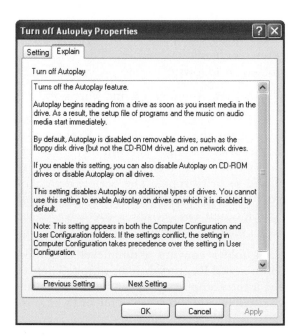

Figure 6-3   Turn off Autoplay Properties dialog box of the Local Computer Policy

Activity 6-7: Exploring Local Computer Policy

ACTIVITY

Time Required: 20 minutes

Objective: Expand each node of the Local Computer Policy snap-in to become familiar with the options available.

Description: There are many nodes and options available in the Local Computer Policy console. It is important to become familiar with these options as they may save time and effort later on. As seen earlier, it was a simple task to insert a legal warning message. However, if you had to do it manually by editing the Registry, the task would be much harder and take longer. This activity is for becoming familiar with what options are available in the Local Computer Policy console.

To explore the Local Computer Policy console:

1. Open the Local Computer Policy snap-in.

2. Expand the **Computer Configuration** node of the Local Computer Policy console.

3. Expand the **Administrative Templates** node.

4. Expand each of the **Windows Components**, **System**, **Network**, and **Printers** subnodes.

5. Select each subnode one by one. Review the control details contained in each.

6. To open the Properties of a control detail, select it, select the **Action** menu, and then click **Properties**.

7. View the Setting and Explain tabs of all control details that interest you. Close **Properties**.

8. Expand the **User Configuration** node and all of its subnodes.

9. Perform the same expansion and exploration as you did under the Computer Configuration node.

10. Select the **Exit** command from the File menu of the MMC to close the utility. Click **No** to discard any changes, if prompted.

The Setting tab on the Properties dialog box for each control offers three settings:

- *Not Configured*—The default for all controls; does not change the existing setting of this control

- *Enabled*—Enables the function or restriction of this control

- *Disabled*—Disables the function or restriction of this control

By carefully reading the materials on the Explain tab, you can learn which of the three settings for each control makes the most sense for the action you want to enforce or allow. In some cases, selecting the Enable control reveals additional controls, such as selection lists, numerical entry fields, or text-entry fields that provide the additional settings required by some controls. For example, the timeout settings require that you enable the control as well as define a time period in minutes or seconds for that timeout period.

Security Configuration and Analysis Tool

The Security Configuration and Analysis tool is an MMC snap-in that can be used to analyze, configure, export, and validate system security based on a security template. A security template is a predefined group policy file with specific levels of security. Security templates can include configuration settings for group policy objects, security policies, system configuration, and even object-level ACLs. There are seven predefined security templates included with Windows XP Professional:

- *compatws*—Configures security of a client to be compatible with most non-certified applications

- *hisecdc*—Configures the security of a domain controller to be at the highest level possible
- *hisecws*—Configures the security of a client to be at the highest level possible
- *rootsec*—Applies default root permissions to the boot partition (the one where the OS primarily resides) and to all child objects within the root
- *securedc*—Configures the security of a domain controller to be at a moderate level
- *securews*—Configures the security of a client to be at a moderate level
- *setup security*—Configures the security of a system to the original default state after a typical installation

The act of analyzing security checks a system's current configuration against a selected security template (or a composite of multiple templates) and produces a report of the discrepancies. The act of configuring a system is the process of applying one or more security templates directly to a system. The configuration defined in the templates is forced onto the target systems. The act of exporting simply creates a security template file based on the configuration of a system. In essence, it produces your own customized templates for application onto other systems or for future analysis of a system's state. The act of validating verifies the syntax and content of a security template. It ensures that the template is internally consistent and without errors.

To learn how to use this tool and to perform the various activities supported by the Security Configuration and Analysis snap-in, visit *www.microsoft.com/technet/treeview/default.asp?url=/technet/prodtechnol/winxppro/proddocs/sag_SCMhowToTN.asp*.

Secedit

While the Security Configuration and Analysis snap-in is useful, most administrators opt to employ secedit instead. Secedit (Security Editor) is the command-line version of the Security Configuration and Analysis tool. It is used to analyze, configure, export, and validate security based on a security template. The same security templates used by the Security Configuration and Analysis MMC snap-in tool can be used with secedit. Secedit is often favored by administrators because it can be run from a command prompt and can be scripted. The four functions of secedit each have their own specific parameters and syntax. The four functions of secedit perform the exact same operations as the Security Configuration and Analysis MMC snap-in.

The syntax and parameters of secedit are as follows:

```
Secedit /analyze /db FileName [/cfg FileName] [/log
FileName] [/quiet]
Secedit /configure /db FileName [/cfg FileName]
[/overwrite]
        [/areas area1 area2] [/log FileName] [/quiet]
Secedit /export [/mergedpolicy] [/db FileName]
[/cfg FileName]
        [/areas area1 area2] [/log FileName] [/quiet]
Secedit /validate FileName
```

- *analyze*—Used to compare the current configuration of a system against a pre-defined security template

- *db FileName*—Defines the path and filename of the security database. If no database file currently exists, the */cfg* parameter must be used in conjunction with */db*.

- *cfg FileName*—Defines the path and filename of the security template that will be imported into the database. This parameter can only be used with */db*. If */cfg* is not used, the action is performed against the security template already loaded into the database.

- *log FileName*—Defines the path and filename of a log file; if unspecified, a default log file is used.

- *quiet*—Suppresses all screen and log output

- *configure*—Used to forcibly apply a security template to a system

- *overwrite*—Indicates whether the imported security template should overwrite any template already stored in the database. If not specified, the imported security template overwrites any existing template in the database. This parameter can only be used with */cfg*.

- *areas area1 area2*—Defines the areas of the security template to be used in the action against the database. Valid area names are: SECURITYPOLICY, GROUP_MGMT, USER_RIGHTS, REGKEYS, FILESTORE, and SERVICES. Multiple area names must be separated by a space. If no areas are specified, all areas are used.

- *export*—Used to create a security template from the current configuration of a system

- *mergedpolicy*—Causes the export function to merge and export local and domain policy settings

- *validate*—Used to verify the syntax of a security template before it is used

- *FileName*—Defines the path and filename of the security template to validate

AUDITING

Auditing is the security process that records the occurrence of specific operating system **events** in a Security log. Every object in the Windows XP system has audit events related to it. These events can be recorded on a success or failure basis, and in some cases based on users or groups. For example, logging all failed logon attempts may warn you when an attack that might breach your security is occurring, or monitoring classified documents for read access can let you know who is accessing them and when. Auditing can provide valuable information about security breaches, resource activity, and user adeptness. Auditing is also useful for investigating performance and planning for expansion.

Auditing is enabled through the local security policy or through a domain policy (see Chapter 5). Once enabled, the audited events are recorded in the Security log in Event

Viewer. **Event Viewer** is accessed through the Administrative Tools applet (accessed from the Start menu or Control Panel) and maintains logs about application, security, and system events on your computer, enabling you to view and manage the event logs, gather information about hardware and software problems, and monitor Windows XP security events. To view the items related to auditing, select the Security Log node (see Figure 6-4).

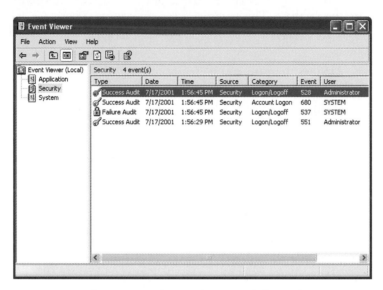

Figure 6-4 The Security log node viewed through Event Viewer

Double-clicking an event opens the Event Properties dialog box (see Figure 6-5).

This particular audit event records the data about a successful logon of the Administrator account on the workstation named WXPPRO-102. Audit entries in the Security log contain information about the event, including user logon identification, the computer used, time, date, and the action or event that instigated an audit.

If you select to audit object access on either a success or failure basis, you can define the actions or activities to audit for objects on an object-by-object basis for each possible action based on that object's type for specific users and groups. For example, you might audit access to certain network resources, such as files or printers by different users and/or groups. To set an object's auditing controls, work through Activity 6-8.

Auditing can be configured only for users and resources that belong to a domain, not a workgroup.

NOTE

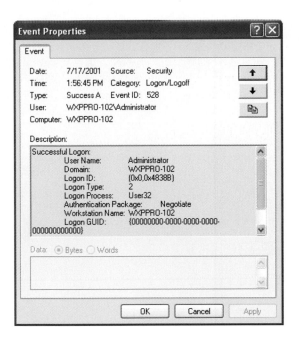

Figure 6-5   Event Properties dialog box

Each of the three logs viewable through Event Viewer can have different log size configuration settings. Opening the Properties for each log file reveals a log-specific Properties dialog box (see Figure 6-6). By default, each log file is assigned a maximum size limit of 512 KB. Once the log file reaches that size, one of three possible actions is taken. The default action is to overwrite any events that are older than seven days. The other two options are to overwrite events as needed, or to not overwrite events. If you elect not to overwrite events, you must manually clear the log (by pressing the Clear Log button) when it reaches capacity. This dialog box also can be used to change the displayed log name and to alter the storage location of the log file itself. The dialog box also displays status information about the log file, such as current size, creation date, last modified date, and last accessed or viewed date.

There is a Registry setting or group policy object setting named CrashOnAuditFail. If this value is set to 1, then when the Security log reaches capacity, only the Administrator is allowed to logon to the system, and the only allowed activities are to clear the Security log file or alter the log file size settings. This security precaution prevents malicious activities from occurring while the Security log is unable to record new events.

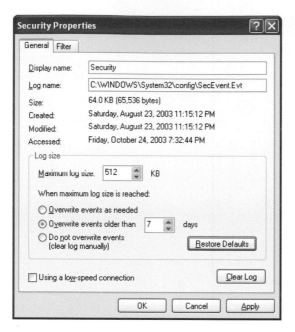

Figure 6-6   The Security Properties dialog box

Activity 6-8: Configuring Auditing

Time Required: 20 minutes

Objective: Configure auditing for success or failure of actions with different objects.

Description: Auditing activity on objects in a network is a good way to see if there is inappropriate activity taking place and who might not be following company policy. Of course, auditing too many items can degrade performance, and if you gather too much information, it is difficult to extract relevant information. In this activity, you set up auditing on a number of objects for either a successful or failed activity.

To set up auditing:

1. Open the **Properties** dialog box for an NTFS object (such as a file, folder, or printer). Right-click the object, then click **Properties** on the shortcut menu.

2. Click the **Security** tab.

3. Click the **Advanced** button.

4. Click the **Auditing** tab. This displays all of the currently defined audit events for this object. It is blank by default.

5. Click the **Add** button.

6. Click the **Advanced** button.

7. Click the **Find Now** button.

8. Select a computer, group, or a user from the Select User, Computer, or Group dialog box.

9. Click **OK**.

10. Click **OK**.

11. Select either **Successful** or **Failed** for any of the listed actions for this object type. The selections made here are the actions that are recorded in the Security log.

If you selected to record only Failures in the Local Security Policy console, selecting Successful actions on this dialog box does not record items in the Security log.

TIP

12. Click **OK**.

13. Repeat Steps 5 through 12 for all users, computers, or groups.

14. Repeat Steps 1 through 13 for all objects.

Auditing numerous objects or events can result in a large Security log and can slow down network or computer performance.

CAUTION

Event Viewer can be configured to monitor the size of the Security log and to take action when it reaches a target size. The actions are Overwrite events as needed, Overwrite events older than *XX* days, or Do not overwrite events. If the maximum size is reached and Do not overwrite events is selected, an alert appears stating that the log must be cleared. To access these controls, select Properties on the menu that appears when right-clicking the Security log node in Event Viewer.

Activity 6-9: Auditing File Access

ACTIVITY

Time Required: 20 minutes

Objective: Use auditing to track activity on a Windows XP computer.

Description: Auditing can be used for several purposes. One purpose may be to see if all members of a workgroup have opened a file that is to be read by all group members. A more common use is to track access to objects to ensure that only authorized users have access. In this activity, you set auditing on a file and verify that access gets logged.

To enable file access auditing:

1. Click **Start, Control Panel**, and click **Switch to Classic View** if you are in Category View.

2. Double-click **Administrative Tools**.

3. Double-click **Local Security Policy**.

4. Expand the **Local Policies** node by double-clicking it.

5. Click the **Audit Policy** node.

6. Double-click the **Audit object access** item.

7. Click the **Success** check box. Click **OK**.

8. Click **Start**, **All Programs**, **Accessories**, **Windows Explorer**.

9. Locate and select any text document on your computer, such as
   %systemroot%\Windows\setuplog.txt.

10. Select **File**, and then click **Properties**.

11. Click the **Security** tab.

12. Click the **Advanced** button.

13. Click the **Auditing** tab.

14. Click **Add**.

15. Click the **Advanced** button.

16. Click the **Find Now** button.

17. Click **Authenticated Users**.

18. Click **OK**.

19. Click **OK**.

20. Click the **List Folder/Read Data** check box under **Successful**.

21. Click **OK**.

22. Click **OK**.

23. Click **OK**.

24. Double-click the text file to open it.

25. Close Notepad by selecting **File**, and then clicking **Exit**.

26. Return to **Administrative Tools** by clicking its button on the taskbar.

27. Double-click **Event Viewer**.

28. Select the **Security** log.

29. Double-click one of the event details.

30. Using the arrow buttons, scroll through the most recent event details to locate an event dealing with the successful reading of the text file.

31. Click **OK** to close the Event detail.

32. Close Event Viewer.

33. Close Administrative Tools by selecting **File**, **Close**.

34. Close Windows Explorer by selecting **File**, **Close**.

35. In the Local Security Settings dialog box, double-click **Audit object access**.

36. Deselect **Success**.

37. Click **OK**.

38. Close the Local Security Settings dialog box.

6

ENCRYPTING FILE SYSTEM

Microsoft has extended the native NTFS file system to include encrypted storage. This new security measure, the **Encrypting File System (EFS)**, allows you to encrypt data stored on an NTFS drive. When EFS is enabled on a file, folder, or drive, only the enabling user can gain access to the encrypted object. EFS is enabled through a check box accessed through the Advanced button on the General tab of an object's Properties dialog box.

EFS uses a public and private key encryption method. The private key is assigned to a single user account. No other user, computer, or operating system can gain access to the encrypted files. For the authorized user (i.e., the user with the correct private key), access to the encrypted files is unhindered. In fact, the entire encryption process is invisible to the user.

Encryption is just another attribute of NTFS; therefore, you should treat encryption in the same manner as attributes and permissions. Any new file created or copied into an encrypted folder assumes the settings of that folder. Moving an encrypted file to a nonencrypted folder allows the file to retain its original settings, but copying the encrypted file causes the file to assume the settings of the destination folder. Because EFS is an additional level of processing required by the operating system to grant access to file-level objects, the performance of the file system can be noticeably impaired when using it. You need to perform your own baseline comparison of your storage system's performance to determine exactly how much degradation is caused by EFS.

If the encryption key is lost or the user account is deleted, there is a mechanism to recover encrypted files. This mechanism is called the Recovery Agent, which is defined through the Group Policy utility found in the Public Key Policies folder. EFS does not function without a Recovery Agent. In fact, Windows XP automatically designates the local Administrator as the Recovery Agent until you specifically define another Recovery Agent. When Windows XP becomes a member of the domain, the Domain Administrators group becomes the default Recovery Agent. To remove the ability to use EFS on a system, simply remove or delete the defined data Recovery Agent from group policy. The Recovery Agent is able to decrypt files by logging onto the system where the files are stored and deselecting the Encrypt check box on the files and folder's Advanced Properties dialog box.

When a user's encryption key is lost, deleted, or corrupted, a Recovery Agent must employ the data recovery agent key to decrypt any files encrypted with the lost key. This is accomplished by logging into the system as the user account, which is designated as the EFS Recovery Agent. Then go to the files and folders that are encrypted and simply clear the encrypt attribute check box. In other words, this process is the same as a typical user decrypting a file; the only difference being the user is the EFS Recovery Agent account. Once the files are recovered, a new key must be assigned to the user for future EFS encryption and decryption activities. For more details on the Recovery Agent, consult the Microsoft Windows XP Professional Resource Kit.

Windows XP includes a command-line tool for batch processing of encryption (i.e., encrypting or decrypting large numbers of files or folders through a command line or batch file). The CIPHER command has the following syntax:

```
CIPHER [/E|/D] [/S[:directory]] [/A] [/I] [/F] [/Q]
       [/H] [pathname [...]]
CIPHER /K
CIPHER /R:pathname
CIPHER /U [/N]
CIPHER /W:directory
```

The following alphabetical list defines each of the CIPHER command's parameters:

- */A*—Forces operation on files and folders
- */D*—Decrypts the listed filename(s)
- */E*—Encrypts the listed filename(s)
- */F*—Forces encryption, even on already encrypted files
- */H*—Shows files with the hidden or system attributes set
- */I*—Ignores errors and proceeds with processing
- */K*—Creates a new encryption key for the user
- */N*—Prevents encryption keys from being updated; must be used with /U
- */Q*—Silences activity except for essential feedback
- */R:pathname*—Generates a Recovery Agent key and certificate into .pfx and .cer files
- */S*—Performs the action on all subcontents
- */U*—Scans for all encrypted files on local drives to update user's encryption key
- */W:directory*—Removes deleted data in the available disk space
- *Pathname*—Specifies a pattern, file, or directory. Wildcards can be used; each pattern must be separated by a space.
- *Directory*—Specifies a directory

When CIPHER is used with only a filename and without parameters, the status of the object is displayed, indicating whether the object is encrypted and whether new files added to a folder will be encrypted.

The primary benefit of EFS is that if your computer is either physically accessed or stolen, the data is protected as long as the malicious user does not gain access to the username and password that holds the private key for the encrypted files. The primary drawback is the increased processing power required to encrypt all writes and decrypt all reads on the fly. This process negatively affects performance to a noticeable extent on many systems.

EFS is supported by Windows 2000 Server, Windows 2000 Professional, Windows XP Professional, and Windows Server 2003. However, each generation of operating system uses a different default cryptography algorithm for EFS. Windows 2000 EFS uses DESX. Windows XP Professional EFS uses 3DES by default, but supports DESX. Windows Server 2003 and Windows XP Professional with Service Pack 1 EFS use AES by default, but support 3DES and DESX. Attempting to decrypt an EFS protect file using a different algorithm than was used to encrypt it may result in a corrupted and destroyed file. Once an encrypted file is corrupted, it cannot be recovered except from a backup. Microsoft Knowledge Base document 329741 (*http://support.microsoft.com/default.aspx?scid=kb;en-us; 329741*) discusses the means by which you can change the default algorithm for EFS for environments where different generations of operating systems are employed.

INTERNET SECURITY

Connecting to the Internet requires that you accept some risk. That risk includes unwittingly downloading Trojan horses or viruses, accepting malicious e-mail, or even (through lack of appropriate safeguards) allowing a remote cracker to take complete control of your computer. Most of the security features used to protect data within a LAN or even on a standalone system can also be leveraged to protect against Internet attacks. Plus, Microsoft has added the Internet Connection Firewall to Windows XP. The Internet Connection Firewall (ICF) is a simple firewall used to protect any network connection, especially dial-up or dedicated Internet links. ICF is discussed, along with other important Internet security issues, in Chapter 8.

CHAPTER SUMMARY

- Windows XP has object-level access controls that provide the foundation on which all resource access rests. By comparing the access control lists associated with individual objects to the access tokens that define the rights of any user process, Windows XP decides which object access requests to grant and which to deny.

- The Windows XP logon process (Winlogon) strictly controls how users identify themselves and logon to a Windows XP machine. The attention sequence (Ctrl+Alt+Delete) prevents an unauthorized user from obtaining system access to domain clients or properly configured standalone clients. Likewise, the Winlogon protected memory structures keep this all-important gatekeeper function from being replaced by would-be system crackers. Authentication can take place using various encryption schemes, including Kerberos, SSL, or NTLM.

❑ Winlogon also supports a number of logon controls: handling of a default logon name, providing security notices, changing the default shell, handling system shutdown options, and enabling automatic logon. Key local computer policy settings can be used to block unauthorized break-in attempts.

❑ The local computer policy controls many aspects of the security system as well as enabling or restricting specific functions and features of the operating system. All in all, Windows XP offers a reasonably secure operating environment that is designed to help administrators keep their important assets safe from harm and unwanted exposure.

❑ You can use Windows XP auditing capabilities to track down errant behavior or detect when system problems may be occurring.

❑ Encrypting File System (EFS) protects your data with an encryption system.

KEY TERMS

access control list (ACL) — A list of security identifiers that are contained by a resource object. Only those processes with the appropriate access token can activate the services of that object.

access token — Objects containing the security identifier of an active process. These tokens determine the security context of the process.

auditing — The process of tracking events by recording selected types of events in the Security log.

authentication — The process of validating a user's credentials to allow access to certain resources.

certificate — An electronic identity verification mechanism. Certificates are assigned to a client or server by a Certificate Authority. When communications begin, each side of the transmission can decide to either trust the other party based on their certificate and continue the communications or not to trust and terminate communications.

domain — A collection of computers with centrally managed security and activities.

domain controller — A specified computer role of Windows NT, 2000, or 2003 Servers that authenticates domain logons and maintains the security policies and the account database for a domain.

domain security — The control of user accounts, group memberships, and resource access for all members of a network instead of for only a single computer.

Encrypting File System (EFS) — A security feature of NTFS under Windows XP that allows files, folders, or entire drives to be encrypted. Once encrypted, only the user account that enabled the encryption has the proper private key to decrypt and access the secured objects.

event — Any significant occurrence in the system or in an application that requires users to be notified or a log entry to be added. Types of events include audits, driver failures, user logon, process launching, system shutdown, etc.

Event Viewer — The utility that maintains application, security, and system event logs on your computer, enabling you to view and manage the event logs, gather information about hardware and software problems, and monitor Windows XP security events.

identification — The process of establishing a valid account identity on a Windows XP machine by supplying a correct and working domain name (if necessary) and an account name.

IP Security (IPSEC) — An encrypted communication mechanism for TCP/IP to create protected communication sessions. IPSec is a suite of cryptography-based protection services and security protocols.

Kerberos version 5 — An authentication encryption protocol employed by Windows XP to protect logon credentials.

local computer policy — A Windows XP security control feature used to define and regulate security-related features and functions.

network authentication — The act of connecting to or accessing resources from some other member of the domain network. Network authentication is used to prove that you are a valid member of the domain, that your user account is properly authenticated, and that you have access permissions to perform the requested action.

NTLM (NT LAN Manager) authentication — The authentication mechanism used on Windows NT that is retained by Windows XP for backward compatibility.

object — Everything within the Windows XP operating environment is an object. Objects include files, folders, shares, printers, processes, etc.

password — A unique string of characters that must be provided before a logon or an access is authorized. Passwords are a security measure used to restrict initial access to Windows XP resources.

process — The primary unit of execution in the Windows XP operating system environment. A process may contain one or more execution threads, all associated with a named user account, SID, and access token. Processes essentially define the container within which individual applications and commands execute under Windows XP.

public key policy — A security control of Windows XP where Recovery Agents for EFS and domain-wide and trusted certificate authorities are defined and configured. These policies can be enforced on a user-by-user basis.

Secure Socket Layer/Transport Layer Security (SSL/TLS) — A mechanism used primarily over HTTP communications to create an encrypted session link through the exchange of certificates and public encryption keys.

security ID (SID) — A unique number that identifies a logged-on user to the security system. SIDs can identify one user or a group of users.

shell — The default user process that is launched when a valid account name and password combination is authenticated by the Winlogon process for Windows XP. The default shell of Windows XP is Windows Explorer. The default shell process manages the desktop, Start menu, taskbar, and other interface controls. The shell process defines a logged on user's runtime environment from this point forward, and supplies all spawned processes or commands with its access token to define their access permissions until that account logs out.

user account — This entity contains all of the information that defines a user to the Windows XP environment.

Winlogon — The process used by Windows XP to control user authentication and manage the logon process. Winlogon produces the logon dialog box where username, password, and domain are selected, it controls automated logon, warning text, the display of the shutdown button, and the display of the last user to logon to the system.

Review Questions

1. Which of the following should be used to define IPSec policies for a domain?
   a. TCP/IP Properties
   b. Local Computer Policy
   c. Event Viewer
   d. group policy

2. All processes in Windows XP require an access token. True or False?

3. A SID is a unique number and is never duplicated. True or False?

4. Permissions that are changed while the user is actively logged on do not take effect until that user logs on to the system again. True or False?

5. The default Windows XP authentication method is to supply valid domain and account names, plus a valid password; however, Windows XP permits use of alternate authentication techniques. True or False?

6. What is the first thing the security system looks for when it scans an ACL for an object?
   a. a Deny to the object for the requested service, at which point access is immediately denied
   b. any Allow permission that provides the requested permission
   c. It checks the default, and if access is permitted thereby, allows the request to proceed.
   d. none of the above

7. What is the default access level that Windows XP assigns to new objects by default?
   a. Restrict
   b. Allow
   c. Legal Access
   d. Illegal Access

8. Which of the following is a good reason for adding DontDisplayLastUserName to the Windows XP Registry? (Choose all that apply.)

   a. to prevent easy discovery of user account names

   b. to improve security on a shared machine

   c. to reduce burnout on the machine's monitor

   d. to force users to provide a valid username in addition to a password to logon

9. The Windows XP authentication process can be automated by adding default user information and the _____ value to the Registry.

   a. DontDisplayLastUsername

   b. AutoAdminLogon

   c. Legal Notice Caption

   d. AutomateLogon

10. Which of the following is the most likely reason for a security notice that appears when users attempt to logon to a Windows XP machine at the National Security Agency?

    a. to make sure that outsiders don't try to break into the system

    b. to inform unauthorized users that they are subject to legal action if they obtain unauthorized access to the system

    c. to remind valid system users about Acceptable Use Policies

    d. none of the above

11. The default shell process for Windows XP is called the _____ .

    a. Windows Explorer

    b. Program Manager

    c. command shell

    d. C shell

12. The _____ is created by the Windows XP security subsystem at logon and identifies the current user to the subsystem.

    a. Access ID

    b. Security ID

    c. Group ID

    d. access token

13. The _____ key sequence initiates the classic logon process.

    a. Ctrl+Esc

    b. Alt+Tab

    c. Ctrl+Break

    d. Ctrl+Alt+Delete

14. An access token is required to access any Windows XP object. True or False?

15. To customize the security structure of your Windows XP system, you can change the behavior of the logon process. True or False?

16. What is the primary protocol that Windows XP uses for authentication?

    a. NTLM

    b. Secure Socket Layer

    c. Kerberos

    d. NetBIOS

17. Which of the following statements are true about the Local Computer Policy snap-in? (Choose all that apply.)

    a. It is used to control aspects of the Windows XP security system.

    b. It is used to assign user accounts to groups.

    c. It can be customized by third-party applications.

    d. It can be superceded by a domain's group policy.

18. What is the special-purpose application the Windows XP attention sequence calls and which serves as the logon process?

    a. Winpopup

    b. Winlogon

    c. Usermgr

    d. Explorer

19. What security feature is included in Windows XP specifically to protect TCP/IP communications between two systems?

    a. Kerberos version 5

    b. IPSec

    c. Strong passwords

    d. EFS

20. What is EFS used to protect?

    a. passwords

    b. data files

    c. group policy

    d. communication sessions

21. If the Windows Explorer shell is replaced with the Program Manager shell, which of the following side effects occur? (Choose all that apply.)

    a. no access to the Start menu

    b. no taskbar

    c. no access to the Task Manager

    d. no more DOS Command prompt

22. Only the user who encrypts a file through EFS can access that file later. True or False?

23. What predefined IPSec policy should you use to employ encryption only when required by a remote system?

    a. Client (Respond Only)

    b. Server (Request Security)

    c. Secure Server (Require Security)

    d. Password (User)

24. Auditing can be defined for an object for specific users and groups for one or more individual services or actions. True or False?

25. Audit events are recorded in the System log. True or False?

CASE PROJECTS

Case Project 6-1

You've been assigned the task of defining a security policy for your company. You've been given basic guidelines to follow. These include preventing users from installing software, securing the logon process, and enforcing disk quotas. Using the Local Computer Policy console, detail the control you should configure and what settings you think would work best to accomplish these goals.

Case Project 6-2

You've recently inherited the responsibility of administering a Windows XP network. The last administrator was rather lax in restricting user access. After working through the data folders to correct the access permissions, you suspect that some users still have access to confidential files. What can you do to determine if this type of access is still occurring? Describe the steps involved in enabling this mechanism and examining the results.

7

WINDOWS XP NETWORK PROTOCOLS

After reading this chapter and completing the exercises, you will be able to:

♦ Understand networking in Windows XP

♦ Understand Windows XP networking protocols

♦ Configure and use TCP/IP protocols and services

♦ Access NetWare servers and services from Windows XP

♦ Understand Windows XP Remote tools

This chapter discusses the networking protocols that Windows XP supports, as well as how and when to use them. This chapter also discusses Transmission Control Protocol/Internet Protocol (TCP/IP)—probably the most important networking protocol used with any version of Windows—and what is required to configure Windows XP to employ this protocol for network communications. Also covered is NWLink, a protocol historically associated with NetWare, but a valid protocol option under Windows XP as well. Finally, other protocols that Windows XP Professional supports are also examined.

WINDOWS XP NETWORK OVERVIEW

Windows XP is the most versatile Windows operating system from Microsoft to date. It is capable of establishing a network connection through a myriad of devices and technologies. Windows XP was designed specifically to offer easy-to-use networking capabilities for inexperienced home users and both enterprise-level networked organizations. Windows XP is able to act as a standalone system for occasional Internet dial-up, as a dedicated workgroup connection-sharing server, and even as a client in a domain network.

Windows XP supports local area network (LAN) connections, which are typically established with an expansion card or a PC card network adapter. The network medium is attached to the network adapter, usually with twisted-pair cabling. Windows XP also supports emerging wireless technologies to eliminate network cables from both home and office networking. Windows XP offers both WAN and LAN support and can establish VPN and IPSec connections with local and remote systems. Windows XP also supports a wide range of MAN and WAN communication devices.

Windows XP has improved on the remote access support found in Windows 9x and Windows 2000. It is easier to create and use dial-up Internet connections than in previous versions. Windows XP also supports dedicated connections, such as cable modems, and specialty connections, such as DSL and ISDN. Through the use of the proper hardware, Windows XP can fully manage any type of remote access connectivity.

Through its implementation of the NWLink protocol, Windows XP continues its support for the Internet Packet eXchange/Sequenced Packet eXchange (IPX/SPX) protocol suite for compatibility with Novell NetWare networks. There is a significant installed user base for NetWare; therefore, support for this type of network transmission is important to overall network connectivity. However, the use of this protocol is declining because most network operating systems (server and client versions) support TCP/IP as their default primary protocol.

Windows XP is designed for networking, with all the elements necessary for interacting with a network without requiring any additional software. Windows XP networking is powerful and efficient, yet is relatively easy to configure and use with a graphical user interface and wizards for configuration support.

Windows XP Professional can function as a network client, as a network server (in a limited sense), or both. It can participate in peer-to-peer, client/server, and terminal/ host environments. Windows XP also has everything needed to access the Internet, including all necessary protocols and client capabilities, a Web browser (Internet Explorer), and other Internet tools and utilities.

In Windows XP, numerous components work together to define its networking capabilities. Each component provides one or more individual network functions and defines an interface through which data moves on its way to and from other system components. This allows Windows XP to support multiple protocols easily and transparently; applications need only know how to communicate through a standard application programming interface

(API), while the modular organization of the operating system shields them from the complex details that can sometimes be involved.

Networking components can be added to or deleted from a Windows XP system without affecting the function of other components, except in those cases where such components are bound to the other components. (Binding is discussed later in this chapter.) Adding new components to Windows XP brings new services, communications technologies, and other capabilities into existing networks and allows additional protocols to join the mix at any time.

NETWORK PROTOCOLS SUPPORTED BY WINDOWS XP

7

Windows XP supports two core network transport protocols. Both of these protocols can be used on any network of any size. The major network protocols are the **Transmission Control Protocol/Internet Protocol (TCP/IP)** and **NWLink** (identified in the Local Area Connection Properties dialog box as the NWLink IPX/SPX/NetBIOS Compatible Protocol). These network protocols have associated advantages and drawbacks, as outlined in the sections that follow.

The following list sums up the important characteristics of each of these protocols:

- TCP/IP works on almost any scale, from a single-segment network to a global scale, as demonstrated by its use on the global Internet. TCP/IP is complicated, yet powerful, and is the most widely used of all networking protocols.

- NWLink works best on networks of medium scope (20 servers or fewer in a single facility). It's also useful on networks that include versions of NetWare that predate NetWare 5.*x* (the first version of NetWare to incorporate full-blown, native TCP/IP support).

TCP/IP

TCP/IP represents an all-embracing suite of protocols that cover a wide range of capabilities. (More than 50 component protocols that belong to the TCP/IP suite have been standardized.)

TCP/IP has also been around for a long time; the original version of TCP/IP emerged from research funded by the Advanced Research Projects Agency (ARPA, a division of the U.S. Department of Defense). Work on this technology began in 1969, continued throughout the 1970s, and became broadly available in 1981 and 1982. Today, TCP/IP is the most common networking protocol in use worldwide, and it is the protocol suite that makes the Internet possible.

TCP/IP has become the platform for a staggering variety of network services, including newsgroups (NNTP), electronic mail (SNMP and MIME), file transfer (FTP), remote printing (the lpr, lpd, and lpq utilities), remote boot (bootp and **Dynamic Host Configuration Protocol [DHCP]**), and the World Wide Web (Hypertext Transfer Protocol [HTTP]).

To provide **Network Basic Input/Output System (NetBIOS)** support using TCP/IP transports, Microsoft includes an implementation of **NBT (NetBIOS over TCP/IP)** with Windows XP. Microsoft extends the definition of NBT behaviors by defining a new type of NetBIOS network node for the NBT environment, called an *H* (for Hybrid) node. An H node inverts the normal behavior of the standard NBT *N* (or network) node. It looks first for a NetBIOS name service (such as a WINS server), and then sends a broadcast to request local name resolution. An N node broadcasts first and then attempts a directed request for name resolution. The Microsoft approach reduces the amount of broadcast traffic on most IP-based networks that use NetBIOS names (as older Microsoft networks that predate Windows 2000 must do).

TCP/IP Advantages

TCP/IP supports networking services better than the other Windows XP protocols through its multiple components (see Figure 7-1). TCP/IP supports multiple routing protocols that in turn support large, complex networks. TCP/IP also incorporates better error detection and handling, and works with more kinds of computers than any other protocol suite.

The components or elements of the TCP/IP protocol stack are shown in Figure 7-1:

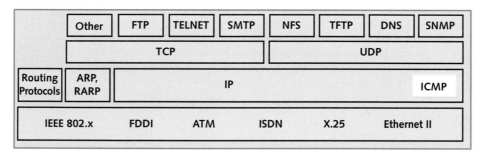

Figure 7-1   TCP/IP protocol stack

The TCP/IP protocol stack components or elements are as follows:

- *Other*—Any of the nearly 40 other service/application-level protocols defined for TCP/IP
- **FTP (File Transfer Protocol)**—The service protocol and corresponding TCP/IP application that permit network file transfer
- *Telnet*—The service protocol and corresponding TCP/IP applications that support networked terminal emulation services.

- ***SMTP (Simple Mail Transfer Protocol)***—The most common e-mail service protocol in the TCP/IP environment. POP3 (Post Office Protocol version 3) and IMAP (Internet Mail Access Protocol) are also involved in a great deal of Internet e-mail traffic.

- *NFS (Network File System)*—A UDP-based networked file system originally developed by Sun Microsystems and widely used on many TCP/IP networks. (Windows XP does not include built-in NFS support, but numerous third-party options are available.)

- ***TFTP (Trivial File Transfer Protocol)***—A lightweight, UDP-based alternative to FTP, designed primarily to permit users running Telnet sessions elsewhere on a network to grab files from their "home machines."

- ***DNS (Domain Name System)***—An address resolution service for TCP/IP-based networks that translates between numeric IP addresses and symbolic names known formally as Fully Qualified Domain Names (FQDNs).

- ***SNMP (Simple Network Management Protocol)***—The primary management protocol used on TCP/IP networks, SNMP is used to report management data to management consoles or applications and to interrogate repositories of management data around a network.

- ***TCP (Transmission Control Protocol)***—The primary transport protocol in TCP/IP, TCP is a robust, reliable, guaranteed delivery, **connection-oriented** transport protocol.

- ***UDP (User Datagram Protocol)***—A secondary transport protocol on TCP/IP networks, UDP is a lightweight cousin of TCP. It is **connectionless**, has low overhead, and offers best-effort delivery rather than the delivery guarantees offered by TCP. It is used for all kinds of services on TCP networks, including NFS and TFTP.

- *Routing protocols*—These embrace several important IP protocols, including the Routing Internet Protocol (RIP), the Open Shortest Path First (OSPF) protocol, the Border Gateway Protocol (BGP), and others.

- ***ARP (Address Resolution Protocol)***—The protocol used to map from a logical IP address to a physical MAC-layer address.

- ***RARP (Reverse Address Resolution Protocol)***—The protocol used to map from a physical MAC-layer address to a logical IP address.

- ***IP (Internet Protocol)***—The primary protocol in TCP/IP, IP includes network-addressing information that is manipulated when a packet is routed from sender to receiver, along with data integrity and network status information.

- ***ICMP (Internet Control Message Protocol)***—The protocol that deals with quality of service, availability, and network behavior information. It also supports the **PING (Packet Internet Groper)** utility, which is often used to inquire if an

7

address is reachable on the Internet, and if so, to provide a measure of the "round-trip time" to send a packet to its destination address, and receive a reply.

- *IEEE 802.X*—Includes the 802.2 networking standard, plus standard networking technologies like Ethernet (802.3) and token ring (802.5), among others

- *FDDI (Fiber Distributed Data Interface)*—A 100 Mbps fiber-based networking technology.

- *ATM (Asynchronous Transfer Mode)*—A cell-oriented, fiber- and copper-based networking technology that supports data rates from 25 Mbps to as high as 2.4 Gbps

- *ISDN (Integrated Services Digital Network)*—A digital alternative to analog telephony, ISDN links can support two or more 64 Kbps channels per connection, depending on type.

- *X.25*—An ITU standard for packet-switched networking, X.25 is very common outside the United States where its robust data-handling capability makes it a good match for substandard telephone networks.

- *Ethernet II*—An older version of Ethernet that preceded the 802.3 specification, Ethernet II offers the same 10 Mbps as standard Ethernet, but uses different frame formats.

In addition to its many services and capabilities, TCP/IP also supports the following:

- Direct Internet access from any TCP/IP-equipped computer, with a link to the Internet by phone, some kind of digital link (frame relay, T1, and so forth), or across any network with routed Internet access.

- Powerful network management protocols and services, such as Desktop Management Interface (DMI), which supports interrogation of desktop hardware and software configuration data.

- Dynamic Host Configuration Protocol (DHCP), which provides unique IP addresses on demand and simplifies IP address management.

- Microsoft **Windows Internet Naming Service (WINS)** to enable IP-based NetBIOS name browsing for Microsoft clients and servers. TCP/IP also supports the Domain Name System (DNS), the most common name resolution service used to map FQDNs to numeric IP addresses throughout the Internet. NetBIOS names are limited to 15 characters. FQDNs or host names are names composed of multiple segments, such as mail.adminsys.microsoft.com.

The Internet Network Information Center (InterNIC) manages all TCP/IP domain names, network numbers, and IP addresses to make the global Internet work correctly and reliably.

TCP/IP Drawbacks

For all the clear advantages of TCP/IP, there are some drawbacks. As network protocols go, TCP/IP is neither extremely fast nor very easy to use. Configuring and managing a TCP/IP-based network requires a fair degree of expertise, careful planning, and constant maintenance and attention. Each of the many services and protocols that TCP/IP supports brings unique installation, configuration, and management chores. In addition, there's a huge mass of information and detail work involved in establishing and maintaining a TCP/IP-based network. In short, it's a demanding and unforgiving environment and should always be approached with great care.

NWLink (IPX/SPX)

NWLink is the Microsoft implementation of Novell's **Internetwork Packet Exchange/ Sequenced Packet Exchange (IPX/SPX)** protocol stack. Rather than supporting the native Novell **Open Datalink Interface (ODI)**, NWLink works with the **Network Device Interface Specification (NDIS)** driver technology that's native to Windows XP; NDIS defines parameters for loading more than one protocol on a network adapter. NWLink is sufficiently complete to support the most important IPX/SPX APIs.

Although IPX/SPX is the default protocol for NetWare prior to version 5, TCP/IP is the default protocol in version 5.

NWLink Advantages

NWLink offers some powerful capabilities, including:

- *SPX II*—SPX II is a new SPX version that has been enhanced to support windowing and can set a maximum frame size.

- *Autodetection of frame types*—NWLink automatically detects which IPX **frame type** is used on a network during initial startup and broadcast advertisement phases. When multiple frame types appear, Windows XP defaults to the industry-standard 802.2 frame type.

- *Direct hosting over IPX*—This is the ability to host ongoing network sessions using IPX transports. Direct hosting over IPX can increase network performance by as much as 20 percent on client computers. This is especially beneficial for client/ server applications.

NWLink Drawbacks

On large networks, IPX may not scale well. IPX lacks a built-in facility for centralized name and address management similar to the service that DNS provides for TCP/IP. This omission allows address conflicts to occur—especially when previously isolated networks that employed identical defaults or common addressing schemes attempt to interoperate. Novell established an address Registry in 1994 (IPX was introduced in 1983), but it is neither generally used nor acknowledged. The InterNIC and its subsequent partners have managed all public IP addresses since 1982. IPX fails to support a comprehensive collection of network management tools. Finally, IPX imposes a greater memory footprint on DOS machines and runs less efficiently across slow serial connections.

NetBEUI and DLC

Both **NetBIOS Extended User Interface (NetBEUI)** and **Data Link Control (DLC)** have been greatly deemphasized in Windows XP. In fact, you won't even find them as available options when attempting to install new protocols. NetBEUI is not often used anymore, owing to its limitations on the number of addressable nodes per network and its inability to be routed. Likewise, DLC has been replaced by SNA for mainframe interaction and TCP/IP or proprietary protocols for network attached printers. If your current network relies on either of these protocols, you must consider alternatives before deploying Windows XP.

NETWORKING UNDER WINDOWS XP

The Windows XP networking system is controlled by a single multifaceted interface that combines networking access for LAN, Internet, and modem. The interface is called Network Connections (see Figure 7-2) and is accessed through Control Panel (in Classic View, or through the Network and Internet Connections category in Category View). A Connect To submenu is added to the Start menu if you create dial-up or VPN connection objects. Through this menu, you can also access the Network Connections tool by selecting the Show all connections command.

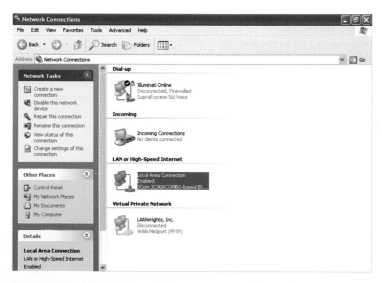

Figure 7-2   The Network Connections utility

Network Connections is used to create and configure network connections. The Create a new connection command in the Network Tasks list starts a wizard that takes the user through the process of establishing new network links. The wizard is used for any network links employing modems, virtual private networks (VPNs) over the Internet, or serial, parallel, or infrared ports. Windows XP automatically enables all normal network links achieved through a network adapter and an attached cable. A Local Area Connection icon is listed in the Network Connections window for each installed adapter card. If there are two or more LAN connections, it is recommended that you rename the Local Area Connection icons to reflect the domain, network, or purpose of the link.

Existing local area connections can be configured by opening the Properties dialog box for a particular object either through the File menu or by right-clicking the object and using the shortcut menu. A typical default configuration of a Local Area Connection Properties dialog box is shown in Figure 7-3, listing the adapter in use as well as all installed protocols and services that can function over this interface. The Configure button is used to access the Properties dialog box for the adapter. Each listed service or protocol has a check box. When checked, the protocol or service is bound to the adapter (that is, it can operate over the network link established by the adapter). When unchecked, the protocol or service is not bound to the adapter.

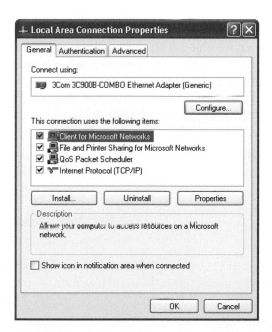

Figure 7-3   A Local Area Connection Properties dialog box, General tab

The Install button is used to add new client interfaces, protocols, and services that any of the Connection objects can use. When a new element is added, all possible bindings are enabled by default. The following available elements can be installed onto Windows XP Professional:

- *Client: Client for Microsoft Networks*—Used to gain access to Microsoft network resources; this component is installed by default

- *Client: Client Service for NetWare*—Used to gain access to NetWare resources

- *Service: QoS Packet Scheduler*—An extension service for Winsock used to reserve bandwidth for communications; this component is installed by default

- *Service: File and Printer Sharing for Microsoft Networks*—Enables a system to share its files and printers with a Microsoft network; this component is installed by default

- *Service: Service Advertising Protocol*—Used by Windows XP to participate actively in NetWare networks

- *Protocol: Internet Protocol (TCP/IP)*—The protocol used on networks connected to the Internet or using Internet Information Services (IIS) privately; this component is installed by default

- *Protocol: Network Monitor Driver*—Driver used to allow full versions of Network Monitor to obtain network activity information from Windows XP Professional systems

- *Protocol: NWLink IPX/SPX/NetBIOS Compatible Transport Protocol*—Protocol most often used on NetWare networks

The Uninstall button is used to remove a client, protocol, or service. Once an element is removed, it is removed for all Connection objects. The Properties button opens the Properties dialog box for the selected installed component (client, service, or protocol). Note that not all components have configurable options. This dialog box also offers an option to display an icon in the status area of the taskbar when the Connection object is in use. The Network Connections interface's File and Advanced drop-down menus include the following functions:

- *File: Disable*—Prevents the selected Connection object from being used to establish a communications link. This command is for automatic connections, such as those for a LAN.

- *File: Enable*—Allows the selected Connection object to be used to establish a communications link. This command is for automatic connections, such as those for a LAN.

- *File: Connect*—Initiates the selected Connection object to establish a communications link. This command is for manual connections, such as those over a modem.

- *File: Status*—Displays a Status window for the selected Connection object that lists whether the object is connected, how long the connection has been active, the speed of the connection, and the packet counts. This window offers Properties and Disable buttons to perform the same functions as the File menu commands.

- *File: Repair*—Attempts to repair a connection object by clearing the ARP cache and resetting the buffers or ports. This is often a good first step to try before changing configuration data. This command also forces a new DHCP lease request if the interface is configured to use DHCP.

- *File: New Connection*—Opens the New Connection Wizard

- *Advanced: Operator-Assisted Dialing*—Used to manually dial a connection number and then have the computer take control of the line once the remote system answers the call.

- *Advanced: Dial-up Preferences*—Opens a dialog box in which RAS-related controls are set (see Chapter 8, "Internetworking with Remote Access").

- *Advanced: Network Identification*—Opens the Computer Name tab of the System applet that displays the current computer name and workgroup/domain name. To join a domain and create a local user, click Network ID.

- *Advanced: Bridge Connections*—Used to create a virtual bridge between two or more network segments

- *Advanced: Advanced Settings*—Opens a dialog box where bindings and provider order can be managed; see the "Managing Bindings" section later in this chapter.

- *Advanced: Optional Networking Components*—Adds other networking components, such as Monitoring and Management Tools, Networking Services, and Other Network File and Print Services.

Some of these commands appear only when a specific Connection object type is selected.

NOTE For most networks, the default Local Area Connection that Windows XP creates automatically is sufficient for LAN activity. As shown earlier, this Connection object is designed to link with a Microsoft-based network (workgroup or domain), allows file and printer sharing, and employs the TCP/IP protocol.

To change TCP/IP settings, select the protocol from the list of components in the Properties window of a Local Area Connection, and then click Properties. This reveals the Internet Protocol (TCP/IP) Properties dialog box (see Figure 7-4). From here, you can easily enable DHCP for this computer, or define a static IP address, subnet mask, and gateway. You can also define the preferred and alternate DNS servers. The Advanced button brings up a multitabbed dialog box in which multiple IP addresses, additional gateways, DNS and WINS functionality, and TCP/IP service extension properties can be defined.

NOTE Some presentations of the Internet Protocol (TCP/IP) Properties dialog box contain an Alternate Configuration tab. The appearance of this feature is explained in the TCP/IP section later in this chapter.

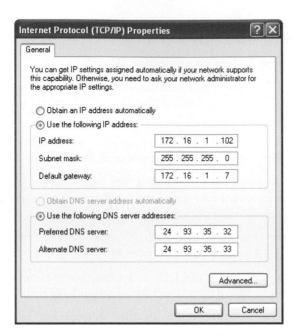

Figure 7-4 The Internet Protocol (TCP/IP) Properties dialog box

Activity 7-1: Local Area Connection Properties

Time Required: 5 minutes

Objective: Use Network Connections in Control Panel to view the properties of the Local Area Connection and the status of the network connection.

Description: A common question is whether a network connection is working properly. With Windows XP, the user can quickly check to see if packets are being sent and received. If communication doesn't seem to be operating properly, the user's next step is to check the properties. In this activity, you view the status of your network connection and the properties for the Local Area Connection configuration.

To view the status and properties of a Local Area Connection:

This activity assumes your Windows XP Professional system is connected to a network.

1. Open the Network Connections dialog box by clicking **Start**, **Control Panel**, **Network Connections**. If the Control Panel is in Category view, select the **Network and Internet Connections** category, and then click the **Network Connections** object.

2. Select the **Local Area Connection** object.

3. Select **File**, **Status**. This reveals the Local Area Connection Status dialog box. Notice the details provided on this dialog box: Connection Status, Duration, Speed, and Packets.

4. Click the **Properties** button. This reveals the Local Area Connection Properties dialog box for this connection. Notice how this dialog box reveals the NIC involved with this connection and all the services and protocols associated with this connection.

5. Click **Cancel** to close the Local Area Connection Properties dialog box.

6. Click **Close** to close the Local Area Connection Status dialog box.

Adding new network interfaces to Windows XP Professional is handled in the same fashion as installing any other piece of hardware: physically install it and allow Windows XP to detect it and install drivers, or use the Add Hardware applet to perform the drive installation manually. Both of these procedures are discussed in Chapter 3, "Using the System Utilities." Once a new NIC is installed, Windows XP automatically creates a new Local Area Connection that you can customize for your networking needs.

7

WIRELESS NETWORKING

Wireless networking allows for reliable network connectivity and communications without being tied down by a network cable. Windows XP Professional includes native support for home and office networking. Microsoft has placed itself firmly behind the IEEE 802.11 wireless standards. In fact, Microsoft is so intent on pushing wireless technologies that it has transformed most of its own Redmond, Washington, campus and many of its branch offices into wireless networks.

Many public facilities, such as airports and hotels, are adopting wireless technologies to offer Internet connectivity and local information to their customers throughout their buildings without tying people down with wires. Once a wireless NIC is installed, you'll find that Windows XP integrates itself easily into a wireless network.

Wireless networks, also known as Wi-Fi networks, consist of two primary components: a base station and a NIC. The base station, or wireless access point, is a wireless hub designed to support one or more network connections for wireless-enabled clients. Each client must have a corresponding compatible wireless network interface card to communicate with the base station and thus participate in the wireless network. A wireless network is exactly the same as a wired network except that instead of communication signals being transmitted over copper wiring, they are transmitted over radio waves.

The latest version of this standard is 802.11g, which supports up to 54 Mbps of throughput. While 802.11g is gaining widespread support, the previous 802.11b standard is still widely deployed. 802.11b supports throughputs up to 11 Mbps. 802.11g is backward compatible with 802.11b, so systems with 802.11b NICs can participate in a wireless network hosted by an 802.11g base station.

Because wireless network communications are broadcast over radio waves, the communications themselves must be protected from interception and eavesdropping. This is done by encrypting the traffic before it is broadcast over the air waves. The standard used by 802.11 to protect wireless communications is known as the Wired Equivalent Privacy (WEP) encryption.

For the most part, installing and setting up a wireless network is the same as creating a wired network. First, purchase a base station and compatible wireless NICs. Next, connect the base station to the existing network or to your Internet access router or broadband modem. Then, install the wireless NIC in your Windows XP Professional computer and install drivers as needed. In most cases, the IP address configuration of the wireless client is assigned automatically by the base station. That's it—you're done.

If you run into any problems, you can use the Windows XP Professional Help and Support Center to access network troubleshooting information. You may also want to review the documentation for the wireless products and possibly contact the vendor if you are having an unresolved issue. If you'd like to read more about wireless networking with Microsoft products, visit *www.microsoft.com/hardware/broadbandnetworking.mspx*.

THE WINDOWS XP NETWORK BRIDGE

Windows XP boasts a networking feature known as network bridge. In essence, network bridge creates a Layer 2 bridge between two or more network interfaces, effectively connecting multiple network segments. A network bridge can connect network segments even if they use different protocols and different topologies. Microsoft has included the network bridging capability in Windows XP to encourage the creation of networks in small offices and at home. Using the Windows XP-based network bridge, there's no need to purchase a separate (and sometimes expensive) hardware bridge or router. Furthermore, no configuration is required. Just select two or more network connections (such as a wired NIC and a wireless NIC), and then issue the Bridge Connections command from the Advanced menu in the Network Connections utility.

Windows XP can support only a single network bridge per system. However, that one bridge can bridge multiple networks together. The only restrictions on connections that may be bridged are to prevent bridging with those objects controlled by the Internet Connection Sharing (ICS) or Internet Connection Firewall (ICF). Another restriction is that only similar interfaces can be bridged. That is, a dial-up connection can be bridged only to other dial-up connections.

 See Chapter 8, "Internetworking with Remote Access," for details on ICS and ICF.

Once a bridge is created, it appears as a connection object named Network Bridge within the Network Connections utility. To add other connections to this bridge, mark their respective check boxes in the list of adapters available in the Properties dialog box of the Network Bridge. To remove a connection from a bridge, deselect the appropriate check box from this dialog box. To remove the bridge altogether, select it within the Network Connections and press the Delete key.

NETWORK SETUP WIZARD

The Network Setup Wizard (previously known as the Home Networking Wizard) is used to configure nondomain networks for small offices or home use of Windows XP. This step-by-step, walk-through tool allows easy configuration of the following:

7

- Friendly computer names, such as "Study Computer" or "Den System"

- Your Internet connection, be it dial-up or dedicated

- Internet Connection Sharing (ICS)

- Internet Connection Firewall (ICF)

- TCP/IP for networking

The Network Setup Wizard can be opened from the network tasks list from within the Network Connection utility (set up for a home or small office network), or through the Network and Internet Connections category of Control Panel. For best results, use the wizard on the system to be the ICS host first. All other systems on the network automatically configure themselves against the ICS host to gain access to the shared Internet link and to share resources between networked systems.

During the Network Setup Wizard's operation, you are asked whether to create a floppy disk to run the Network Setup Wizard on Windows 98, 98 SE, or Me. If you are using any of these systems on your network, creating the floppy disk is a good idea. The wizard does not function on any other system; thus, Windows 2000 and NT systems must be configured manually to participate in this type of network.

MANAGING BINDINGS

Binding refers to the order in which Windows XP networking components are linked. These linkages and the order in which multiple components link to a single boundary layer affect how the systems behave and how well they perform. Binding is defined in the Advanced Settings dialog box (see Figure 7-5). This dialog box is reached by issuing the Advanced Settings command from the Advanced menu of the Network Connections window.

By default, Windows XP binds any two components that share a common boundary layer, unless such bindings are explicitly removed. In fact, Windows XP binds all components that

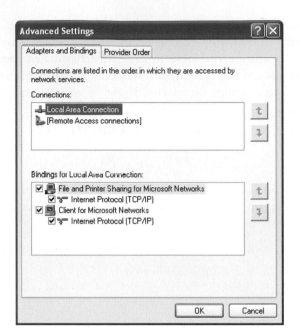

Figure 7-5   The Advanced Settings dialog box, Adapters and Bindings tab

share a common boundary to the boundary layer they share, unless one or more of these bindings is removed manually.

Because this default is known as *complete binding*—that is, all possible bindings are created automatically—it can lead to system inefficiencies, especially when bindings are created that will not be used. Such unused bindings might appear higher in the binding order (as indicated by their position beneath a boundary layer element, where closer indicates higher priority) than bindings that are used. This arrangement can build delays into the system because the MUP attempts to satisfy UNC requests for names it does not recognize in the order in which bindings appear, and unused bindings must time out before the next binding in the order is attempted.

Disabling all protocol bindings that are not needed or used improves system performance and decreases the likelihood of communication errors. It's also important to understand that because clients (in this case Windows XP Professional machines) initiate communications with Windows servers, changing the binding order of protocols on clients is what matters. Servers respond using whatever protocol appears within the transmission, so changing their binding order doesn't do much to improve performance. Changing a client's binding order, on the other hand, can sometimes deliver dramatic performance improvements.

Binding priority affects network performance because Windows XP makes connections in the order in which protocols are bound. For two machines that use IPX/SPX and TCP/IP, Windows XP uses whichever protocol appears higher in the services binding list. If both computers run IPX/SPX and TCP/IP, and IPX/SPX ranks higher than TCP/IP in the binding list, the two machines establish a faster connection (IPX/SPX is faster than TCP/IP) than if the bindings were reversed. To change the priority for any transport protocol, highlight an object on the Adapters and Bindings tab, and then use the arrow buttons to increase (or decrease) its priority level. You can also unbind services and protocols by deselecting the check box in front of the object's name.

The Provider Order tab is used to alter the binding priority of various providers, such as network connectivity or print servers. This is useful only when two or more providers of the same type can be employed by a system. For example, if a computer participates in NetWare and Microsoft networking environments, it can be useful to change the priority of those providers to favor the most often accessed network.

Activity 7-2: Network Bindings

ACTIVITY

Time Required: 10 minutes

Objective: Use the Advanced Settings of the Network Connections object to view the network bindings.

Description: Similar to the bindings between the layers in the OSI model, there are layers of binding on each computer. The NIC is bound to the protocol, which in turn is bound to the service, and so on. In this activity, you view the bindings and see how a service or protocol can be disabled.

To view network bindings:

1. Open Network Connections by clicking **Start, Control Panel, Network Connections**. If Control Panel is in Category view, select the **Network and Internet Connections** category, and then click the **Network Connections** object.

2. Click the **Advanced** menu, and then click **Advanced Settings**. This reveals the Advanced Settings dialog box where bindings are managed.

3. Select a connection from the Connections box.

4. Notice the contents of the lower field where installed services and protocols are listed in their binding order.

5. Notice the items closer to the top of the list are bound in higher priority than those listed lower on the list.

6. Notice the check box beside each item that allows you to disable that service or protocol.

7. Click **Cancel** to ensure you've made no changes.

8. Click **File**, and then click **Close**.

TCP/IP ARCHITECTURE

TCP/IP supports easy cross-platform communications and provides the technical foundation for the worldwide Internet. TCP/IP is actually a suite of protocols; this discussion breaks it down into IP and TCP. Under each of these protocols lie many additional protocols that give the TCP/IP suite such a wide range of functionality.

Internet Protocol

The Internet Protocol (IP) provides source and destination addressing and routing in the TCP/IP suite. IP addresses are logical addresses that are 32 bits (4 bytes) long. Each byte, or octet, is represented by a decimal number from 0 to 255 and separated by a period, for example, 183.24.206.18. IP is a connectionless datagram protocol that, like all connectionless protocols, is fast but unreliable. IP assumes that other protocols are available to ensure reliable delivery of the data.

 NOTE In the final octet of an IP address, the numbers 0 and 255 are reserved for special purposes. In the range of 0–255, the zero address is reserved to identify the network and the 255 address is used for broadcasts that are read by all IP hosts on the network. IP network hosts can use only numbers 1 through 254 in the final octet. "Host" is the IP-specific term that identifies any device on an IP network that is assigned a specific address.

Part of the IP address assigned to a computer designates which network the computer is on; the remainder of the address represents the host ID of that computer. The four bytes that IP uses for addresses can be broken up in multiple ways; in fact, several classes of IP addresses have been defined that use different boundaries for the network part and the host ID part. These are shown in Table 7-1.

Table 7-1   Classes of IP addresses

Class	Network IDs	Host IDs	Usable network IDs
A	126	16,777,214	1.x.y.z–126.a.b.c
B	16,384 (2^14)	65,534	128.1.y.z–191.255.b.c
C	2,097,150	254	192.0.1.z–223.255.254.c

In a Class A address, the first octet is used to identify the network and the three trailing octets are used to identify the hosts. This creates a situation in which a small number of networks (126, to be exact) is possible, but a large number of hosts (over 16 million per network) can be defined on each. Class B addresses split the octets evenly, so the first two identify the network and the second two identify the host. This permits over 16,000 networks with over 65,000 hosts. Class C addresses use the first three octets for the network portion and the final octet for the host portion of an address. This permits over two million networks, but only a maximum of 254 hosts for each Class C network.

For example, if a computer has an address of 183.24.206.18, it is a Class B address because the first two octets fall in the range of 128.1-191.255, as indicated in the fourth column of Table 7-1. Thus, the first two octets represent the network address (183.24) and the host address portion is 206.18. The computer next to it might have the address of 183.24.208. 192, which indicates that it's on the same network (183.24) but has a different host address (208.192).

IP uses a special bit mask called a subnet mask to determine which part of an address denotes the network and which part the host. The job of the **subnet mask** is to block out the network section of the address so that only the host ID portion remains significant. For the addresses on the 183.24 network, the subnet mask can be stated as 255.255.0.0. Notice that the two most significant octets are occupied by a binary value that translates into all ones (255 is 11111111 in binary), while the network portion is all zeros (0 is the same as 00000000 in binary).

A subnet can be written in at least two different ways. Until recently, the most common method was to write out the subnet in dotted-decimal notation, such as 255.255.0.0. This method is the form required when configuring most systems to use TCP/IP. However, a new method for writing the subnet is simply added on to an IP address, such as 172.16.1.1/16. The slash and the number at the end of this IP address indicate the subnet mask used. The number defines the number of bits taken from the 32-bit binary form of the IP address to be used as the subnet mask. So, a /16 is a subnet mask of 255.255.0.0 and a /24 is 255.255.255.0.

NOTE Sometimes, IP network administrators use part of what the IP address class considers the host portion of an address to further subdivide a single Class A, B, or C network. You might see the occasional subnet mask that looks like 255.192 for a Class A network, 255.255.192 for a Class B network, and 255.255.255. 192 for a Class C network. The 192 equals 11000000 in binary; therefore this extends the network portion two digits into the host ID portion of the address. This permits defining of two **subnets** within a single range of host addresses. The top and bottom values (0 and 3, in this case) are reserved to identify the subnetwork and to handle broadcasts, respectively.

Another form of addressing is increasingly used on the IP network, especially when individual networks don't need, or can't use, an entire Class B or Class C address. This technique is called Classless Interdomain Routing (CIDR), pronounced "cider." CIDR uses the same technique described in the preceding paragraph to let Internet service providers carve up their available addresses into more numerous subnetworks and make better use of the IP address space that's still available.

Each TCP/IP address must be unique on the Internet—and in fact, on any IP-based network. If two IP addresses are duplicated, neither machine with that address is able to access the network; therefore, managing IP addresses is very important. All the Class A addresses were handed out years ago, most Class Bs have been allocated, and Class C addresses are becoming scarce. (When you add together all possible networks allowed by all three address classes, you get the maximum number of individual networks on the Internet—2,113,604.) Given the vast number of networks on the Internet and the continuing growth in that arena, it is clear that subnet masking tricks and CIDR represent stopgap measures to extend the current address space as much as possible. At the same time, the standards body that governs the Internet (the IAB, or Internet Activities Board) is working to complete a new version of TCP/IP called IPv6 (the current version is IPv4), which extends the IP address space significantly. (The address space expands to 128 bits with IPv6, compared to the current 32 bits; this is enough to support trillions of networks with trillions of nodes per network.)

 All IP-based devices on a single network segment must use the same subnet mask.

Internet Control Message Protocol

Internet Control Message Protocol (ICMP) is used to send control messages (such as error messages, quality of service information, and confirmations) between IP hosts. PING is used to request a response from a remote host. It uses ICMP to return messages regarding this function, such as whether the response was received or timed out or whether the host was not reachable.

Address Resolution Protocol

The Address Resolution Protocol (ARP) is used to associate a logical (IP) address to a physical (MAC) address. When a system begins a conversation with a host for which it does not have a physical address, the system sends an ARP broadcast packet requesting a physical address that corresponds to the logical address. Given this information, the packet can be correctly sent across a physical network.

 Ethernet is the common form of network in use, and on most networks, the MAC address is identical to the Ethernet address. The Ethernet address takes the form of 00:00:00:00:00:00, or six hexadecimal digits separated by colons. In other words, on an Ethernet network, the physical (or MAC) address is the same as the Ethernet address burned into PROM on the network interface card that attaches a computer to a network. On other types of networks, the interfaces also supply unique MAC layer addresses, but their formats vary according to the kind of network in use.

Dynamic Host Configuration Protocol

Dynamic Host Configuration Protocol (DHCP) is used to automatically configure computers. A DHCP server manages a defined block of IP addresses that can be assigned to computers upon request. Client systems basically take out a lease on an address and can use that address only so long as the lease remains valid. The DHCP server handles granting, renewing, or canceling such leases. It can also block out reserved IP addresses within a numeric range, permitting certain computers that may not be able to communicate with the DCHP server to obtain static, fixed IP address assignments.

Using DHCP makes it easy for network administrators to manage IP addresses and makes it automatic for users to gain access to IP-based resources. DHCP has proven to be a real boon for those reasons, and one of the best features of Windows XP is that it can be configured for TCP/IP by selecting the Obtain an IP address automatically option button in the IP Protocol Properties dialog box.

Transmission Control Protocol

Transmission Control Protocol (TCP) is the primary Internet transport protocol. It accepts messages of any length and provides transportation to a TCP peer on a remote network host. TCP is connection oriented, so it provides more reliable delivery than connectionless IP. When a connection is established, a TCP port number is used to determine which process on the designated host is to receive any particular packet. TCP is responsible for message fragmentation and reassembly. It uses a sequencing function to ensure that packets are reassembled in the correct order and includes mechanisms both to acknowledge successful delivery of correct packets and to request retransmission of damaged or lost packets.

UDP

User Datagram Protocol (UDP) is a connectionless protocol. Due to its reduced overhead, it is generally faster, although less reliable, than TCP. UDP was designed primarily to transport purely local services, where it is relatively safe to assume network reliability. This is one reason it's used for distributed file systems like the Network File System (NFS) and for the Trivial File Transfer Protocol (TFTP), where the underlying assumption is that access is either purely local (NFS) or that guaranteed delivery is not required (TFTP).

FTP

File Transfer Protocol (FTP) provides file transfer services, as well as directory and file manipulation services, such as being able to list directory contents, delete files, and specify file formats.

 A command-line version of FTP is available as part of Windows XP. Type "help" or "?" to see the list of commands. To learn more about this command, open a DOS window, type ftp, and press Enter. This lists all the commands that can be used within FTP. Type quit and press Enter to exit the FTP utility.

Telnet

Telnet is a remote terminal emulation protocol that is primarily used to provide connectivity between dissimilar systems (PC and VAX/VMS, PC and router, and UNIX and VMS), where the remote client works on the Telnet host machine as if it were a terminal attached directly to that host. Using Telnet, remote equipment, such as routers and switches, can be monitored and configured or remote systems can be operated as needed. Despite a primitive, character-oriented interface, Telnet remains one of the most important IP services.

 A 32-bit windowed version of Telnet is available as part of Windows XP. To learn more about this utility, run Telnet from a command prompt or Run command and access its Help utility (type Help at the insertion point).

SMTP

Simple Mail Transfer Protocol (SMTP) is used to provide IP-based messaging services. Although it is not the only e-mail protocol available in the IP environment, most experts regard SMTP as the basis for Internet e-mail.

SNMP

Simple Network Management Protocol (SNMP) is a TCP/IP protocol used for network management. SNMP is an industry-standard protocol supported by most networking equipment manufacturers. SNMP can query collections of management data, called management information bases (MIBs), on networked devices. This permits management applications to use SNMP to poll devices on the network and obtain regular status updates about their operating conditions, network utilization, and quality of service.

In addition, SNMP supports a trap mechanism that permits networked devices to send a message to a management application when specific events or error conditions occur. This capability is quite important because it permits networked devices to report potential or actual problems as soon as they are detected, rather than waiting for a management application to poll the device.

 SNMP services are not activated by default on Windows XP. To enable these services, use the Optional Networking Components command from the Advanced menu of the Network Connections interface.

The Berkeley R Utilities

Among the many enhancements added to the UNIX TCP/IP implementation present in the Berkeley Software Distribution (BSD) in the 1980s was a collection of IP-based network commands collectively known as the "R utilities," where the R stands for remote. This includes such commands as **rsh (remote shell)**, which permits a user on one network host to access shell commands on another network host, and **rexec (remote execution)**, which permits a user on one network host to execute a program remotely across the network on another network host. Windows XP Professional supports both of these R utilities from the client side, but cannot act as an rsh or rexec server to other machines elsewhere on the network.

NOTE   To learn more about rsh and rexec, start a DOS window and enter either rsh ? or rexec ? at the command prompt to access the Help files for these command-line utilities.

route Command

The route command is used to view and manipulate the local IP routing tables. Full use of this utility is beyond the scope of this book and the 70-270 exam. However, there are some basic uses of the route command with which all network users should be familiar, as follows:

- The route print command is used to display all or part of the current routing table used by the local system.

- The route add command is used to define new routes in the routing table. If the -p parameter is employed with the ADD command, the route is made permanent across reboots. Otherwise the added route is dropped at the next system reboot.

- The route change command is used to alter an existing route.

- The route delete command is used to remove routes from the table.

The complete syntax for the route command is as follows:

```
route [-f] [-p] [Command [Destination] [mask Netmask] [Gateway]
[metric Metric]] [if Interface]
```

The following list contains information about the preceding syntax elements:

- –f—Clears out the local routing table. Those routes not removed by this command include all host routes, the loopback network route, and the multicast route. A host route is one with a netmask of 255.255.255.255. The loopback network route has a destination of 127.0.0.0 and a netmask of 255.0.0.0. The multicast route has a destination of 224.0.0.0 and a netmask of 240.0.0.0. If this command is used with other commands, the table is cleared prior to running the command.

- –p—Adds the specified route the Registry (KEY_LOCAL_ MACHINE\ SYSTEM\CurrentControlSet\Services\Tcpip\Parameters\PersistentRoutes) and initiates the IP routing table when used with the add command. It also lists the persistent routes when used with the print command.

- Command—Indicates the desired command to run. Table 7-2 lists valid commands.

Table 7-2 Valid commands for the route command action

Command	Purpose
add	Adds a route
change	Modifies an existing route
delete	Deletes a route or routes
print	Prints a route or routes

- *Destination*—Indicates the route's network destination. A destination can be an IP network address (where the host bits of the network address are set to 0), an IP address for a host route, or 0.0.0.0 for the default route.

- mask *Netmask*—Indicates the netmask or subnet mask for a network destination. Valid masks can be the appropriate subnet mask for an IP network address, 255.255.255.255 for a host route, or 0.0.0.0 for the default route. If a mask is not defined, 255.255.255.255 is used by default.

- *Gateway*—Defines the forwarding address over which specified addresses are reachable.

- metric *Metric*—Defines the cost metric (1 to 9999) for a specific route.

- if *Interface*—Indicates the interface index for the specific interface that must be used to reach a defined destination. Interface indexes can be defined in decimal or hexadecimal (preceded by 0x) values.

tracert command

The tracert (or trace route) command is used to determine the path employed by an ICMP (Internet Control Message Protocol) echo request message (that is, a PING packet). The tracert command displays a list of all encountered routers between the client and the target system along with time to live (TTL) field values.

You will find that tracert is a great tool to employ when attempting to discover at what point between two communication partners network latency is becoming a serious factor in prohibiting or delaying the transmission of network packets. The basic command structure to run a tracert scan is: tracert *TargetName*.

The complete syntax for the tracert command is as follows:

```
tracert [-d] [-h MaximumHops] [-j HostList] [-w Timeout]
[TargetName]
```

The following list contains information about the preceding syntax elements:

- –d—Disables the resolution of IP addresses of intermediary hops to their domain names.

- –h *MaximumHops*—Defines the maximum number of hops to a target before terminating the trace. The default is 30 hops.

- -j *HostList*—Configures the echo request messages to employ the loose source route option in the IP header with the set of intermediate destinations specified in the HostList. The HostList is a series of IP addresses (in dotted-decimal notation) separated by spaces.

- -w *Timeout*—Indicates the timeout period in milliseconds for the trace to wait for an echo response. The default is 4000.

- *TargetName*—Specifies the destination's IP address or host name

PING

Packet Internet Groper (PING) is one of the most colorful acronyms in the TCP/IP utility box. PING is a command-line utility that uses the ICMP protocol to inquire if a designated host is reachable on the network. It also provides information about the round-trip time required to deliver a message to that machine and to receive a reply.

PING is a very useful utility that permits you to see if your own machine is properly attached to the network. You can PING yourself by entering the command PING 127.0.0.1 or PING loopback; in the latter case, this special address is defined as the loopback address, which is the address of your own machine. You can find out if the network itself is working by pinging a nearby machine. Finally, you can determine if a particular machine is reachable by pinging either its host name or the equivalent numeric IP address. All of this capability comes in handy when installing and testing IP on a new machine or when you need to troubleshoot a network connection.

To learn more about PING, launch a DOS window and type ping (with no arguments) at the command prompt to access its online Help file. Note that PING can supply all kinds of routing and quality of service data, as well as simply test for reachability.

Activity 7-3: Testing TCP/IP Communications

Time Required: 5 minutes

Objective: Use the PING command to test the communication with a host address.

Description: The TCP/IP protocol suite has a few commands that can be used to verify your computer's ability to communicate with another host. The PING command sends a "request" to the host or address specified in the command and displays the time taken to respond to the request. In this activity, the PING command is used to verify if the user's computer can communicate with another computer on their mutual network.

To use PING to test TCP/IP communications:

This activity assumes you are connected to a TCP/IP network. You must know the IP address, host name, or FQDN of at least one system on your network (or the Internet if you also have Internet access).

1. Open a Command Prompt window by clicking **Start**, **All Programs**, **Accessories**, **Command Prompt**.

2. Type **PING** **<*IP address or name*>**, where <*IP address or name*> is the IP address of a system on your network, the name of a system on your network, or the domain name of a system on the Internet. Press **Enter**. You should see a statement similar to "Pinging 172.16.1.7 with 32 bytes of data:" followed by four lines listing whether a reply was received or a timeout occurred.

3. Type **exit** and then press **Enter**.

TFTP

Trivial File Transfer Protocol (TFTP) is a lightweight analog of FTP that uses UDP as its transport protocol rather than TCP. TFTP is a much more stripped-down version of file transfer services than FTP; all it basically supports is the ability to communicate with a TFTP server elsewhere on the network and to copy files from the workstation to a remote host, or vice versa. For directory navigation, file grooming, or format translations, FTP is a much better choice.

 To learn more about TFTP, start a DOS window, and enter TFTP ? at the command prompt to view its online Help file.

The HOSTS File

The **HOSTS** file is a static file placed on members of a network to provide a resolution mechanism between host names and IP addresses. The HOSTS file was the name resolution used before DNS was created. HOSTS files are used on small networks where the deployment of a DNS server is unwarranted or for remote systems to reduce traffic over slow WAN links. HOSTS files can also be employed to hard code important systems, such as mission-critical servers. Assigning a static IP address in this way prevents a DNS glitch from inhibiting access. Each line of a HOSTS file contains an IP address followed by one or more corresponding host names to that IP address. A system processes the HOSTS file on a line-by-line basis when attempting to resolve a host name. Once the first match is reached, the resolution process terminates and the acquired IP address is used. HOSTS files are only as useful as they are current. Most administrators update their HOSTS file on a regular basis and have a logon script automatically download the HOSTS file from a central location to remote systems each time they log onto the network.

Windows XP includes a sample HOSTS file in the *%systemroot%*\System32\drivers\etc folder. The HOSTS file is a plain text document that can be edited with Notepad or any other text editor. Basic information about editing the HOSTS file is included in its own header text, but for complete information, please consult the *Microsoft Windows XP Professional Resource Kit*, the *Microsoft Windows Server 2003 Resource Kit*, or a text on the TCP/IP protocol.

DNS

Domain Name System (DNS) is a critical component of the Internet's ability to span the globe. DNS handles the job of translating a symbolic name such as *lanw02.lanw.com* into a corresponding numeric IP address (172.16.1.7). It can also provide reverse lookup services to detect machines that are masquerading as other hosts. (A reverse lookup obtains the symbolic name that goes with an IP address; if the two do not match, some form of deception is at work.)

DNS is a powerful, highly distributed database that organizes IP names (which, for its purposes, must take the form of Fully Qualified Domain Names) into hierarchical domains. When a name resolution request occurs, all the DNS servers that can identify themselves to each other cooperate very quickly to resolve the related address. DNS servers include sophisticated caching techniques that permit them to store recently requested name-address pairs so that users can get to a previously accessed address quickly.

 Windows XP Professional can communicate with DNS servers, but only Windows Server 2003 supports a full-fledged DNS server implementation.

NOTE

The LMHOSTS File

The **LMHOSTS** file is a static file placed on members of a network to provide a resolution mechanism between NetBIOS names and IP addresses. The LMHOSTS file was the name resolution used before WINS was created. Now LMHOSTS files are used only on small networks where the deployment of a WINS server is unwarranted, or for remote systems to reduce traffic over slow WAN links.

Each line of an LMHOSTS file contains an IP address followed by the corresponding NetBIOS name. A system processes the LMHOSTS file on a line-by-line basis when attempting to resolve NetBIOS names. Once the first match is reached, the resolution process terminates and the acquired IP address is used. LMHOSTS files are only as useful as they are current. Thus, most administrators update their LMHOSTS file on a regular basis and have a logon script automatically download the LMHOSTS file from a central location to remote systems each time they log onto the network.

Windows XP includes a sample LMHOSTS file in the *%systemroot%*\System32\drivers\etc folder, which is named LMHOSTS.SAM. The LMHOSTS file is a plain text document that can be edited with Notepad or any other text editor. Basic information about editing the LMHOSTS file is included in its own header text, but for complete information, consult the *Microsoft Windows XP Professional Resource Kit* or the *Microsoft Windows Server 2003 Resource Kit*.

ACTIVITY

Activity 7-4: Name-to-address Resolution

Time Required: 10 minutes

Objective: View the contents of the LMHOSTS and HOSTS files to see how a NetBIOS or host name can be resolved to an IP address.

Description: Names are a friendlier means of referring to computers than numbers, especially for people who are not in a support role. To resolve a user-friendly name to its IP address, LMHOSTS and HOSTS files are used. In this activity, you view a sample of both of these files.

To view the HOSTS and LMHOSTS sample files:

1. Open Notepad by clicking **Start**, **All Programs**, **Accessories**, **Notepad**.

2. Select **File**, **Open**.

3. Use the Open dialog box to locate and select the **\WINDOWS\system32\drivers\etc** directory.

4. Change the Files of type to **All Files** by using the pull-down list.

5. You should see a list of files in this folder. Select **hosts**, and then click **Open**.

6. Scroll down through this file reading the information it provides. Do not make any changes to the file at this time.

7. Select **File**, **Open**. You should still be viewing the \etc directory.

8. Change the **Files of type** to **All Files** by using the pull-down list.

9. You should see a list of files in this folder. Select **LMHOSTS** or **LMHOSTS.SAM**, and then click **Open**.

10. Scroll down through this file reading the information it provides. Do not make any changes to the file at this time.

11. Select **File**, **Exit**.

WINS

Windows Internet Naming Service (WINS) is not a true native TCP/IP service; it is an extension added by Microsoft. As discussed, most of the internal and network communications within a Microsoft network employ NetBIOS; however, on a TCP/IP network, NetBIOS names must be resolved into IP addresses so that packets can be properly delivered to the intended recipient. This process is automated by the WINS service. WINS dynamically associates NetBIOS names with IP addresses and automatically updates its database of associations as systems enter and leave a network, so it does not require ongoing maintenance. WINS is the dynamic service that is used to replace the static mechanism of the LMHOSTS file.

IPCONFIG

IPCONFIG is used to manage and view information related to DHCP and DNS. When used alone without any parameters, IPCONFIG displays the IP address, subnet mask, and default gateway for all network interfaces on the local machine. The syntax and parameters of IPCONFIG are as follows:

```
ipconfig [/all] [/renew [Adapter]] [/release [Adapter]]
[/flushdns] [/displaydns] [/registerdns] [/showclassid
Adapter] [/setclassid Adapter [ClassID]]
```

- /all—Shows all TCP/IP configuration details for all network interfaces. An example of the display is shown in Figure 7-6.

Figure 7-6   The results of an ipconfig /all command

- /renew [*Adapter*]—Forces a renewal of the address lease with the DHCP server; without a specified *Adapter*, the renewal occurs on all DHCP configured network interfaces. The *Adapter* value should be replaced with a name listed when IPCONFIG is executed without parameters.

- /release [*Adapter*]—Releases the address lease with the DHCP server; without a specified *Adapter*, the release occurs on all DHCP configured network interfaces. The *Adapter* value should be replaced with a name listed when IPCONFIG is executed without parameters.

- /flushdns—Clears and resets the DNS client resolver cache. This parameter should be used to remove negative cache entries and dynamically added entries.

- /displaydns—Shows the content of the DNS client resolver cache. The cache includes preloaded entries from the HOSTS file and any resource records still in memory from resolved queries. The cache is used to attempt to resolve new queries locally before contacting a DNS server.

- /registerdns—Forces the system to register all local IP addresses and DNS names with DNS. This parameter should be used to replace a failed automatic DNS registration or resolve a dynamic update problem without needing to reboot. The data on the DNS tab of advanced TCP/IP settings determines the information sent to the DNS server for registration.

- /showclassid *Adapter*—Shows the DHCP class ID for the specified adapter. An asterisk can be used to show DHCP class IDs for all adapters. The *Adapter* value should be replaced with a name listed when IPCONFIG is executed without parameters.

- /setclassid *Adapter* [*ClassID*]—Sets the DHCP class ID for the specified adapter, if the *ClassID* parameter is provided. This parameter clears the DHCP class ID for the specified adapter, if the Class ID is not provided. An asterisk can be used to indicate all adapters. The *Adapter* value should be replaced with a name listed when IPCONFIG is executed without parameters.

Other TCP/IP Command-line Tools

There are a wide range of TCP/IP command-line tools used for network connectivity analysis and troubleshooting. These include NETSTAT and NBTSTAT. NETSTAT displays a list of active TCP connections. This list includes open ports, Ethernet statistics, the IP routing table, and IPv4/IPv6 statistics. The syntax and parameters of NETSTAT are as follows:

```
netstat [-a] [-e] [-n] [-o] [-p Protocol] [-r] [-s] [Interval]
```

- –a—Shows a list of active TCP connections and open TCP and UDP ports

- –e—Shows Ethernet statistics, such as sent and received bytes, unicast packets, nonunicast packets, discards, errors, and unknown protocols; this parameter can be used with –s.

- –n—Shows a list of active TCP connections using IP addresses and port numbers only; no human friendly names are given.

- –o—Shows a list of active TCP connections and shows the process ID (PID) for the active process using the connection. The PID can be used to cross-reference the actual process name on the Processes tab of the Task Manager. This parameter can be used with –a, –n, and –p.

- −p *Protocol*—Lists the connections for the specified *Protocol*. The value of *Protocol* can be *tcp*, *udp*, *tcpv6*, or *udpv6*. If this parameter is used with −s, the value of *Protocol* can be *tcp*, *udp*, *tcpv6*, *udpv6*, *icmp*, *ip*, *icmpv6*, or *ipv6*.

- −r—Shows the IP routing table. This parameter displays the same information as the route print command.

- −s—Lists statistics by protocol. By default, it only displays information for TCP, UDP, ICMP, and IP. If IPv6 is installed, then the displayed statistics are for the v6 version of these protocols. This parameter can be used with −p.

- *Interval*—Configures the system to redisplay the selected information every *Interval* seconds with updated information. CTRL+C terminates the repeated display of data. If this parameter is not used, NETSTAT displays the requested information only once.

The nbtstat command displays protocol statistics for NetBIOS over TCP/IP (NetBT), NetBIOS name tables, and the NetBIOS name cache. nbtstat can also be used to force a refresh of the NetBIOS name cache and names registered with WINS. The syntax and parameters of nbtstat are as follows (note that the parameters of nbtstat are case sensitive):

```
nbtstat [-a RemoteName]  [-A IPAddress]  [-c]  [-n]  [-r]  [-R] [-RR]
[-s]  [-S]  [Interval]
```

- −a *RemoteName*—Shows the NetBIOS name table on a remote computer indicated by the NetBIOS computer name *RemoteName*.

- −A *IPAddress*—Shows the NetBIOS name table on a remote computer indicated by the *IPAddress*.

- −c—Shows the contents of the NetBIOS name cache table of the local system and related IP addresses.

- −n—Shows the NetBIOS name table of the local system.

- −r—Shows NetBIOS names resolution and registration statistics. See Figure 7-7.

- −R—Clears the NetBIOS name cache and rebuilds it by loading the #PRE entries from the LMHOSTS file.

- −RR—Clears and refreshes the NetBIOS names for the local system that are registered with WINS.

- −s—Shows information about NetBIOS connections, such as client and server sessions. Remote hosts are resolved into NetBIOS names when possible.

- −S—Shows information about NetBIOS connections, such as client and server sessions. Remote hosts are displayed only as IP addresses.

- *Interval*—Configures the system to redisplay the selected information every *Interval* seconds with updated information. CTRL+C terminates the repeated display of data. If this parameter is not used, nbtstat displays the requested information only once.

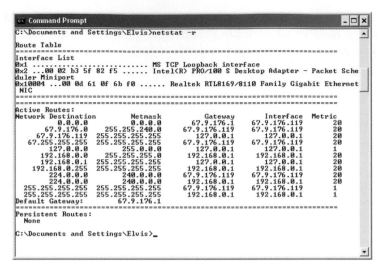

Figure 7-7   The results of a netstat -r command

TCP/IP Configuration

TCP/IP configuration is performed through the Network Connections tool. When configuring TCP/IP for Windows XP Professional, there are many items of information that you need. If the machine uses DHCP, the DHCP server handles all these details. If not, here's a list of items that you might need to obtain from a network administrator (or figure out for yourself, if that's your job):

- A unique IP address for the computer

- The subnet mask for the network to which the computer belongs

- The address of the default gateway, the machine that attempts to forward any IP traffic not aimed at the local subnet (which makes it the gateway to other networks)

- The address of one or more DNS servers, to provide IP name resolution services. This is more important on bigger networks than on smaller ones. If you use an ISP for network access, you probably need to get this address from them.

- On Windows-based networks in particular, you might need to provide an address for a WINS server, which permits NetBIOS name resolution requests to be transported across IP networks (even through routers, if necessary).

When TCP/IP is installed, its default settings are to seek out a DHCP server to provide all configuration settings. If a DHCP server is already present on your network, you do not need to configure TCP/IP to be able to access the network. When an interface is configured to use DHCP, an additional tab, called Alternate Configuration, is revealed. This tab is used to define a set of TCP/IP configurations that can be used in the event that DHCP communication fails. If an alternate configuration isn't manually defined, Windows XP automatically assigns a configuration through APIPA (Automatic Private IP Addressing). This automatic configuration will have an IP address within the range of 169.254.0.1 through 169.254.255.254 and a subnet mask of 255.255.0.0. If you have a NIC that should be assigned its IP configuration by DHCP but it is assigned an APIPA range IP, then you should issue the command IPCONFIG /RENEW to attempt to recommunicate with the DHCP server and obtain the correct configuration.

TCP/IP configuration takes place in the Internet Protocol (TCP/IP) Properties dialog box. (Refer back to Figure 7-4.) You can access the dialog box by clicking the Properties button after selecting TCP/IP from the list of installed components from the Properties dialog box of a Local Area Connection from the Network Connections interface. On a multihomed system (a computer with more than one network interface card), the configuration for each adapter can be different. Be sure to select the correct Local Area Connection object for the adapter you want to modify.

There are two ways to assign an IP address to a computer: manually or through DHCP. As discussed earlier, DHCP is used to automatically configure the TCP/IP settings for a computer. If a DHCP server is available and will be used to configure this computer, select the Obtain an IP address automatically option. If there is no DHCP server available or if the configuration is to be handled manually, select the Use the following IP address option.

Before you can do this, you must obtain a valid IP address from a network administrator or your ISP. If your network does not need to access the Internet directly (or address translation software mediates Internet access on your behalf), you can assign private IP addresses from a number of reserved address ranges that the InterNIC has set aside for this purpose. To learn more about these private address ranges and how to use them, download a copy of RFC 1918 at *www.cis.ohio-state.edu/cs/Services/rfc/rfc-text/rfc1918.txt*.

If you select Use the following IP address, the remaining three boxes become active. When you are finished, the IP Address box should display the correct IP address for that computer.

 If you are entering an IP address into an entry box, press the period key to jump from one octet to the next. This comes in handy when an address does not contain a three-digit number in any octet field. You can also use the right arrow key to advance the insertion point, but do not use the Tab key—it advances the insertion point to the next input field and forces you to backtrack to complete the IP address specification.

As described earlier, the subnet mask defines which part of the IP address represents the network and which part represents the host. You must supply this information or your computer cannot communicate using TCP/IP.

The default gateway for a computer specifies the host, usually a router, to which the computer should send data that is not destined for the computer's subnet. For example, if a computer's address is 156.24.99.10 with a subnet mask of 255.255.255.0, its host address is 10 and its network address is 156.24.99. If this computer had data to send to a computer whose address was 203.15.13.69, it sends the packets to the default gateway for forwarding to the appropriate network. Whenever connectivity to other networks is required, you must provide an IP address for the default gateway on the machine's network segment. If you don't, traffic from your machine cannot get to machines that are not on the same network segment as your computer.

Clicking the Advanced button opens the window shown in Figure 7-8. The IP Addresses section allows you to assign multiple addresses to one network adapter, whereas the Gateways section provides support for multiple router configurations.

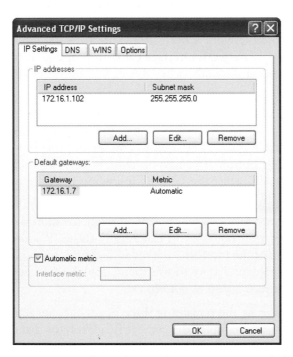

Figure 7-8   The Advanced TCP/IP Settings dialog box, IP Settings tab

By selecting the DNS tab, shown in Figure 7-9, the user is able to configure DNS on his or her computer. Multiple DNS servers can be defined along with setting their use priority. You can also define how incomplete domain names or host names are resolved (e.g., by adding suffixes to create a Fully Qualified Domain Name).

Use the WINS tab (see Figure 7-10) to configure WINS settings. You can define multiple WINS servers and set their use priority. You can also enable or disable the use of an LMHOSTS file. Furthermore, you can enable, disable, or save the setting to the DHCP server regardless of whether this system will use NetBIOS over TCP/IP.

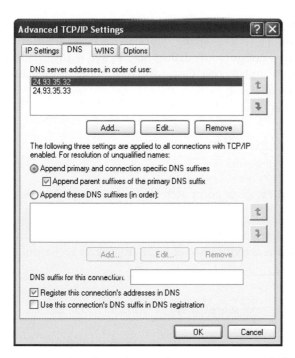

Figure 7-9 The Advanced TCP/IP Settings dialog box, DNS tab

7

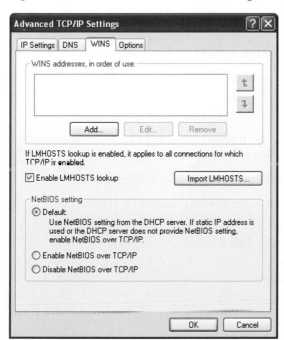

Figure 7-10 The Advanced TCP/IP Settings dialog box, WINS tab

The Options tab lists optional TCP/IP-related services or capabilities. The two default optional items are IP Security and TCP/IP filtering. Selecting a listed item and clicking Properties reveals a service-specific configuration dialog box. IPSec is briefly discussed in Chapter 6, "Windows XP Security and Access Controls." For more information about configuring these and other optional items, consult the *Microsoft Windows XP Professional Resource Kit* or the *Microsoft Windows Server 2003 Resource Kit*.

Activity 7-5: TCP/IP Configuration

ACTIVITY

Time Required: 20 minutes

Objective: Configure the IP address of a computer from the Local Area Connection properties dialog box.

Description: It is important to understand how the address of a computer is configured and how it affects communication. In this activity, you set your IP address to be unique.

To configure TCP/IP:

The IP address of 172.16.1.1 and subnet mask of 255.255.255.0 can be replaced by your own assigned values.

NOTE

1. Open Network Connections by clicking **Start**, **Control Panel**, **Network Connections**.

2. Select the **Local Area Connection** object.

3. Select **File**, **Properties**. This reveals the Properties dialog box for the selected Local Area Connection object.

4. Select the **Internet Protocol (TCP/IP)** in the list of components.

5. Click **Properties**. This reveals the Internet Protocol (TCP/IP) Properties dialog box.

6. Select the **Use the following IP address** option button.

7. Type the IP address of **172.16.1.x** (your instructor can provide you with unique addresses).

8. Type the subnet mask of **255.255.255.0**.

9. Click **OK**.

10. Click **Close**.

11. Click the **File** menu, and then click **Close**. Restart the system for the changes to take effect.

IPv6: Looking to the Future

Researchers have endeavored to update and improve TCP/IP. Of primary importance is the number of available addresses. When TCP/IP was developed using a 32-bit address space, nobody conceived that there could ever be an address shortage. It seemed that over four billion addresses would be enough. This proved to be wrong. IPv6 aims to correct the address shortage and improve other aspects of TCP/IP, including security and efficiency. IPv6 uses a 128-bit address space, which results in over $3.4210^{\wedge}38$ (340,000,000,000,000, 000,000,000,000,000,000,000) addresses.

Microsoft has included preliminary support for IPv6 in Windows XP. This support includes socket extensions and updated RPC systems to handle the 128-bit addresses. Microsoft also included a Developers Edition of the IPv6 protocol, which should be used only for research and testing purposes. Once IPv6 has been finalized, Microsoft will most likely include an IPv6 upgrade in a service pack or other downloadable installation module.

For more information about IPv6, consult the Help and Support Center on the Microsoft Web site. At the time of this writing there were at least three useful resources: *www.ipv6.org*, *www.microsoft.com/windows2000/techinfo/howitworks/communications/nameadrmgmt/introipv6.asp*, and *http://msdn.microsoft.com/downloads/sdks/platform/tpipv6.asp*. However, if these documents are moved, you can always perform a search using IPv6 as the keyword.

Windows XP Remote Tools

Microsoft has aimed to improve remote access to client systems over networks and the Internet. This is evident in two new features: Remote Assistance and Remote Desktop. Remote Assistance allows a distant user to view your desktop and even have control over the mouse and keyboard activities. Remote Desktop enables you to access your client's logon environment from a remote system.

Both of these remote tools are enabled on the Remote tab of the System applet. Once Remote Assistance is enabled, you can also set whether this system can be fully controlled remotely and the maximum lifetime of invitations. Once Remote Desktop is enabled, you can define which users can establish a remote connection.

Remote Assistance

Remote Assistance was designed to simplify the task of training users or walking users through tasks. An administrator or trainer can remotely show the end user the steps required to perform some function right on the user's system. Remote Assistance even supports real-time, two-way chat (text or voice) between the end user and the remote assistant.

To simplify the discussion of this feature, label the end user who needs assistance as the "student" and the person who remotely provides help the "teacher." When a student wants help through Remote Assistance, he or she must send an invitation to the teacher from whom they need help. This is done using Windows Messenger or by e-mailing an invitation script to the teacher. If Windows Messenger is employed, then the student needs either a Net Passport when connected to the Internet or an Exchange account if he or she is not connected to the Internet. It is even possible to save the invitation to a file (named rcBuddy.MsRcIncident) and use some other means to send it to the teacher.

To initiate a Remote Assistance invitation, use the Invite a friend to connect to your computer with Remote Assistance link from within Help and Support. Remote Assistance invitations have an expiration time limit, which you define when sending the invitation. Invitations also can have a password associated with them to prevent unwanted persons from using the invitation to gain access to your system.

Once connected, both participants can chat, exchange files, or disconnect the session. The teacher can take full control of the student's system to demonstrate an activity or perform some action. Remote Assistance is an excellent tool for training and troubleshooting.

Both systems used by the participants must be Windows XP or newer with either Windows Messenger Service or a MAPI-compliant e-mail utility (such as Microsoft Outlook or Outlook Express). Both systems must be able to communicate with each other over a network connection and have Internet access. The faster the connectivity between the two systems, the more responsive is the control. Remote Assistance can be used to link two systems on the same LAN or two systems anywhere in the world over the Internet.

In most cases, Remote Assistance is used by a nonexpert on a network client to request help from an expert. However, by enabling the Remote Assistance - Offer Remote Assistance policy in the domain, site, or OU group policy, an expert user can initiate a Remote Assistance session with a nonexpert user.

Remote Assistance and Remote Desktop both employ the Remote Desktop Protocol (RDP). RDP uses TCP port 3389 for establishing the communication session between the user requesting help and the support personnel providing it. For Windows XP remote capabilities to function across a secured network perimeter, TCP port 3389 must be opened on any firewall, router, or other port-filtering device. On the Internet Connection Firewall, this port is opened by enabling the Remote Desktop service.

For more information on Remote Assistance, see the Help and Support Center, the *Microsoft Windows XP Professional Resource Kit*, or the *Microsoft Windows Server 2003 Resource Kit*.

Activity 7-6: Requesting Remote Assistance

Time Required: 25 minutes

Objective: Use the Windows XP Remote Assistance utility to request remote assistance on your computer.

Description: Many third-party utilities have been developed over the years that allow one person to take remote control over another computer. Microsoft has finally included such a utility in a desktop OS. In this activity, you use the utility to send a request to another user.

To send an invitation for Remote Assistance:

 This activity requires that the system have Outlook Express or other e-mail system configured. This project also requires that each student have an e-mail address (Hotmail, etc.) and that students work in pairs. Remote Assistance should be enabled in Systems Properties on both the "student" and "teacher" machines.

1. Click **Start**, **Help and Support**. The Help and Support Center appears.

2. Click **Invite a friend to connect to your computer with Remote Assistance**. The Remote Assistance Help page appears.

3. Click **Invite someone to help you**. The "Pick how you want to contact your assistant page" appears.

4. In the Type an e-mail address text box, enter the e-mail address of your partner.

5. Click **Invite this person**. The E-mail an invitation page is displayed.

6. In the From field, type the name to appear on the invitation.

7. In the Message field, type a message to the invitee, such as **Please help me**.

8. Click **Continue**.

9. Define the expiration time limit for this invitation, such as 30 minutes.

10. Be sure the **Require the recipient to use a password** check box is checked.

11. Provide a password and confirm the password. Be sure to remember this password and to provide it to the teacher. It is not wise to include the password in the e-mail message.

12. Click **Send Invitation**.

13. A confirmation box may appear asking whether you want to send the message. Click **Send** or **Yes**.

14. The Help and Support Center returns you to the Remote Assistance page. Click **View invitation status**. A listing of the invitation you sent appears.

15. Click the option button beside your invitation, and then click **Details**.

16. A dialog box with complete details about the invitation appears. Click **Close**.

 Do not use any of these options now, but for informational purposes, you should know that the Expire button instantly expires the invitation, the Resend button initiates resending the invitation, and the Delete button removes the invitation.

17. Close the Help and Support Center.

You may have to send the message manually from within Outlook.

Activity 7-7: Providing Remote Assistance

Time Required: 20 minutes

Objective: Respond and take control of a person's computer using the Remote Assistance utility.

Description: By responding to the request for Remote Assistance sent in the previous activity you send a prompt to the requestor to verify whether he or she wants you to take control. In this activity, your partner responds and takes remote control of the computer.

To respond to an invitation for Remote Assistance:

This activity requires that you work from another Windows XP system, that you have received the invitation from Activity 7-6, network connectivity between the first computer (the requestor) and the second computer (the remote controller), and that both computer systems have Internet access.

1. Open the e-mail client on your partner's computer.

2. Locate the e-mail request for Remote Assistance you sent in the previous activity.

3. Open the attachment to initiate Remote Assistance.

The messages and attachments from Remote Assistance are easy to impersonate, so be sure that the attachment you open is a valid Remote Assistance utility and not a malicious hacker tool.

4. The Remote Assistance tool prompts you for the password. Enter the password you created in the previous exercise.

5. Click **Yes**.

6. On your computer, a shortcut dialog box appears asking if you want to allow the partner to connect. Click **Yes**.

7. The Remote Assistance control bar appears on your computer. The Remote Assistance desktop access window and control utility appear on your partner's computer.

8. From either system, type a short message in the Message Entry section, such as **What may I assist you with?**, and then click **Send**.

9. On your partner's computer, click **Take Control** from the top toolbar.

10. On your computer, click **Yes** when prompted whether to grant control of the computer.

11. On your partner's computer, click **OK** when informed you have taken control.

12. On your partner's computer, open and close Windows Explorer. Ensure that you choose the **Start** button on your partner's computer to start Windows Explorer. Notice that the movements made on your partner's computer actually take effect on your computer.

13. On your partner's computer, click **Disconnect** from the top toolbar.

14. On both computers, click **OK** when informed that Remote Assistance has been disconnected.

15. On both computers, close the Remote Assistance interface.

 If time permits, repeat Activities 7-6 and 7-7 with the partners reversing their roles.

Remote Desktop

Remote Desktop is similar to a single client version of Terminal Services. Remote Desktop was developed so that workers can access their work desktops (a.k.a. host clients) from their home systems (a.k.a. remote systems). Through Remote Desktop, you have the same access to your files and applications as you do when you are physically sitting at the system.

Remote Desktop is enabled through a component of IIS, namely Remote Desktop Web Connection. This component need only be installed on the IIS server on the same network as the client, not necessarily on the client itself. Once properly configured, you need to switch to another user or log off the host client. Then, from the remote system, open http://<*servername*>/tsweb/ in Internet Explorer, where <*servername*> is the IIS server, and then provide the IP address or name of the host client. Once connected, you have full control over the host client, just as if you were seated at its keyboard.

A second method to support Remote Desktop connections does not directly involve IIS. The Remote Desktop Connection utility can be installed on a Windows 9*x*, NT, 2000, or 2003 system directly from the Windows XP distribution CD. The Remote Desktop Connection allows a link between a remote system and the client without the need of IIS.

For more information on Remote Desktop, see the Help and Support Center, the *Microsoft Windows XP Professional Resource Kit*, or the *Microsoft Windows Server 2003 Resource Kit*.

WINDOWS XP AND NETWARE NETWORKS

Novell NetWare is designed for file and printer sharing on a network. Because it was one of the first true network operating systems, NetWare garnered a substantial and loyal following throughout the late 1980s and early 1990s. By the mid-1990s, NetWare servers functioned as the backbone for more networks than any other type of server on the market. With the growth of PC capabilities and the advent of the Internet, NetWare has adapted and expanded to provide robust services, while maintaining its solid file and printer sharing performance.

Although servers running Windows NT, Windows 2000, Windows Server 2003, or other versions of Windows account for a growing number of network servers, a large number of companies around the world rely on Novell NetWare for their server requirements. For this reason, Microsoft includes interconnectivity enhancements to allow Windows XP-based computers to connect to and function with NetWare servers. These enhancements include NWLink, Client Service for NetWare, File and Print Services for NetWare, and Gateway Services for NetWare. Of these, only NWLink and Client Service for NetWare are used by Windows XP Professional systems. File and Print Services for NetWare and Gateway Services for NetWare are used by Windows server computers, not on end-user workstation computers.

Beginning with version 1.0, NetWare utilized a datastore called the **bindery**, a proprietary database that contains network resource information, such as user and group names, print server settings, and file server configurations. With NetWare 4.0, Novell introduced **Novell Directory Services (NDS)**. NDS is a hierarchical database used by NetWare 4.0 and newer servers to store network resource and object data, comparable in function to Active Directory in Windows 2000 Server and Windows Server 2003. With this introduction, Novell began the era of object-oriented directory services. In this context, a directory is a dynamic database that contains information for network objects such as printers, applications, and groups. Later sections of this chapter discuss the differences between connecting to bindery (pre-version 4.0) servers and NDS servers.

Because the Professional edition of Windows XP is designed to operate as a network client, it includes features that enable it to connect to a variety of network servers, including NetWare servers. Because both bindery and NDS servers remain in use today, Windows XP is able to connect to both types. Once connected, the Windows XP Professional computer utilizes resources on the NetWare server as if it were actually on a Windows server. In this way, all network resources are accessed using the same methods, thereby making a heterogeneous network appear seamless to its users.

NetWare Compatibility Components

There are two main components that facilitate Windows XP Professional compatibility with NetWare servers: NWLink and Client Service for NetWare. The next sections discuss installing and configuring these components.

NWLink

NWLink is Microsoft's implementation of the IPX/SPX protocol suite and can communicate with all NetWare implementations. Novell and Microsoft approach networking in different ways, meaning that the underlying architecture of each company's network access differs. Novell's specification is called the Open Datalink Interface (ODI). Microsoft's architecture is called the Network Device Interface Specification (NDIS). Strictly speaking, IPX/SPX is ODI-compliant, but not NDIS-compliant. NWLink is the NDIS-compliant implementation of IPX/SPX.

IPX (Internetwork Packet Exchange) is a connectionless protocol that provides quick network transport for most communications on a NetWare network. Because it is connectionless, IPX does not guarantee packet delivery, but it is generally sufficient for network communications. **SPX (Sequenced Packet Exchange)** is a connection-oriented protocol that provides guaranteed packet delivery. However, because it is connection-oriented, it requires higher overhead and is slower than IPX. For this reason, SPX is used in NetWare communications for only certain applications, such as those that manage the server's console.

Installing NWLink

Like all networking components in Windows XP, NWLink is installed through a connection object within Network Connections. From the Connect To item in the Start menu, select the Show all connections entry in the pull-out menu. Then, you can either right-click the connection to which you want to add NWLink and select the Properties entry from the shortcut menu, or double-click that connection and click the Properties button to produce the same window. Either way, you use the Install button to add the NWLink protocol. The Local Area Connection Properties window, shown earlier in Figure 7-3, shows information about the LAN connection on a test machine; note the Install button on the lower-left of the connection items pane.

The Connection Properties window is where you add networking components to Windows XP. If the Typical installation option is selected during the installation process, Client for Microsoft Networks, File and Printer Sharing for Microsoft Networks, the QoS (Quality of Service) Packet Scheduler, and Internet Protocol (TCP/IP) are loaded by default.

To connect to an older NetWare network, the NWLink protocol must be loaded (newer versions of NetWare—5.x or newer—use TCP/IP by default, and probably won't need this protocol). To add a new networking component to the Local Area Connection, click the Install button. You are presented with the Select Network Component Type dialog box, which allows you to install a client, service, or protocol.

Configuring NWLink: Ethernet Frame Types and IPX Network Numbers

After installation is complete, NWLink has three configuration options available: Internal Network Number, Ethernet frame types, and network numbers.

Ethernet can utilize four frame types supported by NWLink, as described in the following list. Note that a packet's frame type defines the structure of the packet and the fields that are included.

- *Ethernet 802.3*—Ethernet 802.3, also known as raw 802.3, is a Novell proprietary Ethernet frame format that Novell implemented prior to the completion of the 802.3 committee's frame format definition efforts. It served as the initial Ethernet frame scheme that Novell used, but seldom appears on networks today. It includes an Institute of Electrical and Electronic Engineers (IEEE) 802.3 Length field but not an IEEE 802.2 (LLC) header. The IPX header immediately follows the 802.3 Length field.

- *Ethernet 802.2*—802.2 is the standard IEEE 802.3 frame format, which includes the IEEE 802.2 (LLC) header.

- *Ethernet II*—Ethernet Version 2 includes the standard Ethernet Version 2 header, which consists of Destination and Source Address fields followed by an EtherType field.

- *Ethernet SNAP*—SNAP extends the IEEE 802.2 header by providing a type code similar to that defined in the Ethernet Version 2 specification.

 It is very important for all computers communicating on the network to use the same frame type to ensure that communication takes place. If frame types do not match, communication is not possible.

By default, Windows XP determines the frame type in use on the network and configures itself accordingly. It does this by accepting the first NWLink packet it receives and using the same frame type. If all computers on the network are set to use autodetection, the Ethernet 802.2 frame type is used because it is the accepted industry standard for NWLink.

Unless there is a specific reason to use some different frame type, it's best to let Windows XP detect the frame type in use on the network. By doing so, potential problems caused by frame type mismatches are eliminated. However, if it is necessary to specify a frame type for the connection, select the appropriate frame from the Frame type drop-down list in the NWLink IPX/SPX/NetBIOS Compatible Transport Protocol Properties dialog box. When a frame type other than Auto Detect is selected, you must specify an IPX **network number** (the network identifier) that the frame type uses (if you don't know this information, you need to get it from your network administrator).

Like TCP/IP, NWLink (IPX) makes a distinction between the computer ID and the network ID on which the connection resides. However, unlike TCP/IP, the computer ID and network ID, or network number, are separate fields in IPX. When the computer is configured to detect the frame type used on the network automatically, it is also able to determine the network number from the frames it receives. However, when a specific frame type is selected, you must also specify the network number to which the computer is attached. If the network number does not match the network number used by other computers on the network, your system will not be able to communicate.

Network numbers on IPX networks are not limited to numerals. Because the IPv4 and IPX addresses are both 32-bits long, IPX administrators can convert IP addresses to hexadecimal notation and use corresponding IP and IPX addresses for the same cable segments. For example, the Class C IP address 192.168.1.0 converts to C0A80100, 192.168.2.0 converts to C0A80200, and so on for the various logical networks that might occur on a corporate LAN.

Part of the design of IPX utilizes a network number assigned to the internal operations of the computer. Under most circumstances, it is not necessary to change this number. However, if the network number that is assigned to the internal network number is in use elsewhere on the network as a normal network number, communication will be sporadic and difficult to troubleshoot.

Activity 7-8: Installing the NetWare Protocol

Time Required: 20 minutes

Objective: Install NWLink, the NetWare-compatible protocol.

Description: Although Microsoft operating systems have seemed to be dominant in the industry for a few years now, there is still a large installed base of Novell networks. To allow communication between Microsoft computers and Novell computers, a similar protocol needs to be used. In this activity, you install and configure the NWLink protocol.

To install NWLink:

1. If you have not already done so, log on to your Windows XP Professional computer as **Administrator**.

2. Click **Start**, right-click **My Network Places**, and then select **Properties**.

3. Right-click **Local Area Connection**, and then select **Properties**.

4. In the Local Area Connection Properties dialog box, click **Install**.

5. Select **Protocol** from the list of available components, and then click **Add**.

6. Select **NWLink IPX/SPX/NetBIOS Compatible Transport Protocol** from the list.

7. Click **OK** to complete the installation. Note that you do not need to restart the computer for this addition to take effect.

8. Click **Close** on the Local Area Connection Properties dialog box.

9. Right-click again on the **Local Area Connection** icon and select **Properties** to configure NWLink. Note that NWLink NetBIOS has been added to the installed components list.

10. Select **NWLink IPX/SPX/NetBIOS Compatible Transport Protocol** from the list, and then click **Properties**.

11. Enter an internal network number for the computer. Use any combination of up to six numbers and the letters A-F. For example, you might use 1FAD or 1999A.

12. Click the down arrow for the **Frame type** drop-down list and select a frame type. If you are in a classroom environment, select the frame type specified by the instructor.

13. Note that you must specify the Network number for the selected frame. Enter a network number in the space provided. If you are in a classroom environment, enter the network number specified by the instructor.

14. Click **OK** and then Close. Note that the changes take effect immediately. If you are in a classroom environment, ensure that communications are available to computers with the same frame type and network number.

15. Close the Network Connections window.

Client Service for NetWare

The Client Service for NetWare (CSNW) component of Windows XP Professional allows a Windows XP computer to access resources on NetWare servers version 2.*x*, 3.*x*, and 4.*x*. CSNW supports full access to NetWare file and print servers, NetWare utilities, bindery connections, and some NDS connections.

NOTE The version of CSNW that is included with Windows XP Professional is not compatible with all features of the NetWare 6.*x* version of NDS. CSNW allows authentication to NetWare 5.0 NDS-enabled servers, but for full functionality, load the 32-bit Windows client software provided with NetWare.

File and Print Servers

To provide access to NetWare file and print servers, CSNW adds a NetWare-focused redirector that acts as an extension of the file system, in much the same way that the native redirector supports access to Microsoft Windows Servers. (Redirectors handle transmission of remote requests across the network so that the requests are filled.) The difference is that CSNW implements **NetWare Core Protocol (NCP)** requests for file and print services, whereas the native redirector uses the **Common Internet File System (CIFS)**, an enhanced version of the Server Message Block (SMB) protocol. Both NCP and SMB perform the same functions, but provide access to different file systems.

Once CSNW is installed, a Windows XP user can use a single logon to access all resources on the network, regardless of the server hosting the resources. In a NetWare-only environment, only CSNW is active and it provides access to resources. However, in a mixed

NetWare/Windows server environment, the appropriate client software is used, depending on the type of server being accessed. (Installation of CSNW is covered in a later section; complete steps are given in Activity 7-9.)

Supported NetWare Utilities

To ensure proper desktop integration in a NetWare server environment, CSNW supports most NetWare utilities and functions. It provides access to character-based NetWare administration utilities, such as SYSCON and PCONSOLE. Many of the utilities are dependent on the versions of NetWare in use. Versions 3.12 and lower support only character-based applications, whereas versions 4.0 and above utilize mainly GUI-based applications. However, even in NetWare 6, certain character-based utilities can be used to manage the server environment.

 By default, NetWare versions before 5.0 do not support long filenames. To ensure that long Windows filenames are not truncated when they are copied to NetWare servers, those servers must load the OS/2 name space. This is done on the NetWare server itself and ensures that all files retain their settings when stored on the server.

NWLink and CSNW also support IPX burst mode, which enhances bulk data transfer over an IPX network. By design, IPX is best suited to handle small to medium-sized packets and numerous network communications. When tasked with transferring large amounts of data, IPX loses efficiency and creates excessive network traffic. Burst mode allows routed network connections to negotiate the largest possible packet size so that fewer packets are sent to transmit large data files. This improves bandwidth utilization and reduces network overhead.

Bindery and NDS Support

To effectively ensure that client computers can attach to any server on the network, Client Service for NetWare includes support for both bindery and NDS servers. As mentioned, versions of NetWare prior to 4.0 used the bindery to store their configuration information, including user and group lists, printers, and security settings. When users log on to a bindery-based NetWare server, they access the bindery for logon authentication, confirmation of security authorizations, group memberships, and so forth. One of the primary limitations of bindery-based NetWare is that each server on the network has its own bindery. Users that access resources on multiple servers are required to logon to each server individually.

NetWare 4.0 uses a Novell Directory Services (NDS) database to store and maintain information that was previously stored in the bindery. The NDS database is much more dynamic and supports enterprise-wide networks. The NDS database is a hierarchical tree stored on many servers on the network that provides single-logon access to resources. In addition, centralized administration and resource management is possible with NDS—a real improvement over earlier versions of NetWare.

Because NDS is a hierarchical database that can be stored on multiple servers on the network, an NDS implementation resembles a tree and is referred to as the **NDS tree**. At the base of the tree is the Root object, which generally represents the largest organization connected to the network, often the entire corporation. Working down through the tree, each department may have a container, and then each group within the department can have another container. In NDS, each network resource, which can be a user, group, file server, printer, or storage area, is represented as an object. Objects are stored in containers representing their function on the network. A network object's location in the NDS tree is called its **context**. Figure 7-11 is an example of an NDS tree.

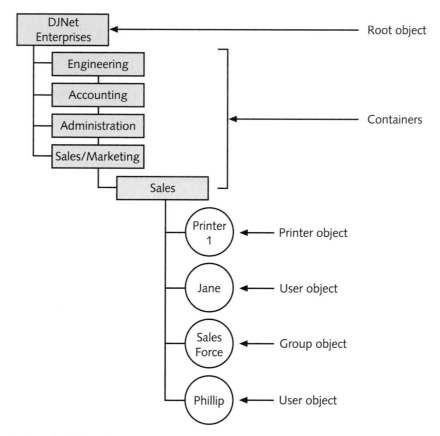

Figure 7-11   Illustration of an NDS tree structure

In Figure 7-11, the Phillip user object resides in the Sales container, which in turn resides in the Sales/Marketing container, which resides under the DJNet Enterprises Root object. The context for the Phillip user is DJNet Enterprises.Sales/Marketing.Sales.

Installing and Configuring Client Service for NetWare

Like NWLink, installation of Client Service for NetWare occurs in the Local Area Connection Properties dialog box. Once in that window for the appropriate connection object, click Install; you are asked whether to install a Client, Service, or Protocol. As its name implies, Client Service for NetWare is a client component. Select Client and click Add. If the default configuration is installed, the only client available for installation is CSNW. Ensure that Client Service for NetWare is selected and click OK to continue the installation. Once installation is complete, you are asked to restart your computer. You must do so before CSNW can be used. Click Yes to restart your computer.

Client Service for NetWare relies on NWLink to operate. If NWLink is not loaded when CSNW is installed, it is installed automatically.

Assigning a Default Tree and Context Using CSNW

After the computer has restarted, you are presented with the Select NetWare Logon dialog box. It is through this dialog box that you assign a default NetWare tree and context on the NDS-enabled NetWare network to which the Windows XP Professional computer will connect. Unlike most areas of Windows XP, you cannot browse for tree and context data. You must have this information available to type into the dialog box. If this information is not available the first time the computer is restarted, you can click Cancel and enter the information later.

Unlike many networking components, CSNW is not configured through the Local Area Connection Properties dialog box. When CSNW is installed, a separate utility, represented by the CSNW icon, is placed in Control Panel. If at any point you need to change the default tree and context settings, or any CSNW settings, double-click the CSNW icon to access the Client Service for NetWare configuration dialog box. When accessed by this method, additional configuration options are available, as discussed in later sections of this chapter.

The CSNW applet appears in Control Panel only in Classic view; it is not available in Category view.

Preferred Server Versus Directory Tree

Should you need to connect a Windows XP Professional computer to a bindery-based NetWare server, you must use the Preferred Server configuration options available in the Client Service for NetWare applet (see Figure 7-12). Unlike the Default Tree and Context settings where you must type the tree and context manually, clicking the down arrow next to the Preferred Server box displays a list of all servers that advertise themselves on your network. From that list, select the name of the NetWare server to which you want to attach. You can also enter the server's name in the Preferred Server box directly. If making a manual entry, be sure the server's name is spelled correctly. If an incorrect server name is entered, the dialog box shown in Figure 7-13 appears, informing you that you could not be authenticated on the selected server because the network path could not be found. Clicking No returns you to the Select NetWare Logon dialog box, whereas clicking Yes accepts the configuration anyway.

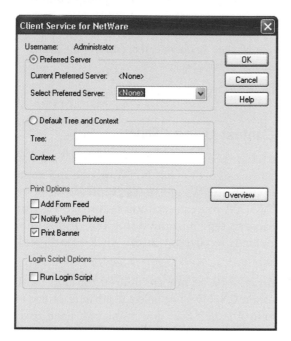

Figure 7-12   The Client Service for NetWare applet

Figure 7-13   Client Service for NetWare error (incorrect server path)

Regardless of the configuration changes you make, a message box notifies you that the changes will take effect the next time you log on. Click OK to continue. The computer must be restarted manually, because the configuration program does not automatically restart the computer after the dialog box is closed.

Other Configuration Settings

When you use the Client Service for NetWare applet to configure networking components, configuration options are available that are not presented when the client is first installed. As shown in Figure 7-12, these options make up the bottom half of the dialog box, in the Print Options and Login Script Options sections.

The settings available in the Print Options section determine whether a computer sends a form-feed command to the printer when the print job is finished, sends a notification message to the user when the print job is complete, or prints a banner before the print job itself. Form-feed commands are generally necessary only on older printers, usually those that use tractor-feed paper; most laser and inkjet printers do not require form-feed commands to end a print job. If this option is used on a laser printer, for example, a blank sheet of paper is ejected from the printer after the job. Many users in a networked environment are not within eyesight of the printers they are using. For that reason, the Client Service for NetWare can be configured to send a network notification to the user after a job is complete. If that option is selected, a message box appears on the user's computer when the print job is done. The banner page is also used in many larger networks. A banner page identifies the user who initiated the print job and the name of the job. Thus, users can easily identify their print jobs when they go to pick them up from the printer.

When the Run Login Script option is selected, the computer runs the NetWare logon script specified for the user by the administrator. This preserves logon scripts that network administrators have developed for their clients and provides easy, centralized administration for all client computers. This is especially important to standardize client behavior, regardless of the client type. However, many of the functions that logon scripts provide also work using such Windows XP functions as Map Network Drive. As more client computers are converted to Windows XP Professional, it may no longer be necessary to use logon scripts, and this option can be disabled.

Note that Novell uses the terms "log in" and "login," whereas Microsoft uses "log on" and "logon."

Activity 7-9: Client Service for NetWare

Time Required: 25 minutes

Objective: Install Client Service for NetWare so that the Windows XP computer can be a NetWare client.

Description: There are many companies that run more than one type of network because of business needs. In the event that workstations are Windows XP and the servers are NetWare, using Client Service for NetWare is a requirement. In this activity, you configure a computer with CSNW so that it can connect to the NetWare services.

To install and configure Client Service for NetWare:

1. If you have not already done so, log on to your Windows XP Professional computer as **Administrator**.

2. Click **Start**, right-click **My Network Places**, and then select **Properties**.

3. Right-click **Local Area Connection**, and then select **Properties**.

4. In the Local Area Connection Properties dialog box, click **Install**.

5. Select **Client** from the list of available components and then click **Add**. Note that the only client available to be installed is Client Service for NetWare.

6. Select **Client Service for NetWare** and then click **OK**. Click **Yes** to restart your computer when prompted to do so.

7. Log on to the computer as Administrator.

8. When prompted in the Select NetWare Logon window, follow your classroom instructions. You'll either click the Default Tree and Context option button, and enter the default tree and context for your computer on the network, or provide a name for the Preferred Server to which the computer will connect (this latter element is selected by default).

9. Wait a moment while the configuration changes are made, and then, if prompted, click **Yes** to restart the computer.

10. After the computer has restarted, log on to your Windows XP Professional computer as **Administrator**.

11. Open Control Panel by selecting **Start**, **Control Panel**. Note that the CSNW icon appears.

12. Double-click the **CSNW** icon to open the Client Service for NetWare dialog box. Adjust the Print Options and Login Script Options as desired and click **OK**.

13. Note that you receive a message box telling you that the changes will take effect the next time you log in. Click **OK** to continue.

14. Close Control Panel.

CONNECTING TO NETWARE RESOURCES

Because Client Service for NetWare integrates so closely with Windows XP, connecting to NetWare resources works the same way as connecting to other resources. Most often, this is accomplished through My Network Places. In an NDS environment, if the resources to which you are connecting are in the same NDS tree, your initial logon provides you access to available resources. However, on bindery-based networks, you must log on to each server to access the resources on that server. Once you have logged on to the appropriate server or directory tree, the NetWare security system determines whether you should be granted access to the requested resources.

Through the Computers Near Me icon in My Network Places, you can connect to resources on servers or trees to which you have already logged on. To search for other servers or NDS trees, double-click the Entire Network icon, and click the Entire Contents link shown in the lower-left corner.

After clicking the link, you are presented with icons for each type of client installed, usually Microsoft Windows Network and NetWare or Compatible Network. To browse for additional NetWare resources, double-click the NetWare or Compatible Network icon.

Choosing Appropriate NetWare Client Software

Because Novell also offers its Novell 32-bit client for Windows, you may sometimes find yourself forced to choose between the Microsoft client for NetWare networks or the Novell equivalent when setting up Windows XP Professional workstations for network access. In that case, consider the following list of factors to help you choose an appropriate client:

- On networks where NetWare servers outnumber Windows servers, or where clients need native NDS or NetWare-aware applications support, it's sensible to use the Novell 32-bit client for Windows.

- On networks where Windows servers outnumber NetWare servers, or where clients need native Active Directory and Windows applications support, it may make more sense to use the Microsoft client for NetWare networks.

- In situations where an equal number of servers of each type occur, or where NDS or NetWare-aware applications aren't necessary, it's far easier to install and use the Microsoft client for NetWare networks.

- When all that's required for Windows XP clients is access to file and print services on NetWare servers, you may want to consider installing Gateway Services for NetWare on Windows servers, because they can mediate access to NetWare file and print services. In that case, no NetWare client software of any kind is needed.

If you let your circumstances dictate the choice of client, remember also the principle of "least administrative effort." This means that you should evaluate which approach involves the least amount of effort to implement and weigh its pros and cons very carefully. Only when the balance firmly tilts toward the cons should you consider a different implementation approach!

NOTE

If you decide to install the Novell 32-bit Windows client, you may not also install NWLink or CSNW. (In fact, if you've installed those Microsoft components, you must first uninstall them before you attempt to install the Novell components.)

INTERPROCESS COMMUNICATION

In addition to the high-level functionality of Windows XP networking and the utilities and interfaces used to manage and configure networking, there are a few other nuts and bolts issues with which you should be familiar. This section and the following section on redirectors are included to provide you with additional details regarding networking functions within Windows XP and to inform you about a few issues that may appear on the Microsoft certification exam for Windows XP.

In the Windows XP environment, communication among processes—interprocess communication—is quite important because of the operating system's multitasking, multi-threaded architecture. **Interprocess communication (IPC)** defines a way for such processes to exchange information. This is a general-purpose mechanism so it doesn't matter whether such communications occur on the same computer or between networked computers. IPC defines a way for client computers to request services from some servers and permits servers to reply to requests for services. As shown in Figure 7-14, IPC operates directly below the redirector on the client side and the network file system on the server side to provide a standard communications interface for handling requests and replies.

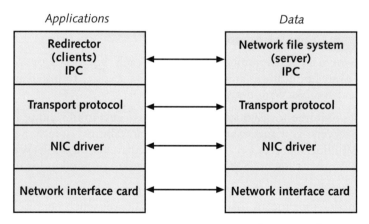

Figure 7-14   Interprocess communication between client and server

In Windows XP, IPC mechanisms fall into two categories: programming interfaces and file system mechanisms. Programming interfaces permit general, open-ended client/ server dialogue, as mediated by applications or system services. Normally, such dialogue is not strictly related to data streams or data files. File system mechanisms support file sharing between clients and servers. Where programming interfaces are concerned, individual APIs differ depending on what kinds of client/server dialogue they support. Where file systems are concerned, they must behave the same way, no matter how (or where) they employ Windows XP networked file systems and services.

The following sections discuss each mechanism in turn.

IPC File System Mechanisms

Windows XP includes two IPC interfaces for file system access: named pipes and mail slots. These mechanisms work through the Windows XP redirector, which distinguishes between local and network resource requests. This process permits one simple set of file I/O commands to handle both local and network access to file system data.

Named Pipes

Named pipes support a connection-oriented message-passing service for clients and servers. To be connection-oriented, a message's receiver must acknowledge each message it receives. Named pipes offer a reliable method for clients and servers to exchange requests, replies, and associated files. Named pipes provide their own methods to ensure reliable data transfer, which makes them a good match for lightweight, unreliable transport protocols like the User Datagram Protocol (UDP). In short, named pipes delivery guarantees make transport-level delivery guarantees less essential.

The Windows XP version of named pipes includes a security feature called impersonation, which permits the server side of the named pipes interface to masquerade as a client that requests a service. This allows the interface to check the client's access rights and to make sure that the client's request is legal, before returning any reply to a request for data.

Mail Slots File System

Mail slots are like a connectionless version of named pipes; mail slots offer no delivery guarantees, nor do they acknowledge successful receipt of data. Windows XP uses mail slots internally to support nonessential system-to-system communications. Such things as registering names for computers, domains, and users across a network, passing messages related to the Windows XP browser service, and providing support for broadcasting text messages across the network fall into this category. Outside such lightweight uses, mail slots are used less frequently than named pipes.

IPC Programming Interfaces

For communications to succeed, the client and server sides of an application must share a common programming interface. Windows XP offers a number of distinct interfaces to support IPC mechanisms for various kinds of client/server applications. Windows XP supports several programming interfaces, including NetBIOS, Windows Sockets, RPC, NetDDE, DCOM, Wnet, and WinInet.

NOTE

External applications can support other programming interfaces or implement private interfaces.

NetBIOS

NetBIOS is a widely used, but simple PC client/server IPC mechanism. Because it is so easy to program, it has remained quite popular since IBM published its definition in 1985. NetBIOS services are required to permit older Windows networks to operate, or to permit older clients and servers (those that predate Windows 2000 and Windows XP) to operate on a Microsoft Windows network.

Fortunately, NetBIOS works with all TDI-compliant transports, including NWLink (Net-BIOS over NWLink, or NWNBLink) and TCP/IP (NetBIOS over TCP/IP, or NBT). Windows XP uses TCP/IP as its primary network protocol by default, but Windows XP may also use NBT. By default, Windows XP TCP/IP is configured to use the NetBIOS setting defined by a local DHCP server. However, when statically defined IP addresses are used, NetBIOS is enabled by default. This setting is configured on the WINS tab of the Advanced TCP/IP Properties dialog box. The options here are:

- Use NetBIOS setting from the DHCP server. If a static IP address is used or the DHCP server does not provide NetBIOS setting, enable NetBIOS over TCP/IP (selected by default).
- Enable NetBIOS over TCP/IP.
- Disable NetBIOS over TCP/IP.

Windows Sockets

Windows Sockets (Winsock) define a standardized and broadly deployed interface to network transports such as TCP/IP and IPX. Winsock was created to migrate UNIX applications written to the Berkeley Sockets specification into the Windows environment. Winsock also makes it easier to standardize network communications used on multiple platforms because one socket interface is much like another, even if one runs on UNIX and the other on some variety of Windows (such as Windows XP, where Winsock 2.0 is the standard sockets API).

Windows Sockets appear in many programs that originated as UNIX programs and include the majority of Internet utilities, especially the most popular IP utilities, such as Web browsers, e-mail software, and file transfer programs.

RPC

Remote Procedure Call (RPC) implements IPC tools that can use separate programs on remote computers, supply them with input, and collect whatever results they produce. This permits the distribution of a single processing task among multiple computers, a process that can improve overall performance and help balance the processing load across numerous machines.

RPC is indifferent to where its client and server portions reside. It's possible for both client and server portions of an application to run on a single computer. In that case, they communicate using local procedure call (LPC) mechanisms. This makes building such applications easy because they can be constructed on one computer, while allowing processing to be distributed on one machine or across many machines, as processing needs dictate. This creates an environment that is both flexible and powerful.

RPC consists of four basic components:

- A remote stub procedure that packages RPC requests for transmission to a server. It's called a stub because it acts as a simple, extremely compact front end to a remote process that may be much larger and more complex elsewhere on the network.

- An RPC runtime system to pass data between local and remote machines or between client and server processes

- An application stub procedure that receives requests from the runtime RPC system. Upon such receipt, this stub procedure formats requests for the designated target RPC computer and makes the necessary procedure call. This procedure call can be either a local procedure call (if both client and server components are running on the same computer) or a remote procedure call (if client and server components are running on two machines).

- One or more remote procedures that may be called for service (whether locally or across the network)

NetDDE

Network Dynamic Data Exchange (NetDDE) creates ongoing data streams called exchange pipes (or simply, pipes) between two applications across a network. This process works just like Microsoft's local **Dynamic Data Exchange (DDE)**, which creates data exchange pipes between two applications on the same machine. DDE facilitates data sharing, object linking and embedding (OLE), and dynamic updates between linked applications. NetDDE extends local DDE across the network.

NetDDE services are installed by default during the base Windows XP installation, but they remain dormant until they are started explicitly. NetDDE services must be started using the Services control in Computer Management, where they appear under the headings Network DDE (the client side of NetDDE) and Network DDE DSDM (DDE Share Database Manager, the server side of NetDDE).

Distributed Component Object Model

Distributed Component Object Model (DCOM) (previously known as Network OLE) is a protocol that facilitates the communication of application components over a network by providing a reliable, secure, and efficient mechanism for exchanging information. DCOM can operate over most network transport mechanisms, including HTTP. Microsoft based its implementation of DCOM on the Open Software Foundation's DCE-RPC specification, but expanded its capabilities to include Java and ActiveX support.

Windows Network Interface

The Windows Network (Wnet) interface allows applications to take advantage of Windows XP networking capabilities through a standardized API. This means that the application does not require specific control data about the network provider or implementation, allowing applications to be network-independent while still able to interact with network-based resources.

Win32 Internet API

The Win32 Internet API (WinInet) is a mechanism that enables applications to take advantage of Internet functionality without requiring extensive proprietary programming. Through WinInet, applications can be designed to include FTP, Web, and Gopher support with a minimum of additional coding. WinInet makes interacting with Internet resources as simple as reading files from a local hard drive without requiring programming to Winsock or TCP/IP.

REDIRECTORS

A redirector examines all requests for system resources and decides whether such requests are local (they can be found on the requesting machine) or remote. The redirector handles transmission of remote requests across the network so that the requests are filled.

The following components are redirectors that operate at this level: Workstation service, Server service, **Multiple Universal naming convention Provider (MUP)**, and **Multi-Provider Router (MPR)**. All of these system components take client requests for service and redirect them to an appropriate network service provider. Redirectors interact and interface directly with user applications. The sections that follow explain more about each of these components and their roles in the Windows XP networking environment.

NOTE Windows XP file and print sharing are regarded as the most important functions supplied by any network operating system. Windows XP delivers these services through two critical components: the Workstation service and the Server service. Both of these services are essentially file system drivers that operate in concert with other file system drivers that can access local file systems on a Windows XP machine.

Workstation Service

The Workstation service supports client access to network resources and handles functions such as logging in, connecting to network shares (directories and printers), and creating links using Windows XP IPC options. The Workstation service has two elements, the user mode interface and the redirector. The User mode interface determines the particular file system that any User mode file I/O request is referencing. The redirector recognizes and translates requests for remote file and print services and forwards them to lower-level boundary layers aimed at network access and delivery.

This service encompasses a redirector file system that handles access to shared directories on networked computers. The file system is used further to satisfy remote access requests, but if any request uses a network name to refer to a local resource, it instead passes that request to local file system drivers.

The Workstation service requires that at least one TDI-compliant transport and at least one MUP be running. Otherwise, the service cannot function properly because it supports connections with other Windows XP machines (through their Server services), LAN Manager, LAN Server, and other MS-Net servers, which require an MUP to be running. The Workstation service, like any other redirector, communicates with transport protocols through the common TDI boundary layer.

Server Service

The Windows XP Server service handles the creation and management of shared resources and performs security checks against requests for such resources, including directories and printers. The Server service allows a Windows XP computer to act as a server on a client/server network, up to the maximum number of licensed clients. This limits the number of simultaneous connections possible to a Windows XP Professional machine to 10, in keeping with its built-in connection limitations.

Just as with the Workstation service, the Server service operates as a file system driver. Therefore, it also uses other file system drivers to satisfy I/O requests. The Server service is also divided into two elements:

- *Server.exe*—Manages client connection requests
- *Srv.sys*—The redirector file system that operates across the network and that interacts with other local file system drivers when necessary

Multiple Universal Naming Convention Provider

Windows XP supports multiple redirectors that can be active simultaneously. As an example, both the Workstation and Server services and the NetWare redirector built into Windows XP **Client Service for NetWare (CSNW)** can be active at the same time. Like the Server service, the NetWare redirector handles Microsoft Windows Network shares, but exposes them to NetWare clients instead of Microsoft clients. As with other boundary layers, the ability to support multiple clients uniformly is possible because a common provider interface allows Windows XP to treat all redirectors the same way.

The boundary layer, called the Multiple Universal naming convention Provider (MUP), defines a link between applications that make UNC requests for different redirectors. MUP allows applications to remain oblivious to the number or type of redirectors that might be in use. For incoming requests, the MUP also decides which redirector should handle that request by parsing the UNC share name that appears within the request.

Here's how it works: When the I/O subsystem receives any request that includes a UNC name, it turns over that request to the MUP. The MUP first checks its internal list of recently accessed shares, which it maintains over time. If the MUP recognizes the UNC name, it immediately passes the request to the required redirector. If it doesn't recognize the UNC name, the MUP sends the request to each registered redirector and requests that it service the request.

The MUP chooses redirectors on the basis of the highest registered response time. The response time is how long the redirector takes to connect to a UNC name. Response times are cached until no activity occurs over a specific redirector for 15 minutes. This can make trying a series of redirectors incredibly time-consuming and helps explain why the binding order of protocols is so important. It also influences the order in which name resolution requests are handled.

Universal Naming Convention Names

Universal Naming Convention (UNC) names represent the format used in NetBIOS-oriented name resolution systems. UNC names precede the computer portion of a name with two backslashes, followed by a backslash that precedes (and separates elements of) the share name and the directory path, followed by the requested filename. Thus, this string:

\\computername\sharename\dir-path\filename.ext

represents a valid UNC name. In this example, the name of the computer is *computername*, the name of the share is *sharename*, the directory path is named *dir-path*, and the file is named *filename.ext*.

Multi-Provider Router

Not all programs use UNC names in the Windows XP environment. Programs that call the Win32 API must use the file system service called the Multi-Provider Router (MPR) to designate the proper redirector to handle a resource request. The MPR lets applications written to older Microsoft specifications behave as if they were written to conform to UNC naming. The MPR is able to recognize the UNCs that represent drive mappings, so it can decide which redirector can handle a mapped network drive letter (such as X:) and make sure that a request that references that drive can be properly satisfied. The MPR handles all Win32 Network API calls, passing resource requests from that interface to those redirectors that register their presence through special-purpose dynamic link libraries (DLLs). That is, any redirector that wants to support the MPR must provide a DLL that communicates through the common MPR interface. Normally, this means that whichever network developer supplies a redirector must also supply this DLL. Microsoft implemented CSNW as a DLL that supports this interface. This allows the NetWare redirector to provide the same kind of transparent file system and network resource access as other Windows XP redirectors.

CHAPTER SUMMARY

❏ Windows XP Professional provides network access primarily by using TCP/IP. TCP/IP is routable, supports enterprise-level networks, and has been designed to interconnect dissimilar types of computers, which helps explain why it's the protocol of choice on the Internet.

❏ TCP/IP is an industry-standard protocol that provides easy cross–platform communication. Windows XP is specifically designed and engineered to take full advantage of this protocol and the networking capabilities made possible through its use.

❏ A thorough knowledge of TCP/IP is important. This includes understanding IP addressing, subnetting, default gateways, routing, private IP addresses, and APIPA.

❏ Windows XP supports and employs numerous subprotocols and utilities associated with TCP/IP, including the following: FTP, Telnet, SMTP, SNMP, ROUTE, TRACERT, PING, TFTP, HOSTS, DNS, LMHOSTS, WINS, NETSTAT, NBSTAT, and IPCONFIG.

❏ Windows XP includes a number of applications that utilize TCP/IP and provide Internet connectivity. In spite of TCP/IP's complexity, configuring Windows XP to employ this protocol is not difficult.

❏ Windows XP includes several new networking features and utilities; these include network bridging, Remote Assistance, Remote Desktop, greater support for wireless networking, and support for the upcoming IPv6 protocol.

❏ Windows XP includes the NWLink protocol and Client Service for NetWare (CSNW) to enable users to access resources and services from NetWare-based networks. This implementation supports older, bindery-based NetWare servers (3.x and older) as well as newer, Novell Directory Services-based NetWare servers (4.x and newer).

❏ When choosing NetWare client software for use on Windows XP clients, pick the client that fits the majority of servers in use or that provides native support for the most important directory and application services.

KEY TERMS

ARP (Address Resolution Protocol) — The IP protocol used to resolve numeric IP addresses into their MAC-layer physical address equivalents.

bindery — The database used by versions of NetWare before 4.0 to store network resource configuration information.

binding — The process of developing a stack by linking together network services and protocols. The binding facility allows users to define exactly how network services operate for optimal network performance.

Client Service for NetWare (CSNW) — Service included with Windows XP Professional that provides easy connection to NetWare servers.

Common Internet File System (CIFS) — An enhanced version of SMB used for file and print services.

connectionless — A class of network transport protocols that makes only a "best-effort" attempt at delivery and that includes no explicit mechanisms to guarantee delivery or data integrity. Because such protocols need not be particularly reliable, they are often much faster and require less overhead than connection-oriented protocols.

connection-oriented — A class of network transport protocols that includes guaranteed delivery, explicit acknowledgment of data receipt, and a variety of data integrity checks to ensure reliable transmission and reception of data across a network. However, reliable, connection-oriented protocols can be slow because of the overhead and extra communication.

context — The location of an NDS object in the NDS tree.

Data Link Control (DLC) — A network transport protocol that allows connectivity to mainframes, printers, and servers running remote program load software.

DNS (Domain Name System) — The TCP/IP service that is used to resolve names to IP addresses.

Dynamic Data Exchange (DDE) — A method of interprocess communication within the Windows operating system.

Dynamic Host Configuration Protocol (DHCP) — An IP-based address management service that permits clients to obtain IP addresses from a DHCP server. This allows network administrators to control and manage IP addresses centrally, rather than on a per machine basis.

FTP (File Transfer Protocol) — The protocol and service that provides TCP/IP-based file transfer to and from remote hosts and confers the ability to navigate and operate within remote file systems.

frame type — One of four available packet structures supported by IPX/SPX and NWLink. The four frame types supported are Ethernet 802.2, Ethernet 802.3, Ethernet II, and Ethernet SNAP.

HOSTS — A static file placed on members of a network to provide a resolution mechanism between host names and IP addresses.

ICMP (Internet Control Message Protocol) — The protocol in the TCP/IP suite that handles communication between devices about network traffic, quality of service, and requests for specific acknowledgments (such as those used in the PING utility).

IPX (Internetwork Packet Exchange) — The protocol developed by Novell for its NetWare product. IPX is a routable, connectionless protocol similar to TCP/IP but much easier to manage and with lower communication overhead.

Internetwork Packet Exchange/Sequenced Packet Exchange (IPX/SPX) — The name of the two primary protocols developed by Novell for its NetWare network operating system. IPX/SPX is derived from the XNS protocol stack and leans heavily on XNS architecture and functionality. See also *IPX* and *SPX*.

IP (Internet Protocol) — The protocol that handles routing and addressing information for the TCP/IP protocol suite. IP provides a simple connectionless transmission that relies on higher layer protocols to establish reliability.

interprocess communication (IPC) — The mechanism that defines a way for internal Windows processes to exchange information.

LMHOSTS — A file that is used in Microsoft networks to provide NetBIOS name-to-address resolution.

mail slots — A connectionless version of named pipes; mail slots offer no delivery guarantees, nor do they acknowledge successful receipt of data.

Multiple Universal naming convention Provider (MUP) — A Windows XP software component that allows two or more UNC providers (for example, Microsoft networks and NetWare networks) to exist simultaneously. The MUP determines which UNC provider handles a particular UNC request and forwards the request to that provider.

Multi-Provider Router (MPR) — A file system service that can designate the proper redirector to handle a resource request that does not use UNC naming. The MPR lets applications written to older Microsoft specifications behave as if they used UNC naming. The MPR is able to ensure that those UNCs that correspond to defined drive mappings receive copies of the domain security database or Active Directory.

named pipes — Provide support for a connection-oriented message-passing service for clients and servers.

NDS tree — The hierarchical representation of the Novell Directory Services database on NetWare 4.0 and higher networks.

NetBIOS Extended User Interface (NetBEUI) — A simple transport program developed to support NetBIOS installations. NetBEUI is not routable, so it is not appropriate for larger networks.

NBT (NetBIOS over TCP/IP) — A network protocol in the TCP/IP stack that provides NetBIOS naming services.

NetWare Core Protocol (NCP) — The protocol used by CSNW to make file and print services requests of NetWare servers.

Network Basic Input/Output System (NetBIOS) — A client/server interprocess communication service developed by IBM in 1985. NetBIOS presents a relatively primitive mechanism for communication in client/server applications, but allows an easy implementation across various Microsoft Windows computers.

Network Device Interface Specification (NDIS) — Microsoft specification that defines parameters for loading more than one protocol on a network adapter.

Network Dynamic Data Exchange (NetDDE) — An interprocess communication mechanism developed by Microsoft to support the distribution of DDE applications over a network.

network number — The specific network identifier used by IPX for internal and network communication.

Novell Directory Services (NDS) — The hierarchical database used by NetWare 4.0 and higher servers to store network resource object configuration information.

NWLink — The Microsoft implementation of Novell's IPX/SPX protocol suite.

Open Datalink Interface (ODI) — Novell's specification for network device communication.

PING (Packet Internet Groper) — An IP-based utility that can be used to check network connectivity or to verify whether a specific host elsewhere on the network can be reached.

RARP (Reverse Address Resolution Protocol) — The IP protocol used to map from a physical MAC-layer address to a logical IP address.

rexec (remote execution) — The IP-based utility that permits a user on one machine to execute a program on another machine elsewhere on the network.

rsh (remote shell) — The IP-based utility that permits a user on one machine to enter a shell command on another machine on the network.

SPX (Sequenced Packet Exchange) — A connection-oriented protocol used in the NetWare environment when guaranteed delivery is required.

SMTP (Simple Mail Transfer Protocol) — The IP-based messaging protocol and service that supports most Internet e-mail.

SNMP (Simple Network Management Protocol) — The IP-based network management protocol and service that makes it possible for management applications to poll network devices and permits devices to report error or alert conditions to such applications.

subnet — A portion of a network that might or might not be a physically separate network. A subnet shares a network address with other parts of the network but is distinguished by a subnet number.

subnet mask — The number used to define which part of a computer's IP address denotes the host and which part denotes the network.

Telnet — The TCP/IP-based terminal emulation protocol used on IP-based networks to permit clients on one machine to attach to and operate on another machine on the network as if the other machines were terminals locally attached to a remote host.

Transmission Control Protocol/Internet Protocol (TCP/IP) — A suite of Internet protocols upon which the global Internet is based. TCP/IP is the default protocol for Windows XP.

TCP (Transmission Control Protocol) — The reliable, connection-oriented IP-based transport protocol that supports many of the most important IP services, including HTTP, SMTP, and FTP.

TFTP (Trivial File Transport Protocol) — A lightweight alternative to FTP, TFTP uses UDP to provide only simple get-and-put capabilities for file transfer on IP-based networks.

Universal Naming Convention (UNC) — A multivendor, multiplatform convention for identifying shared resources on a network.

UDP (User Datagram Protocol) — A lightweight, connectionless transport protocol used as an alternative to TCP in IP-based environments to supply faster, lower overhead access, primarily (but not exclusively) to local resources.

Windows Internet Naming Service (WINS) — A service that provides NetBIOS-name-to-IP-address resolution.

REVIEW QUESTIONS

1. The _____ enables a system to determine which part of an IP address represents the host and which part represents the network.

2. _____ is a TCP/IP service used to resolve host or domain names to addresses.

3. The _____ service can be used to automatically assign IP configurations to a computer.

4. The _____ file provides NetBIOS name-to-IP address resolution.

5. _____ is a TCP/IP protocol that is used for file manipulation.

6. By changing the _____ , you alter the order in which services are accessed.

7. _____ is the Microsoft service that provides NetBIOS name-to-address resolution.

8. The current version of TCP/IP (IPv4) uses a(n) _____ -bit addressing scheme.

9. NDIS allows any number of adapters to be bound to any number of transport protocols. True or False?

10. Which of the following new networking features of Windows XP cannot be used on systems that are domain clients?
    a. network bridging
    b. Remote Assistance
    c. Remote Desktop
    d. wireless networking

11. What are the restrictions for making a network connection part of a network bridge on Windows XP?
    a. not a dial-up connection
    b. not controlled by ICF
    c. not a wireless connection
    d. not controlled by ICS

12. Which Windows XP networking component allows a system to access shared resources?
    a. TCP/IP
    b. Workstation service
    c. RPC
    d. NetDDE

7

13. If you are assigned the IP address 172.16.1.1, what full-class subnet mask is most likely the correct one to use?

    a. 255.0.0.0

    b. 255.255.0.0

    c. 255.255.255.0

    d. 255.255.255.255

14. Which class of IP addresses offers the most flexibility with regard to subnetting by providing for the most number of hosts?

    a. Class A

    b. Class B

    c. Class C

    d. Class D

15. What should be placed on remote systems that connect to routed networks over slow WAN links?

    a. NWLink

    b. LMHOSTS

    c. DNS

    d. HOSTS

    e. WinInet

16. Which TCP/IP command was designed to test the presence of a remote system?

    a. Telnet

    b. PING

    c. ARP

    d. ROUTE

17. Which of the following is the static, text-based equivalent of the Windows XP NetBIOS name to IP address resolution service?

    a. HOSTS

    b. LMHOSTS

    c. DNS

    d. WINS

18. If your network hosts the appropriate automatic addressing service, you do not need to manually configure TCP/IP to participate in a network. True or False?

19. Which of the following protocols is used to inquire if an address is reachable on the Internet?

    a. SMTP

    b. UTP

    c. PING

    d. IMAP

20. What IPC interfaces are used by Windows XP for file system access? (Choose all that apply.)

    a. Winsock

    b. named pipes

    c. mail slots

    d. OLE

21. Network bridging offers what benefits?

    a. filtering

    b. communication between subnets without expensive hardware

    c. communication between networks of differing media and protocol

    d. full routing control

22. Remote Desktop can be used to invite another user to interact with your desktop environment to demonstrate how to perform some activity. True or False?

23. NDIS and ODI are technologies that provide for _____ .

    a. dynamic client configuration

    b. distribution of driver software

    c. binding of multiple protocols to multiple adapters

    d. resolution of names to IP addresses

24. Which of the following most reduces broadcasts in a TCP/IP environment?

    a. DNS

    b. WINS

    c. NWLink

    d. DLC

25. TCP/IP is the most widely used protocol in the world. True or False?

26. All versions of NetWare utilize NDS. True or False?

27. Which of the following elements is part of the Microsoft NetWare environment for Windows XP Professional? (Choose all that apply.)

    a. NWLink

    b. CSNW

    c. GSNW

    d. NetWare File and Print Services

7

28. For IPX/SPX communication to succeed on a network, all computers must use the same frame type. True or False?

29. Which of the following NetWare protocols provides guaranteed packet delivery?

a. NWLink

b. IPX

c. SPX

d. NCP

30. When choosing a NetWare client for Windows XP, which of the following conditions should guide that choice? (Choose all that apply.)

a. Always use the Microsoft Client for NetWare networks.

b. Always use the Novell 32-bit Windows client.

c. If there are more NetWare servers than Windows servers, or if native support for NDS and NetWare-aware applications is required, use the Novell 32-bit Windows client.

d. If there are more Windows servers than NetWare servers, or if native support for Active Directory and Windows applications is required, use the Microsoft Client for NetWare Networks.

CASE PROJECTS

Case Project 7-1

Describe the functions and features of TCP/IP included with Windows XP.

Case Project 7-2

As a network administrator at XYZ Corp., you always hear about it when performance problems arise on the network. In the past two weeks, you've been involved in switching the network over from using NWLink exclusively to a mixture of NWLink and TCP/IP. You've installed TCP/IP on all Windows 2000 Server and Windows XP Professional systems and made sure that all the machines are properly configured. Because the network is growing and an additional cable segment has been added, with more planned for the future, you plan to switch entirely from NWLink to TCP/IP over time. All of a sudden, your users complain that the network has slowed dramatically. What steps can you take that might improve performance speed? On which machines should you make changes and why?

8

INTERNETWORKING WITH REMOTE ACCESS

After reading this chapter and completing the exercises, you will be able to:

♦ Understand remote access under Windows XP

♦ Configure various remote access connection types for a Windows XP Professional system

♦ Install remote access hardware

♦ Understand remote access security

♦ Understand the Internet Options applet

♦ Implement Internet Connection Sharing and the Internet Connection Firewall

♦ Understand the native Internet tools and utilities

♦ Troubleshoot remote access problems

Not all network access occurs from computers that are directly attached to the network where the resources and data reside. For roaming workers, such as salespeople and field engineers, and increasingly for telecommuters, the ability to gain access to a network remotely—that is, from some location other than where the network physically resides—is crucial. This is an area where Windows XP really shines; it is one of the few major network operating systems that includes remote access capabilities with the core software at no additional charge. For Windows XP Professional, this means that part of the package is a single dial-in or dial-out connection that can use a **modem** over a **PSTN (Public Switched Telephone Network)** connection, DSL (Digital Subscriber Line), cable modem, an **ISDN (Integrated Services Digital Network)** line, frame relay, or any of the other more exotic digital remote link technologies. A modem is a device that allows a computer to make a communication connection with a remote system over normal telephone lines. PSTN is a formal name for normal telephone service. ISDN is a digital high-speed communications line that can support computer transmissions as well as voice calls. Since Windows NT became a force to be reckoned with when Windows NT 3.51 was released in 1995, remote access services have played a central role in the operating system's burgeoning popularity and widespread acceptance up to and including the current Windows XP release.

REMOTE ACCESS

You can use **Remote Access Service** to log on to a Windows XP system for user or administrative access while you're away from the office. For example, a user can access the system from a hotel room while traveling on business. Remote access can be used to dial into another system or to answer incoming connections. A client system is any system that initiates access to a Windows XP system established as a remote access server.

A Windows XP remote access configuration includes the following components:

- *Clients*—Windows XP, Windows 2000, Windows NT, Windows 95/98, Windows for Workgroups, MS–DOS (with Microsoft network client software installed), and LAN Manager remote access clients can all connect to a Windows XP remote access server. "Clients" can also mean any client of a platform that supports the Point-to-Point Protocol (PPP).

- *Protocols*—Windows XP remote access servers support PPP, enabling any PPP client to use TCP/IP (Transmission Control Protocol/Internet Protocol) or NWLink (IPX/SPX). Windows XP as a dial-up client can also access the installed base of SLIP (Serial Line Internet Protocol) remote access servers. However, SLIP cannot be used to connect to a Windows XP remote access server system.

- *WAN connectivity*—Clients can dial in using standard telephone lines with a modem or modem pool employing legacy analog or the new DSL technology. Faster links are possible using ISDN or T-carrier lines. Remote access clients can also be connected to remote access servers using **X.25**, ATM (Asynchronous Transfer Mode), or an RS-232C null modem. X.25 is a communications technology widely used in Europe. Windows XP also allows for channel aggregation with PPP Multilink. Windows XP does support cable modems; however, in most cases proprietary software and drivers from the vendor are used to establish connections over these network adapter-like devices, because they function differently from a modem.

- *Security*—Windows XP logon and domain security, support for security hosts, data encryption, Internet Connection Firewall (ICF), IPSec (IP Security), and callback provide secure network access for remote clients. With Windows XP, you also have the option of separating LAN traffic from remote access traffic with the Point-to-Point Tunneling Protocol (PPTP) or the Layer Two Tunneling Protocol (L2TP).

- *Server*—As a remote access server, Windows XP Professional supports only one inbound connection at a time. However, most Windows server operating systems permit up to 256 remote clients to dial in. The remote access server can be configured to provide access to an entire network or restrict access to the remote access server.

- *LAN protocols*—Internet Protocol support permits accessing a TCP/IP network such as the global Internet. NWLink (IPX/SPX) protocol support enables remote clients to access NetWare servers and printers. You can use NetBIOS applications over IPX or TCP/IP. Also, Windows Sockets applications over TCP/IP or IPX, named pipes, Remote Procedure Call (RPC), and the LAN Manager API are also supported.

Note that remote control and remote access are control technologies that work in different ways. Remote control employs a remote client as a dumb terminal for the answering system, whereas remote access establishes an actual network connection between a remote client and the answering computer system, using a link device (such as a modem) as a network adapter. Remote access keyboard entries and mouse movements occur locally; with remote control, these actions are passed to a host system. Using remote access, computing operations are executed on the client; remote control computing operations are executed on the host with the resulting video signal sent to the client.

Remote access and Terminal Services are also different mechanisms. Terminal Services allows thin clients—basic computers consisting of a display, keyboard, and mouse, with only enough capability to connect to the terminal server host—to participate in a rich computing environment. Basically, the terminal server host acts as the CPU for the thin client. All operations and calculations are performed on the terminal server host; only display changes are sent to the client and only keyboard and mouse information is sent back to the terminal server. Terminal Services are often employed in situations where budget restrictions prevent the purchase of fully capable desktop systems or when complete security is required (i.e., when data cannot exist outside the secure server). Remote access is a mechanism by which remote computers that exist as independent systems are able to make connections over some type of communication link to a system or standalone machine. This link is used to access data or to gain further access to linked networks.

FEATURES OF REMOTE ACCESS IN WINDOWS XP

Remote access is a standard component of Windows XP and does not require a manual service installation. Some of the impressive features of remote access under Windows XP are discussed in the following sections.

PPP Multilink

Remotely accessing resources through PPP Multilink allows you to increase overall throughput by combining the bandwidth of two or more physical communication links, such as analog modems, ISDN, and other analog/digital links. PPP Multilink is based on Internet Engineering Task Force (IETF) standard RFC 1717, "The PPP Multilink." RFC stands for Request for Comments, designating official standards documents published by the IETF. This standard is located on the Web at *http://www.faqs.org/rfcs/rfc1717.html*.

VPN Protocols

Windows XP supports two Virtual Private Network (VPN) protocols: Point-to-Point Tunneling Protocol and Layer Two Tunneling Protocol. **Point-to-Point Tunneling Protocol (PPTP)** is a networking technology that supports multiprotocol VPNs, allowing users to access corporate networks securely through the Internet. Clients using PPTP can access a corporate LAN by dialing an ISP or by connecting directly through the Internet. In both cases, the PPTP tunnel is encrypted and secure and works with any protocol.

Cisco Systems developed a PPTP alternative called **Layer Two Tunneling Protocol (L2TP)**. Similar to PPTP, L2TP encapsulates PPP frames for transport over various networks, including IP, X.25, Frame Relay, and ATM. L2TP is used in combination with IPSec to provide a secure encrypted VPN link over public networks.

Restartable File Copy

The restartable file copy feature automatically retransmits incomplete file transfers produced by interruption of remote access connectivity. This feature provides the following:

- Faster transmission of large files over lower-quality connections
- Reduced cost from avoiding retransmission of the whole file
- Reduced frustration from interrupted transfers

Idle Disconnect

The idle disconnect feature breaks off a remote access connection after a specified period of inactivity. This feature reduces the costs of remote access, helps you troubleshoot by closing dead connections, and frees up inactive remote access **ports**. A port is any physical communication channel to which a modem, direct cable, or other device can be connected to enable a link between two computers.

Autodial and Logon Dial

You can configure remote access to automatically connect and retrieve files and applications stored on a remote system. Users do not have to establish a remote access connection each time they want to transfer a remote object; Windows XP quickly and efficiently handles all remote access events. By maintaining a virtual database of mappings between resources and connection objects, Windows XP remote access is able to reestablish links when previously accessed resources are rerequested.

Client and Server Enhancements

Windows XP remote access includes a number of client and server components that allow third-party vendors to develop remote access and dial-up networking applications.

Look and Feel

Windows XP remote access has undergone some changes since Windows 2000 and is significantly different from similar utilities in Windows NT and Windows 95/98. Remote access capabilities have now been integrated with the networking components, resulting in Network Connections, a multipurpose management interface where both standard LAN networking links and remote access links are established and configured. Just about everything related to remote access is controlled through this interface. The only exception is that all remote access hardware (such as modems) are installed through the Add Hardware applet if they were not installed automatically by Plug and Play at system startup.

8

Callback Security

You can control access to the system from specified phone numbers by using the callback feature. Calls may originate only from known phone number locations, or the remote access client can set the phone number dynamically. Callback is configured on the Callback tab of the Dial-up Preferences dialog box, accessed through the Advanced menu of the Network Connections utility. There are three options: No callback, Ask me during dialing when the server offers, and Always call me back at the number(s) below. Allowing the number to be set dynamically (i.e., during the connection) does not provide any security; security is enforced only when predefined callback numbers are used. Callback forces the remote server to disconnect from the client calling in, and then to call back the client computer. One reason for using this feature is to have the bill for the phone call charged to a company phone number, rather than the phone number of the user who called in.

WAN Connectivity

Wide area networks (WANs) link sites that are often a considerable physical distance apart. Using remote access, Windows XP enables you to create a WAN by connecting existing LANs through remote access over telephone, ISDN, cable modems, campus networks, or other communication lines. This is a cost-effective solution if you have minimal to moderate network traffic between sites. You can improve the performance of remote access-based WANs in one of three ways:

- Increasing bandwidth of the remote access connection
- Multilinking communication links using PPP Multilink
- Implementing PPTP over the Internet

INTERNET NETWORK ACCESS PROTOCOLS

Windows XP remote access supports all standard protocols for remote Internet access as well as **PPP Multilink**, a variation of PPP that enables you to create one large high-bandwidth pipe by banding together multiple PPP channels. The remote access protocol used in establishing and maintaining a WAN link is dependent on the client and server OS and LAN protocols. Windows XP-supported remote access protocols are outlined in the following sections.

PPP

Point-to-Point Protocol (PPP) is the current standard for remote access. Remote access protocol standards are defined in RFCs published by the IETF and other groups. The RFCs supported in Windows XP remote access are:

- *RFC 1661*—The Point-to-Point Protocol (PPP)
- *RFC 1549*—PPP in HDLC Framing
- *RFC 1552*—The PPP Internetwork Packet Exchange Control Protocol (IPXCP)
- *RFC 1334*—PPP Authentication Protocols
- *RFC 1332*—The PPP Internet Protocol Control Protocol (IPCP)

Microsoft recommends using PPP because it is flexible and it is the industry standard, which means continued compatibility with client and server hardware and software in the future. Remote clients connecting to third-party PPP servers might need to use a postconnect terminal script to log on to the PPP server.

 When using a non-Microsoft PPP stack to dial into a Windows server that is a part of a domain and not a domain controller, the server looks only to its local accounts for the account name and password you specified on dial-in. If the server doesn't find the name and password locally, it won't check the domain accounts; it simply denies access. Because a domain controller does not have local accounts that it can use for verification, it uses the accounts in the domain's Active Directory database to grant or deny access.

PPTP

Point-to-Point-Tunneling Protocol (PPTP) is one of the most interesting features of Windows XP. It allows you to establish a secure remote access pipeline over the Internet and to "tunnel" IPX or TCP/IP traffic inside PPP packets. PPTP can provide real benefits for companies with numerous remote users who subscribe to a local Internet service provider (ISP) for e-mail and Internet access and who use the same connection to access the corporate LAN. These VPNs can support the IPX and TCP/IP LAN protocols and provide private network access from any Internet connection point.

PPTP's significant features include:

- *Transmission costs*—Uses the Internet as the primary long-distance connection medium rather than leased lines or long-distance telephone lines, reducing the cost of establishing and maintaining a remote access connection

- *Hardware costs*—Requires less hardware by letting you locate modems and ISDN hardware on a network rather than directly attaching them to the remote access server

- *Administrative overhead*—Permits centralized management of remote access networks and users

- *Improved security*—Connections over the Internet are encrypted and secure.

L2TP is a similar protocol developed by Cisco for use with IPSec to support secure VPN links. From a user's perspective, it operates in the same manner as PPTP.

PPP-MP

The PPP Multilink Protocol (PPP-MP) combines two or more physical remote access links (modem, ISDN, or X.25 links) into one logical bundle with greater bandwidth. Multilink can combine analog and digital links in the same logical bundle. The only drawback to multilinking is that all connections to be aggregated must be of the same technology type. For example, ISDN and modem links cannot be aggregated, but three ISDN lines can.

 Because only one phone number can be stored in a user account, Multilink does not function with the callback security feature.

SLIP

Serial Line Internet Protocol (SLIP) was one of the first protocols developed specifically for TCP/IP support over dial-up connections. Though SLIP is rarely used (PPP offers much more power and flexibility), Microsoft has included it in Windows XP for backward-compatibility with older systems. SLIP does not support the **Dynamic Host Configuration Protocol (DHCP)**, so a static IP address must be assigned to every SLIP client, making IP address administration more difficult. DHCP is a network service which can be used to automatically configure IP addressing for systems. Unlike PPP, SLIP does not support IPX. SLIP's biggest drawback is that it does not support encrypted passwords; SLIP passwords are passed as plain text. Windows XP remote access does not offer a SLIP server, but supports SLIP as a client.

The RFCs related to remotely access SLIP are:

- *RFC 1144*—Compressing TCP/IP Headers for Low-Speed Serial Links

- *RFC 1055*—A Nonstandard for Transmission of IP Datagrams Over Serial Lines: SLIP

IPSec

IP Security (IPSec) is a security measure added to TCP/IP to protect communications between two systems using that protocol. IPSec negotiates a secure encrypted communications link between a client and server through public and private encryption key management. IPSec can be used over an RAS/WAN link or within a LAN. In either case, IPSec creates a secured point-to-point link between two systems. IPSec offers protection against a wide range of security problems, including: eavesdropping, data modification, identity spoofing, password attacks, denial-of-service attacks, man-in-the-middle attacks, compromised security keys, sniffer attacks, and Application-layer attacks.

IPSec and IP Security policies were discussed in detail in Chapter 6, "Windows XP Security and Access Controls."

Telephony Features

TAPI, the remote access Telephony API, supplies a uniform way of accessing fax, data, and voice. TAPI is part of the Windows Open System Architecture (WOSA) developed to aid third-party vendors in designing powerful, integrated telephony applications. TAPI enables communication between a TAPI-aware computer and telephone hardware, such as PBX, modems, and fax machines. TAPI treats a telephone network as a system resource using standard APIs and device drivers; so once installed, TAPI applications have seamless access to phone features and server-based communications.

REMOTE ACCESS CONFIGURATION

As stated previously, remote access is an integrated default component of Windows XP, and no additional service installation is required. Remote access is configured and managed from the Network Connections window (see Figure 8-1). The basic functions of this window were discussed in Chapter 7, "Windows XP Network Protocols" (refer to that discussion for general interface information). This interface window is accessed through the Start menu by selecting Start, Control Panel, clicking Network and Internet Connections (if in Category view), and then clicking Network Connections.

All remote access or remote links must be created. Clicking the Create a new connection link in the Network Tasks list starts the New Connection Wizard. The second page of this Wizard offers three remote connection options (see Figure 8-2):

- *Connect to the Internet*—Creates a connection object to connect to an ISP
- *Connect to the network at my workplace*—Creates a connection object to connect to a network through dial-up or VPN
- *Set up an advanced connection*—Creates a connection object using a serial, parallel, or infrared port connection, or configures the system to answer incoming connections

Figure 8-1   Network Connections

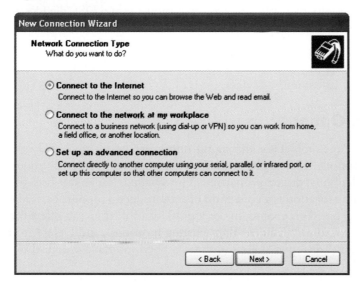

Figure 8-2   New Connection Wizard

Only three options appear in this dialog box when Windows XP is installed in a domain. If the workstation is installed as a standalone machine or as part of a workgroup, a fourth option, Set up a home or small office network, is available.

Establishing remote access connection objects using the wizard is very simple and quick. The following sections look at the step-by-step process for each of these connection types and the postcreation properties you can manipulate.

All the network connection object types require that the hardware device used to establish the remote access link be installed and configured before creating the connection object. This includes modems, cable modems, ADSL devices, infrared ports, and so on.

Installing Remote Access Hardware

Before any remote access connection can be established, the hardware required by that connection must be physically present and its drivers properly installed. Under Windows XP, the process of installing hardware is often simple and requires little user input. Upon system startup, Windows XP inspects the hardware and attempts to identify any new devices. If a device is recognized, Windows XP attempts to locate and install drivers for it. In some cases, you are prompted for additional paths to search for drivers. When Windows XP is unable to identify a device, you are either prompted to provide a path for the drivers or you need to use the Add/Remove Hardware applet or the Phone and Modem Options applet to install the drivers. For some specialty hardware, such as cable modems and DSL devices, you might need to use the vendor-supplied installation routine to install the correct drivers.

Because of the wide range of remote access-related devices, it is recommended that you consult the device's manual or contact the vendor for further aid with installation; this is necessary only for a few uncommon devices.

Phone and Modem Options

The primary Control Panel applet for managing remote access devices and operations is Phone and Modem Options. This applet is used to control dialing rules, configure remote access devices, and telephony driver properties. The Dialing Rules tab lists the defined dialing location. A dialing location is a collection of remote access properties used to govern how links are established based on geographic or logical location. This tab offers the controls of New (to create new locations), Edit (to alter existing locations), and Delete (to remove a location). Both New and Edit open the same three-tabbed interface where the default or existing settings for a location can be altered.

When a new location is being created (New) or an existing location is being modified (Edit), a three-tabbed interface used to define the settings for a location is displayed. On the General tab of the Edit Location dialog box (see Figure 8-3), the following information items can be defined or changed:

- Location name
- Country/region
- Area code

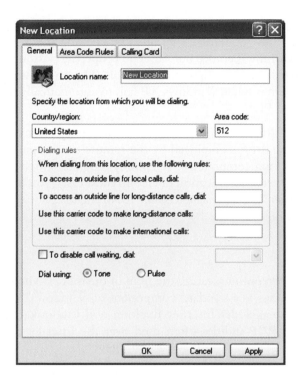

Figure 8-3   The Edit Location dialog box, General tab

- Number to dial to gain access to an outside line for local calls
- Number to dial to gain access to an outside line for long-distance calls
- Use this carrier code to make long-distance calls
- Use this carrier code to make international calls
- Disable call waiting
- Dial using pulse or tone

The Area Code Rules tab is used to define how numbers that exist within or outside the current area code are dialed. These rules include which prefixes (the first three numbers of a seven-digit phone number) are included in an area code (and thus are local calls), whether to dial 1 (one) first when calling certain prefixes, and whether to include the area code when dialing certain prefixes.

The Calling Card tab is used to specify a method for charging long-distance calls to a credit card or dialing card. There are dozens of predefined cards that require you to provide only your account number and PIN, or you can define your own calling card billing rule.

Once you've created an alternate location by setting the dialing rules, this location appears in a pull-down list on most connection object connect interfaces. You can select the location profile to use each time you initiate a remote access link.

The Modems tab of the Phone and Modem Options applet lists all currently installed modems and their attached ports. New modems are installed by clicking the Add button; existing modems can be deleted with the Remove button. The Properties button is used to access device/driver-specific properties and configuration controls. The only time you ever need to use this tab to install a modem is when Windows XP fails to automatically recognize and install drivers through Plug and Play.

The Advanced tab of the Phone and Modem Options applet lists all the telephony providers present on the system. These are the drivers employed by the remote access system to link communication devices and networking components. Telephony providers are the interface between the operating system and the communication device. In most cases, you'll never use this tab. Consult the *Microsoft Windows XP Professional Resource Kit* or the telephone provider's vendor for configuration information.

Connecting to the Internet

The Internet has quickly become the communication medium of the masses. Microsoft had the foresight to include Internet access as a standard component of Windows XP remote communications. Windows XP also includes Internet Explorer and Outlook Express, in addition to the other common TCP/IP utilities often used over the Internet (e.g., FTP, Telnet, ping, tracert, and so on).

You can choose from the following options in the Connect to the Internet Wizard:

- *Choose from a list of Internet service providers (ISPs)*—Establish a new account through MSN or an ISP that services your area.

- *Set up my connection manually*—Set up an ISP connection manually whether connecting using a dial-up phone number (such as analog modem, ISDN, or DSL) or a broadband always-on connection (such as cable modem).

- *Use the CD I got from an ISP*—Start an ISP installation from a vendor-provided CD.

Transferring an existing MSN account to this computer involves the use of the Files and Settings Transfer Wizard as discussed in Chapter 5, "Users, Groups, Profiles, and Policies."

Activity 8-1: Dial Up to an ISP

Time Required: 20 minutes

Objective: Create a dial-up object for connecting to an ISP.

Description: Most home users have an account with an ISP. Although many people are starting to use high-speed connections, such as cable modems, there are still many people using standard modems for dialing in to an ISP over a telephone line. This may not be the fastest connection method, but it is the most economical. In this activity, you create an object for connecting to an ISP using a modem.

To create a dial-up connection object to connect to an ISP:

This activity assumes that a modem is installed. This lab performs a manual ISP configuration, which requires a phone number and valid username and password. If this lab is to be used as a demonstration only, use 555-1212 as the phone number.

1. Click **Start**, **Control Panel**. Click **Switch to Classic View** if Control Panel is currently in Category view.

2. Double-click **Network Connections**.

3. Start the New Connection Wizard by clicking the **Create a new connection** link in the Network Tasks Quick List.

4. The first page of the wizard is a welcome message. Click **Next**.

5. On the Network Connection Type page, select **Connect to the Internet**. Click **Next**.

6. On the Getting Ready page, click **Set up my connection manually**. Click **Next**.

7. On the Internet Connection page, click **Connect using a dial-up modem**. Click **Next**.

8. If you have two or more dial-up devices installed on your system, you will see the Select a Device page. Otherwise, skip to Step 9. On the Select a Device page, select the communication device(s) for this connection object. This object will use devices with a marked check box; devices with an empty check box will not be used. If you select multiple devices, the system attempts to aggregate the links through Multilink. Click **Next**.

9. On the Connection Name page, provide a name for this connection object, such as **Lab ISP1**. Click **Next**.

10. On the Phone Number to Dial page, provide the dial-up number for your ISP. Click **Next**.

11. On the Connection Availability page, select whether this connection will be available for Anyone's use or My use only. Click **Next**. Note that if you are working from a system that is a standalone computer (rather than a member of a network), the Connection Availability page may not appear.

12. On the Internet Account Information page, provide the username and password for the ISP account.

13. By default, the selections of Use this account name and password when anyone connects to the Internet from this computer, Make this the default Internet connection, and Turn on Internet Connection Firewall for this connection are marked. If this is acceptable, click **Next**.

14. Click **Finish**. The New Connection Wizard finishes creating the connection object (i.e., it now appears in the Network Connections window), but instead of returning you to the Network Connections window, the wizard starts the new connection object for the first time.

15. In the Connect dialog box, double-check the name of the user account you need to employ when connecting to the ISP.

16. If you want the system to retain your password, select the **Save this user name and password for the following users** check box, then select **Me only** or **Anyone who uses this computer**. If you decide not to check this box, you have to provide the password each time this connection object is used to establish the remote access link.

17. Double-check that the listed phone number in the Dial field is correct. If not, change it to the correct number.

18. To initiate the connection, click **Dial**. If this project is being performed as an example rather than a real-life implementation, skip this step.

Once a connection object is created, the Connect dialog box is automatically opened and offers four action buttons at the bottom of its display (Figure 8-4). The Dial button initiates this connection and attempts to establish a connection using the current settings. The Cancel button closes the Connect dialog box and discards any changes made. The Properties button opens the multitabbed Properties dialog box for this connection object. The Help button opens the Windows XP Help system in the Network Connections context section.

In most cases, you want to click Dial to test the new object. If your modem was properly configured, your phone line attached, and the service was not offering a busy signal, you should have established an Internet connection, and the default home page should be displayed in Internet Explorer. Close Internet Explorer by selecting Close from the File menu. You might be prompted to terminate your connection; choose No to keep the connection active for now. Notice the connection icon in the status area of the taskbar—it's the one with the two overlapping monitors that blink. Double-clicking this icon opens the connection status dialog box (see Figure 8-5). You can terminate the connection at any time by clicking the Disconnect button in this dialog box. Double-clicking a connection object from the Network Connections utility can access this same connection status dialog box.

Figure 8-4   Connect dialog box

Figure 8-5   Connection status dialog box

The connection status dialog box's General tab displays connection status, duration, speed, packets (LAN connections), bytes (dial-up connections), compression (dial-up connections), and errors (dial-up connections). From this tab, you can access the connection object's Properties or disconnect the link. The Details tab lists data relevant to the connection, such as server type, protocols, and IP addresses of server and client.

If your system employs a proxy server to gain Internet access over a LAN, you do not see a connection object representing the proxy connection in the Network Connections window, nor does a connection icon appear in the status area of the taskbar. Proxy connections are defined through the LAN Settings button on the Connections tab of the Internet Options applet (the Internet Options applet is accessed through Control Panel or the Tools menu in Internet Explorer). Any changes to your proxy settings should be made through the LAN Settings dialog box.

The connection object functions on default settings in most cases, but you might want to fine-tune your connection to improve performance or add capabilities.

The Properties dialog box for a connection object can be accessed through a variety of means:

- Select the connection object in the Network Connections window, then select Properties from the File menu or right-click the icon and select Properties from the shortcut menu.

- If the connection object is already in use, right-click the icon in the status area of the taskbar and select Properties from the shortcut menu.

- If the connection object is already in use, double-click the icon in the status area of the taskbar, and then click the Properties button in the Status dialog box.

No matter how you get there, the Properties dialog box (see Figure 8-6) for an Internet connection object is used to configure a wide variety of settings that were not offered by the New Connection Wizard.

The General tab is used to configure devices and dial-up numbers. The Connect using field lists all installed communication devices. Those devices with a marked check box are employed by the connection object in an attempt to establish a connection. The listed devices can be ordered to give priority to the faster or more reliable devices. By default, all devices dial the same phone number. By deselecting the All devices call the same numbers check box, the Phone number group becomes dependent on the selected device. The Phone number area includes settings for the area code, phone number, country/ region code, and dialing rules (see the Phone and Modem Options section earlier in this chapter). Clicking the Configure button when a device is selected can configure individual devices. This opens a device-specific configuration dialog box where elements such as communication speed, modem protocols, hardware features, terminal window, logon scripts, and modem speaker are configured.

Settings in the connection object's Properties dialog box apply only to the selected device. The Show icon in notification area when connected check box enables an icon for this connection to appear in the status area of the taskbar. This icon is used for quick access to connected links.

Figure 8-6   A connection object's Properties dialog box, General tab

The Options tab (see Figure 8-7) configures the behavior of the connection object while establishing a connection. The settings are:

Figure 8-7   A connection object's Properties dialog box, Options tab

- *Display progress while connecting*—Provides a status report of the connection establishment process; default is selected.

- *Prompt for name and password, certificate, etc.*—Forces access credentials before opening the connection object; default is selected.

- *Include Windows logon domain*—Forces the connection to request logon domain information from the remote access server; default is not selected.

- *Prompt for phone number*—Forces the connection object always to prompt for phone number verification before attempting to establish a connection; default is selected.

- *Redial attempts*—Sets the number of retries the system makes when a connection cannot be established with the remote system; default is three retries.

- *Time between redial attempts*—Sets the time period between redials; default is one minute.

- *Idle time before hanging up*—Sets the inactivity disconnect time period; default is never.

- *Redial if line is dropped*—Forces the connection object to attempt to reconnect if the link is broken for any reason; default is enabled.

- *Multiple devices*—Enables multilinking; default is Dial all devices. Other settings include Dial only first available device (establishes a single link with the remote system) and Dial devices only as needed (establishes activity-based dialing). Clicking the Configure button for the latter selection opens the Automatic Dialing And Hanging Up dialog box (Figure 8-8), which is used to define when additional devices are dialed or disconnected based on the level and time period of traffic. Defaults are dial new devices when current bandwidth has been at 75% utilization for two minutes, and to disconnect when utilization has been less than 10% for two minutes. This option is only available if there is more than one dialog device (modem) installed in the computer.

- *X.25*—Opens the configuration dialog box for X.25 connections, through which you can define the X.25 network type in use, your X.25 address, and the two optional settings of user data and facilities. For more information on X.25, consult the *Microsoft Windows Server 2003 Resource Kit*.

The Security tab (see Figure 8-9) is used to define the connection object's security requirements. This tab offers two top-level security settings: Typical (recommended settings) and Advanced (custom settings). The default setting is Typical, which allows unsecured passwords. This top-level setting has two other options: Require secured passwords and Use smart cards (available in the pull-down selection list). Two check boxes further define these alternate security options. The Automatically use my Windows logon name and password (and domain if any) check box should be used when your local and remote logon credentials are identical (this check box is enabled only when Require secured password is used). The

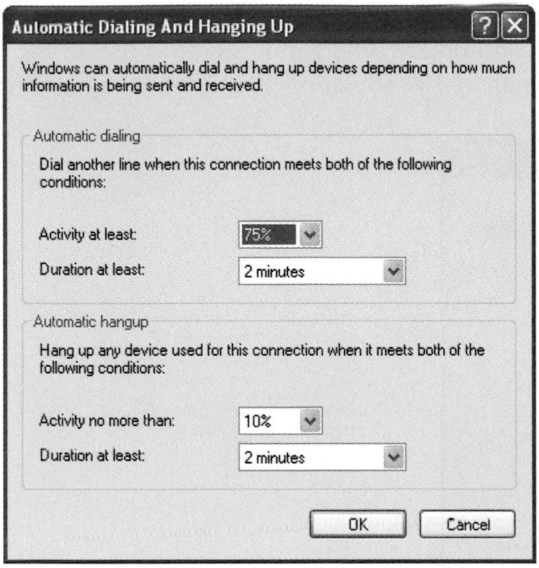

Figure 8-8   The Automatic Dialing And Hanging Up dialog box

Require data encryption (disconnect if none) option protects not just the authentication process but all data transferred over the link (this check box is not enabled when Allow unsecured password is used).

Figure 8-9   A connection object's Properties dialog box, Security tab

The second top-level security setting, Advanced (custom settings), is used to specify exactly the level of security for this connection object. The Settings button reveals the Advanced Security Settings dialog box (see Figure 8-10), which offers the following settings:

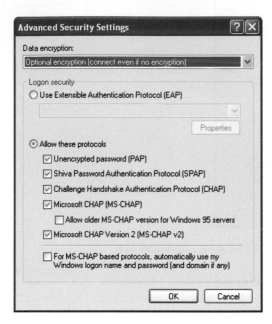

Figure 8-10   The Advanced Security Settings dialog box

- *Data encryption*—Defines the encryption requirements. Selections are No encryption allowed (server disconnects if it requires encryption), Optional encryption (connect even if no encryption), Require encryption (disconnect if server declines), and Maximum-strength encryption (disconnect if server declines).

- *Use Extensible Authentication Protocol (EAP)*—Enables smart card or third-party security mechanisms to be required. The Properties button accesses mechanism-specific configuration settings. Windows XP includes default drivers for smart card readers and MD5-challenge mechanisms. See the *Microsoft Windows Server 2003 Resource Kit* for more details on smart cards and third-party security mechanisms.

- *Allow these protocols*—Selects the encryption protocols allowed over this connection object, including PAP (i.e., unencrypted clear text), SPAP, CHAP, MS-CHAP, MS-CHAP from Windows 95, and MS-CHAP v.2.

- *For MS-CHAP-based protocols, automatically use my Windows logon name and password (and domain if any)*—Uses local logon credentials over the connection object.

To force the use of a specific authentication protocol, mark only the check box beside the single specific authentication protocol desired.

The bottom of the Security tab (as was shown in Figure 8-9) controls whether to open a terminal window and run a script after a connection is established. These settings apply to all devices used by this connection object. To define device-specific items, use the Configure button on the General tab. In most cases, terminal windows and logon scripts are unnecessary; however, depending on the type of server you are connecting to and the security mechanisms employed, you might need to alter these settings. A terminal window allows you to enter keystrokes directly to the authentication mechanism on the remote server. Some systems require multiple passwords, selecting a logon method from a menu, or issuing protocol run commands. If the logon requirements of a system can be automated, you can create a logon script that provides these items automatically without requiring a terminal window and user input each time the connection is established. Dial-up logon scripts can be as complex as necessary, including branching decision trees based on data from the remote server. Windows XP includes several sample scripts in the %systemroot%\ system32\ras\ folder that you can customize for your own purposes. For details on creating and modifying logon scripts, consult the content of the sample scripts (which include useful details in the form of context-specific comments).

The Networking tab (see Figure 8-11) is used to configure the network communication components employed by the connection object. As you can see, this tab is very similar to the Properties of a Local Area Connection object. Because a remote access connection is the same as a local connection and differs only in speed, this similarity is not surprising.

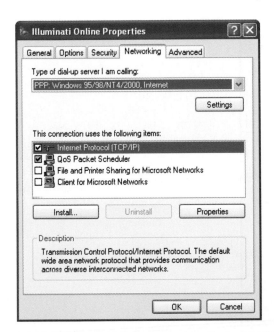

Figure 8-11   A connection object's Properties dialog box, Networking tab

The most important setting on this tab is the type of dial-up server. Your options are PPP and SLIP. Because Windows remote access servers can accept only inbound PPP connections, you most likely want to select PPP. However, if you are connecting to an older UNIX system, you might need to employ SLIP. If you don't know, try PPP first, because it is the standard remote link connection technology.

Note that PPP offers three further configuration details through the Settings button: enabling LCP extensions, enabling software compression, and negotiating multilink for single-link connections. In most cases, the default settings are correct, but when connecting to older UNIX systems or other platforms, these PPP settings can prevent stable communications.

The remaining portion of this tab is used to enable, install, and configure networking components. Enabling and disabling a component applies only to this connection object, but installing or removing a component applies to all connection objects. By default, only the Internet Protocol (TCP/IP) and QoS Packet Scheduler components are enabled; the File and Print Sharing for Microsoft Networks component is disabled. For information on configuring networking components, refer to Chapter 7.

The Advanced tab (see Figure 8-12) is used to configure Internet Connection Firewall (ICF) and Internet Connection Sharing (ICS) for this connection object. ICF offers a reliable level of security for Internet connections. ICS is used to share a single Internet connection with other computers on your network.

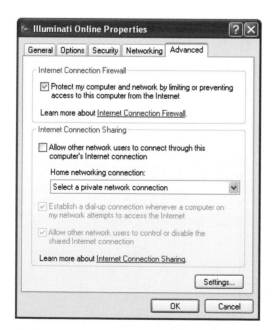

Figure 8-12   A connection object's Properties dialog box, Advanced tab

Internet Connection Sharing

Internet Connection Sharing (ICS) is used to share a single network connection with a small group of networked computers. The shared connection can be a link to the Internet or any type of network. ICS is enabled on the Advanced tab of a connection object's Properties dialog box. By enabling sharing for a connection object, you allow other computers on your network to access resources over that external link.

Internet Connection Sharing incorporates the Network Address Translation (NAT) function, a Dynamic Host Configuration Protocol (DHCP) address allocator, and a Domain Name System (DNS) proxy. The mechanism hides your internal network configuration (keeping this information secure), provides automatic assignment of unregistered, non-routable IP addresses to internal clients, and provides a forwarding handoff procedure for all requests for external services. Basically, Internet Connection Sharing transforms your Windows XP system into a limited DHCP proxy server. After ICS is enabled, you must set all other clients to use DHCP in order to take advantage of the shared connection.

Activity 8-2: Internet Connection Sharing

Time Required: 10 minutes

Objective: Configure Windows XP Professional to be able to share an Internet connection with other computers on a network.

Description: People with home networks are typically on a limited budget. Rather than paying for multiple ISP accounts, many people are taking advantage of the ability to have one computer connect to the Internet and then share that connection with other computers on the local network. In this activity, you configure your computer to allow Internet Connection Sharing.

To configure Internet Connection Sharing:

This activity requires that a network connection already be defined.

1. Click **Start**, **Control Panel**. Click **Switch to Classic View** if Control Panel is currently in Category view.

2. Double-click **Network Connections**.

3. Select the dial-up connection created in Activity 8-1 in the Network Connections window.

4. Select **File, Properties**.

5. Click the **Advanced** tab.

6. Click the **Allow other network users to connect through this computer's Internet connection** check box under Internet Connection Sharing.

7. A message dialog box might appear stating that a username and password are not stored for this connection. Click **OK**.

8. Click the **Settings** button.

9. Click the **Services** tab.

10. Select the **Remote Desktop** option.

11. Click **OK**.

12. Click **OK**.

Once Internet Connection Sharing is enabled, you can also select whether to enable on-demand dialing. This feature automatically reestablishes the remote link when a client attempts to access external resources over your system through the currently offline connection object. Microsoft recommends using ICF on each ICS link for added security.

Troubleshooting the Internet Connection Service involves two distinct activities. First, verifying that the connection is active and functioning is usually accomplished using a Web browser. Second, verifying that communication from other clients can access your system over the network is achieved either by pinging or by attempting to access a shared resource from your client.

Once ICS is enabled, you can also define which services running on your internal network are accessible to external Internet users. This is performed through the Settings button on the Advanced tab, which opens the Advanced Settings dialog box. If you have enabled only ICS, then the Advanced Settings dialog box has a single tab—Services. However, if you have enabled ICF, then this dialog box has three tabs. Windows XP is configured by default to allow access to L2TP, PPTP, and IKE (i.e., IPSec) resources. This allows external VPN clients to establish a connection into the network over the dial-up link. If you want to share other resources, you can enable FTP, IMAP, SMTP, POP, Remote Desktop, Telnet, and HTTP. Other services can be defined by using the Add or Edit buttons.

ICS should not be used on any network with domain controllers, DNS servers, **gateway** systems, DHCP servers, or with clients that must have static IP addresses. A gateway is a computer that serves as a router, a format translator, or a security filter for an entire network. ICS is designed for use on small workgroup networks, not within domains. ICS and normal DHCP interfere with each other. ICS uses the 192.168.x.x network to assign IP addresses to clients and does not support statically configured clients. For sharing an Internet connection with a domain, use the proxy routing and NAT capabilities of a Windows server product.

Internet Connection Firewall

The Internet Connection Firewall (ICF) is a security measure for protecting network connections from unwanted traffic. ICF can set restrictions on traffic in and out of your network to an external network or the Internet. Microsoft recommends that ICF be used on each ICS link, but ICF can be used on LAN connections as well. In fact, Microsoft recommends using ICF on every network connection to an external network except those that host VPN links. ICF is a much-needed feature for systems that employ shared broadband connections, such as cable modems or even campus networks. On shared broadband connections, the potential exists for one client customer to infiltrate another client's system. Only a secure personal firewall can prevent such infiltration.

ICF is a stateful firewall, which means each packet that passes ICF is inspected to determine its source and destination addresses. This allows ICF to prevent any external traffic not requested by an internal client from entering the private network. Because ICF is configured by default to block most incoming traffic, especially traffic that is not a response to an internally issued request, you may experience some communication problems. For example, if ICF is enabled with its default settings, you are unable to obtain echo responses when attempting to ping the ICF protected system. In fact, you receive an error message from PING stating that the request timed out. Fortunately, Microsoft foresaw this issue and built in a workaround. See the paragraph in this section discussing the ICMP tab.

However, ICF can also be configured to allow specific types of traffic to enter the private network without a corresponding internal client request. These features are defined on the Services tab of the Advanced Settings dialog box (see Figure 8-13), which is accessed through the Settings button on the Advanced tab of a connection object's Properties dialog box.

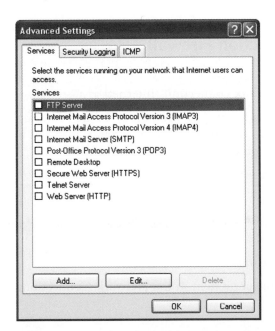

Figure 8-13   Advanced Settings dialog box, Services tab

The Services tab lists nine predefined, commonly used information service types that you may want to allow external users to access. These services include FTP, e-mail (SMTP, IMAP3, IMAP4, POP3), Web Server regular and secure (HTTP, HTTPS), Telnet, and remote desktop. If you are using a standalone system it is unlikely that you are offering services to Internet users, thus all of these services are disabled by default. To enable access to these services, simply mark the respective check box. This effectively opens the corresponding service port in ICF so external users can access the network service. If the specific service you wish to offer is not listed, then use the Add button to create your own service definition.

By default, ICF silently drops all traffic that is not allowed to enter the private network. In other words, it does not record a log file of dropped packets. If you want a record of dropped packets or successful connections, logging can be enabled on the Security Logging tab. You can use the logging ICF actions to determine which ports or services are outside sources attempting to connect and which are succeeding. You might find some surprising footprints in the logs. One such example would be finding out that you have a Web server running on the default port 80 and some external user is regularly connecting to it. Rogue connections into your system, whether over a LAN or Internet connection, can significantly reduce the performance of your system and compromise your security.

The ICMP tab is used to configure to which ICMP requests from an external system the ICF-protected system will respond. For example, if you want to allow other systems to ping your ICF protected system and receive an echo response, you must enable the Allow incoming echo request setting on this tab.

ACTIVITY

Activity 8-3: Internet Connection Firewall

Time Required: 10 minutes

Objective: Configure the dial-up network connection (Internet) as a firewall.

Description: Windows XP Professional has built-in firewall capabilities. Although it is not as robust as third-party firewall products that are available, it is better than not having any firewall. In this activity, you configure some basic firewall settings.

To configure Internet Connection Firewall:

This activity requires that a network connection already be defined.

1. Click **Start**, **Control Panel**. Click **Switch to Classic View** if Control Panel is currently in Category view.

2. Double-click **Network Connections**.

3. Select the predefined dial-up connection item in the Network Connections window.

4. Select **File**, **Properties**.

5. Click the **Advanced** tab.

6. Click the **Protect my computer and network by limiting or preventing access to this computer from the Internet** option under Internet Connection Firewall.

7. Click **Settings**.

8. On the Services tab, mark any service that you want ICF to pass without restriction.

9. Click the **Security Logging** tab.

10. Click the **Log dropped packets** option.

11. Click the **ICMP** tab.

12. Make sure that all check boxes are cleared.

13. Click **OK**.

14. Click **OK** again.

If your organization allows notebooks or other portable systems running Windows XP Professional to leave the security of your network for mobile activities, you should seriously consider employing ICF whenever connecting to an Internet service provider or any other network. However, ICF can cause some problems when these portable systems reconnect to your primary network. For the most part, the problems are related to network users accessing shared resources on the reconnected portable system. By default, ICF blocks external access to shared resources. One way around this issue is to disable ICF whenever the system is connected to the primary network. This can be done manually or through a group policy. The group policy control entry of Prohibit the use of ICF on your DNS domain network disables ICF when connected to the network and allows ICF to run at all other times. If by some strange configuration you need the ability to dial out to another network while connected to your primary network and you want to protect the dial-out connection with ICF, you will be unable to use the group policy control because it prevents the use of ICF on all connections from the portable system, not just the one with the primary network. In such situations, you need to manually configure ICF to allow access to your shared resources or disable ICF on your primary network interface.

Connecting to the Network at My Workplace

Telecommuters and mobile personnel often need to communicate with the office LAN for a wide variety of purposes. Because a remote access link supports all network functions (access to files, printers, proxied Internet access, security control, service access, network application interaction, etc.) with only a change in the speed (based on the connection technology), remote connections to the LAN are very useful. Many organizations are taking advantage of the ease of distance communications offered by Windows XP, Windows 2000, Windows Server 2003, Windows NT, and Windows 9x to reduce office space costs and increase the productivity of their employees.

Virtual Private Networking (VPN) is a trend in mobile computing that employs the Internet as a long-distance carrier to enable distant, secure LAN connections. VPNs enable mobile or remote computers to establish a connection with a LAN over a local connection to an ISP. In other words, you can connect to the Internet anywhere in the world through a local access point, then use Windows XP VPN technology to link to your LAN. Such a remote access link offers you all of the functionality of a network client, with only slightly reduced speed. Furthermore, Windows XP VPN encrypts not just your authentication credentials, but all of the data transferred as well, thus ensuring private, secure, confidential long-distance computing.

The Connect to the network at my workplace option on the second page of the New Connection Wizard is used to create direct dial-up and VPN connections to an office LAN. Keep in mind that a VPN link establishes a PPTP or L2TP communication pipeline over an existing network connection between two systems. Thus, you must either have a dedicated LAN or use a dial-up connection to establish the network between the two systems to be linked.

Activity 8-4: Dial Up to a Private Network

Time Required: 20 minutes

Objective: Create a dial-up object for remotely connecting to a private network.

Description: A modem and telephone line can be used to connect to a number of different resources. In this activity, the user creates an object that can be used for connecting to a private network through a dial-up connection.

To create a dial-up connection object to connect to a private network:

This activity assumes that a modem is installed. You need the phone number of a remote access server to contact. If this lab is to be used as a demonstration only, use 555-1212 as the phone number.

1. Click **Start**, **Control Panel**.

2. Click **Switch to Classic View** if Control Panel is currently in Category view.

3. Double-click **Network Connections**.

4. Start the New Connection Wizard by clicking the **Create a new connection** link in the Network Tasks Quick List.

5. The first page of the wizard is a welcome message. Click **Next**.

6. On the Network Connection Type page, select **Connect to the network at my workplace**. Click **Next**.

7. On the Network Connection page, select **Dial-up connection**. Click **Next**.

8. If you have two or more dial-up devices installed on your system, you see the Select a Device page. Otherwise, skip to Step 9. On the Select a Device page, select the communication device(s) for this connection object. Devices with a marked check box are used by this object; devices with an empty check box are not. If you select multiple devices, the system attempts to aggregate the links through Multilink. Click **Next**.

9. On the Connection Name page, provide a name for this connection object, such as Act 8-4. Click **Next**.

10. On the Phone Number to Dial page, provide the dial-up number for your remote access server. Click **Next**.

11. On the Connection Availability page, select whether this connection will be available for Anyone's use or My use only. Click **Next**. Note that if you are working from a system that is a standalone computer (rather than a member of a network), the Connection Availability page may not appear.

12. Click **Finish**. The New Connection Wizard finishes creating the new connection object (i.e., it now appears in the Network Connections window), but instead of returning you to the Network Connection window, the wizard opens the new connection object for the first time.

13. In the Connect dialog box, provide the name of the user account to employ when connecting to the remote access system.

14. In the Password field, type the password for that user account. Your keystrokes will be echoed with dots instead of the actual character you typed to prevent over-the-shoulder theft of your password.

15. If you want the system to retain your password, select **Save this user name and password for the following users**, then select **Me only** or **Anyone who uses this computer**. If you decide not to check this box, you have to provide the password each time this connection object is used to establish the remote access link.

16. Double-check that the listed phone number in the Dial field is correct. If not, change it to the correct number.

17. To initiate the connection, click **Dial**. If this project is being performed as an example rather than a real-life implementation, skip this step.

The Properties dialog box of a network dial-up connection object is substantially the same as that of an Internet ISP connection object. The only real difference is that the network dial-up connection object has the Client for Microsoft Networks component enabled on the Networking tab, and the ISP connection object does not. Refer to the previous connection object section for details on the Properties dialog box for the network dial-up connection object.

The Properties dialog box of a VPN connection object is similar to that of an Internet ISP connection object, with a few distinct differences. The General tab lists the IP address or host name of the VPN server and controls whether an Internet connection is dialed before attempting the VPN connection. The Options tab does not include X.25 options. The Security tab does not include terminal window and script options, but does include a button to enter the IPSec Security preshared authentication key. The Networking tab defines the type of VPN to establish; the options are Automatic, PPTP VPN, and L2TP IPSec VPN.

Activity 8-5: VPN Connection

Time Required: 20 minutes

Objective: Configure a VPN connection.

Description: To provide a more secure connection, and to allow home users to connect to their private network at a minimal cost, a Virtual Private Network can be configured. This allows a user to dial up an ISP and then connect to their private network with reasonable security. In this activity, you create a VPN connection object.

To create a VPN connection object:

This activity performs a VPN configuration, which requires a host name or IP address of the remote system to connect to. If this lab is to be used as a demonstration only, use 172.16.1.1 as the IP address of the remote system.

1. Click **Start**, **Control Panel**. Click **Switch to Classic View** if Control Panel is currently in Category view.

2. Double-click **Network Connections**.

3. Start the New Connection Wizard by clicking the **Create a new connection** link in the Network Tasks Quick List.

4. The first page of the wizard is a welcome message. Click **Next**.

5. On the Network Connection Type page, select **Connect to the network at my workplace**. Click **Next**.

6. On the Network Connection page, select **Virtual Private Network connection**. Click **Next**.

7. On the Connection Name page, provide a name for this connection object, such as Lab VPN 1. Click **Next**.

8. On the Public Network page, select **Do not dial the initial connection**. If you want this VPN connection to establish an Internet connection automatically before initiating the VPN link, then select **Automatically dial this initial connection** and make a choice from the pull-down list. Click **Next**.

9. On the VPN Server Selection page, provide the host name or IP address of the remote system to connect to. Click **Next**.

10. On the Connection Availability page, select whether this connection will be available for Anyone's use or My use only. Click **Next**. Note that if you are working from a system that is a standalone computer (rather than a member of a network), the Connection Availability page may not appear.

11. Click **Finish**. The New Connection Wizard finishes creating the the connection object (i.e., it now appears in the Network Connections window), but instead of returning you to the Network Connections window, the wizard starts the new connection object for the first time. If your connection was closed during this procedure, you may be prompted about whether to reestablish your connection. Click **Yes** to reestablish the connection.

12. In the Connect dialog box, provide the username and password needed to authenticate to the remote system.

13. If you want the system to retain your password, select the **Save this user name and password for the following users** check box, then select **Me only** or **Anyone who uses this computer**. If you decide not to check this box, you have to provide the password each time this connection object is used to establish the remote access link.

14. To initiate the connection, click **Connect**. If this project is being performed as an example rather than a real-life implementation, skip this step.

The remote access server to which you are connecting must be preconfigured to accept VPN connections. See the Setting Up An Advanced Connection section to learn how to configure a Windows XP system to accept inbound connections.

Setting Up an Advanced Connection

The Set Up An Advanced Connection option on the second page of the New Connection Wizard can be used to establish a direct connection between two systems or to configure the system to answer inbound dial-up calls. Because these are very different activities, they are discussed in the following sections.

Accepting Incoming Connections

Windows XP Professional, although designed as a network client, can act as a remote access server for a single incoming connection. This connection can be made over a modem, an existing Internet/network connection (i.e., a VPN link), or a direct access cable. In most cases, you use this feature only for special-purpose applications. For example, accepting a dial-in connection can be used to access your home system while traveling or to simplify technical support help for telecommuters.

Activity 8-6: Incoming Connections

Time Required: 15 minutes

Objective: Create an incoming connection object for remote connection to the workstation.

8

Description: There may be times when a user wants to have others remotely connect to their computer. If the computer is in a small peer-to-peer network, one or all machines may be configured to allow designated people to dial in to the network through their computer. In this activity, you configure your computer to accept a remote connection.

To create an incoming connection object:

This activity assumes that a modem is installed.

1. Click **Start**, **Control Panel**. Click **Switch to Classic View** if Control Panel is currently in Category view.

2. Double-click **Network Connections**.

3. Start the New Connection Wizard by clicking the **Create a new connection** link in the Quick List.

4. The first page of the wizard is a welcome message. Click **Next**.

5. On the Network Connection Type page, select **Set up an advanced connection**. Click **Next**.

6. On the Advanced Connection Options page, select **Accept incoming connections**. Click **Next**.

7. On the Devices for Incoming connections page, select the communication device(s) for this connection object. Devices with a marked check box will be used by this object; devices with an empty check box will not. Click **Next**.

8. On the Incoming Virtual Private Network (VPN) Connection page, select whether to allow VPN connections or not. Click **Next**.

9. On the User Permissions page, select users to be allowed to connect over this incoming connection object. Only these selected users will be able to use this connection object. Click **Next**.

10. On the Networking Software page, select those components to bind to the incoming connection object. The defaults are usually satisfactory. Click **Next**.

11. Click **Finish**. The new incoming connection object is added to the Network Connections utility awaiting a dial-in attempt.

The process of configuring an incoming connection object includes the selection of the devices that answer incoming calls, whether to allow VPN links, which users can dial in, and which networking components (protocols, clients, and services) are supported over a dial-in link. Once that's completed, the incoming connection object is added to the Network Connections window. Opening this object's Properties reveals a three-tabbed dialog box. The General tab (see Figure 8-14) is used to select the devices for this object and enable VPN connections. The Users tab is used to select which users can connect to this system over the incoming connection object. Furthermore, you can select the Require all users to secure their passwords and data option and whether to allow directly connected devices to connect without providing a password. By opening the Properties for a specific user, you can change that user's full name and password and set the callback options. The Networking tab is where the networking components are enabled and configured.

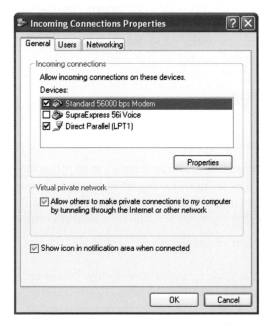

Figure 8-14   The Incoming Connections Properties dialog box, General tab

Once an incoming connection object is created, the devices selected for that object are placed in answer mode. When that device receives a call, Windows XP automatically answers the call and attempts to authenticate the connection. When a device is placed into answer mode, it can only be used by one process for incoming connections, but such a device can be used to establish outbound calls. In other words, creating an incoming connection object for your modem won't prevent you from using that modem to establish a connection with your ISP or office LAN. However, it does prevent you from running two answering processes at the same time, such as remote access and fax.

Connecting Directly to Another Computer

All too often you discover that you need to move several megabytes of data from one system to another when one or both of the systems has no network interface. In such cases, you have only a few reasonable options: Use a floppy spanning tool, purchase and install a NIC, purchase and install removable media devices (such as Zip drives), or create a direct cable connection. Obviously, spanning floppies is often a doomed task, especially when working with more than 3 MB of material. If you had the budget for a NIC or a removable media device, you probably would have them installed already. The best option is to use a **serial** or parallel cable (or even infrared port if already present on both systems), directly connecting the computers, which you probably already have on hand or can purchase for less than $10. A serial connection is a method of communication that transfers data across a medium one bit at a time, usually adding start and stop bits to ensure reliable delivery.

To employ the direct connection, first attach the cable (or orient the infrared devices) between the two systems. Next, you need to create a direct connection object on both systems; one acts as the host and the other acts as the guest. Just be sure to select the correct link type based on your hardware (i.e., serial, parallel, or infrared).

Activity 8-7: Direct Connections

Time Required: 20 minutes

Objective: Create a direct connect connection object.

Description: There may be a time when a computer may have a modem, but does not have a NIC. To enable the transfer of larger files without having to use a dial-up connection, a Windows XP computer can be configured to connect directly to another computer through either a parallel or serial port. In this activity, you set up a direct connect connection.

To create a direct connect connection object:

 This activity requires two systems in close proximity. One system should be labeled as the host or server; the other system should be labeled as the guest or client. A connecting parallel or serial cable or properly oriented infrared link must be present between the two systems.

1. Go to the system that will act as the host in the direct connection pair. Typically, the host system has the resource that needs to be transferred or accessed by the guest system.

2. Click **Start**, **Control Panel**. Click **Switch to Classic View** if Control Panel is currently in Category view.

3. Double-click **Network Connections**.

4. Start the New Connection Wizard by clicking the **Create a new connection** link in the Quick List.

5. The first page of the wizard is a welcome message. Click **Next**.

6. On the Network Connection Type page, select **Set up an advanced connection**. Click **Next**.

7. On the Advanced Connection Options page, select **Connect directly to another computer**. Click **Next**.

8. On the Host or Guest? page, select **Host**. Click **Next**.

9. On the Connection Device page, select the link device type (serial, parallel, infrared, etc.) from the pull-down list. Click **Next**.

10. On the User Permissions page, select the user(s) that can connect over this link. Click **Next**.

11. Click **Finish**.

12. Go to the system that will act as the guest in the direct connection pair.

13. Click **Start**, **Control Panel**. Click **Switch to Classic View** if Control Panel is currently in Category view.

14. Double-click **Network Connections**.

15. Start the New Connection Wizard by clicking the **Create a new connection** link in the Quick List.

16. The first page of the wizard is a welcome message. Click **Next**.

17. On the Network Connection Type page, select **Set up an advanced connection**. Click **Next**.

18. On the Advanced Connection Options page, select **Connect directly to another computer**. Click **Next**.

19. On the Host or Guest? page, select the **Guest** option. Click **Next**.

20. On the Connection Name page, provide a name for this connection object, such as **Lab direct guest 1**. Click **Next**.

21. On the Select a Device page, select the link device type (serial, parallel, infrared, etc.) from the pull-down list. Click **Next**.

22. On the Connection Availability page, select whether this connection will be available for Anyone's use or My use only. Click **Next**. Note that if you are working from a system that is a standalone computer (rather than a member of a network), the Connection Availability page may not appear.

23. Click **Finish**. The New Connection Wizard finishes creating the connection object (i.e., it now appears in the Network Connections window), but instead of returning you to the Network Connection window, the wizard opens the new connection object for the first time.

24. The Connect dialog box appears. Provide a username and password (for a user account granted access to connect back in Step 10). Click **Connect**.

 You can create the host connection object through either the Accept incoming connections or the Connect directly to another computer suboptions of the Set up an advanced connection option. But you can create the guest or connecting object only through the Connect directly to another computer option.

Once the link is established, you have the same link to the other system as if you were both members of the same workgroup connected by normal network cables.

The Properties dialog box for a host direct connection object is the same as that of an incoming connection object. The Properties dialog box for a guest connection object is the same as that of any dial-out connection object, with the General tab offering control over the connection device.

ALTERNATE IP CONFIGURATION

Windows XP Professional supports a feature called Alternate Configuration. This feature is available whenever a networking connection object uses DHCP (i.e., obtains an IP address automatically). Alternate configuration allows you to preconfigure an alternate default IP configuration if DHCP fails. This prevents an APIPA address from being assigned in case of such a failure.

On the Internet Protocol (TCP/IP) Properties dialog box, when the Obtain an IP address automatically option button is selected, the Alternate Configuration tab appears (see Figure 8-15). This tab has an option button with two selections: Automatic private IP address (APIPA) and User configured. If you select User configured, you can define a complete IP address configuration to use in the event of a DHCP assignment failure.

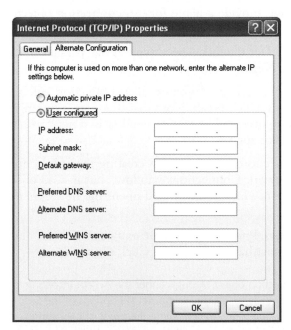

Figure 8-15 Internet Protocol (TCP/IP) Properties dialog box, Alternate Configuration tab

REMOTE ACCESS SECURITY

Remote access security is built on Windows XP local and network security. A remote access connection is simply another type of network connection. This means that remote users still must pass logon authentication and have the correct user/group permissions to gain access to shared resources. However, remote access boasts several additional security measures to aid in keeping break-ins and unauthorized access to a minimum. Remote access connections can be protected from unwanted traffic by using the Internet Connection Firewall (discussed earlier in this chapter).

Dial-up connection objects have authentication and encryption security options. These are defined on the Security tab of their Properties dialog boxes, and were discussed earlier in the Connecting to the Internet section. Basically, they define whether a password can be transmitted in plain text (i.e., without encryption) or requires encryption, what encryption methods can be used, whether data encryption is required, and whether a smart card is required.

Remote access does not restrict the ability to dial out from a Windows system. As long as there is a modem and a defined connection object, any user of the system can initiate a dial-out connection. However, there is a strict limitation on who can dial into a Windows system. As discussed earlier in regard to accepting incoming connections, only selected users are authorized to connect when they attempt to dial in. For each user that is granted dial-in access, you can also define callback security. Furthermore, the incoming connection can require that all passwords and data be secured with encryption.

In addition to these security controls, remote access can be further secured using a VPN protocol. Whether the Internet is involved or not, PPTP or L2TP can be used to establish a secured and encrypted communication pipeline between the client and answering system. L2TP offers encryption using IPSec. For more information on IPSec, see the IP Security Policies section of Chapter 6, "Windows XP Security and Access Controls."

CERTIFICATES

Certificates provide proof of identity for network and Internet communications. Certificates allow systems to trust unknown online parties for the purposes of exchanging information, data, or performing e-commerce. A certificate, also called a public-key certificate or a digital certificate, is a digitally signed statement that is used for authentication and to aid in providing secured communications.

Certificates are a product of a cryptographic mechanism known as public key infrastructure (PKI). PKI is the idea of a secured environment where identity is proven by an independent third party. This system is known as a trusted third-party solution. The trusted third party in a PKI environment is called a Certificate Authority or CA. A CA is responsible for creating, issuing, managing, and revoking certificates.

The details of establishing, maintaining, and administering a PKI environment are far beyond the scope of this book and the Microsoft 70-270 exam. However, you need to understand a few basics about CAs, certificates, and trust.

A CA can be a server computer system within your organization's network or a service offered by an independent third-party organization. For communications over the Internet, the CA is almost always an independent third-party organization. These entities are known as public CAs. One of the most well-known and widely used public CAs is VeriSign (*www.verisign.com*).

A CA that is used for internal purposes only within a specific organization is called a private CA.

Certificates are used to provide trust using a third party. For example, if trust exists between user A and VeriSign and trust exists between company B and VeriSign, then company B can trust user A and vice versa. But do keep in mind that this trust extends only to identity; it does not guarantee that a malicious act won't occur or that services or products will perform as expected.

It is the responsibility of a CA to investigate the identity of all the individuals and organizations to which they assign a certificate. Because certificates are used to prove identity online, the CA must first prove your identity in reality. Sometimes this can be as little as a quick challenge-response e-mail or a phone call. Other times this can be as extensive as a credit check, an FBI background check, calling references, visiting your place of employment, checking with the Better Business Bureau, and so on. The greater the requirements and qualifications to obtain a certificate, the more trust you can place in the identity provided by a certificate.

For the most part, as a typical Internet user, you can obtain a certificate from VeriSign simply by asking. You are asked to provide personal information such as phone number, e-mail address, mailing address, and so on. Usually, VeriSign sends a confirmation e-mail to ensure your online contact information is valid before issuing you a certificate. Personal certificates are usually available at no cost. However, certificates for profit organizations must be purchased.

Certificates have a defined valid lifetime. Once a certificate's lifetime has expired, it must be replaced. To obtain a new certificate, a new request and a new background check must be performed. If a new certificate is requested before the current certificate expires, a new certificate can be generated based on the current certificate. This is known as renewal. Renewal does not require a new background check as long as the current certificate is valid.

A CA can revoke a certificate at any time. Usually reasons to revoke certificates include the certificate holder performing an illegal or malicious activity or a significant change in the identity of the certificate holder (e.g., domain name change, mailing address change, name change, etc.). Once a certificate is revoked, it is placed on the Certificate Revocation List (CRL) maintained by the CA. Whenever your system is offered a certificate to prove the identity of your communication partner, your system first checks the certificate's lifetime value then it checks the CA's CRL. If the certificate is still valid and not revoked, you are prompted whether to accept the certificate or not. In many cases you can elect to select the certificate this one time only or for all future events when this certificate is presented (with the caveat that the lifetime value and CRL is rechecked in each case).

For a certificate solution to function, you must have a trust relationship with the issuing CA of certificates you are likely to receive. Internet Explorer is preconfigured with a trust list that includes those CAs that Microsoft deems safe to trust. This trust list is known as the Trusted Root Certificate Authorities. If a specific issuing CA is not listed in this list, then your system will not accept any certificates from that CA.

To view the current Trusted Root Certificate Authorities list, open Internet Options, select the Content tab, click the Certificates button, then click the Trusted Root Certificate Authorities tab in the Certificates dialog box. When you encounter a certificate that is issued by a CA that you do not already trust, you must add that CA to your Trusted Root Certificate Authorities list in order to accept its certificates. This can be done through the Certificates dialog box or through the dialog box that appears when an unknown CA's certificate is presented to your system. Adding a CA through the Certificates dialog box requires a certificate file from the CA. Adding a CA through the dialog box is as simple as clicking Yes when prompted whether to add the CA to your Trusted Root Certificate Authorities list.

The Certificates dialog box has five tabs. The Personal tab lists any certificates assigned to the currently logged on user. The Other People tab lists any certificates installed for other users of the system. The other three tabs of Intermediate Certification Authorities, Trusted Root Certification Authorities, and Trusted Publishers (see Figure 8-16) list the CAs that your system trusts.

For more information on certificates and Certificate Authorities, please see the *Microsoft Windows XP Professional Resource Kit*, *Microsoft Windows 2000 Server Resource Kit*, or *Microsoft Windows Server 2003 Resource Kit*.

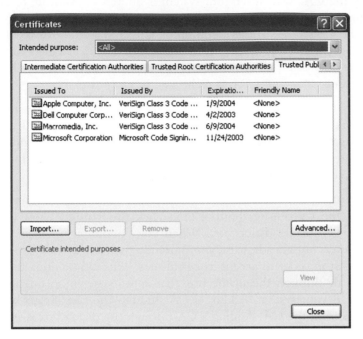

Figure 8-16   Certificate dialog box

INTERNET OPTIONS APPLET

The Internet Options applet (see Figure 8-17 and note that the dialog box is titled Internet Properties) is used to define settings for Internet Explorer and general Internet access. This applet has seven tabs, as follows:

- The General tab sets the home page, temporary file cache, URL history, colors, fonts, languages, and accessibility options.

- The Security tab defines the security level for four Web zones. The security level determines whether software is automatically downloaded, form data is submitted, or cookies (text scripts that a Web browser sends to a server to customize a user's browsing experience) are used.

- The Privacy tab is used to set the level of personal information that is shared or restricted when communicating with a Web site.

- The Content tab is used to configure the Content Advisor (a content-based site blocker), identity certificates, AutoComplete, and your online identity.

- The Connections tab is used to define how Internet Explorer and other online tools access the Internet through a LAN or dial-up network connection, which is often used for home Internet service connections.

Figure 8-17   Internet Options applet

- The Programs tab is used to specify which helper applications are used for HTML editing, e-mail, newsgroups, Internet calls, calendar, and contacts.

- The Advanced tab is used to set advanced features, such as browsing functions, HTTP 1.1, multimedia, printing, searching, security, and accessibility.

The four Web zones controlled on the Security tab are Internet, Local intranet, Trusted sites, and Restricted sites. Each zone can have a predefined default level or a customized level of security restrictions placed on that zone. The predefined default security levels are High, Medium, Medium-low, and Low. The security restrictions for each of these are as follows:

- *Low*—Provides minimal safeguards and warning prompts, most content is down-loaded and run without prompts, all active content can run, and appropriate for sites that you absolutely trust. This is the default security level of the Trusted sites zone.

- *Medium-low*—Same as Medium without prompts, most content will be run without prompts, unsigned ActiveX controls will not be downloaded, and appro-priate for sites on your local network (intranet). This is the default security level of the Local Intranet zone.

- *Medium*—Provides for safe browsing and still is functional, prompts before down-loading potentially unsafe content, unsigned ActiveX controls will not be down-loaded, and appropriate for most Internet sites. This is the default security level of the Internet zone.

- *High*—This is the safest way to browse, but also the least functional. Less-secure features are disabled, and this is appropriate for sites that might have harmful content. This is the default security level of the Restricted zone.

The content of this bulleted list is taken directly from the Security tab of the Internet Options dialog box of Windows XP Professional. Copyright is held by Microsoft.

These restrictions can include controls set for Disable, Enable, or Prompt (or possible custom settings based on security control) over downloading signed ActiveX controls, downloading unsigned ActiveX controls, running ActiveX scripts not marked as safe, running ActiveX controls and plug-ins, running ActiveX scripts marked as safe, file downloads, font downloads, Java permissions, and so on.

The Internet zone contains all sites on the Internet or local intranet that have not been placed in any of the three other zones. The Local intranet zone contains those sites within your local intranet. This list is created automatically based on include/exclude selections of three controls: all local sites not in other zones, all sites that bypass the proxy server, and all network UNC paths. The Trusted sites zone includes only those sites that you add to this zone specifically. You should only add sites to this zone that you highly trust. You can force HTTPS server verification for all sites in this zone (enabled by default). The Restricted zone includes only those sites that you specifically add to this zone. You should add any site you discover that attempts to cause harm.

The Content Advisor—accessed from the Content tab of the Internet Options dialog box—is used to control site access based on RSACi content ratings. You are able to select the level of language, nudity, sex, and violence which users are allowed to see. Preapproved sites can be defined using the site's URL as always accessible or never accessible. You can allow users to view all nonrated sites; however, this option is disabled by default. You can also define a supervisor password that allows access to all previously restricted content.

For details on configuring Internet Explorer, consult the Internet Explorer Help file or the Internet Explorer Web site at *http://www.microsoft.com/windows/ ie/default.asp.*

WINDOWS XP AND THE INTERNET

Windows XP Professional features a number of tools to help you access the vast resources of the Internet: Internet Explorer, Outlook Express, FTP client, Telnet client, and Internet Information Server (IIS). Connections can be established through Network Connections to the Internet or an Internet access point (such as a LAN with a proxy server).

Internet Explorer

Microsoft Internet Explorer (IE) version 6.0 is included with the Windows XP operating system (this was the current release of Internet Explorer when Windows XP was developed). Newer versions of Internet Explorer can be obtained from the Microsoft Web site at *www.microsoft.com/ie/*.

Internet Explorer is a state-of-the-art Web browser. In addition to being powerful and easy to use as a Web-surfing tool, Internet Explorer is tightly integrated with other Windows applications; it can call up Word to open .doc files or Excel to open .xls files across the Web. The program also includes advanced support for newsgroups and FTP and is tightly integrated with Outlook Express.

Internet Explorer offers a wide range of security related configuration options. These are discussed in earlier sections under the headings of Certificates and Internet Options.

Internet Explorer can be used as an FTP client. To connect to an FTP site, simply provide the domain name of the FTP site as the URL or create a complete URL using the following syntax: ftp://*domainname*/. Internet Explorer prompts you for logon credentials for the FTP site. If the FTP site is configured to allow only anonymous connections, the contents of the FTP root directly are displayed in Internet Explorer's main window as files and folders in the default Icons view. If the FTP site requires authentication, then a dialog box appears, prompting you for your logon credentials. You can provide the username and password in the fields provided and then click Log On. In this logon dialog box are two additional check boxes. One is to save the password to facilitate automatic logon the next time you access this FTP site. The other is to log on to the site anonymously. It is also possible to submit logon information to an FTP site by constructing the URL with the following syntax: ftp://*username:password@domainname*/.

Internet Explorer can also be used to access files stored locally on the hard drive or network shares. To access local or network files, either use the File, Open command, then click Browse to select the file or construct a URL. The correct URL syntax to access a file from the local network is: file://*sharename/path/filename*. If the file is stored on a local hard drive, the URL syntax is: file://*driveletter*;*path\filename*.

Outlook Express

One of the most popular e-mail client utilities is Outlook, a part of the suite of applications known as Microsoft Office. To tempt you with its features and offer you a taste of a multifunction e-mail client, Microsoft has included Outlook Express in Windows XP. Outlook Express is limited only by the types of messaging it supports—it can manage only Internet e-mail involving POP3, IMAP, and SMTP services. Outlook Express can be used to read and write e-mail, file and sort messages, and more. It can act as a contact management tool, is integrated with Internet Explorer for easy task switching, and offers customizable interfaces and rules (actions to be performed on messages automatically).

If "free" is your first criterion when choosing an e-mail package, Outlook Express is no slouch. However, if you are not above spending a few dollars for a worthwhile product, Outlook is worth the upgrade. For more information on Outlook and Outlook Express, visit *www.microsoft.com/outlook/*.

FTP Client

As mentioned earlier, FTP is an IP-based Application-layer protocol that handles file transfer and remote file system access and manipulation functions. Microsoft includes a command-line implementation of an FTP client as part of the Windows XP operating system. This client is installed automatically when TCP/IP is installed.

 To learn more about this program, launch a DOS window and enter ftp at the command line. When the ftp> prompt appears, enter the word help to read the program's associated list of commands (enter help *<command>* to obtain information about a specific command, where you replace *<command>* with the name of an actual FTP command, such as "get" or "put").

Even though the command-line version of FTP included with Windows XP is perfectly adequate, there are numerous freeware and shareware GUI implementations of FTP that can take its place and are much easier and friendlier to use. For a complete listing of such utilities, visit either of these Web sites, select Windows as the platform, and use "FTP" or "FTP client" as your search string:

- *www.shareware.com*
- *www.download.com*

Telnet Client

Telnet is the text-based remote interaction tool commonly used on older UNIX systems to gain access to shell accounts. Some ISPs still offer shell access to customers. The Telnet client included with Windows XP is a simple tool that attempts to establish a Telnet session with a remote system based on domain name or IP address. You can alter the display fonts and record the session for later perusal (it's all text anyway). For more information on Telnet, type "telnet" at a command prompt, and then type "help" at the Microsoft Telnet> prompt.

Internet Information Server

A reduced functionality version of Internet Information Server (IIS) is included with Windows XP Professional to allow a system to host Web and FTP services. In most cases, IIS on a client system (such as Windows XP Professional) is used for site development and testing before deployment on an IIS system (such as Windows NT Server, Windows 2000 Server, or Windows Server 2003). When hosted by Windows XP Professional, IIS is limited to the same 10 simultaneous connections as Windows XP Professional itself. Thus, it is not a platform designed or intended for public Web/FTP site hosting.

Perhaps the most important and widely recognized function of IIS is the WWW (World Wide Web) Service. This service allows the user to publish Hypertext Markup Language (HTML) documents for use on the Web. Web browsers such as Internet Explorer use the Hypertext Transfer Protocol (HTTP) to retrieve HTML documents from servers.

Overlooking limitations on the number of simultaneous users and the omission of certain site management tools, the two environments (IIS on Windows XP Professional and IIS on a Windows server) are nearly identical. They are certainly adequate to facilitate Web site development on a Windows XP Professional system with IIS intended for ultimate deployment on a Windows server system with IIS.

The FTP Server installed with IIS is used to transfer files from the server to remote computers. Most installations of FTP on the Internet are used to download drivers and other data or software files.

NOTE

This code module represents the server side of FTP, whereas the software mentioned earlier in the chapter covered the client side of FTP. In other words, this module permits machines elsewhere on the network to upload files to or download files from a Windows XP Professional system. The client-side software only permits the system to perform the same activities with other FTP servers elsewhere on the network or the Internet.

Web server resources are managed similarly to any other network resource. You should think of Web and FTP services as a type of share for Internet clients. Thus, troubleshooting Web resource access problems is like troubleshooting typical network shared resource access problems. You need to manage file permissions on an NTFS file object level, and general access to resources through the share (or, in this case, Web or FTP services). If a user is unable to gain access to a resource through the Web or FTP, check the NTFS file object-level permissions first on the file/object/resource itself, then on all of its parent containers. Next, check the setting on the Web or FTP service itself. To access resources over Web or FTP, the user must have at least Read access granted through the service and at least Read access on the file or resource based on group memberships. Keep in mind that most Web access is anonymous, whereas many FTP sites require user authentication for access. However, the logon credentials for FTP are transmitted in clear text. The anonymous user account IUSR_<computername> is a member of the Everyone and the Authenticated Users groups. This account is used to "authenticate" anonymous users on both Web and FTP sites hosted by IIS. Be sure to check the permissions for these groups as well.

A single Windows XP Professional system can be assigned multiple IP addresses. When a system has multiple IP addresses and is the host of IIS as a Web server, each Web site can be assigned its own IP address. Assigning each Web site a different IP address is handled on the Web Site tab of the Properties dialog box. Just set the IP Address field to the specific IP address you want a particular Web site to use.

If you want to host multiple Web sites from a system that has only a single IP address, you must employ host headers. Host headers are defined through the Advanced button located alongside the IP Address field on the Web Site tab of the Properties dialog box of a Web site. Each unique Web site should be assigned its own host header. A host header is usually a word, short phrase, domain name, or title that the administrator of the Web site wants to use as the distinguishing element for that site. The Web user never sees the host header. If host headers are not used, a Web user would always see the first or default Web site hosted by the one-IP address IIS Web server. This would occur even if they used the URL or domain name of any other Web site hosted by that Web server.

Activity 8-8: Internet Information Server

Time Required: 20 minutes

Objective: Install Internet Information Server on Windows XP Professional.

Description: Windows XP Professional is considered a more robust and secure operating system than previous versions of Microsoft desktop operating systems. As such, it is more likely that someone may want to set up his or her computer as a Web server, where an actual server is not available or required. In this activity, you install Internet Information Server on the computer.

To install Internet Information Server on a Windows XP Professional system:

1. Click **Start**, **Control Panel**. Click **Switch to Classic View** if Control Panel is currently in Category view.

2. Double-click **Add or Remove Programs**.

3. Select the **Add/Remove Windows Components** item in the left column. This starts the Windows Components Wizard.

4. Select the check box beside Internet Information Services (IIS). Click **Next**.

5. When prompted, provide the path to the Windows XP Professional CD. This can involve just inserting the CD into the drive and clicking **OK** or using a Browser dialog box to locate the \i386 directory on the CD.

6. The installation wizard copies files to your system. This can take several minutes. You might be prompted for the path to the CD a second time. Eventually, click **Finish**.

7. Click **Close** to terminate the Add or Remove Programs applet.

8. Close Control Panel by selecting **File**, **Close**.

Activity 8-9: Managing Web Resources

Time Required: 20 minutes

Objective: Create a default Web page using a text editor.

Description: Each Web site has a default page. In this activity, you use a text editor (Notepad) to create a simple default page for your Internet Information Server.

To manage resources hosted by a Web server:

1. Click **Start**, **Control Panel**. Click **Switch to Classic View** if Control Panel is currently in Category view.

2. Double-click **Administrative Tools**.

3. Double-click **Internet Information Services**.

4. Expand the left node items by double-clicking them until you can see Default Web Site.

5. Click **Default Web Site**.

6. Click **Action**, **Properties**.

7. Click the **Home Directory** tab.

8. In the box labeled **Local Path**, take note of the directory path listed there. It is most likely c:\inetpub\wwwroot. This is the top-level root directory for your Web site.

9. Click **OK**.

10. Select **File**, **Exit** to close the IIS tool.

11. Open **Windows Explorer** by clicking **Start**, **All Programs**, **Accessories**, **Windows Explorer**.

12. Locate the top-level root directory for your Web site and select it in the left pane of Windows Explorer.

13. In the right pane of Windows Explorer, right-click an empty area, select **New** from the shortcut menu, and then select **Text Document** from the submenu.

14. Type the filename **default.htm**, and press **Enter**. If prompted about whether to change the filename extension, click **Yes**.

15. Open **Notepad** by clicking **Start**, **All Programs**, **Accessories**, **Notepad**.

16. Select **File**, **Open**.

17. Change the Files of type in the pull-down list to **All Files**.

18. Locate and select the **default.htm** document.

19. Click **Open**.

20. Type the following into the body of this document: **<HTML><BODY><P>This is the default document.</P></BODY></HTML>**.

21. Select **File**, **Save**.

22. Select **File**, **Exit**.

23. Double-click **Internet Explorer** on the desktop or open it from the Start menu.

24. Select **File**, **Open**.

25. Type **localhost** and click **OK**.

8

26. The Web browser should display the default document you created by showing a line stating "This is the default document."

27. Select **File**, **Close**.

28. Delete the **default.htm** file you created.

ORDER PRINTS ONLINE

Order Prints Online is a feature of the My Pictures folder and any media folder defined as an image repository (see the Working with Media Folders and the Customize Tab section in Chapter 4, "Managing Windows XP File Systems and Storage"). This command starts the Online Print Ordering Wizard, which walks you through the process of submitting digital images to a printing company. You select the images to print, the sizes, quantities, and billing and shipping information. The wizard requires that Internet access be available. If you need help with the wizard, use the Help and Support Center of Windows XP.

CLIENT VS. SERVER-BASED REMOTE ACCESS

Choosing which platform to use as a remote access server is usually straightforward. Windows XP Professional is limited to a single incoming dial-up connection and can support only 10 simultaneous network connections (including LAN and VPN). Windows 2000 Server and Windows Server 2003 both support up to 256 concurrent incoming dial-up connections and have no hard restriction on the number of simultaneous network connections (restricted by license for LAN and hardware for VPN or Internet connections). Windows XP Professional can share an Internet link with a workgroup, but the workgroup is forced to use DHCP, and the range of IP addresses is assigned by ICS. Windows servers offer Internet Connection Sharing through a proxy router that does not restrict the clients to DHCP or a specified IP address range. Windows XP Professional lacks a full-featured version of IIS, which is integrated into Windows server products.

From these issues, it is clear that a small workgroup network can use Windows XP Professional as its remote access server if it can operate within the connection limitations. If an organization requires greater flexibility and connectivity, a Windows server should be selected to act as the remote access server.

REMOTE ACCESS TROUBLESHOOTING

Remote access problems can be fairly elusive, but there are several commonsense first steps and several useful Windows XP tools to simplify the process of troubleshooting. Your first approach to a remote access problem should include considerations for:

- Physical connections (phone lines, serial cables, etc.)
- Power to external devices
- Properly installed and updated drivers
- Properly configured settings
- Correct authentication credentials
- Similar encryption or security requirements
- Proper protocol requirements and settings

If reviewing these items still fails to uncover the problem, there are several log files you can examine to hopefully glean more specific information. There are three logs related to remote access events. The first log is a file containing all communications made between the OS and the modem device during connection establishment. This log must be enabled through the Diagnostics tab of the modem's Properties on the Modems tab of the Phone and Modem Options applet. Once enabled, a text file named after the modem (in the format "ModemLog_Practical Peripherals PC288LCD V.34.txt") is stored in the main Windows XP directory. Simply clicking View Log next to the enable check box on the Diagnostics tab allows you to view the file with Notepad.

The second log file, PPP.LOG, records the communications involved in the setup, management, and continuity of a PPP connection. Editing the Registry enables this log. The PPP value in the HKEY_LOCAL_MACHINE\SOFTWARE\Microsoft\Tracing\ Registry key should be set to 1 (one) to start the logging. This file is stored in the %systemroot%\ tracing folder.

The final log is the System log as viewed through the Event Viewer. This log often records events related to remote access connection failures. By combining data gleaned from these logs, you should be able to determine the cause of your connection problem and easily discover a simple resolution.

CHAPTER SUMMARY

- ☐ This chapter introduced you to the Windows XP Remote Access Service, including the significant features, services, and protocols of remote access in Windows XP.
- ☐ This chapter examined remote access WAN connections and protocols, how to install and configure remote access, and how to take full advantage of remote access dial-up networking and security features.

❑ Internet Connection Sharing can be used to share a single ISP link with a small network.

❑ Internet Connection Firewall is used to protect systems against unwanted traffic from the Internet or untrusted network connections.

❑ Certificates are used to prove identity and support secured online transactions.

❑ This chapter discussed the Internet access features built into Windows XP and how they can be employed to gain access to vast public and private resources.

❑ Windows XP is also designed to participate in Virtual Private Networking (VPNs) by establishing an encrypted link between two systems over the Internet.

❑ Internet Information Server can be used to host Web and FTP sites for others to access.

KEY TERMS

Dynamic Host Configuration Protocol (DHCP) — A method of automatically assigning IP addresses to client computers on a network.

gateway — A computer that serves as a router, a format translator, or a security filter for an entire network.

ISDN (Integrated Services Digital Network) — A direct, digital dial-up PSTN Data Link-layer connection that operates at 64 KB per channel over regular twisted-pair cable between a subscriber site and a PSTN central office.

Layer Two Tunneling Protocol (L2TP) — A VPN protocol developed by Cisco Systems to improve security over Internet links which employs IPSec for data encryption.

modem — A Data Link-layer device used to create an analog signal suitable for transmission over telephone lines from a digital data stream. Modern modems also include a command set to negotiate connections and data rates with remote modems and to set their default behavior.

Point-to-Point Protocol (PPP) — A Network-layer transport that provides connectivity over serial or modem lines. PPP can negotiate any transport protocol used by both systems involved in the link and can automatically assign IP, DNS, and gateway addresses when used with TCP/IP.

Point-to-Point Tunneling Protocol (PPTP) — A protocol used to connect to private networks through the Internet or an ISP.

port — Any physical communication channel to which a modem, direct cable, or other device can be connected to enable a link between two computers.

PPP Multilink — A remote access capability to aggregate multiple data streams into one network connection for the purpose of using more than one modem or ISDN channel in a single connection.

PSTN (Public Switched Telephone Networks) — A global network of interconnected digital and analog communication links originally designed to support voice communication between any two points in the world, but quickly adapted to handle digital data traffic.

Remote Access Service — The service in Windows XP that allows users to log into the system remotely.

serial — A method of communication that transfers data across a medium one bit at a time, usually adding start and stop bits to ensure reliable delivery.

Serial Line Internet Protocol (SLIP) — An implementation of the IP protocol over serial lines. SLIP has been made obsolete by PPP.

wide area network (WAN) — A geographically dispersed network of networks connected by routers and communications links. The Internet is the largest WAN.

X.25 — A standard that defines packet-switching networks.

REVIEW QUESTIONS

1. You have configured a Windows XP Professional client to dial up and establish a connection to a Windows server computer. The user adds a dial-up connection object, sets the proper network configuration, and the modem is functioning properly. The user submits the username and password correctly. Unfortunately, the user is unable to authenticate properly. What might be causing this problem?

   a. The user did not configure the gateway properly.

   b. The user was not granted the appropriate dial-in permissions.

   c. The user was not added to the dial-in users group.

   d. Internet Connection Firewall is blocking the authentication.

2. DHCP is the option for automatically assigning IP configuration to TCP/IP dial-up clients. True or False?

3. Windows XP Professional supports PPP logon scripts. True or False?

4. Which of the following remote access-related logs are enabled by default?

   a. PPP.LOG

   b. Modemlog_<modem name>.txt

   c. System log

5. Which of the following encrypted authentication options does Windows XP Professional support through remote access? (Choose all that apply.)

   a. PAP

   b. SPAP

   c. DES-3

   d. MS-CHAP

   e. PGP

8

6. The special protocol _____ allows multiple channels to be aggregated to increase bandwidth.

   a. PPP Multilink

   b. PPTP

   c. PPP

   d. SLIP

7. Where in Windows XP Professional do you specify which users have dial-in permissions to the remote access server?

   a. Network Connections

   b. Control Panel

   c. Remote Access Admin Tool

   d. My Computer

8. Which remote access security option also has an additional option to encrypt data?

   a. Require encrypted authentication

   b. Require C2 encrypted authentication

   c. Require B encrypted authentication

   d. Require Microsoft Encrypted Authentication

9. Which remote access callback option provides the greatest level of security?

   a. Set by Caller

   b. Set by Server

   c. Preset to

   d. Call back and confirm remote access password

10. Which of the following protocols are supported by both Windows XP remote access clients and servers?

    a. SLIP

    b. PPP

    c. none of the above

    d. all of the above

11. Which of the following are similar technologies used to establish secured WAN links over the Internet?

    a. MPPP

    b. PPTP

    c. SLIP

    d. L2TP

12. Help-U-Sell has just opened a new office in Cedar Park, Texas. They have a small workgroup network of eight computers. A cable modem has been installed. Which of the following technologies should be used to provide each system in the office with Internet access and prevent as much unwanted traffic as possible?

    a. IPSec

    b. ICS

    c. ICF

    d. callback

    e. L2TP

13. Which connection protocol can be used by Windows XP Professional to connect to remote systems over standard telephone lines?

    a. SLIP

    b. PPP

    c. DLC

    d. PPTP

14. By default, Internet Connection Firewall blocks traffic of which service type if it originates from the Internet instead of responding to a request by an internal client?

    a. FTP

    b. L2TP

    c. POP3

    d. IKE

    e. Remote Desktop

    f. Telnet

    g. HTTP

15. The New Connection Wizard from Network Connections is used to create both remote access connections and standard LAN connections. True or False?

16. If you want to connect only to servers that offer secured data transmission, which of the following encryption settings should you define for your connection object?

    a. No encryption allowed (server disconnects if it requires encryption)

    b. Optional encryption (connect even if no encryption)

    c. Require encryption (disconnect if sever declines)

17. Windows XP supports Direct Cable Connections under remote access using:

    a. RS-232 null modem cables

    b. APC UPS cables

    c. LapLink cables (i.e. parallel pass-through cables)

    d. printer cables

8

18. Remote access is remote control for Windows XP. True or False?

19. Internet Connection Sharing can be used to share which of the following types of connections with a workgroup network?

    a. Internet

    b. LAN dial-up

    c. VPN

    d. incoming

    e. bridge connection

20. You can connect to another computer from a remote access client using resources in the same manner as if you were connected on a LAN. True or False?

21. Dialing rules or dialing locations are used to define the geographic location of a mobile computer to prescribe the dialing procedures. True or False?

22. The modem-specific log file is enabled through what utility?

    a. Computer Management

    b. Phone and Modem Options

    c. Network Connections

    d. Server applet

23. Which of the following are Internet utilities included with Windows XP Professional?

    a. Internet Explorer

    b. Internet Information Server

    c. Outlook

    d. Telnet

    e. FTP client

24. In which of the following situations is the use of Windows XP Professional as a remote access server a reasonable option?

    a. A single telecommuter needs to connect to the office network.

    b. A domain network needs Internet access.

    c. A SOHO network needs Internet access.

    d. A high-traffic, e-commerce Web site needs hosting.

    e. A private network needs internal Web documentation access.

25. Offline Files are cached locally at logoff, are accessed in the same way as the original files, and are automatically synchronized by default. True or False?

CASE PROJECTS

Case Project 8-1

1. Your organization has decided to allow several employees to work from home. With Windows XP Professional on the telecommuters' systems, describe your configuration and setup options, including how you can deal with security and nondedicated connections.

2. After installing a new modem, none of your connection objects function, even after you've re-created them. Describe the process to troubleshoot this problem.

8

9

PRINTING AND FAXING

After reading this chapter and completing the exercises, you will be able to:

- ◆ Understand Windows XP print terminology and architecture
- ◆ Work with the Windows XP print subsystem architecture
- ◆ Work with printer driver software
- ◆ Print across the network and understand the printing process
- ◆ Install and manage printers
- ◆ Configure a printer and manage the print server
- ◆ Troubleshoot printing
- ◆ Configure Windows XP fax capabilities

Printing is an integral part of any operating system. Often, people do not understand a concept or layout until they see it on hard copy.

In this chapter, you are introduced to some of the concepts associated with Windows XP printing, and then you will learn what is involved in installing and configuring printers for Windows XP. Although this may sound somewhat simplistic, because of the many options that are available when accessing printers in the Windows XP environment, this topic is more complex than it may at first appear. For example, it is important to understand the distinction between printers that are directly attached to a computer and those with built-in network interfaces that are attached directly to a networking medium. You will also learn how to troubleshoot common printing-related problems on Windows XP-based networks and systems. Finally, you will learn how to install and configure the Windows XP fax components.

WINDOWS XP PRINTING TERMINOLOGY

As is the case in other areas of Windows XP system architecture and behavior, Microsoft uses its own unique and specialized terminology to describe and explain how printers interact with the Windows XP system, and how its overall printing capabilities work. For the best results with the Microsoft certification tests, it is important to understand Microsoft's printing subsystem concepts, architecture, and behavior, which is why this chapter begins with a vocabulary list of Microsoft print terminology before discussing the key components of the Microsoft print architecture and behavior. For convenience, these terms are presented in alphabetical order in the following list:

- *Client application*—An application or service that creates print jobs for output, which can be either end-user-originated or created by a print server (see also print client).

- *Connecting to a printer*—The negotiation of a connection to a shared printer through the browser service from a client or service across the network to the machine where the shared printer resides.

- *Creating a printer*—The process of using the Add Printer Wizard in the Printers and Faxes applet (Start, Printers and Faxes) to name and define settings for a print device in a Windows XP-based network.

- *Direct-attached printer*—A print device attached directly to a computer, usually through a parallel port (see also network interface printer).

- *Network interface printer*—A print device attached directly to the network medium, usually by means of a built-in network interface integrated within the printer, but sometimes by means of a parallel-attached network printer interface.

- *Print client*—A network client machine that transmits print jobs across the network to a printer for spooling and delivery to a designated print device or printer pool.

- *Print device*—In everyday language, a piece of equipment that provides output service—in other words, a printer; however, in Microsoft terminology, a printer is a logical service that accepts print jobs and delivers them to some print device for output when that device is ready. Therefore, in Microsoft terminology, a print device is any piece of equipment that can produce output, so this term also describes a plotter, a fax machine, or a slide printer, as well as a text-oriented output device, such as an HP LaserJet.

- *Print job*—The contents of a completely or partially interpreted data file that contains text and control characters that will ultimately be delivered to a print device to be printed or otherwise rendered in some tangible form.

- *Print resolution*—A measurement of the number of dots per inch (dpi) that describes the output capabilities of a print device; most laser printers can produce output at 300 to 600 dpi if not greater. In general, the larger the dpi rating for a device, the better looking its output is (but high-resolution devices cost more than low-resolution ones).

- *Print server*—A computer that links print devices to the network and shares those devices with client computers on the network. In the Windows XP environment, Windows XP Professional, Windows 2000, and Windows Server 2003 can function as print servers.

- *Print Server services*—A collection of named software components on a print server that handles incoming print jobs and forwards them to a print spooler for postprocessing and delivery to a print device. These components include support for special job handling that can enable a variety of client computers to send print jobs to a print server for processing.

- *Print spooler*—A collection of Windows XP dynamic link libraries (DLLs) used to acquire, process, catalog, and dispense print jobs to print devices. The print spooler manages an area called the spool file on a print server that acts like a holding tank; pending print jobs are stored there until they have been successfully output. The term "despooling" refers to the process of reading and interpreting what is in a spool file for delivery to a print device.

- *Printer (logical printer)*—In Microsoft terminology, a printer is not a physical device, but rather a named system object that communicates between the operating system and a print device. The printer handles the printing process for Windows XP from the time a print command is issued until a print job has been successfully output. The settings established for a printer in the Add Printer Wizard in the Printers and Faxes applet (Start, Printers and Faxes) not only indicate which print device (or devices, in the case of a printer pool) handles print output, but also provide controls over how print jobs are handled (banner page, special postprocessing, and so forth). Adding a local printer is detailed in Activity 9-1. Removing a printer is covered in Activity 9-7.

- *Printer driver*—The special-purpose software components that manage communication between the Windows XP I/O Manager and a specific print device. Ultimately, printer drivers make it possible for Windows XP to despool print jobs and send them to a print device for output services. Modern printer drivers also allow the printer to communicate with Windows XP, and to inform it about print job status, error conditions (out of paper, paper jam, and so forth), and print job problems.

- *Printer pool*—A collection of two or more identically configured print devices to which one or more Windows XP printers direct their print jobs. Basically, a printer pool permits two or more printers to act in concert to handle high-volume printing needs.

- *Queue (print queue)*—A series of files stored in sequential order waiting for delivery from a spool file to a print device.

9

- *Rendering*—Windows XP produces output according to the following sequence of steps: (1) A client application or a service sends file information to a software component called the **Graphical Device Interface (GDI)**. (2) The GDI accepts the data, performs any necessary local processing, and sends the data to a designated printer. (3) If this printer is local, the data is directed to the local print driver; if the printer is remote (located elsewhere on the network), the data is shipped to a print server across the network. (4) Either way, the driver then takes the print job and translates it into the mixture of text and control characters needed to produce output on the designated print device. (5) This file is stored in a spooling file until its turn for output comes up, at which point it is shipped to a print device. (6) The target device accepts the input data and turns it into the proper low-level format for rendering on that machine, on a page-by-page basis. (7) As each page image is created, it is sent to the printer's print engine, where it is output on paper (or whatever medium the print device may use).

- *Spooling*—One of the functions of the print spooler, this is the act of writing the contents of a print job to a file on disk so the print jobs are not lost if the print server is shut down before the job is completed.

Familiarity with these terms is helpful when interpreting questions about Windows XP printing on the certification exam, and in selecting the proper answers to such questions. Testing considerations aside, some familiarity with this lexicon makes it much easier to understand Microsoft Help files and documentation on this subject as well.

WINDOWS XP PRINT SUBSYSTEM ARCHITECTURE

Given all this specialized terminology, it is essential to put it into context within the Windows XP environment, which is why the architecture of this subsystem is described next. The Windows XP print subsystem architecture consists of several components that turn print data into a printable file, transfer that file to a printer, and manage the way in which multiple print jobs are handled by a printer. These components are:

- GDI
- Printer driver
- Print spooler

Each of these elements is described in the subsections that follow.

Graphical Device Interface

The Graphical Device Interface (GDI) is the portion of Windows XP that begins the process of producing visual output, whether that output goes to the screen or to the printer; it is the part of Windows XP that makes WYSIWYG (what-you-see-is-what-you-get) output possible. In the case of screen output, the GDI calls the video driver; in the case of printed output, it calls a printer driver and provides information about the targeted print device and what type of data must be rendered for output.

Printer Driver

A printer driver is a Windows XP software component that enables an application to communicate with a printer through the IP Manager in the Executive Services module in the Windows XP kernel. A printer driver is composed of three subcomponents that work together as a unit:

- *Printer graphics driver*—Responsible for rendering the GDI commands into **Device Driver Interface (DDI)** commands that can be sent to the printer. Each graphics driver renders a different printer language; for example, Pscript.dll handles PostScript printing requests, Plotter.dll handles the HPGL/2 language used by many plotters, and Rasdd.dll deals with printer languages based on raster images (that is, those based on bitmapped images, which are collections of dots). Rasdd.dll is used by PCL (Printer Control Language) and most dot matrix printers.

- *Printer interface driver*—You need some means of interacting with the printer, and the role of the printer interface driver is to provide that means; it provides the interface you see when you open the Printers and Faxes applet (Start, Printers and Faxes).

- *Characterization data file*—Provides information to the printer interface driver about the make and model of a specific type of print device, including its features, such as double-sided printing, printing at various resolutions, and accepting certain paper sizes.

Printer drivers are not compatible across hardware platforms, so although some client types (including Windows XP Professional, Windows Server 2003, Windows 2000 Professional and Server, Windows NT 4.0, 3.51, 3.5, and 3.1 Workstation and Server, and Windows 95 and 98) can print to a Windows XP print server without first installing a local printer driver—they'll download the driver from the print server—you must make sure that necessary drivers are available for the proper platforms.

Print Spooler

The print spooler (Spoolsv.exe) is a collection of DLLs and device drivers that receives, processes, schedules, and distributes print jobs. The spooler is implemented as part of the Spooler service, which is required for printing. By default, the Spooler service is installed as part of the base Windows XP installation process (to check its status, look at the Print Spooler entry in the Services window, or look for Spoolsv.exe in the list on the Processes tab in the Task Manager). The Spooler includes the following components:

- Print router

- Local and remote print providers

- Print processors

- Print monitor

The print spooler can accept data from the print provider in two main **data types**: enhanced metafile (EMF) or RAW. **Enhanced metafile (EMF)** spool files are device-independent files used in Windows XP to reduce the amount of time spent processing a print job—all GDI calls needed to produce the print job are included in the file. **RAW** spool files are device-dependent output files that have been completely processed (usually by their sending application or service) and are ready for output on the targeted print device. After a spool file has been created, control is restored to the application that created the print job, and other processing can resume in the foreground.

 EMF spool files are normally smaller than RAW spool files.

RAW spool files are used for local print jobs, for Encapsulated PostScript (.eps) print jobs, or when specified by the user. Unlike EMF spool files, which still require some rendering once it is determined to which printer they're going, RAW spool files are fully defined when created. The Windows XP print processor also recognizes plain ASCII text files, which may be submitted by other clients (especially UNIX machines); the name of this spool file type is TEXT.

Print Router

The **print router** sends print requests from clients to the print server, so the requests can be routed to the appropriate print provider. When a Windows XP client computer connects to a Windows XP print server, communication takes place in the form of remote procedure calls from the client's print router (Winspool.drv) to the server's print router (Spoolss.dll), at which point the server's print router passes the print request to the appropriate print provider: the local print provider if it's a local job, and either the Windows XP or the NetWare print provider if it is sent over the network.

Print Provider

The **print provider** is server-side software that sends a print job to the proper server in the format required by that server. When a client sends a print job to a remote printer, the print router polls the remote print providers on the client computer and passes control of the print job to the first computer that recognizes the name of the specified printer. Windows XP uses one of the two following print providers:

- *Windows XP print provider (Win32Spl.dll)*—Used to transfer print jobs to Windows network print servers
- *NetWare print provider (Nwprovau.dll)*—Used to transfer print jobs to NetWare print servers

If the Windows XP print provider recognizes the printer name, it sends the print job along in one of two ways, depending on the operating system on the print server. If the print server is running a compatible network operating system (such as Windows NT 3.*x*, Windows for Workgroups, or LAN Manager), the print job is routed by NetBIOS to the print server. If the print server is running Windows XP or Windows NT 4.0, the print provider contacts the Spooler service on the print server, which then passes it to the local print provider.

The local print provider writes the contents of the print job to a spool file (which has the extension .spl) and tracks administration information for that print job. By default, all spool files are stored in the %*systemroot*%\System32\Spool\Printers directory. You can change that location if desired, (perhaps if you've installed a faster drive) by adjusting the print server settings in the Printers and Faxes utility from the Start menu or from Control Panel. (You practice changing the location of the spool file in Activity 9-6.)

Spool files are normally deleted after the print job to which they apply is completed because they only exist to keep the print job from getting lost in case of a power failure that affects the print server. However, you can configure the spooler to retain all print jobs, even after they are printed. This control is accessed on a per-printer basis on the Advanced tab of the printer's Properties dialog box.

If a NetWare print provider recognizes the printer name, it passes the print job along to the NetWare workstation service, which then passes control of the print job to the NetWare redirector for transfer to the NetWare print server.

NOTE To send print jobs from a Windows XP client to a NetWare server, you must have Client Service for NetWare (CSNW) installed on the client computer (see Chapter 7, "Network Protocols"). To route print jobs through a Windows Server computer to a NetWare print server, the Windows Server must have the Gateway Services for NetWare (GSNW) installed.

Print Processor

A **print processor** works with the printer driver to despool spool files during playback, making any needed changes to the spool file according to its data type. The print processor itself is a PostScript program that understands the format of a document image's file and how to print the file to a specific PostScript printer or class of printers. Windows 2000 Server and Windows Server 2003 support two print processors: one for Windows clients and one for Macintosh clients (Sfmpsprt.dll), which is normally installed only after the Services for Macintosh are installed. Remember that Services for Macintosh is included only with Windows Server products, which is why this isn't an issue on Windows XP Professional machines.

The built-in Windows print processor in Windows XP Professional understands EMF data files, three kinds of RAW data files, and text files. However, the Macintosh print processor that's installed on a Windows Server when Services for Macintosh is installed understands only Pstscrpt1, which signifies that the spool file contains PostScript code from a Macintosh

9

client, but that the output is not destined for delivery to a PostScript printer. In actuality, this data type lets the print processor know that a postprocessing job must be performed to translate the PostScript into the equivalent RAW data for output on the target printer before the print job can be spooled to the targeted print device.

 Windows XP uses a raster image processor to send print jobs from a Macintosh client to a printer. The limitations of this processor mean that print jobs can have a maximum resolution of 300 dpi and must be printed in monochrome, regardless of the capabilities of the targeted printer. However, there are third-party raster image processors available for those who want to use the full capabilities of their printers even when printing through Services for Macintosh.

Print Monitor

The print monitor is the final link in the chain of the printing process. It is actually two monitors: a language monitor and a port monitor. The **language monitor**, created when you install a printer driver if a language monitor is associated with the driver, comes into play only if the print device is bidirectional, meaning that messages about a print job's status may be sent both to and from the computer. Bidirectional capabilities are necessary to transmit meaningful error messages from the printer to the client. If the language monitor has a role, it sets up the communication with the printer and then passes control to the port monitor. The language monitor supplied with Windows XP uses the Printer Job Language. The **Printer Job Language** provides printer control at the print-job level and enables users to change printer default levels, such as number of copies, color, and printer languages. If a manufacturer creates a printer that speaks a different language, it would need to define another language monitor, because the computer and print device must speak the same language for communication to work.

The **port monitor** transmits the print job either to the print device or to another server. It controls the flow of information to the I/O port to which the print device is connected (a serial, parallel, network, or SCSI port). The port monitor supplied with Windows XP controls parallel and serial ports. If you want to connect a print device to a SCSI port or network port, you must use a port monitor supplied by the vendor. Regardless of type, however, port monitors interface with ports, not printers, and are in fact unaware of the type of print devices to which they are connected. The print job is already configured by the print processor before it ever reaches the output port.

Windows XP supports the following port monitors:

- Local port monitor (Localmon.dll)
- Hewlett-Packard network port monitor (Hpmon.dll)
- Line printer (LPR) port monitor (Lprmon.dll)
- AppleTalk port monitor (Sfmmon.dll)
- DEC network port monitor (Decpsmon.dll)

- Lexmark Mark Vision port monitor (Lexmon.dll)

- NetWare port monitor (Nwmon.dll)

- Standard TCP/IP port monitor (SFM)

- Hypertext Transfer Protocol (HTTP) port monitor

- PJL monitor (Pjlmon.dll)

By default, only the local print monitor is installed. To use another monitor, you have to create a new port when configuring a printer from the Printers icon.

At this point, you've now been exposed to the unique Microsoft printing terminology and to the architecture of the Windows XP print subsystem. Now, you can learn how to work with printers and to define and configure them.

In the Windows XP world, the focus is on printers, not print devices. As you've seen, in Windows XP parlance, printers are logical constructs—named combinations of output ports, a print driver, and configuration settings that can involve one or more print devices, the physical output devices—such as laser, ink-jet, or dot matrix printers, plotters, fax modems, or slide makers. All the configuring and manipulation you do in Windows XP is done to printers, not to the print devices.

PRINTER DRIVER SOFTWARE

The function of a printer driver is to provide an interface between the client and the printer, whether that printer is connected to a print server or directly to the client. In other words, the job of printing software is to insulate applications from having to incorporate the logic and understanding necessary to communicate with a large collection of printers. That's why the functions that take application-specific file data and translate them into formats suitable for printing are included in the printer drivers themselves.

Because selecting a particular printer for output is part of the Windows printing process, it makes perfect sense to put this intelligence into the driver. That's because you must indicate what kind of device to which you want to send a print job as a part of instructing an application to print to a specific printer. Because print devices differ so much from manufacturer to manufacturer, and even from model to model, the right place to bury the details is in the printer driver itself. Not only does this shield application developers from having to write code to drive every kind of print device imaginable, it also puts the task of building the file translation routines on the print device manufacturers because they're the usual source of driver software.

PRINTING ACROSS THE NETWORK

Few organizations can afford to give each user his or her own printer, which explains why printing to a remote printer across the network is by far the most common print scenario on Microsoft networks. (In fact, many experts argue that sharing printers was one of the original primary justifications for networking.) Two typical options for printing across the network exist for Microsoft network clients, including Windows XP Professional clients:

- You can print to a printer connected to a print server through a parallel or serial port.
- You can print to a printer connected directly to the network.

The main reason to connect a printer directly to the network is for convenience, because the printer doesn't have to be located near the print server. A print server must still provide drivers and print job management.

The Printing Process

Now that you're familiar with the components of the printing process, here is how they fit together when printing from a Windows XP Professional client:

1. The user chooses to print from an application, causing the application to call the GDI. The GDI, in turn, calls the printer driver associated with the target print device. Using the document information from the application and the printer information from the printer driver, the GDI renders the print job.

2. The print job is passed to the spooler. The client side of the spooler makes a remote procedure call to the server side, which then calls the print router component of the server.

3. The print router passes the job to the local print provider, which spools the job to disk.

4. The local print provider polls the print processors, passing the job to the processor that recognizes the selected printer. Based on the data type (EMF or RAW) used in the spool file, any necessary changes are made to the spool file to make it printable on the selected print device.

5. If desired, the separator page processor adds a separator page to the print job.

6. The print job is despooled to the print monitor. If the printer device is bidirectional, the language monitor sets up communication. If not, or after the language monitor is done, the job is passed to the port monitor, which handles the job of getting the print job to the port to which the print device is connected.

7. The print job arrives at the print device and is printed.

INSTALLING AND MANAGING PRINTERS

The Printers and Faxes window is the starting point for all printer installation and management. To reach it, select Start, Printers and Faxes. If there are no printers installed, click the Add a printer command in the Quick List to create a printer (add a local printer definition) or connect to one across the network. After you have created or connected to a printer, it appears in this window with its own icon, as the example in Figure 9-1 shows. To set its properties, right-click the printer and choose Properties from the shortcut menu that appears.

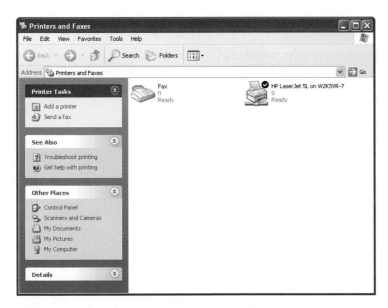

Figure 9-1   The Printers and Faxes window

Creating a Local Printer

In Windows XP jargon, "creating a printer" means that you're setting up a printer for local use. To do so, click the Add a printer command in the Printers and Faxes window and answer the questions as prompted, including the following:

- Is the attached printer Plug and Play compatible?
- Is the printer local or on the network?
- To which port will the printer be connected?
- What is the make and model of the printer?
- What do you want the printer to be named?
- Do you want the printer to be the default for all print jobs?
- Should the printer be shared with the network?

If you're not sure whether your printer requires some fine-tuning (such as port configuration), you can create the printer and adjust its properties later.

After you have answered all the questions and supplied the needed files for the installation, you can choose to print a test page to make sure you have set up the printer properly.

Activity 9-1: Add a Local Printer

Time Required: 10 minutes

Objective: Install the drivers required to create a local printer.

Description: To set up a printer on a computer, the associated drivers must be installed locally. In this activity, you will install the required drivers and create a local printer.

To create a local printer:

This activity does not require a physical printer.

1. Click **Start**, **Printers and Faxes**.
2. Click **Add a printer** in the Printer Tasks column.
3. Click **Next** in the Add Printer Wizard dialog box.
4. Select **Local printer attached to this computer**.
5. Deselect the Automatically detect and install my Plug and Play printer check box if it is selected.
6. Click **Next**.
7. In the Use the following port pull-down list, ensure that **LPT1** is selected.
8. Click **Next**.
9. From the list of manufacturers, locate and select **HP**.
10. From the list of printers, locate and select **HP LaserJet 5**.
11. Click **Next**.
12. If the required printer driver is already present on the system, a prompt is displayed asking whether to keep or to replace the existing driver. Select to replace the driver, and then click **Next**.

13. Provide a name for this printer and select **Yes** for this printer to be the default if prompted.

14. Click **Next**.

15. Select **Do not share this printer** if it is not already selected.

16. Click **Next**.

17. Select **No** to printing a test page if it is not already selected.

18. Click **Next**.

19. Click **Finish**.

20. The newly added printer is displayed in the Printers and Faxes window (you may need to refresh the display by pressing F5).

Connecting to a Remote Printer

Connecting to a remote printer is even simpler than creating a printer. Once again, click the Add a printer link in the Printers and Faxes window, but this time choose to connect to a network printer instead of creating one locally. You are presented with a list of shared printers to which to connect, and have the option of making that printer the default. Select to connect to it, and your work is done. Because Windows XP clients download printer drivers from the print server, you don't have to install drivers locally.

 Windows XP print servers, by default, automatically host and install drivers for Windows XP and Windows 2000. They can also host and install drivers for Windows 95/98/ME, Windows NT 4.0 Intel or Alpha, or Windows XP IA64 if an administrator adds the appropriate drivers. Note that most Windows 2000 drivers also function for Windows Server 2003.

Managing Print Jobs

The Printers and Faxes window comes into play not only when installing and managing printers, but also when managing print queues (see Activity 9-2). To manage print jobs, open the Printers and Faxes window and double-click the icon for the printer in question. When you do so, you see a window (similar to the one shown in Figure 9-2) that displays all current print jobs for the selected print device.

To manage a print job, select it and then choose the appropriate menu option. For example, to delete a print job, choose Cancel from the Document menu, and the print job is deleted, allowing the next job in the queue to begin. Alternatively, you can right-click the print job's list entry, and select Pause or Cancel. If the job has already been partially or completely spooled to the printer, it continues printing until the print device has finished with the spooled data. No more data is sent to the printer after you cancel the job.

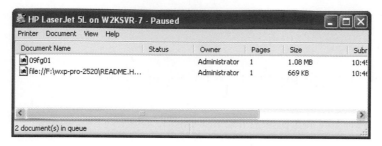

Figure 9-2   A printer's queue window

Activity 9-2: Managing Print Queues

Time Required: 15 minutes

Objective: Become familiar with the options available for managing print queues.

Description: The more print jobs that are sent to a printer, the more important it becomes to be able to manage the print queue. There are often jobs that need to be paused, restarted, or deleted. In this activity, you will perform steps to carry out these functions.

To pause a print queue, see documents, delete documents, and restart a print queue:

1. Click **Start**, **Printers and Faxes**, and then double-click your default printer (the one with the circled check mark).

2. From the Printer menu, select **Pause Printing**.

3. Open any application, such as Notepad or Word. Print three documents.

4. Return to the open print queue.

5. Double-click any of the print jobs now appearing in the queue.

6. Explore the information for this document.

7. Click **OK**.

8. Highlight any of the documents in the queue.

9. From the Document menu, select **Pause**.

10. Select a different document in the queue.

11. From the Document menu, select **Cancel**. Select **Yes** to confirm the cancellation if prompted.

12. Select the paused document in the queue.

13. From the Document menu, select **Resume**.

14. From the Printer menu, select **Cancel All Documents**.

15. Click **Yes** to confirm the deletion of print jobs if prompted.

16. From the Printer menu, select **Pause Printing**.

17. From the Printer menu, select **Close**.

 To delete print jobs, you need Manage Documents or Manage Printers permissions or ownership of the print job. Administrators and Power Users have Print, Manage Printers, and Manage Document permissions over printers by default.

The functions or commands available through the Printer menu of the print queue window are:

- *Connect*—Used to connect to shared printers when the printer share has been dragged and dropped into the Printers and Faxes applet instead of configured using the Add Printer Wizard

- *Set As Default Printer*—Sets the system to use this printer as the primary printer choice

- *Network Tasks Preferences*—Opens the Printing Preferences dialog box for this printer. This is the same dialog box reached by clicking the Printing Preferences button on the General tab of the printer's Properties dialog box.

- *Pause Printing*—Halts the printing of all print jobs through this logical printer. When deselected, printing continues from the same point where it was paused.

- *Cancel All Documents*—Deletes all print jobs in the queue

- *Sharing*—Opens the printer's Properties dialog box with the Sharing tab selected

- *Use Printer Offline*—Turns a local printer queue "off" in much the same way as the offline status of a physical print device

- *Properties*—Opens the Properties dialog box for the printer

- *Close*—Closes the printer window

The options available from the Document menu are as follows:

- *Pause*—Pauses the print job. If the print job is already in the process of being sent to the printer, no other print jobs can be sent to the printer until it is resumed or canceled. If the print job is still in the queue, other print jobs will bypass it on their way to be printed.

- *Resume*—Resumes printing of a paused print job

- *Restart*—Prints jobs again from the beginning

- *Cancel*—Removes a print job from the print queue

- *Properties*—Opens the Properties dialog box for the selected print job

The Properties dialog box of a print job displays details, such as size, pages, data format type, owner, time submitted, layout, and paper tray selection. It also allows you to change the printing priority of the print job and to redefine the schedule. The schedule is the same type of control as a printer's activity time period, meaning that you can set it to either no restriction or define a time within which the print job can be sent to the printer.

CONFIGURING A PRINTER

After the printer is created, configuring it is easy. The following sections explain the options on each tab of the printer Properties dialog box that appears when you right-click a printer in the Printers and Faxes window and choose Properties.

NOTE You can create more than one logical printer for a single print device, so you can set up different configurations for the same print device. Different configurations might include setting up one printer to print high-priority jobs immediately, whereas another might be configured to print low-priority jobs during nonbusiness hours. Just be sure to tell your users to which printer they should connect, so they get the configurations they need.

General Tab

The General tab (see Figure 9-3) in a printer's Properties dialog box contains a variety of controls that you can use to not only create a text comment that shows up in the Browse list entry for that printer, but also to create a separate entry to identify the printer's location. This tab also displays the features and paper sizes currently available for this printer. The Printing Preferences button brings up a dialog box (see Figure 9-4) in which orientation, duplexing, page order, pages per sheet, color, and paper source tray (Paper/Quality tab) are defined. The Print Test Page button sends a default test page to the printer.

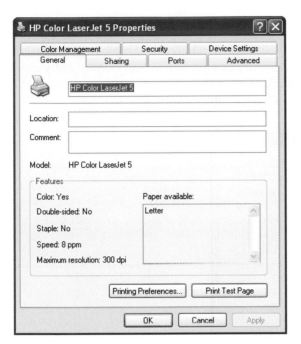

Figure 9-3 A printer's Properties dialog box, General tab

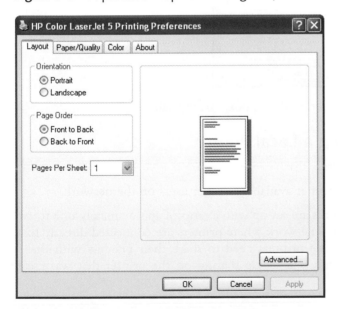

Figure 9-4 The Printing Preferences dialog box

Sharing Tab

The Sharing tab (shown in Figure 9-5) works much like the Sharing tab used when creating a shared directory. Simply select the Share this printer option button and provide a Share name for the printer. To install additional drivers for several client types that are connecting to the printer, click the Additional Drivers button.

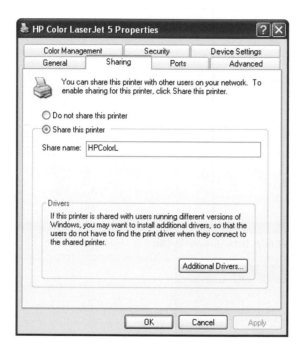

Figure 9-5   A printer's Properties dialog box, Sharing tab

Activity 9-3: Sharing a Local Printer

Time Required: 5 minutes

Objective: Make a local printer available to other users on the network.

Description: Most networks are set up with a ratio of approximately one to two printers for every 10 computers. In a network where printers are connected directly to a workstation, the individuals with the printers need to share their printers with the rest of the network. In this activity, you will set up sharing on the printer that was created in the previous activity.

To share a printer with the network:

This activity requires that you complete Activity 9-1.

1. If necessary, click **Start**, **Printers and Faxes**. Right-click the printer created in Activity 9-1, and select **Sharing** from the resulting menu. The printer's Properties dialog box appears with the Sharing tab selected.

2. Click the **Share this printer** option button.

3. Provide a name for the share.

4. Click **OK**.

Ports Tab

On the Ports tab (shown in Figure 9-6), you can adjust settings (including interrupts and base I/O addresses) for the ports selected for use with a particular print device. You can also add port monitors by clicking the Add Port button. The bidirectional printing option should be checked for printers that are able to send status information back to the print monitor, where it can provide the basis for user notifications (print job complete, out of paper, paper jam, and so forth).

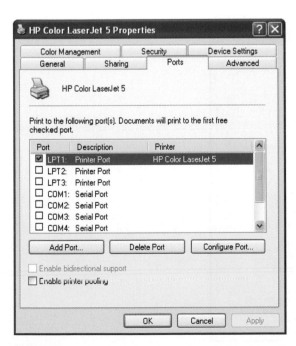

Figure 9-6 A printer's Properties dialog box, Ports tab

This tab is also used to set up a printer pool, in which more than one print device (the physical printer) is assigned to a single printer (the logical printers construct). This option, which works best with identical print devices, even to the amount of memory installed in each, can reduce waiting time on heavily used printers by sending jobs to whichever print device is least busy.

Select print devices that are in close physical proximity to each other for pooling. Users will not be able to tell to which pooled print device a print job went, and they're not going to like running all over to find their print jobs. Also, if there's any difference in speed among the pooled printers; pool the fastest printer first because the pooling software checks the first-pooled printer first.

Advanced Tab

Use the Advanced tab (shown in Figure 9-7) to set the hours during which the printer is available, set printer priority, and define spooling options. The availability hours are used to enable a printer only within a specified time frame. All print jobs sent to the printer outside this time frame are spooled and printed when the start time is reached. The **printer priority** setting determines which logical printer is given first access to a printer. This setting is used to grant privileged, faster access to a busy printer for an individual or small group, the higher the number, the higher the priority, ranging from 1 to 99. The default is 1. From this tab, you can also select the printer driver to use or install an updated or alternate driver by clicking the New Driver button.

Figure 9-7   A printer's Properties dialog box, Advanced tab

The spooling options define how print jobs are managed. In most cases, the default options will work well for you, because they'll start the printing process quickly and restore control to the application as rapidly as possible. However, here's what the options mean:

- If you choose to print directly to the printer instead of spooling documents, your application won't regain control until the print job is fully sent to the printer, but it completes the print job faster.

- Waiting to print until the document has completely spooled to the printer does not hold up the application the way printing to the printer does, but it does delay the printing process commensurately with the size of the print job.

- **Mismatched documents** are those for which the page setup and printer setup are incompatible. Holding mismatched documents prevents only those documents from printing, without affecting any others. This setting is useful because it prevents wasted resources, such as printing one character per page, when such documents are sent.

- If you choose to print spooled documents first, the order in which documents spool to the print device overrides any print priorities that you have in place. By default, this option is disabled, so printer priority controls the order in which jobs print.

- If you want to be able to print a document again without resubmitting it from the application, choose to keep documents in the spooler after they've printed. (*Warning*: Retaining the spooled print jobs consumes drive space at a rapid pace. Be sure to monitor the free space on your print server.)

- Enabling advanced printing features activates functions, such as page order, booklet printing, and pages per sheet, that are only available on specific printers (and enabled on the Device Settings tab and the Printing Preferences button on the General tab).

At the bottom of the Advanced tab are three buttons: Printing Defaults, Print Processor, and Separator Page. The Printing Defaults button accesses the same dialog box as the Printing Preferences button on the General tab. The Print Processor button is used to select an alternative printing processor and data type format (RAW, EMF, or TEXT). The selections offered are based on the installed printer drivers and associated printer services. In most cases, you will not change these settings unless specified by a proprietary application or printing procedure.

Separator pages are extra pages printed before each print job. They are used to clearly identify details about a printed document, such as to which user it belongs. Separator pages can be handy when several people are using the same printer, and you want to be sure that documents from different users don't get mixed up. Windows XP comes with several separator page files: Pcl.sep, Pscript.sep, Sysprint.sep, and Sysprtj.sep, but you can create custom pages in Notepad. Start off the document by putting a character on a line of its own, then use the codes in Table 9-1 to create separator files with the information that you need.

You can define any character as the lead character for the codes, but in this example, the exclamation point (!) is used.

Save the separator page file with a .sep extension in the %*systemroot*%\System32 directory, and it will be among the options available when you configure the separator page through the Advanced tab.

Table 9-1   Separator page code

Code	Function
!B!M	Prints all characters as double-width block characters until the !U code is encountered
!B!S	Prints all characters as single-width block characters until the !U code is encountered
!D	Prints the date the job was printed, using the format in the Regional and Language Options settings in Control Panel
!E	Ejects a page from the printer
!Fpathname	Prints the contents of the file specified in *pathname*, without any formatting
!Hnn	Prints a printer-specific control sequence, indicated by the hexadecimal number *nn*. Check your printer manual to get the numbers.
!I	Prints the job number (every print job is assigned a number)
!L	Prints all the characters following it until reaching another escape code (!)
!N	Prints the username of the person submitting the job
!*n*	Skips *n* number of lines, where *n* is a number between 0 and 9
!T	Prints the time the job was printed, using the format specified in the Regional and Language Options settings in Control Panel
!U	Turns off block character printing
!Wnn	Specifies a certain width for the page (counted in characters). The default is 80; the maximum is 256.

Color Management Tab

The Color Management tab is used to associate a color profile with a color printer. A color profile is used to control how color is produced by the printer. A color profile takes into account the printer's configuration and the type of media (i.e., paper, film, etc.) being used. This tab is only used by printers supporting color. In most cases, the Automatic selection determines the best color profile to use. However, you can manually install and choose alternative color profiles. Consult your color printer's manual for more information on managing color.

Security Tab

The Security tab (shown in Figure 9-8) contains options quite similar to those used to set up secure files and directories. Here you can set permissions for printers. The Add and Remove buttons are used to alter the list of users and groups with defined permissions for this printer. The Permissions frame lists the permission types (Print, Manage Printers, Manage Documents, and Special Permissions) and offers check boxes to Allow or Deny individual permissions for the selected user or group.

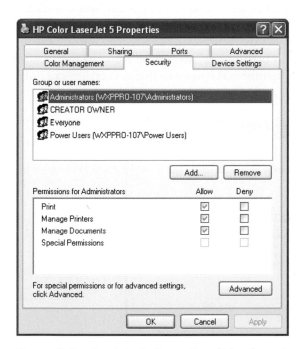

Figure 9-8   A printer's Properties dialog box, Security tab

The three main permissions for printers—Print, Manage Documents, and Manage Printers—encompass the following capabilities:

- *Print documents*—Print, Manage Documents, Manage Printers

- *Pause, resume, restart, and cancel owned document*—Print, Manage Documents, Manage Printers

- *Connect to a printer*—Print, Manage Documents, Manage Printers

- *Control settings for any print job*—Manage Documents, Manage Printers

- *Pause, resume, restart, and cancel all documents*—Manage Documents, Manage Printers

- *Cancel all documents*—Manage Printers

- *Share a printer*—Manage Printers

- *Delete a printer*—Manage Printers
- *Change permissions*—Manage Printers

The Advanced button reveals another dialog box where more detailed permissions, auditing, and ownership are controlled. In this dialog box (see Figure 9-9), permissions are added on a user or group basis for the detailed permissions of Print, Manage Printers, Manage Documents, Read Permissions, Change Permissions, and Take Ownership. These permission settings can be defined for each user to apply to this printer only, Documents only, or both. The Auditing tab is a control interface similar to the permissions interface where the same types of actions granted through permissions can be set so you can audit them. The audit events created through this object are recorded in the Security log and viewed through the Event Viewer. The Owner tab is used to take ownership for your user account or one of your groups (of which you are a member). Remember that ownership can only be taken, it cannot be given.

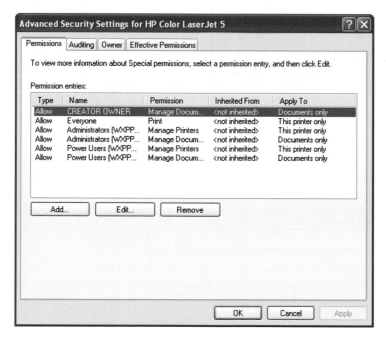

Figure 9-9   The Advanced Security dialog box, Permissions tab

Activity 9-4: Managing a Printer

Time Required: 5 minutes

Objective: Control access to a printer by changing the printer permissions.

Description: Managing a printer is somewhat different than managing print queues. Managing queues refers to the individual print jobs, whereas managing a printer refers to controlling the access to the printer. In this activity, you will set the permissions for a specific group to access the printer.

To change printer permissions:

This activity requires that you complete Activity 9-1.

1. If necessary, click **Start**, **Printers and Faxes**. Right-click the printer created in Activity 9-1, and select **Properties** from the resulting menu.

2. Select the **Security** tab from the printer's Properties dialog box.

3. Select the **Power Users** group.

4. Deselect the **Allow** check box for Manage Printers.

5. Click **OK**.

Device Settings Tab

The final tab in the Properties dialog box (shown in Figure 9-10), the Device Settings tab, is used to make sure that the print device itself is configured properly. Most of these settings shouldn't need to be adjusted if you chose the proper printer driver during setup, but these items may be subject to change as you upgrade your printer:

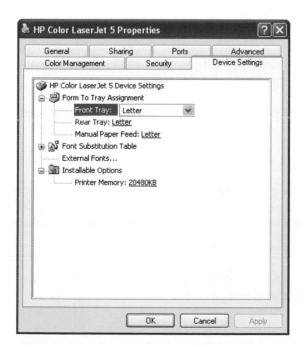

Figure 9-10   A printer's Properties dialog box, Device Settings tab

- *Memory*—Be sure that the amount of memory listed on this tab is equal to that installed in the printer. Too little, and you will not get the performance of which your printer is capable. Too much, and the printer may try to take on more than it can handle.

- *Paper trays and other accessories*—Some printers may be upgraded with particular paper trays. If you install one, or rearrange existing ones, you need to update the settings here.

There may be other options and functions listed on this tab that are printer model-specific. When these appear, consult the printer's user manual for information on modifying these settings.

PRINTERS AND THE WEB

Windows XP includes Web support in its print subsystem, which allows remote users to submit print jobs for printing, view printer queues, and download print drivers. These features are afforded through the **Internet Printing Protocol (IPP)**. The Web-based features are accessible only when the print server is running Internet Information Server (IIS).

IPP offers two main benefits. First, it enables Web-based distribution of printer drivers. Second, it offers Web-based print queue management.

To download a printer driver, simply use a URL as the network path when connecting to a network printer. The URL should be formatted as: http://*printservername*/printers/*printersharename*/.printer.

To access a print queue through the Web, open a URL with the following formatting: http://*printservername*/printers/. Select a printer from the list, then use the Web-based menu to perform print queue management. The operations and commands are the same as those accessed through a normal printer queue window.

Activity 9-5: Internet Printing

Time Required: 15 minutes

Objective: Install a printer that is located on the Internet.

Description: To meet the needs of remote printing on distributed networks, it is possible to install a printer that is located somewhere on the Internet (as long as the user has permission). In this activity, you will create a printer that is located on the Internet.

To connect to an Internet printer:

This activity requires that a Windows XP system running IIS is present and a shared printer is installed on the IIS host.

1. If necessary, click **Start**, **Printers and Faxes**.

2. Click **Add a printer** in the Printer Tasks columns.

3. Click **Next**.

4. Select a network printer, or a printer attached to another computer, and then click **Next**.

5. Select the **Connect to a printer on the Internet or on a home or office network** option button.

6. Type the **URL** to your printer in the form of http://*servername*/printers/ *sharedname*/.printer where *servername* is the name of the IIS/PWS host/printer server and *sharedname* is the name of the printer share.

7. Click **Next**.

8. If prompted for authentication, provide a name and password with access permissions to this printer.

9. Select whether to configure this printer as the default printer for your client. Click **Next**.

10. Click **Finish**.

Managing the Print Server

In addition to the configurable properties of each logical printer, the print server itself can be fine-tuned. Selecting Server Properties from the File menu from the Printers and Faxes window reveals the Print Server Properties dialog box (see Figure 9-11).

The Forms tab of this dialog box is used to define paper sizes. The Ports tab lists all known ports and installed printers on those ports (if any). On this tab, you can add new ports, delete existing ports, or configure individual ports. The Drivers tab lists the installed printer drivers. On this tab, you can add, remove, replace, or configure printer drivers. The Advanced tab offers control over the spool file location and several events:

- Log spooler error events
- Log spooler warning events
- Log spooler information events
- Beep on errors of remote documents
- Show informational notifications for local printers
- Show informational notifications for network printers
- Notify when remote documents are printed
- Notify computer, not user, when remote documents are printed

9

Figure 9-11   The Print Server Properties dialog box, Forms tab

All of these events, when selected, appear in the System log, viewed through the Event Viewer. The default location for the spool files is *%systemroot%*\System32\Spool\Printers.

Activity 9-6: Print Spool Location

ACTIVITY

Time Required: 5 minutes

Objective: Use the Print Server Properties dialog box to set a new location for the spool files.

Description: If a workstation is being used as a print server, the workstation performance can be adversely affected by all of the disk activity required to perform the spooling process. If the workstation has separate disk controllers, or at least two separate disks, performance can be improved by moving the spooling folder to the disk that does not have the system and boot files on it. In this activity, you will change the spool location to a different folder.

To change the location of the spool files:

1. If necessary, click **Start**, **Printers and Faxes**. From the File menu, select **Server Properties**.

2. Select the **Advanced** tab of the Print Server Properties dialog box.

3. Change the Spool folder field to **c:\temp\spooler** (or something similar that matches an existing folder on your computer).

4. Click **OK**, and then click **Yes** to confirm the changes to the spool folder.

TROUBLESHOOTING PRINTING PROBLEMS

Printing from Windows XP is usually a trouble-free process, but there's always something that can go wrong. Microsoft recommends following these steps when troubleshooting printing problems:

1. Identify which of the seven components of the printing process is failing (printer creation and configuration, connecting to a shared printer, creating a print job, sending the print job to the spooler, processing the spooled job, sending the processed job to the print device, or printing at the device). To find the correct one:
   a. Analyze the symptoms of the problem.
   b. Change the configuration as applied to that part of the process.
   c. Test the configuration to see if the print job works.
   d. If the print job now works, you found the right part. If not, then it's time to start over.

2. After you identify the problem, look for documented solutions online, in the manuals that ship with Windows XP or the printer, or in the Microsoft Knowledge Base (*http://support.microsoft.com/search/*).

3. Implement a short-term solution.

4. Implement a long-term solution, if possible.

Troubleshooting Printing in General

When deciding on your method of attack for a systematic troubleshooting response to a printing problem, try the following:

- Check the physical aspects of the printer—cable, power, paper, toner, and so on.
- Start and restart the spooler (discussed later in this chapter).
- Terminate and reshare the printer on the print server.
- Try using a different application, user account, or computer to print to the same printer.
- Check for stalled print jobs.
- Make sure the printer is online (a device setting).
- Remove or uninstall, and then reinstall the print driver. Check with the vendor for a new or updated print driver.
- Check the free space on the drive where the spooler is directed; at least 75 MB is recommended.
- Delete and then re-create the logical printer on the client.
- Try using the Print Troubleshooter by selecting Start, Help and Support, clicking Fixing a problem, and then clicking Printing problems.

Activity 9-7: Removing a Printer

Time Required: 5 minutes

Objective: Delete a printer from the computer configuration.

Description: Occasionally, it is necessary to delete a printer. There are many possible reasons, such as the incorrect printer was installed, or the printer was exchanged for a new model, and so on. In this activity, you will delete the printer that was installed in Activity 9-1.

To delete a printer:

This activity requires that you complete Activity 9-1.

1. If necessary, click, **Start**, **Printers and Faxes**. Select the printer created in Activity 9-1.

2. From the **File** menu, select **Delete**.

3. Click **Yes** to confirm the deletion.

4. Click **OK** on the warning that the printer has been removed.

5. In the Printers and Faxes applet, select **File**, **Close**.

Troubleshooting Network Printing

When troubleshooting network printing problems, add the following steps to your troubleshooting checklist:

1. Verify basic network connectivity, making sure you can see and connect to the print server from your workstation. Try copying a file to or from the server. If you can't do this, the print server itself may be inaccessible.

2. Create a local printer and redirect its port to a network printer. This will determine whether there's a problem copying files from the server to the workstation, as is done when you connect to a shared printer.

3. Print from a DOS-based program using the NET USE command to connect to the printer. If the print job works, this may indicate that the connection to the printer is not persistent and needs to be adjusted.

4. If using TCP/IP printing or connecting to a printer attached directly to the network, try pinging the printer's IP address (by opening a Command Prompt window and typing PING followed by the printer's IP address) to make sure that the printer is functioning. Also, create an LPR port to the printer and connect to that port to allow the computer to act as the printer's queue.

Stopping and Restarting the Print Spooler

The Spooler service is required for printing. Like other services, it's stopped and started—and its startup configured—from the Services tool in Administrative Tools (from Control Panel). By default, the Spooler service is set to begin automatically when the system starts. To stop it, select it from the list of services (it's called Print Spooler—see Figure 9-12) and click the Stop button or select Stop from the Action menu. To start the Spooler service again, select it from the list (it remains on the list even when stopped) and click Start. Sometimes, stopping and restarting the Spooler service can clear up problems that are difficult to troubleshoot.

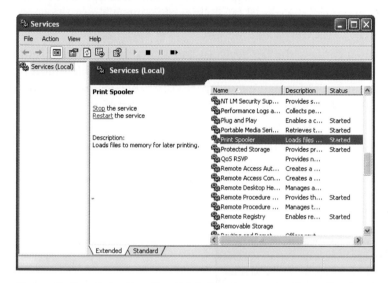

Figure 9-12   Selecting the Print Spooler service from the Services applet

For more information on troubleshooting the printing process, see Chapter 15, "Troubleshooting Windows XP."

FAX SUPPORT

Windows XP Professional supports native fax features and operations. The Printers and Faxes applet in Control Panel is used to install and configure the fax components of Windows XP as well as printers. Faxing is not enabled by default, therefore to initiate faxing, click Install a local fax printer in the Printer Tasks list. You must have a fax-capable device installed in order to configure faxing. This action installs the required components for faxing. A Fax icon will appear in the Printers and Faxes window. Even after the fax service is installed, it is by default initially enabled only for sending faxes. You must manually configure faxing in order to receive faxes.

Opening the Properties dialog box for the Fax icon reveals a multitabbed dialog box very similar to that of a printer. In fact, the General and Security tabs are exactly alike.

The Sharing tab is blank when the fax device is a fax modem. Fax modems cannot be shared under Windows XP. The Sharing tab functions normally for fax devices that are not fax modems but multifunction print/fax devices.

The Fax Security tab is very similar to the Security tab. However, the permissions it controls are Fax, Manage Fax Configuration, Manage Fax documents, and Special Permissions. The permissions on this tab control the special capabilities of faxing, whereas the permissions on the Security tab control the printerlike queue of the fax device.

The Devices tab is used to view the fax device(s) and access the fax-related settings of the device. Those settings include: enable send, Transmitting Subscriber Identification (TSID), banner, retries, retry time delay, discount toll periods, enable receive, Called Subscriber Identification (CSID), answer mode, answer ring number, automatic print, automatic save to file, and delete old faxes after a time period.

The Tracking tab (see Figure 9-13) is used to define the notification and monitoring settings of the fax device. These include notification of the progress of a sent or received fax, as well as the success or failure of incoming and outgoing faxes. You can also configure the Fax Monitor to open whenever a fax is sent or received and to play a sound for various fax events.

Figure 9-13   The Tracking tab of the Fax Properties dialog box

The Archives tab defines the storage location for incoming and outgoing faxes. You may also select not to store faxes.

The first time you double-click the Fax icon from the Printers and Faxes window, you may be prompted for your area code, and then the Fax Configuration Wizard appears. This wizard is used to define sender information details (see Figure 9-14) and set the fax device. After this wizard has been executed once, it won't appear again. Instead, subsequent double-clicks to the Fax icon open the Fax Console. This console is used to manage incoming and outgoing faxes in much the same way as a standard printer queue. Through this tool, you can also create custom cover pages and alter your sender information.

Figure 9-14 The Sender Information page of the Fax Configuration Wizard

To send a fax from Windows XP, you can either print a document from any application or select Fax as the printer. Or, you can issue the Send a fax command from the Quick List of the Printers and Faxes window. In either case, the Send Fax Wizard walks you through the process of sending a fax.

Activity 9-8: Fax Printing

Time Required: 15 minutes

Objective: Configure the Windows XP workstation to answer incoming fax calls.

Description: In an effort to reduce the number of hardware devices that are purchased for small offices, many people are turning to using their PCs to combine a number of functions. In this activity, you will install a fax printer and configure your Windows XP Professional computer to answer fax calls.

To enable fax receiving:

NOTE

This activity requires that a fax modem be already present and installed on the system.

1. Click **Start**, **Printers and Faxes**.
2. Click **Install a local fax printer** from the Printer Tasks column. Windows XP installs the necessary foundation components for fax services.
3. A Fax icon appears in the Printers and Faxes window; double-click it.
4. If prompted, provide your area code, and then click **OK**.
5. The Fax Configuration Wizard appears. Click **Next**.
6. Fill in all the requested sender information, and then click **Next**.
7. Use the pull-down list to select your fax device. Mark both the **Enable Send** and **Enable Receive** check boxes.
8. Set the Rings before answer to **1**.
9. Click **Next**.
10. Provide a TSID, such as **Lab Fax 2**, and then click **Next**.
11. Provide a CSID, such as **Lab Fax 2**, and then click **Next**.
12. Make no changes on the Routing Options page. Click **Next**.
13. Click **Finish**. Your Windows XP system is now configured to answer incoming fax calls.

Troubleshooting fax problems is accomplished through a few simple actions. First, check the physical connections of the phone line from the wall to the computer's fax device. Second, verify the driver is properly installed through the Device Manager. Third, check to make sure you have enabled send and/or receive capabilities for that modem. Fourth, check the Receive options to ensure you are handling inbound faxes as you actually intend.

Chapter Summary

- The Windows XP print subsystem architecture consists of several components that turn print data into a printable file, transfer that file to a printer, and manage the way in which multiple print jobs are handled by a printer. These components are the GDI, printer driver, and print spooler.
- Microsoft uses a special vocabulary for printing-related services, software and hardware components, and activities. It is important to grasp this vocabulary to be able to interact with and troubleshoot the Windows XP print subsystem.

◻ You use the Add Printer Wizard in the Printers and Faxes applet to create, share, and connect to print devices, whether directly attached to a local machine or shared elsewhere on the network.

◻ You also use the Add Printer Wizard to configure a print device, including the selection of the driver, output configuration, and postprocessing options, and for working with two or more identically configured printers to establish a printer pool.

◻ It is important to fine-tune the printing process for various situations, including managing priorities for print jobs, and setting up multiple printers with differing priorities so that multiple-user communities can share a single print device, yet give one community preferential access to the device.

◻ The most common causes of printing problems in the Windows XP environment were discussed, along with suggestions for how to isolate and identify their causes, and take the right kinds of corrective actions to resolve them.

◻ Faxing has been thoroughly integrated with the Windows XP's printing system. Faxing is natively supported and requires only a few easy configuration steps to enable faxing from any print-capable application.

9

KEY TERMS

characterization data file — The file responsible for rendering the GDI commands into DDI commands that can be sent to the printer. Each graphics driver renders a different printer language.

client application — An application or service that creates print jobs for output, which can be either end-user-originated or created by a print server itself (see also print client).

connecting to a printer — The negotiation of a connection to a shared printer through the browser service from a client or service across the network to the machine where the shared printer resides.

creating a printer — The process of setting up a printer for local use.

data type — The format in which print jobs are sent to the spooler. Some data types are ready for printing (RAW) and some require further preparation (EMF).

Device Driver Interface (DDI) — A specific code component that handles the translation of generic print commands into device-specific equivalents, immediately prior to delivery of a spool file to a print device.

direct-attached printer — A print device attached directly to a computer, usually through a parallel port (see also network interface printer).

enhanced metafile (EMF) — The device-independent spool data used to reduce the amount of time spent processing a print job. Once it's queued, EMF data requires additional processing to prepare it for the printer.

Graphical Device Interface (GDI) — The portion of the Windows XP operating system responsible for the first step of preparing all graphical output, whether it is sent to a monitor or to the printer.

Internet Printing Protocol (IPP) — A new Windows XP protocol that adds Web support to the print subsystem. IPP allows remote users to submit print jobs for printing, view printer queues, and download print drivers.

language monitor — The part of the print monitor that sets up bidirectional messaging between the printer and the computer initiating the print job.

mismatched document — A document with incompatible printer and page settings (that is, the page settings are impossible to produce given the existing printer settings).

network interface printer — A print device attached directly to the network medium, usually by means of a built-in network interface integrated within the printer, but sometimes by means of a parallel-attached network printer interface.

port monitor — The part of the print monitor that transmits the print job to the print device through the specified port. Port monitors are actually unaware of print devices as such, but only know that something is on the other end of the port.

print client — A network client machine that transmits print jobs across the network to a printer for spooling and delivery to a designated print device or printer pool.

print device — In everyday language, a piece of equipment that provides output service—in other words, a printer. However, in Microsoft terminology, a printer is a logical service that accepts print jobs and delivers them to some print device for output when that device is ready. Therefore, in Microsoft terminology, a print device is any piece of equipment that can produce output, so this term would also describe a plotter, a fax machine, or a slide printer, as well as a text-oriented output device, such as an HP LaserJet.

print job — The contents of a completely or partially interpreted data file that contains text and control characters that are ultimately delivered to a print device to be printed, or otherwise rendered in some tangible form.

print processor — The software that works with the printer driver to despool files and make any necessary changes to the data to format it for use with a particular printer. The print processor itself is a PostScript program that understands the format of a document image file and how to print the file to a specific PostScript printer or class of printers.

print provider — The server-side software that sends the print job to the proper server in the format that it requires. Windows XP supports both Windows network print providers and NetWare print providers.

print resolution — A measurement of the number of dots per inch (dpi) that describes the output capabilities of a print device; most laser printers usually produce output at 300 or 600 dpi. In general, the larger the dpi rating for a device, the better looking its output is (but high-resolution devices cost more than low-resolution ones).

print router — The software component in the Windows XP print subsystem that directs print jobs from one print server to another, or from a client to a remote printer.

print server — A computer that links print devices to the network and shares those devices with client computers on the network.

Print Server services — A collection of named software components on a print server that handles incoming print jobs and forwards them to a print spooler for postprocessing and delivery to a print device. These components include support for special job handling that can enable a variety of client computers to send print jobs to a print server for processing.

print spooler — A collection of Windows XP DLLs used to acquire, process, catalog, and dispense print jobs to print devices. The spooler acts like a holding tank, in that it manages an area on disk called the spool file on a print server, where pending print jobs are stored until they've been successfully output. The term "despooling" refers to the process of reading and interpreting what's in a spool file for delivery to a print device.

printer (logical printer) — In Microsoft terminology, a printer is not a physical device, but rather a named system object that communicates between the operating system and some print device. The printer handles the printing process for Windows XP from the time a print command is issued, until a print job has been successfully output. The settings established for a printer in the Add Printer Wizard in the Printers and Faxes applet (Start, Printers and Faxes) not only indicates which print device (or devices, in the case of a printer pool) handles print output, but also provides controls over how print jobs are handled (banner page, special postprocessing, and so forth).

printer driver — The special-purpose software components that manage communications between the I/O Manager and a specific print device. Ultimately, printer drivers make it possible for Windows XP to despool print jobs, and send them to a print device for output services. Modern printer drivers also allow the printer to communicate with Windows XP, and to inform it about print job status, error conditions (out of paper, paper jam, and so forth), and print job problems.

printer graphics driver — The part of the printer driver that renders GDI commands into Device Driver Interface commands that may be sent to the printer.

printer interface driver — The part of the printer driver that provides an interface to the printer settings.

Printer Job Language — A specialized language that provides printer control at the print-job level and enables users to change printer default levels, such as number of copies, color, printer languages, and so on.

printer pool — A collection of two or more identically configured print devices to which one or more Windows XP printers direct their print jobs. Basically, a printer pool permits two or more printers to act in concert to handle high-volume printing needs.

printer priority — The setting that helps to determine which printer in a pool receives a given print job. The printer with the higher priority is more likely to receive the print job.

queue (print queue) — A series of files stored in sequential order waiting for delivery from a spool file to a print device.

RAW spool file — The device-dependent spool data that is fully ready to be printed when rendered.

rendering — The process of graphically creating a print job.

spooling — One of the functions of the print spooler, this is the act of writing the contents of a print job to a file on disk so the contents are not lost if the print server is shut down before the job is completed.

REVIEW QUESTIONS

1. In the Windows XP print model, the hardware used to produce printed output is called a _____ .

2. What is a print device connected to a computer through a parallel cable known as?

   a. logical printer

   b. network-attached printer

   c. print processor

   d. direct-attached printer

3. Which of the following is software that enables the operating system to communicate with a printer?

   a. printer driver

   b. print provider

   c. print monitor

   d. print router

4. The service implements the part of the printing software that receives, processes, schedules, and distributes print jobs. True or False?

5. Because they're device independent, EMF spool files are generally smaller than RAW spool files. True or False?

6. Which of the following statements are true about network-attached printers? (Choose all that apply.)

   a. They can be a member of a printer pool.

   b. They can use TCP/IP to receive print jobs.

   c. They can only be serviced by a single logical printer.

   d. They require a print server to operate.

7. Spool files are normally deleted after the print job they prepared is completed. True or False?

8. Which software must you have installed to access a NetWare print server through a Windows Server machine?

   a. Client Services for NetWare

   b. File and Print Services for NetWare

   c. Internet Printing Protocol

   d. Gateway Services for NetWare

9. Which tool or mechanism is used to grant one user or group faster printing than others?

    a. print resolution

    b. print priority

    c. printer availability

    d. printer pools

10. To delete a print job, you must have Manage Documents permissions. True or False?

11. Auditing can be defined on a permission and user detail level. True or False?

12. What is the function of the .sep files stored in the \System32 directory?

    a. to create custom graphics banner pages for print jobs

    b. to provide templates for separator pages

    c. to provide standard separator pages for immediate use

    d. none of the above

13. When you have more than one printer set up for the same print device, what is this known as?

    a. print sharing

    b. printer pooling

    c. printer porting

    d. none of the above

14. Ownership of a printer can be assigned to any group. True or False?

15. If you choose to print directly to ports, what happens?

    a. The job can print only if it can fit all at once into printer memory.

    b. The application stalls until the print job is completed.

    c. The application stalls until the print job is fully spooled to the printer.

    d. Complex pages may not print correctly.

16. Clients connecting to a network over RAS links do not have the ability to print. True or False?

17. What must all logical printers for a single print device have in common?

    a. priority

    b. access time window

    c. driver

    d. paper tray source

    e. none of the above

18. The one restriction on the members of a printer pool is that all print devices must be the exact same model. True or False?

19. When pages print only after being fully loaded into printer memory, page protection is _____ .

20. The spool files are stored in which location by default?

    a. \Documents and Settings\Printers\Spooler

    b. *%systemroot%*\System32\Spooler\Printers

    c. *%systemroot%*\System32\Printers\Spooler

    d. \Temp\Spooler

21. Print queues cannot be managed from a Web browser. True or False?

22. After sending several print jobs to a printer, you discover that they have not printed. You look at the print queue and the only items there are your print jobs. You attempt to delete them but are unable to do so. What can you do to resolve this?

    a. Make sure the printer is not paused.

    b. Cycle the power on the printer.

    c. Restart the print spooler.

    d. Create a new shared printer on the print server.

23. Which printer permission level has the ability to print documents, connect to a printer, and share a printer?

    a. Print

    b. Manage Documents

    c. Manage Printers

24. What is the first step in troubleshooting network printer problems?

    a. Re-create the local logical printer.

    b. Print from a DOS application.

    c. Change client computers.

    d. Verify that you can see and connect to the print server.

25. Windows XP printer settings include both the native internal default controls of the Windows XP print system and device-specific proprietary controls of the physical device. True or False?

CASE PROJECTS

Case Project 9-1

Your workgroup has a single physical printer. One person in the workgroup generates many memos and other short documents, while another produces very long documents that are (usually) less time-sensitive than the memos. You can't add another printer to the network, and both users must be able to print throughout the workday. How can you make sure that the memos are printed in a timely fashion?

Case Project 9-2

Documents sent to your locally attached printer no longer print. Explain the basic troubleshooting steps you can take to resolve the problem.

9

10

PERFORMANCE TUNING

After reading this chapter and completing the exercises, you will be able to:

- ◆ Create a performance baseline
- ◆ Understand the performance and monitoring tools found in Windows XP Professional
- ◆ Log and use logged activity
- ◆ Use performance tuning in the system applet
- ◆ Detect and eliminate bottlenecks
- ◆ Boost Windows XP Professional performance
- ◆ Optimize performance for mobile Windows XP users

Once you have installed and configured Windows XP Professional, connected it to the network, and set up printers, you are ready to optimize your computer's performance. Windows XP includes several tools for monitoring your computer's performance and tuning it for the best output, including the Performance Monitor Event Viewer, and Task Manager.

This chapter introduces these tools and discusses specific system objects and counters that are worth monitoring. You learn what combinations of counters can be used to analyze system slowdowns and how to isolate, identify, and correct system bottlenecks. Very few operating systems include the kinds of tools that Windows XP Professional offers to help inspect and analyze system performance. In this chapter, you learn how to use these Windows XP Professional monitoring tools to good effect.

Establishing a Baseline

To recognize bottlenecks, it is first necessary to establish some feeling for what is normal on your system. You need a **baseline** against which you can measure system behavior. Key elements in a baseline include recorded observations about the characteristics and behavior of the computer system.

If you think back to the architectural overview of the Windows operating system given in Chapter 1, "Introduction to Windows XP Professional," you should recall that Windows XP is an object-oriented operating system in which all user-accessible system resources, files, folders, processes, threads, and so forth take the form of specific object instances. In object-oriented parlance, **objects** have properties; in Windows operating systems, some of these properties are called **counters** because they count, average, or otherwise monitor specific events, activities, or behavior of the objects with which they're associated. Counters make it quite easy to gather data about the system while it is running, and they impose surprisingly little overall performance overhead on a system.

Baselines can be recorded by creating a Counter log for whatever list of performance object counters you consider important and collecting that data at regular intervals over a period of time. This helps you establish a definition of what a normal load looks like—which is what a baseline is supposed to convey—and provides points of comparison with future system behavior.

Of course, you want to make sure that your system baseline itself doesn't indicate existing bottlenecks. If you discover unacceptably long queues or evidence of memory problems when you create your baseline, you'll want to address these bottlenecks right away. The sections that follow discuss how you can do this for common Windows XP Professional subsystems.

Monitoring and Performance Tuning

When it comes to system analysis, there are two primary activities involved in tackling performance-related issues:

- *Monitoring*—Requires a thorough understanding of system components, their behavior, and how they interact, as well as continued observation of those components and how they behave on a regular (preferably scheduled) basis
- *Performance tuning*—Consists of changing a system's configuration systematically and carefully observing performance before and after such changes. Changes that improve performance should be left in place; those that make no difference—or that make things worse—should be reversed. There are many ways to improve Windows XP Professional performance. The more useful approaches or configuration changes are covered in this chapter.

In many ways, Windows XP Professional does a remarkable job of tuning itself. It is capable of managing both its physical and virtual memory quite well. It also adjusts allocation of memory dynamically and effectively among a variety of uses, including file caching, virtual memory, system kernel, and applications. Because its self-tuning features manage resources so effectively, Windows XP Professional offers a more limited set of tools and utilities to monitor and alter system performance than do older operating systems, such as Windows NT. Changing the default Windows XP Professional operating system configuration is rarely required. Instead, you learn how to recognize and react to system bottlenecks that can limit a system's overall performance and respond to the need for tuning and manual optimization only when it's required.

Task Manager

Windows Task Manager, shown in Figure 10-1, provides an overview of the current state of a computer. You can access the Task Manager in one of three ways:

- Press Ctrl+Alt+Delete.
- Press Ctrl+Shift+Esc.
- Right-click any unoccupied area on the Windows XP taskbar and select Task Manager from the menu that appears.

Figure 10-1   Windows Task Manager, Applications tab

The first tab in Task Manager is the Applications tab, which is shown in Figure 10-1. This tab displays all programs currently running on the computer and the status of those programs (usually "Running"). You can use this tab to halt an application by highlighting an entry in the list and clicking the End Task button. To switch to a specific task, highlight an entry and click the Switch To button. To launch a new application, click the New Task button and provide the name of an executable program or command in the Create New Task dialog box that appears.

The Processes tab offers information about all currently active processes, including Process ID number (PID), CPU usage (CPU), and Memory Usage. A **process** is an environment that defines the resources available to threads, which are the executable parts of an application. This display is an excellent instant diagnostic tool to show when ill-behaved applications take up an inordinate amount of CPU time. If this happens at the moment you use Task Manager, you'll see the process's CPU usage spike above 90%. Even if an application is not currently hogging the CPU, the CPU time entry might be high enough (above 80%) to stick out like a sore thumb.

On a system with two CPUs, it is possible to set processor affinity. Processor affinity is assigning a process to execute only on a specific CPU or multiple CPUs. By default, processes in Windows XP Professional execute on any CPU. This can result in poor performance in some situations; therefore, to assign a process to a specific CPU, right-click over it and select Set Affinity from the shortcut menu. Then click on one or more processors to assign to this process. Setting processor affinity only affects the one process that is configured. All other processes use CPUs as they would normally by default.

You can change the columns displayed on the Processes tab by choosing Select Columns in the View menu. The Processes tab lists all processes that contribute to the operation of Windows XP Professional, including Winlogon.exe and Lsass.exe. You can stop any process by selecting it from the list, then clicking the End Process button. However, use this capability with caution. You may inadvertently terminate a process and lose data you have not saved. Fortunately, the system prevents you from stopping system-critical services.

Be wary of ending Windows XP processes; you can cripple or disable a system by ending processes that are required for proper system operation. That's why Microsoft recommends terminating applications rather than processes. However, sometimes the only way to access a rogue system component is through the Processes tab.

The Performance tab, shown in Figure 10-2, provides a graphical representation of cumulative CPU usage and memory usage. The four text windows at the bottom of the screen provide detailed information on the total number of handles, threads, and processes (Totals) active on the system, the amount of memory allocated to application programs or the system (Commit Charge), the amount of physical memory installed on your computer (Physical Memory), and the memory used by the operating system for internal processes (Kernel

Memory). A **thread** is the minimal unit of system execution and corresponds roughly to a task within an application, within the Windows XP Professional kernel, or within some other major system component. A **handle** is an internal identifier for some kind of system resource, object, or other component that must be accessed by name.

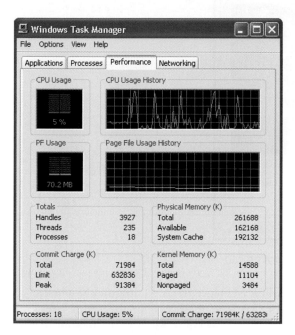

Figure 10-2   Task Manager, Performance tab

The Networking tab in Task Manager shows current levels of network utilization, on a per-interface basis, as shown in Figure 10-3. For computers with more than one network interface, you must select a specific Adapter Name in the section underneath the utilization graph to view its corresponding chart. Note also that by default the Auto Scale option is selected; because the network in view is only lightly utilized, the graph shows only utilizations between 0 and 1 percent.

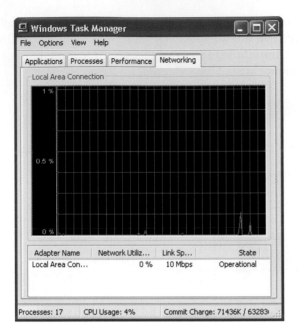

Figure 10-3   Task Manager, Networking tab

You can use the Performance tab in Task Manager to ascertain quickly whether a computer is performing optimally. If the total CPU usage shown in the status bar is consistently high—say over 70%—you can use the Processes tab to identify the process that is monopolizing the CPU and take corrective action.

There is a fifth tab called Users in Task Manager (see Figure 10-4), but it only appears under special circumstances on Windows XP Professional machines. The only machines that have this tab are those that belong to a Windows workgroup or have been set up to run as standalone machines with no networking capabilities. You must also run the User Accounts utility in Control Panel (Start, Control Panel, User Accounts, Change the way users log on or off) and select the Use the Welcome screen and Use Fast User Switching check boxes. This facility permits one user to take over a Windows XP machine temporarily (without logging off the other user or changing active applications, settings, and so forth), execute a few commands or a program, and then return control to the original user. This facility is provided as a convenience for home and small office use where multiple users must share a single machine. This facility does not work in a domain environment.

Figure 10-4   Task Manager, Users tab

System Monitor

The performance monitoring tool included with Windows XP Professional can monitor and track many different areas of system performance. Called **System Monitor**, this tool is used to monitor and record the same system measurements as in Windows 2000 systems (prior to that, the program was called Performance Monitor or Perfmon). As shown in Figure 10-5, System Monitor is a graphical tool that can monitor many different **events** concurrently. By using System Monitor, you can analyze network operations, identify trends and bottlenecks, determine system capacity, notify administrators when thresholds are exceeded, track the performance of individual system devices, and monitor either local or remote computers. To start System Monitor, first open Control Panel through the Start button by selecting Start, Control Panel. Then open Administrative Tools in Classic View by double-clicking its icon. Finally, double-click Performance to launch the Performance Console, which contains System Monitor.

The performance tools in Windows XP can perform a wide range of monitoring functions, including realtime monitoring, recording logs for future examination, and generating performance threshold alerts. Through proper use of these functions, system administrators can effectively monitor their systems for bottlenecks, extract historical trends, and receive notification of abnormal activities. All of these uses are discussed in the following sections.

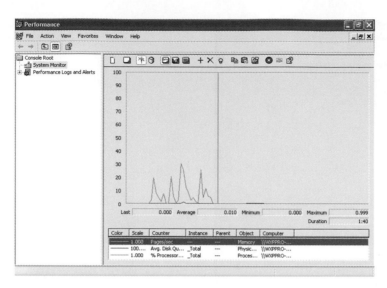

Figure 10-5 System Monitor displays memory pages accessed, disk queue length, and CPU utilization by default

Activity 10-1: Monitoring the System

Time Required: 25 minutes

Objective: Use System Monitor to view the activity of physical devices on the computer.

Description: It is important to understand how a computer reacts when commands are executed. In this activity, you will select a number of objects to be viewed while normal computer activity takes place.

To use System Monitor to monitor performance of memory, processor, disks, network, and applications:

1. Click **Start**, **Control Panel**.

2. In Classic View, double-click **Administrative Tools**.

3. Double-click **Performance**.

4. Select the **System Monitor** node in the MMC console.

5. Click **Add** on the toolbar (the plus sign).

6. Use the Performance object pull-down list to select the **Memory** object.

7. Select the **Available KBytes** counter, if necessary.

8. Click **Add**.

9. Click **Explain**. Read the detail about the selected counter and close it when done.

10. Repeat Steps 7 through 9 to add some or all of the following counters (if multiple instances of these objects are present, select one or more instances and/or the _Total instance):

- *PhysicalDisk*—Current Disk Queue Length
- *PhysicalDisk*—%Disk Time
- *PhysicalDisk*—Avg. Disk Bytes/Transfer
- *Memory*—Available Bytes
- *Memory*—Cache Faults/sec
- *Memory*—Page Faults/sec
- *Memory*—Pages/sec
- *Network Interface*—Bytes Total/sec
- *Network Interface*—Current Bandwidth
- *Network Interface* Output Queue Length
- *Network Interface*—Packets/sec
- *Processor*—Interrupts/sec
- *System*—Processor Queue Length
- *Thread*—% Processor Time
- *Thread*—Priority Current
- *Process*—% Processor Time
- *Process*—Elapsed Time
- *Process*—Page Faults/sec
- *Process*—Thread Count

11. Click **Close**.

12. Start and close **Windows Explorer** or any other application several times, read files from disk, access network resources, and so on to cause system activity.

13. Notice how the respective lines of the selected counters change according to system activity.

Realtime Monitoring

Realtime monitoring is the process of viewing the measured data from one or more counters in the System Monitor display area. System Monitor can display realtime and logged data in one of three formats: graph (see Figure 10-5), histogram (thermometer bars), or report (text-based instant values). You can select these views or displays by clicking the View Graph (default), View Histogram, or View Report buttons on the toolbar. (ScreenTips appear and explain these buttons to you if you leave the cursor over these buttons for more than a second or two.)

To begin monitoring a particular counter, click the Add Counters button, which looks like a plus sign on the toolbar. You see the Add Counters dialog box, shown in Figure 10-6. This dialog box reveals the object-oriented architecture of the Windows XP Professional system as a whole, and of performance monitoring in general. From this dialog box, you select counters based on the following:

- *Local or network-accessible computer*—Counters can be read from the local system or any accessible system over a network.

- *Performance object*—A **performance object** is a component of the Windows XP Professional system environment that can register with System Monitor for tracking; performance objects range from devices to services to processes.

- *Counter*—Counters are aspects or activities of a performance object that can provide measurable information.

- *Instance*—An **instance** is a selection of a specific performance object when more than one (such as multiple CPUs or hard drives) is present on the monitored system.

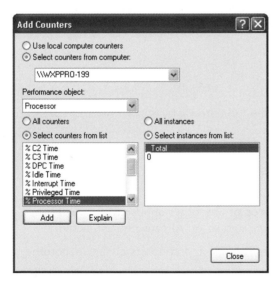

Figure 10-6   Add Counters dialog box

The Add Counters dialog box also allows you to select all counters for a specific performance object or all instances of a performance object at once. Once you've selected your host computer, object, counter (one or all), and instance (one or all), click the Add button to add the counter(s) and instance(s) to the list. If you need more information on any selected counter, click the Explain button. This reveals a floating window (see Figure 10-7) with additional information about the selected counter. Once you've added all the counters you are interested in monitoring, click Close to return to System Monitor.

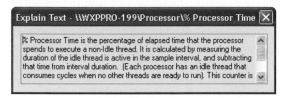

Figure 10-7   The Explain Text window provides additional information about the counter selected in the Add Counters dialog box

As you'll discover if you spend any time with System Monitor, its counters are numerous. A standard Windows XP Professional installation makes it possible to monitor hundreds of such counters. In practice, however, there are only a handful of performance objects and associated counters that you must work with regularly (some more often than others). The following list outlines the performance objects and counter pairs that are worth memorizing, as well as several others that you may find useful when evaluating performance on your systems and networks. The list deals with six kinds of objects: LogicalDisk (the divisions of a drive into partitions or dynamic storage units), Memory (RAM), Network, PhysicalDisk (the actual hard disk as a whole), Processor (CPU), and System. For convenience, they are presented in alphabetical order, listed in the form *Performance Object: Counter*.

- *LogicalDisk: Current Disk Queue Length*—This counter indicates how many system requests are waiting for disk access. If the queue length is greater than two for any logical drive, that drive is probably suffering from congestion. If you can't redistribute the load across multiple logical disks, consider upgrading your disk subsystem. Always check the corresponding PhysicalDisk counter when examining LogicalDisk counters.

- *LogicalDisk: %Disk Time*—This counter measures the percentage of time that a disk is busy handling read or write requests. It's rare for this percentage to hit 100; it's unusual for this level to be sustained at 80% or higher. If this occurs, redistribute files in an attempt to spread the load across multiple logical drives. Always check the corresponding PhysicalDisk counter.

- *LogicalDisk: Avg. Disk Bytes/Transfer*—This counter measures the average number of bytes transferred between memory and disk during read and write operations. If the value hovers at or near 4 KB (4086 bytes), this can indicate excessive paging activity on that drive. In general, a larger number indicates more efficient transfers than a smaller one, so look for declines against your baseline.

- *Memory: Available Bytes*—This counter measures the number of bytes of memory available for use on the system at any given moment. Microsoft recommends that this value always be 4096 KB or higher. If values hover at or below this threshold, your system will definitely benefit from additional RAM. You can obtain this number from the Task Manager Performance tab (it's the Available entry in the Physical Memory pane) without having to run System Monitor.

- *Memory: Cache Faults/sec*—This counter measures the number of times that the Windows XP cache manager must ask the system to bring in a file's page from the disk or locate it elsewhere in memory. Higher values indicate potential performance problems, because a system's performance is best when cache hit rates are not too high. Establishing a baseline on a lightly loaded system can help you recognize when this counter begins to climb into risky regions (double the values that appear in the baseline or higher). As with monitoring other memory counters, the proper response is to add more memory; in this case, adding more L2 cache is even better than adding main RAM.

- *Memory: Page Faults/sec*—This counter returns the average number of page faults per second for the current processor instance. A page fault occurs whenever a memory page not already loaded in RAM is referenced. When this happens, the Virtual Memory Manager (VMM) must bring in that page from the disk and possibly make room for it by swapping an old page out to the disk. Understanding this process helps to explain how memory congestion sometimes manifests itself in excessive disk activity. If this value increases to more than double what you observe in a lightly loaded baseline, it can indicate a need for more RAM.

- *Memory: Pages/sec*—This counter tracks the number of pages written to or read from disk to satisfy requirements of the VMM, and also includes paging traffic for the system cache to access file data for applications. Memory: Pages/sec can indicate that paging levels are slowing the system down. If its number increases to more than double what you observe in a light-load baseline (or, in most instances, goes above 20 for a sustained period of time), there is a strong need for additional RAM.

- *Network Interface: Bytes Total/sec*—This counter presents the total amount of traffic through the computer's network adapter, including all inbound and outbound data (framing characters as well as payload data). When the total amount of traffic begins to approach the practical maximum for the type of media in use—for example, 5.5 Mbps on on-switched 10 Mbps Ethernet—potential bandwidth saturation might be a problem. Fixing this problem might require an upgrade to a faster type of network such as 100 Mbps Ethernet. It may also require the installation of switched Ethernet hubs so that each pair of machines can use the entire 10 Mbps bandwidth that Ethernet can supply when there's no competition for the medium. Another solution is to distribute the machine's load across multiple network segments (and, therefore, multiple adapters) to balance the traffic load.

- *Network Interface: Current Bandwidth*—This measures the current utilization levels of the network medium and provides a background count against which to evaluate the monitored machine's adapter. The same observations about loading and distribution apply to this counter as to Bytes total/sec, except that Current

Bandwidth may indicate the need to partition the network to which this machine is attached to lower the total traffic on individual cable segments.

- *Network Interface: Output Queue Length*—This counter keeps track of the number of packets that are queued up for transmission across the network pending access to the medium. As with most other Windows XP queues, if more than two packets are queued, network delays are likely and the bottleneck should be removed, if at all possible.

- *Network Interface: Packets/sec*—This counter monitors the number of packets sent and received across a specific network adapter. Comparison with a baseline indicates when this value is getting out of hand. The observations that apply to the Bytes Total/sec counter also apply to this counter.

- *PhysicalDisk: Current Disk Queue Length*—PhysicalDisk counters track hard disk activity on a per-disk basis and provide much the same kind of information as the LogicalDisk counters. However, calculating acceptable queue lengths for physical disks is different than for logical ones. Here, the threshold for trouble is two more than the number of spindles on the hard drive. For ordinary drives, this is the same as for logical disks, but for RAID arrays (which Windows 2000 treats as a single drive, but are not supported by Windows XP), the threshold is two more than the number of drives in the array.

- *PhysicalDisk: % Disk Time*—This counter records the percentage of time that a hard drive is kept busy handling read or write requests. For Windows XP machines, you may see peaks as high as 100%, but the sustained average should not exceed 80%. High-sustained averages are not worrisome unless the corresponding queue length numbers are in the danger zone as well.

- *PhysicalDisk: Avg. # Disk Bytes/Transfer*—This counter keeps track of the average number of bytes that read or write requests transfer between the drive and memory. Smaller values are more worrisome than larger ones here because they can indicate inefficient use of drives and drive space. If this behavior is caused by applications, try increasing file sizes. If paging activity is the culprit, an increase in RAM or cache memory is a good idea.

- *Processor: % Processor Time*—This counter tracks the percentage of time that the CPU is busy handling nonidle threads—in other words, doing real work. Sustained values of 85% or higher indicate a heavily loaded machine. Consistent high readings indicate that a machine needs to have its load reduced or its capabilities increased with a new machine, a motherboard upgrade, or a faster CPU. See the Eight Ways to Boost Windows XP Professional Performance section later in this chapter for a discussion of these performance improvements.

- *Processor: Interrupts/sec*—This counter calculates the average number of times per second that a device requesting immediate processing interrupts the CPU. Network traffic and system clock activity establish a kind of background count for comparison. Pathological increases occur when a malfunctioning device begins to generate false interrupts or when excessive network traffic overwhelms a network adapter. In both cases, this usually creates a count that's five or more times greater than a lightly loaded baseline.

■ *System: Processor Queue Length*—This counter records the number of execution threads that are waiting for access to a CPU. If this value increases to more than double the number of CPUs present on a machine (two for a single-processor system), this machine's load should be distributed across other machines or its capabilities increased, usually by adding an additional CPU or by upgrading the machine or the motherboard. (Increasing CPU speed does not increase performance as much as you might think, because it does nothing for the machine's cache or its memory and bus transfer capabilities.)

NOTE Where it is indicated that more than one counter is worth watching for a particular performance object (for instance, there are four network-related counters), it's more significant when all counters experience a dramatic change in status simultaneously than when only one or two such counters show an increase. Across-the-board changes are more likely to indicate a bottleneck than are more localized changes (because they are more likely to be caused by applications or by shifts in local conditions, traffic levels, and so forth).

You can customize the display of System Monitor through its Properties dialog box. Access the System Monitor Properties dialog box by selecting System Monitor in the left pane, then right-clicking in the right pane and selecting Properties from the shortcut menu. Alternatively, you can click the Properties button, which looks like a hand holding a piece of paper, in System Monitor's toolbar. The General tab (shown in Figure 10-8) offers the following controls:

■ Set the view to Graph, Histogram, or Report (that is, the same function as the toolbar buttons).

■ Enable the Legend, Value bar, and Toolbar items.

■ Set the report and histogram data to Default, Current, Average, Minimum, or Maximum.

■ Set the appearance to 3D or Flat.

■ Set the border to None or Fixed Single.

■ Set the update/measurement interval in seconds; default is one second.

■ Allow duplicate counter instances.

The Source tab (see Figure 10-9) is used to specify whether the displayed information is pulled from realtime measurements, from a Counter log (Counter logs are discussed in the Logging and Using Logged Activity section later in this chapter), or from a DSN (data source name) database (if available). If a Counter log is used, you must also define the time range.

Use the Data tab to add or remove counters and to alter the color, scale, width, and style (all using pull-down lists) for each counter's chart line. The Graph tab defines a title and vertical

Figure 10-8   System Monitor Properties, General tab

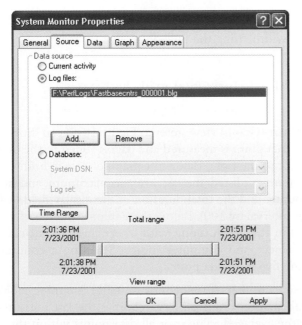

Figure 10-9   System Monitor Properties, Source tab

axis label, enables vertical and horizontal grid lines, indicates whether to display vertical scale numbers, and sets the vertical maximum and minimum scale. The vertical maximum and minimum scales are used to focus or expand the display to make counter measurements more informative. For example, if several counters display measurements within .3 deviations of the 80 mark, setting the maximum to 85 and the minimum to 75 expands the displayed information to grant an order of magnitude of greater detail. The Appearance tab includes a Color pane where you can define the colors for the various components of System Monitor. Likewise, the Font pane on the Appearance tab allows you to choose the font used to display text information.

ACTIVITY

Activity 10-2: Customizing the System Monitor Display

Time Required: 10 minutes

Objective: Modify the display within System Monitor to provide more useful information.

Description: Whenever data is being gathered, it is important to determine what and how much information is useful. The user makes changes to better view important data at a glance.

To use System Monitor to alter the display parameters:

1. Click the **Properties** button on the toolbar (or press **Ctrl+Q**).
2. Change Sample automatically from every **1** second to **2** seconds.
3. Select the **Data** tab.
4. Select the **\Memory\Pages/sec** counter.
5. Change the color and width, using the pull-down lists.
6. Select the **Graph** tab.
7. Select the **Vertical grid** and **Horizontal grid** check boxes.
8. Click **OK** to close the System Monitor Properties dialog box.

The System Monitor display in Chart (Graph) view (refer to Figure 10-5) can show 100 data points from left to right. As each data point is measured and data is added to the display, the event horizon line moves one point to the right. Below the graph of data in both Chart and Histogram views, five metadata items are listed: the last, average, maximum, and minimum measurements of the selected counter and the total duration of the display field (calculated by multiplying the measurement interval by 100). Below these items is the counter legend, which lists all counters displayed in the graph, along with information about color, scale, counter name, instance, parent, object, and computer source. Selecting a counter in the legend changes the content of the five metadata points.

Report view displays all selected counters grouped by instance, counter, object, and computer in text form. The information displayed in a report is the last measured value when viewing realtime data, or the averaged value over all data points within the selected time range (selected on the Source tab of the System Monitor Properties dialog box) when viewing logged data.

LOGGING AND USING LOGGED ACTIVITY

The Windows XP Professional Performance tool offers two types of logging capabilities. A **Counter log** records data from selected counters at regular, defined intervals, allowing you to define exactly which counters are recorded (based on computer, performance object, counter, and instance). A **Trace log** records nonconfigurable data from a designated provider (such as the kernel) only when an event occurs (such as process creation, thread deletion, disk I/O, and page fault). Trace logs are operating system environment status dumps more similar to the memory dump written when a Stop error occurs than a log of performance statistics. You can review Counter log files using System Monitor. Trace logs differ from Counter logs in that they measure data continually rather than taking only periodic samples.

Using Counter logs is fairly simple. First, select the Counter Logs item beneath the Performance Logs and Alerts node of the Performance tool (see Figure 10-10). Notice that a Counter log named System Overview is already defined by default. You can use this predefined Counter log to get a basic look at the performance of the system. It's a basic look because it looks at only three counters—memory, storage, and CPU. Creating your own Counter log requires selecting counters (based on computer, object, counter, and instance), setting the measurement interval, providing file storage information, and setting start and stop times.

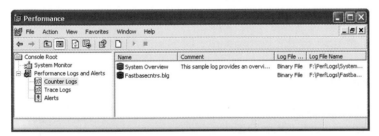

Figure 10-10   The Counter Logs node in the Performance tool

NOTE   Counter logs record data at regular intervals; all counters in a Counter log use the same interval. The default interval is 15 seconds, but you can define intervals from 1 second to 999,999 days.

The Properties dialog box for Counter logs has three tabs. The General tab shows the filename of the selected log, lists all counters included in the log, allows adding and removing counters, and sets the measurement interval. The Log Files tab sets the file type (comma-delimited, tab-delimited, binary, or SQL database) and defines the filename extension. By clicking the Configure button, you can change the name and location of the file and set the maximum file size in kilobytes or available drive space. The Schedule tab defines the start and the stop times for the log (either manual or at a specified time). You can terminate a log manually or set termination to occur after a specified length of time, at a specified time, or when the file is full. Once a log file closes, you can run a command (such as a batch file) or start a new log file (if drive space is available).

Once you define a Counter log, you can either wait for the defined start time or issue the Start command from the Action menu to begin recording data. Once you start recording, the Counter log continues to collect data until you stop the recording manually (by issuing the Stop command from the Action menu) or a defined stop event occurs (such as after a time period, a specific time, or when the log is full). The Counter log records data even when the Performance tool is closed. While a Counter log is recording data, the log icon beside the name is green. When the recording stops, the icon turns red.

Activity 10-3: Creating a Counter Log

Time Required: 20 minutes

Objective: Use the Performance tool to schedule the creation of a Counter log.

Description: Performance data can be tracked in real time, but there is the potential that running System Monitor may skew the results. To best track the performance, a counter log can be created without having the System Monitor running. In this activity, you will create a counter log to track performance of the processor.

To create, start, and stop a Counter log:

1. Launch the Performance tool if it is not still open from the previous activity.

2. Click the plus sign next to the Performance Logs and Alerts node to expand its contents.

3. Select the **Counter Logs** item.

4. Select **New Log Settings** from the Action menu.

5. Type a name, such as **Set1**. Click **OK**.

6. Click the **Add Objects** button on the General tab, select the **Processor** object in the Performance objects pane, then click **Add** to add the object, and **Close** to close the window.

You can use this method to select entire objects for monitoring, or you can add counters one at a time. To prevent seeing an error message in Step 7, click the Remove button in the Counters list in the Set1 window before proceeding to Step 7.

7. Click the **Add Counters** button, select the **% Processor Time** counter in the Select counters from list pane (this is easy; it's selected by default), and then click the **Add** button to add this counter to the log. Click the **Close** button.

8. Change the Interval from **15** seconds to **2** seconds in the Sample data every text box.

9. Click **OK** to save your counter log definition. (If you receive an error message, click **Yes** to create the log now.)

10. Right-click the **Set1** Counter log and select **Properties** from the shortcut menu.

11. Select the **Log Files** tab. Review its controls, but don't make any changes.

12. Select the **Schedule** tab.

13. If you are prompted that the log file path does not exist but can be created, select **Yes** to create the path.

14. In the Start log area, select the **At** option and change the start time to **3** minutes from the present.

15. In the Stop log area, select the **After** option and change the time to **4** minutes.

16. Click **OK**.

17. Notice that the new log appears in the list. Within three minutes, its icon will turn green.

18. After the icon turns green, start and terminate Windows Explorer several times to cause system activity.

19. After four minutes the icon turns back to red. (Do not go on with the next activity until the icon is red.)

Once you've recorded a log file, it can be used in System Monitor. To do so, open the Properties dialog box for System Monitor and go to the Source tab (refer to Figure 10-9). Select the Log files option button, click the Add button, and then provide the path to the Counter log file (by default, such logs are stored in *%systemroot%\PerfLogs*). Next, click the Time Range button to reveal the start and stop time stamps for the recorded data. Next use the sliding endpoints to click and drag the view range. Time Range is used to focus the display around important data. Keep in mind that the display area can reveal only 100 measurement points. If you select more than 100 data points, System Monitor will resample the data down to 100 points. For example, if you have 300 points, every three data items will be averaged to produce a single point. System Monitor retains all 300 data points, but only the average points appear. If fewer than 100 data points are selected in the time range, the data is displayed without any extrapolation.

ACTIVITY

Activity 10-4: Viewing a Counter Log

Time Required: 20 minutes

Objective: Use the System Monitor tool to open a previously captured Counter log.

Description: Numerous Counter logs can be captured during different days of the week and different times of the day to get a true sample of activity on a computer. In this activity, you will open a previously captured Counter log and view the data.

To view data from a Counter log with System Monitor:

1. Start the Performance tool if it is not still open from the previous activity.

2. Select the **System Monitor** node.

3. Right-click the right pane and select **Properties** from the shortcut menu.

4. Select the **Source** tab.

5. Select the **Log files** option.

6. Use the **Add** button to locate and select the Counter log created in Activity 10-3. Click **Open**.

7. Click **OK** in the System Monitor Properties dialog box.

8. Click the **New Counter Set** button in the toolbar (the blank page with a sparkle on the upper-right corner).

9. Click the **Add** button (the plus sign) on the toolbar.

10. Click **Add** to add the % Processor Time Counter to the System Monitor display. Note the Counter log recorded in the previous activity has only this one counter so it is selected by default.

11. Click **Close**.

12. Because the Counter log recorded measurements every 2 seconds for 4 minutes, there are 120 data points that are compressed and averaged to create the display you see. To prevent compression of data, you must select a time range of 100 data points or fewer.

13. Click the **Properties** button on the toolbar.

14. Select the **Source** tab.

15. Click the **Time Range** button to refresh the Counter log data.

16. Click and drag the right slider so that only 198 seconds separate the start and stop ends of the view range.

17. Click **OK**. Notice that now 99 data points are displayed.

Alerts

An **alert** is an automated watchdog that informs you when a counter crosses a defined threshold, high or low. An Alert object can consist of one or more counter/instance-based alert definitions. For example, you can configure an alert to be sent if the CPU goes above 99% usage, which is a possible indicator of CPU overload (see Figure 10-11). The individual alert definitions within an Alert object share the same sample interval, action triggers, and stop/start settings, but operate as distinct alert events. More than one Alert object can be created to assign different sample rates, action triggers, and stop/start settings.

Figure 10-11 Setting a CPU threshold alert

An alert is defined on a counter/instance basis as are counters for the Counter log and System Monitor. An alert definition focuses on one or all counters of one or all objects on the local or networked computer. Each alert definition is assigned a threshold and told whether to issue an alert when the measured value is under or over that threshold. An alert event is triggered only when the measured value of the specific counter at the time of alert sampling has crossed the threshold. Counter levels between samplings have no effect on alerts, because those levels are unknown to the alert-monitoring system. The sampling interval of an Alert object is the same as that of Counter logs—one second to 999,999 days.

Activity 10-5: Counter Alerts

Time Required: 15 minutes

Objective: Set the Performance tool to alert the user when a counter exceeds a threshold.

Description: Counter logs are useful in tracking activity, but there are also times when an administrator needs to know if limits are exceeded and when that takes place. In this activity, you will set a threshold for a specific counter.

To create an Alert object:

1. Launch the Performance tool if it is not still open.

2. Select the **Alerts** node.

3. Select **New Alert Settings** from the Action menu.

4. Type a name such as **Set2**. Click **OK**.

5. Click **Add**.

6. Click **Add** to add the % Processor Time counter to the alert. Note that this counter is selected by default.

7. Click **Close**.

8. Ensure that **Over** in the Alert when the value is pull-down box is selected.

9. Type in **50** in the Limit box.

10. Change the sample Interval to **1** second.

11. Select the **Action** tab.

12. Select the **Send a network message to** check box.

13. Type the username of the account with which you are currently logged on.

14. Select the **Schedule** tab.

15. Select the **Manually (using the shortcut menu)** option in the Start scan area.

16. Click **OK**.

17. Select the new **Alert object** that appears in the list of alerts.

18. Select the **Start** command from the Action menu. The Alert object's icon will be green when active.

19. Start and terminate Windows Explorer several times to force system activity. When the % Processor Usage crosses the 50 percent threshold, a network message appears on your screen. Click **OK** to close it.

20. Select the **Delete** command from the Action menu. Click **OK** to confirm the deletion if prompted. This deletes the Action object.

When an alert is triggered, any of the following four actions can occur. These are enabled and defined on the Action tab of an Alert object's Properties dialog box, as shown for the CPUthresh Alert object in Figure 10-12.

- *Log an entry in the application event log*—You can view the event detail through Event Viewer.

- *Send a network message to*—A single NetBIOS name for a user, group, or computer can be defined. When an alert occurs, a message regarding the alert and the measured counter level is sent to the designated entity.

- *Start performance data log*—Starts the recording of a Counter log.

- *Run this program*—Used to execute a program with command-line options or to call up a batch file. When this action is used, a string of performance-related information can be included at the end of the defined command line in the form. You can choose to have a single argument string with all data points separated with commas, or individual strings with the data elements of date/time, measured value, alert name, counter name, limit value, and a custom text string.

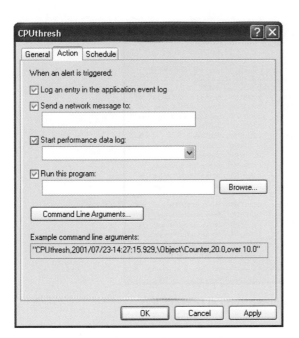

Figure 10-12   The Action tab controls actions taken for Alert objects when thresholds are passed or when specific events occur

The Schedule tab in an Alert event's Properties dialog box is similar to that for a Counter log. Use this tab to define a start event that is either manual or at a specified time and a stop event that can be manual, after a period of time, or at a specified time. Similar to Counter logs, Alert events function even when the Performance tool is closed.

Event Viewer

The Windows XP Professional **Event Viewer** is another useful tool for examining the performance and activities on a system. The Event Viewer tracks all events generated by the operating system as well as security and application events. An event is anything that causes an event detail to be created in one of the logs that the Event Viewer manages. Failure of a device to load, an unsuccessful logon, or a corrupt database file can all be recorded by Event Viewer and viewed through one of three log files: System, Application, or Security. Access the Event Viewer through the Administrative Tools in Control Panel. Figure 10-13 shows Event Viewer displaying a typical System log.

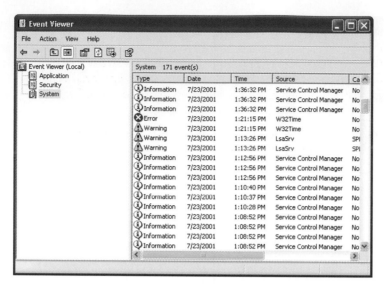

Figure 10-13   Event Viewer displaying a typical System log

Activity 10-6: Tracking Activity with Event Viewer

Time Required: 10 minutes

Objective: Use Event Viewer to view the details of System Monitor.

Description: Event Viewer can also be used to see details of what has been monitored on the system. In this activity, you will view what counter was tracked and see when exactly the alert took place.

To use Event Viewer to view an event detail:

1. Click **Start**, **Control Panel**.

2. Open the **Administrative Tools** by double-clicking its icon in Control Panel.

3. Open **Event Viewer** by double-clicking its icon in the Administrative Tools window.

4. Select the **Application log**.

5. Locate and select an Information detail with a SysmonLog source.

6. Double-click the item to open the event detail.

7. Notice that the Description includes information about the counter and the measured level that caused the alert.

8. Click **OK**.

9. Close Event Viewer.

Three types of System and Application log events and two types of Security log events are recorded in Event Viewer, as follows:

- *Information*—A System and Application log event that signifies rare but significant events about successful operation of internal services and drivers, indicated by the *i* icon. For example, when a database program loads successfully, it may generate an Information event.

- *Warning*—A System and Application log event that signifies potential problems although there is no present danger, indicated by an *!* (exclamation point) icon. For example, if disk space is running low, a Warning event may be logged.

- *Error*—A System and Application log event that signifies the presence of significant problems requiring immediate attention, indicated by a white *x* in a red circle. For example, if a driver fails to load correctly, an Error event is issued.

- *Success Audit*—A Security log event that indicates that an event selected for audit has taken place. For example, when a user successfully logs on to a system, a Success Audit event is logged. A gold key icon represents success audits.

- *Failure Audit*—A Security log event that indicates when an audited event has failed. For example, an unsuccessful attempt to access a network drive is logged as a Failure Audit event. A gold lock icon represents failure audits.

The System log is the primary log file for most system services, drivers, and processes. Typical System log events occur when device drivers fail to load or load with errors, when system services fail to start, when system service errors or failures occur, or when auditing is enabled and system-related events flagged for audit occur. The Application log contains event messages that can be generated by Windows XP Professional native applications or services. Unlike the System and Application logs, the Security log does not automatically track events. It records audit events, such as logon, resource access, and computer restart and shutdown. Auditing must be enabled and configured (for details see Chapter 6, "Windows XP Security and Access Controls").

All Event log entries include the event's date and time, source, category (such as Logon or Logoff), an event number, the name of the account that generated the event, and the name of the computer on which the event occurred. You can use Event Viewer to view logs on other computers. To access log files on other computers, select the Connect to another computer command in the Action menu while Event Viewer (Local) is highlighted.

Each Event Viewer log has customizable properties. Access a log's Properties dialog box by highlighting that log, then selecting the Properties command from the Action menu. The System Properties dialog box (see Figure 10-14) has two tabs. Use the General tab to set properties, such as the displayed name, the maximum file size, action to take when log is full (overwrite as needed, overwrite only events older than a specified number of days, or do not overwrite), and whether to manually clean out the log. Use the Filter tab to reduce the number of events displayed. Filter options include sorting by the five event types, source of the event, event category, event ID, user, computer, and date range.

10

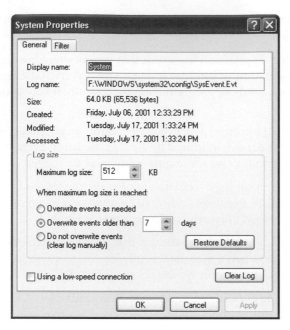

Figure 10-14   System Properties, General tab

Performance Options

You use the Performance Options dialog box (see Figure 10-15) to adjust system performance based on applications and virtual memory. Access this dialog box by clicking the Settings button in the Performance pane on the Advanced tab of the System applet found inside Control Panel. From there, click the Advanced tab in the Performance Options window.

In the Performance Options dialog box, you can perform three tasks. First, you can optimize processor scheduling by indicating whether the computer is used primarily for user or interactive programs or background services (the default is programs, as you'd expect for a desktop operating system). The option button selection of Programs boosts the priority of foreground processes, whereas Background services balances the use of processor resources for foreground and background processes.

Second, you can optimize memory usage in much the same way by indicating whether memory should favor programs or the system cache. The option button selection of Programs grants more memory to foreground programs; choosing System cache gives the operating system more latitude in managing memory allocations (here again, the default is Programs, as you'd expect for a desktop operating system).

Third, you can manage the size of the paging file—that portion of disk space where the operating system stores memory pages not in active use to extend the capacity of memory beyond what physical RAM in the system allows—in the virtual memory pane. In most

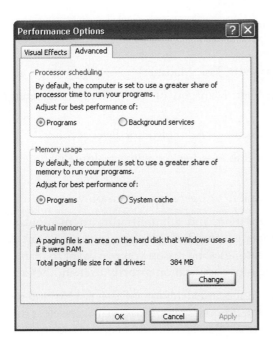

Figure 10-15   The Performance Options dialog box (Advanced tab) offers controls for processor scheduling, memory usage, and virtual memory

cases, the Windows XP automatic paging file selection should be adequate, but if System Monitor shows excessive hard page faults, increasing the size of this file (if hard disk space allows) or adding physical RAM can improve system performance. By default, the paging file size is set between 1.5 and 3.0 times the amount of RAM in the system or 192–384 MB, whichever number is greater.

Use the Change button on the Performance Options dialog box to access the Virtual Memory dialog box, where the size and location(s) of the paging file may be defined.

Setting Application Priority

Windows XP Professional uses 32 levels of application priority, numbered 0 (zero) to 31, to determine which process should gain access to the CPU at any given moment. Users have only minimal control over the initial startup priority level for any task begun. The following list indicates important ranges and specific priority levels:

- *0–15*—User-accessible process priorities
- *16–31*—System-accessible process priorities
- *0–6*—Low user range
- *4*—Low value (as set in Task Manager, or with /low parameter to Start command)
- *5*—BelowNormal value (as set in Task Manager)

- *7*—Normal (default setting for user processes)

- *8–15*—High user range

- *10*—AboveNormal value (as set in Task Manager)

- *13*—High value (as set in Task Manager, or with /high parameter to Start command)

- *16–24*—Realtime values accessible to Administrator-level accounts

- *24*—Realtime value (as set in Task Manager, or with /realtime parameter to Start command)

- *25–31*—Realtime values accessible to operating system only

There are two techniques available to users and administrators to manipulate process priorities: manage already running processes using Task Manager or use the Start command to start processes with specific priority settings. One reason you may want to manipulate the priority of a process is to give a time-sensitive application priority over another application.

To use Task Manager, right-click any unoccupied region of the taskbar and select Task Manager from the shortcut menu. On the Processes tab of Task Manager, select the name of the desired process (usually this is the name of an .exe file that corresponds to the process), and then right-click that process to produce another menu. From this menu, select the Set Priority item. This is where you can pick one of the predefined priority settings—Low, BelowNormal, Normal, AboveNormal, High, or Realtime. The current setting is the entry marked with a bullet symbol to the left. You must be logged on with Administrator privileges to use the Realtime setting.

You can use the Start command from a command prompt to open a new application at some priority level other than the default. You can enter this command from either a command prompt or the Run command. The Start command follows this general syntax:

```
Start /priority-level program
```

where */priority-level* must be one of /low, /belownormal, /normal, /abovenormal, /high, or /realtime, and *program* is a valid path plus filename for the program you want to start at the specified priority level. For more details on the Start command, enter start /? from a command prompt.

PERFORMANCE TUNING IN THE SYSTEM APPLET

The System applet in Control Panel includes an Advanced tab that addresses several Performance entries. To access this utility, follow this menu sequence if you're using the Category View: Start, Control Panel, Performance and Maintenance, then click the System icon in the Control Panel section. The Windows Classic view is simpler: Start, Control Panel, System. Next, select the Advanced tab, and then click the Settings button in the

Performance pane. You should see a display like the one shown in Figure 10-16, where the Visual Effects tab is selected by default. An Advanced tab is also available, as shown in Figure 10-17.

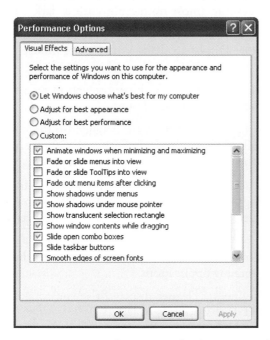 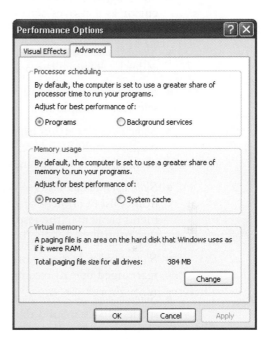

Figures 10-16 and 10-17 The System Applet's performance controls include Visual Effects and Advanced tabs, respectively

The Visual Effects Tab

The Visual Effects tab permits you to control how Windows XP handles your computer display when managing screen output. By default, the Let Windows choose what's best for my computer setting is selected, and permits the computer to trade performance against appearance as the system load increases. You can instruct Windows XP to always Adjust for best appearance or to always Adjust for best performance if you prefer to lock the system into a completely consistent mode of graphics operation. Finally, for those who love to tweak and tune their systems, the Custom setting permits 16 different visual effects to be manipulated separately:

- *Animate windows when minimizing and maximizing*—Shows visual effects when minimization and maximization controls are used.

- *Fade or slide menus into view*—Enables a smooth visual effect when menus are opened for display.

- *Fade or slide ToolTips into view*—Enables a smooth visual effect when tool tips are displayed.

- *Fade out menu items after clicking*—Enables a smooth visual effect to remove menus from display after a selection is made.

- *Show shadows under mouse pointer*—Produces a drop shadow beneath the mouse cursor as it moves across the desktop (most noticeable with a dark cursor on a white background).

- *Show shadows under mouse pointer*—Displays a shadow under the mouse pointer in order to enhance the 3-D effect.

- *Show translucent selection rectangle*—Displays a translucent selection rectangle while selecting multiple items in a window or on the desktop.

- *Show window contents while dragging*—As windows are dragged on the desktop, the window outline and some or all of its contents follow the cursor, where the level of detail displayed depends on the speed of motion and the overall processing load.

- *Slide open combo boxes*—When selecting a menu choice involves picking an item from a list of choices or opening a secondary menu (as is the case with some Start menu elements), the resulting text box is sometimes called a combo box. Enabling this control causes the boxes to slide open from left to right.

- *Slide taskbar buttons*—Enables a smooth visual effect when taskbar buttons are rearranged due to closing or opening applications.

- *Smooth edges of screen fonts*—Produces a cleaner display of screen fonts by adding shaded pixels around the jagged or sharp edges of letters.

- *Smooth-scroll list boxes*—When text boxes contain too many items to fit in the display, you must scroll up or down to view additional elements. Smooth-scrolling means that elements move up or down smoothly, rather than popping one or more list elements up or down at a time. When this control is turned off, lists jump up and down in a more jerky fashion.

- *Use a background image for each folder type*—Associates a more specific image with folders based on their type and contents, rather than using a simpler, more generic icon.

- *Use common tasks in folders*—Drives the task-oriented displays in the left-hand pane of most Windows XP windows and creates the linkage between task data and the window itself to permit that data to be displayed. Disabling this control eliminates display of task information.

- *Use drop shadows for icon labels on the desktop*—Displays a shadow under desktop icons in order to enhance the 3-D effect.

- *Use visual styles on windows and buttons*—Instructs Windows XP to use shading, 3-D effects, and edge shading on windows and buttons to give them a more realistic appearance. Disabling this control gives such elements a flat, 2-D appearance.

Although these controls may not seem terribly performance-oriented, keep in mind that drawing the desktop and managing how windows, buttons, and icons appear is a big part of what Windows XP does. By deselecting elements that require more computation or lookup (tasks, visual styles, background images, and so forth), you reduce the burden on the CPU. It won't double the speed of a computer, but it does speed things up somewhat. Notice, for example, that selecting the Adjust for best performance option turns off all settings in the Custom combo box, thereby disabling all visual effects.

The Advanced Tab

The Advanced tab consists of the following three panes:

- *Processor scheduling*—Permits wholesale manipulation of the priority granted to applications versus services. Because Windows XP Professional is a desktop operating system, it should come as no surprise that the default option here is to select Programs (applications running on the desktop, presumably at your command) over Background services (system and other services usually intended to respond to requests for services from other remote users). This means that the assumption is that most Windows XP machines should prioritize applications over services. Change this setting only on machines where services are not just installed but used regularly by others. This setting routinely boosts the default thread priority for the item chosen by two.

- *Memory usage*—Prioritizes allocating memory to applications rather than to the system cache, again in keeping with the Windows XP Professional primary role as a desktop operating system (where its normal task is to run applications for users). Normally, the System Cache option button is selected only on a server or on a desktop machine where applications themselves require large amounts of system cache (as they would indicate in their documentation or Help files).

- *Virtual memory*—By default, Windows XP sets its paging file at 1.5 times the amount of RAM installed, with an upper limit of three times that amount. Figure 10-18 shows a default setup on a system with 256 MB of RAM installed (which explains the paging file size of 384–768 MB). The Virtual Memory window can be used to situate and distribute a Windows XP paging file across multiple drives. To achieve maximum performance from a Windows XP paging file, follow as many of these rules as you can when altering the default setup:

  - Avoid placing the bulk of the paging file on the system and boot partitions whenever possible. If other partitions share a controller with the boot partition, performance benefits are diminished, because system disk calls and paging calls must use the same disk controller. To enable crash dumps, it remains necessary to create a minimal paging file on the boot partition, the size of which matches the configuration information on the Advanced tab of the System applet (click the Settings button in the Startup and Recovery pane).

  - Spread the paging file across as many drives as possible. If such drives share a controller, performance benefits are less than if they have separate controllers.

  - There's no performance benefit to spreading paging files across multiple RAID arrays; if you have more than one RAID array on your system, you can safely situate the paging file on any single RAID array.

10

- If the paging file is of insufficient size for your system and normal work activities, you see an error stating that the system is low on virtual memory. If free space is available, the system automatically enlarges the paging file. However, this action may take 10 to 30 seconds and significantly slows down the performance of the system during this process. To avoid this issue in the future, reconfigure the paging file size.

- There are three options for how the paging file size is managed: custom size, system managed size, and no paging file. Custom size allows you to specifically define where and how large the paging file is. System managed size allows the OS to manage the paging file as it sees fit. However, it keeps the entire paging file on the boot partition. The selection of No paging file will completely remove the paging file from the system and will force the OS to rely upon physical RAM only. Select this option only if you have 1 GB of RAM or greater.

- The Custom size option allows you to configure an initial and a maximum size for the paging file. The initial size is the amount of drive space the OS will be preallocated as the paging file upon boot up of the system. No other file is allowed to consume space from this preallocation even if the system is not using the entire allotment. The maximum size is how large the paging file is allowed to grow if the system deems it necessary to expand the size of the paging file. The additional space (i.e., the difference between the initial size and maximum size values) is not preallocated. Other files may consume this space. If the drive is approaching maximum capacity, the OS will be unable to expand the paging file.

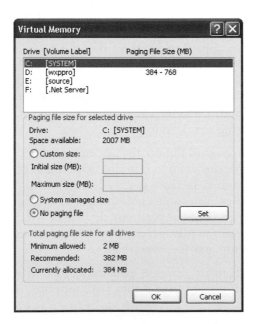

Figure 10-18   A Windows XP Professional default setup

Under most circumstances, the defaults for these three settings work nicely on Windows XP machines. Only when the machine acts primarily as a server should the Processor Scheduling and Memory Usage settings be changed. Similarly, only on systems where applications make unusually heavy demands on memory or the operating system should it be necessary to change page file locations and sizes.

RECOGNIZING AND HANDLING BOTTLENECKS

A **bottleneck** occurs when a limitation in a single component slows down an entire system. The first thing to remember about bottlenecks is that they always exist in any computer. Applications, hard drives, operating systems, and network interfaces might all act as bottlenecks from time to time, but for any given configuration, it is always possible to identify one component that slows down the others the most.

There is no single bottleneck monitor that can easily identify all possible problems. However, by using the monitoring tools included with Windows XP Professional, you can identify possible bottlenecks and make necessary adjustments. The goal when tuning a workstation for performance is to make bottlenecks unnoticeable for everyday functions. A computer used for CAD requires much greater throughput than a computer used primarily for word processing. Ideally, a computer should be waiting for user input rather than making users wait for the computer's response; the user becomes the bottleneck.

Although the details vary from situation to situation, the method of finding and fixing computer system bottlenecks follows a reasonably consistent course, as shown in the following:

1. Create a baseline for a computer. For Windows XP Professional, this includes observations of memory usage, disk usage, CPU usage, operating system resource usage and activity, and network utilization, at the barest minimum.

2. The first step in identifying potential bottlenecks is to compare baseline observations to current system behavior. In most cases, one or more of the baseline values will have changed for the worse. These changes indicate further areas for investigation.

3. Investigate the more common causes of system problems (some of these for Windows XP Professional are documented later in this chapter) to see if any match the symptoms your computer is exhibiting. If you have a match, the causes of bottlenecks are easy to identify and fixes are easy to apply.

4. If the list of usual suspects does not produce an obvious culprit, further analysis is required. You can obtain more details of system behavior from System Monitor and other performance tools, analyze their reports and statistics, and pinpoint potential bottlenecks. Use the general analytical techniques and combinations of objects and counters described in this chapter to help in isolating and identifying bottlenecks.

10

5. Once a potential bottleneck is identified, you make changes to the system configuration to correct the situation. Sometimes, this involves software configuration changes; other times, it can involve adding or replacing specific hardware components or subsystems.

6. Always test the impact of any fix you try. Compile a new set of statistics and compare them to the same system measurements before the fix was applied. Sometimes, the fix does the trick and values return to normal, or at least come closer to acceptable levels. If the fix doesn't make a difference, further analysis, other fixes, and more testing are required. It's important to keep at the job until something improves the bottleneck.

Although bottlenecks can always be fixed, some fixes are more expensive than others. Remember, you can always replace an overloaded server or workstation with another bigger, faster system, or you can spread the load from a single overloaded system across multiple systems to reduce the impact on any single machine. These kinds of fixes are a great deal more expensive than tweaking system settings or adding more memory or disk space to a machine. However, in some cases, such drastic solutions are necessary. If you monitor performance correctly, such radical changes needn't take anyone by surprise.

Common Bottlenecks

This section explains how to use the counters you have chosen to watch, either alone or in combination, to determine what kinds of bottlenecks might be present on a system. Also discussed are the steps you might consider taking to correct such bottlenecks.

Disk Bottlenecks

Disk bottlenecks are the most likely problem when disk-related counters increase more dramatically than other counters (or when compared to your baseline) or when disk queue lengths become unacceptably long. Windows XP Professional collects information about the performance of physical disks (the actual devices) by default.

If Disk Queue Length and % Disk time values remain consistently high (1.5 or higher and more than 80%, respectively), it's probably time to think about adding more disk controllers or drives, or possibly switching existing drives and controllers for newer, faster equivalents (such as UltraWide SCSI or a storage area network, or SAN). This costs money, but can provide dramatic performance improvements on systems with disk bottlenecks. Adding a controller for each drive can substantially improve performance, and switching from individual drives to disk (RAID) arrays can also improve performance on such systems. Because high-end disk controllers often include onboard memory that functions as yet another level of system cache, they can confer measurable performance benefits. But unless users need extremely fast disks for 3-D ray tracing, CAD applications, modeling, or other data-intensive applications, this is probably overkill for most conventional desktops.

Software can also contribute to disk bottlenecks through poor design, configuration settings that affect disk performance, or outdated drivers. Because tweaking an application's source code is beyond the reach of most system administrators, inspect the application to see if you can increase the size of the files it manipulates directly or the size of data transfers it requests. Larger and fewer data transfers are faster and more efficient than smaller, more frequent transfers. You should also defragment your hard drives regularly to optimize their performance.

Memory Bottlenecks

Windows XP Professional is subject to various kinds of **memory bottlenecks**. To begin with, it's important to make sure that the paging file is working as efficiently as possible; that is, its size is 1.5 to 3 times the amount of physical RAM on a machine (see Chapter 3, "Using the System Utilities"). On machines with more than one drive, Microsoft recommends situating the paging file somewhere other than the boot partition (where the Windows system files reside) or the system partition (where the boot loader and other startup files reside). If multiple drives are available, it's a good idea to spread the paging file evenly across all such drives (except a drive with the system or boot partition). Better yet is for each drive to have its own disk controller, which allows Windows XP Professional to access all drives in parallel.

You can detect excessive paging activity by watching the page-related counters mentioned earlier and by observing the lowest number of Available Bytes over time. (Microsoft recommends that this number never dip below 4 MB or 4096 KB.) Excessive disk time and disk queue lengths can often mask paging problems, so be sure to check paging-related statistics when disk utilization zooms. Adding more memory can fix such problems and improve overall system performance.

Processor Bottlenecks

Processor bottlenecks are indicated when the Processor object's % Processor time counter stays consistently above 80% or when the System object's Processor Queue Length counter remains fixed near a value of 2 or more. In both cases, the CPU is being overworked. However, occasional peaks of 100% for processor time are not unusual (especially when processes are being started or terminated). The combination of consistently high utilization and overlong queues is a more common indication of trouble than an occasional high utilization spike.

Even on machines that support multiple CPUs, it's important to recognize that performance doesn't scale arithmetically as additional CPUs are added. A second CPU gives a more dramatic incremental improvement in performance than a third or fourth; however, two CPUs do not double performance. You're often better off responding to CPU bottlenecks by redistributing a machine's processing load, upgrading its CPU, memory, and motherboard, or replacing the machine altogether. Simply upgrading or adding another CPU neither increases the amount of cache memory on a system nor improves the system's underlying CPU-to-memory data transfer capabilities, both of which often play a crucial role in system performance.

10

When there is more than one CPU on a system, you can choose to monitor their activity on an individual basis or as a group. To monitor a single CPU, select the individual instance of the CPU. The first CPU is instance 0; the second CPU is instance 1. To monitor the activity of all CPUs as a whole, select the _Total instance.

Network Bottlenecks

Network bottlenecks are not typical on most Windows XP Professional machines, because end users seldom load the network sufficiently to experience performance problems. However, it is worth comparing how much traffic is passing through a workstation's network adapter with the traffic through the networking medium to which it is attached. Excessive activity can indicate a failing adapter (sometimes called a "jabbering transceiver") or an ill-behaved application. In both cases, the fix is relatively straightforward—replace the NIC or the application, respectively.

Occasionally, however, the network itself may be overloaded. This situation is indicated by utilization rates that exceed the recommended maximum for the medium in use. (For example, Ethernet should not be loaded more heavily than 56% utilization, but Token Ring can function adequately at loads as high as 97%.) When this happens, as a network administrator you have two options: divide the network into segments and balance traffic so that no segment is overloaded, or replace the existing network with a faster alternative. Neither of these options is especially fast, cheap, or easy, but the former is cheaper than the latter, and may give your network—and your budget—some breathing room before a wholesale upgrade is warranted.

ACTIVITY

Activity 10-7: Create a Baseline

Time Required: 1 hour 30 minutes

Objective: Use Counter logs to create a baseline.

Description: Baselines can be very useful for troubleshooting. They can be used to compare performance to see if problems are real or perceived. In this activity, you will create a baseline to be used for comparison purposes.

To create and view a baseline:

1. Click **Start**, **Control Panel**.
2. Double-click **Administrative Tools**.
3. Double-click **Performance**.
4. Click the plus sign next to the Performance Logs and Alerts node to expand its contents.
5. Select the **Counter Logs** item.
6. Select **New Log Settings** from the Action menu.

7. Type a name, such as **Baseline1**. Click **OK**.

8. Click the **Add Counters** button on the General tab.

9. Click **Explain** to open the Explain Text window.

10. Use the **Performance object** pull-down list to select the **Memory** object.

11. Select the **Pages/sec** counter in the list under the **Select counters from list** option button.

12. Read the details in the Explain Text window about the selected counter.

13. Click **Add**.

14. Repeat Steps 10 through 13 to add some or all of the following counters (if multiple instances of these objects are present, select one or more instances and/or the _Total instance):

    - PhysicalDisk: %Disk Time
    - Memory: Available Bytes
    - Network Interface: Bytes Total/sec
    - Processor: % Processor Time
    - System: Processor Queue Length

15. Click **Close**.

16. Change the Interval from **15** seconds to **30** seconds.

17. Select the **Log Files** tab. Review its controls, but don't make any changes.

18. Select the **Schedule** tab.

19. If you are prompted that the log file path does not exist but can be created, select **Yes** to create the path.

20. In the Start log area, select the **At** option and change the start time to **3** minutes from the present.

21. In the Stop log area, select the **After** option and change the time to **2** days.

22. Click **OK**. You may have to click **Yes** to create the log.

23. Notice the new log appears in the list. Within three minutes, its icon will turn green.

24. After the icon turns green, continue performing normal or typical work on this system until two days have passed.

25. After two days, the icon turns back to red. *Do not go on with the remaining part of this activity until the icon is red again.*

26. Select the **System Monitor** node in the Performance tool.

27. Right-click the **right pane** and select **Properties** from the shortcut menu.

28. Select the **Source** tab.

29. Select the **Log files** option.

30. Use the **Add** button to locate and select the Counter log created in Step 7. Click **Open**.

31. Click **OK** in the System Monitor Properties dialog box.

32. Click the **New Counter Set** button in the toolbar (the blank page with a sparkle on the upper-right corner).

33. Click the **Add** button (the plus sign) on the toolbar.

34. Use the **Performance object** pull-down list to select the **Memory** object.

35. Select the **Pages/sec** counter in the list under the **Select counters from list** option button.

36. Read the details in the Explain Text window about the selected counter.

37. Click **Add**.

38. Repeat Steps 34 through 37 to add some or all of the following counters (if multiple instances of these objects are present, select one or more instances and/or the _Total instance):

    - PhysicalDisk: %Disk Time

    - Memory: Available Bytes

    - Network Interface: Bytes Total/sec

    - Processor: % Processor Time

    - System: Processor Queue Length

39. Click **Close**.

40. Click the **View Report** button from the toolbar. The values listed are an average of all measurements over the entire time period recorded in the log file.

41. Click the **Properties** button on the toolbar.

42. Select the **Source** tab.

43. Click the **Time Range** button to refresh the Counter log data.

44. Click and drag the right and left sliders so that they encompass a time period of 8 hours, such as 9 AM to 5 PM.

45. Click **OK**.

46. Notice that new averaged data points are displayed.

47. Take note of the values seen here; be sure to indicate the time range used for each measurement.

48. Repeat Steps 41–47 for the time ranges of 5 PM to 10 PM, 10 PM to 6 AM, 6 AM to 9 AM, and then hourly for each hour of the typical work day (i.e., 9 AM to 10 AM, then 10 AM to 11 AM, and so on).

49. Click the **File** menu, and then select **Save As**.

50. Using the Save As dialog box, select a folder and provide a filename to save the console configuration, such as **baseline view1.msc**. Click **Save**.

51. Close the Performance tool by clicking the **File** menu and then clicking **Exit**.

52. At a later date, reopen the Performance tool (see Steps 1 through 3).

53. Click the **File** menu, and then select **Open**.

54. Using the Open dialog box, locate and select the file saved in Step 50. Click **Open**.

55. The view should return to that seen in your final action of Step 48.

56. The saved data in the first Counter log is your baseline. To use the baseline, you must record a new log file over a similar time period, and compare the new data points with the old data points.

57. Click the plus sign next to the Performance Logs and Alerts node to expand its contents.

58. Select the **Counter Logs** item.

59. Click to select the Counter log created in Step 7.

60. Right-click over this Counter log and select **Properties** from the shortcut menu.

61. Select the **Log Files** tab. Notice the Start numbering at field has been incremented.

62. Repeat Steps 18 through 48.

63. Compare the measurements you wrote down from the first baseline Counter log with the most recent Counter log. Any discrepancies may indicate a change in system activity or may point toward a developing bottleneck.

10

Eight Ways to Boost Windows XP Professional Performance

Although there are many things you can do to deal with specific system bottlenecks, there are eight particularly useful changes in system components, elements, approaches, or configuration that are likely to result in improved performance by Windows XP Professional. Though these are listed in approximate order of their potential value, all elements on this list are worth considering when performance improvements are needed.

■ *Buy a faster machine*—It takes only a year or so for a top-of-the-line, heavily loaded PC to become obsolete these days. When you find yourself considering a hardware upgrade to boost performance, compare the price of your planned upgrade to the cost of a new machine. If you're planning on spending more than half the cost of a newer computer (and can afford to double your expenditure), buy the newer, faster machine. Otherwise, you may be facing the same situation again in a few months. The extra cost buys you at least another year before you must go through this exercise again.

- *Upgrade an existing machine*—You might decide to keep a PC's case, power supply, and some of the adapter cards it contains. As long as the price stays below half the cost of a new machine, replacing a PC's motherboard not only gets you a faster CPU and more memory capacity (both cache and main memory), but it can also get you more and faster bus slots for adapter cards. While you're at it, be sure to evaluate the costs of upgrading the disk controller and hard drives, especially if they're more than twice as slow as prevailing access times. (As we write, garden-variety drives offer average access times of around 8 milliseconds, and fast drives offer average access rates of 2 to 3 milliseconds.)

- *Install a faster CPU*—As long as you can at least double the clock speed of your current CPU with a replacement, such an upgrade can improve performance for only a modest outlay. Be sure to review your memory configuration (cache and main memory) and your disk drives at the same time. A faster CPU on an otherwise unchanged system can't deliver the same performance boost as a faster CPU with more memory and faster drives.

- *Add more L2 cache*—Many experts believe that the single most dramatic improvement for an existing Windows XP PC comes from adding more L2 cache to a machine (or to buy only machines with the maximum amount of L2 cache installed). The CPU can access L2 cache in two CPU cycles, whereas access to main RAM usually takes 8 to 10 CPU cycles. This explains why adding L2 cache to a machine can produce dramatic performance improvements. Although cache chips are quite expensive, they provide the biggest potential boost to a system's performance, short of the more drastic—and expensive—suggestions detailed earlier in this list.

- *Add more RAM*—Windows XP Professional is smart about how it uses main memory on a PC; it can handle large amounts of RAM effectively. It has been widely observed that the more processes that are active on a machine, the more positive the impact of a RAM increase. For moderately loaded workstations (six or fewer applications active at once), 128 MB of RAM is recommended. For heavily loaded workstations, 256 MB or more may improve performance significantly.

When you add RAM to a Windows XP Professional machine, be sure to resize the paging file to accommodate the change properly.

- *Replace the disk subsystem*—Because memory access occurs at nanosecond speeds, and disk access occurs at millisecond speeds, disk subsystem speeds can make a major impact on Windows XP performance. This is particularly true in cases where applications or services frequently access the disk, when manipulating large files, or when large amounts of paging activity occur. Because the controller and the drives both influence disk subsystem speeds, it is recommended that you use only Fast Wide SCSI drives and controllers (or the latest of the EIDE drives and controllers) on Windows XP Professional machines. However, it's important to recognize that a slow disk controller can limit a fast drive and vice versa. That's why upgrading the entire subsystem is often necessary to realize any measurable performance gains.

■ *Increase paging file size*—Whenever System Monitor indicates that more than 10% of disk subsystem activity is related to paging, check the relationship between the Limit and Peak values in the Commit Charge pane in Task Manager. (Right-click any empty portion of the taskbar, select Task Manager, and then select the Performance tab and check the lower-left corner of the display.) If the Peak is coming any closer than 4096 KB to the limit, it's time to increase the size of this file. Use a figure somewhere between twice and three times the amount of RAM installed in the machine.

■ *Increase application priority*—On machines where a lot of background tasks must be active, you can use the Task Manager's Processes tab to increase the priority of any already running process. Highlight the process entry, and then right-click to produce a menu that includes a Set Priority entry. This entry permits you to set the priority to High or Realtime, either of which can improve a foreground application's performance. Set only critical applications to Realtime, because they can interfere with the functioning of the operating system. To start an application with an altered priority level, refer to the Setting Application Priority section earlier in this chapter.

CAUTION

Only users with administrator-level access to Windows XP Professional can run processes at a Realtime priority level. Be aware that raising the priority of a single process causes other background processes to run more slowly. The other performance improvements in this list should improve system performance across the board; this improvement affects only those processes whose priorities are increased.

OPTIMIZING PERFORMANCE FOR MOBILE WINDOWS XP USERS

Basically, managing performance for mobile Windows XP machines is substantially the same as managing performance for network-connected Windows XP machines. The same observations about optimizing key system resources—particularly RAM, disk, CPU, and communications—still apply, even though the circumstances sometimes differ.

Key differences are related to how mobile users access shared resources, such as redirected files and IntelliMirror, and how they use and synchronize Offline Files. Here, common sense goes a long way. If you follow these simple rules, you'll be able to avoid most potential performance problems that offline or remote use can cause, and you should be able to get the best possible results for your mobile users when they're disconnected from the network:

■ Make sure the network interface appears higher in the binding order than a modem or other slower link device. Although users incur an extra timeout when they fire up a remote link for the first time, once that link is active, the delay

10

disappears. Because network interfaces are much faster than modems, this binding order ensures the best overall performance.

■ Make sure that file synchronization settings for folder redirection and Offline Files do not require machines to synchronize when running on battery. File synchronization can take a while and can consume significant power. Though some risk may be involved—along with a need for user education about those risks—users working on battery power will generally be happier if shutting down a system or exiting some application does not automatically perform file synchronization.

■ Make sure your mobile users understand how to use hibernate and standby modes on their battery-powered machines. It's both faster and significantly less power-consumptive to "wake up" from hibernate or standby mode than it is to reboot from a machine that has been shut down.

■ Make sure that all Offline Files a user might need are copied to his or her machine before they leave the network environment. The default is to make local copies only for recently accessed files; under some circumstances, this may not be acceptable—particularly when a slow link is the only way to grab missing items while a mobile user operates off the local network.

■ Refresh rates also apply to group policy, which defaults to 90 minutes on Windows XP. For machines operating off the network (particularly using modems), refresh rates should be extended to avoid unnecessary network access.

■ To prevent file synchronization over slow links, configure group policy's Configure Slow link speed control (located in Computer Configuration, Administrative Templates, Network, Offline Files) to define the threshold at which a link is considered slow as opposed to fast. File synchronization cannot occur over slow links.

By reviewing how networked machines normally work on a Windows network, and taking the special needs (and slower speeds) associated with remote access or off-network operation into account, you should be able to formulate a series of policies and settings that will help your mobile users obtain the best possible performance when they're not directly attached to their home networks.

CHAPTER SUMMARY

❏ Windows XP Professional provides a number of tools to monitor system performance. By using these tools, it is easy to examine the effects of bottlenecks and to improve system response time.

❏ You can use Task Manager to view applications, processes, and overall system performance, or to stop applications and processes (an efficient way to regain control from an application that is experiencing problems). The default configuration of the Processes tab displays imagename (i.e., processname), user name, CPU, and memory usage.

Other columns, such as Virtual Memory Size and Thread count, can be added to the Processes tab.

❏ The Performance console is an exceptionally useful collection of tools that includes System Monitor, log files, and alerts. System Monitor is used to watch realtime performance or review data collected in log files. Log files record performance data for one or more counters over a specified period of time. Alerts inform administrators when specific counters cross defined threshold levels.

❏ EventViewer is a less dynamic but equally important tool that tracks logs generated by the system. EventViewer monitors three different logs: System, Application, and Security. The System log records system information and errors, such as the failure of a device driver to load. The Application log maintains similar information for programs, such as database applications. The Security log monitors system security events and audit activities.

❏ Finally, you should keep an eye on logs and performance counters to isolate any bottlenecks that occur in the system. Once you identify the bottleneck, take the steps necessary to remove it and get the system running more smoothly. In addition, try the recommendations listed in this chapter for improving overall system performance.

10

KEY TERMS

alert — A watchdog that informs you when a counter crosses a defined threshold. An alert is an automated attendant looking for high or low values, and can consist of one or more counter/instance-based alert definitions.

baseline — A definition of what a normal load looks like on a computer system; it provides a point of comparison against which you can measure future system behavior.

bottleneck — A system resource or device that limits a system's performance. Ideally, the user should be the bottleneck on a system, not any hardware or software component.

counter — A named aspect or activity that the Performance tool uses to measure or monitor some aspect of a registered system or application object.

Counter log — A log that records measurements on selected counters at regular, defined intervals. Counter logs allow you to define exactly which counters are recorded (based on computer, object, counter, and instance).

disk bottleneck — A system bottleneck caused by a limitation in a computer's disk subsystem, such as a slow drive or controller, or a heavier load than the system can handle.

event — A system occurrence that is logged to a file.

EventViewer — A system utility that displays one of three event logs: System, Security, and Application, wherein logged or audited events appear. EventViewer is often the first stop when monitoring a system's performance or seeking evidence of problems, because it is where all unusual or extraordinary system activities and events are recorded.

handle — A programming term that indicates an internal identifier for some kind of system resource, object, or other component that must be accessed by name (or through a pointer). In Task Manager, the number of handles appears on the Performance tab in the Totals pane.

A sudden increase in the number of handles, threads, or processes can indicate that an ill-behaved application is running on a system.

instance — A selection of a specific object when more than one is present on the monitored system, as in multiple CPUs or hard drives.

memory bottleneck — A system bottleneck caused by a lack of available physical or virtual memory that results in system slowdown or (in extreme cases) an outright system crash.

network bottleneck — A system bottleneck caused by excessive traffic on the network medium to which a computer is attached, or when the computer itself generates excessive amounts of such traffic.

object — See performance object.

performance object — A component of the Windows XP Professional system environment; objects range from devices to services to processes.

process — An environment that defines the resources available to threads, the executable parts of an application. Processes define memory available, show where the process page directory is stored in physical memory, and other information that the CPU needs to work with a thread. Each process includes its own complete, private 2 GB address space and related virtual memory allocations.

processor bottleneck — A system bottleneck occurs when demands for CPU cycles from currently active processes and the operating system cannot be met, usually indicated by high utilization levels or processor queue lengths greater than or equal to two.

System Monitor — The utility that tracks registered system or application objects, where each such object has one or more counters that can be tracked for information about system behavior.

thread — In the Windows XP Professional runtime environment, a thread is the minimum unit of system execution and corresponds roughly to a task within an application, the Windows XP kernel, or within some other major system component. Any task that can execute in the background can be considered a thread (for example, runtime spell checking or grammar checking in newer versions of MS Word), but it's important to recognize that applications must be written to take advantage of threading (just as the operating system itself is).

Trace log — A log that records nonconfigurable data from a designated provider only when an event occurs.

REVIEW QUESTIONS

1. Monitoring is the act of changing a system's configuration systematically and carefully observing performance before and after such changes. True or False?

2. In a system that is performing optimally, the user should be the bottleneck. True or False?

3. Which of the following can Task Manager monitor?
   a. application CPU percentage
   b. total CPU percentage
   c. process CPU percentage
   d. all of the above

4. The longer a system is in productive use, the more its performance
   _____ .

5. Which of the following are methods to access Task Manager? (Choose all that apply.)
   a. Ctrl+Alt+Delete
   b. executing "taskman" from the command prompt
   c. Ctrl+Shift+Esc
   d. Control Panel

6. In System Monitor, the counters are the same for all objects. True or False?

7. A(n) _____ event is issued when a driver fails to load.

8. The _____ provides a detailed description of a counter.

9. To record log files the Performance tool must be open. True or False?

10. A Counter log can include which of the following?
    a. one or more counters
    b. counters from multiple computers
    c. different intervals for each counter
    d. a stop time defined by a length of time

11. A(n) _____ occurs when a system resource limits performance.

12. Which of the following objects can be disabled to prevent performance measurements from being taken?
    a. Memory
    b. LogicalDisk
    c. RAS port
    d. System

13. In general, a bottleneck might exist if a queue counter is consistently _____ than the total number of instances of that object.

10

14. Which one of the following counters is the most likely indicator of a high level of disk activity caused by too little RAM?

    a. Memory: Pages/sec

    b. Memory: Page Faults/sec

    c. Memory: Cache Faults

    d. Memory: Available bytes

15. Which of the following tools can monitor another computer's information?

    a. System Monitor

    b. Task Manager

    c. Event Viewer

16. The _____ on the Source tab is used to select a window of data from a Counter log.

17. The _____ is used to generate system performance reports.

18. What parameter should be used with diskperf to disable only the PhysicalDisk object?

    a. –yd

    b. –yv

    c. –nd

    d. –nv

19. The System Monitor can display only _____ data points.

20. The _____ and _____ event types are available only in the Security log.

21. Of the following commands, which gives the Test.exe application the highest priority level available to ordinary users (not administrators)?

    a. start /abovenormal test.exe

    b. start /normal test.exe

    c. start /high test.exe

    d. start /realtime test.exe

22. Which of the following activities can occur when an alert is triggered? (Choose all that apply.)

    a. an alert to a NetBIOS name

    b. shutdown of the system

    c. start the recording of a Counter log

    d. write an event to the Application log

23. The _____ feature of Event Viewer can be used to quickly locate all audit details for a specific user.

24. The Start command can be used to alter the priority of active processes. True or False?

25. What change to a system is most effective in producing a performance improvement?

    a. adding RAM

    b. replacing network cables

    c. adding more processors

    d. updating drivers

CASE PROJECTS

Case Project 10-1

Performance on a Windows XP Professional system used by the Accounting Department has been slowly degrading. You recently added a 100-Mbps network card, thinking that would correct the problem. To your knowledge, no other hardware has been added to the server, but you suspect someone has been adding software.

Describe the steps to determine what is causing the system to slow down, including which monitoring applications you will use and on which computer they will be run.

Case Project 10-2

You are considering upgrading your Windows XP Professional hardware, including memory, hard drive controller, and video card. The only things you are planning to keep are your hard drive, motherboard, and CPU.

Outline the tools and utilities you will use to measure the performance increase or decrease as each new component is added. Include information on expected performance changes and actual changes.

11

WINDOWS XP PROFESSIONAL APPLICATION SUPPORT

> **After reading this chapter and completing the exercises, you will be able to:**
>
> ♦ Understand the Windows XP Professional system architecture
>
> ♦ Deploy Win32 applications
>
> ♦ Fine-tune the application environment for DOS and the virtual DOS machine
>
> ♦ Fine-tune the application environment for Win16
>
> ♦ Work with Windows application management facilities

In this chapter, you encounter the pieces of the Windows XP Professional operating system that endow it with its exceptional power and flexibility. Its numerous runtime environments include limited support for DOS and 16-bit Windows applications, as well as more modern 32-bit Windows applications. Here, you'll have a chance to examine the various subsystems that Windows XP Professional provides to support DOS applications, plus 16-bit and 32-bit Windows applications, and understand how they work. You'll also have a chance to learn about the Windows XP mechanisms to ensure compatible operation of multiple applications on a single machine.

WINDOWS XP PROFESSIONAL SYSTEM ARCHITECTURE

Fundamentally, the Windows XP Professional operating system incorporates two primary components, namely the environment subsystem and Executive Services, which provide an environment that supports user applications (see Figure 11-1).

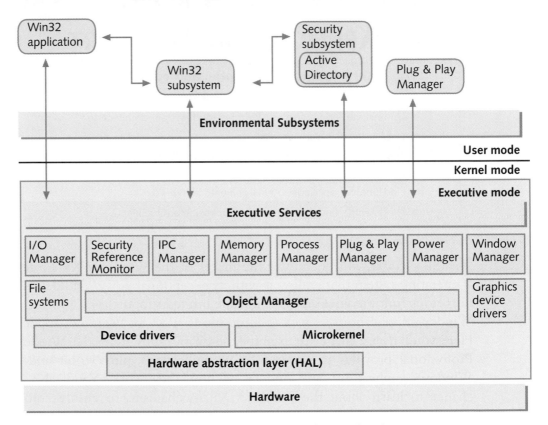

Figure 11-1   Components of the Windows XP Professional architecture

- **Environment subsystems** offer runtime support for a variety of different kinds of applications, under the purview of a single operating system. A **subsystem** is an operating environment that emulates another operating system (such as DOS or 16-bit Windows) to provide support for applications created for that environment, or a set of built-in programming interfaces that support the native Win32 (Windows 32-bit) runtime environment. Just like the applications they support, Windows XP Professional environment subsystems run in user mode, which means that they must access all system resources through the operating system's kernel mode.

- Windows XP Professional **Executive Services** and the underlying Windows XP **kernel** define the kernel mode for this operating system and its runtime environment. **Kernel mode** components are permitted to access system objects and resources directly, and provide the many services and access controls that allow multiple users and applications to coexist and interoperate effectively and efficiently.

User applications provide the functionality and capabilities that rank Windows XP Professional among the most powerful network operating systems in use today. All such applications run within the context of an environment subsystem in Windows XP user mode. Applications and the subsystems in which they run have a mediated relationship because the client application asks the subsystem to perform activities for it, and the subsystem complies with such requests (or denies them if the requester lacks sufficient privileges).

To understand how these components fit together, the following sections review some important concepts, starting with kernel and user modes.

Kernel Mode Versus User Mode

The main difference between the two modes lies in how memory is used by user mode components and kernel mode components.

In **user mode**, each process perceives the entire 4 GB of virtual memory available to Windows XP as its exclusive property—with the condition that the upper 2 GB of addresses are normally reserved for operating system use. This perception remains unaltered, no matter on what kind of hardware Windows XP may run. Note also that this address space is entirely virtual, and must operate within the confines of whatever RAM is installed on a machine and the amount of space reserved for the paging file's use. Although the upper limit for Windows XP virtual memory addresses may be 2 GB (or 4 GB, for system purposes), the real upper limit for Windows XP physical memory addresses is always the sum of physical RAM size plus the amount of space in the paging file.

Although processes that operate in user mode may share memory areas with other processes (for fast message passing or sharing information), they, by default, do not do this. This means that one user mode process cannot crash another, or corrupt its data. This is what creates the appearance that applications run independently, and allows each one to operate as if it had exclusive possession of the operating system and the hardware it controls.

 If a user mode parent process crashes, it will, of course, take its child processes down with it. (Parent and child processes are discussed later in this chapter.)

Processes running in user mode cannot access hardware or communicate with other processes directly. When code runs in the Windows XP kernel mode, on the other hand, it may access all hardware and memory in the computer (but usually through an associated

Executive Services module). Thus, when an application needs to perform tasks that involve hardware, it calls a user mode function that ultimately calls a kernel mode function.

Because all kernel mode operations share the same memory space, one kernel mode function can corrupt another's data and even cause the operating system to crash. This is the reason that the environment subsystems contain as much of the operating system's capabilities as possible, making the kernel itself less vulnerable. For this reason, some experts voiced concern about the change in the Windows 2000 design that moved graphics handlers to the kernel. But because those graphics components were originally part of the Win32 environment subsystem—which must be available for Windows XP Professional to operate properly—a crash in either implementation could bring down the system. That's why this change has had little effect on the reliability or stability of Windows 2000 or Windows XP Professional.

 For a review of the user mode and kernel mode architecture of Windows XP Professional, refer to Chapter 1.

NOTE

Processes and Threads

From a user's point of view, the operating system exists to run programs or applications. But from the view of the Windows XP Professional operating system, the world is made of processes and threads. A **process** defines the operating environment in which an application or any major operating system component runs. Any Windows XP process includes its own private memory space, a set of security descriptors, a priority level for execution, processor-affinity data (that is, on a multiprocessor system, information that instructs a process to use a particular CPU), and a list of threads associated with that process. A list of currently active processes can be seen on the Processes tab of Task Manager (see Figure 11-2). You access Task Manager in any of several ways:

- Pressing Ctrl+Alt+Delete and clicking the Task Manager button (in normal Windows logon mode only)

- Pressing Ctrl+Alt+Delete (in Windows Welcome mode only)

- Right-clicking an unoccupied area of the taskbar on your display, and selecting Task Manager from the resulting shortcut menu

- Pressing Ctrl+Shift+Esc

The basic executable unit in Windows XP is called a **thread**, and every process includes at least one thread. A thread consists of placeholder information associated with a single use of any program that can handle multiple concurrent users or activities. Within a multithreaded application, each distinct task or any complex operation is likely to be implemented in its own separate thread. This explains how Microsoft Word, for instance, can perform spelling and grammar checks in the background while you're entering text in the input window in

Figure 11-2   The Processes tab in Task manager displays all currently active Windows XP Professional processes

the foreground: two threads are running—one manages handling input, and the other performs these checks.

Applications must be explicitly designed to take advantage of threading. Although it's safe to assume that most new 32-bit Windows applications—and the Windows XP operating system itself—are built to use the power and flexibility of threads, older 16-bit Windows and DOS applications are usually single threaded. Also, it is important to understand that threads are associated with processes and do not exist independently. Processes themselves don't run—they merely describe a shared environment composed of resources that include allocated memory, variables, and other system objects; threads represent those parts of any program that actually run.

Processes can create other processes, called **child processes**, and those child processes can inherit some of the characteristics and parameters of their **parent process**. (A child process is a replica of the parent process and shares some of its resources, but cannot exist independently if the parent is terminated.) The parent-child relationship between pairs of processes usually works as follows:

- When a user logs on to Windows XP Professional successfully, a shell process is created inside the Win32 subsystem within which the logon session operates. The Win32 subsystem is an operating environment that supports 32-bit Windows applications; this subsystem is required to run Windows XP. This process is endowed with a security token used to determine if subsequent requests for system objects and resources may be permitted to proceed. This shell process defines the Win32 subsystem as the parent process for that user.

■ Each time a user launches an application or starts a system utility, a child process is created within the environment subsystem where that application or utility must run. This child process inherits its security token and associated information from the parent user account, but is also a child of the environment subsystem within which it runs. This "dual parentage" (security information from the user account and runtime environment from the environment subsystem) explains how Windows XP can run multiple kinds of applications in parallel, yet maintain consistent control over system objects and resources to which any user process is permitted access.

For example, each of the environment subsystems discussed in the following sections is an executable file—a combination of processes and threads running within the context of those processes (a **context** is the current collection of Registry values and runtime environment variables in which a process or thread runs). When an application runs in a Windows XP Professional subsystem, it actually represents a child of the parent process for the environment subsystem, but one that is endowed with the permissions associated with the security token of the account that starts the process. Whenever a parent process halts or is stopped, all child processes stop as well.

Environment Subsystems

Windows XP Professional offers support for various application platforms. Although primarily designed for 32-bit Windows applications, Windows XP Professional includes limited support and backward compatibility for 16-bit Windows and DOS applications.

Windows XP Professional's support for multiple runtime environments, also known as environment subsystems, confers numerous advantages, including:

■ It permits users to run more than one type of application concurrently, including 32-bit Windows, 16-bit Windows, and DOS applications.

■ It makes maintaining the operating system easier, because the modularity of this design means that changes to environment subsystems require no changes to the kernel itself, as long as interfaces remain unchanged.

■ Modularity makes it easy to add or enhance Windows XP—if a new OS is developed in the future, Microsoft could decide to add a subsystem for that OS to Windows XP without affecting other environment subsystems.

The catch to using an architecture that supports multiple environment subsystems is in providing mechanisms that permit those subsystems to communicate with one another when necessary. In the Windows XP environment, each subsystem runs as a separate user-mode process, so that subsystems cannot interfere with or crash one another. The only exception to this insulation effect occurs in the Win32 subsystem: Because all user-mode I/O passes through this subsystem, the Win32 subsystem must be running for Windows XP to function properly. If the Win32 subsystem's process ends, the whole operating system goes down with it. This explains why you can shut down processes associated with 16-bit Windows or DOS applications on a Windows XP machine without affecting anything other than those processes (and any related child processes) themselves.

Applications and the subsystems in which they run have a client/server relationship, in that the client application asks the server subsystem to do things for it, and the subsystem complies. For example, if a Win32 client application needs to open a new window (perhaps to create a Save As dialog box), it doesn't create the window itself, but asks the Win32 subsystem to draw the window on its behalf. If the 16-bit Windows on Windows (WoW) environment is running and another 16-bit Windows application is started, it runs within the existing 16-bit Windows environment by default.

The client issues the request through a mechanism known as a **local procedure call (LPC)**. The serving subsystem makes its capabilities available to client applications by linking them to a **dynamic link library (DLL)**. Think of a DLL as a set of buzzers, where each one is labeled with the capabilities it provides. Pushing a specific buzzer tells the server subsystem to do whatever the label tells it. This form of messaging is transparent to the client application (as far as it knows, it's simply calling a procedure). When a client pushes one of those buzzers (requests a service), it appears as if the act is handled by the DLL; no explicit communication with a server subsystem is needed. If a service isn't listed in the library, an application can't request it; thus, a word processor running in a command-line environment as a DOS application, for example, can't ask that subsystem to draw a window.

Message passing is a fairly time-consuming operation, because any time the focus changes from one process to another, all the information for the calling process must be unloaded and replaced with the information for the called process. In operating system lingo, this change of operation focus from one process to another is called a **context switch**. To permit the operating system to run more efficiently, Windows XP avoids making context switches whenever possible. To that end, Windows XP includes the following efficiency measures:

- It caches attributes in DLLs to provide an interface to subsystem capabilities, so that (for example) the second time Microsoft Word requests a window to be created, this activity may be completed without switching context to the Win32 subsystem.

- It calls Executive Services (the collection of kernel-mode Windows XP operating system components that provides basic system services, such as I/O, security, object management, and so forth) directly, to perform tasks without requesting help from an underlying environment subsystem. Because the kernel is always active in another process space in Windows XP, calling for kernel-mode services does *not* require a context switch.

- It batches messages so that when a server process is called, several messages can be passed at once—the number of messages has no impact on performance, but a context switch does. By batching messages, Windows XP allows a single context switch to handle multiple messages in sequence, rather than requiring a context switch for each message.

When LPCs must be used, they're handled as efficiently as possible. Likewise, their code is optimized for speed, and special message-passing functions can be used for different situations, depending (for example) on the size of the messages passed, or the circumstances in which they're sent.

The Win32 Subsystem

As the only subsystem required for the functioning of the operating system, the **Win32 subsystem** handles all major interface capabilities. In early versions of Windows NT, the Win32 subsystem included graphics, windowing, and messaging support, but since Windows NT 4.0 was released, these have been moved to the kernel and are now part of Executive Services. This applies equally to Windows 2000 and Windows XP Professional.

In Windows XP, user-mode components of the Win32 subsystem consist of the console (text window support), shutdown, hard-error handling, and some environmental functions to handle such tasks as process creation and deletion. The Win32 subsystem is also the foundation upon which **virtual DOS machines (VDMs)** rest. These permit Windows XP to deliver both DOS and Win16 subsystems, so that DOS and Win16 applications can run on Windows XP unchanged (VDMs and the DOS and Win16 subsystems are discussed later in this chapter).

WIN32 APPLICATIONS

So far, this chapter has examined the components of the Windows XP Professional operating system kernel. Now, it's time to see how applications run under that operating system.

The Environment Subsystem

As mentioned, the Win32 subsystem is the main environment subsystem under Windows XP, and the only one required for operation. Strictly speaking, even the other environment subsystems (the scaffolding that supports DOS and 16-bit Windows applications) are Win32 applications that run as child processes to the main Win32 process and support application environments called virtual DOS machines (VDMs) that run under Win32 to support DOS applications. (VDMs and DOS application support are explained in more detail later in this chapter.)

Multithreading

When a program's process contains more than one thread of execution, it's said to be a **multithreaded process**. The main advantage of multithreading is that it provides multiple threads of execution within a single memory space without requiring that messages be passed between processes or that local procedure calls be used, thus simplifying thread communication. Threads are easier to create than processes because they don't require as much context information, nor do they incur the same kind of overhead when switching from one thread to another within a single process.

Some multithreaded applications can even run multiple threads concurrently among multiple processors (assuming a machine has more than one). One more advantage to threading is that it's *much* less complicated to switch operation from thread to thread than to switch from one process to another. That's because every time a new process is scheduled for execution, the system must be updated with all the process's context information. Also, it's often necessary to remove one process to make room for another, which may require writing large amounts of data from RAM to disk for the outgoing process, before copying large amounts of data from disk into RAM to bring in the incoming process.

As a point of comparison, a thread switch can normally be completed somewhere between 15 and 25 machine instructions, whereas a process switch can take many thousands of instructions to complete. Because most CPUs are set up to handle one instruction for every clock cycle, this means that switching among threads is hundreds to thousands of times faster than switching among processes.

The big trick with multithreading, of course, is that the chances that one thread could overwrite another are increased with each additional thread, so this introduces the problem of protecting shared areas of memory from intraprocess thread overwrites. Windows XP manages access to memory very carefully, and limits which sections of memory any individual thread can write to by locking them, as you'll see in the next section. This largely avoids the problems associated with shared access to a single set of memory addresses.

Memory Space

Multithreaded programs must be designed so that threads don't get in each other's way, and they do this by using Windows XP **synchronization objects**. A section of code that modifies data structures used by several threads is called a **critical section**. It's very important that a critical section never be overwritten by more than one thread at once. Thus, applications use Windows XP synchronization objects to prevent this from happening, creating such objects for each critical section in each process context. When a thread needs access to a critical section, the following occurs:

1. A thread requests a synchronization object. If it is unlocked (not suspended in a thread queue), the request proceeds. Otherwise, go to Step 2.

2. The thread is suspended in a thread queue until the synchronization object is unlocked for its use. As soon as this happens, Windows XP releases the thread and locks up the object.

3. The thread accesses the critical section.

4. When the thread is done, it unlocks the synchronization object so that another thread may access the critical object.

Thus, multithreaded applications avoid accessing a single data structure with more than one thread at a time by locking its critical section when it is in use and unlocking it when it is not.

Input Message Queues

One of the roles of the Win32 subsystem is to organize user input and get it to the thread to which that input belongs. It does this by taking user messages from a general input queue, and distributing them to the **input message queues** for the individual processes.

As discussed later in this chapter, Win16 applications normally run within a single process, so they share a message input queue, unlike Win32 or DOS applications with their individual queues.

Base Priorities

When a program is started under Windows XP Professional, its process is assigned a particular priority class, generally Normal—but there is a range of options (see Figure 11-3). The priority class helps determine the priority at which threads in a process must run, on a scale from 0 (lowest) to 31 (highest). In a process with more than one active thread, each thread may have its own priority, which may be higher or lower than that of the original thread, but that priority is always relative to the priority assigned to the underlying process, which is known as the **base priority**. Managing priorities may be accomplished in one of several ways, and can sometimes provide a useful way to improve application performance. These include Task Manager and the Start command, as discussed in Chapter 10, "Performance Tuning."

Figure 11-3   The Task Manager Processes tab with priority options on display

DOS AND THE VIRTUAL DOS MACHINE

DOS and Win16 applications work somewhat differently from Win32 applications. Rather than each running in the context of its own process, these applications run within a virtual DOS machine (VDM), a special environment process that simulates a DOS environment so that non–Win32 Windows applications can run under Windows XP. In fact, it's reasonable to describe two separate operating environments that can run within a VDM: one supports straightforward DOS emulation and may be called the **DOS operating environment**; the other supports operation of Win16 applications within a VDM, and may be called the **Win16 operating environment**.

Any DOS operating environment under Windows XP occurs within a Win32 process named ntvdm.exe (see the top entry in Figure 11-4). The ntvdm process creates the environment wherein DOS applications execute. Each DOS application that is initiated executes within a separate emulation environment. Thus, if you start three DOS applications, three instances of ntvdm appear in the process list. Once a DOS application terminates, Windows XP also shuts down the emulation environment for that application by terminating the associated instance of ntvdm. This frees its system resources for reuse.

NOTE   The environment created in a VDM is not the same as that available to Win32 applications. Instead, it is equivalent to the environment of Windows 3.x enhanced mode, in which each DOS application has access to 1 MB of virtual memory, with 1 MB of extended memory and expanded memory if necessary.

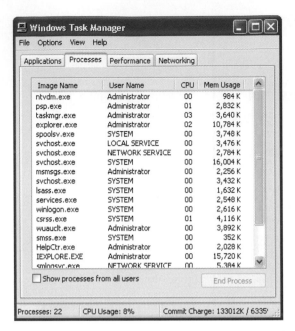

Figure 11-4   The Task Manager's Processes tab shows ntvdm.exe running when a 16-bit DOS application is loaded

By default, all DOS applications run in their own VDMs. By default, all Win16 applications share a single VDM (just as they do in "real Windows 3.x" environments).

VDM Components

The VDM runs using the following files:

- *Ntio.sys*—The equivalent of Io.sys on MS-DOS machines; runs in **real mode** (real mode is a mode of operation for *x*86 CPUs wherein they can address only 1 MB of memory, broken into sixteen 64-KB segments). It provides "virtual I/O" services to the DOS or Win16 applications that run in a VDM.

- *Ntdos.sys*—The equivalent of Msdos.sys; runs in real mode. It provides basic DOS operating system services to the DOS or Win16 applications that run in a VDM.

- *Ntvdm.exe*—A Win32 application that runs in kernel mode. This is the execution file that provides the runtime environment within which a VDM runs. If you look at the list on the Processes tab of Task Manager, you see one such entry for each separate VDM that's running on your machine.

- *Ntvdm.dll*—A Win32 dynamic link library that runs in kernel mode. Ntvdm.dll provides the set of procedure stubs that fool DOS and Win16 programs into thinking they're talking to a real DOS machine with exclusive access to a PC, when in fact they're communicating through a VDM with Windows XP Professional.

■ *Redir.exe*—The virtual device driver (VDD) redirector for the VDM. This software forwards I/O requests from programs within a VDM for I/O services through the Win32 environment subsystem to the Windows XP I/O Manager in Executive Services. Whenever a DOS or Win16 program in a VDM thinks it's communicating with hardware, it's really communicating with Redir.exe.

Activity 11-1: VDM Applications

Time Required: 20 minutes

Objective: Use Task Manager to learn how Windows XP handles DOS applications.

Description: There are numerous types of applications that can be run on Windows XP, including DOS, Win16, and Win32. In this activity, you use Task Manager to better understand how Windows XP handles the different types of applications.

To view the effects of various VDM-based applications on Windows XP:

1. Restart your Windows XP system and log on.

2. Open Task Manager by pressing **Ctrl+Shift+Esc**.

3. Select the **Processes** tab.

4. Next, run Edit.com, which is a DOS application. To do so, click **Start**, and then click **Run**. In the Run dialog box type **c:\WINDOWS\system32\Edit.com**, and then click **OK**. Notice in the list of processes through Task Manager that ntvdm has appeared, but the name of the DOS application itself has not.

5. Click **File**, **Exit**. Once the application terminates, notice that ntvdm no longer appears in the process list on the Processes tab of Task Manager.

6. Next, run Winhelp.exe, which is a Windows 16 bit application. To do so, click **Start**, and then click **Run**. In the Run dialog box, type **c:\WINDOWS**\winhelp.exe, then click **OK**. Notice in the list of processes through Task Manager that ntvdm appears along with Wowexec.exe and Winhelp.exe as subitems.

7. Click **File**, **Exit**. Notice in the list of processes that ntvdm and wowexec remain.

8. Select **wowexec** and click **End Process** to terminate that process.

9. Click **Yes** to confirm termination. Notice that both ntvdm and wowexec are no longer listed in the processes.

10. Close Task Manager by selecting **File**, **Exit Task Manager**.

Virtual Device Drivers

DOS applications do not communicate directly with Windows XP drivers. Instead, a layer of **virtual device drivers (VDDs)** underlies these applications, and they communicate with Windows XP 32-bit drivers. Windows XP supplies VDDs for the mouse, the keyboard, any printers and communication ports, as well as file system drivers (including one or more network drivers, each of which is actually implemented as a file system driver).

AUTOEXEC.BAT and CONFIG.SYS

When a DOS application is started, Windows XP runs the files specified in the application's program information file (PIF) or in Autoexec.nt (see Figure 11-5) and Config.nt (see Figure 11-6), the two files that replace Autoexec.bat and Config.sys for VDMs. Autoexec.nt installs CD-ROM extensions and the network redirector. By default, Windows XP provides DOS Protected Mode Interface (DPMI) support, to permit DOS and Win16 applications to access more than 1 MB of memory within a virtual (or real) DOS machine. Config.nt loads into an upper memory area for its VDM, and supports HIMEM.SYS by default to enable extended memory; it also sets the number of files and buffers available to DOS or Win16 programs, and provides necessary details to configure expanded memory.

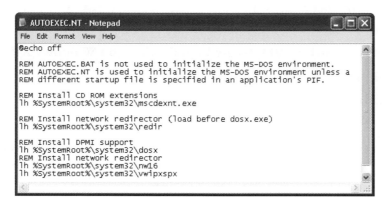

Figure 11-5   AUTOEXEC.NT as it appears in Notepad

```
CONFIG.NT - Notepad                                          [_][□][X]
File  Edit  Format  View  Help
REM application, any running TSR may be disrupted. To ensure that only
REM MS-DOS-based applications can be started, add the command dosonly to
REM CONFIG.NT or other startup file.
REM
REM EMM
REM You can use EMM command line to configure EMM(Expanded Memory Manager)
REM The syntax is:
REM
REM EMM = [A=AltRegSets] [B=BaseSegment] [RAM]
REM
REM     AltRegSets
REM         specifies the total Alternative Mapping Register Sets you
REM         want the system to support. 1 <= AltRegSets <= 255. The
REM         default value is 8.
REM     BaseSegment
REM         specifies the starting segment address in the Dos conventional
REM         memory you want the system to allocate for EMM page frames.
REM         The value must be given in Hexdecimal.
REM         0x1000 <= BaseSegment <= 0x4000. The value is rounded down to
REM         16KB boundary. The default value is 0x4000
REM     RAM
REM         specifies that the system should only allocate 64Kb address
REM         space from the Upper Memory Block(UMB) area for EMM page frame
REM         and leave the rests(if available) to be used by DOS to support
REM         loadhigh and devicehigh commands. The system, by default, woul
REM         allocate all possible and available UMB for page frames.
REM
REM     The EMM size is determined by pif file(either the one associated
REM     with your application or _default.pif). If the size from PIF file
REM     is zero, EMM will be disabled and the EMM line will be ignored.
REM
dos=high, umb
device=%SystemRoot%\system32\himem.sys
files=40
```

Figure 11-6 CONFIG.NT as it appears in Notepad

11

Activity 11-2: The DOS Environment

Time Required: 10 minutes

Objective: View CONFIG.NT and AUTOEXEC.NT to see how Windows XP sets up the operating environment for DOS applications.

Description: DOS applications cannot recognize the resources that are available to Windows applications. Therefore, they must have an environment set up for them that they can recognize. In this activity, you open CONFIG.NT and AUTOEXEC.NT to become familiar with how the environment is configured.

To view the Windows XP AUTOEXEC.NT and CONFIG.NT files:

1. Open **Notepad** by selecting **Start, All Programs, Accessories, Notepad**.

2. Select **File, Open**.

3. Change directories to **C:\WINDOWS\system32**.

4. Change the Files of type to **All Files**.

5. Locate and select **AUTOEXEC.NT**.

6. Click **Open**. View the contents of this file (refer to Figure 11-5).

7. Select **File, Open**.

8. Change the Files of type to **All Files**.

9. Locate and select **CONFIG.NT**. (*Hint:* Type **c*.nt** into the File name text box to limit the list of files displayed to something close to the one you want!)

10. Click **Open** and view the contents of this file (refer to Figure 11-6).

11. Close Notepad by selecting **File**, **Exit**.

NOTE

CONFIG.SYS isn't used at all by Windows XP, whereas Autoexec.bat is only used at system startup to set path and environment variables for the Windows XP environment. Neither file is consulted when it comes to running applications or initializing drivers; those settings must exist in the system Registry to work at all.

Once read from Autoexec.bat, path and environment variables are copied to the Registry, to HKEY_LOCAL_MACHINE\System\CurrentControlSet\Control\Session Manager\Environment (see Figure 11-7).

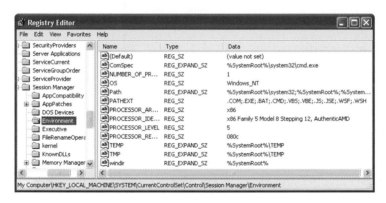

Figure 11-7 The Registry key shows the variables defined within the ...\Environment subkey

Custom DOS Environments

Windows XP offers customizable environment controls for its DOS runtime environment. These controls can be used to fine-tune or simply to alter how any DOS application functions. To customize a DOS application's execution parameters, open the Properties dialog box for that executable (.exe or .com) file. Right-clicking an executable file and selecting Properties from the resulting menu performs this.

The Properties dialog box for a DOS executable file has numerous tabs. The General tab lists the same data items as any other file within the Windows XP Professional environment. The Program tab (see Figure 11-8) offers controls over the following elements:

- *Filename text box (this label is not shown on the tab)*—The name of the file

- *Cmd line text box* —Used to add command-line parameter syntax

- *Working text box* —Used to define the working directory, which is the directory from which the application loads files and where it saves files

Figure 11-8   MASTMIND.EXE Properties dialog box, Program tab

- *Batch file text box* —Used to run a batch file before running the executable file
- *Shortcut key text box*—Used to define a keystroke that runs the executable file
- *Run text box* —Used to define the window size of the DOS environment— normal, maximized, or minimized
- *Close on exit check box*—Informs the OS to close the DOS window when the application terminates
- *Advanced button*—Allows you to define the path to alternative AUTOEXEC.NT and CONFIG.NT files
- *Change Icon button*—Changes the icon displayed for the executable file

The Font tab is used to define the font used by the DOS application. The Memory tab is used to define the memory parameters for the DOS environment that the corresponding ntvdm creates. These controls include settings for conventional memory, expanded memory (EMS), extended memory (XMS), and DOS Protected Mode Interface (DPMI) memory.

The Screen tab is used to define whether the DOS application loads as a full screen or in a window. It also indicates if the ntvdm should emulate fast ROM, and whether it should allocate dynamic memory.

The Misc tab (see Figure 11-9) is used to define the following:

- Whether to allow a screen saver over the DOS window
- Whether the mouse is used by the DOS application
- If the DOS application is suspended when in the background
- Whether or not to warn if the DOS application is active when you attempt to close the DOS window
- How long the application waits for I/O before releasing CPU control
- Whether to use fast pasting (a quick method for pasting information into the application; this doesn't work with some programs, so disable this check box if information does not paste properly)
- Which Windows shortcut keys are reserved for use by Windows XP Professional instead of the DOS application

Figure 11-9   MASTMIND.EXE Properties dialog box, Misc tab

The Security tab provides access to standard user and group information, along with permissions data for each user and group named. The Summary tab provides access to file description and attribution information. This is primarily to provide better information for searching your file system for specific keywords or categories. For older files—especially DOS files—this kind of information is usually undefined.

The Compatibility tab provides access to modes of screen operation that are no longer available on the Settings tab in the Display applet. This tab only appears on executables from previous versions of Windows, not on DOS applications. Here's where you can emulate screen behavior like that found in Windows 95, Windows 98, Windows NT 4, and Windows 2000 (using the Compatibility mode check box and its associated pull-down menu). You can also revert to older VGA emulation, including 640 x 480 resolution, 256 colors, and disable visual themes (none of which is accessible through the Display applet any more, either).

Once you alter any portion of one of these tabs (except Security, which is a general-purpose NTFS file object control), a new shortcut for the application is created that retains whatever changes you make. Thus, you can reuse and fine-tune your custom DOS environment settings for each application, and even for multiple instances of the same application, if need be.

ACTIVITY

Activity 11-3: DOS Application Properties

11

Time Required: 10 minutes

Objective: View and become familiar with the properties of a DOS application.

Description: The properties of a DOS application are quite different than those of a Win32 application. In this activity, you view the different components of a DOS application in the Properties dialog box.

To explore the Properties configuration for a DOS application:

1. Open Windows Explorer.

2. Locate the DOS application, **edit.com**. (*Hint:* You can use the Search function: Select All files and folders as the search target, specify edit.com as the filename to search for, and then select Local Hard Drives as the search domain.)

3. Right-click **edit.com** and select **Properties** from the resulting menu.

4. View the details provided on the General tab (see Figure 11-10).

5. Click the **Program** tab and view the details provided.

6. Click the **Advanced** button and view the details provided.

7. Click **Cancel**.

8. Click the **Font** tab and view the details provided.

9. Click the **Memory** tab and view the details provided.

10. Click the **Screen** tab and view the details provided.

11. Click the **Misc** tab and view the details provided.

12. Explore other tabs in your Properties dialog box.

13. Click **Cancel** to close the Properties dialog box and discard any changes.

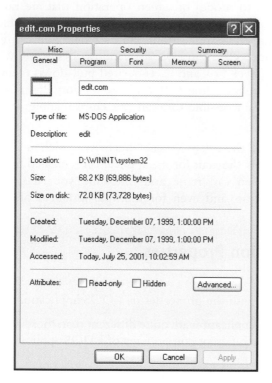

Figure 11-10   The General tab of a DOS application's properties

WIN16 CONCEPTS AND APPLICATIONS

Like DOS applications, Win16 applications also run in a VDM, although unlike DOS applications, which by default run in their own individual address spaces, all Win16 applications run in the same VDM unless you specify otherwise. This permits them to act like Win32 applications, and lets multiple Win16 applications interact with one another within a single VDM. This creates the appearance that multiple applications are active simultaneously. (Usually, only one Win16 application in a VDM can be active at any given moment, but this form of **multitasking**—which Microsoft calls cooperative multitasking—creates a convincing imitation of the more robust and real multitasking available to Win32 applications.) The **Win16-on-Win32 (WOW)** VDM runs as a multi-threaded application, where each Win16 application occupies a single thread (see Figure 11-11), but where all such threads run by default in the context of a single VDM.

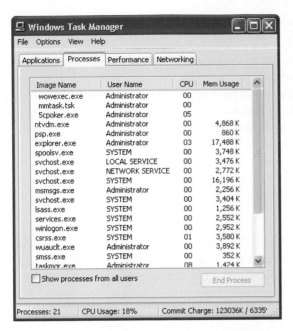

Figure 11-11 The Task Manager's Processes tab showing the wowexec environment

Win16-on-Win32 Components

The WOW VDM includes the following components:

- *Wowexec.exe*—Handles the loading of 16-bit Windows–based applications
- *Wow32.dll*—The dynamic link library for the WOW application environment
- *Mmtask.tsk*—This is a multimedia background task module brought over from Windows Millennium Edition (Me) into the Windows XP Professional environment. It is used to handle multimedia and video effects for graphical WOW applications. As Figure 11-11 indicates, this item shows up within the wowexec. exe environment in Task Manager.
- *Ntvdm.exe, ntvdm.dll, ntio.sys*, and *redir.exe*—Run the VDM
- *Vdmredir.dll*—The redirector for the WOW environment
- *Krnl386.exe*—Used by WOW on *x*86-based systems
- *Gdi.exe*—A modified version of Windows 3.*x* Gdi.exe
- *User.exe*—A modified version of Windows 3.*x* User.exe

Calls made to 16-bit drivers are transferred ("thunked") to the appropriate 32-bit driver without the application having to call that driver directly (or even know what's going on). Similarly, if a driver needs to return information to an application, it must be thunked back again. This back and forth translation helps explain why many Win16 applications run more slowly in a VDM on Windows XP, 2000, and Windows NT, than they do on other versions of Windows (even Windows 95), where no such translations are required.

Once a WOW environment is created, Windows XP sustains that environment until the system is restarted or you manually terminate the Wowexec.exe task (through the Task Manager Processes tab). Creating new WOW environments each time a Win16 application is started was deemed more costly in terms of resources and CPU time than maintaining a WOW environment once it had been created throughout a boot session. Thus, if you use Win16 applications often, this function offers you some modest performance benefits. But if you seldom use Win16 applications, you'd be better off terminating the WOW environment after you finish using the 16-bit application.

Memory Space

By default, all Win16 applications run as threads in a single VDM process. However, it might be a good idea not to permit this, because multiple threads running in a single process can affect the performance of each application. This mixture of applications can also make tracking applications more difficult, because most monitoring in Windows XP takes place on a per-process basis, not on a per-thread basis. Finally, running all Win16 applications in a single VDM means that if one of those applications goes astray and causes the VDM to freeze or crash, all applications in that VDM will be affected.

Separate and Shared Memory

The "lose one, lose them all" effect of a single shared VDM explains why you might choose to run Win16 applications in separate VDMs. That way, you can increase the reliability of those applications as a whole, and one errant application won't take down all the other Win16 applications if it crashes. Likewise, you can make preemptive multitasking possible (that is, one busy application won't be able to hog the processor), and you can take advantage of multiple processors if you have them, because all the threads in a single VDM process must execute on the same processor.

The disadvantages of running Win16 applications in separate memory spaces hinge on memory usage and interprocess communications. Each additional process running on a machine requires about 2 MB of space in the paging file and 1 MB of additional working set size. The working set size is the amount of data that the application keeps in memory at any given moment. Also, those older Win16 applications that don't support Dynamic Data Exchange (DDE) or Object Linking and Embedding (OLE) won't be able to communicate with each other if they run in separate VDMs.

It's also important to recognize that running Win16 applications as processes instead of threads increases the time it takes to switch from one application to another, because each switch requires a full context switch from one process to another. The best way to observe the impact of this separation is to try it the default way (wherein all Win16 applications share a single VDM), and then set up those Win16 applications in separate VDMs and compare the performance that results from each such scenario.

To run a Win16 application in a separate memory space, you must first create a shortcut to the executable. Then edit the properties of the shortcut and select the Run in separate memory space check box. You can also start 16-bit applications in their own address spaces using the /separate command-line switch. The proper syntax is: start /separate [*16-bit program executable name*].

The Run command in Windows XP Professional, Windows 2000, and Windows Server 2003 does not have a Run in separate memory space check box like Windows NT 4.0 did; thus, a Win16 application cannot be run in a separate memory space using the Run command.

Activity 11-4: Separate Memory Space for Win16 Applications

Time Required: 15 minutes

Objective: Run Win16 applications in their own memory space.

Description: To provide a stable environment, it is recommended that you run Win16 applications in their own memory space. In this activity, you start a couple of Win16 applications and then view the processes running in Task Manager.

11

To run a Win16 application in its own address space:

1. Open Windows Explorer.

2. In the right pane, double-click the drive letter that hosts your Windows XP main directory. If necessary, click **Tools, Folder Options**, click the **View** tab, and then click **Show hidden files and folders** to see the files in this volume. Click **OK**.

3. In the right pane, double-click the **Windows XP main folder** (this is windows by default). If necessary, repeat the instructions in the preceding step to view the files in this folder.

4. Scroll down the right pane to locate winhelp.exe (it may help to select the **Details** menu item in the **View** menu, rather than sticking with the default icon-based display).

5. Select **winhelp.exe**.

6. Right-click **winhelp.exe** and select **Create Shortcut** from the resulting menu.

7. Select **Shortcut to winhelp.exe**.

8. Right-click **Shortcut to winhelp.exe**, and select **Properties** from the resulting menu.

9. By default, the Shortcut tab is selected. Click the **Advanced** button to open the Advanced Properties window, and then click the **Run in separate memory space** check box (see Figure 11-12).

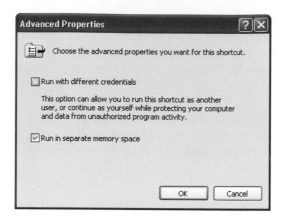

Figure 11-12   Configuring an application to run in a separate memory space from the Advanced Properties dialog box for a shortcut

Depending on your system settings, the file extensions may not appear.

10. Click **OK** twice to close the Advanced Properties window and apply the settings.

11. Double-click **winhelp.exe**. (This runs one instance of the 16-bit program.)

12. Double-click **Shortcut to winhelp.exe**. (This runs a second instance.)

13. Open Task Manager by pressing **Ctrl+Shift+Esc**.

14. Click the **Processes** tab.

15. Notice that two WOW environments exist, each hosting an instance of winhelp. exe. Close Task Manager by selecting **File**, **Exit Task Manager**.

16. Close both instances of Windows Help by selecting **File**, **Exit**.

Message Queues

As mentioned earlier, the Win32 subsystem is responsible for collecting user input and getting it to those applications that need it. However, unlike Win32 applications, all Win16 applications running in a single process share a message queue. Therefore, if one application becomes unable to accept input, it blocks all other Win16 applications in that VDM from accepting further input as well.

Threads

As mentioned earlier, Win16 threads that run in a VDM do not multitask like threads running in the Win32 subsystem. Instead of being preemptively multitasked, so that one thread can push another aside if its priority is higher, or so that any thread that's been taking up too much CPU time can be preempted, all application threads within a WOW VDM are cooperatively multitasked. This means that any one thread—which corresponds to any Win16 application—can hog the CPU. This is sometimes called the "good guy" scheduling algorithm, because it assumes that all applications will be well behaved and relinquish the CPU whenever they must block for I/O or other system services. The net effect, however, is that WOW VDMs behave as if they have only a single execution thread to share among all applications within that VDM.

Activity 11-5: Processes and Threads

Time Required: 15 minutes

Objective: Use Task Manager to view the processes and threads that are active.

Description: Most users assume that if they are running an application that a single process or thread is being used. By using Task Manager, you can see how some applications may involve one or more processes, which in turn may also have one or more threads.

To view the number of threads used by processes under Windows XP:

1. Open Task Manager by pressing **Ctrl+Shift+Esc**.

2. Click the **Processes** tab.

3. Select **View**, **Select Columns**.

4. Select the **Thread Count** check box (as shown in Figure 11-13).

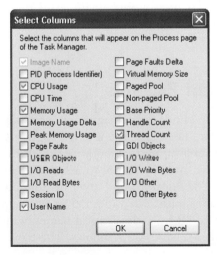

Figure 11-13   Select Columns dialog box

5. Click **OK**.

6. Maximize the Task Manager window.

7. Notice the number of threads for each of the currently active processes. (*Note:* You may have to resize the Task Manager display, or scroll to the right, to see this column; you can also click the Threads entry in the columns above the display area to list processes ordered by thread count.)

8. Close Task Manager by selecting **File**, **Exit Task Manager**.

Using Only Well-behaved DOS and Win16 Applications

Many DOS applications, as well as numerous older Win16 applications, often take advantage of a prerogative of DOS developers—namely, the ability to access system hardware directly, bypassing any access APIs or drivers that the system might ordinarily put between an application and the underlying hardware. Although such applications work fine in DOS, Windows 3.*x*, and even Windows 98, this is not the case with Windows XP. The division into user mode and kernel mode in Windows XP means that any application that attempts to access hardware directly is shut down with an error message to the effect of "illegal operation attempted."

In Windows XP terminology, any application that attempts direct access to hardware is called "ill behaved." Such applications do not run in a VDM. On the other hand, any Win16 or DOS application that uses standard DOS or Windows 3.*x* APIs instead of attempting direct access to hardware does work in a VDM. Such applications are called "well behaved." Unfortunately, there is no list of well-behaved applications available, so the only way to tell the difference is to test the ones you'd like to use with Windows XP and see what happens. If an application doesn't perform properly, it shouldn't be deployed on your system. It is recommended that you deploy only well-behaved applications for use with Windows XP, and that you seriously consider replacing any ill-behaved applications you may find in your current collection of programs.

OTHER WINDOWS APPLICATION MANAGEMENT FACILITIES

Windows XP Professional supports additional methods for managing or accessing applications over and above what's been covered so far. These include a new Program Compatibility Wizard that supports installation of older applications that require APIs, DLLs, or other components from previous releases of Windows, and the ability to assign and/or publish applications using Group Policy Objects from a Windows 2000 Server or Windows Server 2003. Windows XP also offers an interesting and sophisticated method to resolve problems related to programs that use different versions of DLLs with identical names, which was a source of difficult compatibility issues with earlier versions of Windows. These methods are covered in the following sections.

Program Compatibility Wizard

The Program Compatibility Wizard is specifically designed to support the installation of older Windows applications that may occasionally cause problems or fail to work altogether when installed on Windows XP. To access this tool, click the program compatibility link located at the bottom of the Compatibility tab of a program's Properties dialog box. Clicking the Start the Program Compatibility Wizard link opens the wizard. This produces the Program Compatibility Wizard's welcome screen, as shown in Figure 11-14.

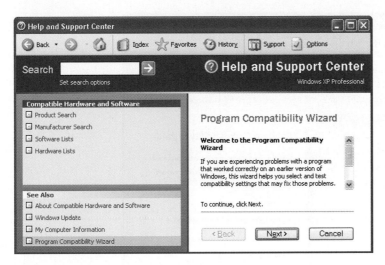

Figure 11-14   Program Compatibility Wizard

After clicking Next, you can select an option to help manage compatibility issues for older applications, as follows:

- *I want to choose from a list of programs*—Produces a list of applications from a scan of your hard drives. From here, you can select any single program to proceed with the wizard's assistance. The next choice is a compatibility mode setting, which is discussed later in this section; here, the point is that you can rely on an automated scan of your drives to show you which executable files might need compatibility setting changes.

- *I want to use a program in the CD-ROM drive*—Points the automatic scan at a particular CD-ROM player in your machine instead of your hard drives, but otherwise works the same as the preceding option.

- *I want to locate the program manually*—Permits you to browse your hard drives to locate some particular program in a specific location. Thus, the wizard provides a browse control, so you can select a single entry from the list of programs that resides in whichever directory you choose in response.

After selecting a program, the wizard displays a list of compatibility settings with option buttons from which you can make a single selection, as depicted in Figure 11-15. The choices shown are as follows:

- Microsoft Windows 95
- Microsoft Windows NT 4.0 (Service Pack 5)

- Microsoft Windows 98/Microsoft Windows Me

- Microsoft Windows 2000

- Do not apply a compatibility mode

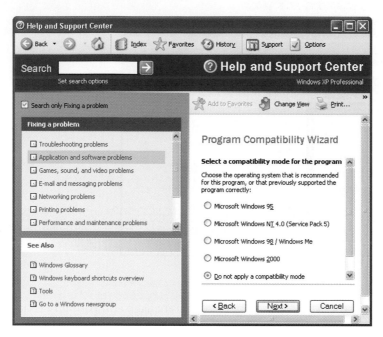

Figure 11-15   Compatibility mode settings are selected from a specific list of available options

By default, the final element in the list—namely, Do not apply a compatibility mode—is selected. Unless you're sure which mode you need, you may have to follow a process of trial and error to determine which compatibility mode to use. The next screen in the wizard permits you to alter default display settings, which is often a requirement to make older programs work (because they were designed for environments where lower screen resolutions and reduced color levels were all that was available). This screen provides a set of options to permit you to limit the display to 256 colors, set resolution at strict 640 x 480 VGA resolution, and to disable Windows XP visual themes (so that older programs won't be adversely influenced by those settings).

Next in this process, the wizard shows a screen that lists the mode and display settings you've chosen. These are the same mode and display settings that are available through the Properties dialog box of the application, as shown in Figure 11-16. It then gives you the option to test the program against these settings. If the program performs an illegal instruction during the test, the test window closes itself rather than displaying the executing application. Such experiences are common for older applications that include illegal access to hardware (in other words, for ill-behaved DOS and Windows applications). When you work with the wizard, it is highly recommended that you test the default settings first, then work your way through the list of other options from the top down.

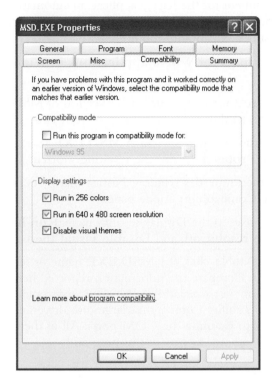

Figure 11-16 MSD.EXE Properties dialog box, Compatibility tab

In the next stage of the wizard, the program may request permission to send the compatibility settings it establishes to Microsoft. You may choose to allow this information to be transmitted or not at your discretion.

Note that whatever compatibility settings occur in the wizard can subsequently be viewed and changed through the Compatibility tab in the program's Properties window. To access this window, right-click the program name or icon (depending on your current view in Windows Explorer/My Computer), and then click the Compatibility tab (as shown in Figure 11-16).

The Learn more about application compatibility hyperlink on the Compatibility tab in the Properties window for any executable file takes you directly to the Help files on this subject.

Activity 11-6: Compatibility Mode

Time Required: 20 minutes

Objective: Use compatibility mode to run 16-bit (or earlier) applications.

Description: Running old applications has always been a challenge for Windows NT kernel operating systems (NT, 2000). Windows XP has a newer feature where the operating system tries to set up the proper environment for the legacy application automatically. This may or may not work, depending on how the application itself functions. In this activity, you attempt to run a 16-bit application using compatibility mode.

To manage compatibility mode settings for Win16 applications in Windows XP Professional:

1. Obtain information from your instructor to copy the 16-bit version of MSD.EXE or some other executable to your local hard disk, in a directory of your choosing.

2. Use My Computer to navigate to the directory in which **MSD.EXE** resides. Right-click its name or icon, and choose **Properties** from the resulting shortcut menu.

3. Select the **Compatibility** tab in the Properties window. Notice that by default no operating system is selected in the Compatibility mode pane.

4. Check the following three check boxes in the Display settings pane: **Run in 256 colors**, **Run in 640 x 480 screen resolution**, and **Disable visual themes**.

5. Click **OK** to accept your settings. Double-click the **MSD.EXE** name or icon to run the program and observe the results. Compare the information reported here to that available from winmsd.exe (located in *%systemroot%*\WINDOWS\System32). Notice that the age of the program limits its ability to recognize large disk drives, newer CPUs, and that it crashes if you try to examine the COM ports. All of these behaviors reflect outmoded notions implemented as part of this program!

 Steps 6 and 7 are optional; if you want to conclude this project, skip directly to Step 9.

NOTE

6. Repeat Steps 2 and 3. Deselect the **Display settings** check boxes, and then click **OK**. Restart **MSD.EXE** and observe the results.

7. Repeat Steps 2 and 3. Check the **Run this program in compatibility mode for:** check box in the Compatibility mode pane, select **Windows 95** as the compatibility target, and then click **OK**. Restart MSD.EXE and observe the results.

8. Ask your instructor if he or she has any other older applications with which you can experiment. Try working with various display settings and compatibility mode selections.

9. Close all open applications to complete this activity.

Assigning and Publishing Applications on Windows XP Professional

In the Windows 2000 Server and Windows Server 2003 environments, you can use group policies to assign or publish programs to users or computers in a domain, site, or organizational unit. It's especially useful to control access to programs through group memberships. Because it's easier to manage users in a group rather than one at a time, this permits administrators to control access to applications through group management, thereby making it easy to establish which applications users can run by virtue of the groups to which they belong.

When you assign a program in the Windows environment, you're really assigning a Windows Installer package to some group or user. A Windows Installer package is nothing more than a complete set of software installation and configuration instructions. This provides an easy mechanism to manage access to software within an organization. When a user clicks an icon for an assigned application, the action automatically uses the necessary instructions to install and configure the software on the computer where the user is working (assuming, of course, that he or she has the right group membership or user permissions to allow the request to proceed). Publishing a program requires some additional work to properly construct the collection of files and instructions so that installation can occur upon demand.

Users who want to access assigned and published applications must belong to a Windows 2000 Server or Windows Server 2003 domain. Of course, a domain administrator must also create an appropriate Windows Installer (MSI) package to handle the job as well. In fact, only someone with administrative privileges to a domain can configure a Group Policy Object for software assignment and publishing. The Microsoft Installer tool is not included as part of the Windows XP Professional release, and is most commonly used passively (and perhaps even unknowingly) by ordinary users. A file that contains instructions for the Windows Installer is called a **package**, and normally ends with the extension .msi. From an administrator's standpoint, it is necessary to create a network share that contains whatever Windows Installer packages (.msi files) are needed, plus any additional customizations that may apply to those basic .msi files, called **transforms** (.mst files), plus all necessary program files and related components.

NOTE

Additional information on working with the Windows Installer is covered in the discussion of IntelliMirror management technologies in Chapter 14. Numerous articles on the Windows Installer, and on building and deploying related packages, may be accessed in the Microsoft Knowledge Base, which is available online at *support.microsoft.com/* or on the TechNet CDs. Also, an especially good white paper titled "Windows Installer Service Overview" appears online at *http://www.microsoft.com/windows2000/techinfo/howitworks/ management/installer.asp.*

If an application does not have an installer package (i.e., an .msi file), you can create a .zap file to perform the same function. In almost all cases, the .msi files are created by the vendor and included on the distribution medium (such as the CD). A .zap file is a text file with the .zap extension. A .zap file is basically a batch file that contains commands to start the setup or installation routine of the application. .zap files should only be created and used when an .msi file is not available. .zap files are more restrictive than .msi files because they do not execute with elevated privileges for the installation process, do not support incremental or partial installs, do not provide automated rollback capabilities, and do not support automated customized installations.

To assign a program to a group within a Windows 2000 Server or Windows Server 2003 domain, it is necessary to construct the necessary .msi and .mst files (if needed), and to create a shared folder that contains those files plus all necessary program files and components with appropriate user and group permissions. From a logon with domain administrator privileges, creating the necessary Group Policy Object (GPO) occurs within the Active Directory Users and Computers MMC snap-in. From that point, follow these general steps to assign a program to a group:

1. Select a directory container (domain, site, or organizational unit, also known as an OU) to which the GPO should be linked.

2. Create a new GPO for your MSI package; be sure to give that object a self-documenting name (e.g., InstallOfficeXP).

3. Select the new GPO and click Edit to start the Group Policy snap-in so that you can edit your new GPO.

4. Open and then right-click the Software Installation entry in the GPO (it is located under Software Settings in both the Computer Configuration and User Configuration sections), and then click New Package.

5. When prompted for the path to the Windows Installer file (.msi file), browse to the network share where that file resides, click the file, and then click Open. When selecting files on a local hard drive, use a UNC name (e.g., \\computername\path); otherwise, other computers will look for the package on their local drives rather than on the machine where the share resides!

6. In most cases, choose the Assigned item instead of the Advanced Published or Assigned option that's presented next (unless, as Microsoft points out, you have the necessary knowledge and need to use Advanced options). This should create a software package element in the right pane in the Group Policy snap-in.

7. From the Active Directory Users and Computers snap-in, select the container to which you linked your package GPO. Right-click the container, click Properties, and then click the Group Policy tab. Next, click your new GPO, and then click Properties.

8. Click the Security tab, and remove Authenticated Users from the list of assigned users and groups. Use the Add button to select whichever security group or groups to which you want to grant access to the GPO, set the access level to Read, and then select the Apply Group Policy permissions.

NOTE Changes to a GPO are not immediately imposed on affected computers; instead, they're applied during the next group policy refresh interval. If necessary, you can use the secedit.exe command-line tool to impose such changes immediately; consult Microsoft Knowledge Base Article 227448 for the details on how to do so. To access the Knowledge Base online, please visit *http://search.support.microsoft.com/kb/c.asp*, or use the TechNet CDs.

In some situations, the deployment of new software through a GPO may be hindered. In fact, it may take several logons before newly deployed software is actually installed onto the target workstations. This is due to the default activity of Windows XP. After the initial logon of a user to a workstation, the Fast Logon Optimization feature takes over. This feature attempts to shorten the logon process by granting the user access to their desktop before the network is fully initialized, and often logs the user on using cached credentials. When this occurs, changes to the applicable GPOs, such as new software installation packages, are not immediately applied to the workstation. In fact, changes to the Software Installation and Folder Redirection sections of the GPO take at least two logons before being applied when Fast Logon Optimization is enabled. To disable the Fast Logon Optimization feature, enable the Always wait for the network at computer startup and logon control located in the Computer Configuration section of a GPO under Administrative Templates, System, Logon.

11

Resolving DLL Conflicts in Windows XP

Windows XP includes a remarkable new technology called Windows Side by Side (WinSxS) isolation support. All versions of Windows have been prey to a problem that can occur when application installers blindly copy files onto a Windows machine without checking for potential compatibility problems. This can be particularly galling for a special kind of Windows code file called a dynamic link library (DLL), which is designed to be shared by multiple instances of the same program, or multiple programs, because it contains common interface objects, code elements, controls, and so forth. In many cases, different programs require different versions of the same DLLs, but, by default, whichever installer ran most recently overwrites the version of a DLL necessary for some particular program with another version of the same DLL necessary for another particular program.

By default, Windows checks DLLs and other common code components before installing them on a computer. If it finds potential conflicts, it automatically makes the Registry modifications necessary to point to alternate versions of DLLs and other shared objects in a special directory named *%systemroot%*\WINDOWS\WinSxS. Then, when any program that requires a particular version of some DLL or other shared object runs, it automatically uses the correct file to do its job properly.

This is a great improvement over earlier versions of Windows (including Windows 2000), where extensive analysis and comparison of DLL files was required, and hand-editing of a special Registry key named r1dllHell was also required to inform those versions of Windows that alternate versions of the files were to be used. Because this process is now completely automated in Windows XP Professional (and in Windows Server 2003), this once vexing problem has been solved.

 For information on resolving DLL compatibility issues in other versions of Windows, consult the Knowledge Base Article Q247957, titled "Using DUPS to Resolve DLL Compatibility Problems" (DUPS stands for DLL Universal Problem Solver). You can access the Microsoft Knowledge Base online at *http://support. microsoft.com/kb/c.asp*, or on the TechNet CDs.

CHAPTER SUMMARY

- Windows XP Professional is divided into three main parts: environment subsystems, Executive Services, and user applications. The environment subsystems provide support for applications written for a variety of operating systems, not just for Windows XP. The Executive Services define the Windows XP runtime environment, and user applications provide additional functionality for a variety of services, such as word-processing and e-mail applications.

- In addition to the basic Win32 subsystem, two special-purpose operating environments (VDM and WOW) also run within that subsystem to provide limited backward compatibility for DOS and Win16 applications.

- Of these subsystems, only Win32 is crucial to the functioning of Windows XP as a whole. The other subsystems start up only as they're needed, but once started, the WOW environment remains resident until the machine is shut down and restarted, or its parent VDM process is manually terminated within Task Manager.

- Windows XP includes some interesting additional application management facilities. The Program Compatibility Wizard may be used to manage compatibility modes and display settings for older Win16 or DOS applications. Specific Group Policy Objects to assign and publish Windows applications within Windows 2000 Server or Windows Server 2003 domains may be configured and controlled to permit members of groups with proper permissions to access and use such applications. Finally, Windows XP includes powerful, automated facilities to recognize and resolve potential conflicts with DLLs and other shared code objects without requiring user involvement.

KEY TERMS

base priority — The lowest priority that a thread may be assigned, based on the priority assigned to its process.

child process — A process spawned within the context of some Windows XP environment subsystems (Win32, OS/2, or POSIX) that inherits operating characteristics from its parent subsystem and access characteristics from the permissions associated with the account that requested it be run.

context — The collection of Registry values and runtime environment variables in which a process or thread is currently running.

context switch — The act of unloading the context information for one process and replacing it with the information for another, when the new process comes to the foreground.**critical section** — In operating system terminology, this refers to a section of code that can be accessed only by a single thread at any one time; this prevents uncertain results from occurring when multiple threads attempt to change or access values included in that code at the same time.

DOS operating environment — A general term used to describe the reasonably thorough DOS emulation capabilities provided in a Windows XP virtual DOS machine (VDM).

dynamic link library (DLL) — A collection of virtual procedure calls, also called procedure stubs, that provide a well-defined way for applications to call on services or server processes within the Win32 environment. DLLs have been a consistent aspect of Windows since Windows 2.0.

environment subsystem — A miniature operating system running within Windows XP that provides an interface between applications and the kernel.

Executive Services — A set of kernel-mode functions that control security, system I/O, memory management, and other low-level services.

input message queue — A queue for each process, maintained by the Win32 subsystem, that contains the messages sent to the process from the user, directing its threads to perform a task.

kernel — The part of Windows XP composed of system services that interact directly with applications; it controls all application contact with the computer.

kernel mode — The systems running in kernel mode that are operating within a shared memory space and with access to hardware. Windows XP Executive Services operates in kernel mode.

local procedure call (LPC) — A technique to permit processes to exchange data in the Windows XP runtime environment. LPCs define a rigorous interface to let client programs request services, and to let server programs respond to such requests.

multitasking — The sharing of processor time between threads. Multitasking may be preemptive (the operating system may bump one thread if another one really needs access to the processor) or cooperative (one thread retains control of the processor until its turn to use it is over). Windows XP uses preemptive multitasking except in the context of the WOW operating environment, because Windows 3.*x* applications expect cooperative multitasking.

multithreaded process — A process with more than one thread running at a time.

package — The name of the collection of installer files, transforms, and other code components that support automated deployment of Windows programs. This term may also be applied to the .msi files associated with the Microsoft Installer facility used to drive automated installations through the Microsoft Installer itself.

parent process — The Windows XP environment subsystem that creates a runtime process and imbues that child process with characteristics associated with that parent's interfaces, capabilities, and runtime requirements.

process — An environment in which the executable portion of a program runs, defining its memory usage, which processor to use, its objects, and so forth. All processes have at least one thread. When the last thread is terminated, the process terminates with it. Each user-mode process maintains its own map of the virtual memory area. One process may create another, in which case the creator is the parent process and the created process is the child process.

real mode — A DOS term that describes a mode of operation for x86 CPUs wherein they can address only 1 MB of memory, broken into sixteen 64-KB segments, where the lower ten such segments are available to applications (the infamous 640 KB), and the upper six segments are available to the operating system or to special application drivers—or, for Windows XP, to a VDM.

subsystem — An operating environment that emulates another operating system to provide support for applications created for that environment.

synchronization object — Any of a special class of objects within the Windows XP environment that are used to synchronize and control access to shared objects and critical sections of code.

thread — The executable portion of a program, with a priority based on the priority of its process—user threads cannot exist external to a process. All threads in a process share that process's context.

transform — A specific type of Microsoft Installer file that usually ends in .mst and that defines changes or customization to an existing Microsoft Installer package, and the .msi file in which the base installer instructions reside. Because most vendors (and Microsoft) define .msi files for their programs and systems, it's often easier to customize an existing .msi file with an .mst transform, rather than defining a new installer package from scratch.

user mode — Systems running in user mode are operating in virtual private memory areas for each process, so that each process is protected from all others. User-mode processes may not manipulate hardware, but must send requests to kernel-mode services to do this manipulation for them.

virtual device driver (VDD) — A device driver used by virtual DOS machines (VDMs) to provide an interface between the application, which expects to interact with a 16-bit device driver, and the 32-bit device drivers that Windows 2000 provides.

virtual DOS machine (VDM) — A Win32 application that emulates a DOS environment for use by DOS and Win16 applications.

Win16 operating environment — The collection of components, interfaces, and capabilities that permits Win16 applications to run within a VDM within the Win32 subsystem on Windows XP.

Win16-on-Win32 (WOW) VDM — The formal name for the collection of components, interfaces, and capabilities that permits the Win32 subsystem to provide native support for well-behaved 16-bit Windows applications.

Win32 subsystem — An operating environment that supports 32-bit Windows applications and that is required to run Windows XP.

REVIEW QUESTIONS

1. Which of the following is not an environment subsystem in Windows XP Professional? (Choose all that apply.)

    a. Win32

    b. Windows on Windows (WOW)

    c. OS/2

    d. POSIX

2. If the threads in a process always run on the same CPU in a multiprocessor system, that process is said to have a(n) _____ for that processor.

3. Which of the following statements about process termination are true? (Choose all that apply.)

    a. When a process's last thread is terminated, the process is terminated as well, unless it creates another thread within a certain interval.

    b. When a process terminates, all of its child processes terminate with it.

    c. A process must have at least one thread at all times.

    d. If a parent process terminates, its threads may be taken over by a child process.

4. Which of the following is not a reason to use the environment subsystem/kernel model?

    a. speed

    b. modularity

    c. subsystem protection

    d. ease of communication

5. The _____ subsystem is required for the functioning of the Windows XP operating system.

6. Applications and the subsystems in which they run have a(n) _____ , in that the client application asks the server subsystem to do things for it, and the subsystem complies.

7. When an application stops operating in user mode and begins operating in kernel mode, this is called a context switch. True or False?

8. Which of the following does not represent or result from an attempt to speed up subsystem/user application communications?

    a. LPCs

    b. caching services provided by the subsystem

    c. batching messages

    d. calling kernel services directly

11

9. Which two parts of the kernel were part of the Win32 subsystem prior to Windows NT 4.0?

   a. GDI

   b. I/O Manager

   c. device drivers

   d. Windows Manager

10. User applications always operate in user mode. True or False?

11. To access Windows program compatibility settings, you can: (Choose all that apply.)

   a. Run the Program Compatibility Wizard.

   b. Use the application compatibility tool (Apcompat.exe).

   c. Access the Compatibility tab in the program's Properties window.

   d. none of the above

12. The Windows XP Executive Services belong to the kernel mode of this operating system and its runtime environment. True or False?

13. Windows XP Professional automatically detects and handles potential DLL conflicts. True or False?

14. Each time you start a DOS application under Windows XP, it runs in its own VDM. True or False?

15. Which of the following statements are true regarding LPCs, or local procedure calls? (Choose all that apply.)

   a. used to inform the CPU of I/O

   b. code optimized for speed

   c. supports specialized message passing functions

   d. employed only by the GDI portion of the OS

16. A child process can inherit the security token of its parent, or it can obtain a new security token by querying the Security Accounts Manager. True or False?

17. Windows 16-bit applications rely on which of the following? (Choose all that apply.)

   a. ntvdm

   b. POSIX

   c. WOW

   d. Win32

18. Under Windows XP, what do Win16 applications all share by default? (Choose all that apply.)

   a. working directory

   b. message queue

    c. address space

    d. NTFS file permissions

19. Which of the following are true statements about Win16? (Choose all that apply.)

    a. Wowexec.exe functions directly within a Win32 VM.

    b. When Wowexec.exe terminates, its NTVDM host also terminates.

    c. By default, all Win16 applications run within the same Wowexec.exe context.

    d. Only a single instance of wowexec.exe can be run at the same time.

20. Win16 applications can be opened into a separate memory space from the Run command within Windows XP. True or False?

21. In Windows XP, DOS applications can be opened into DOS environments with customized memory configurations. True or False?

22. All multithreaded applications running under Windows XP could be designed to operate on multiple processors for greater efficiency. True or False?

23. The first 16-bit application always runs in a separate memory space by default, whereas all subsequent 16-bit applications run by default in the same memory space as other applications of their kind. True or False?

24. A section of code that modifies data structures used by several threads is called a

    _____ .

25. Neither AUTOEXEC.BAT nor CONFIG.SYS has any role in determining Windows XP system configuration. True or False?

11

CASE PROJECTS

Case Project 11-1

CASE PROJECTS

To avoid the need to reimplement old code for your user community, which is in the process of upgrading from Windows 98 to Windows XP Professional, you decide to allow your users to run your company's homegrown application, Teller.exe, which is a well-behaved 16-bit Windows application, on their machines. Because this program sometimes hangs for as much as two or three minutes while computing end-of-day balances, it may cause problems for other 16-bit Windows applications that your users might need to run. What can you do to insulate these other applications from Teller.exe? How might you run this program to accomplish this goal?

Case Project 11-2

CASE PROJECTS

Provide a complete list of steps that you must complete to install two or more applications on a Windows XP machine, where such applications share a common DLL, but use different versions of that code. Explain exactly what you must do to create the proper Registry entries to resolve any potential DLL conflicts.

Case Project 11-3

Given a list of DOS and 16-bit Windows applications that you may want to use on a Windows XP machine, what is the proper method to ensure that each of them will (or won't) work with this operating system? What happens if any of these applications is ill behaved?

12

WORKING WITH THE WINDOWS XP REGISTRY

After reading this chapter and completing the exercises, you will be able to:

♦ Understand the function and structure of the Registry

♦ Describe the purpose of the Registry keys and the hive files to which some of them map

♦ Use the Registry editor and various other Registry tools

♦ Work with Registry storage files and fault tolerance

♦ Restore and protect the Registry

♦ Work with Registry tools in the Microsoft Windows XP Professional Resource Kit

Windows XP is a complex operating system that relies upon a dynamic data structure to maintain its configuration and operational parameters. This structure is the hierarchical database known as the **Registry**, which contains most of the control and functional settings for Windows XP core elements, services, and native applications, as well as many Microsoft and third-party add-on software products. In this chapter, you learn about the Registry, its structure, tools to edit and manage it, and values you may consider altering to improve or configure system operation.

Windows Registry Overview

The Registry provides Windows XP with a hierarchical database of information about a system's configuration. The Registry stores information essential to Windows XP itself, native applications, added services, and most add-on software products from Microsoft and third-party vendors. The information stored in the Registry is comparable to that stored in initialization files (.ini, .dat, .bat, .sys, and so on) in Windows 3.*x* or even Windows 95/98 (which used both the Registry and .ini files). For native 32-bit Windows applications, the Registry database takes the place of .ini files and stores all configuration information. The Registry is not a text file, such as WIN.INI or CONFIG.SYS, but is rather a multifaceted branchlike grouping of data.

Although most Windows XP Professional configurations can be performed using the Control Panel applets and the Administrative Tools (in fact, changes made to system configurations through these tools are applied to the Registry database), some settings can be established or changed only by editing the Registry directly. To edit the Windows XP Registry, you must use the Registry editor, which is launched by executing Regedit. This tool is discussed in detail later in this chapter.

 CAUTION Microsoft warns that editing the Registry directly should only be performed when absolutely necessary. If possible, use Control Panel applets or Administrative Tools to make system modifications rather than manipulating values directly in the Registry. Improper editing of the Registry can cause system malfunctions and can even render the system completely inoperable.

The Registry was designed for programming ease and speed of interaction for processes. The Registry's structure, although a bit daunting, is understandable if broken down into its component parts. The Registry is divided into keys and subkeys. Each Registry **key** is similar to a bracketed heading in an .ini file and represents a top-level container in the Registry hierarchy. There are five of these highest-level, or root, keys; their names start with HKEY to designate their highest-level status. Each key may contain one or more lower-level keys called **subkeys**. Within each subkey, one or more values or subkeys can exist.

A **value entry** is a named parameter or placeholder for a control setting or configuration data. A value entry can hold a single binary digit, a long string of ASCII characters, or a hexadecimal value. The actual piece of data held by a value entry is known as the **value**. Figure 12-1 shows the structure of the Registry contents in Regedit. The left pane shows three of the five root keys, with subkeys displayed for the HKEY_LOCAL_MACHINE key. The right pane shows the value entries for the SYSTEM\ControlSet002\Control subkey.

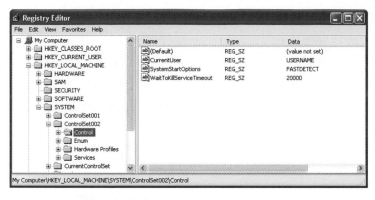

Figure 12-1   View of the hierarchical Registry structure, including three primary keys

 A discrete body of Registry keys, subkeys, and values stored in a file is also known as a **hive**. Such files reside in the *%systemroot%*\system32\config directory and normally correspond to some of the root keys shown in Figure 12-1 (for example, the file named "system" corresponds to the HKEY_LOCAL_ MACHINE\SYSTEM root key). For a complete listing of all hives on your system, use Regedit.exe to inspect the contents of the HKLM\SYSTEM\ CurrentControlSet\Control\hivelist subkey.

Value entries within the Registry are composed of three parts: name, type, and data (value). A Registry value entry's name is typically a multiword phrase, without spaces, with title capitalization, such as AutoAdminLogon in Figure 12-2. The data type of a value entry informs the Registry how to store the value. The **data type** defines whether the piece of data is a text string or a number and gives the numerical base (radix) of that number. Radix types supported by Windows XP are decimal (base 10), hexadecimal (base 16), and binary (base 2). All hexadecimal values are listed with the prefix "0x" to identify them clearly (as in 0xF for 15).

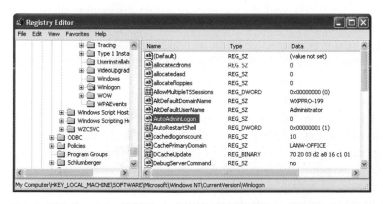

Figure 12-2   AutoAdminLogon value entries

The data types supported by Windows XP are:

- *Binary*—Binary format

- *DWORD*—Binary, hex, or decimal format

- *String*—Text-string format

- *Multiple String*—Text-string format that contains multiple human-readable values separated by NULL characters

- *Expandable String*—Expandable text-string format containing a variable that is replaced by an application when used (*%systemroot%*\File.exe)

Once a value entry is created and its data type defined, that data type cannot be changed. To alter a value's data type, you must delete the value entry and re-create it with a new data type.

Important concepts to keep in mind about the Registry are:

- Keys are the top-level, or root, divisions of the Registry.

- Keys contain one or more subkeys.

- Any subkey can contain one or more subkeys.

- Any subkey can contain one or more value entries.

Also note that the Registry is not a complete collection of configuration settings. Instead, it holds only the exceptions to the defaults. Processes within Windows XP operate with their own internal defaults unless a value in the Registry specifically alters that default behavior. This makes working with the Registry difficult: very often, the control you need is not present in the Registry because internal defaults are in use. To alter such a setting, you need to add a new value entry to the Registry. To accomplish this, you must know the exact syntax, spelling, location, and valid values; otherwise, you are unable to alter the default behavior. Keep in mind that failing to use the exact syntax, spelling, location, or valid values can result in malfunctions, possibly resulting in an inoperable system. So always edit with extreme care. The Microsoft Windows XP Professional Resource Kit includes a Help file named Regentry.chm, which lists all possible Registry entries and valid values. This is an invaluable tool when attempting to modify existing Registry entries or when adding new ones.

Each time Windows XP starts, the Registry is loaded into memory from files (see the Registry Storage Files section later in this chapter) stored on the hard drive. Each time Windows XP shuts down, the Registry is written from memory back to the files. While Windows XP is operating, the Registry remains in memory. This makes the Registry easy to access and quick to respond to control queries, and it is the reason why changes to the Registry take effect immediately. Only in extreme cases does Windows XP require you to restart the system to enforce changes in the Registry.

IMPORTANT REGISTRY STRUCTURES AND KEYS

In the following sections, you will look at various keys and subkeys in the Registry and learn their functions.

HKEY_LOCAL_MACHINE

The **HKEY_LOCAL_MACHINE** key contains the value entries that control the local computer. These configuration items include information about hardware devices, applications, device drivers, kernel services, and physical settings. These data are used to establish the configuration of the hardware and operating system environment. The content of this key is not dependent on the currently logged-on user, or the applications or processes in use; it is dependent only on the physical composition of the hardware and software present on the local computer.

This key has five subkeys (see Figure 12-3): HARDWARE, SAM, SECURITY, SOFTWARE, and SYSTEM, which are described in the following sections.

Figure 12-3 The HKEY_LOCAL_MACHINE key

HKEY_LOCAL_MACHINE\HARDWARE

The HKEY_LOCAL_MACHINE\HARDWARE subkey, as shown in Figure 12-4, is the container for data related directly to physical devices installed on a computer. This subkey stores configuration data, device driver settings, mappings, linkages, relationships between kernel-mode and user-mode hardware calls, and IRQ hooks. This subkey is re-created each time the system starts and is not saved when the system shuts down. That explains why this subkey does not map to a specific hive file in the *%systemroot%*\system32\config directory.

The HKEY_LOCAL_MACHINE\HARDWARE subkey contains three subkeys: DESCRIPTION, DEVICEMAP, and RESOURCEMAP. The DESCRIPTION subkey stores data extracted from a device's own firmware or onboard BIOS. The DEVICEMAP subkey stores information about device driver paths, locations, and filenames. The RESOURCEMAP subkey stores information about the mappings between system

12

Figure 12-4   The HKEY_LOCAL_MACHINE\HARDWARE subkey

resources (I/O ports, I/O memory addresses, interrupts, and direct memory access [DMA] channels) and device drivers. When certain bus types are present in the computer, a fourth subkey named OWNERMAP stores association information about the bus type and device drivers.

The HKEY_LOCAL_MACHINE\HARDWARE subkey contains a fourth subkey if your system contains software that supports the Advanced Configuration and Power Interface (ACPI). The ACPI subkey contains all of the operational parameters for that feature.

The contents of the HARDWARE subkey should not be manipulated. This key contains data read from the state of the physical devices and associated device drivers. There should be no need or reason to alter the data because they should always present a proper reflection of the state of the system. Second, these data are most often in binary format; so deciphering the data is difficult, if not impossible, for most users. If you want to view the data contained in this key, you can do so using the System Information tool. To use this tool go to Start, Help and Support, then click Support, and then choose Advanced System Information from the See Also task items. Alternatively, you can go to Start, Run, and then type msinfo32.exe in the Open text box or run it from the Start menu (Start, All Programs, Accessories, System Tools, System Information).

HKEY_LOCAL_MACHINE\SAM

The subkey HKEY_LOCAL_MACHINE\SAM is a hive that contains data related to security. The **Security Accounts Manager (SAM)** database is stored in this key and is where local user accounts and group memberships are defined. The entire security structure of your Windows XP system is stored in this key. In most cases, these data are not accessible from a Registry editor, but instead reside in a file named SAM in the *%systemroot%* system32\config directory.

CAUTION

This is another area of the Registry that you should not normally attempt to modify. Most of the data contained in this subkey are in binary or encrypted format. You should employ the user manager tools (that is, the Local Users and Groups section of the Computer Management tool) to manipulate the data stored in this subkey. Additionally, to prevent you from editing it, this subkey has a security setting such that only the System (or the System utility) has rights to read and alter its contents.

HKEY_LOCAL_MACHINE\SECURITY

The subkey HKEY_LOCAL_MACHINE\SECURITY is the container for the local security policy, which defines control parameters, such as password policy, user rights, account lockout, audit policy, and general security options for the local machine. This subkey maps to a hive file named SECURITY in the *%systemroot%*\system32\config directory.

CAUTION

This is yet another area of the Registry that you should not attempt to modify. Most of the data contained in this subkey are in binary format or are encrypted. You should employ the Local Security Policy tool to manipulate the data stored in this subkey (see Chapter 5, "Users, Groups, Profiles, and Policies" and Chapter 6, "Windows XP Security and Access Controls"). Additionally, to prevent you from editing this subkey, it has a security setting such that only the System utility has rights to read and alter its contents.

HKEY_LOCAL_MACHINE\SOFTWARE

The subkey HKEY_LOCAL_MACHINE\SOFTWARE is the container for data about installed software and mapped file extensions. These settings apply to all local users. The \Software\Classes subkey contains the same information as the HKEY_CLASSES_ROOT key; in fact, the HKEY_CLASSES_ROOT key is created by copying the data from the \Software\Classes subkey. The subkey maps to a hive file named SOFTWARE in the *%systemroot%*\system32\config directory.

HKEY_LOCAL_MACHINE\SYSTEM

The subkey HKEY_LOCAL_MACHINE\SYSTEM is the container for the information required to boot Windows XP. This subkey stores data about startup parameters, loading order for device drivers, service startup credentials (settings and parameters), and basic operating system behavior. This key is essential to the start process of Windows XP. It contains subkeys called control sets that include complete information about the start process for the system. This subkey resides in a hive file named "system" in the %*systemroot*%\system32\config directory.

This subkey also contains additional subkeys with settings for storage devices (such as MountedDevices) and control set boot status (Select), and possibly subkeys left over from upgrading from Windows NT 4.0 (Disk and Setup). The control set keys are named and numbered; for example, ControlSet001 and ControlSet002. In most cases, there are only two control sets numbered 001 and 002. These two sets represent the original (001) system configuration set and a backup (002) of the last functioning system configuration set. Thus, there is always a functioning configuration to allow the operating system to start (see Chapter 13, "Booting Windows XP").

Each control set has four subkeys (refer to Figure 12-1):

- *Control*—This is the container for data related to controlling system startup, boot parameters, computer name, and necessary subsystems to initiate.

- *Enum*—This is the container for data regarding required device drivers and their configuration.

- *Hardware Profiles*—This is the container for data specific to the hardware profile currently in use.

- *Services*—This is the container for data about drivers, services, file systems, applications, and other required hardware components necessary to load all installed and active services during bootup. This subkey also defines the order in which services are called and the way that one service can call or query other services.

The value entries under the HKEY_LOCAL_MACHINE\SYSTEM\Select subkey are used to define how Windows XP uses its control. The four value entries are shown in Figure 12-5.

- *Default*—Defines which control set will be used during the next bootup

- *Current*—Lists the control set that was used to start the current session

- *LastKnownGood*—Indicates the control set last used to boot and successfully log on a user (see later in this chapter for details and use)

- *Failed*—Lists the control set that was replaced by the control set from the Last-KnownGood control set because of a failure to start

The HKEY_LOCAL_MACHINE\SYSTEM\CurrentControlSet subkey is a redirector to the actual ControlSet### currently in use rather than a truly distinct subkey (where ### is the three-digit number representing the control set version). This symbolic link is used to simplify the programming interface for applications and device drivers that need information from the active control set. Because of this redirection, when you need to make modifications to the control set, you should use the CurrentControlSet subkey to direct your changes to the active control set properly.

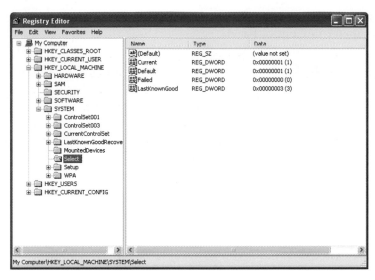

Figure 12-5   The HKEY_LOCAL_MACHINE\SYSTEM\Select subkey

HKEY_CLASSES_ROOT

12

The **HKEY_CLASSES_ROOT** key (see Figure 12-6) is the container for information pertaining to application associations based on file extensions and COM object data. The contents of this key are copied from the HKEY_LOCAL_MACHINE\ SOFTWARE\Classes subkey. This key is maintained for backward compatibility with legacy applications and device drivers and is not strictly required by Windows XP.

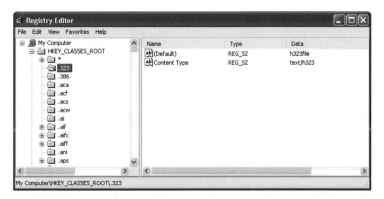

Figure 12-6   HKEY_CLASSES_ROOT contains file extension and COM object settings and associations

As with other binary or protected keys, do not edit the contents of this key, or the HKEY_LOCAL_MACHINE\SOFTWARE\Classes subkey, directly. Instead, use the File Types tab of the Folder Options dialog box. To access this dialog box, select the Folder

Options command from the Tools menu in Windows Explorer or My Computer or by using the Folder Options applet in Control Panel.

HKEY_CURRENT_CONFIG

The **HKEY_CURRENT_CONFIG** key (see Figure 12-7) is the container for data that pertain to whatever hardware profile is currently in use. This key is just a link to the HKEY_LOCAL_MACHINE\SYSTEM\CurrentControlSet\HardwareProfiles\Current subkey. This key is maintained for backward compatibility with legacy applications and device drivers and is not strictly required by Windows XP.

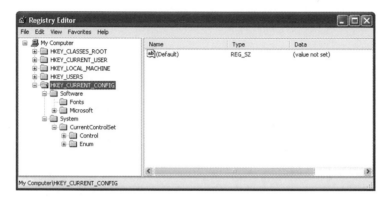

Figure 12-7   THE HKEY_CURRENT_CONFIG/ key is maintained in Windows XP for backward compatibility

The contents of this key, and the HKEY_LOCAL_MACHINE\SYSTEM\ CurrentControlSet\Hardware Profiles\Current subkey, should not be edited directly. Instead, the Hardware Profiles interface or Device Manager should be used. The Hardware Profiles interface is accessed by clicking the Hardware Profiles button on the Hardware tab of the System applet in Control Panel. Device Manager is accessed by clicking the Device Manager button on the Hardware tab of the System applet in Control Panel or by selecting the Device Manager node from the Computer Management utility in Administrative Tools.

HKEY_CURRENT_USER

The **HKEY_CURRENT_USER** key (see Figure 12-8) is the container for the profile for whichever user is currently logged on. The contents of this key are built each time a user logs on by copying the appropriate subkey from the HKEY_USERS key. The contents of this key should not be edited directly; instead, you should modify a user's profile through conventional profile management techniques (see Chapter 5 for more information on profile management).

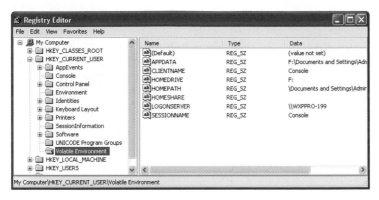

Figure 12-8   HKEY_CURRENT_USER contains data for whichever user is currently logged onto the system

HKEY_USERS

The **HKEY_USERS** key (see Figure 12-9) contains profiles for all users who have ever logged onto this system and the default user profile. The contents of this key are built each time the system boots by loading the default file and the locally stored copies of Ntuser.dat or Ntuser.man from user profiles (see Chapter 5). These locally stored copies are found in the \Documents and Settings*username* directory on a Windows XP Professional system. To remove a user profile from this key, use the User Profiles tab of the System applet in Control Panel. To alter the contents of a profile, use conventional profile management techniques (see Chapter 5 for more information on profile management) instead of attempting to edit this key directly. Note also that subkeys in this key use Windows Security IDs (SIDs) to identify users, rather than account names, which explains their cryptic alphanumeric names.

12

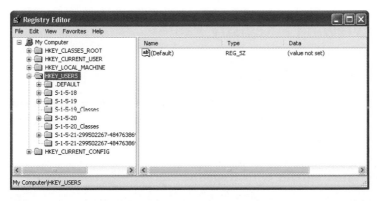

Figure 12-9   HKEY_USERS contains data for any user who has ever logged onto the system, plus a default user profile

HKEY_DYN_DATA

In some Registries, you may occasionally run across another main key named HKEY_DYN_DATA. This root or main key appears only on machines with Windows 95 or Windows 98 applications that use older versions of Plug and Play to detect and track hardware devices as they enter or leave a system. Because Windows XP Professional's Plug and Play implementation is vastly superior to these older versions, this entry exists solely to help the operating system maintain backward compatibility with older versions of Windows.

REGISTRY EDITORS

Because the structure of the Registry is so complex, special tools are required to operate on it directly. The primary Registry editor for Windows XP is launched by executing either Regedit.exe or Reg.exe.

Regedit (see Figure 12-10) offers global searching, security manipulation, and combines all of the keys into a single display.

Figure 12-10   Regedit is the older Registry editor that suffices for most uses

Activity 12-1: Viewing a Registry Value

Time Required: 10 minutes

Objective: Use the Registry editor to view information storage locations.

Description: Almost all system information is stored in the Registry, from the value of the IP address of the computer, to the name of the computer, even to what wallpaper is displayed. In this activity, you use the Registry editor to view the key value for the logged-on person's name.

To view Registry value entries with Regedit:

1. Select **Start**, **Run**.

2. Type **regedit**, and then click **OK**. The Registry editor opens.

3. Double-click **HKEY_LOCAL_MACHINE**.

4. Locate and double-click **SOFTWARE** under HKEY_LOCAL_MACHINE.

5. Locate and double-click **Microsoft** under SOFTWARE.

6. Locate and double-click **Windows NT** under Microsoft.

7. Locate and double-click **CurrentVersion** under Windows NT.

8. Locate and select **Winlogon** under CurrentVersion.

9. In the right pane, locate and select **DefaultUserName**.

10. From the **Edit** menu, select **Modify**.

11. Notice that the value of this value entry is the name of your current user account.

12. Click **Cancel**.

13. In the left pane, scroll up until you see HKEY_LOCAL_MACHINE.

14. Double-click **HKEY_LOCAL_MACHINE**. Leave the system as is for the next activity.

Reg.exe (see Figure 12-11) is the Console Registry tool for Windows, a command-line utility that permits users, batch files, or programs to operate on the Registry, but that supports no attractive graphical user interface like that for Regedit.

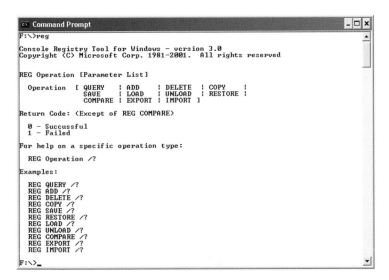

Figure 12-11   Reg.exe is a command-line utility that permits users, batch files, or programs to operate on the Registry

Because it is a command-line utility and does not display the Registry's hierarchical organization in an easy-to-grasp form, Reg.exe is not as convenient or friendly as Regedit. exe. However, both editors can be used to view keys and values, perform searches, add new subkeys, value entries, alter the data in value entries, and import or export keys and subkeys. For most purposes, however, Regedit should be your primary Registry inspection and editing tool.

Activity 12-2: Search for a Registry Key or Value

Time Required: 10 minutes

Objective: Use the Find command to quickly locate a key or value.

Description: The entries within the Registry number in the thousands and increase with every application installed, account created, and so on. It would be difficult to manually look for a key or value if you did not know the general location of it. In this activity, you use the Find command to locate the DefaultUserName.

To search for a value entry with Regedit:

This activity requires that Activity 12-1 be completed. The Regedit application is used to locate a key or value without knowing its path within the Registry. The search begins at the system status point where Activity 12-1 ended.

1. From the **Edit** menu, select **Find**.

2. In the Find what field, type **DefaultUserName**.

3. Click **Find Next**. Regedit locates the first key, value, or data containing that string.

4. Notice that the first found match is AltDefaultUserName (be patient; this first search may take as long as a minute to complete).

5. From the **Edit** menu, select **Find Next** (or click the hotkey equivalent, **F3**). This is the actual DefaultUserName value entry that you viewed in Activity 12-2.

6. In the left pane, scroll up until you see HKEY_LOCAL_MACHINE.

7. Double-click **HKEY_LOCAL_MACHINE**. Leave the system as is for the next activity.

Activity 12-3: Command-line Registry Editor

Time Required: 15 minutes

Objective: Use Reg.exe from a command prompt to edit the Registry.

Description: Regedit.exe is the GUI interface for editing the Registry. Reg.exe is the command-line version. In this activity, you use Reg.exe to view the contents of DefaultUserName.

To use Reg.exe, the Windows Console Registry tool:

1. Select **Start**, **All Programs**, **Accessories**, **Command Prompt**.

2. Type **reg** and press **Enter** to produce the basic documentation for the utility.

3. Notice that each major key may be abbreviated for compactness.

4. Type **reg query "HKLM\SOFTWARE\Microsoft\Windows NT\CurrentVersion\Winlogon" /v DefaultUserName** to display the contents of that value entry (it should match your current logon name). Press **Enter**.

As already noted many times in this chapter, editing the Registry directly should not be undertaken without forethought and planning. It is possible to alter the Registry, whether on purpose or accidentally, in such a way as to render a system completely unrecoverable. If you don't know exactly what you are doing, *don't do it!* Please also note that although earlier versions of Windows included another GUI Registry editor called Regedt32.exe, that program is no longer available as part of Windows XP Professional. However, executing Regedit32 starts the existing Registry editor tool.

Even when you do think you know exactly what you want to change in the Registry, it is always a good idea to take precautions, such as the following:

- Back up all important data on the computer before editing the Registry.

- Make a distinct backup of all or part of the Registry. Saving each key or subkey individually is recommended (see Activity 12-4). Saving parts of the Registry to files enables you to restore parts of the Registry instead of the entire Registry. Store the backup files on local drives, network drives, and floppies or other removable media to ensure access.

- Restart the machine before editing the Registry.

- Perform only a single Registry modification at a time. Test the results before proceeding.

- Restart immediately after each change to force full system compliance with the new settings in the Registry. This is not strictly necessary, but has often proved to be prudent.

- Always test changes on a nonproduction system hosting noncritical services before deploying on production systems.

REGISTRY STORAGE FILES

The files in which static images of the Registry are stored reside in the *%systemroot%*\system32\config and *%systemroot%*\repair directories of the boot partition (see Figure 12-12). The Registry is not stored in files that match one-to-one with the top-level keys, as is explained shortly, but there is plenty of Registry data mapped into files for safekeeping (and to maintain backup or rollback versions of these data).

The Registry is stored in various subkey, logging, and backup files, as indicated in Table 12-1.

12

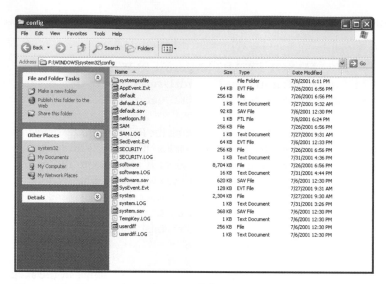

Figure 12-12   Explorer listing of the …\system32\config folder shows various Registry file types and instances

Table 12-1   Registry storage files

Registry key/subkey	Subkey, logging, and backup files,
HKEY_LOCAL_MACHINE\SAM	Sam, Sam.log, Sam.sav
HKEY_LOCAL_MACHINE\SECURITY	Security, Security.log, Security.sav
HKEY_LOCAL_MACHINE\SOFTWARE	Software, Software.log, Software.sav
HKEY_LOCAL_MACHINE\SYSTEM	System, System.alt, System.log, System.sav
HKEY_USERS\.DEFAULT	Default, Default.log, Default.sav
(Not directly associated with a Registry key)	Userdiff, Userdiff.log
HKEY_CURRENT_USER	Ntuser.dat, Ntuser.dat.log

NOTE   Note that only two of the HKEY_LOCAL_MACHINE subkeys, the Default subkey of the HKEY_USERS key, and the HKEY_CURRENT_USER key are stored in files. All of the other keys and subkeys are either built "on the fly" when the system starts or are copies of a subsection of HKEY_LOCAL_MACHINE.

The HKEY_USERS key is built from the default file (which represents the default user profile's Ntuser.dat file) and copies of profiles for all users who have ever logged onto the computer. These profiles are cached locally in the \Documents and Settings*username* directory. A copy of the Ntuser.dat or Ntuser.man file is copied into the repair directory for the currently logged-on user.

Notice that four extensions are used by the Registry storage files to identify the purpose or function of the file:

  ■ *No extension*—The storage file for the subkey itself, also known as a hive file.

- *.alt*—The backup file for the subkey. Note that only the HKEY_LOCAL_ MACHINE\SYSTEM subkey has a backup file.

- *.log*—A file containing all changes made to a key. This file is used to verify that all modifications to the Registry are properly applied.

- *.sav*—Copies of keys in their original state as created at the end of the text portion of Windows XP installation.

NOTE TechNet now includes a wonderful *Windows NT Magazine* article titled "Inside the Registry" by Mark Russinovitch, a leading Windows expert. Online, you can find this article at *www.microsoft.com/technet/treeview/*default.asp? url=/TechNet/prodtechnol/winntas/tips/winntmag/inreg.asp. Note that even though the article is somewhat outdated, it's still a worthwhile read.

Under Windows NT 4.0, the Registry files stored in the \Config directory were used to build the emergency repair disk (ERD). Under Windows XP, 2000, and 2003, these files are no longer copied onto the ERD when it is created. However, you can create your own custom ERD by manually copying the files in the \Config directory to a formatted floppy. You may find having a complete copy of the Registry quite handy when you need to perform a system repair or restore any portion of the Registry because of corruption or human error. If you need to use those files, you can always use the Import command in Regedit to restore that data to a damaged Registry.

12

REGISTRY FAULT TOLERANCE

If the Registry becomes corrupted or destroyed, Windows XP cannot function or even start. Several mechanisms have been established to prevent the Registry from becoming damaged or to repair minor problems automatically. The fault tolerance of the Registry is sustained by its structure, memory residence, and transaction logs. These mechanisms ensure that all changes or operations performed on the Registry either succeed or fail. This prevents any partially applied alterations that could result in an invalid value entry or entries. Thus an "all or nothing" guarantee is supported no matter what method of alteration is used, including using a Registry editor or the Administrative Tool or alterations by an application. If the change action is interrupted (by power failure, too little CPU time, hardware failure, and so on), the Registry remains intact, even if the desired change was not implemented.

As mentioned, when a value entry is altered in the Registry, that change applies to the copy of the Registry stored in active memory; this means that the change affects the system immediately in most cases. A change to the Registry is only made permanent when key files are copied back to the hard drive. This activity occurs during a **flush**, a copy procedure to update the files on the hard drive with the new settings stored in the memory-resident version of the Registry. A flush occurs at shutdown, when forced by an application, or just after a Registry alteration.

Transaction logs are files wherein the system records edits, changes, and alterations to the Registry, similar to a list of orders or commands. When a flush occurs, the transaction log is updated to record all changes currently in memory, which will be written to the Registry storage files. This log is used by the system to automatically verify that all Registry changes are correct as the flush concludes.

A flush includes the following sequence of steps:

1. All alterations to a key are appended to that key's transaction log file (.log).
2. The key file is marked as being in transition.
3. The key file is updated with the new data from memory.
4. The key file is marked as complete.

If a system failure occurs between the time that the key file is marked as in transition and when it is marked complete, the original state of the key is recovered using the data from the transaction log. If the flush finishes uninterrupted, the system continues to perform normally.

The flush operation is performed on all keys except the SYSTEM subkey. This subkey contains system-critical data and is a major ingredient in a successful start of Windows XP. For this reason, recovery cannot rely upon transaction logs. Instead, Windows XP updates the SYSTEM subkey using a different method:

1. The system file is marked as being in transition.
2. The system file is brought up to date with the state of the Registry from memory.
3. The system file is marked as being complete.
4. The System.alt file is marked as being in transition.
5. The System.alt file is brought up to date with the state of the Registry from memory.
6. The System.alt file is marked as being complete.

This dual-file process, with its primary and backup copies of the SYSTEM subkey file, ensures that no matter at which stage the update process might be interrupted, a complete and functional copy of the SYSTEM subkey file is available. If the failure occurs within the first three steps, the nonupdated System.alt file is used to start the system. If the failure occurs within the last three steps, the updated system file is used to start the system. Once booting is complete after a failure, Windows XP performs the update again to ensure that both copies of the SYSTEM subkey are exactly the same. However, if the failure occurs during the first three steps, any changes made to the system will have been lost.

Though Windows XP automatically manages the safety of the Registry through its fault-tolerance mechanisms (.log and .alt files), it is still important for you to take proactive measures to back up the Registry. There are several ways to create reliable Registry backups:

- Most Windows XP backup applications (for example, the built-in Backup tool and third-party products, such as Veritas Backup Exec and UltraBac) include support for full Registry backups. With these products, you can back up the Registry as part of your daily automated backup or as a distinct Registry-only procedure. Backing up the Registry with most of these products consists of selecting a "Back up the Registry" or "System State" check box when you make file/folder selections before initializing a backup.

- Regedit can be used to save all or part of the Registry to distinct files. This tool offers an Export command, which may be used to save the entire Registry, a single key, or any portion of a key to a file.

- Make a copy of the *%systemroot%*\system32\config and *%systemroot%*\repair directories manually. Just copy the contents to another location on your local computer, on a drive elsewhere on your network, or to a floppy disk (if size allows) or recordable CD.

- Employ the Microsoft Windows XP Professional Resource Kit tools, such as Regback.exe. This tool offers command-line scripting capabilities. Explore the Microsoft Windows XP Professional Resource Kit for ideas on how to best employ these tools. You can see a syntax parameter listing for these and most command-line tools by issuing a "/?" parameter after the command from a command prompt (that is, *reg /?*, or *reg /? more*, if more than one screen's worth of data is displayed).

12

No matter which backup method you employ, take the time to make two copies or perform the backup twice. This provides additional insurance in case your first backup fails.

Activity 12-4: Registry Backup

Time Required: 20 minutes (depending on the size of the Registry and the portion that is backed up)

Objective: Use the Regedit application to back up a portion of the Registry.

Description: Before giving any direction as to the editing of the Registry, Microsoft always states first that the Registry should only be edited when absolutely necessary. This is because if an error is made, the system may be rendered useless. To provide a level of protection, it is possible to back up the Registry prior to editing. The ability to make backups of the Registry also offers you an additional level of support in the event of a system problem or a human error in regard to the Registry. In this activity, you perform a backup of a portion of the Registry.

To back up a Registry key:

 This activity begins at the system status point where Activity 12-2 ended.

1. Expand the **HKEY_USERS** key, if necessary, and select the .DEFAULT subkey.

2. From the **File** menu, select **Export**.

3. Select a destination folder (such as **c:\temp**) of your choice in the Save in pull-down list.

4. Provide a filename, such as **HKUDsave.reg**.

5. Make sure the **Selected branch** option button at the bottom of the Export Registry File dialog box is selected and that **HKEY_USERS\.DEFAULT** is listed in the text field.

6. Click **Save**.

7. The Regedit tool creates a backup file of the selected key. Leave the system as is for the next activity.

This procedure can be used to back up the entire Registry or just a small subset of subkeys, simply by selecting different keys or subkeys.

RESTORING THE REGISTRY

Obviously, if you are going to take the time to create backups of the Registry, you must understand how to restore it. You have several options for restoring the Registry, depending on the method used to make a backup. Windows XP itself attempts to maintain a functional Registry, using its own internal automatic fault-tolerance mechanisms. If the automatic restoration process fails, you can first attempt to restore the Last Known Good Configuration. The **Last Known Good Configuration (LKGC)** is the state of the Registry stored in one of the control sets (covered earlier in this chapter) when the last successful user logon occurred. If the Registry is damaged in a way that it cannot fully start or won't allow a user to log on, the LKGC option can restore the system to its prior working state.

This boot option is accessed by pressing F8. Windows XP starts and the boot menu is displayed. Don't worry; the basic boot menu even prompts you to press F8 if you need an alternative boot method. Pressing F8 reveals a new selection menu similar to the following:

```
Windows Advanced Options Menu
Please select an option:
Safe Mode
Safe Mode with Networking
Safe Mode with Command Prompt

Enable Boot logging
Enable VGA Mode
Last Known Good Configuration (your most recent settings
   that worked)
Directory Services Restore Mode (Windows domain
   controllers only)
Debugging Mode

Start Windows Normally
Reboot
Return to OS Choices Menu

Use the up and down arrow keys to move the highlight to
   your choice.
```

Use the arrow keys to highlight the Last Known Good Configuration selection, and then press Enter. Keep in mind that any changes made to the system between the time the LKGC was stored and its use to restore the system will be lost. If the LKGC fails to restore normal system functions, you have only two options:

1. Use your backup software to restore the Registry files. This is only possible if your backup application offers a DOS-based restore mechanism that can bypass NTFS write restrictions. In other words, the backup software must operate without a functional Windows XP environment when launched from a bootable floppy. This type of software lets you restore files to the boot and system partitions (such as the Registry) so you can return to a functional OS. Unfortunately, these applications are few and far between. One such product is UltraBac (*www.ultrabac.com*).

2. Reinstall Windows XP, either fully or as an upgrade. An upgrade may replace the section of the Registry that is causing the problems, allowing you to retain most of your configuration, but this is not guaranteed. A full, new installation of Windows XP returns the system to a preconfigured state and requires you to repeat all postinstallation changes you may have made.

If you are able to boot into the system, but things are not functioning the way they should; or if services, drivers, or applications are not loading or operating properly, you may need to restore the Registry in part or whole from backup. Simply use the same tool employed to create the backup to restore the Registry. Keep in mind that some tools allow you to restore portions of the Registry instead of the whole thing.

No matter what method you employ to restore the Registry, it's always a good idea to reboot the system to ensure that the restore operation completed successfully and that the system is using only working (or more correctly, reverted-to) settings. It's also a good idea to retain the copies of the old Registry until you are confident that the system is functioning normally and you have had the opportunity to create new backups. In other words, don't throw away the disks, erase the drives, or format the tapes containing the Registry backup; keep a few generations of Registry backups on hand, just in case.

Activity 12-5: Registry Restore

Time Required: 20 minutes

Objective: Use Regedit to restore all or a portion of the Registry.

Description: There may several reasons to restore all or parts of a Registry file. For instance, you may need to restore a portion of the Registry because a portion was edited incorrectly. In another instance, you may want to restore a Registry file on another machine to ensure that the settings on both machines are identical. In this activity, you restore the Registry using the backup file that was created in the previous activity.

To restore a Registry key:

This activity requires that Activity 12-4 be completed. It begins at the system status point where Activity 12-4 ended.

1. From the **File** menu, select **Import**.

2. Locate and select your **HKUDsave.reg** file.

3. Click **Open**.

Performing this activity may result in an error stating that the file cannot be imported. Even if this activity fails in this instance, you can still see the process of how to import saved Registry keys.

4. After a few moments of importing, a message stating whether the import succeeded is displayed; click **OK**.

5. From the **File** menu, select **Exit**.

As with backing up a Registry key, this procedure can be used to restore the entire Registry or just a small subset of subkeys simply by selecting different keys or subkeys. However, it does require that the same amount or even more data be backed up for the material to be restored.

PROTECTING THE REGISTRY

As Microsoft often warns, the Registry should only be edited by a qualified person. This may not necessarily stop a person from going into the Registry and making changes on their own, however. To protect the Registry from being edited by certain individuals or groups, or to allow a person to view the Registry without making changes to it, permissions can be assigned to the hives and keys within the Registry. The method of applying the permissions is almost identical to assigning permissions and protecting files and folders on an NTFS partition.

In most cases, only privileged groups and users are allowed to edit and view the Registry, but there may be instances in which users are given administrative rights to their own workstations. In this type of scenario, it may save time and trouble if the Registry was protected by either restricting the users altogether or to allow them read-only access.

ACTIVITY

Activity 12-6: Regedit Security

Time Required: 20 minutes

Objective: Set permissions within Regedit to restrict access to editing the Registry.

Description: The quickest way to disable a computer is to allow a person to edit their Registry if they don't know what they are doing. Deleting files from a local computer is not normally debilitating. However, if a person has just enough knowledge to be dangerous and decides to edit the Registry, it can be almost impossible to determine what is wrong with their computer. In this activity, you view the permissions that can be set in Regedit.exe.

To view security permissions with Regedit:

1. Click **Start**, **Run**, type **regedit**, and then click **OK**. The Registry editor opens.

2. Select **HKEY_USERS**.

3. From the **Edit** menu, select **Permissions**. Notice the Permissions dialog box for the Registry is identical to that used elsewhere in Windows XP.

4. Select each of the groups displayed and view the permissions that are assigned to each.

5. Select the **Advanced** button to see if the permissions are inherited and if they apply to the current key and subkeys or just subkeys.

6. Select the **Edit** button to view all of the possible permissions that could be applied to a key. You'll notice that the options are very similar to those that can be applied to an NTFS object. Also notice that there is a check box that can be selected if the permissions are to be applied to objects or containers within the current object.

7. Select **Cancel** three times to return to the Registry Editor window.

8. From the **File** menu, select **Exit**.

12

Windows XP Professional Resource Kit Registry Tools

The Microsoft Windows XP Professional Resource Kit includes several tools that can be used to manipulate the Registry: The Microsoft Windows XP Professional Resource Kit is a Microsoft product separate from the Windows XP Professional operating system. The Microsoft Windows XP Professional Resource Kit has additional documentation on Windows XP Professional, its operations, and its use, as well as a host of useful tools and utilities not included with the standard operating system software. You can purchase the Microsoft Windows XP Professional Resource Kit from Microsoft or from most software or book vendors.

Because many of these tools are command-line tools or require perusal of significant ancillary materials, it is recommended that you read over the Microsoft Windows XP Professional Resource Kit documentation yourself before actually using these tools. Some of the key utilities include:

- *Regdump.exe*—A command-line tool used to dump all or part of the Registry to Stdout (this is an abbreviation for the standard output file, where the system creates output by default; normally, this sends the output to a file whose name you specify when you run the command). The output of this tool is suitable for the Regini.exe tool. This tool is useful when you need to create scripts based on Registry content by creating a dump of existing settings.

- *Regfind.exe*—A command-line tool used to search the Registry for a key, value name, or value data based on keywords

- *Compreg.exe*—A GUI tool used to compare two local or remote Registry keys and highlight all differences

- *Regini.exe*—A command-line scripting tool used to add keys to the Registry

- *Regback.exe*—A command-line scripting tool used to back up keys from the Registry

- *Regrest.exe*—Another command-line scripting tool used to restore keys to the Registry

- *Scanreg.exe*—A GUI tool used to search the Registry for a key, value name, or value data based on keywords

Chapter Summary

- ❑ The Windows XP Registry is a complex structure consisting of keys, subkeys, values, and value entries.

- ❑ The Registry should be manipulated with extreme caution. Unless absolutely necessary, the Registry should not be edited directly; instead, employ the Control Panel applets and Administrative Tools to modify system settings.

❑ Windows XP maintains a functional Registry through several fault-tolerant measures, including transaction logs and backup of key files.

❑ The Registry is divided into five main keys. The primary and most important key is HKEY_LOCAL_MACHINE, because it hosts data ranging from system startup information to driver settings to the security database. For some, but not all, of these main keys, Windows XP Professional writes them to files in the %*systemroot*%\system32\config directory that are called hives or hive files.

❑ Windows XP includes two Registry editors, the graphical Regedit.exe and the command-line Reg.exe utility. The former is useful for global searches and general inspection or quick edits, the latter for performing systematic or comprehensive user- or program-driven Registry edits.

❑ As part of your normal system maintenance and administration, you should create copies of the Registry. Backing up the Registry often is the only way to ensure you have a functional Registry to restore in the event of a failure.

KEY TERMS

12

Binary — A Registry value entry data type that stores data in binary format.

DWORD — A Registry value entry data type that stores data in binary, hexadecimal, or decimal format.

data type — The setting on a Registry value entry that defines the data format of the stored information.

Expandable String — A Registry value entry data type that stores data in expandable text-string format containing a variable that is replaced by an application when used (for example, %*systemroot*%\File.exe).

flush — Forcing the memory-resident copy of the Registry to be written to files stored on the hard drive. A flush occurs at shutdown, when forced by an application, or just after a Registry alteration.

hive — A discrete body of Registry keys, subkeys, and values stored in a file.

HKEY_CLASSES_ROOT — This Registry key contains the value entries that control the relationships between file extensions (and therefore file format types) and applications. This key also supports the data used in object linking and embedding (OLE), COM object data, and file-class association data. This key actually points to another Registry subkey named HKEY_LOCAL_MACHINE\SOFTWARE\Classes and provides multiple points of access to make itself easily accessible to the operating system itself and to applications that need access to the compatibility information already mentioned.

HKEY_CURRENT_CONFIG — This Registry key contains the value entries that control the currently active hardware profile; its contents are built each time the system is started. This key is derived from data stored in the HKEY_LOCAL_MACHINE\SYSTEM\CurrentControlSet\HardwareProfiles\Current subkey. HKEY_CURRENT_CONFIG exists to provide backward-compatibility with Windows 95/98 applications.

HKEY_CURRENT_USER — This Registry key contains the value entries that define the user environment for the currently logged-on user. This key is built each time a user logs on to the system. The data in this key are derived from the HKEY_USERS key and the Ntuser.dat and Ntuser.man files of a user's profile.

HKEY_LOCAL_MACHINE —This Registry key contains the value entries that control the local computer. This includes hardware devices, device drivers, and various operating system components. The data stored in this key are not dependent on a logged-on user or the applications or processes in use.

HKEY_USERS — This Registry key contains the value entries that define the user environments for all users who have ever logged on to this computer. As a new user logs on to this system, a new subkey is added for that user that is built either from the default profile stored in this key or from the roaming user profile associated with the domain user account.

key — A top-level division of the Registry. There are five keys in a Windows XP Registry. A key can contain subkeys.

Last Known Good Configuration (LKGC) — The state of the Registry stored in one of the control sets when the last successful user logon was performed. If the Registry is damaged in a way that it will not fully start or will not allow a user to log on, the LKGC option can restore the system to a previous state. Keep in mind that any changes made to the system between the time the LKGC was stored and its use to restore the system will be lost.

Multiple String — A Registry value entry data type that stores data in text-string format containing multiple human-readable values separated by null characters.

Reg.exe — A special command-line utility that users, programs, or the operating system can use to access, inspect, create, or modify Registry keys.

Regedit — The 16-bit Registry editor. Regedit offers global searching and combines all of the keys into a single display. It can be used to perform searches, add new subkeys and value entries, alter the data in value entries, and import and export keys and subkeys.

Registry — The hierarchical database of system configuration data essential to the health and operation of a Windows XP system.

Security Accounts Manager (SAM) — The database of user accounts, group memberships, and security-related settings.

String — A Registry value entry data type that stores data in text-string format.

subkey — A division of a Registry key, such as HKEY_LOCAL_MACHINE. A subkey can contain other subkeys and value entries.

transaction log — A file created by Windows XP to record Registry changes. These files, with a .log extension, are used to verify that changes to the Registry are made successfully.

value — The actual data stored by a value entry.

value entry — A named Registry variable that stores a specific value or data string. A Registry value entry's name is typically a multiword phrase without spaces and with title capitalization.

REVIEW QUESTIONS

1. The Registry is the primary mechanism for storing data about Windows XP. Which of the following are configuration files used by other Microsoft operating systems and may still exist on Windows XP for backward compatibility? (Choose all that apply.)

   a. Win.ini

   b. Autoexec.bat

   c. System.ini

   d. Config.sys

2. The Registry is only used to store configuration data for native Windows XP applications, services, and drivers. True or False?

3. Which of the following tools is most highly recommended by Microsoft for editing the Registry? (Choose all that apply.)

   a. Control Panel applets

   b. Regedit

   c. Reg.exe

   d. Administrative Tools

4. The Registry is an exhaustive collection of system control parameters. True or False?

5. When editing the Registry, especially when attempting to alter the unseen defaults, which of the following pieces of information are important? (Choose all that apply.)

   a. syntax

   b. spelling

   c. subkey location

   d. valid values

   e. time zone

6. Changes made to the Registry never go into effect until the system is restarted. True or False?

7. The Windows XP Professional Registry has how many default keys?

   a. 2

   b. 4

   c. 5

   d. 6

12

8. Which of the following can host subkeys or values?

    a. data type

    b. key

    c. subkey

    d. value data

9. Each of the highest-level keys of the Registry are stored in a distinct file on the hard drive. True or False?

10. Which Registry key contains the value entries that control the local computer?

    a. HKEY_LOCAL_MACHINE

    b. HKEY_CLASSES_ROOT

    c. HKEY_CURRENT_CONFIG

    d. HKEY_USERS

11. Which Registry key contains the value entries that define the user environment for the currently logged-on user?

    a. HKEY_LOCAL_MACHINE

    b. HKEY_CLASSES_ROOT

    c. HKEY_CURRENT_CONFIG

    d. HKEY_CURRENT_USER

12. Which Registry key contains the value entries that control the relationships between file extensions (and therefore file format types) and applications?

    a. HKEY_LOCAL_MACHINE

    b. HKEY_CLASSES_ROOT

    c. HKEY_CURRENT_CONFIG

    d. HKEY_USERS

13. Which Registry key contains the value entries that control the currently active hardware profile?

    a. HKEY_LOCAL_MACHINE

    b. HKEY_CLASSES_ROOT

    c. HKEY_CURRENT_CONFIG

    d. HKEY_CURRENT_USER

14. From which key can you delete subkeys using the System applet?

    a. HKEY_LOCAL_MACHINE

    b. HKEY_CLASSES_ROOT

    c. HKEY_CURRENT_CONFIG

    d. HKEY_USERS

15. Some Windows 95 or 98 applications require a sixth Registry key. Windows XP adds the _____ key, which is actually a redirector rather than an actual key, to maintain backward compatibility.

16. After you've created a value entry, you can easily change its data type by using the Edit dialog box. True or False?

17. The value entry data type that can store binary-, hexadecimal-, or decimal-formatted data is:

    a. String

    b. DWORD

    c. Multiple String

    d. Expandable String

18. Where are the files used to load the Registry at bootup stored on a Windows XP system?

    a. %systemroot%\config

    b. %systemroot%\system32\config

    c. %systemroot%\system\config

    d. %systemroot%\system32\repair

19. Which subkey of HKEY_LOCAL_MACHINE is the only subkey to have a backup file?

    a. SAM

    b. SOFTWARE

    c. SYSTEM

    d. SECURITY

20. The process of pushing Registry changes from memory to a hard drive file is known as _____ .

21. Which type of file (specified by file extension) does Windows XP use to record the changes to the Registry for verification purposes?

    a. .alt

    b. .sav

    c. .dat

    d. .log

12

22. Assume that your system is performing an update to the SYSTEM subkey. While altering the system file, before working on the System.alt file, a system crash occurs. When the system restarts, which of the following occurs?

    a. You'll be prompted whether to use the system or System.alt set of configuration parameters.

    b. The state of the Registry before changes to the SYSTEM subkey is restored.

    c. The state of the Registry after changes to the SYSTEM subkey is restored.

    d. The system fails to boot because of a corrupt SYSTEM subkey.

23. Which subkey usually cannot be edited with a Registry editor?

    a. HARDWARE

    b. SOFTWARE

    c. SAM

    d. CurrentControlSet

24. Which control set subkey is the container for data related to controlling system startup, boot parameters, computer name, and necessary subsystems to initiate?

    a. Control

    b. Enum

    c. Hardware Profiles

    d. Services

25. Which subkey of HKEY_LOCAL_MACHINE\SYSTEM\Select indicates the control set that was last used to boot and successfully log on a user?

    a. Default

    b. Current

    c. LastKnownGood

    d. Failed

CASE PROJECTS

Case Project 12-1

Describe the actions that you can perform manually or that are performed automatically to provide protection or fault-tolerance mechanisms for the Windows XP Registry.

Case Project 12-2

You have been asked to perform several Registry modifications to fine-tune an application. You'll be following detailed instructions from the vendor. What steps can you take to ensure that even if the vendor's instructions fail, you'll be able to return to a functioning Windows XP system?

CHAPTER

13

BOOTING WINDOWS XP

After reading this chapter and completing the exercises, you will be able to:

♦ Understand the Windows XP boot process

♦ Work with the Windows XP boot phase

♦ Understand troubleshooting and advanced startup options

♦ Understand boot configuration and selecting an operating system

♦ Edit the Boot.ini file

♦ Understand the XP load phase

♦ Understand multiple-boot systems

On the surface, booting a computer might seem simple. But in reality, it is a complex process. In fact, it is critically important to your success as an IT professional to understand each step of the process by which an inert hunk of metal becomes a computer running Windows XP. This understanding is essential for the Microsoft certification exam, and for troubleshooting a system that won't boot properly.

In this chapter, you learn the steps that Windows XP takes to successfully complete a boot process. The process begins with the initial operation of the hardware, as it finds pointers to the software that ultimately lead to the choice of which operating system to run (and as it goes through the process of loading and starting Windows XP). The process culminates when the logon dialog box appears. It is only at this point that the Windows XP boot process is considered to be complete. All computers, whether hosting Windows XP or another operating system, go through a similar boot process when they are turned on. This chapter includes discussion of this process, troubleshooting boot problems, using advanced startup options, managing booting, and working with multiple operating systems on the same computer.

WINDOWS XP BOOT PHASE

In Windows XP, the **boot process** is broken down into two major phases: the boot phase and the load phase. The **boot phase** takes place when the computer is first powered on, and when you choose Restart from the Turn Off Computer dialog box. This dialog box appears when you select Turn Off Computer from the Start menu. As soon as the boot phase is completed and a configuration is selected, the **load phase** begins.

The six steps of the Windows XP boot phase are as follows:

1. Power-on self test (POST)
2. Initial startup
3. Boot loader
4. Selecting the operating system
5. Detecting hardware
6. Selecting a configuration

Power-on Self Test

The **power-on self test (POST)** is the first step in the boot sequence for any computer with an operating system. The POST determines the amount of real memory that exists, and whether or not all necessary hardware components, such as a keyboard, are present. The actual tests can differ, depending on how the **BIOS (Basic Input/Output System)** is configured. If the tests are successful, the computer boots itself. If the tests are unsuccessful, the computer reports the error by emitting a series of beeps and possibly displaying an error message and code on the screen. The number of beeps indicates the error; however, the number of beeps differs from one BIOS to another. The software for the POST resides in a special, battery-powered chip called the **CMOS (complementary metal oxide semiconductor)**. This chip can store not only the software necessary to conduct the POST, but also basic configuration information that the POST uses to check the amount of RAM installed in a system, along with other key information. Figure 13-1 shows a typical screen that results from the successful completion of the POST on an Intel PC.

After the system POST is completed, each adapter card in the system performs its own self-test. For example, if a computer has a SCSI card installed in addition to its own built-in adapter cards, it checks its internal configuration and any related devices it sees when it runs its own POST. At the same time, a report on what it finds during this process appears on the computer monitor in text-only form (because there is no real operating system running at this point, screen output at this stage of the boot process is kept as simple and direct as possible). The screen shown in Figure 13-2 adds the report from an Adaptec 2940 SCSI controller to the information already supplied by the POST routine.

```
American Megatrends
AMIBIOS (c) 1995. American Megatrends Inc.,
TAC960209B

65152KB OK

Wait..
Primary Master HDD: P0IRA74B IBM-DJAA-3170
Secondary Master HDD: 07-07-01 ST32140A




(C) American Megatrends Inc.,
51-0000-001223-00111111-101094-INTEL-FX-F
```

Figure 13-1   The POST display on a PC

```
American Megatrends
AMIBIOS (c) 1995. American Megatrends Inc.,
TAC960209B

65152KB OK

Wait..
Primary Master HDD: P0IRA74B IBM-DJAA-3170
Secondary Master HDD: 07-07-01 ST32140A

Adaptec AHA-2940 BIOS v1.11
(c) 1994 Adaptec. All Rights Reserved.

>>> Press <CTRL><A> for SCSISelect(tm) utility <<<


(C) American Megatrends Inc.,
51-0000-001223-00111111-101094-INTEL-FX-F
```

Figure 13-2   Output from the BIOS on an Adaptec 2940 SCSI controller

Initial Startup

The initial startup sequence involves numerous files and initialization procedures. The first sector of the hard disk contains the Master Boot Record (MBR) and the partition table. The **Master Boot Record (MBR)** begins the boot process by looking up the partition table to determine which partition to use for booting. If you are booting from a floppy disk, the first sector contains the **partition boot sector**.

Table 13-1 outlines the startup files for Windows XP on x86 computers.

Table 13-1   Windows XP startup files

Filename	Location	Explanation
Ntldr	Root of startup disk	Windows XP boot loader for PC machines
Boot.ini	Root of startup disk	Windows XP PC boot menu information
Bootsect.dos	Root of startup disk	DOS boot information for dual-boot PCs
Ntdetect.com	Root of startup disk	Windows XP hardware detection program
Ntbootdd.sys	Root of startup disk	Lets Windows XP access SCSI drives on PCs with SCSI controller with onboard BIOS disabled
Ntoskrnl.exe	%systemroot%\System32	Windows XP operating system kernel
Hal.dll	%systemroot%\System32	Hardware abstraction layer code (CPU driver for x86 chips)
SYSTEM key	%systemroot%\System32	Key Windows XP Registry data
Device drivers	%systemroot%\System32	PC-specific device drivers for Windows XP use

When the POST has successfully concluded, the BIOS tries to locate the startup disk. The BIOS represents a chip-based set of routines that DOS and Windows 95/98 use to drive all system input and output, including access to peripheral devices. Windows XP, on the other hand, uses its own built-in input/output logic and drivers, and ignores whatever BIOS is installed in a computer. By doing this, Windows XP is able to manage I/O more carefully than earlier Windows and DOS operating systems. It also helps to explain why applications that attempt to access drivers or the computer's BIOS or hardware directly are treated as ill behaved in the Windows XP environment.

If a floppy disk is in drive A when the BIOS checks that drive, it might use that drive as the startup disk (this decision depends on how the boot sequence has been configured in the PC's CMOS). If there is no floppy disk in that drive, or if the CMOS has been configured to boot from a hard disk, it uses the first hard disk it finds as the boot disk. Of course, if drive A is enabled for booting, and the floppy disk you have inserted in that drive does not have a partition boot sector, you get a "Non-system disk or disk error: Replace and press any key when ready" message, and the system won't start. This is one of the most common causes of boot failure in the Windows XP environment.

NOTE   If you get the "Non-system disk or disk error" message because the system attempted to boot from a non-system floppy, remove the floppy and cycle the power off and on again. It is important to do this (rather than restarting with Ctrl+Alt+Delete) to avoid transferring boot-sector viruses to the computer.

When the BIOS uses the hard disk as its startup disk, it reads the MBR and loads that into memory. The BIOS then transfers system control to the MBR. The MBR scans the partition table to locate the system partition. When the MBR locates the system partition, it loads sector 0 of the partition into memory, and executes it. Sector 0 (zero) can contain a diagnostic program, a utility such as a virus scanner, or a partition boot sector that contains the startup code for the operating system. If the computer boots from a floppy, only the partition boot sector is used.

In general, the MBR is independent of the operating system. For example, the same MBR is used in *x*86 systems to boot to Windows 95, 98, MS-DOS, Windows 2000, Windows Server 2003, Windows NT, Windows XP, and Windows 3.*x*.

The partition boot sector is completely dependent on the operating system and file system in use. For example, the partition boot sector in a Windows XP computer is responsible for a number of functions that are specific to the operating system. The partition boot sector must understand enough of the file system in use to find **Ntldr** (the program that locates and loads the Windows XP operating system files in the root folder). On a hard drive with a FAT partition, the partition boot sector is generally one sector long, and points to another location on the disk that ultimately permits the computer to find and launch Ntldr. On an NTFS partition, because the partition boot sector can be as many as 16 sectors long, it can contain all the necessary file system code needed to locate and launch Ntldr, without requiring transfer of control to another area on the disk. Thus, the partition boot sector is responsible for loading a boot loader (Ntldr) into memory and initiating boot loader execution.

At this point, the **system partition**, the partition that contains the MBR and partition boot sector, must be on the first physical hard drive in the system. However, the **boot partition**—the partition that contains the Windows XP files—can be on the same partition, a different partition on the same drive, or on another drive entirely within the local computer. In other words, you boot Windows XP from the system partition, and run the operating system from the boot partition.

 This terminology seems counterintuitive, but is important to remember for Microsoft exams. One way to keep the terms straight is that the files needed to choose the operating system (Ntldr, Bootsect.dos, and so on) are located on the system partition and the files for booting the chosen operating system (Windows NT, Windows XP, and so on) are on the boot partition.

Boot Loader

The boot loader is the collection of files on the system partition that is used to initiate the loading of the operating system. The boot loader will display a boot menu if more than one OS is present or if an advanced boot option is needed. Once an OS or boot option is selected, it commences the loading of the specific operating system from the boot partition. On PCs, once the boot OS is selected from the Boot.ini menu, Ntldr controls the operating system selection and hardware detection processes before the Windows XP kernel is initialized.

Ntldr, Boot.ini, Bootsect.dos, Ntdetect.com, and Ntbootdd.sys may all be present in the root directory of the startup disk (also known as the system partition; see Figure 13-3). Some files might be dimmed because they have the read-only attribute. The partition hosting the boot loader can be formatted with FAT, FAT32, or NTFS. Of this collection of files, Ntldr,

Ntdetect.com, and Boot.ini must always be present for Windows XP to boot (the other two are optional, and depend on the configuration of the particular machine in use).

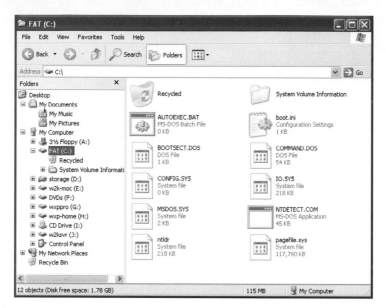

Figure 13-3   The system partition on a typical Windows XP system

 The Folder Options applet must be configured to show all hidden and system files; otherwise, most of these boot files will not be shown.

 Bootsect.dos appears only if the machine has been configured to dual-boot between Windows XP/ 2003/2000/NT and DOS, Windows 3.*x*, or Windows 9*x*. Ntbootdd.sys appears only when a SCSI controller has its built-in BIOS controller disabled; this file supplies the necessary controller driver that the hardware would otherwise provide.

At this point, Ntldr switches the processor into 32-bit flat memory mode. When an *x*86 computer starts, it is running in real mode, which means it is functioning as an old-fashioned 8088 or 8086 computer. Because Ntldr is a 32-bit program, it must change the processing mode to support the 32-bit flat memory model it uses before it can perform any further processing.

Next, Ntldr starts the appropriate file system. The code to access both FAT and NTFS file systems is programmed into Ntldr so that it can read, access, and copy files on either type of file system.

Selecting the Operating System

Ntldr reads the Boot.ini file and displays the operating system selections it contains. The screen that appears at this point is usually called the boot loader screen or the **boot selection menu**, and represents the point at which users can select which operating system they want to load (or which form of Windows XP graphics operation they want to use).

A typical boot selection menu appears in Figure 13-4. Notice the prompt to access troubleshooting and advanced startup options by pressing F8. These options are discussed in the Troubleshooting and Advanced Startup Options section of this chapter.

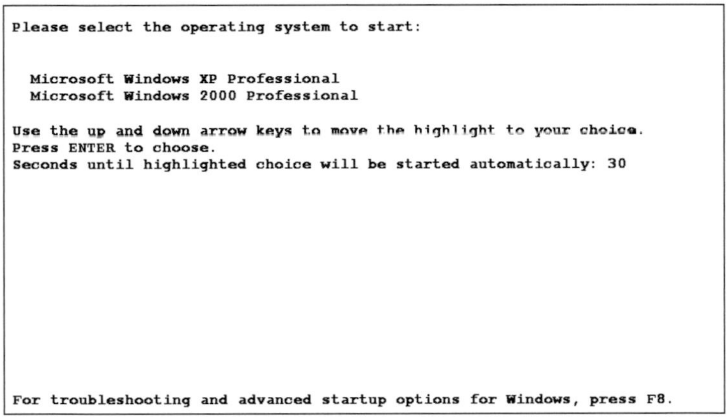

```
Please select the operating system to start:

  Microsoft Windows XP Professional
  Microsoft Windows 2000 Professional

Use the up and down arrow keys to move the highlight to your choice.
Press ENTER to choose.
Seconds until highlighted choice will be started automatically: 30




For troubleshooting and advanced startup options for Windows, press F8.
```

Figure 13-4   A typical Windows XP boot selection menu

Notice on this particular system, Windows XP Professional is present with Windows 2000 Professional. In fact, Windows XP can coexist with numerous other operating systems, including those that depend on DOS for their underpinnings.

When you do not manually alter the highlighted selection of the boot menu, a line below the menu displays a counter: "Seconds until highlighted choice will be started automatically: 30." If a selection is not made before the counter reaches zero, the highlighted operating system starts automatically. To change the default operating system to load or the amount of time to wait before automatically loading the highlighted operating system, change the settings in the Boot.ini file, which is discussed in greater detail in the Editing Boot.ini section in this chapter. In addition, pressing the up arrow or down arrow key halts the timer.

If the user selects an operating system other than Windows XP or Windows NT, the boot loader loads Bootsect.dos and hands over control of the system. The other operating system then starts normally because Bootsect.dos contains the partition boot sector for that operating system. However, if the user selects a version of Windows XP, the boot loader executes Ntdetect.com to gather hardware information.

The remaining functions of Ntldr (operating system selection, hardware detection, and configuration selection) are discussed later in this section. For now, note that Ntldr maintains control of the computer until it loads Ntoskrnl.exe and passes the hardware information and system control to that program.

Detecting Hardware

Ntdetect.com is executed by the boot loader and is used to collect a list of hardware currently installed in the computer. Ntdetect checks the computer ID, bus/adapter type, video, keyboard, communication ports, parallel ports, floppy disks, and mouse or pointing devices. Ntdetect creates a system profile that is later compared to Windows XP Registry entries that describe the system so that the operating system can look for discrepancies or potential problems.

Selecting a Configuration

Once hardware is detected, the system needs to select a system configuration, otherwise known as a hardware profile. If a single hardware profile is defined, this is the one that is used. If two or more hardware profiles are present, the system attempts to select a profile based on detected hardware. If the system cannot make an automatic selection, you are prompted to manually select a hardware profile.

TROUBLESHOOTING AND ADVANCED STARTUP OPTIONS

Windows XP has combined the boot and recovery options of Windows NT and Windows 95/98. The result is a more robust operating system and additional options to restore a malfunctioning system to a functional state. To access the additional startup options, when the boot menu appears, press F8 before the timer expires. Once F8 is pressed, the Windows Advanced Options Menu appears (see Figure 13-5).

```
Windows Advanced Options Menu
Please select an option:

   Safe Mode
   Safe Mode with Networking
   Safe Mode with Command Prompt

   Enable Boot Logging
   Enable VGA Mode
   Last Known Good Configuration (your most recent settings that worked)
   Directory Services Restore Mode (Windows domain controllers only)
   Debugging Mode

   Start Windows Normally
   Reboot
   Return to OS Choices Menu

Use the up and down arrow keys to move the highlight to your choice.
```

Figure 13-5   The Windows Advances Options menu

The contents of this menu are somewhat dependent on installed components, such as the Remote Installation Service, but it typically contains the following items:

- *Safe Mode*—Boots Windows XP with only the minimum required system files and device drivers. Safe Mode does not load networking components.

- *Safe Mode with Networking*—Boots Windows XP in the same manner as Safe Mode, but adds networking components

- *Safe Mode with Command Prompt*—Boots Windows XP in the same manner as Safe Mode, but boots to a command prompt instead of to the GUI environment

- *Enable Boot Logging*—Enables or disables the boot process and writes details to a log file regarding drivers and services. The log file is located at *%systemroot%* Ntbtlog.txt.

- *Enable VGA Mode*—Boots Windows XP normally, but uses only the basic VGA video driver

- *Last Known Good Configuration*—Boots Windows XP with the **Last Known Good Configuration (LKGC)**, the state of the Registry as it was recorded during the last successful user logon. After each successful boot sequence, Windows XP makes a copy of the current combination of driver and system settings and stores it as the Last Known Good Configuration.

- *Directory Services Restore Mode*—(Valid only on Windows XP domain controllers) Boots Windows XP and restores Active Directory

- *Debugging Mode*—Boots Windows XP normally, but sends debugging information to another system over a serial cable. Details about using this option are included in the *Microsoft Windows XP Professional Resource Kit.*

Advanced Options for booting can be used to recover from a wide variety of system problems or failures. Safe Mode offers the ability to boot into a functioning system even when specific drivers are corrupted or failing. This includes bypassing bad video drivers, network drivers, and GUI controls by booting into Enable VGA Mode, Safe Mode (without networking support), and/or Safe Mode with Command Prompt, respectively. In most cases, this allows you to replace or remove the problematic driver before rebooting back into Normal Mode.

NOTE

If a problem is occurring and you are unable to discern its exact cause or nature, you might want to choose Enable Boot Logging from the Advanced Options Menu to record the process of steps performed between the boot menu and the logon prompt. The resultant file, *%systemroot%*\Ntbtlog.txt, can provide clues as to the driver, system, or procedure that is causing the system malfunction.

13

If you've recently installed a driver or entire software product, or just modified the Registry, and the result is a system that does not fully boot, the Last Known Good Configuration is a great first step in returning the system to a functional state. The LKGC returns the system to the state of the Registry at the time of the last successful logon.

Activity 13-1: Safe Mode Booting

Time Required: 10 minutes

Objective: Use the Windows Advanced Options Menu to boot the computer with minimal drivers loaded.

Description: A computer that won't boot can be extremely frustrating for both the user and the support person. To see if the problem is a corrupt, missing, or incorrect driver, it is useful to try booting with only the essential drivers being loaded. In this activity, you reboot your computer using Safe Mode so that only those drivers that are required are loaded.

To reboot Windows XP into Safe Mode:

1. Restart Windows XP by selecting **Start**, **Turn Off Computer** (or **Shut Down**). Select **Restart**. Click **OK** (assuming Classic logon mode).

2. As Windows XP reboots, watch for the boot selection menu. As soon as it appears, press **F8**. This reveals the Windows Advanced Options Menu. (Refer to Figure 13-5.)

3. Use the arrow keys on the keyboard to select **Safe Mode** from the list of options. This is usually selected by default.

4. Press **Enter**, and allow the boot process to continue to completion. If dual-boot, you may have to select your OS, then log in.

5. Your system boots with minimal drivers and without network support. Click **Yes** to clear any warning, if necessary.

6. Repeat Step 1, and allow your machine to reboot normally.

Activity 13-2: Boot with Minimal Video

Time Required: 15 minutes

Objective: Use VGA Mode to boot the computer when video problems occur.

Description: Even if the wrong video driver is installed or the incorrect resolution is chosen, VGA Mode allows you to install the proper driver or modify the resolution. In this activity, you boot your computer in VGA Mode.

To reboot Windows XP with minimal VGA support:

This boot method should be used when a bad video driver is present or incorrect resolution has been set.

1. Restart Windows XP by selecting **Start**, **Turn Off Computer** (or **Shut Down**). Select **Restart**. Click **OK** (assuming Classic logon mode).

2. As Windows XP reboots, watch for the boot selection menu. As soon as it appears, press **F8**. This reveals the Windows Advanced Options Menu (refer to Figure 13-5).

3. Use the arrow keys on the keyboard to select **Enable VGA Mode** from the list of options.

4. Press **Enter**, and allow the boot process to continue to completion. If dual-boot, you may have to select your OS, then log in.

5. Your system boots normally, but uses the standard VGA video drivers at 640 × 480 with a color depth of 16 or 256 (depending on your video card). This allows you to correct your display resolution or replace the bad video driver.

Activity 13-3: Boot in Safe Mode with Networking

13

Time Required: 15 minutes

Objective: Use the Windows Advanced Options Menu to boot the computer with minimal drivers and network support loaded.

Description: Being able to boot your computer with minimal drivers can help you find where a problem lies on a computer. However, most network administrators keep the drivers and install files on a network server. To simplify getting the files loaded onto the computer, it is useful to load network drivers as well. In this activity, you boot in Safe Mode with Network Support.

To reboot Windows XP into Safe Mode with Networking:

1. Restart Windows XP by clicking **Start**, **Turn Off Computer** (or **Shut Down**). Select **Restart**. Click **OK** (assuming Classic logon mode).

2. As Windows XP reboots, watch for the boot selection menu. As soon as it appears, press **F8**. This reveals the Windows Advanced Options Menu (refer to Figure 13-5).

3. Use the arrow keys on the keyboard to select **Safe Mode with Networking** from the list of options.

4. Press **Enter**, and allow the boot process to continue to completion. If dual-boot, you may have to select your OS, then log in.

5. Your system boots with minimal drivers but includes network support. This boot method is useful when attempting to troubleshoot a system that requires network access to tools, data files, or traffic. Click **Yes** to clear any warning, if necessary.

If none of these options provides you with a method to restore your system, you do have one final option from the Windows Advanced Options Menu, namely Debugging Mode. This mode is used in conjunction with a second computer connected by a serial cable. Debugging Mode causes the boot process to send detailed information on activities to the companion system. This information can be used to determine at what point in the boot process problems are occurring. The information created by Debugging Mode is rather complex and is typically used only by high-end programmers. If you want more details on the Debugging Mode process and how to interpret the extracted data, consult the Microsoft Windows XP Professional Resource Kit.

BOOT CONFIGURATION AND SELECTING AN OPERATING SYSTEM

The Windows XP boot configuration can be controlled through its configuration file, Boot.ini. As previously mentioned, Boot.ini is located in the root directory of the system partition and is used by the boot loader to display the list of available operating systems. This file consists of two sections: [boot loader] and [operating systems]. A typical Boot.ini file is shown in Figure 13-6.

The following sections discuss [boot loader] and [operating systems] and also discuss a related topic: advanced RISC computing pathnames.

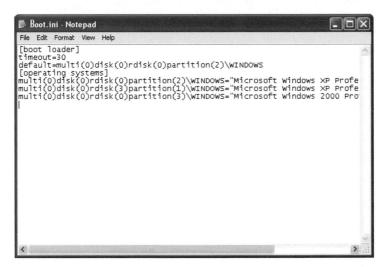

Figure 13-6   Boot.ini viewed through Notepad

[boot loader]

The [boot loader] section of the Boot.ini file contains two items: timeout and default. The timeout setting defines the number of seconds the system waits for the user to select an operating system before loading the default operating system. If timeout is set to zero, Ntldr immediately loads the default operating system without displaying the boot loader screen. To cause the system to wait indefinitely for a selection, set the timeout to –1. This setting, however, can only be altered by using a text editor, because it is an illegal value for the setting from the System applet in Control Panel. (See the Editing Boot.ini section later in this chapter. It explains how to edit this file and what kind of text editor to use.) The default setting in Boot.ini lists the path to the default operating system.

[operating systems]

The [operating systems] section of Boot.ini lists the available operating systems. Each listing contains the path to the boot partition for the operating system, the text displayed in the boot loader screen, and optional parameters. The text is clipped in the screen capture in Figure 13-6, but here's what it looks like in its entirety:

```
multi(0)disk(0)rdisk(0)partition(2)\WINDOWS="Microsoft
Windows XP Professional"
/fastdetect
multi(0)disk(0)rdisk(3)partition(1)\WINDOWS="Microsoft
Windows XP Professional" /fastdetect
multi(0)disk(0)rdisk(0)partition(3)\WINDOWS="Windows 2000
Professional"
```

The following list details some of the switches that can be added to the end of entries in the [operating systems] section of Boot.ini. In most cases, you want to employ the F8 Windows Advanced Options Menu (see the description earlier in this chapter) to access troubleshooting boot methods. However, you can employ the following switches and switch combinations to mimic the Windows Advanced Options Menu selections in your Boot.ini file:

- */BASEVIDEO*—Starts Windows XP in standard VGA mode (640 × 480) with 16 colors

- */BAUDRATE=n*—Sets the baud rate for the serial connection used in kernel debugging (the default is 9600; a setting of up to 115,200 can be used)

- */BOOTLOG*—Enables boot logging

- */CRASHDEBUG*—Loads the kernel debugger but remains inactive until a STOP error occurs

- */DEBUG*—Loads the debugger and allows access by a host debugger connected to the computer

- */DEBUGPORT={com1 | com2 | 1394}*—Sets the port for debugging

- */FASTDETECT={com1 | com2 | ...}*—Specifies a serial port to skip during bootup hardware scanning; if no com port is specified, all ports are skipped. This switch is included in every entry in the BOOT.INI file by default.

- */MAXMEM=n*—Sets the maximum amount of RAM the OS can consume

13

- */NOGUIBOOT*—Boots without showing the splash screen; does not determine whether Windows XP GUI environment or command prompt is booted

- */NODEBUG*—Disables the debugger

- */NUMPROC=n*—Sets the number of processors on a multiprocessor system the OS is allowed to use

- */SAFEBOOT:MINIMAL*—Boots into Safe Mode

- */SAFEBOOT:NETWORK*—Boots into Safe Mode with Networking

- */SAFEBOOT:MINIMAL(ALTERNATESHELL)*—Boots into Safe Mode with Command Prompt

- */SOS*—Displays the device driver names when they are loaded

 The switches used in the Boot.ini file are not case sensitive.

Advanced RISC Computing Pathnames

In the Boot.ini file, the path pointing to the \windows directory is written using the **Advanced RISC Computing (ARC) pathname** naming conventions. These pathnames are as follows:

- *scsi(n) or multi(n)*—This portion of the path indicates the type of device on which the operating system resides. *scsi* is used if the operating system is on a SCSI hard disk that is connected to a SCSI adapter that has a disabled built-in BIOS. *multi* is used for other hard disks, including IDE, EIDE, and SCSI with a built-in BIOS. The *(n)* indicates the hardware adapter from which to boot. It is replaced with a number corresponding to the correct hardware adapter, numbered ordinally (starting with zero).

- *disk(n)*—This portion of the path indicates which SCSI bus number should be used. The *(n)* always equals zero when the adapter is a multiadapter (that is, the ARC path starts with multi(*n*)); otherwise, it is numbered ordinally.

- *rdisk(n)*—This portion of the path indicates the SCSI LUN number or selects which of the hard disks attached to the adapter contains the operating system. *(n)* always equals zero when the adapter is SCSI; otherwise, it is numbered ordinally.

- *partition(n)*—This portion of the path selects the disk partition that contains the operating system files. Partition is numbered cardinally (starting with 1).

- *\path*—The final portion of the path indicates the directory on the partition in which the operating system files are found. The default path for Windows XP is \WINDOWS.

EDITING BOOT.INI

To make changes to a Boot.ini file, the user has two options: use Control Panel to edit this file indirectly, or use a text editor to change the file directly.

Using Control Panel

Using Control Panel to make changes to Boot.ini is the safest way to proceed. By opening the System applet in Control Panel (Classic View), selecting the Advanced tab, and then clicking the Settings button in the Startup and Recovery section (see Figure 13-7), you can make certain changes to your setup. The Startup and Recovery dialog box (shown in Figure 13-8) allows you to choose a default boot selection and to select a delay interval before the boot selection starts automatically. This delay time corresponds to the timeout value set in Boot.ini. These options are depicted in the System startup section in the Startup and Recovery dialog box. Notice also that the options that control debugging output for system failures appear in this dialog box as well; this information often comes in handy when severe problems occur.

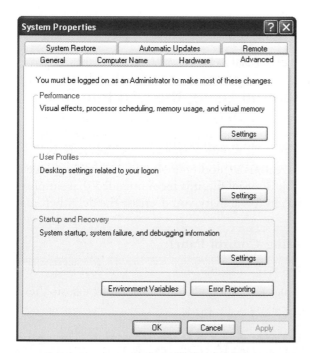

Figure 13-7 The Advanced tab of the System applet

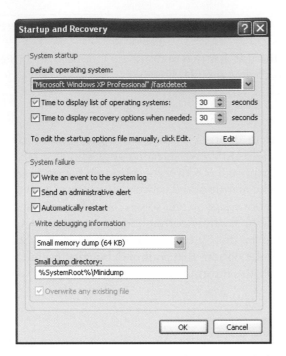

Figure 13-8   The Startup and Recovery dialog box

ACTIVITY

Activity 13-4: Modify Boot.ini Using the GUI Interface

Time Required: 15 minutes

Objective: Use the advanced System settings to modify the boot process (Boot.ini).

Description: There may be many reasons to modify the boot process. To reduce the chance of incorrectly typing an entry in the Boot.ini file, it is recommended that simple changes be performed using the GUI interface. In this activity, you decrease the delay before the default operating system is started.

To modify the Boot.ini file using Control Panel:

1. Click **Start**, **Control Panel**.

2. Double-click the **System** applet (assuming Control Panel is in Classic View).

3. Select the **Advanced** tab (refer to Figure 13-7).

4. Click the **Settings** button in the Startup and Recovery section. This reveals the Startup and Recovery dialog box (refer to Figure 13-8).

5. Notice that the System startup section defines the default operating system for the computer. Select another operating system from the drop-down list.

6. To modify the amount of time the list appears when the system is booted, change the Time to display list of operating systems option. Change this setting to **10** seconds by clicking the down arrow beside the field.

7. The remaining options define the action for the kernel to take when a STOP error occurs. In most situations, these should not be changed.

8. To save the configuration to Boot.ini, click **OK**. Click **OK** again to close the System Properties dialog box.

9. To see the effect of the changes you made, restart the computer.

Using a Text Editor

You can use Notepad or any other text editor to edit Boot.ini. As with any initialization file, you should be careful when editing the file. If you configure the file incorrectly, Windows XP might not boot. You should always create a backup copy of the file and name it Boot.bak before you make any changes.

ACTIVITY

Activity 13-5: Modify Boot.ini Manually

Time Required: 15 minutes

Objective: Manually modify the Boot.ini file using a text editor.

Description: In the previous activity, you learned that there are settings that can be modified using a GUI interface. However, there may be instances in which the option the person wants to implement is not one of the options displayed. In those cases, the Boot.ini file needs to be modified manually. In this activity, you use a text editor to set the default timeout back to the original setting.

To change the Boot.ini settings using a text editor:

1. To view Boot.ini, open Windows Explorer and select **Tools**, **Folder options**, and select the **View** tab. Select the **Show hidden files and folders** option button and deselect the **Hide extensions for known file types** and **Hide protected operating system files (Recommended)**. Click **Yes** on the confirmation dialog box that appears. Click **OK** to save these changes and close the Folder Options dialog box.

2. First create a backup copy of the Boot.ini file: in **Windows Explorer** select the root of drive C in the left pane. Right-click the **Boot.ini** entry, select the **Copy** option, click the current drive, and then press **Ctrl+V** (paste). This creates a file named "Copy of boot.ini" in that directory. Rename the file to **Boot.bak**. Click **Yes** in the confirmation dialog box that appears. This information can come in handy in case something goes wrong later.

3. Open the **Boot.ini** file in Notepad by selecting **Start**, **Run**, typing **notepad c:\boot.ini** in the text box provided, and then clicking **OK**. Notepad opens with the Boot.ini file displayed (refer to Figure 13-6).

13

4. Restore the timeout to 30 seconds by changing the timeout= value to **30**.

5. Save the file by selecting **File**, **Save**.

6. Exit Notepad by selecting **File**, **Exit**.

7. Reboot the computer to deploy your changes.

WINDOWS XP LOAD PHASE

The Windows XP load phase begins when the kernel assumes control of the machine. It consists of the following five stages:

- Loading the kernel
- Initializing the kernel
- Services load
- Windows XP system startup
- Logging on

Loading the Kernel

Once you've selected the option to boot into Windows XP, a brief "Starting Windows..." text message is displayed before the full Windows XP splash screen is shown. While you are "entertained" by the image, the boot loader loads the Windows XP kernel (Ntoskrnl.exe) and the hardware abstraction layer (HAL; file Hal.dll) into memory. However, these programs are not executed at this time. Before executing the programs, the boot loader loads the Registry key HKEY_LOCAL_MACHINE\ SYSTEM from the *%systemroot%* system32\Config\ directory.

At this point, the boot loader retrieves the configuration you selected from the Registry subkey HKEY_LOCAL_MACHINE\SYSTEM\Select. Based on the ControlSet00x setting in the subkey, the boot loader knows which ControlSet00x to use. For example, if you chose the Last Known Good Configuration option during the configuration selection process, the **control set** may be ControlSet003 rather than ControlSet001, which is the default configuration. Notice the values of the Current, Default, Failed, and LastKnownGood value entries in Figure 13-9. (Working with the Registry and the contents of Registry keys is covered in Chapter 12.)

The boot loader then loads the drivers listed in the Registry subkey HKEY_LOCAL_ MACHINE\SYSTEM\CurrentControlSet\Services. These drivers are loaded and/or initialized according to their settings in the Registry.

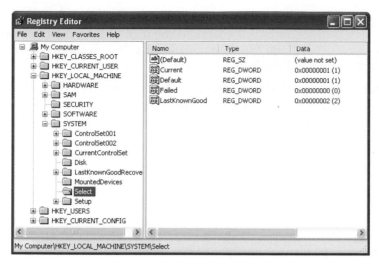

Figure 13-9   The HKEY_LOCAL_MACHINE\SYSTEM\Select subkey viewed through Regedit

Initializing the Kernel

After its initialization, the kernel creates the Registry key HKEY_LOCAL_MACHINE\ HARDWARE using the information received from the boot loader. This key contains the hardware information that is computed when the system is started up, and includes information about components on the system board and the interrupts used by specific hardware devices.

The kernel also creates the CloncControlSet by making a copy of the CurrentControlSet. The Clone set is never modified, because it is intended to be an identical copy of the data used to configure the computer and should not be modified during the startup process.

The kernel then initializes the drivers that were loaded by the boot loader. If drivers experience errors as they load, they send conditions to the kernel that determines how the error is treated. The error levels are as follows:

- *Ignore*—The error is ignored and no message is displayed to the user, if the ignore condition is sent to the kernel.

- *Normal*—The boot process continues, but a message is displayed to the user if the device driver returns the normal error condition.

- *Severe*—The management of this error depends on whether the Last Known Good Configuration is in use or not. If the LKGC is not being used, then the error is displayed to the user, and the boot process restarts using the LKGC. If the LKGC is already in use, then the message is displayed and the boot process continues.

- *Critical*—The management of this error depends on whether the LKGC is in use or not. If not, then the error is displayed to the user, and the boot process restarts using the Last Known Good Configuration. If the LKGC is already in use, then the message is displayed and the boot process fails.

All such events are saved automatically in the System log, and produce on-screen messages as well. The System log is available as one of the views in the Windows XP Event Viewer, and should always be checked whenever errors are reported during the boot process. Because that process cannot be interrupted, however, it's necessary to wait and inspect the log after the bootup phase is complete.

Services Load

During the services load phase, the kernel starts the Session Manager, which reads the entries that are stored in the Registry key, which is HKEY_LOCAL_MACHINE\ SYSTEM\CurrentControlSet\Control\Session Manager.

It then starts programs that correspond to the key entries under this Registry key: HKEY_LOCAL_MACHINE\SYSTEM\CurrentControlSet\Control\Session Manager\BootExecute.

The default entry for this key is *autocheck autochk* *. Autocheck makes sure that the files stored on your hard drive are always consistent. It detects and attempts to repair damaged files and directories. As with any repair utility, it cannot guarantee that all files can be fixed or retrieved.

Once Autocheck is complete, the paging files are set up. These are stored under HKEY_ LOCAL_MACHINE\SYSTEM\CurrentControlSet\Control\Session Manager\Memory Management.

The Session Manager then writes the CurrentControlSet and the CloneControlSet to the Registry, and, finally, loads the subsystems that are defined in the Registry.

HKEY_LOCAL_MACHINE\SYSTEM\CurrentControlSet\Control\Session Manager\ Subsystems contains the subsystem information. The Windows (Win32) subsystem is the default subsystem for Windows XP, and is also the subsystem within which the default user shell always executes.

Windows XP System Startup

Once the Windows XP services have all started, and the elements in the group of processes that are configured to launch on startup are fired off, the Windows XP system can be considered to be fully started. This brief but meaningful phase of the process is signaled by the appearance of the Windows XP logon screen as the Win32 subsystem starts winlogon. exe, and that process automatically launches the Local Security Authority (Lsass.exe) process.

Logging On

Until a user successfully logs on, the boot process is not complete until the Clone control set is copied to the Last Known Good control set. This procedure provides the values to be used the next time the machine is powered up, if the user elects to use the Last Known Good Configuration.

Activity 13-6: Last Known Good Configuration

Time Required: 10 minutes

Objective: Boot the computer using only the drivers that were loaded during the last successful boot.

Description: Microsoft creates a set of criteria that they want vendors to follow when developing hardware and software. In most cases, the conflicts between products are minimal. There are instances in which a new driver is installed that conflicts with existing products and the computer does not boot properly. In this case, you can reboot the computer and select to use the Last Known Good Configuration. In this activity, you boot the computer using the Last Known Good Configuration.

To reboot Windows XP with the Last Known Good Configuration:

Performing this project causes all changes made to the system since the last successful logon to be discarded.

1. Restart Windows XP by selecting **Start**, **Turn Off Computer** (or **Shut Down**). Select **Restart**. Click **OK** (assuming Classic logon mode).

2. As Windows XP reboots, watch for the boot selection menu. As soon as it appears, press **F8**. This reveals the Windows Advanced Options Menu (refer to Figure 13-5).

3. Use the arrow keys on the keyboard to select **Last Known Good Configuration** from the list of options.

4. Press the **Enter** key, and allow the boot process to continue to completion. If dual-boot, you may have to select your OS, then log in.

5. Your system boots with the state of the Registry recorded at the last successful logon.

MULTIPLE-BOOT SYSTEMS

One of the biggest advantages of the Windows XP operating system is its ability to peacefully coexist with other operating systems. Each operating system uses one or more file systems to organize the data within the volumes. Some operating systems can use the same file system, whereas others are incompatible. For example, MS-DOS, Windows 95/98, Window NT, Windows 2000, Windows Server 2003, and Windows XP are able to share files through FAT volumes, and Windows NT, Windows 2000, Windows 2003, and Windows XP are able to share files through NTFS volumes. Windows XP and UNIX do not have a common file system, although it is possible for Linux to access FAT volumes.

In addition to the file system issue, you must also keep in mind that only Windows 2000, Windows Server 2003, and Windows XP support dynamic disks. All other operating systems cannot see the volumes on dynamic disks nor any of the resources stored on them. Even from within Windows 2000, Windows Server 2003, or Windows XP, you must import the foreign dynamic disk before you can access its contents.

When selecting a file system to format a partition, keep in mind the capabilities of each OS. MS-DOS, Windows 3.1, and Windows 95 support only FAT. Windows 95 OSR2 and Windows 98 support only FAT and FAT32. Windows NT (SP4+), Windows 2000, Windows Server 2003, and Windows XP support FAT, FAT32, and NTFS. To install MS-DOS, Windows 3.1, Windows 95, OSR2, or Windows 98 in a multiboot configuration with Windows NT, 2000, 2003, or XP, the boot partition must be formatted with FAT.

Multiple Windows Operating Systems

Windows 3.1, Windows 3.11, Windows 95/98, Windows NT, Windows 2000, and Windows Server 2003 can all exist on the same system as Windows XP. When Windows XP is to be installed on a system with another operating system—especially some previous version of Windows—it is important to specify a different installation partition. Unless you want to upgrade the computer (that is, install Windows XP over an existing OS), always define a new main directory and partition different from the one already in use. Different versions of Windows XP can also be installed on the same computer, but, again, each must have a separate partition.

If you plan to use applications from the different versions of Windows you have installed, you must install the application from each operating system. For example, if you intend to use Microsoft Word from both Windows 98 and Windows XP, you must run the Word setup program while the computer is booted to each operating system.

Multiple Installation Order

When installing multiple operating systems on *x*86-based computers, the order in which you install the operating systems is important. When installing Windows XP and MS-DOS, it is best to install MS-DOS first, then Windows XP. Windows XP sees the DOS operating system and leaves it intact. The same guideline applies to installing Windows XP and Windows 95/98 or Windows 2000/2003. At this time, the recommended installation order is: older Windows products first, then Windows XP. If you plan on running all three operating systems (MS-DOS, Windows 98, and Windows XP), they should be installed in that order: MS-DOS, then Windows 98, and Windows XP last. When installing multiple versions of Windows XP or Windows 2000/2003 onto the same system, it really doesn't matter which one is installed first. As a general rule, install the newest operating system last and the oldest first.

CHAPTER SUMMARY

☐ The Windows XP boot process can be daunting, but it is not nearly as mysterious as one first supposes. It follows the same general boot steps as any other operating system, and, in fact, "plays well with others." After the POST (power-on self test), the BIOS loads the Master Boot Record (MBR), which then loads the partition boot sector. Then, the boot loader takes control of the system and begins the true Windows XP boot. The user is presented with options for choosing the operating system to load, and—if he or she chooses Windows XP—the configuration to use.

☐ When the boot menu appears, you can press F8 to access the Windows Advanced Options Menu. The advanced options are alternative boot methods that can bypass certain types of drivers or subsystems to aid in troubleshooting. Advanced options include, among others, Safe Mode, Enable VGA, Enable Boot Logging, and Last Known Good Configuration.

☐ After the boot loader, the kernel is loaded into memory and is granted control of the computer. The kernel loads the operating system files and device drivers before finally allowing the user to log on. When the user successfully logs on to the computer, it is considered a good startup and the configuration is saved to the Registry.

☐ The boot process can be altered by changing the Boot.ini file. This includes information such as the default operating system, its location, and the amount of time to wait before automatically loading the default OS. The type of information displayed and the debugger setting can be changed by adding switches to the configurations in the Boot.ini file.

☐ Windows 3.1, Windows 3.11, Windows 95/98, Windows NT, Windows 2000, and Windows Server 2003 can all exist on the same system as Windows XP. You can configure Windows XP to offer the choice of booting to other operating systems. In a multiboot system, it's generally best to install the operating systems in chronological order, from older to newer ones.

13

KEY TERMS

Advanced RISC Computing (ARC) pathname — The naming convention used in the Boot.ini file to define the particular hard disk and partition where Windows XP operating system files reside.

BIOS (Basic Input/Output System) — A special PC ROM chip that contains sufficient program code to let a computer perform a POST routine, check its hardware components, and operate basic input and output routines for keyboard or mouse input, and screen output.

boot partition — In Windows XP, the disk that contains the Windows XP operating system files.

boot phase — Any of a number of stages in the Windows XP boot process, starting with the POST, through initial startup activities, to activation of a boot loader program, to selection of the operating system (or version) to boot, to hardware detection (Ntdetect), to selecting a configuration.

boot process — The process of bringing up a completely functional computer, starting from initial power-up (or reboot) through the boot phases and load phases involved in starting the hardware, finding a boot loader, and then loading and initializing an operating system.

boot selection menu — The list of bootable operating systems (or versions) that Boot.ini provides for display at the end of the Windows XP boot phase.

CMOS (complementary metal oxide semiconductor) — A special, battery-powered chip that can store not only the software necessary to conduct the POST, but also the basic, nonvolatile configuration information that POST uses to check the RAM installed in a system, the number and type of hard drives, the type of keyboard and mouse, and so forth.

control set — A special set of Registry values that describes a Windows XP machine's startup configuration that is saved each time a Windows machine is shut down (as the current configuration) and each time a user successfully logs on for the first time after bootup (as the Last Known Good Configuration).

Last Known Good Configuration (LKGC) — The control set for Windows XP that is automatically saved by the system in a special set of Registry keys the first time a user logs on successfully to a system immediately after it has booted up. This information provides a safe fallback to use when booting the system the next time, if changes made to the Registry in the interim cause problems with booting (or if changes have been introduced that a user does not want to retain on that system).

load phase — The Windows XP load phase begins when the kernel assumes control of the machine, and consists of the following five steps: (1) loading the kernel, (2) initializing the kernel, (3) loading services, (4) starting the Windows XP system, and (5) logging on. All five steps must be completed successfully for a complete load to occur.

Master Boot Record (MBR) — The partition table for a disk, and the code that permits that partition table to be read. A functioning MBR is required to boot a hard disk.

Ntldr — The Windows XP loader program that manages the boot and load phases of Windows XP on a PC.

partition boot sector — The partition that contains the information the file system uses to access the volume, including a physical description of the disk, the name and version of the operating system files, the bootstrap code, and an instruction that allows the Master Boot Record to find all this information.

power-on self test (POST) — The system check performed by all computers when they are turned on.

system partition — In Windows XP, the partition or volume that contains the MBR and partition boot sector.

REVIEW QUESTIONS

1. Which of the following partitions contain the files that load the initial components of the operating system?

   a. boot partition

   b. system partition

   c. start partition

   d. kernel partition

2. What program has control of an *x*86 computer when the user is able to choose which operating system to boot?

   a. Ntldr

   b. Osloader

   c. Boot.ini

   d. Ntbootdd.sys

3. When configuring an *x*86 computer for multiple operating systems, _____ should always be loaded last.

4. When booting an *x*86 computer, the boot loader must be installed on a(n) _____ file system. (Choose all that apply.)

   a. NTFS

   b. HPFS

   c. FAT

   d. FAT32

5. Which Boot.ini file setting defines the operating system that is automatically loaded?

   a. [operating systems]

   b. [system loader]

   c. [boot loader]

   d. default=

6. When a Windows XP Professional system is not installed as a domain client, the _____ logon method is used by default. True or False?

7. What is the primary boot loader for *x*86-based systems?

   a. Ntldr

   b. Osloader.exe

   c. Bootdd.sys

   d. Bootsect.dos

8. The timeout option is in the _____ section of the Boot.ini file.

13

9. What portion of a computer system startup is the same on all computers?

   a. POST

   b. initial startup

   c. boot loader

   d. OS selection

10. The Boot.ini file can be changed by two methods. What are they?

    a. Control Panel System applet

    b. Control Panel Startup applet

    c. Windows XP Configuration Manager

    d. using a text editor

11. Which of the following files is accessed only when SCSI disks with onboard BIOS disabled are used?

    a. Multidisk.sys

    b. Scsildr.sys

    c. Rdisk.sys

    d. Ntbootdd.sys

12. Which of the following are selections listed on the Windows Advanced Options Menu when you press F8 during the boot menu display? (Choose all that apply.)

    a. Safe Mode with Command Prompt

    b. Enable VGA Mode

    c. NTFS Transfer Mode

    d. Debugging Mode

13. Which ARC settings are used only for SCSI controllers without an enabled onboard BIOS? (Choose all that apply.)

    a. multi()

    b. scsi()

    c. rdisk()

    d. disk()

14. The Ntoskrnl.exe file is located in the _____ directory on an *x*86 system.

15. The Last Known Good Configuration is accessed by pressing the spacebar after the operating system is selected from the boot menu. True or False?

16. You recently installed a new video driver and a new networking interface driver, and now your system does not boot, or at least you never see the logon prompt. Which of the following advanced options should you use to attempt to return to a fully functional system?

    a. Safe Mode

    b. Safe Mode with Networking

    c. Safe Mode with Command Prompt

    d. Enable VGA Mode

    e. Enable Debugging Mode

    f. Enable Boot Logging

17. What are the Boot.ini parameter switches that mimic the Safe Mode with Networking Windows Advanced Options Menu selection?

    a. /SAFEBOOT:MINIMAL(ALTERNATESHELL)/ SOS/ BOOTLOG /NOGUIBOOT

    b. /SAFEBOOT:DSREPAIR /SOS

    c. /SAFEBOOT:NETWORK /SOS /BOOTLOG /NOGUIBOOT

    d. /BOOTLOG

18. Which of the following Boot.ini switches displays the names of the device drivers as they are loaded?

    a. /B

    b. /AT

    c. /SOS

    d. /DRV

19. The Last Known Good Registry key is written or updated after _____ .

20. The _____ partition contains the Windows XP operating system files.

    a. system

    b. boot

    c. start

    d. kernel

21. If the system and boot partitions are the same and reside on an IDE hard drive, which of the following ARC names appear in Boot.ini?

    a. scsi(0)disk(0)rdisk(1)partition(1)

    b. multi(0)disk(0)rdisk(0)partition(1)

    c. multi(0)disk(1)rdisk(0)partition(1)

    d. multi(0)disk(0)rdisk(1)partition(1)

13

22. Windows XP uses its own built-in input/output logic and drivers, and ignores whatever BIOS is installed in a computer. True or False?

23. The presence of a floppy in drive A can cause which of the following situations? (Choose all that apply.)

    a. booting from the floppy to whatever OS is installed there

    b. failure to boot due to a missing boot sector on the floppy

    c. "Non-system disk or disk error: Replace and press any key when ready" error message

    d. normal booting from the hard drive

24. The same MBR is found on Windows 95, MS-DOS, Windows NT, Windows 2000, Windows Server 2003, Windows XP, and Windows 3.x systems. True or False?

25. Ntbootdd.sys appears on a system when which of the following operating systems is present in a multiboot configuration with Windows XP?

    a. MS-DOS

    b. Windows 3.x

    c. Windows 98

    d. none of the above

Case Projects

Case Project 13-1

The Engineering Department in your company has decided to update their computers to Windows XP Professional. They currently have four PCs, two running Windows 3.11 and two running Windows 95. They want to retain their current configurations and programs. Outline the steps necessary to install Windows XP on their systems and explain what configurations will be available after the update is complete.

Case Project 13-2

After installing a new graphics controller on a Windows XP Professional machine, you start up the system, but when the boot process is complete, you see nothing on the monitor except a small dot of light in the exact center. What boot option can you use to see enough of the screen to try a different driver, or to change display settings in the Control Panel Display applet?

Case Project 13-3

By default, the Boot.ini entry for Windows 95 in the boot selection menu reads "MS Windows." How might you edit Boot.ini to change this value to read "Windows 95 Rules!" instead? What part of the Boot.ini file does the appropriate entry reside in, and which entry should you edit?

WINDOWS XP PROFESSIONAL FAULT TOLERANCE

> **After reading this chapter and completing the exercises, you will be able to:**
>
> ♦ Define IntelliMirror technology and describe its key features
>
> ♦ Back up data and settings on Windows XP Professional
>
> ♦ Work with the Microsoft Backup Utility
>
> ♦ Perform preventive maintenance
>
> ♦ Repair an installation of Windows XP Professional

Disaster recovery involves minimizing the amount of time a computer is nonfunctional in the event of a disaster, which can include anything from corrupt system files to a hardware failure. Although Windows XP includes several disaster recovery features, Microsoft IntelliMirror technologies and built-in backup mechanisms help to minimize the chances of such a loss. IntelliMirror and new and enhanced disaster protection and recovery options allow Windows XP Professional users and system administrators to rest assured that their information and configurations are backed up and ready to be restored at a moment's notice. This chapter discusses IntelliMirror and backup technologies, as well as various disaster recovery methods, including remote OS installation.

Microsoft IntelliMirror

IntelliMirror is a term used to describe features of Windows XP that help ensure the availability of a user's data and computer configuration. The following list includes the three key elements of IntelliMirror and an explanation of how each relates to disaster protection and recovery:

- *User data management*—Data backup
- *User settings management*—PC configuration recovery
- *Software installation and maintenance*—Application installation and repair

IntelliMirror greatly reduces the need for and cost of administrative intervention. Therefore, IntelliMirror plays a crucial role in both disaster protection and disaster recovery. If, for any reason, a user loses data or deletes required operating system or application files, that information can be recovered easily, sometimes seamlessly, with little or no action by an administrator. At the same time, the Administrators group's central administration capabilities allow it to manage users' machines centrally. Therefore, both end users and the administrative team benefit.

IntelliMirror is not a cure-all, nor is it a complete disaster recovery solution. It is simply an additional tool that can be used to provide a means to protect against disasters and establish a process by which some data can be recovered when a disaster occurs. IntelliMirror must be configured by an administrator; it is not fully enabled and configured by default.

Data Backup and Data Management

As users work at various computers on a network or take their computers home, IntelliMirror can manage their documents and data for them. If a user's machine crashes, or the user is away from his or her primary computer, he or she can still access any needed data. Using the user data management feature of IntelliMirror also means that if a user's data is corrupted on one machine, it can be restored using the copy of the data on the network.

IntelliMirror technologies in Windows XP enable users to store and synchronize their data easily in a specified network location. **Folder redirection** can be completed seamlessly through the use of a group policy, or a user can set it up manually (see Figure 14-1). Typically, a user's My Documents folder or other important data folders are redirected to a share on a Windows server on the network. In this case, when a user on the network saves a document to the My Documents folder, it is automatically saved not only on the local machine, but also on the network share. If the user is not on the network, the document is saved only to the user's hard drive. This process is part of the Windows XP Offline Files feature, discussed in detail in Chapter 4, "Managing Windows XP File Systems and Storage." When the user rejoins the network, the local version of the document is automatically synchronized with the network version. If the network version of the document also has been modified during that time, the user is prompted as to whether to overwrite the local version, overwrite the network version of the document, or save both copies of the document. To synchronize a file or folder manually when a user rejoins the network, he or she can highlight the file or folder to be synchronized in Windows Explorer. Then, the user must select Synchronize from the Tools menu.

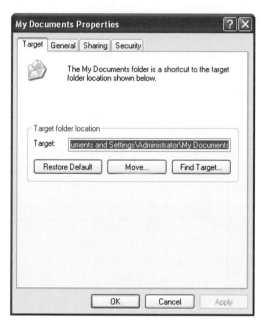

Figure 14-1   The My Documents Properties dialog box, Target box

If one of the copies becomes corrupt or is missing, it is automatically restored from the existing version of the document. This recovery is transparent to the user.

NOTE Administrators must consider the cost of hardware and maintenance of the servers that back up user data. A network's bandwidth could also be affected by the synchronization of user data; that is, the synchronization process can increase network traffic, thus slowing down the network.

ACTIVITY

Activity 14-1: Synchronizing Files

Time Required: 20 minutes

Objective: Use the Synchronize utility to synchronize files on the local machine with the network version of the files.

Description: For people who do not always have access to the network file server, it is important that files which are stored on the network are synchronized with the files that are on the local disk drive. An example of this type of user might be a laptop owner who does a lot of work at home or away from the office. In this activity, you configure the Synchronize utility to automatically synchronize the files at log on and log off.

To enable your files to be synchronized with the network's copy of your files when you log off:

1. Open **Synchronization Manager** by clicking **Start**, **All Programs**, **Accessories**, **Synchronize**.

2. Click **Setup**, and then click the **Logon/Logoff** tab (see Figure 14-2).

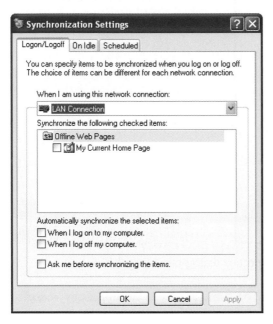

Figure 14-2 Synchronization Settings dialog box, Logon/Logoff tab

3. In the When I am using this network connection list, select the network connection you want to use.

4. In the Synchronize the following checked items list, select the files or folders you want to synchronize when you log on and log off the network.

5. Under Automatically synchronize the selected items, select both **When I log on to my computer** and **When I log off my computer**.

6. Click **OK**, and then click **Close** to close the Items to Synchronize box.

7. Verify file synchronization by creating and saving a Notepad document on your system, and then log off.

8. Go to the server system or another client and check to see that the document was automatically stored on the network server. The location of the files can be determined by right-clicking **My Documents** in Windows Explorer and clicking

Properties. The My Documents Properties dialog box displays the location of the files in the Target field.

PC Configuration Recovery

Personalized machine settings can be accessed by Windows XP Professional users from whatever machine they use on the network, through the user settings management feature of IntelliMirror. Therefore, if a user's machine crashes or is unavailable, its user environment configuration can be easily transferred to a new machine. Personalized settings are customizations of the operating system and applications, including language settings, desktop schemes, and custom dictionaries, and are provided to users when they log on to the system, regardless of which physical computer they use. Essentially, this is the same thing as a roaming profile.

Application Installation and Repair

If users inadvertently remove essential application or system files, or if their systems crash, they can use the software installation and maintenance feature of IntelliMirror to rebuild their machines with the same applications they had previously. By using the **Windows Installer Service (WIS)**, users can reinstall their applications and repair applications seamlessly. Restorable applications include software, software upgrades, and even operating system upgrades.

 NOTE Windows Installer Service can also be used to create a software package for end users. Review Windows XP Help and Support and the Microsoft Windows XP Professional, Windows 2000, and Windows Server 2003 Resource Kits for additional details.

The Windows Installer program is included with Windows XP, as it was with Windows 2000, as Msiexec.exe. This command-line tool is used to install and configure software (with the /i parameter), repair software (/f), uninstall software (/x), apply patches (/p), and more. Windows Installer can apply three types of software packages to a system: .msi (software installation), .msp (patches, service packs, and software updates), and .mst (transformation or modification files, used to customize an installation). These installer packages can be found in the distribution set of many full-size applications, such as Microsoft Office XP. You can also create custom installer packages using third-party tools, such as VERITAS WinIN-STALL LE, InstallShield, Wise Solutions, or Microsoft Visual Studio Installer.

Most of the Msiexec.exe functions are performed using simple, single parameter syntax. For example, installing a program can be performed using msiexec /i gensoft.msi. However, repairing software using Msiexec.exe is a bit more complex. There are 10 types of repair actions Msiexec.exe can use against a software product; these include reinstall if file is missing (p), reinstall if file is missing or a different version is installed (d), force all files to

14

be reinstalled (a), and rewrite all requires user-specific Registry entries (u). These additional syntax elements for repairing are added onto the /f repair parameter, such as msiexec/fdu gensoft.msi.

Activity 14-2: Removing an Application

Time Required: 30 minutes

Objective: Use the Add/Remove applet in Control Panel to remove an application.

Description: The Add/Remove applet in Control Panel is a central location for removing applications and Windows components. Some applications provide an Uninstall icon within their application group in the Start menu, but not always. In this activity, you first install Adobe Acrobat Reader and then use the Add/Remove applet to uninstall it.

This activity requires that the user has access to the Internet or that the install files for Adobe Acrobat Reader be available on the local server. It is also assumed that Control Panel is in Classic View.

To install Adobe Acrobat Reader so that it can be removed:

1. Download and install Adobe Acrobat Reader from *www.adobe.com/products/acrobat/readstep2.html*.

2. Follow the instructions on the page to download and install Acrobat Reader.

   To remove applications and repair applications:

3. Click **Start**, **Control Panel**.

4. Double-click **Add or Remove Programs**.

5. Select the **Change/Remove** button for Acrobat Reader.

6. Select **Yes** to completely remove Acrobat Reader and all of its components. Most applications don't have an option for Change and simply go directly to uninstalling the application.

7. Follow the prompts to remove the application.

8. Close any open dialog boxes or windows and the Add/Remove Programs applet. Restart your computer if prompted.

MICROSOFT BACKUP UTILITY

Microsoft IntelliMirror technologies are quite effective in backing up user data, applications, and personalized settings, using network shares and policies. However, there are also methods of backing up a PC by using external tools, such as the following:

- Tape drives
- External hard disks (i.e., network drives)

- Zip or Jaz drives
- Recordable CD-ROM drives
- Logical drives

The **Backup utility** in Windows XP provides the easiest method of backing up or restoring data (including the system configuration) onto any one of these media or onto a server on a network (see Activity 14-3). There are three main functions within Backup (located on the Welcome tab of the Backup utility, and accessed by clicking the labeled button):

- Back up programs and files
- Restore programs and files
- Create an ASR (Automated System Recovery) data set

Figure 14-3 shows the Welcome tab of the Backup utility. Using this tool is a good precautionary element in the disaster recovery process. The restore and repair options are discussed later in this chapter.

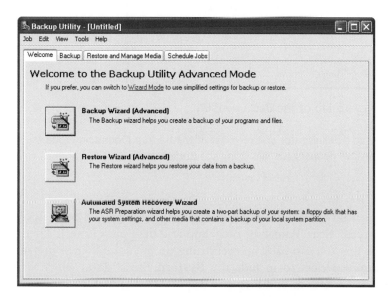

Figure 14-3   The Welcome tab of the Backup Utility

The Windows XP Professional native Backup tool is similar to the one in Windows NT, Windows 2000, and Windows Server 2003, but is significantly different from the versions in Windows 98, 98 SE, and ME. The backup media sets created by the Windows 98 Backup utility are incompatible with the Backup utility found in Windows XP, NT, 2000, and Server 2003. Thus, the only method by which you can extract data from a Windows 98 backup media for a Windows XP system is to perform the restore from a Windows 98 system and move the files to the Windows XP system.

The Backup utility provides two methods to back up your data. You can use the Backup Wizard, or you can click the Backup tab to set your backup options manually (see Figure 14-4). The wizard guides you through the process of defining and scheduling (if necessary) your backups and is launched automatically by default when you open the Backup utility.

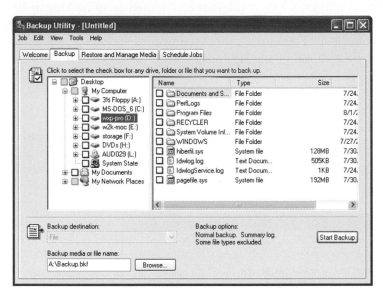

Figure 14-4   The Backup tab of the Backup Utility

NOTE

You must be an Administrator or a member of the Backup Operators group to back up or restore nonpersonal files using the Backup utility.

To start the Backup utility, select Start, All Programs, Accessories, System Tools, Backup (alternately, you can select Start, Run, type ntbackup, and then press Enter). Then, you must choose what to back up. You can back up everything on the computer or just specific files and folders. You can also elect to include the **System State data**, which includes the system's boot files, COM settings, and Registry data.

ACTIVITY

Activity 14-3: Windows Backup

Time Required: 20 minutes

Objective: Back up and restore files using the Windows XP Backup utility.

Description: Files on workstations are not normally backed up by the central backup infrastructure. To protect data on a standalone or mobile computer without purchasing a lot of expensive equipment, basic backups can be accomplished with the built-in utility. In this activity, you use the Windows XP Backup utility to back up a folder to a local file and then restore the folder again.

To back up the contents of your My Documents folder using the Windows Backup utility:

1. Select **Start**, **All Programs**, **Accessories**, **System Tools**, **Backup**.

2. If the tool launched in wizard mode, click the **Advanced Mode** link to switch to the utility interface.

3. Click the **Backup** tab.

4. Check the check box next to **My Documents**. Notice that a gray check mark automatically appears next to the drive containing My Documents and that the check boxes next to each of the subdirectories under My Documents are automatically checked.

5. In the bottom-left corner, change the path in the Backup media or file name field to **c:\backup.bkf**.

6. Look over your options, and then click **Start Backup**.

7. The Backup Job Information dialog box appears. Click **Start Backup**.

8. When the backup is complete, click **Close** to exit the Backup Progress dialog box.

To restore your files:

1. Click the **Restore and Manage Media** tab.

2. Expand the left pane listing of File to view the drive-level contents of the backup you just performed.

3. Mark one or more check boxes beside folders or files within the backup.

4. Click **Start Restore**.

5. Click **OK** to initiate restore without viewing Advanced options.

6. Once the Restore is complete, close all dialog boxes and close the Backup utility.

In addition to choosing what to back up, you can also specify the **backup type**:

- *Copy backup*—Backs up all selected files but does not mark them as being backed up (i.e., the archive bit is not cleared)

- *Normal (or full) backup*—Backs up all selected files and marks them as being backed up (i.e., the archive bit is cleared)

- *Daily backup*—Backs up only the selected files that have been created or modified the day that the backup is being performed but does not mark the files as being backed up (i.e., the archive bit is not cleared)

- *Differential backup*—Backs up only the selected files that have been created or modified since the last full or incremental backup but does not mark the files as being backed up (i.e., the archive bit is not cleared)

■ *Incremental backup*—Backs up only the selected files that have been created or modified since the last normal or incremental backup and marks the files as being backed up (i.e., the archive bit is cleared)

 When you use the Backup Wizard and choose either the Back up everything option or the Back up selected files option, the backup type defaults to Normal or Incremental, respectively. You can change the backup type from the Completing Backup Wizard dialog box by clicking the Advanced button.

 You must have the correct permissions over the backup media location (whether local hard drives, network mapped drives, or removable media) to write, format, and eject media through the Backup utility.

Most backup schemes combine the use of weekly full backups with either incremental or differential daily backups. Using incremental daily backups makes the daily backup operation run quicker, but requires a longer restore period. The size of the backed up files will be roughly the same every day that an incremental backup is performed. To restore data to its most current backed up state, you must first restore the full backup and then restore every daily incremental backup in the original order that they were performed. Using differential backups causes a longer and longer backup period each day. This also requires increased storage space on the backup media each day as well. However, the restore time is greatly reduced in comparison with incremental. To restore data to its most current backed up state, you must first restore the full backup, and then only the last differential backup.

As mentioned, backing up the System State data protects the Registry, the COM+ Class Registration database, and system boot files. By backing up these files, you can restore your PC's configuration to its original state if necessary. If you back up to a network drive, you must have a system boot disk with network drivers in order to attach to the network share and restore files.

 When the System State data is backed up, a copy of your Registry files (by default, SAM, SECURITY, SOFTWARE, and SYSTEM) is also saved in the \WINDOWS\Repair\ Regback directory. Advanced users can use these files to restore their Registry files manually without restoring the entire System State. (See Chapter 12, "Working with the Windows XP Registry," for more information.)

Automated System Recovery (ASR) can restore essential system files in the event of a severe system failure. ASR won't protect your personal data or even application configuration settings; it creates a backup of only those files essential to the boot process. The ASR media set consists of a backup floppy and one or more backup tapes or other media. To restore a system using ASR, start the system using the original system CD or the boot floppies. When prompted, press F2 to initiate the ASR restore process, and provide the ASR floppy and the backup media when requested. ASR is accessed on the Welcome tab of the Backup utility by clicking the ASR button.

ACTIVITY

Activity 14-4: Scheduled Backups

Time Required: 20 minutes

Objective: Use the Backup utility to schedule a backup job.

Description: It is often best to perform administrative work when a computer is not actively being used. In this activity, you set up a daily incremental backup of a folder on your computer.

To schedule a backup of your My Documents folder, using the Windows Backup utility:

1. Select **Start, All Programs, Accessories, System Tools, Backup**.

2. If the Backup or Restore Wizard does not load, click **Tools, Switch to Wizard Mode**.

3. The Backup or Restore Wizard Welcome dialog box appears. Click **Next**.

4. At the Backup or Restore dialog box, select the **Back up files and settings** option button. Click **Next**.

5. Select the **My documents and settings** option button. Click **Next**.

6. Click the **Browse** button to locate the drive and/or folder to store your backup. Click **Cancel** to get past the prompt to insert a floppy disk.

7. Select the root of drive C: (C:\) from the drop-down menu.

8. Accept the name for this backup in the File name field, as **backup.bkf**. Click **Save**, and then click **Next**.

9. On the Completing the Backup or Restore Wizard dialog box, click the **Advanced** button and select **Incremental** from the pull-down list. Click **Next**.

10. Read through your verification and compression options. Click **Next**.

11. Select **Replace the existing backups**. Notice that the option at the bottom is no longer dimmed. Check the check box so that only the owner and Administrator can access the backups. Click **Next**.

12. In the When to Back Up dialog box, choose **Later**.

13. In the Job name field, type **Daily Backup of My Documents**. Then click **Set Schedule**.

14. Under Schedule Task, choose **Daily** from the drop-down list and set the start time for **5** minutes from now.

15. Click the **Settings** tab to review your options, but accept the defaults. Click **OK** to continue. Click **Next**.

16. When prompted for your account information, enter a username and password of an

14

Administrator or Backup Operator. Click **OK**. Click **OK** again, if necessary, in the dialog box that reads, "Make sure that the specified account can access the backup selection file for this job."

17. Review your settings, and then click **Finish** to schedule the backup.

PREVENTIVE MAINTENANCE

Windows XP includes several mechanisms to reduce the number of problems commonly experienced by users. These range from removing bad device drivers to installing system updates. Each of these useful mechanisms is covered in the following sections.

Device Driver Rollback

You should already be familiar with the concept of device driver signing from Windows 2000 and its discussion in Chapter 3, "Using the System Utilities." A new feature of this technology to help prevent problems related to faulty device drivers is the ability to roll back device drivers. Device driver rollback removes the current driver for a device and reinitializes the previous driver, which Windows XP retained when the new driver was installed. To use device driver rollback, open the Driver tab (see Figure 14-5) of a device's Properties dialog box (typically through the Device Manager), and click the Roll Back Driver button.

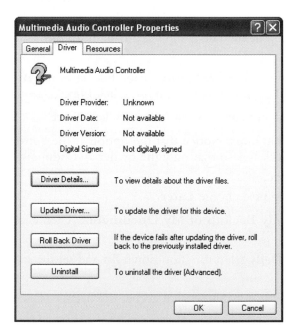

Figure 14-5   The Driver tab of a device's Properties dialog box

Windows File Protection

Windows File Protection (WFP) was included in Windows 2000 and has been retained by Windows XP. WFP ensures that the correct and uncorrupted version of certain core files is retained on the system at all times. These files include .sys, .dll, .exe, and .ocx files native to Windows XP and several True Type font files that are critical to system operation. Native files are those included on the original distribution CD or those updated by Microsoft-approved and distributed updates and service packs.

WFP protects its list of sacred files from changes due to application installation, virus infection, and even human error. WFP works in the background, watching for attempted writes to its monitored files. If a write occurs, the resultant file is compared to its signature in a database of known files. If there is a mismatch, the altered file is replaced. The replacement file is pulled either from the WINDOWS\system32\dllcache folder, the original distribution files from the Windows XP Professional CD, a local copy of this CD, or on a network share. WFP operates invisibly to the user in most cases. In the event of a change to a critical core file, you might be prompted to restart the system.

The key to the operation of WFP is the System File Checker (SFC) tool, which actually performs the inspection and replacement of monitored files. Although WFP uses SFC automatically when needed, SFC also can be executed manually from a command prompt. All of its parameters and syntax can be accessed by issuing the SFC /? command. In addition to inspecting and replacing suspect files, it can also be used to purge and rebuild the DLLCACHE and set the size of the DLLCACHE folder. By default, this folder has a limit of 50 MB.

Automatic Updates and Windows Update

Even after the final release of a product, Microsoft continues to improve the code by fixing problems. Such code is made available online and can be accessed through the Windows Update command on the Start menu and on the Tools menu of Internet Explorer. Windows XP has improved upon software update functionality by offering a configuration for updating the system. The Automatic Updates tab of the System applet is used to define whether the OS automatically checks, downloads, and installs updates, notifies you when updates are available, or leaves all updating processes up to you to perform manually. The specific configuration options are to enable or disable automatic updates as a whole. If enabled, you can then select one of three options:

- Notify before downloading any updates and notify me again before installing them on my computer.

- Download the updates automatically and notify me when they are ready to be installed.

- Automatically download the updates, and install them on the schedule that I specify.

14

When you choose manual or notify, you reserve the option to refuse or decline offered updates. If you decline an update, this tab offers the ability to reaccess or restore declined updates.

After you complete the installation of Windows XP, usually with the first logon session, the system prompts you to configure Automatic Update if you have not already done so through the System applet.

You can access the Windows Update Web site at any time using the Windows Update command from the All Programs submenu of the Start menu or the Tools menu of Internet Explorer. The Windows Update Web site inventories your system and informs you of any updates available from Microsoft that your system is lacking. You can select these missing updates and elect to download and install them immediately.

Desktop Cleanup Wizard

The Desktop Cleanup Wizard is nothing more than a nag that asks your permission to remove unused icons from the desktop. This tool launches automatically every 60 days and prompts you to allow it to move all icons that have not been used in the last 60 days to the Unused Desktop Items folder, which is added to your desktop after the first item is moved.

This feature can be disabled by opening the Display applet, selecting the Desktop tab, clicking Customize Desktop, selecting the General tab, and then deselecting the Run Desktop Cleanup Wizard every 60 days check box.

Hibernate vs. Standby

Hibernate and standby are commonly used terms or features that often confuse users. Windows XP supports both, so it is a good idea to understand them clearly. Hibernation under Windows XP saves the contents in memory to the hard drive and performs a system shutdown. Upon restarting the system, the system is restored to its state at the moment hibernation was activated. If the user account is protected by a password, you are prompted to provide it before access to the system is restored. Hibernation restores the user environment to its exact state, including open applications and dialog boxes.

Standby is a feature added to a system through support for APM (Advanced Power Management) or ACPI (Advanced Configuration and Power Interface). Typically, one or both of these is supported by notebook or portable systems; however, there are now many desktop systems that support these power-saving options. Standby retains the contents of memory in RAM instead of saving it, allowing for very fast restoration to the user environment. However, if the system loses power, the data saved in RAM is lost; the next time the system is powered up, the system starts normally. If power is maintained, the stored user environment is instantly restored when the user reactivates the system (with either a quick press of the power key, pressing a key, or just opening the display lid). If the user account is protected by a password, you must provide it before access is granted.

Standby mode can be configured to begin automatically when you close the display lid of your notebook computer.

When shutting down a domain client system, hibernate and standby options (if supported by the system) appear in the pull-down list on the Shut Down Windows dialog box. The Shut Down Windows dialog box appears when the Start, Shut Down command is issued. On nondomain clients in Welcome screen logon mode, only the Start, Turn Off Computer command reveals a three-button dialog box. The first button displays hibernate or standby. If your system supports both, you must press Shift to switch the button to the other feature.

REPAIRING WINDOWS XP PROFESSIONAL

Although disaster prevention is important, you still need to be prepared for the worst. If system files become corrupt or are accidentally deleted, or if certain drivers or services are keeping the operating system from loading, you have several options for repairing or restoring your PC:

- Safe Mode (discussed in Chapter 13, "Booting Windows XP")
- System Restore
- Emergency repair process
- Recovery Console
- Remote OS installation

14

System Restore

Windows XP boasts a new mechanism for maintaining a functioning user environment: System Restore can be used to return the OS to a previously saved state. It can reverse system configuration settings and Registry changes or even undo the changes made by installed software, all without altering personal files or e-mail. System Restore can undo a botched alteration if you can gain access to the System Restore interface. If you cannot start the system, you need to employ some other recovery technique.

Basically, System Restore automatically creates restoration points during critical system changes. You can even initiate the creation of a restoration point manually. System Restore is controlled and managed through two interfaces: the System Restore tab of the System applet and the System Restore tool (see Figure 14-6).

The System Restore tab of the System Properties applet is used to enable or disable the storage of restore points on a systemwide or drive-by-drive basis. The amount of space that can be consumed by the System Restore files can also be configured. If a drive is not configured to host restore information, any changes to files hosted by that drive won't be included in a restore point. Also, if there is not sufficient space, some files might not be included in the restore point, or the oldest existing restore point is deleted.

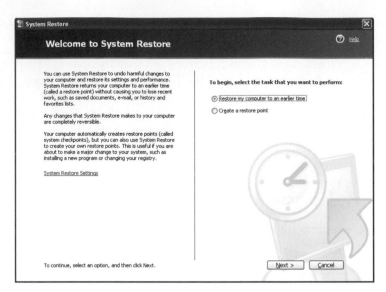

Figure 14-6   The System Restore tool

Windows XP creates restore points automatically for a wide number of events, including:

- The first bootup
- Every 24 hours of calendar time or 24 hours of uptime
- The installation of an application through Install Shield or Windows Installer (*Note*: Some applications do not use either of these to manage their installation.)
- Automatic updates
- Any restore operation using the Backup utility
- Installing unsigned device drivers
- Any System Restore operation

The System Restore tool (found in Start, All Programs, Accessories, System Tools, System Restore) is a wizard that walks you through the process of creating a new restore point or reestablishing an existing restore point.

The System Restore mechanism repairs the changes made by the installation of an application, but it does not delete the files associated with that application. You should use the Add or Remove Programs applet to uninstall an application if the application itself does not provide an uninstall function.

Emergency Repair Process

If your problem is caused by corrupt or missing system files, your startup environment, or your partition boot sector, you might want to use the emergency repair process. You must restart your machine with the Windows XP Setup disks or the Windows XP Professional CD. Setup asks if you would like to install Windows XP. Press Enter to start the installation process. Then you are prompted whether you want to reinstall Windows XP or repair an existing version of Windows XP. Press R to repair Windows XP. Press R again to repair your system using the emergency repair process. You then have two options for repairing Windows XP:

- *Fast repair*—Requires no user interaction; automatically attempts to repair problems related to the Registry, system files, the boot volume, and your startup environment

- *Manual repair*—Enables the user to choose to repair the Registry, system files, the boot volume, or startup environment

If the emergency repair process is successful, the PC reboots automatically, and everything should be in working order again. As a last resort, if the emergency repair process cannot repair the system, you might consider reinstalling Windows XP. However, this method is time consuming, and you might need to reinstall many of your applications and upgrades.

Recovery Console

Expert users and system administrators might want to use the Windows XP **Recovery Console** for more precise control over the troubleshooting and repair process. If you know which services or drivers might be causing the problem, instead of running the PC in Safe Mode, you can simply use the Recovery Console to disable those specific services or drivers. You can also use the Recovery Console to repair a corrupted Master Boot Record or to copy needed files to your PC from a floppy disk, CD-ROM, or a network share.

You can access the Recovery Console in one of two ways:

- From a command prompt, change directories to your Windows XP CD. Run /i386/winnt32.exe/cmdcons to install the Recovery Console. When you restart your machine, you'll notice a new option for starting Windows XP Professional with the Recovery Console.

- Use the Windows XP CD or startup disks to start your computer. Select the Recovery Console option when you are prompted to choose repair options.

Activity 14-5: Recovery Console

Time Required: 15 minutes

Objective: Install and view the options available within the Recovery Console.

Description: There are times when it is necessary to recover files from a system that has corrupted or missing files. This often means booting from a floppy disk. In this activity, you install and view the options that are available within the Windows XP Recovery Console.

14

To install the Recovery Console:

1. From a command prompt (**Start**, **All Programs**, **Accessories**, **Command Prompt**), browse to the i386 folder of your Windows XP Professional CD.

2. Run **winnt32 /cmdcons**.

3. You are prompted by a Windows XP Setup dialog box that explains how to use the Recovery Console. Click **Yes** to install it.

4. The necessary files are copied to your system. When finished, click **OK**.

5. Choose **Start**, **Turn Off Computer** (or **Shut Down**). Choose **Restart** from the menu, and then click **OK**.

6. When prompted, choose **Microsoft Windows Recovery Console** from the list of available operating systems and then press **Enter**.

7. You are prompted to select which operating system you'd like to log onto. Type the number for your operating system and press **Enter**.

8. You are then prompted for the local administrator password. Type that password. Press **Enter**.

9. Type **help** at the command prompt for a list of commands that you can use in the Recovery Console and press **Enter**. Scroll through the help options using the space bar until you are back at the command prompt or press **Esc** to return to the command prompt.

10. Type **exit** and press **Enter** at the command prompt to exit and restart Windows. This time, choose your Windows XP operating system to start the system.

When the Recovery Console opens, you must specify the Windows XP client you want to log onto and log on as Administrator. The following commands are available from the Recovery Console. To view the command-line parameters and uses for each of these commands, see the Recovery Console commands section in the Windows XP Professional online Help.

- *attrib*—Changes the attributes of a file or directory
- *batch*—Executes the commands specified in a text file
- *bootcfg*—Boot file configuration and recovery
- *chdir (cd)*—Changes directories or displays the current directory name
- *chkdsk*—Checks and reports on the status of the disk
- *cls*—Starts Windows XP while logging all of the drivers and services that were and were not loaded during the boot process
- *copy*—Copies files
- *delete (del)*—Deletes files
- *dir*—Displays the directory structure

- *disable*—Disables a service or driver

- *diskpart*—Manages partitions

- *enable*—Enables or starts a service or driver

- *exit*—Exits the Recovery Console and restarts the computer

- *expand* — Extracts files from compressed files

- *fixboot* — Writes a new partition boot sector onto the system partition

- *fixmbr*—Repairs the Master Boot Record

- *format* — Formats a disk

- *help*—Displays a list of commands available in the Recovery Console

- *listsvc*—Lists the services available

- *logon* — Logs onto Windows XP

- *map*—Displays the drive letter mappings

- *mkdir (md)*—Creates a new folder

- *more*—Displays a text file

- *net use (net)*—Connects a network share to a local drive letter

- *rename (ren)*—Renames a file

- *rmdir (rd)*—Deletes a folder

- *systemroot* — Sets the current folder to the Systemroot folder

- *type*—Displays the contents of a text file

The Recovery Console can be employed to correct a wide range of problems. For example, if a device driver is corrupted but you are unable to boot into the GUI, you can use the Recovery Console to replace the corrupted file with a new version off a floppy disk. If your boot.ini file is damaged, you can re-create it using the bootcfg /rebuild command. If a service is causing a system lockup, you can disable it using the disable command. If your system drive no longer allows booting, you can repair the boot section using the fixboot command.

Activity 14-6: Remove Recovery Console

Time Required: 15 minutes

Objective: Delete hidden and protected files while editing the Boot.ini file to remove Recovery Console.

Description: It may be annoying to have the Recovery Console appear as an option each time the computer is started. The installation of the product is quite simple, but the removal is not. In this activity, you remove Recovery Console.

14

To uninstall the Recovery Console:

Before continuing, copy your Boot.ini file and rename the copy Boot.bak. You can use this file later should the Boot.ini file become damaged. Be extra careful with the next step to make sure that you delete only the line for the Recovery Console. An incorrect Boot.ini file could keep your computer from restarting.

1. Click **Start, My Computer**. Choose **Tools, Folder Options**. Click the **View** tab.

2. Click **Show hidden files and folders** and clear the **Hide protected operating system files** check box. Click **Yes**, and then click **OK**.

3. Browse to the root directory and delete the **\cmdcons** folder and the file called **cmldr**.

4. Using Notepad (**Start, All Programs, Accessories, Notepad**), open the **Boot.ini** file in the root directory. Remove the entry for the Recovery Console. For example, you would need to delete the last line in the following sample Boot.ini file:

```
[boot loader]
timeout=10
default=multi(0)disk(0)rdisk(0)partition(1)\WINDOWS
[operating systems]
multi(0)disk(0)rdisk(0)partition(1)\WINDOWS= "Microsoft
Windows XP Professional" /fastdetect
C:\CMDCONS\BOOTSECT.DAT="Microsoft Windows Recovery
Console" /cmdcons
```

5. Save the file and close it.

6. Close any open windows.

Using the Recovery Console is a better way to restore a damaged Registry than running an emergency repair. This is because the Registry files in the *%systemroot%*\Repair folder are from the original installation of Windows XP Professional so any changes made after the initial operating system installation are lost when you use the emergency repair process.

Remote OS Installation

Administrators can also enable **remote OS installation**, which can be used along with the Microsoft IntelliMirror technologies to recover an entire PC, including a user's data, individual configurations, and applications. Remote OS installation is a component of the optional Windows Server **Remote Installation Services (RIS)** (see Chapter 2, "Installing Windows XP Professional"), which allows a user to rebuild the computer's entire image remotely across the network. No on-site technical support is necessary, minimizing both administrative costs and user downtime.

Client computers that can participate in a remote OS installation must have a **PXE (Preboot Execution)** environment. Network PCs and computers that comply with an industry-standard hardware guide called PC98 have this ROM. If a computer does not have the PXE remote-boot ROM, an RIS remote-boot disk can be used with a supported PCI-based network interface card (NIC). These client machines must also use a DHCP (Dynamic Host Configuration Protocol) server on the network.

When a user starts a client with either the PXE remote-boot ROM or an RIS remote-boot disk, the client can request an installation of Windows XP Professional from a remote RIS server. The server, in turn, provides one of the following types of installations:

- *CD-based*—Similar to installing the OS with a CD, but the source files are on another machine (the RIS server) on the network

- *Remote Installation Preparation (RIPrep) desktop image*—After installing Windows XP Professional, installing applications, and making configuration changes on one workstation, an administrator clones the image of that machine and replicates it on an RIS server. The entire **Remote Installation Preparation (RIPrep)** image can then be deployed to other workstations with remote OS installation.

Once the images are on the RIS server, the server can be used to install those images to any client that is remote-boot enabled. A user can initiate a network service boot by pressing the F12 key when starting the system, at which time the RIS server installs the Client Installation Wizard. This wizard uses group policies to give the user a list of available installation options from Active Directory. If there is only one installation option, the user is simply prompted with a confirmation dialog box, and the installation begins. Otherwise, the four installation options are:

- *Automatic Setup*—Prompts the user with a list of OS options if there is more than one OS installed, and then an unattended installation begins

- *Custom Setup*—Allows the user to specify the computer name and the location where the computer account should reside in Active Directory

- *Restart a Previous Setup Attempt*—Restarts the remote OS installation process if a previous installation attempt failed

- *Maintenance and Troubleshooting*—Provides the user with access to third-party maintenance, pre-OS installation maintenance, and troubleshooting tools

14

CHAPTER SUMMARY

- IntelliMirror consists of a set of features within Windows XP utilizing user and group policies, folder redirection, and the Windows Installer Service (WIS) for backing up and restoring users' data, personalized settings, and applications.

- Windows XP includes built-in backup features. You should thoroughly understand the Backup utility and how it can be used to back up and restore a PC.

❑ You can use the emergency repair process or ASR to repair a system that has failed.

❑ You can use the System Restore feature to return the system to a previously saved state.

❑ You can use driver rollback to remove a bad driver and return to a previously functioning driver.

❑ You can rely upon WFP to keep your system files in working order.

❑ You can use the Automatic Updates feature to keep your system in line with the latest patches from Microsoft.

❑ You can install and use the Recovery Console to recover user settings in the event of a system failure.

❑ You can use the Remote Installation Services (RIS) for a complete remote system restoration.

KEY TERMS

backup type — A backup configuration that determines how often data is backed up and how old and new files are handled. The types of backups are copy, daily, differential, incremental, and normal.

Backup utility — The Windows XP built-in tool that enables users to back up and restore their data and system configurations in case of a hardware or software failure.

copy backup — A method of backing up all selected files without marking them as being backed up.

daily backup — A method of backing up only the selected files that have been created or modified on the day that the backup is being performed. They are not marked as being backed up.

differential backup — A method of backing up selected files that have been created or modified since the last full backup. They are not marked as being backed up.

folder redirection — A component of IntelliMirror technologies that uses group policies to place specified user folders on a share on the network.

incremental backup — A method of backing up selected files that have been created or modified since the last normal or incremental backup. These files are marked as being backed up.

IntelliMirror — A set of features within Windows XP that utilizes policies, folder redirection, and the Windows Installer Service (WIS) for backing up and restoring users' data, personalized settings, and applications.

normal (or full) backup — A method of backing up all selected files and marking them as being backed up.

PXE (Preboot Execution) — A standard environment in PC98-compliant computers and network computers that can be used for a remote OS installation.

Recovery Console — A command-line interface that provides administrative tools useful for recovering a system that is not booting correctly.

Remote Installation Preparation (RIPrep) — A type of installation used with remote OS installation whereby an administrator can take an entire image of one Windows XP Professional machine and install it onto other workstations. That image can include the OS as well as installed applications and configuration settings.

Remote Installation Services (RIS) — An optional service in Windows Server that works with various other services to enable remote installations, including a remote operating system installation.

remote OS installation — A component of Remote Installation Services (RIS) that can install Windows XP Professional on remote-boot-enabled PCs across a network.

System State data — A collection of system-specific data that can be backed up and restored using the Windows XP Backup utility.

Windows Installer Service (WIS) — A Windows XP component that manages the installation and removal of applications by applying a set of centrally defined setup rules during the installation process.

REVIEW QUESTIONS

1. Which of the following types of media can be used to back up a user's data? (Choose all that apply.)

    a. tape drives

    b. external hard drives

    c. logical drives

    d. network shares

2. The Recovery Console can be used to stop and start services. True or False?

3. Which of the following could *not* participate in remote OS installation?

    a. a network computer with no RIS remote-boot disk

    b. a PC with a PXE-based remote-boot ROM, but with no RIS remote-boot disk

    c. a PC with an RIS remote-boot disk, but with no PXE-based remote-boot ROM

    d. an undocked laptop with a RIS remote-boot disk

4. Which of the following backup types backs up only the selected files that have been created or modified since the last normal or incremental backup? (Choose all that apply.)

    a. normal

    b. daily

    c. differential

    d. incremental

14

5. Windows XP automatically records new restoration points at which of the following events?

   a. 24 hours of computer uptime

   b. every logon

   c. application installation through Install Shield

   d. unsigned driver installation

6. Which of the following boot options is used to send troubleshooting and system status information from one computer to another on the network?

   a. Last Known Good Configuration

   b. Safe Mode with Networking

   c. Enable Boot Logging

   d. Debugging Mode

7. The WFP automatically protects core system files, which includes some font files. True or False?

8. Which of the following IntelliMirror technologies is associated with recovering a user's personal desktop settings?

   a. user data management

   b. software installation

   c. user setting management

   d. user desktop management

9. Which of the following items are backed up when backing up the System State data, using the Backup utility? (Choose all that apply.)

   a. COM+ Class Registration database

   b. Registry files

   c. system boot files

   d. the \system32 directory

10. Folder redirection is set up using the Synchronization Manager. True or False?

11. When the _____ repair option is run, the system automatically attempts to repair problems related to the Registry, system files, the boot volume, and the startup environment.

12. Which of the following backup types marks backed up files as being backed up? (Choose all that apply.)

    a. copy

    b. daily

    c. differential

    d. incremental

    e. normal

13. Which of the following users can use the Backup utility to back up secured files on a Windows XP Professional computer? (Choose all that apply.)

    a. a member of the Administrators group

    b. a member of the Backup Operators group

    c. any user that has Log On Locally rights

    d. a member of the Backup Utility group

14. The Windows XP Automatic Update feature is configured to install new updates automatically by default. True or False?

15. ASR is used to perform what action?

    a. Restore the entire system from backup initiated with a floppy.

    b. Recover lost administrator passwords.

    c. Restore system files required for booting.

    d. Repair a damaged Registry.

16. You can install the Recovery Console by using the WINNT32.exe program on the Windows XP CD with the _____ switch.

17. Driver rollback is part of which Windows XP tool?

    a. ASR

    b. Device Manager

    c. System Restore

    d. Recovery Console

18. The Desktop Cleanup Wizard automatically launches every 30 days. True or False?

19. _____ can be used along with IntelliMirror technologies to recover an entire PC's image.

20. In order to use the Remote Installation Services (RIS), a machine must be a DHCP client. True or False?

21. Which of the following are types of installations that an RIS server can offer a client?

    a. client based

    b. RIPrep desktop image

    c. CD based

    d. network based

22. A user can initiate a network service boot by pressing the _____ key when booting up.

14

23. When a client PC requests a remote OS installation, which of the following tools does an RIS server install first on the client?

   a. Recovery Console

   b. Client Installation Wizard

   c. Windows XP Professional

   d. PXE remote-boot ROM

24. Which of the following setup options can an RIS server provide for a remote OS installation through the Client Installation Wizard? (Choose all that apply.)

   a. Automatic Setup

   b. Custom Setup

   c. Restart a Previous Setup Attempt

   d. Maintenance and Troubleshooting

CASE PROJECTS

Case Project 14-1

You're in charge of backing up all of your organization's data stored on Windows XP Professional machines. Your organization consists of 2500 users, 500 of whom usually dial in from home. All of your users use Windows XP Professional. Which of the following backup methods will you use across your organization? Choose all that apply, and justify your choice(s).

   a. tape backups

   b. Zip drives

   c. folder redirection

   d. remote OS installation

Case Project 14-2

Describe the three key features of IntelliMirror and a scenario for each feature that explains how that feature reduces the total cost of ownership (TCO).

Case Project 14-3

Describe a situation in which it would make more sense to use the Recovery Console than the emergency repair process.

15

TROUBLESHOOTING WINDOWS XP

> **After reading this chapter and completing the exercises, you will be able to:**
>
> ◆ Understand the general principles of troubleshooting
> ◆ Use troubleshooting tools
> ◆ Troubleshoot installation and printer problems
> ◆ Troubleshoot RAS and network problems
> ◆ Troubleshoot disk problems and other issues
> ◆ Apply services packs and hot fixes
> ◆ Understand the use of Microsoft troubleshooting references

Troubleshooting Windows XP Professional, as with any operating system, is an important and vast subject area. In this chapter, you learn how to detect, isolate, and eliminate problems with installation, printing, remote access, networking, disks, and other aspects of a Windows XP Professional system.

In addition to the techniques discussed in this chapter, important troubleshooting options and features of Windows XP Professional have already been covered in previous chapters. The Registry is a common location for problems as well as a source for implementing solutions. The Registry is discussed in Chapter 12, "Working with the Windows XP Registry." The Windows boot process can sometimes be prey to problems as well. These problems and related solutions are covered in Chapter 13, "Booting Windows XP." Catastrophic events, virus infections, worms, or simple hardware failure can leave you without a functioning system. To help combat these issues, fault tolerance, system recovery, and working with backups are discussed in Chapter 14, "Windows XP Professional Fault Tolerance." Keep the troubleshooting advice in these chapters in mind as you attempt to prevent and resolve problems involving Windows XP Professional.

GENERAL PRINCIPLES OF TROUBLESHOOTING

When troubles arise in Windows XP Professional, you must take action to resolve the issues at hand as quickly as possible. Troubleshooting is the art and science of systematically diagnosing and eliminating problems in a computer system. Although troubleshooting may sound exciting, in reality it is usually a fairly tedious process. The following sections present some procedures and commonsense guidelines that should improve your troubleshooting skills and help you keep downtime to a minimum.

Collect Information

The first rule of troubleshooting is this: you can never have too much information. In fact, information is your best weapon not just for resolving problems, but also for preventing them in the first place. Useful, detailed information typically falls into three areas: your system (hardware and software); previous troubleshooting, maintenance, and configuration activities; and the current problem.

Collecting information about your system's hardware and software is preventive maintenance. All pertinent information, kept in an accessible form and location, is called a **computer information file (CIF)**. A good CIF provides detailed information about the hardware and software products that make up your computer (and even your entire network). A CIF is not just a single file, but an ever-expanding accumulation of data sheets sorted into related groupings. Your CIF should be stored in a protected area (such as a safe or fireproof vault) that can be accessed in the event of an emergency (a bank's safety deposit box won't allow you to get at the information at 3:00 in the morning). Obviously, constructing a CIF from scratch is a lengthy process, but one that will be rewarded with problems solved, easy reconfigurations, or simplified replacement of failed components.

Here are some of the important elements you want to include in your CIF:

- Platform, type, brand, and model number of each component
- Complete manufacturer specifications
- Configuration settings, including jumpers and dip switches, as well as what each setting means, including IRQs, DMA addresses, memory base addresses, port assignments, and so forth
- The manual, user's guide, or configuration sheets
- Version of BIOS, driver software, patches, fixes, and so on, with floppy copies
- Printed and floppy copies of all parameter and initialization files
- Detailed directory structure printout
- Names and versions for all installed software
- Network-assigned names, locations, and addresses
- Status of empty ports or slots, upgrade options, or expansion capabilities

- System requirements, such as the manufacturer's listed minimum system requirements for its operating system, drivers, applications, hardware, etc.

- Warranty information, such as service phone numbers and e-mail addresses, and support Web sites

- Complete technical support contact information

- Error log with detailed and dated entries of problems and solutions

- Date and location of the last complete backup

- Location of backup items and original software

- Network layout and cabling map

- Copies of all software, the operating system, and driver installation or source CDs and/or floppies

Each of these items should be dated and initialed. However, your CIF is not complete if it contains only hardware and software details. You should also include the nonphysical characteristics of your system, such as:

- Information services present, such as Web, FTP, e-mail, newsgroups, message boards, and so on

- Important applications, such as productivity suites (Microsoft Office), collaboration utilities, whiteboard applications, video conferencing, and so on

- Plans for future service deployments

- A mapping or listing of related hardware and software with each service or application present on the system

- Structure of authorized access and security measures

- Training schedule

- Maintenance schedule

- Backup schedule

- Contact information for all system administrators

- Personnel organization or management hierarchy

- Workgroup arrangements

- Online data storage locations

- In-house content and delivery conventions

- Authorship rights and restrictions

- Troubleshooting procedures

15

Neither of these lists is exhaustive. As you operate and maintain your systems, you'll discover numerous other important items to add to the CIF. Don't be bashful about customizing these lists to meet your particular needs and circumstances—if it doesn't work for you, it doesn't work at all.

TIP

Remember, if you don't document it, then you won't be able to find it when you really need it. A good way to keep any CIF current is to add to, remove, or modify its contents each time you make a system modification. Performing a quarterly or semiannual audit of each CIF is not a bad idea, either.

It is essential that the contents of the CIF be complete and up to date. Without thorough, specific, and accurate information about the products, configuration, setup, and problems associated with your network, the CIF will be all but useless. Keep in mind that the time you spend organizing your CIF reduces the time required to locate information when you really need it. It is wise to create a correlation system so you can easily associate items in the CIF with the actual component, such as an alphanumeric labeling system.

It is recommended that you maintain both a printed or written version and an electronic version of this material. Every time a change, update, or correction occurs, it should be documented in the electronic version, and a printout made and stored. Murphy's Law guarantees that the moment you need your electronic data most, your system will not function.

ACTIVITY

Activity 15-1: Computer Information File

Time Required: 15 minutes

Objective: View the system information of the computer and save it to a file.

Description: Knowing what hardware and software is installed and their configurations can be very useful when troubleshooting problems. Not only does the System Information window provide you with a list of hardware and software, but it provides details of what drivers are loaded, whether they are signed, IRQs that are assigned, and so on. In this activity, you view the detail that is provided in the System Information window and then save it to a CIF.

To extract information for a CIF:

NOTE

This activity suggests a method to obtain some information about your system for a CIF; it does not constitute a complete or exhaustive collection of data. This activity is only one part of the task of creating a CIF.

1. Click **Start**, **All Programs**, **Accessories**, **System Tools**, **System Information**. You will see a window similar to the one shown in Figure 15-1.

2. Expand **Hardware Resources**, **Components**, **Software Environment**, and **Internet Settings** in the left pane by clicking the plus sign to the left of each unexpanded node.

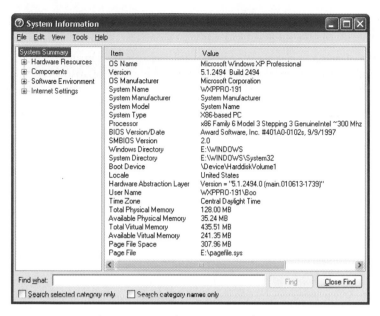

Figure 15-1　The System Information tool

3. Take the time to expand and select every item in the resulting node hierarchy. As you view each page of data, consider the value of this data for future troubleshooting and decide whether to print or save the information.

4. To print a page, click the **Print** entry on the **File** menu in the menu bar.

5. To save a page, click the **Save** entry on the **File** menu in the menu bar (this produces text-only .nfo or information files for later examination and use).

6. When you have finished examining your system information, close the utility.

Use Common Sense Troubleshooting Guidelines

When problems occur, you would like to be at your sharpest. However, as a corollary to Murphy's Law, you'll probably find that problems tend to occur when you are stressed, short on time, or when it is just generally inconvenient. If you take the time now to keep your CIF up to date and heed the following commonsense guidelines, you'll take some of the headache out of troubleshooting, and you'll be better prepared to resolve problems quickly. Although common sense is sometimes in short supply, it is a key ingredient for successful troubleshooting.

- *Be patient*—Anger, frustration, hostility, and frantic impatience usually cause problems to intensify rather than dissipate.

- *Be familiar with your system's hardware and software*—If you don't know what the normal baselines for your system are, you may not know when a problem is solved or when new problems surface. (See Chapter 10, "Performance Tuning" for information on creating baselines.)

- *Attempt to isolate the problem*—When possible, eliminate segments or components that are functioning properly, thus narrowing the range of suspected sources for a problem or failure.

- *Divide and conquer*—Disconnect, one at a time, as many nonessential devices as possible to narrow the scope of your investigation.

- *Eliminate suspects*—Move suspect components, such as printers, monitors, mice, or keyboards, to a known working computer to see if they work in their new location. If they work, they're not at fault; if they don't, they may very well be involved in the problem you're trying to solve.

- *Undo the most recent change*—If you have recently made a change to your system, the simplest fix may be to back out of the most recent alteration, upgrade, or change made to your system.

- *Investigate common points of failure first*—The most active or sensitive components also represent the most common points of failure—including hard drives, cables, and connectors.

- *Recheck items that have caused problems before*—As the old axiom goes, history does repeat itself (and usually right in your own backyard).

- *Try the easy and quick fix first*—Try the easy fixes before moving on to the more time-consuming, difficult, or even possibly destructive measures.

- *Let the fault guide you*—The adage "Where there is smoke, there is fire" applies not only to the outside world, but to computer problems as well. Investigate components and system areas associated with the suspected fault.

- *Make changes one at a time*—A long flight of stairs is best traversed one step at a time; attempting to leap several or all of the steps may result in injury or death. When troubleshooting, a step-by-step process enables you to identify the solution clearly when you stumble upon it.

- *Repeat the failure*—Often repeating an error is the only way to identify it. Transient and inconsistent faults are difficult to diagnose until you see a pattern in their occurrence.

- *Keep a detailed log of errors and attempted solutions*—Keep track of everything you do (both successful and failed attempts). This will prove an invaluable resource when an error recurs on the same or a different system, or when the same system experiences a related problem.

- *Learn from mistakes (your own and others')*—Studying the mistakes of others can save you from repeating them; a wise person uses failures to find a better solution.

- *Experiment*—If your diagnosis is inconclusive, try tasks similar to the ones that provoke the problem to see if a pattern develops.

There is probably not much in this list of commonsense items that you don't already know. The hardest part is remembering these in the heat of a crisis.

TROUBLESHOOTING TOOLS

Becoming familiar with the repair and troubleshooting tools native to Windows XP Professional can save you countless hours when troubleshooting. The next sections detail the use of the Event Viewer and the Computer Management tools.

Event Viewer

The **Event Viewer** is used to view system messages regarding the failure and/or success of various key occurrences within the Windows XP Professional environment (see Figure 15-2). The items recorded in the Event Viewer's logs inform you of system drivers or service failures as well as security problems or misbehaving applications.

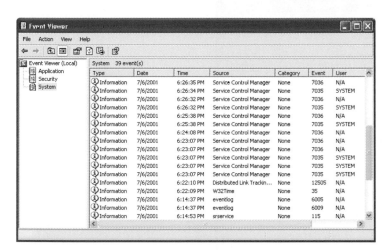

Figure 15-2   Event Viewer with System log selected

Located in the Administrative Tools section of Control Panel, the Event Viewer is used to view the logs that Windows XP Professional creates automatically:

- *System log*—Records information and alerts about Windows XP Professional internal processes, including hardware and operating system errors, warnings, and general information messages

- *Security log*—Records security-related events, including audit events for failed logons, user rights alterations, and attempted object accesses without sufficient permissions

- *Application log*—Records application events, alerts, and some system messages

15

- *Directory service*—Records events related to the directory service
- *DNS Service*—Records events related to the DNS Service.
- *File Replication Service*—Records events related to the File Replication Service

Each log records a different type of event, but all the logs collect the same metainformation about each event: date, time, source, category, event, user ID, and computer. Each logged event includes some level of detail about the error, from an error code number to a detailed description with a memory HEX buffer capture. For example, Figure 15-3 shows the properties of a logged event related to the workstation's attempt to register a DNS address, or an A record, with an unreachable directory server. Most system errors, including stop errors that result in the blue screen, are recorded in the System log, allowing you to review the time and circumstances of a system failure. The details in the Event Viewer can often be used as clues in your search for the actual cause of a problem. However, most event log details offer little information on resolving the problems they document.

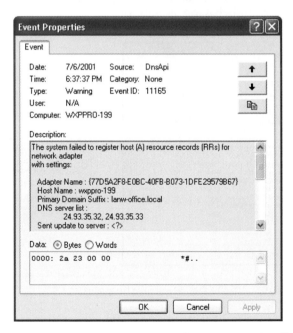

Figure 15-3   Event Viewer's Event Properties dialog box with logged event details

Activity 15-2: Viewing the System Log

Time Required: 15 minutes

Objective: View the System log to read and understand the type of information written to the logs.

Description: The Event Viewer can be very useful in viewing what has been taking place in your computer. This should be one of the first places to look when troubleshooting a potential problem. In this activity, you open the System log and review the details of some of the events that have been recorded.

To use the Event Viewer:

1. Open the Event Viewer from the Start menu (**Start**, **Control Panel**, double-click **Administrative Tools**, double-click **Computer Management**, **Event Viewer** to display the list of available logs).

2. Select the **System** log from the list of available logs in the left pane.

3. Notice the various types of events that appear in the right pane.

4. Select an event in the right pane.

5. Select **Action**, **Properties** (or more simply, double-click the event entry).

6. Review the information presented in the Event Properties dialog box. Try to determine on your own what types of errors, warnings, or information are presented in the detail and why the detail was created.

7. Click the up and down arrows to view other event details.

8. Click **OK** to close the event detail.

9. Select **File**, **Exit** to close Event Viewer.

Computer Management Tool

Windows XP Professional builds on the robustness of Windows 2000, and on the convenience of its Plug-and-Play-assisted configuration capabilities. In Windows XP, these same capabilities provide easy access to troubleshooting tools for nearly every aspect of the operating system. A large number of these tools are collected into a single interface called the Computer Management tool (see Figure 15-4), found in the Administrative Tools application within Control Panel.

The Computer Management tool includes many tools identical to those in Windows 2000; there are some new entries, but some entries have been dropped (system information and logical drives are the most noteworthy in this group). Grouping these utilities in a single interface makes locating and resolving problems on key system components easier than ever before. The Computer Management console is divided into three sections: System Tools, Storage, and Services and Applications.

15

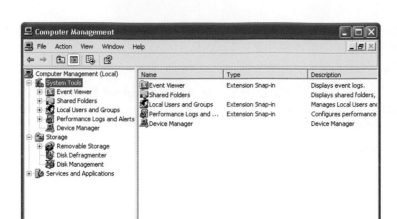

Figure 15-4 The Computer Management tool

The System Tools section contains five individual tools:

- *Event Viewer*—Used to view system messages regarding the failure or success of various key occurrences within the Windows XP Professional environment. Details of system errors, security issues, and application activities are recorded in the logs viewed through the Event Viewer. See the description of the Event Viewer earlier in this chapter.

- *Shared Folders*—Used to view shared folders defined on the local system. This interface shows hidden and public shares, current sessions, and open files, and also allows you to view and alter the share configuration settings for user limits, caching, and permissions.

- *Local Users and Groups*—Used to create and manage local user accounts and groups. (This tool is disabled when Active Directory is present.) Details on use, examples, and activities for this tool are included in Chapter 5, "Users, Groups, Profiles, and Policies."

- *Performance Logs and Alerts*—Used as another means to access the Performance Monitor tool of Windows XP. (The use of this tool in troubleshooting is rather tedious and complex; see Chapter 11, "Windows XP Professional Application Support," for examples and activities involving this tool.)

- *Device Manager*—Used to view and alter current hardware configurations of all existing devices. Details on use, examples, and activities for this tool appear in Chapter 3, "Using the System Utilities."

The Storage section of Computer Management presents three tools for administering storage devices. Details on use, examples, and activities appear in Chapter 4, "Managing Windows XP File Systems and Storage."

- *Removable Storage*—Manages removable media, such as floppy disks, tapes, and Zip drives.

- *Disk Defragmenter*—Improves the layout of stored data on drives by reassembling fragmented files and aggregating unused space.

- *Disk Management*—Views and alters the partitioning and volume configuration of hard drives.

The Services and Applications section contains management controls for various installed and active services and applications. Though the actual contents of this section depend on what is installed on your system, some common controls include:

- *Services*—Stops and starts services and configures the startup parameters for services (such as whether to initiate the service when the system starts and whether to employ a user account security context to initiate the service).

- *WMI Control*—Configures and controls the Windows Management Instrumentation service, a service designed for Web-based or network access. This tool allows network management systems (or related software) to interact with agent software on a Windows XP Professional machine to install, set up, or update system or application software and related configuration data.

- *Indexing Service*—Defines the corpus (collection of documents indexed for searching) for the Indexing service. For information on using this tool, consult the *Microsoft Windows 2000 Server Resource Kit*.

15

Activity 15-3: Workstation Services

Time Required: 10 minutes

Objective: Use the Computer Management tool to view the services on the system and determine whether they are started or stopped.

Description: When there is an issue with an application or utility, it is often a good practice to see if the service or services required for that function are started. Sometimes, simply choosing to start the service is all that is required. Other times, it may be that a file is missing or corrupted, and is preventing the service from starting. In this activity, you use the Computer Management tool to verify that services are started, and then start them if they aren't.

To verify that the Workstation and Server services are running after the system starts:

1. Open **Control Panel** (**Start, Control Panel**).

2. Double-click **Administrative Tools**.

3. Double-click **Computer Management**.

4. Expand the **Services and Applications** section by clicking the plus sign next to the node name if it is not already expanded.

5. Select the **Services** object.

6. Scroll down in the right pane to locate the Workstation service.

7. Notice the item in the Status column. If it says "Started," you can skip to Step 9.

8. If the Status column is blank for the Workstation service, it failed to run at startup. To attempt to start the service, select it, click the **Action** menu, and then click **Start**.

9. Scroll up in the right pane to locate the Server service.

10. Notice the item in the Status column. If it says "Started," you can skip to Step 12.

11. If the Status column is blank for the Server service, it failed to run at startup. To attempt to start the service, select it, click the **Action** menu, and then click **Start**.

12. Close the Computer Management console.

Troubleshooting Wizards

Continuing the trend established in Windows 2000, Windows XP Professional includes many troubleshooting Wizards associated with specific system components or services. For example, the Settings tab in the Display Properties applet (most easily accessed by right-clicking any unoccupied spot on the desktop and then selecting the Properties entry in the resulting shortcut menu) includes a Troubleshoot button, as shown in Figure 15-5. Clicking that button brings up the Video Display Troubleshooter depicted in Figure 15-6; selecting any of its entries leads you through a series of questions with answers and explanations that deal very effectively with common sources of trouble. Similar buttons for other system controls, including Phone and Modem Options (which also has a Troubleshoot button) or the Local Area Connection Properties, might be labeled "Repair" instead, but they offer similar kinds of guided troubleshooting support.

As you investigate the management utilities or Control Panel applets for the system aspects or components you're troubleshooting, don't overlook the kinds of help that the system itself can provide. One of the biggest changes from Windows 2000 to Windows XP Professional is the adoption of a task-oriented metaphor to provide help and guidance, where troubleshooting tasks figure prominently in the lists of tasks for which help and support are available. In other words, Windows XP Professional interfaces, wizards, and help information focus on accomplishing tasks or activities rather than just providing you with factual information.

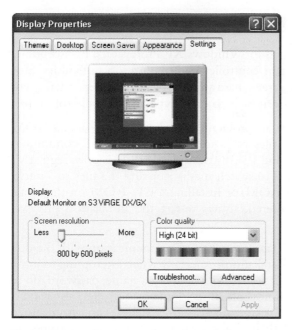

Figure 15-5   Settings tab in the Display Properties applet

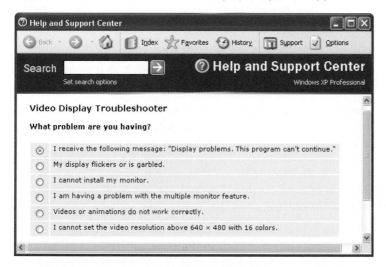

Figure 15-6   The Video Display Troubleshooter

15

TROUBLESHOOTING INSTALLATION PROBLEMS

Unfortunately, the installation process for Windows XP Professional is susceptible to several types of errors: media errors, domain controller communication difficulties, Stop message errors or being hung up on a blue screen, hardware problems, and dependency failures. The following list contains a short synopsis of each error type and possible solutions:

- *Media errors*—Media errors are problems with the distribution CD-ROM itself, the copy of the distribution files on a network drive, or the communication link between the installation and the distribution files. The only regularly successful solution to media errors is to switch media: copying the files to a network drive, linking to a server's CD-ROM, or installing a CD-ROM on the workstation. If media errors are encountered, always restart the installation process from the beginning.

- *Domain controller communication difficulties*—Communication with the domain controller is crucial to some installations, especially when attempting to join a domain. Most often, this problem is related to mistyping a name, password, domain name, and so on, but network failures and offline domain controllers also can be involved. Verify the availability of the domain controller directly and from other workstations (if warranted), and then check that no entries were mistyped during the installation process.

- *Stop message errors or halting on the blue screen*—Using an incompatible or damaged driver is the most common cause of Stop messages and halting on the blue screen during installation. If any error information is presented to you, try to verify that the proper driver is in use. Otherwise, double-check that your hardware has the drivers necessary to operate under Windows XP Professional.

- *Hardware problems*—If you failed to verify your hardware with the HCL (Hardware Compatibility List), or a physical defect has occurred in a previously operational device, strange errors can surface. In such cases, replacing the device in question is often the only solution. Before you go to that expense, however, double-check the installation and configuration of all devices within the computer. Sometimes, manual resolution of conflicts that Plug and Play is unable to resolve automatically can cure hardware problems.

- *Dependency failures*—The failure of a service or driver owing to the failure of a foundation class, or of some other related service or driver, is called a dependency failure. An example is the failure of Server and Workstation services because the NIC fails to initialize properly. Often, Windows XP Professional starts despite such errors, so check the Event Viewer for more details (see Figure 15-7 for an example of an error reported because a common service proves to be unavailable). Most dependency errors usually appear immediately after installing the operating system or new software, or after altering the system configuration.

Figure 15-7   Event Properties dialog box

Just knowing about these installation problems can help you avoid them. However, successfully installing Windows XP Professional does not eliminate the possibility of further complications. Fortunately, Microsoft has included several troubleshooting tools that can help locate and eliminate most system failures (see the Troubleshooting Tools section earlier in this chapter).

If you make any significant changes to the core hardware components of your computer, you may need to repair or replace your hardware access list (HAL). Installing additional CPUs, replacing the motherboard, upgrading the motherboard's BIOS, changing the type of physical RAM installed, and even reconfiguring the motherboard (via CMOS) may all cause the existing HAL to no longer function properly. If significant alteration has taken place, a STOP error occurs. The STOP error message will be similar to 0:000000079HAL_ MISMATCH. To recover from this problem, start the system from the Windows XP Professional CD and select the Repair the installation option.

If your computer contains nonstandard core hardware (such as motherboard, CPU, drive controller, and so on), hardware released after the initial release of Windows XP Professional, or hardware with new or updated drivers, you can install the drivers for this hardware during the initial portion of setup. At the beginning of the text-only portion of setup, the status line at the bottom of the screen prompts you to press F6 to install OEM drivers. The drivers must be on a floppy to install them using this method.

15

TROUBLESHOOTING PRINTER PROBLEMS

Problems with network printers can often bring normal activity to a halt. They can occur anywhere between the printer's power cable and the application that's attempting to print. Systematic elimination of possible points of failure is the only reliable method for eliminating such errors. Here are some useful tips for troubleshooting common printer problems:

- Always check that the physical components of the printer—cable, power, paper, toner, and so on—are present, properly loaded, or connected, as appropriate.

- Make sure the printer is online. There is typically a light or an LCD message to indicate this. You may need to press the Reset button or an Online button to set or cycle the printer into online mode.

- Make sure the printer server for the printer is booted.

- Verify that the logical printer on both the client and server sides exists, and check their configuration parameters and settings. For details on logical printers and their multitudes of controls, see Chapter 9, "Printing and Faxing."

- Check the print queue for stalled jobs (see Figure 15-8, which shows a printing job in progress).

 If a print job does not show an explicit status, such as waiting, paused, printing, and so on, you can assume it is stalled. The print queue is accessed by clicking the Start menu, selecting Printers and Faxes, selecting the printer whose queue you want to examine, and then clicking the See what's printing entry in the Printer Tasks list.

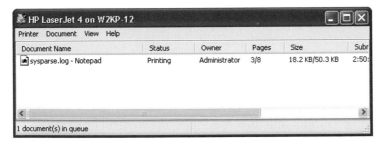

Figure 15-8   The default window for any printer shows its print queue contents

- Reinstall or update the printer driver in case it is corrupt or incorrect.

- Attempt to print from a different application or a different client.

- Attempt to print using Administrator access.

- Stop and restart the spooler using the Services tool found through Computer Management.

- Check the status and CPU usage of the Spoolsv.exe process using the Task Manager (see Figure 15-9). If the spooler seems to be stalled—it will either not obtain any CPU time at all or consume most of the CPU—you should stop and restart the spooler service (Spoolsv.exe).

Figure 15-9 The Windows Task Manager, Processes tab

- Check the free space on the drive where the print spool file resides, and change its destination if less than 100 MB of free space is available. The amount of free space that a spooler file needs is a function of the size and number of print jobs and the logical printer's settings, but in most cases, 100 MB is sufficient. You should change the spool file host drive if there is insufficient space or you suspect the drive is not fast enough. Make this change on the Advanced tab of the Server Properties dialog box accessed on the File menu in the Printer Folder. See Chapter 9 for more information. Table 15-1 lists some common network printing problems and their solutions.

Table 15-1   Printer troubleshooting

Network printing problem	Solutions
Pages print, but only a single character appears on each page —or— Pages print but they include control codes —or— Pages print, but they show random characters instead of the desired document	1. If the job has not completed printing, delete it from the print queue to prevent wasting more paper. 2. Remove and reinstall the logical printer and/or the printer driver on the client (if only a single workstation experiences the problem) or on the server (if all workstations experience the problem). 3. Verify that the data type set in the logical printer is correct for the application used, printer driver installed, and capabilities of the physical print device. 4. Stop and restart the spooler service (Spoolsv.exe).
An Access denied or No access available message is displayed when a print job is submitted	This is typically caused by improper permissions defined on the printer share. Double-check the permission settings. You may also need to review the group memberships of the affected users if you are employing any Deny permissions on the printer share.
A network attached printer shows an error light on the network interface	A network communication or identification error has occurred. Cycling the power on the printer may resolve the problem. If not, try disconnecting then reconnecting the network media while the printer is powered off.
No documents are being created by the physical print device, but the print queue shows that the job is printing	1. View the print queue to see if a print job is stalled or paused; if so, delete or resume the print job. 2. If no other print job is present, delete the current print job and resubmit it from the original application. 3. Stop and restart the spooler service (Spoolsv.exe).
The printer share is not visible from a client (i.e., does not appear in Network Neighborhood or My Network Places)	1. The client system may not be properly connected to the network. Shut down the client, check all physical network connections, and restart. Test whether you can access any other network resources. 2. Check the installed protocol and its settings, especially if TCP/IP is being used. 3. Check the domain/workgroup membership of the client.
On larger print jobs, pages from the end of the print job are missing from the printed document	This can occur when insufficient space is available on the drive hosting the spooler file; either free some space on the host drive or move the spooler file to a drive with more available space.

This list covers most common print-related problems. For more tips on troubleshooting, consult the *Microsoft Windows XP Professional Resource Kit*.

ACTIVITY

Activity 15-4: Computer Management

Time Required: 10 minutes

Objective: Become familiar with the components that make up the Computer Management utility.

Description: The Computer Management utility provides you with a way to perform a quick check on the "health" of the computer. In this activity, you are asked to go through and view all of the information available in the Computer Management utility.

To explore the Computer Management utility:

For this activity, it is assumed that Control Panel is in Classic View.

1. Open the **Control Panel** (**Start**, **Control Panel**).

2. Double-click **Administrative Tools**.

3. Double-click **Computer Management**.

4. Notice that the left pane hosts three divisions: System Tools, Storage, and Services and Applications.

5. Expand the **System Tools** entry (if not already expanded) by clicking the plus sign located to the left of the node name.

6. Explore the contents of the Event Viewer, Performance Logs and Alerts, Shared Folders, Device Manager, and Local Users and Groups sections by expanding them one at a time. To view the contents of any item, select it in the left pane so its contents appear in the right pane.

7. Once you've viewed the contents of the System Tools section, view the contents of the Storage section. This section includes Disk Management, Disk Defragmenter, and Removable Storage.

8. Once you've viewed the contents of the Storage section, view the contents of the Services and Applications section. The items in this section vary based on installed applications and services but can include WMI Control, Services, and Indexing Service.

9. Once you've viewed the contents of the Services and Applications section, close the Computer Management utility.

15

TROUBLESHOOTING RAS PROBLEMS

Remote Access Service (RAS) is another area with numerous points of possible failure—from the configuration of the computers on both ends, to the modem settings, to the condition of the communications line. Unfortunately, there is no ultimate RAS troubleshooting guide, but here are some solid steps in the right direction:

- Check all physical connections.
- Check the communication line itself, with a phone if appropriate.

- Verify the RAS configuration and the modem setup by attempting to establish a connection to another server or by deleting and re-creating the connection object. For detailed examples and activities, see Chapter 8, "Internetworking with Remote Access."

- Check that both the client and the server dial-up configurations match, including speed, protocol, and security. See Figure 15-10 for an example of the security settings for a dial-up connection. You'll need to view the other tabs to compare and confirm speed, protocol, and other connection settings.

Figure 15-10   Setting Security options

- Verify that the user account has RAS privileges.

- Inspect the RAS-related logs: Device.log and Modemlog.txt. Look for errors involving failure to connect, failure to dial, failure to authenticate, failure to negotiate encryption, failure to establish a common protocol, and link termination.

- Remember that multilink and callback do not work together; you must select one or the other. Because nobody has developed technology to perform multiline callbacks, only single-line callbacks are possible. Figure 15-11 shows a configuration setting on a connection object that allows the caller to define a specific callback number to complete a dial-up connection. (To access the window shown, select Start, Control Panel, Network Connections, select the connection, and then select the Dial-up Preferences entry in the Advanced menu at the top of the Network Connections window.)

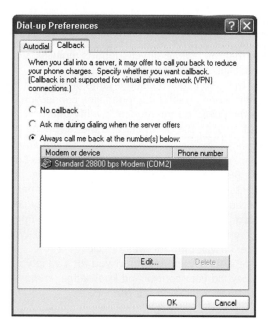

Figure 15-11 Dial-up Preferences, Callback tab

- Autodial and persistent connections may cause a computer to attempt RAS connection with each logon; in some cases, you may need to disable such settings to permit easier troubleshooting of connection problems.

15

TIP Most RAS problems are related to misconfiguration. For more details on RAS, refer to Chapter 8 or the *Microsoft Windows XP Professional Resource Kit*. Table 15-2 lists some common remote printing problems and their solutions.

Table 15-2 RAS troubleshooting

Network printing problem	Solutions
The connection object fails to establish a network link with the remote server	1. Check the username, password, and phone number. 2. Verify that the modem device is powered on and properly connected to the computer and the phone line. You should also check the installed driver and update it if necessary. 3. Verify that the security settings match those required by the remote server. 4. Verify that the protocol settings match those required by the remote server.

Table 15-2   RAS troubleshooting (continued)

Network printing problem	Solutions
The client has multilink enabled and has three identical modems for the connection, but only one modem establishes a network link with the remote server	1. Verify that the remote server supports multilink and that it has multilink connections enabled. 2. Verify that you need to dial the same or different phone numbers when establishing a multilink connection. 3. Cycle the power on the modems; verify that they are properly attached to the computer and the telephone line.
A network link is broken during a remote session after a successful link is established	1. Your phone line probably has call waiting and another call came in; disable call waiting through the connection object. 2. If your telephone line quality is poor (old wiring, phone lines pass by electrical interference, or the weather is bad), connection interruptions are common. You may need to upgrade your internal wiring, request a service upgrade from the telephone company, reroute wiring to avoid interference, or wait until the weather clears. 3. Remote systems can disconnect you for a variety of reasons, most beyond your control and knowledge; in most cases, simply try to reestablish the connection.

TROUBLESHOOTING NETWORK PROBLEMS

Network problems range from faults in the network cables or hardware, to misconfigured protocols, to workstation or server errors. As with all troubleshooting, attempt to eliminate the obvious and easy (such as physical connections and permissions) before moving on to more drastic, complex, or unreliable measures (such as IP configuration, routing, and domain structure). Cabling, connections, and hardware devices are just as suspect as the software components of networking. Verifying hardware functionality involves more than just looking at it; you may need to perform some electrical tests, change physical settings, or even update drivers or ROM BIOS settings. Table 15-3 lists some common network connectivity problems and their solutions.

Commonsense first steps include the following:

- Check to see if other clients or servers or subnets are experiencing the same problem.

- Check physical network connections, including the NIC, media cables, terminators, and logically proximate network devices (such as hubs, repeaters, routers, and so on).

- Check protocol settings.

- Restart the system.

- Verify that the NIC drivers are properly installed. Use the self-test or diagnostic tools or software for the NIC if available.

- Verify the domain/workgroup membership of the client.

Table 15-3   Network connection troubleshooting

Connectivity problem	Solutions
The client does not seem to connect to the network (i.e., no objects are visible in the Network Neighborhood) —or— The client is unable to authenticate with the domain	1. Use the Event Viewer to look for errors in the System log; resolve any issues discovered. 2. Check the physical network connections, including the NIC, media, and local network devices. 3. Check the NIC driver; update or replace if necessary. 4. Check the installed protocol and its configuration settings. 5. Check the domain/workgroup membership. 6. Restart the client.
A system disconnects from the network randomly or when other computers connect to the network	1. Check to see that you are not violating the length, segments, or nodes-per-segment limitations on the network media in use. 2. Verify that all systems have unique address assignments and system computer names. 3. Check for breaks in the network media or the proximity of electrical or magnetic interference.
Shared network resources, such as folders and printers, cannot be accessed from a client	1. Check the assigned permissions on the share itself and on the object (if applicable). 2. Check group memberships for Deny permissions. 3. Attempt to access the resources using a different user account or client. 4. Check that the computer is connecting to the network.

TROUBLESHOOTING DISK PROBLEMS

15

The hard drive is the component on your computer that experiences the most activity, even more than your keyboard or mouse. It should not be surprising that drive failures are common. Windows XP Professional maintains and tunes its file system automatically (see Chapter 4), but even a well-tuned system is subject to hardware glitches. Most partition, boot sector, and drive configuration faults can be corrected or recovered using the Disk Management tool in the Computer Management utility in Administrative Tools (for detailed information on using this tool and on troubleshooting disk problems, see Chapter 4). However, the only reliable means of protecting data on storage devices is to maintain an accurate and timely backup, as discussed in Chapter 14.

MISCELLANEOUS TROUBLESHOOTING ISSUES

The following is a grab bag of troubleshooting tips that don't fit into the other categories described in this chapter.

Permissions Problems

Permissions problems (problems with accessing or managing system resources, such as folders, files, or printers) usually occur when a user is a member of groups with conflicting permissions or when permissions are managed on a per-account basis. To test for faulty permission settings, attempt the same actions and activities with Administrator privileges. Double-check a user's group memberships to verify that Deny access settings are not causing the problem. This means examining the access control lists (ACLs) of the objects and the share, if applicable (see Figure 15-12).

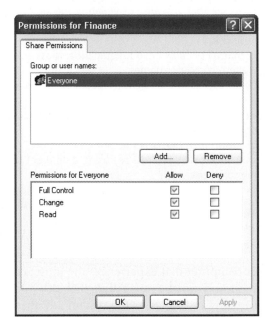

Figure 15-12 Setting Share Permissions

NOTE It is important to remember that any changes to the access permissions for individual users or groups do not affect those users until the next time they log on. The access token used by the security system is created each time a user logs on, but is not altered as long as they stay logged on. This means that any time you need to make sweeping changes to a file system or share permissions, it is a good idea to do so when few users are logged on, and to disconnect those users to force them to log back on under the new permissions regime!

ACTIVITY

Activity 15-5: Troubleshooting Resource Access

Time Required: 20 minutes

Objective: Troubleshoot a resource access issue using different accounts and group memberships.

Description: From time to time, a person may not be able to access a resource (file, folder, share, and so on) when he or she is supposed to have access. The permission might be set incorrectly; the person may not have been added to the correct group, or the person is simply not supposed to have access. In this activity, you try to resolve a problem using basic troubleshooting techniques.

To troubleshoot permission problems:

This activity is not an exhaustive process for permission troubleshooting; it includes only some of the high-frequency actions that may be required to resolve permission problems.

1. If a user cannot access a resource to which they should have access, first restart the system (**Start**, **Shut Down**). Select **Restart** from the pull-down menu, and then click **OK**.

2. After restarting, log back on as the user. Test to see if you can access the resource.

3. If the resource is still not accessible, log off and log back on as an administrator: Press **Ctrl+Alt+Delete** at the logon prompt, and then provide the user account name for the administrator and the associated password. Click **OK**.

4. Once logged on as the administrator, attempt to access the resource. If the resource can be accessed, the problem is with the assigned permissions for the user account. Most likely, the user account is not a member of the proper group or is a member of a group that has Deny access permissions set for that resource.

5. If the resource cannot be accessed by the administrator, the problem may lie with the system itself. This could include network communications, domain membership, or corrupted system drivers and files. You need to troubleshoot these other possible causes of the problem.

6. If you discover that group membership is the problem, make the appropriate group membership changes, and then have the user log off and log back on (changes do not take effect until the next logon).

Activity 15-6: Troubleshooting Printing

Time Required: 15 minutes

Objective: Troubleshoot a printing problem using the available tools.

Description: Most network administrators agree that two of the most common problems that cause user complaints are password issues and printing problems. To provide timely service to your users, proficiency in resolving printer issues is a necessity. In this activity, you perform some of the basic steps to resolve a printing problem.

To troubleshoot a printer problem:

This activity is not an exhaustive process for printer troubleshooting; it includes some of the actions that may be required to resolve a printer problem.

1. First, check that the printer is online, has power, has paper, and has toner. Check the printer's own error-reporting center (often a light or an LCD) for any possible hardware errors.

2. Open the Printers applet (**Start**, **Printers and Faxes**).

3. Double-click the installed printer that you suspect is having a problem to display the print queue window.

4. If any documents appear in the print queue window, select the top document, and then select **Document**, **Restart**.

5. If the printer still fails to function, go to Control Panel (**Start**, **Control Panel**).

6. Double-click the **Administrative Tools** icon.

7. Double-click **Computer Management**.

8. Navigate down the hierarchy of the left pane to locate and select the Services tool (**Computer Management**, **Services and Applications**, **Services**).

9. Locate and select the **Print Spooler** service in the Extended tab (see Figure 15-13).

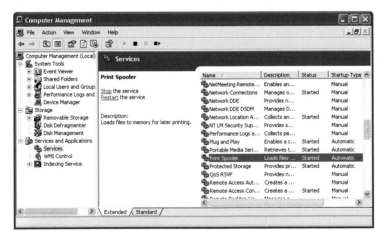

Figure 15-13   Services in the Computer Management tool

10. Select **Action**, **Stop**.

11. Select **Action**, **Start**.

12. Close the Computer Management utility.

13. Close the Administrative Tools.

14. If the printer still fails to function, return to the print queue window that was left open.

15. Select the top document in the print queue.

16. Click the **Document** menu, then select **Cancel** to remove the print job from the queue.

17. If this was the only print job in the queue, print another document. If this was not the only print job in the queue, wait to see if the remaining print jobs print.

 Consult Chapter 9 for more details on managing printers.

Master Boot Record Problems

As you learned in Chapter 13, the **Master Boot Record (MBR)** is the area of a hard drive that contains the data structure for initiating the boot process. However, if the MBR fails, the emergency repair disk (ERD) cannot be used to repair it. Instead, you must use a recovery tool of some kind, for which there are several approaches:

■ Boot from the Windows XP Professional boot floppies (all six of them), use F8 to select the alternate boot menu, and then select Recovery Console from that menu.

■ Reconfigure your system BIOS to boot from your CD player, and then boot from the Windows XP Professional installation CD. Here, you can select Repair damaged installation as an option, and also access the Recovery Console.

■ If neither of the preceding methods works, you need to use a DOS 6.0 (or later) bootable floppy to boot into DOS.

If you can access the Recovery Console, use the FIXMBR command to repair the MBR. If you are forced to boot into DOS, then use the FDISK/MBR command. At that point, execute the command *fdisk/mbr*, which re-creates the drive's MBR and restores the system correctly. If you don't have access to the FDISK, you have to perform a complete install/ upgrade of Windows XP Professional to allow the setup routine to re-create the MBR.

Using the Dr. Watson Debugger

Windows XP Professional has an application error debugger called **Dr. Watson**. This diagnostic tool detects application failures and logs diagnostic details. Data captured by Dr. Watson is stored in the Drwtsn32.log file. Dr. Watson can also be configured to save a memory dump of the application's address space for further investigation. However, the information extracted and stored by Dr. Watson is really only useful to a technical professional well versed in the debugger's cryptic logging syntax.

Windows XP Professional automatically starts Dr. Watson when an application error occurs. To configure Dr. Watson, however, you need to start it from the Start, Run command with *drwtsn32.exe*. Figure 15-14 shows the configuration dialog box for Dr. Watson. As you can see, this dialog box lists the configuration items for the following:

- Log File Path, which is the storage location of the Dr. Watson log file
- Crash Dump, which is the dump location for an application's virtual machine's address space
- Number of Instructions
- Number of Errors To Save
- Crash Dump Type
- Options of what to include in the log file and how to notify the user of an application fault
- A list of previous Application Errors, with access to the log file details

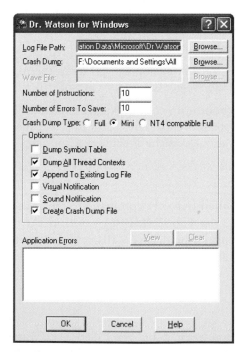

Figure 15-14 Dr. Watson configuration dialog box

APPLYING SERVICE PACKS AND HOT FIXES

A **service pack** is a collection of code replacements, patches, error corrections, new applications, version improvements, or service-specific configuration settings from Microsoft that corrects, replaces, or hides the deficiencies of the original product, preceding service packs, or hot fixes. A **hot fix** is similar to a service pack, except that it addresses only a single problem, or a small number of problems, and may not be fully tested (and is not normally supported, unless you have a special service agreement with Microsoft).

You should apply a hot fix only if you are experiencing the problem it was created to solve; otherwise, the hot fix may cause other problems. Most production environments avoid using hot fixes whenever possible in favor of waiting until the next service pack rolls them up in a form that is fully tested and better supported. The exception to this rule is security-related hot fixes, in which case the affected machine might remain vulnerable to a documented threat or attack if the hot fix is not applied.

Service packs are cumulative. For example, Service Pack 3 (SP3) for Windows 2000 Professional contains SP2 plus all post-SP2 hot fixes. Thus, the latest service pack is all you need to install.

Take the time to review the documentation included with the latest Windows XP Professional service pack.

It is common practice among production networks to wait one to three months after the release of a new service pack before deploying it. This gives the installed community time to test and provide feedback about the patch. The track record of service packs from Microsoft is not perfect, so it's better to wait for verification of a service pack's reliability than to deploy it immediately after its release and live to regret it.

Important points to remember about patches, such as service packs and hot fixes, include:

- Always make a backup of your system before applying any type of patch; this gives you a way to restore your system if the fix damages the OS.

- Be sure you've retrieved a patch for the correct CPU type and language version.

- Always read the readme file and Knowledge Base Q documents for each patch before installing it.

- Update your emergency repair disk (ERD) both before and after applying a patch.

- Make a complete backup of the Registry using the Registry Editor or the REGBACK utility in the *Microsoft Windows XP Professional Resource Kit*.

- Export the disk configuration data from Disk Administrator.

15

- Because service packs rewrite many system-level files, you must disconnect all current users, exit all applications, and temporarily stop all unneeded services before installing any service pack or patch.

To locate Microsoft Knowledge Base documents, visit or use one of these resources:

- Web site: *http://support.microsoft.com/*
- TechNet CD
- Microsoft Network
- Resource Kit documentation (online help file)

Service packs and hot fixes can be retrieved from:

- Microsoft FTP site: *ftp.microsoft.com/bussys/winnt/winnt-public/fixes/usa/*
- The Download section of the Microsoft Windows Web site: *www.microsoft.com/downloads/*

To determine which service packs have been applied to your system, you can use one of the following techniques:

- Enter *WINVER* from a command prompt to view an About Windows dialog box.
- Select Help, About Windows on the menu bar of any native tool, such as My Computer or Windows Explorer.
- Use the Registry Editor to view the CSDVersion value in the HKEY_LOCAL_MACHINE\SOFTWARE\Microsoft\WindowsNT\CurrentVersion.

Service packs can be integrated into the installation files so that a completely integrated installation can be performed. An integrated installation is one in which the completed installation process includes the operating system with the service pack already fully installed. This is also known as slipstreaming a service pack. In order to perform a integrated installation of a service pack, you must download the network installation version of the service pack. There is one important caveat to performing integrated installations: you cannot uninstall any service pack that is applied in this manner.

Activity 15-7: Prepare an Integrated Installation of a Service Pack

Time Required: 15 minutes

Objective: Create a set of installation files with an integrated service pack.

Description: When deploying new systems and installing the OS for the first time, using an integrated installation set simplifies and speeds the installation procedure. Service packs can be integrated into the installation files so that a completely integrated installation can be performed. An integrated installation is one in which the completed installation process includes the operating system with the service pack already fully installed.

To prepare an installation file set with an integrated service pack:

1. Obtain the network installation version of the service pack from the Microsoft Windows XP Web area (*www.microsoft.com/windowsxp/*).

2. Create a new folder on a network server, such as c:\winxpi.

3. Copy the entire contents of the Windows XP Professional CD into the new folder (i.e., c:\winxpi). The command-line command to perform this action is: xcopy d:\ c:\winxpi /e.

4. Unpack the service pack into a temporary directory. The command-line command to perform this action is: xpsp1.exe /x:c:\temp /u.

5. Once extracted, integrate the service pack files into the duplicated Windows XP Professional CD files using the following command: c:\temp\update\update. exe/s:c: \winxpi.

6. Share the c:\winxpi folder with the network.

7. To start an integrated setup, follow the network installation instructions discussed in Chapter 2, "Installing Windows XP Professional."

Activity 15-8: Applying Service Packs

Time Required: 20 minutes (depending on the size of the service pack)

Objective: Update your computer to the latest service levels by installing a service pack.

Description: With the number of security issues being discovered on a daily basis, it is important that everyone keep his or her computer updated with the latest service packs. In this activity, you install a service pack.

15

To apply a service pack:

1. Move or copy the service pack (SP) file into an empty directory as follows. From within Windows Explorer, create a new directory on a volume with at least 100 MB of free space (more may be required depending on the size of the service pack). Move or copy the service pack into the new empty directory.

2. Close all applications, especially debugging tools, virus scanners, and any other non-Microsoft or third-party tools.

3. Locate and execute **Update.exe** with the **Start**, **Run** command.

4. Follow any prompts that appear. If you want the ability to uninstall the service pack, be sure to select the option to store uninstall information.

You must select the Archive Files option during the initial application of the service pack in order to have the option to uninstall it later.

5. When instructed, restart your system.

6. After restarting, you can delete the service pack files and the temporary directory from your hard drive.

Activity 15-9: Uninstalling Service Packs

Time Required: 20 minutes

Objective: Use the uninstall files utility to remove a service pack.

Description: If you chose to be able to uninstall a service pack when it was originally installed, you should be able to uninstall the service pack. In this activity, you uninstall the service pack that you installed in Activity 15-8.

To uninstall a service pack:

You must have selected the Archive Files option during the initial application of the service pack in order to uninstall it.

1. Extract the original service pack archive into an empty directory. If you retained the service pack archive and temporary directory from the installation procedure, you do not need to repeat this activity. The default location for uninstall information for service packs is: *%systemroot%*\$NTServicePackUninstall$.

2. Locate and execute **Update.exe**.

3. Click the **Uninstall a previously installed service pack** button.

4. Follow the prompts.

5. Restart.

MICROSOFT TROUBLESHOOTING REFERENCES

Several Microsoft resources can aid you in troubleshooting and working with Windows XP Professional:

- *The Microsoft Windows Web site*—www.microsoft.com/windowsxp/

- *The Knowledge Base*—The predecessor to and a resource for the TechNet CD is the online Knowledge Base. This resource can be accessed by several means, as detailed earlier in this chapter.

- *TechNet*—The best periodic publication from Microsoft is TechNet. This multi-CD collection is an invaluable resource for white papers, FAQs, trouble-shooting documents, book excerpts, articles, and other written materials, plus utilities, patches, fixes, upgrades, drivers, and demonstration software. At only $300 per year (as of this writing), it is well worth the cost. It is also available online in a limited form at *technet.microsoft.com/*.

- *Resource Kits*—The Resource Kits are useful information sources. These are available in electronic form through the CD-based version of TechNet in their entirety, and through the online version of TechNet in portions. Resource Kits document material above and beyond what's contained in the manuals and online help files, and often include additional software utilities to enhance product use. These Resource Kit Utilities (as they're called) often provide valuable administrative functionality not available from built-in consoles and utilities. They are also available in book form through Microsoft Press.

CHAPTER SUMMARY

- No matter what problems or errors are discovered on your computer system, there are several commonsense principles of troubleshooting you should always follow. These include performing one task at a time, remaining calm, isolating the problem, and performing the simplest fixes first.

- Information is the most valuable troubleshooting tool. Making sure you have the best information includes maintaining a computer information file and a detailed log or history of troubleshooting activities.

- The Windows XP Professional tools most often used for troubleshooting are the Event Viewer and the Computer Management tool.

- There are five common installation problems: media errors, domain controller communication difficulties, stop message errors or halting on a blue screen, hardware problems, and dependency failures.

- Printer problems are most often associated with physical configuration or spooling problems.

- RAS and network problems may be caused by several types of issues, but the most common types arise from misconfiguration.

- Service packs and hot fixes are used to repair portions of Windows XP Professional after its release.

- Microsoft has provided several avenues to access information about the operation and management of Windows XP, including a substantial collection of troubleshooting documentation. Much of this is available at no charge from the Microsoft Web site.

15

KEY TERMS

Application log — A log that records application events, alerts, and system messages.

computer information file (CIF) — A detailed collection of all information related to the hardware and software products that make up your computer (and even your entire intranet).

Dr. Watson — An application error debugger. This diagnostic tool detects application failures and logs diagnostic details.

Event Viewer — The utility used to view the three logs automatically created by Windows XP: the System log, Application log, and Security log.

hot fix — Similar to a service pack, except that a hot fix addresses only one problem, or a small number of problems, and may not be fully tested.

Master Boot Record (MBR) — The area of a hard drive that contains the data structure that initiates the boot process.

Security log — A log that records security-related events.

service pack — A collection of code replacements, patches, error corrections, new applications, version improvements, or service-specific configuration settings from Microsoft that corrects, replaces, or hides the deficiencies of the original product, preceding service packs, or hot fixes.

System log — A log that records information and alerts about Windows XP Professional internal processes.

REVIEW QUESTIONS

1. When approaching a computer problem, which of the following should you keep in mind? (Choose all that apply.)

   a. how the problem was last solved

   b. what changes were recently made to the system

   c. information about the configuration state of the system

   d. ability to repeat the failure

2. If a media error occurs during installation, which of the following steps should you take to eliminate the problem? (Choose all that apply.)

   a. Attempt to recopy or reaccess the file that caused the failure.

   b. Switch media sources or types.

   c. Open Control Panel and reinstall the appropriate drivers.

   d. Restart the installation from the beginning.

3. Which of the following Windows repair tools can be used to gain information about drivers or services that failed to load?

   a. Event Viewer

   b. Registry

   c. System applet

   d. Dr. Watson

4. In addition to the Event Viewer and the System Information tool, which of the following are useful tools in general troubleshooting? (Choose all that apply.)

   a. Advanced Options Boot Menu

   b. Registry Editors

   c. backup software

   d. Time/Date applet

5. Your best tool in troubleshooting is:

   a. a protocol analyzer

   b. information

   c. administrative access

   d. redundant devices

6. Which of the following are possible troubleshooting techniques for eliminating printer problems? (Choose all that apply.)

   a. Check the physical aspects of the printer: cable, power, paper, toner, and so on.

   b. Check the print queue for stalled jobs.

   c. Attempt to print from a different application or a different client.

   d. Stop and restart the spooler using the Services tool.

   e. Disconnect from the network.

7. Which of the following are common RAS problems?

   a. Telco service failures

   b. misconfiguration

   c. user error

   d. communication device failure

8. A user's ability to access a resource is controlled by access permissions. If you suspect a problem with a user's permission settings, what actions can you take? (Choose all that apply.)

   a. Attempt the same actions and activities with the Administrator account.

   b. Delete the user's account and create a new one from scratch.

   c. Double-check group memberships to verify that Deny access settings are not causing the problem.

   d. Grant the user Full Access to the object directly.

15

9. What application automatically loads to handle application failures?

   a. Event Viewer

   b. System applet

   c. Computer Management

   d. Dr. Watson

10. If you are going to create a CIF, which of the following is the most important?

    a. Include the vendor's mailing address.

    b. Keep everything in electronic form.

    c. Update the contents often.

    d. Use nonremovable labels on all components.

11. Which of the following are important actions to perform before installing a service pack or a hot fix? (Choose all that apply.)

    a. Make a backup of your system.

    b. Read the readme file and Knowledge Base Q documents.

    c. Make a complete backup of the Registry.

    d. Enable virus protection.

12. What are some commonsense approaches to troubleshooting?

    a. Understand TCP/IP routing table configuration.

    b. Know your system.

    c. Undo the last alteration to the system.

    d. Replace all server hardware when one device fails.

    e. Let the fault guide you.

13. You can often resolve problems or avoid them altogether if you take the time to write out a history or log of problems and both failed and successful solution attempts. True or False?

14. When installing a new Windows XP Professional system into an existing domain, you can experience communication problems with the domain controller. After you've verified that the domain controller is online and properly connected to the network, what other items should be considered as possible points of failure? (Choose all that apply.)

    a. Shorten the computer name from 12 to 10 characters.

    b. subnet mask

    c. password

    d. domain name

15. Blue screen or Stop errors are often caused by a system when one or more devices are not found on the HCL. True or False?

16. If the driver for your network interface card fails, which other components of your system are most likely to fail due to dependency issues? (Choose all that apply.)

    a. network protocol

    b. Client Services for NetWare

    c. video driver

    d. WinLogon

17. Errors involving internal processes such as hardware and operating system errors, warnings, and general information messages are recorded in the Application log of the Event Viewer. True or False?

18. Which of the following are valid methods for resolving hardware problems? (Choose all that apply.)

    a. Restart the installation from scratch without any other modifications.

    b. Press and hold the Ctrl key during the installation.

    c. Remove or replace the non-HCL hardware.

    d. Recopy the distribution files.

19. An event detail viewed from the Event Viewer's logs provides specific information on the time, location, user, service, and resolution for all encountered errors. True or False?

20. The Computer Management tool offers links to several important administrative and management utilities including: (Choose all that apply.)

    a. Control Panel

    b. Event Viewer

    c. Performance Monitor

    d. Local Security Policy

    e. Local Users and Groups

21. The Storage section of the Computer Management tool offers utilities to perform which types of operations? (Choose all that apply).

    a. Defragmentation

    b. Partitioning

    c. Managing removable storage

    d. Compressing floppies

22. When a printer fails to print your documents, which of the following is a useful first step in troubleshooting?

    a. Replacing the printer

    b. Restarting the spooler

    c. Reinstalling the operating system

    d. Deleting and re-creating the shared printer

15

23. Both printers and RAS connections can suffer from the most common problem—physical connection interruptions. True or False?

24. When a user complains about being unable to access a resource that other users of similar job descriptions are able to access, what should you consider when attempting to troubleshoot this issue? (Choose all that apply.)

    a. group memberships

    b. ACL on the object

    c. domain membership

    d. speed of network connection

25. When you alter the group memberships of a user, how do you ensure that the changes take effect?

    a. Restart the server.

    b. Enable auditing on file objects.

    c. Restart the messaging and alert services.

    d. Log the user account off, then allow the user to log back on.

CASE PROJECTS

CASE PROJECTS

Case Project 15-1

After installing a new drive controller and a video card, along with their associated drivers, Windows XP Professional refuses to boot, and booting with the Last Known Good Configuration (LKGC) option does not result in an operational system.

Required Result:

❑ Return the system to a bootable and operational state.

Optional Desired Results:

❑ Retain the Security ID.

❑ Retain most, if not all, of the system's configuration.

Proposed solution:

❑ Perform a complete reinstallation of Windows XP.

Which results does the proposed solution produce?

    a. The proposed solution produces the desired result and produces both of the optional desired results.

    b. The proposed solution produces the desired result, but only one of the optional desired results.

c. The proposed solution produces the desired result, but neither of the optional desired results.

d. The proposed solution does not produce the desired result.

Case Project 15-2

Describe the common problems associated with installing Windows XP Professional and the appropriate steps to either avoid these problems or resolve them once encountered.

15

A

Exam Objectives Tracking for MCSE Certification Exam #70-270 Installing, Configuring, and Administering Microsoft Windows XP Professional

INSTALLING WINDOWS XP PROFESSIONAL

Objective	Chapter Section
Perform and troubleshoot an attended installation of Windows XP Professional.	Chapter 2: Upgrading versus Installing; Planning the Installation; Important Setup Option Differences; Advanced Customized Installation Options; WINNT and WINNT32; Windows XP Professional Setup: Step by Step from Floppies or from a Bootable CD
Perform and troubleshoot an unattended installation of Windows XP Professional.	Chapter 2: Unattended Installations
Install Windows XP Professional by using Remote Installation Services (RIS).	Chapter 2: Using Remote Installation Service (RIS)
Install Windows XP Professional by using the System Preparation Tool.	Chapter 2: Using SYSPREP
Create unattended answer files by using Setup Manager to automate the installation of Windows XP Professional.	Chapter 2: Unattended Installations
Upgrade from a previous version of Windows to Windows XP Professional.	Chapter 2: Upgrading Versus Installing Chapter 5: Files and Settings Transfer Wizard
Prepare a computer to meet upgrade requirements.	Chapter 1: Windows XP Professional Hardware Requirements; Chapter 2: Upgrading Versus Installing
Migrate existing user environments to a new installation.	Chapter 2: Upgrading Versus Installing
Perform postinstallation updates and product activation.	Chapter 2: Activating Windows XP; Chapter 14: Automatic Updates and Windows Update
Troubleshoot failed installations.	Chapter 15: Troubleshooting Tools

IMPLEMENTING AND CONDUCTING ADMINISTRATION OF RESOURCES

Objective	Chapter Section
Monitor, manage, and troubleshoot access to files and folders.	Chapter 4: File System Object Level Properties; Managing NTFS Permissions; Managing Shared Folders; Troubleshooting Access and Permission Problems
Configure, manage, and troubleshoot file compression.	Chapter 4: File Compression
Control access to files and folders by using permissions.	Chapter 4: File System Object-level Properties; Managing NTFS Permissions; Managing Shared Folders; Troubleshooting Access and Permission Problems
Optimize access to files and folders.	Chapter 4: File System Object-level Properties; Managing NTFS Permissions; Managing Shared Folders

A

Objective	Chapter Section
Manage and troubleshoot access to shared folders.	Chapter 4: File System Object-level Properties; Managing NTFS Permissions; Managing Shared Folders; Troubleshooting Access and Permission Problems
Create and remove shared folders.	Chapter 4: File System Object-level Properties; Managing NTFS Permissions; Managing Shared Folders
Control access to shared folders by using permissions.	Chapter 4: File System Object-level Properties; Managing NTFS Permissions; Managing Shared Folders
Manage and troubleshoot Web server resources.	Chapter 8: Internet Information Server
Connect to local and network print devices.	Chapter 9: Printing Across the Network; Installing and Managing Printers
Manage printers and print jobs.	Chapter 9: Printing Across the Network; Installing and Managing Printers
Control access to printers by using permissions.	Chapter 9: Installing and Managing Printers
Connect to an Internet printer.	Chapter 9: Printers and the Web
Connect to a local print device.	Chapter 9: Installing and Managing Printers
Configure and manage file systems.	Chapter 4: File Storage Basics; File Systems; Disk Management Actions
Convert from one file system to another file system.	Chapter 4: Converting File Systems
Configure NTFS, FAT32, or FAT file systems.	Chapter 4: File Storage Basics; File Systems; Disk Management Actions
Manage and troubleshoot access to and synchronization of offline files.	Chapter 4: Using Offline Files

IMPLEMENTING, MANAGING, MONITORING, AND TROUBLESHOOTING HARDWARE DEVICES AND DRIVERS

Objective	Chapter Section
Implement, manage, and troubleshoot disk devices.	Chapter 4: File Storage Basics; Drive Configurations; Disk Management Actions
Install, configure, and manage DVD and CD-ROM devices.	Chapter 3: Add Hardware; Chapter 4: File Storage Basics; Drive Configurations; Disk Management Actions
Monitor and configure disks.	Chapter 4: File Storage Basics; Drive Configurations; Disk Management Actions
Monitor, configure, and troubleshoot volumes.	Chapter 4: File Storage Basics; Drive Configurations; Disk Management Actions

Objective	Chapter Section
Monitor and configure removable media, such as tape devices.	Chapter 4: File Storage Basics; Drive Configurations; Disk Management Actions; Removable Media
Implement, manage, and troubleshoot display devices.	Chapter 3: Add Hardware; Display; Device Manager
Configure multiple-display support.	Chapter 3: Add Hardware; Display; Device Manager
Install, configure, and troubleshoot a video adapter.	Chapter 3: Add Hardware; Display; Device Manager
Configure Advanced Configuration Power Interface (ACPI).	Chapter 3: Power Options, Chapter 14: Hibernate vs. Standby
Implement, manage, and troubleshoot input and output (I/O) devices.	Chapter 3: Add Hardware; Device Manager
Monitor, configure, and troubleshoot I/O devices, such as printers, scanners, multimedia devices, mouse, keyboard, and smart card reader.	Chapter 3: Add Hardware; Device Manager; Chapter 9: Installing and Managing Printers; Troubleshooting Printing Problems
Monitor, configure, and troubleshoot multimedia hardware, such as cameras. Install, configure, and manage modems.	Chapter 3: Add Hardware; Device Manager Chapter 3: Add Hardware; Device Manager; Phone and Modem Options; Chapter 8: Remote Access Configuration; Phone and Modem Options
Install, configure, and manage Infrared Data Association (IrDA) devices.	Chapter 3: Add Hardware; Device Manager
Install, configure, and manage wireless devices.	Chapter 3: Add Hardware; Device Manager
Install, configure, and manage USB devices.	Chapter 3: Add Hardware; Device Manager
Install, configure, and manage handheld devices.	Chapter 3: Add Hardware; Device Manager
Install, configure, and manage network adapters.	Chapter 3: Add Hardware; Device Manager; Chapter 7: Networking Under Windows XP; TCP/IP Configuration
Manage and troubleshoot drivers and driver signing.	Chapter 3: Add Hardware; Device Manager; Driver Signing
Monitor and configure multiprocessor computers.	Chapter 1: Multiple Processors; Chapter 2: Planning the Installation; Chapter 10: Processor Bottlenecks

Monitoring and Optimizing System Performance and Reliability

Objective	Chapter Section
Monitor, optimize, and troubleshoot performance of the Windows XP Professional desktop.	Chapter 10: Monitoring and Performance Tuning; Recognizing and Handling Bottlenecks; Eight Ways to Boost Windows XP Professional Performance

A

Objective	Chapter Section
Optimize and troubleshoot memory performance.	Chapter 10: Monitoring and Performance Tuning; Recognizing and Handling Bottlenecks; Eight Ways to Boost Windows XP Professional Performance; Memory Bottlenecks
Optimize and troubleshoot processor utilization.	Chapter 10: Monitoring and Performance Tuning; Recognizing and Handling Bottlenecks; Eight Ways to Boost Windows XP Professional Performance; Processor Bottlenecks
Optimize and troubleshoot disk performance.	Chapter 10: Monitoring and Performance Tuning; Recognizing and Handling Bottlenecks; Eight Ways to Boost Windows XP Professional Performance; Disk Bottlenecks
Optimize and troubleshoot application performance.	Chapter 10: Monitoring and Performance Tuning; Recognizing and Handling Bottlenecks; Eight Ways to Boost Windows XP Professional Performance; Chapter 11: Other Windows Application Management Facilities
Configure, manage, and troubleshoot scheduled tasks.	Chapter 3: Scheduled Tasks
Manage, monitor, and optimize system performance for mobile users.	Chapter 3: Hardware Profiles; Chapter 10: Monitoring and Performance Tuning; Recognizing and Handling Bottlenecks; Eight Ways to Boost Windows XP Professional Performance
Restore and back up the operating system, System State data, and user data.	Chapter 14: Data Backup and Data Management
Recover System State data and user data by using Windows Backup.	Chapter 14: Data Backup and Data Management; Microsoft Backup Utility
Troubleshoot system restoration by starting in safe mode.	Chapter 13: Booting Windows XP; Chapter 14: Repairing Windows XP Professional
Recover System State data and user data by using the Recovery Console.	Chapter 14: Recover Console; Repairing Windows XP Professional

CONFIGURING AND TROUBLESHOOTING THE DESKTOP ENVIRONMENT

Objective	Chapter Section
Configure and manage user profiles and desktop settings.	Chapter 5: User Profiles
Configure support for multiple languages or multiple locations.	Chapter 3: Regional and Language Options; Chapter 9: FAX Support
Enable multiple-language support.	Chapter 3: Regional and Language Options
Configure multiple-language support for users.	Chapter 3: Regional and Language Options
Configure local settings.	Chapter 3: Regional and Language Options

Objective	Chapter Section
Configure Windows XP Professional for multiple locations.	Chapter 3: Regional and Language Options
Manage applications by using Windows Installer packages.	Chapter 14: Application Installation and Repair

Implementing, Managing, and Troubleshooting Network Protocols and Services

Objective	Chapter Section
Configure and troubleshoot the TCP/IP protocol.	Chapter 7: TCP/IP; TCP/IP Architecture; TCP/IP Configuration
Connect to computers by using dial-up networking.	Chapter 7: Networking under Windows XP; Chapter 8: Remote Access; Remote Access Configuration
Connect to computers by using a Virtual Private Networking (VPN) connection.	Chapter 7: Networking under Windows XP; Chapter 8: Remote Access; Remote Access Configuration
Create a dial-up connection to connect to a remote access server.	Chapter 7: Networking under Windows XP; Chapter 8: Remote Access; Remote Access Configuration
Connect to the Internet by using dial-up networking.	Chapter 7: Networking under Windows XP; Chapter 8: Remote Access; Remote Access Configuration
Configure and troubleshoot Internet Connection Sharing (ICS).	Chapter 7: Networking under Windows XP; Chapter 8: Remote Access; Remote Access Configuration; Internet Connection Sharing
Connect to resources by using Internet Explorer.	Chapter 8: Internet Explorer
Configure, manage, and implement Internet Information Services (IIS).	Chapter 8: Internet Information Server
Configure, manage, and troubleshoot Remote Desktop and Remote Assistance.	Chapter 7: Windows XP Remote Tools
Configure, manage, and troubleshoot Internet Connection Firewall (ICF).	Chapter 7: Networking under Windows XP; Chapter 8: Remote Access; Remote Access Configuration; Internet Connection Firewall

Configuring, Managing, and Troubleshooting Security

Objective	Chapter Section
Configure, manage, and troubleshoot Encrypting File System (EFS).	Chapter 6: Encrypting File System
Configure, manage, and troubleshoot a security configuration and local security policy.	Chapter 5: Application of Group Policy; Chapter 6: Local Computer Policy

Objective	Chapter Section
Configure, manage, and troubleshoot local user and group accounts.	Chapter 5: Windows XP Professional User Accounts
Configure, manage, and troubleshoot auditing.	Chapter 5: Audit Policy; Chapter 6: Auditing
Configure, manage, and troubleshoot account settings.	Chapter 5: Windows XP Professional User Accounts
Configure, manage, and troubleshoot account policy.	Chapter 5: Password Policy; Account Lockout Policy
Configure, manage, and troubleshoot user and group rights.	Chapter 5: User Rights Assignment
Troubleshoot cached credentials.	Chapter 5: Troubleshooting Cached Credentials
Configure, manage, and troubleshoot Internet Explorer security settings.	Chapter 8: Internet Options Applet

B

Detailed Lab Setup Guide

HARDWARE

Classroom PCs should be configured as follows:

- Intel Pentium or better, AMD K6 or better, with a 233-MHz processor or faster
- At least 64 MB of RAM, but 128 MB is recommended
- At least 1.5 GB of available hard disk space
- Keyboard and mouse (or some other compatible pointing device)
- Video adapter and monitor with Super VGA (800 × 600) or higher resolution
- Sound card (for Activity 3-7)
- Self-powered/amplified speakers or headphones (for Activity 3-7)
- Recordable CD or DVD drive (for Activity 4-18)
- Internal or external fax/modem (for Activities 8-1 through 8-6, and 9-8)
- Ethernet network interface controller
- 3.5-inch disk drive

To perform network-related activities, you also need the classroom PCs to be connected via a network. This requires the following equipment:

- An Ethernet hub or switch with at least as many ports as there are PCs in the classroom
- One twisted-pair Category 5 straight-through cable per PC
- An additional PC running Windows 9x, NT, or 2000 (for Activity 5-13)
- An additional PC running Windows XP Professional and Internet Information Server (for Activity 9-5)
- An additional PC running Novell Netware that is network-accessible from the student PCs (Activity 7-9)

Consumable items that students should bring to class:

- Two blank CD-R or CD-RW disks
- Five blank 3.5-inch disks

SOFTWARE

The following software is needed:

- Microsoft Windows XP Professional operating system (one CD media per student)
- Adobe Acrobat Reader (version 4 or later)

- Latest Microsoft-recommended updates, patches, and service packs from the *http://windowsupdate.microsoft.com* Web site, except Windows XP Service Pack 2

- Novell Netware OS (Activity 7-9); Windows NT, 9x, or 2000 (Activity 5-13)

B

SETUP INSTRUCTIONS

To successfully work on the materials in this book, students need to have administrative privileges over their respective PCs. These privileges will allow students the freedom to make administrative-level configuration changes. If performed incorrectly, these changes can render a PC unbootable or otherwise unusable for participation in the classroom. However, a student's mistakes should never impede completion of lab assignments. In this light, the lab should have a data recovery system and working backups that are both easy to use and reliable.

There are a number of commercial products that are available to make data recovery a swift and painless process. When properly implemented, they can even place the recovery procedure into the hands of the students instead of requiring dedicated lab personnel.

While researching a backup strategy, look specifically for products that employ disk-imaging technology. These products allow you to create a snapshot (or disk image file) of the hard disk(s) you wish to back up. Although there are many different types of backup utilities, those capable of producing disk images are most suitable for classroom use. It is their ability to copy and recreate the entire disk structure (including the partition table and master boot record) that sets them apart as the backup technology of choice in this application.

The most straightforward method of data recovery is the reinstallation of the operating system from the original operating system CDs. This method of installation is covered in Chapter 2. However, having to reinstall the operating system in this way every time a student corrupts his or her system can prove to be time consuming and frustrating. In addition, any added software would also need to be reinstalled and configuration settings repeated. Therefore, to ensure rapid and reliable data recovery, consider the following guidelines when setting up the lab:

1. Although the students will be performing the operating system install as an assigned activity, consider performing the activity yourself and then making a backup of your working installation.

2. This backup can be used to bring corrupted PCs back into a working state. The method that is used to perform the recovery will depend on the utility software used to create the backup.

3. If using commercial disk-imaging software, you can create a reference image file that contains all of the data on the disk. Some imaging software can produce an image file of the entire hard disk or just a select partition. In the case of a complete hard disk image, the file may even contain the partition table along with the master boot record. Restoring data from such an image file brings the

machine back into its original state at the time the backup was created. Formatting and partitioning of the target hard disk drive is generally not necessary because these are automatically executed as part of the restoration process.

4. When creating a reference image file, it is important to remember that the file is a copy of the reference computer's hard disk drive. This means that data such as the NetBIOS computer name and SID (security identifier) is preserved as it was on the reference PC. It also means that unless further steps are taken, all PCs that are imaged from this reference image will have the *same* NetBIOS computer name, SID, and perhaps even IP address (if the IP addresses were set up statically). Using a classroom network of identically named PCs will prevent the success of most network-related activities. You may be able to get away with all the SIDs being the same, but it is advisable to keep them unique. You especially do not want identical SIDs in an environment that employs Active Directory domains.

5. To speed up the process of copying the reference image to many student PCs, consider using a technology known as multicasting. Some commercial packages employ this technology, which allows you to distribute a single reference image to multiple student PCs in the same amount of time it takes to distribute to one PC. Although the technical details of multicasting are beyond the scope of this book, think of it as being analogous to the relationship between a radio station and its listeners. A radio station can have thousands of individuals listening to its single broadcast. Any additional individuals can listen in on the broadcast without adding any extra load to the radio station. In much the same way a multicast-enabled file server can transmit a single image file to many client PCs much more efficiently than sending each client its own separate copy.

6. To make a classroom of uniquely identifiable PCs, utilities such as Microsoft's Sysprep (covered in Chapter 2) may be executed to change the NetBIOS name and SID. If you don't need to change the SID, an alternate method of changing the NetBIOS name is as follows:

   a. Right-click the My Computer icon on the desktop.
   b. Click Properties.
   c. In the window that opens, click the Computer Name tab.
   d. Click the Change button.
   e. In the window that opens, type in the desired NetBIOS computer name in the Computer name field.
   f. When finished, click OK in both the Computer Name Changes and the Computer Properties windows.

To recap, your lab setup procedure should include the following:

1. Performing a fresh install of Windows XP Professional onto one of the student PCs (see Chapter 2). The base hardware of this PC should match as closely as possible all the PCs in the classroom—with emphasis on the motherboard make and model.

2. Installing all Microsoft-recommended updates, patches, and service packs from the *http://windowsupdate.microsoft.com* Web site except, Windows XP Service Pack 2.

3. Installing Adobe Acrobat Reader (*www.adobe.com*).

B

4. Installing any other software you may have purchased and have the legal right to use.

5. Restarting the PC to verify it boots up correctly and then restarting the PC again to create an image of this working configuration. Depending on what software you choose to perform this task, refer to the manufacturer's documentation on creating the necessary boot disks and server setups to perform the backup.

6. Distributing the reference image to all other student PCs. The method you use will be determined by the backup/restore utility you choose. Consider using multicasting if your software allows it.

7. Changing the NetBIOS computer name and SID to make each PC unique on the network. You can automate this task by writing batch scripts that execute automatically after the imaging process. Most commercial imaging packages lend themselves very well to automation.

C

EXPANDED CHAPTER SUMMARIES

CHAPTER 1 SUMMARY

Microsoft has designed Windows XP for multiple types of users by creating multiple versions. It has five different versions available, with Home Edition and Professional being the most popular. The other versions are Tablet PC Edition, Media Center Edition, and a 64-Bit Edition. For the most part, businesses and power users use XP Professional, and home users use Windows XP Home Edition. The other versions are used, but not as widely as the most popular version.

The Windows XP versions are not all that different from each other. To create different editions or versions, Microsoft enabled (or disabled) certain features and also gave the ability to support more hardware. For example, Windows XP Professional supports up to two processors, Remote Desktop, and the ability to join a domain. Windows XP Home Edition can have only a single processor and doesn't have the ability to use Remote Desktop or join a domain.

All versions of Windows XP support three file systems: FAT, FAT32, and NTFS. The FAT and FAT32 files systems provide no local security and also have limits on the size of volumes that you can create on them. FAT volumes cannot exceed 2 GB, while FAT32 volumes cannot exceed 32 GB in size. The FAT file systems were included for backward compatibility with computers that have older operating systems on them and may be upgraded to Windows XP. NTFS allows users to assign permissions to secure resources that take effect locally and over the network. If a volume is formatted with NTFS, you can use Encrypting File System (EFS) and disk quotas with it. Volumes formatted with NTFS can be as large as 2 TB (terabytes).

In all versions of Windows XP, you have two ways to receive help. The first is through Remote Assistance. Remote Assistance allows a user to send an invitation to another user that then allows the second user to connect to the first user's computer. The second user can chat with the first user, view the first user's screen, and even, with permission, take control of the computer. The second way to receive help is through Help and Support Services. This utility can search the Help files installed on the computer and, if there is Internet access, it can scour the Microsoft Web site for answers.

One of the main differences between Windows XP and previous versions of Microsoft operating systems is in the intelligent user interface. Microsoft spent a lot of time designing the user interface, and you will notice widespread changes. You also have the ability to customize your desktop environment, from the Start menu to the notification area. Windows XP also comes preinstalled with some additional utilities such as Windows Media Player 8, Windows Messenger, and Windows Movie Maker.

Microsoft designed Windows XP to work with a broad range of hardware components. Microsoft has published a Hardware Compatibility List (HCL) on the installation CD and on their Web site to identify hardware devices that work properly with Windows XP. The system on which you install Windows XP needs to meet these minimum requirements:

233-MHz CPU, 64 MB of RAM, and 1.5 GB of free disk space. While you wouldn't be able to run many applications with this minimum hardware, it still allows you to install Windows XP.

Windows XP was built to work within a network and to be able to communicate with other computers. With networking you have two methods, workgroups or domains. Workgroups are great if you have a small number of computers that need to share resources. The other option is to join your computer to a domain. This way, all of the accounts are stored in a centralized database called Active Directory. The downside with this is that you need someone who is knowledgeable to manage the day-to-day operations of a domain.

The architecture of Windows XP was built upon the stable and reliable Windows NT/2000 architecture. Windows XP has two modes, user mode and kernel mode. As the name implies, user mode is where users run applications. Depending on the edition of Windows XP you are using, you have the ability to run 16-bit, 32-bit, and/or 64-bit applications. Part of the Windows XP user mode is the security subsystem, which takes care of the logon process. Kernel mode is a privileged area that blocks direct access from applications to hardware. All the processes that run here have a higher priority than processes that are started in user mode.

The area known as the Executive Services is the bridge from user mode to kernel mode. Some of the modules that you can find here are the File Systems Manager, Plug and Play Manager, and the Virtual Memory Manager (VMM)—to name a few.

Within Executive Services, the hardware abstraction layer (HAL) is used to isolate hardware-dependent code to prevent direct access to hardware. By preventing direct access to hardware, Windows XP becomes more stable, and there are less system crashes. The memory architecture manages all physical memory and the page file. So when your system is running low on physical memory, it uses the hard drive as temporary storage. This is called paging and can slow system performance considerably.

CHAPTER 2 SUMMARY

Chapter 2 delves into the many ways to install the Windows XP operating systems.

If you decide to upgrade, then you must have an operating system that can be upgraded to Windows XP. The following OSs can be upgraded to Windows XP Professional:

- Windows 95 OSR2, Windows 98, Windows 98 SE, and Windows ME
- Windows NT 4.0 Workstation with Service Pack 6
- Windows 2000 Professional
- Windows XP Home
- Windows 95 (upgrades do not retain all information)

The following is a list of supported operating systems that can be upgraded to Windows XP Home:

- Windows 98
- Windows 98 SE
- Windows ME

Regardless of the operating system to which you upgrade, you must ensure that you back up any important data that you store on your computer in case of a system failure during the upgrade. Make sure not to compress the backup because many older backup programs' compression does not work with Windows XP. Note that if you upgrade from Windows 9x and keep the existing file system as FAT, you can roll back that upgrade through the Add/Remove Programs feature in Control Panel. However, if you convert the file system to NTFS after the upgrade, you don't have this option.

A clean installation installs the Windows XP operating system into its own directory and is used most of the time with new computers. It is possible to perform a clean install on an existing computer, but it may not retain any of the existing files.

Microsoft has provided a tool to help upgrade your system. The tool is called the Upgrade Advisor, and it lets you know if your hardware and software is compatible with Windows XP. This tool must be downloaded from the Microsoft Web site and should be run while you are still connected to the Internet so that it can receive any updates from Microsoft.

Windows XP also gives you the ability to install multiple operating systems on one computer. This is called a dual boot system. When you install multiple operating systems on the same computer, you cannot run them concurrently. You also may have to install the same applications multiple times per operating system. If you are using any of the older 9x operating systems with Windows XP, then you have to keep the file system formatted with FAT or FAT32. If you convert it to NTFS while you are booted into Windows XP, then the 9x operating system cannot boot up because it cannot read volumes formatted with NTFS.

Once you decide whether to upgrade or perform a clean install, you have to decide how you will perform the install. You can perform installations in the following ways:

- Attended (manual)
- Over the network
- Automated (unattended)
- Remote Installation Services

A manual install is one of the most common methods of installing an operating system for a single or multiple computers. This method involves placing the Windows XP CD-ROM in the CD drive and running Setup.

If you decide to install Windows XP over the network, you need to have a share available that has the Windows XP source files (from the i386 directory on the XP CD-ROM). The only permission that you need to those files over the network is ??Read. This method is used when you have network connectivity available and do not want to carry the XP CD-ROM with you to each install.

Automated installations are sometimes called unattended installations. This occurs when the installation is scripted from a file called UNATTEND.TXT that answers common questions presented during the install, such as FullName, OrgName, ProductKey, and AdminPassword. This method works well if you have a lot of computers that need to be installed because you don't have to be present to answer the prompts; they are answered by the answer file.

In the past, it was difficult to get the syntax of UNATTEND.TXT correct. However, there is now a tool called Setup Manager that runs a wizard and asks you to fill in the answers for the questions you would be asked during the installation. Once Setup Manager is done, it creates the UNATTEND.TXT file with all the appropriate syntax.

To run the installation of Windows XP, you must use the correct command, which is either WINNT or WINNT32. WINNT is intended to be run from DOS and older Windows 3.x operating systems. WINNT32 is for 32-bit operating systems, which are Windows 95 or newer. Once you determine the correct command, you have to choose the correct switch. To start an unattended install while using the WINNT command, use the /U and /S switches; the WINNT32 command uses the /UNATTENDED and /S switches. The /S switch is used to locate the Windows XP source files that would come from either a CD drive or a network location.

Companies use imaging programs to image a base computer and then push or pull that image to other computers in their network. This is a fast way to deploy your operating system to many computers and have a common look and feel. Microsoft has included with their server operating system an imaging application called Remote Installation Services (RIS) that can easily deploy Windows XP. When you use RIS, each computer must have a unique security identifier (SID). To create a unique SID, you run a utility called SYSPREP. SYSPREP takes an existing setup and wipes away any identifying info. By using SYSPREP, you can image a computer and deploy the image using RIS. The next time a computer starts up with that image, it automatically generates a new SID. RIS relies on DHCP, DNS, and Active Directory to work properly. One common problem with RIS deployments is that when you configure applications to work with the RIS image, the applications are installed under the local administrator. You must copy the local administrator's profile to the default user profile so that every user has access to the applications.

The Windows Installer Service is available to install applications on new clients. You can also use Systems Management Server (SMS) to install and configure applications. SMS can also be configured to upgrade an older operating system to Windows XP, but it cannot be used to do a clean install.

One of the first things you will notice after you install an operating system is the Microsoft product activation. This is how Microsoft tries to prevent software piracy. Microsoft gives you a 30-day grace period to activate your version of Windows XP. You can either activate over the Internet or by phone. Activation is considered mandatory. If you don't activate Windows XP within the deadline, you cannot log on to the system until you activate it by phone. If you make significant changes to the hardware in your computer, then you may have to reactivate your copy of Windows XP.

Chapter 3 Summary

Control Panel has a new Category view. Those who prefer the old view that shows icons of all the Control Panel applets can select Classic view.

The Accessibility Options applet offers the ability to fine-tune the Windows XP operating system to help with visually, aurally, or movement-impaired users. The options configure keyboard settings, sound options, display settings, and mouse movements, among others.

The Add Hardware applet allows users to install new hardware that may not have been detected as Plug and Play (PnP). This applet scans a system and detects any additions that may have been made to your system.

The Add or Remove Programs applet shows you all of the applications that you have installed on your machine and sorts them by name, size, frequency of use, and date last used. These features help you to see if you have an application that is taking a lot of space and you haven't used it in some time. Each installed application gives you specific options, such as the ability to remove it or even change how it is installed on your computer.

Inside the Add or Remove Programs applet is an option for you to install new applications from a CD-ROM or floppy disk. This is also the applet you use to install or remove additional Windows components, such as the calculator, built-in games, fax services, Windows Media player, and others.

One of the most powerful applets in Control Panel is Administrative Tools. This is where local administrators can perform administrative tasks such as creating users and shares, setting security options, and using Event Viewer.

The Date and Time applet allows you to alter the way Windows XP represents dates and time. This is important for individuals who travel to different parts of the world, because they can change the time zone on the computer as needed.

The Display applet allows you to change how Windows XP is displayed. From this applet, you can set up your screensaver, the power options for your laptop, the desktop wallpaper, the appearance of icons, and your screen resolution. You can also work with display adaptors drivers, uninstall them, roll them back to a previous version, or update them. If you have multiple display adaptors or one that has multiple inputs, then you can control the Windows XP multiple monitor settings from here as well.

The Folders Options applet gives you the ability to alter how your folders look once they are open. You can display icons in list mode or in details mode. You can also select if you want to show hidden files and folders, or hide or show extensions for known file types.

Control Panel has many different applets. They can be used to configure elements such as fonts, game controllers, Internet Options to help with settings in Internet Explorer, and keyboard and mouse settings.

Mobile users will find the Power Options applet helpful when configuring settings to conserve battery life. You can configure different power schemes based on how you are using your computer. There are timed settings that will turn off your monitor and hard drive. Alarms can be set when you are nearing the end of battery life. A power meter is available to provide information about your battery life. Windows XP supports two mobile states: one is called standby, and the other hibernation. Standby puts your computer into a lower power mode that keeps your applications open. However, if you lose power, you lose all unsaved data. Hibernation mode stores your system state into a temporary data file on your hard drive that can save your current applications as is. This mode takes longer to boot up than standby, but it does not consume battery life.

Printers and faxes can be installed, configured, and shared from Control Panel. There is also an option for configuring regional and language settings.

Another powerful applet to use in Control Panel is the System applet. This applet tells you what operating system you are running, the amount of RAM available, the CPU speed, the computer name, and whether the computer is joined to a domain or workgroup. From this applet, you can access Device Manager and hardware profiles. The System applet lets you configure how your automatic updates are going to be downloaded and installed. It also gives you the ability to let others connect to your machine through Remote Desktop and offer Remote Assistance. On the Advanced tab, you can define startup and recovery options, settings to help configure for performance, and settings to configure user profiles.

Device Manager is an applet you can use to configure devices currently connected to your computer. By selecting a device, you have many options that include updating drivers, uninstalling drivers, and configuring IRQ, I/O ports, Direct Memory Access, and the physical memory that is used. Your system can also be set up to use different hardware profiles that can enable and disable certain hardware devices, depending on how you start your system.

The Startup and Recovery options allow you to set startup parameters and configure how STOP errors are handled. You can configure how long Windows XP displays a list of operating systems before booting into one. This option directly edits the BOOT.INI file.

The Microsoft Management Console (MMC) is a common interface for you to snap in, or link, administrative tools in a common interface. In other words, the MMC by itself is just an empty console and does not give you the ability to perform any administrative tasks; you must add tools to it. Microsoft initially released the MMC with some administrative tools in

Windows NT; however, it was not until Windows 2000 that Microsoft offered users the ability to add whatever snap-ins were wanted, whether from Microsoft or third-party vendors.

Administrative Tools is a collection of utilities that are very powerful and require a special location. One of the most powerful of these utilities is the Local Security Policy snap-in. This tool allows you to configure security settings on the local computer. The Microsoft Management Console contains several tools to help troubleshoot and administer Windows XP. It is divided into three sections: System Tools, Storage, and Services and Applications.

CHAPTER 4 SUMMARY

With basic storage you have the ability to create partitions. There are two types of partitions: primary or extended. A primary partition can be marked active, which means that you can boot an operating system from it. You are limited to four primary partitions per system. If you need to have more than four partitions, then you need to create extended partitions. Extended partitions cannot be marked as active, but you can create logical partitions inside extended partitions.

By default, when you install Windows XP, it installs into a single partition, which is the C: drive. During setup, you have the option to change where Windows XP will be installed. The default directory is C:\WINDOWS. This directory is called the boot partition, and it contains system files. The C:\ drive is known as the system partition, and it contains boot files.

Windows XP also supports dynamic storage. These are the same type of disks as basic disks, except Windows XP made a software change in how the disks are viewed. For a disk to become a dynamic disk, you must convert the entire disk through the Disk Management tool. After a disk is converted to a dynamic disk, you no longer have to reboot the system to make changes, and during the disk conversion, any existing partitions are converted to volumes that were created on that disk.

Windows XP supports several different types of drive configurations. Windows XP can import drives from older operating systems and can support both basic and dynamic drives. The following volume types are supported under Windows XP:

- Simple
- Spanned
- Striped

Note that FTONLINE is a support tool included on the Windows XP CD-ROM in the SUPPORT.CAB file. FTONLINE allows you to mount a failed drive and access information on it.

C

Managing basic and dynamic disks is only one task that is needed to manage your storage options. After you have decided on the type of disk that you will use, you then need to format that partition or volume with the appropriate file system. Your choices are FAT, FAT32, or NTFS.

The FAT file system was developed to support DOS. FAT was included in Windows XP only for backward compatibility and has some serious limitations, for example no file-level security and it supports volumes up to only 4 GB. FAT32 is an enhancement that was released with Windows 95 OSR2 and overcame the 4 GB limitation and bumped it up to 32 GB. There is still no file- or folder-level security.

The NTFS file system was released with Windows NT 4 and has evolved to the version that is now included with Windows XP. This version supports volumes up to 2 TB, file-level security, disk quotas, and compression.

If a drive is formatted with the FAT file system, it can be converted to NTFS without losing data. If a drive is formatted with NTFS, you cannot convert it to FAT. The only way to convert an existing NTFS volume to FAT is to reformat it and then restore files from backup. The NTFS file system includes a feature to compress files and folders. To be able to compress a file or folder, you must have full control over that object.

Disk management tasks include creating, converting, extending, and deleting volumes. You may also have to import foreign disks and reactivate them. A common disk management function is changing the drive letter of a device. This can be done through the Disk Management tool. The drive's properties are available through Device Manager. From Device Manager, you can see information on the type, status, and capacity of the drive. Similar information can be gained regarding volumes or partitions through My Computer by right-clicking the drive letter and making the appropriate selection. Quotas can be enabled per volume to restrict how much disk space can be used by users.

You can set limits and you can configure warnings to notify users that they are approaching their limit. Mount points give you an alternate to drive letters. You can use mount points to connect volumes to an empty NTFS volume. Over time, your disks fill up with files. You can use the Disk Cleanup tool to free up space by removing deleted, orphaned, temporary, or downloaded files.

As files are written to the hard disk and removed, the drive becomes fragmented. Windows XP comes with a Disk Defragmenter tool that can be used to eliminate fragmentation. FSUTIL (file system Utility) is a command-line utility that performs a lot of disk administration functions.

Folder Options allows you to enable or disable the display of common tasks. It also allows you to set how files and folders are viewed in Windows Explorer and My Computer. Each file and folder has specific information, such as name, type, location, and size, that can be displayed through their respective properties.

As an administrator, you can grant users, groups, or even computers access to specific files and folders stored on a particular system. When assigning permissions, ensure that only the needed permission is granted and nothing more. If an NTFS permission does not allow the right type of access, then use a detailed NTFS permission. Detailed NTFS permissions are just subsets of the NTFS permissions. For example, the read NTFS permission is more than just read; there are detailed NTFS permissions that combine to make the NTFS read permission. Detailed NTFS permissions such as the read attribute and read extended attribute make up the standard Read permission.

File- and folder-level security determines who can do what to files stored on the volume. NTFS has both NTFS and detailed NTFS permissions. The NTFS permissions are as follows:

- Read
- Write
- List Folder Contents (folders only)
- Read & Execute
- Modify
- Full Control

When you want to make a folder accessible over a network, you need to create a new shared folder for that folder. This allows others to see that folder when they connect to your computer. Shared folders have their own set of permissions that are much simpler than NTFS permissions. The share permissions are as follows:

- Full Control
- Change
- Read

Media folders are special folders that are used as default storage locations for documents, music files, and images. The Customize tab is used to define the type of folder by defining a folder template, picture, and icon.

Windows XP can compress files and folders to make it easier to move files. Windows XP also has the ability to burn CDs.

Mobile users of Windows XP can use the Offline Files feature. Offline Files allows users to cache files that are stored on remote shared folders to their local computer. Then, they can still work on those files even though they may not be connected to the network. When using Offline Files, mobile users synchronize their files when they reconnect to the network.

Folder Redirection gives you the ability to alter where a folder is stored. It appears as if it is physically stored on your computer but it actually is stored on a network server. This can be used through a local policy, or, in larger networks, it can be configured through Group Policy. Windows XP supports several different formats of removable media, including tape devices, DVD and CD-ROM drives, optical drives, Zip, and Jaz drives.

CHAPTER 5 SUMMARY

This chapter introduces you to users, groups, profiles, and policies. Each person who logs on to a Windows XP computer should have his or her own user account created on it. This way, all of the settings and applications he or she has set up will stay that way—no matter who else logs on to the same computer.

User accounts created on a Windows XP computer are known as local user accounts. These users are granted the right to log on locally and access files and folders on that computer. If the machine is shared by multiple users, then it is a good idea to create an individual account for each person. If you have multiple computers, then you have to create an individual local user account for each person on each computer.

Local user accounts are not the only type of user accounts you can create. If your computer is a member of a domain, then you need to log on using a domain user account. Because the computer is a member of a domain, you can log on to any client computer with the same domain user name and password, as long as that computer is also a member of the same domain.

When supporting multiple users, you may find it easy to manage them with groups. Groups can be created on the local machine or in the domain. Groups provide a way for you to organize users who need similar permissions to resources such as files, folders, or printers.

Selecting the appropriate way for users to log on to their computers is important for security reasons. If your computer is a member of a workgroup instead of a domain, you can choose to use the Windows Welcome logon. This screen appears after you restart your computer and lists all of the user accounts on the machine. You simply click your account and then type your password. For security reasons, this isn't the best option, because it shows all the user account names on the computer.

You can change your logon method to the classic logon, which forces users to press Ctrl+Alt+Del to open the logon window. They then type their user names and passwords. This is the only method available for computers that are joined to a domain. When Windows XP is installed, there are two default users created: the Administrator and the Guest. The Administrator account is the most powerful account on the computer and has the ability to do anything on that computer. The Guest account is the least privileged account and is disabled by default.

Before creating accounts, it is a good practice to come up with a common naming convention. Common user account naming conventions use a combination of first and last names. User accounts are not the only accounts that should have a naming convention; groups and computers also should follow a convention. When creating local user accounts, you use the User Accounts applet in Control Panel. You can create Standard, Restricted, and Other types of user accounts on a local machine. If you need to create local groups, a great tool to use is the Computer Management console. Through this tool, you also have the ability to create local user accounts.

Every installation of Windows XP has default groups. These default groups were created by Microsoft and are given specific rights and permissions to the computer. Instead of creating a new group, you can add users to one of these default groups if there is a task you want them to be able to accomplish. However, there may be times where you have to create a new group and give it specific permissions.

Backup Operators is a default group that gives members the right to back up files and folders and also to restore files. If you need a group that does only backups and another that does only restores, you have to create two new groups, assign those rights to them, and then add members to those groups.

Windows XP Professional can be a member of an Active Directory domain. This allows for centralized control of accounts and security. There are two methods for joining a domain. The first method involves an administrator creating a computer account ahead of time in Active Directory. The second method is to use your logon credentials to manually join the domain. Once a computer is joined to the domain, it may have group policies applied to it. This can impose restrictions on the workstation, and some features of the operating system may no longer be available.

The first time a user logs on to a Windows XP computer, a new user profile is created based on the default user profile. A user profile stores settings specific to that user. Some of the settings defined in profiles are the following:

- Application data
- Desktop preferences
- Favorites
- Start menu

Administrators can force users to load mandatory settings that can restrict their computers. To create a mandatory profile, you need to change the name of the Ntuser.dat file to Ntuser.man. Now users who get this profile can make changes, but those changes revert to whatever was set up by the administrator the next time they log on.

When the user logs off, changes the user has made are saved to his or her unique profile, which is stored in the C:\Documents and Settings\%*username*% folder. These are known as local profiles and are stored only on that machine.

A user with a domain account has the ability to have his or her profile follow him or her to any computer to which he or she logs on. This profile is called a roaming profile and is set up with the Domain Account properties. The drawback to this profile is that it copies the user's entire profile to each computer to which he or she logs on. This process uses valuable network bandwidth, and potentially wastes a lot of space on that computer.

Windows XP clients can be secured by using Group Policy. Group policies can be defined at the site and organizational unit level. These policies apply settings to the Windows XP operating system. If a computer is a member of a domain, Windows refreshes its group policies every 90 minutes to get changes. Policy settings for groups include Password policies, Account Lockout settings, Audit policies, User right assignments, and Security settings.

From time to time, you may have users who need to upgrade their computers from old slow ones to new fast ones. In the past, moving files and settings was a difficult task; however, Windows XP now includes a tool that helps with that process. This tool is the Files and Settings Transfer (FAST) Wizard. It copies all settings and files that you define to a CD, DVD, or network location for importing into a new computer. This application is customizable and allows you to add new file types that may not be included in the FAST Wizard by default. In addition, it is a great tool for moving Files and Settings on a small number of computers.

There is also a command-line version called User State Migration Tool (USMT) that can be used with scripting to move several computers' files and settings to a network location. With USMT, you can use ScanState, which scans computers and stores the information on a network share. LoadState copies that information to the new computers.

CHAPTER 6 SUMMARY

Every user who logs on to a Windows XP computer has to enter a unique user ID and password to gain access to the computer's resources. When a user logs on, they let Windows XP know who they are.

After you successfully log on, you are granted an access token, which includes your SID, any SIDs from groups of which you are a member. The token also includes any user rights you have been assigned. Now when you try to access resources, Windows XP checks your access token to see if you have been granted access to the resource. Access to resources in Windows XP is controlled through the object. Objects that are considered resources are files, folders, processes, user accounts, printers, computers, and so forth.

Windows XP can assign permissions at the object level. The level of access to an object is defined by NTFS permissions. When a user logs on to a Windows XP computer, he or she is granted access to objects. If users don't log on, they do not have access to any resources.

There are different security settings associated with the logon process. To practice good security, you should investigate configuring the following settings:

- Disable the default username
- Add a logon security warning
- Disable the Shutdown button
- Automatic account lockout

For users who will be logging into an Active Directory domain, the security is even tighter. Active Directory uses an authentication protocol called Kerberos, which is used for mutual authentication between the client and server. This process is invisible to the user and looks just like logging onto the local computer.

Basic Web traffic uses HTTP, which transmits all data in clear text. If users need to log on to Web sites or enter personal information onto these sites, you must secure this information. To secure this type of traffic, you use Secure Sockets Layer/Transport Layer Security (SSL/TLS), which uses an encryption key to initiate a communication session with both computers. This creates an encrypted communication link that only the client and server can read.

One of the best ways to secure a Windows XP computer is through its local computer policy. Every Windows XP computer has its own local computer policy that can lock down the user environment for any user who logs on to that computer. In the Local Computer Policy MMC, there are two areas that you can configure: Computer Configuration and User Configuration.

The local computer policy includes a Software Settings node that is used to deploy software. The Computer Configuration portion has most of the security settings for Windows XP, and you can locate them under the Windows Settings folder, Security Settings node. The areas that you can configure in this folder are the following:

- Account Policies
- Local Policies
- Public Key Policies
- Software Restriction Policies
- IPSec Security Policies on Local Computer

Also included under the Computer Configuration section is the Administrative Templates folder. The controls in this folder give you complete control on how the environment appears for the computer. You can change Registry settings, IE settings, disk quotas, and printer settings, to name just a few.

IP Security (IPSec) is used to secure TCP/IP communication between two systems. IPSec can be used in private networks or over public ones. When two clients are configured to use IPSec, they create a secure tunnel between each other to pass all TCP/IP traffic. Windows XP comes with three built-in IPSec policies:

- Client (Respond Only)
- Server (Request Security)
- Secure Server (Require Security)

Windows XP and the other system with which it wants to communicate using IPSec must agree upon an authentication protocol. IPSec supports the following authentication methods:

- Kerberos
- Public key certificate
- Preshared key

The Users Configuration portion is structured the same as the Computer Configuration portion, but its settings pertain to the users that log on to one specific computer.

There are several tools included with Windows XP that help secure the operating system. The Security Configuration and Analysis tool can analyze a computer to a template and then configure the computer to match those settings in the template. The Security Editor (Secedit) is a command–line version of Security Configuration and Analysis. Auditing can be configured to show users who have logged on incorrectly. After configuring auditing, you can view your logs through the security logs through Event Viewer.

If you have a volume that is formatted with NTFS, you have the ability to encrypt local files and folders by using the encrypting file system (EFS). Using EFS allows only the users that have been authorized to access the encrypted file the ability to view those resources. All of this is done transparently to the users.

CHAPTER 7 SUMMARY

Microsoft has made Windows XP easy to set up in a networked environment. Windows XP supports multiple networking protocols, including TCP/IP and NWLink.

After Windows XP is installed, TCP/IP is installed and working. TCP/IP consists of more than 50 component protocols. TCP/IP was created in the late 1960s and became broadly available in the early 1980s. Without TCP/IP, the Internet would not be possible. One major drawback to TCP/IP is that it is difficult to configure large networks.

If you are in a network that is running a version of NetWare that predates version 5, you may have to install and configure NWLink. This is the Microsoft implementation of Novell's IPX/SPX protocol. IPX does not work well on larger networks, and does not include support for name resolution and address management.

Windows XP can accept many types of network connections, including connecting to a local area network (LAN) or a dial-up connection. When using any of these connection methods, a wizard can walk you through configuring the settings. For example, the wizard allows you to name your computer and connect to the Internet through a LAN or dial-up connection.

Windows XP networking is controlled through an interface that can be accessed through Control Panel. Using this interface, you can configure access to LAN, Internet, and modem connections. Network Connections allows you to create new connections to virtual private networks (VPN). Each network connection has the option to install new clients, protocols, and services. You can also uninstall clients, protocols, and services. Each network client, protocol, and service also gives you the ability to configure it by selecting the Properties button in the Network Connections dialog box.

Windows XP supports wireless networks that follow the IEEE 802.11 wireless standard. Windows XP works in a wireless network as long as there is a wireless network card and a wireless access point. Wireless networks are broadcast over radio waves, and because of this, they must be protected from eavesdropping. Windows XP supports the Wired Equivalent Privacy (WEP) protocol for encrypting wireless traffic.

Because multiple protocols, services, and network clients can be installed on Windows XP, it is important to manage your bindings correctly. Binding is the order in which Windows XP networking components are linked. The order affects network performance because you are indicating which protocol, service, and network client will be used first to communicate.

This chapter also goes into great detail on the TCP/IP architecture and how IP addresses can easily be turned into binary. Subnetting is something you need to learn on your journey to becoming an MCSA/MCSE, but it is not discussed in great detail in this chapter nor must you know about it for this exam. TCP/IP networks can utilize any of the component protocols to help manage and configure IP hosts. Such component protocols include the Dynamic Host Configuration Protocol (DHCP), which can configure TCP/IP settings. The File Transfer Protocol (FTP) can be used for transferring files. Telnet is a remote terminal protocol that allows configuration of dissimilar systems such as routers and UNIX terminals. TCP/IP supports the Simple Mail Transfer Protocol (SMTP) to allow for messaging services.

As networks grow, it becomes more and more difficult to communicate with computers based on their IP addresses. Windows XP can use name resolution protocols such as the Domain Name Service (DNS) and Windows Internet Naming Service (WINS) to allow users to connect to resources based on names and not IP addresses, as follows:

- DNS resolves Fully Qualified Domain Names (FQDN) to IP addresses.

- WINS is a NetBIOS name resolution service that maps computer names to IP addresses.

When working with TCP/IP, it is important to be able to manage and view information related to it. One of the best tools to use is a command-line tool called IPCONFIG. IPCONFIG allows you to see the current TCP/IP settings and release and renew addresses if the client is a DHCP client. Another great tool is NETSTAT, which allows you to analyze and troubleshoot network connectivity.

Windows XP has support for two remote tools: one that allows users to connect to other machines remotely, and another that offers assistance when needed, as follows:

- Remote Assistance is a new Windows XP feature that allows users to request assistance from knowledgeable and trusted individuals. There are several ways a user can request remote assistance, including e-mail or chatting using Windows Messenger. Once the "teacher" gets this invitation, he or she needs to input a special password that the troubled user creates for this invitation only. Once connected, the teacher can view the desktop of the troubled user and have the ability to chat about the issue. The teacher can offer the option to take control, which gives the teacher access to the troubled user's mouse and keyboard. This feature is supported on all versions of Windows XP.

C

- Remote Desktop is supported only on Windows XP Professional, and it gives users the ability to connect to their Windows XP from a remote location. This is much like a light version of the Terminal Services component that runs on Windows servers. By using the Remote Desktop Client that comes with Windows XP, you have the ability to share drives, printers, and sound between the host and remote computers.

Windows XP has the ability to communicate within a Novell NetWare network. This feature is included with Windows XP to provide for interoperability with a Novell bindery database or Novell Directory Service (NDS). Windows XP can either use NWLink for older Novell networks, or TCP/IP with NetWare 5.x or newer to communicate with other hosts on these networks. When Windows XP is configured to use NWLink, it automatically detects the NWLink frame type that is being used on the network and configures itself to use that frame type. If Windows XP is going to use NWLink and communicate with resources on a NetWare network, then it may be best to install the Client Service for NetWare (CSNW). CSNW allows a user to log on to either an NDS tree or bindery preferred server.

CHAPTER 8 SUMMARY

Remote access can serve many needs in the corporate environment. The Remote Access Service allows administrative access to remote machines as well as user access. This enables a user to gain access to resources when traveling.

The configuration for remote access includes the following:

- Clients, which can include those with platforms that support Point-to-Point Protocol.
- Protocols are the second element, and Windows XP supports PPP as well as NWLink.
- WAN connectivity is the third common element, allowing clients using dial-up access, ISDN lines, and other methods to connect remotely to a Windows XP remote access server.
- Windows XP also has built-in security capabilities to allow for secure inbound connections.
- Because its primary use is as a desktop operating system, Windows XP is limited to a single inbound connection.
- LAN protocols, such as TCP/IP and IPX/SPX, which are most commonly used, are also supported.

Additional features supported by Windows XP include advanced options such as PPP Multilink, which allows a user to increase his or her network bandwidth by combining multiple connections.

VPN connections are also supported, using industry standards such as Point-to-Point Tunneling Protocol and Layer Two Tunneling Protocol (L2TP). If a remote access user is transferring files, the restartable file copy feature allows the transmission to be resumed if it is interrupted. This can dramatically improve performance and reduce frustration for end users accessing the server from a low-quality link.

Additional features include autodial and idle disconnect, as well as features that allow Windows XP to more easily integrate with applications and tools provided by third-party vendors.

Security features include callback security, which allows an administrator to specify callback numbers, and enhances security. These are used in conjunction with a user name and password, as well as possible encryption and privacy added by VPN connections and technologies such as IPSec.

Windows XP provides support for many standard Internet protocols. For Internet access, support for dial-up connections is included, using PPP and SLIP, as well as the multilink protocol, PPP-MP. VPN support via PPTP, L2TP, and IPSec is also available, an important feature when allowing secure access from remote locations to a corporate network.

For configuration, the Phone and Modem Options applet in Control Panel allows control over most features of the telephony system. End users can modify these settings to control dialing behavior for the modem, set area code settings, and even create dialing rules for remote access connections.

Another remote connection feature is the ability to share it with other hosts on the local area network. This feature, Internet Connection Sharing (ICS), allows the Windows XP host to act as a router for other computers on the LAN, allowing them to access the Internet through the single connection of the Windows XP host. Keep in mind, however, that ICS is intended as a solution for the smallest network, and it is generally not appropriate in a domain environment.

Windows XP also includes, for the first time, a limited-capability firewall, the Internet Connection Firewall (ICF). ICF is not as full featured as an advanced firewall product. It doesn't provide granular control for filtering IP addresses, a common firewall feature. However, it does provide protection for end users, and Microsoft made strides to improve its effectiveness since the release of Windows XP.

While not the fastest method to connect remotely, the modem is still in widespread use. For mobile users in remote connections, dial-up connections are often still necessary. Most locations have at least dial-up Internet access, and with this, an end user can make a remote access connection via a VPN to securely access a Windows XP machine remotely over the Internet.

To make creating connections easier, Microsoft improved the wizards in Windows XP for remote access. Advanced features allow creation of dial-up connections for VPN access as well as dial-up Internet access. Various connection types can be used, including advanced connections and connections to other computers.

Advanced options are also available, including the capability to directly connect to another computer and the options to specify alternate IP configurations for computers.

Certificates provide proof of identity between two entities on the network. This enables trusted communications to occur. Certificates and the support hierarchy, the Public Key Infrastructure (PKI), provide a means to create trusted communications. Certificates can authenticate and ensure the authenticity, confidentially, and integrity of communications between parties.

Other important configuration options reside in the Internet Options applet. Several important settings that control a user's experience can be set through this applet. The General tab allows home page settings and file settings. The Security tab defines security levels for different Web zones. The Privacy tab allows more granular control over cookie options and other personal information. The Content tab allows control of the Content Advisor settings, based on the RSACi standard. The Connections tab includes information regarding how Internet Explorer connects to the Internet. Default programs can be assigned through the Programs tab, and the Advanced tab grants granular control over several browser functions.

IE is included with XP and available by default. Outlook Express is a highly functional e-mail and newsgroup reader and meets the needs of most home users. In a corporate environment, Microsoft Outlook is typically a better choice because it has advanced calendaring and task features.

In Windows XP, command-line tools are also available, including an FTP client and a Telnet client. Each of those is a client-oriented tool.

On the server end, Windows XP includes a limited version of Internet Information Server (IIS), which is the Web and FTP server included with the Windows Server family of operating systems. When using Windows XP, IIS is limited to 10 incoming connections. Therefore, IIS on Windows XP is ideally suited for smaller workgroups or individual sites with low usage. However, beyond the connection limit, IIS has many useful features for hosting a single Web site and performs the task well.

Chapter 9 Summary

Understanding Microsoft's usage of print-related terminology is the first step to understanding printing with Microsoft systems. The following are some of the most common terms encountered and their meanings:

- *Direct-attached printer*—This is a print device attached directly to a computer, usually through a parallel port.

- *Network interface printer*—This is a print device attached to the network directly, most commonly through Ethernet, but possibly through a parallel printer cable attached to a print server.

- *Print device*—Most commonly referred to as a "printer" in everyday terminology, Microsoft refers to the peripheral as a "print device."

- *Print server*—This is a computer that provides network services for printing with a print device.

- *Printer (logical printer)*—This is a printer is the software interface between the computer and the printer.

- *Printer driver*—The printer driver contains the computer files and driver files that allow the print device and Windows XP to communicate properly.

- *Printer pool*—A printer pool is a collection of physical print devices that can be utilized by a single printer. It can ease the workload of a single printer and improve printing efficiency.

- *Queue (print queue)*—These are the print jobs that have been submitted to the print server to be printed by the print device.

- *Spooling*—Spooling is the process that occurs when a print job is sent to a printer. It is the preparation of the print job to be submitted for printing to the print device.

Windows XP incorporates a feature known as the graphical driver interface. This capability allows tools such as word processors to display documents as they will appear when they are printed. This is also referred to as WYSIWYG—What You See Is What You Get.

The print spooler service (spoolsv.exe) has the responsibility for receiving, processing, scheduling, and sending print jobs from users to print devices.

Print driver software may be included with Windows XP or can be provided by the print device manufacturer. Print drivers allow Windows XP to properly interface with a print device. Drivers may also enable special features and capabilities of the print device.

The steps necessary for creating a local printer through the Printers and Faxes window begin with using the Add a printer command. Additional information is typically printer specific, so when setting up a printer, be certain to know the answers to key questions, as follows:

- Is the attached printer compatible with Plug and Play standards?

- Is the printer local or on the network?

- To which port will the printer be connected?

- What is the make and model of the printer?

- What do you want the printer to be named?

- Do you want the printer to be the default for all print jobs?

- Should the printer be shared with the network?

These settings can almost always be adjusted after creation of the printer if you are uncertain of the appropriate setting or if the appropriate setting is changed.

If a local printer is not available, then a remote printer should be added for printing. This can also be done through the wizard. In addition, drivers for the print device are automatically downloaded from the print server, which speeds the installation process.

To manage printers and print jobs, you can employ the Printers and Faxes window. This window allows you to manage print queues by double-clicking the icon representing the printer with the print job. From this window, you have the option to delete, cancel, or simply pause print jobs. You can also use this window to manage the print server's properties, to take the printer offline, or to resume or restart print jobs.

You can go to the printer's Properties dialog box to manage the configuration options for a printer. Options include allowing some users priority access over other users to a particular print device. Also, printers can be shared over the network through the Properties dialog box. Additional ports can be added to set up printer pooling, which makes more efficient use of printers. The Security tab can be used to limit the users who have access to a printer and to grant greater control to a group of users who may need to administer the printer and all of its print jobs.

To fax from Windows XP, a fax-enabled device, such as a fax modem, must be connected. Once it is set up properly, the device can send faxes. With additional manual configuration, the device can be set up to receive faxes as well.

Windows XP has well-developed printing and fax capabilities, which are easy to set up and configure. This allows administrators and end users to most efficiently manage and configure their print devices.

CHAPTER **10** SUMMARY

The first step in performance tuning is establishing a baseline. A baseline is a standard against which you can measure the system's performance. A baseline includes recorded observations regarding a computer system's behavior. Having a baseline allows you to identify bottlenecks, or areas of the system, that slow the overall performance of the operating system.

Performance measurements rely on objects and counters. Objects are items with properties that are measurable, and the measurements are counters. For instance, counters can be checked for items related to the system's hard drives, processor, and network performance.

When analyzing the system, there are two main areas you can investigate:

- *Monitoring*—To be effective, a thorough understanding of several aspects of the system is required. In addition, periodic regular reviews and observation are required.

- *Performance tuning*—This is best accomplished as a result of monitoring, by systematically observing performance and changing the system's configuration, and then observing the results.

Task Manager is provided with Windows XP and provides excellent information regarding the system. Task Manager has the following tabs to provide system information:

- The Applications tab displays information regarding currently running programs and allows you to start and end applications. It also informs you if a program appears to be unresponsive to the operating system.

- The Processes tab gives a detailed view of the processes running in the background on your system. Information provided includes the Process ID number, CPU usage, CPU time, and Memory usage. Additional information can be added along with these default options. In addition, processor affinity can be set here. Processor affinity allows the user to assign a process to a single CPU or to multiple CPUs on a multiprocessor system.

- The Performance tab gives a graphical view of CPU and memory utilization.

- The Users tab is not present in all configurations. It appears only in workgroup configurations and nonnetworked machines.

- The Networking tab displays the computer's network bandwidth usage. It can give a general view of the available network bandwidth for a given computer; however, it cannot identify which system components and processes are using the bandwidth.

System Monitor is the performance monitoring tool in Windows XP. It allows monitoring of multiple aspects of the Windows XP operating system and of hardware performance. System Monitor is the primary tool used to identify trends and bottlenecks, and to generate alerts when defined thresholds are exceeded.

Real-time monitoring is possible by viewing the data provided by counters in the System Monitor display area. This information can be displayed in real time and as logged data in graph, histogram, or report form.

Counters can be selected based on the following information groupings in the Add Counters dialog box:

- *Local or network-accessible computer*—These counters are accessible to the local computer as well as over the network.

- *Performance object*—A performance object is used to provide performance information regarding components of Windows XP. Performance objects provide data to System Monitor that can be used in monitoring and performance tuning.

- *Counter*—Counters are a specific aspect of a performance object that can be quantified and reported to System Monitor.

- *Instance*—If there are multiple instances of a performance object, an individual item can be monitored by selecting the appropriate instance.

Windows XP allows monitoring of a variety of aspects of the system. The following counters give an excellent overall picture of a system's health and performance:

- *LogicalDisk: Current Disk Queue Length*—This indicates the queue of requests for disk access. Values greater than 2 indicate possible congestion problems.

- *LogicalDisk: %Disk Time*—This counter measures how busy the drive is that is performing read and write requests. A value consistently over 80% indicates problems.

- *Avg. Disk Bytes/Transfer*—This counter indicates the number of bytes transferred between the computer's memory and disk systems during read and write operations. A value around 4 KB (4086 bytes) is indicative of excessive paging activity.

- *Memory: Available Bytes*—This counter tracks the available bytes of memory for the system. If it drops below 4096 KB, this value indicates performance problems.

- *Memory: Cache Faults/sec*—This counter indicates how often each second the Windows XP cache manager requests that the system retrieves a file's page from the disk or locate it elsewhere in memory. A high value indicates potential performance problems, and a low value indicates that the system is performing optimally.

- *Memory: Page Faults/sec*—Page faults indicate the system's inability to locate information where it expects it. If this occurs with great frequency, performance will suffer. Page faults indicate a page that is not already in RAM is requested.

- *Memory: Pages/sec*—This is the number of pages read from or written to disk. Paging operations result when information is not readily available in RAM. Paging is done to satisfy the needs of the VMM.

Along with these options, administrators can set alerts when values exceed certain pre-defined thresholds. This allows an administrator to respond to a potentially critical situation. The alert is triggered, and an administrator can be notified to respond to a condition that may be a predecessor to performance problems or outages.

Performance logs help administrators create a historical record of a system's performance. Counter logs can record data from counters and objects that an administrator wants to record. These logs can then be viewed to note trends in a system's performance. This is invaluable information for tasks such as capacity planning.

By carefully monitoring your system, examining performance issues, and identifying bottle-necks, you can realize true performance gain and cost savings. This is an often-underutilized skill and one that many administrators lack. However, it has the potential to differentiate your skill set from other administrators and support engineers.

CHAPTER 11 SUMMARY

Windows XP has two primary components, the environment subsystem and Executive Services. The environment subsystem offers support for applications. For instance, it can emulate another operating system, such as DOS or 16-bit windows. Native Win32 applications also fall under its support. The environment subsystems run under user mode, and all resource access must go through kernel mode. Windows XP Executive Services and XP's kernel mode define the kernel mode and the runtime environment.

The Windows XP operating systems uses two modes of operation. These two modes, kernel mode and user mode, separate functions and capabilities as follows:

- Kernel mode allows operating system components to access system objects and resources directly. It also provides services and access controls that allow Windows XP to have multiple users and applications work together efficiently.

- User mode gives each process 4 GB of virtual memory and allows each process to believe it is the sole owner of that space. The upper 2 GB of space is typically reserved for operating system use. This process is hardware independent.

To Windows, running applications means handling processes and threads (threads are defined below). A process defines the operating environment in which an application or any major operating system component runs. You can access Task Manager to view the processes running on a Windows XP computer. Task Manager can be accessed using the following methods:

- Pressing Ctrl+Alt+Del and clicking the Task Manager button (in normal Windows logon mode only)

- Pressing Ctrl+Alt+Del (in Windows Welcome mode only)

- Right-clicking an unoccupied area of the taskbar, and selecting Task Manager from the resulting shortcut menu

- Pressing Ctrl+Shift+Esc

Along with processes, Windows XP sees threads. The basic executable unit in Windows XP is called a thread, and every process includes at least one thread. A thread consists of information associated with a single use of any program that can handle multiple concurrent users or activities.

Processes can spawn additional processes. These new processes are called child processes and are present with the same characteristics and parameters of the parent process, including the rights associated with the user context under which the parent is running.

Environment subsystems give Windows XP flexibility. They are designed with 32-bit applications in mind, but also grant limited functionality for 16-bit applications. Through this, key features of Windows, such as multitasking, are implemented. In addition, it allows Windows XP to be more modular.

The key subsystem is the Win32 subsystem. This is required by Windows XP, and it handles all major interface capabilities. The Win32 subsystem is the foundation for virtual DOS machines (VDMS). This allows XP to use DOS and Win16 subsystems so that those applications can successfully run on Windows XP.

Processes are more efficient when used with multithreading, which is the execution of multiple threads by a single process. This is more efficient, as it provides for multiple threads within a single memory space, which therefore increases performance. The environment system supports multithreading for the Win32 subsystem.

To run a DOS environment, a Win32 process is started. The process is called ntvdm.exe (NT Virtual DOS Machine). Each DOS application resides in its own virtual space, and a separate instance of ntvdm.exe runs for each DOS application. The Virtual DOS machine requires these key files:

- *Ntio.sys*—The equivalent of IO.SYS on MS-DOS machines; runs in real mode, a mode of operation for x86 CPUs wherein they can address only 1 MB of memory, broken into sixteen 64-KB segments. It provides "virtual I/O" services to the DOS or Win16 applications that run in a VDM.

- *Ntdos.sys*—The equivalent of MSDOS.SYS; runs in real mode. It provides basic DOS operating system services to the DOS or Win16 applications that run in a VDM.

- *Ntvdm.exe*—A Win32 application that runs in kernel mode. This execution file provides the runtime environment within which a VDM runs. Look at the list on the Processes tab of Task Manager, and you will see one such entry for each separate VDM running on your machine.

- *Ntvdm.dll*—A Win32 dynamic link library that runs in kernel mode. Ntvdm.dll provides the set of procedure stubs that fool DOS and Win16 programs into thinking they're talking to a real DOS machine with exclusive access to a PC, when in fact they're communicating through a VDM with Windows XP Professional.

- *Redir.exe*—The virtual device driver (VDD) redirector for the VDM. This software forwards I/O requests from programs within a VDM for I/O services through the Win32 environment subsystem to the Windows XP I/O Manager in Executive Services. Whenever a DOS or Win16 program in a VDM thinks it's communicating with hardware, it's really communicating with Redir.exe.

Some DOS applications rely on settings in the Autoexec.bat and Config.sys files of a typical DOS machine. However, in Windows XP, these files are not present. Instead, you need to modify the AUTOEXEC.NT and CONFIG.NT files. Alterations to these files can be done through Notepad.

Other Windows application tools include the Program Compatibility Wizard, which includes additional features designed to get older applications working under Windows XP.

Keep in mind, however, that it is almost always preferable to use a newer version of an application, if available. It should be one that is fully supported on the Windows XP operating system.

Group Policy options are also available for assigning and publishing of applications. This gives administrators the ability to install applications remotely on users' machines, by default, or on an as needed basis. Group Policy is an Active Directory domain feature, so a Windows 2000 or Windows Server 2003 domain controller is necessary. Administrators can then bundle applications together to deploy software packages to the enterprise. Users can access these applications through various means: they can be automatically installed, installed on first use, or available through the Control Panel's Add/Remove programs feature.

Windows XP was designed to offer maximum flexibility when running applications. The architecture is designed to support newer and older applications. With the numerous tools available to an administrator, many options are available that allow an administrator to maximize the use of applications in the Windows XP operating system environment.

CHAPTER **12** SUMMARY

The Registry is a dynamic data structure used to maintain the operating system's configuration and operating parameters. It includes information regarding hardware and drivers, software applications, and user preferences, for Windows as well as third-party applications. It contains a wealth of information, and Windows XP includes tools to manage, edit, and restore the Registry.

There are five main root keys in the Registry. These key name values start with HKEY, and organize the Registry into five discrete parts. Subkeys are located beneath each of these main keys. Under the subkeys, there are value entries, which contain specific values or configuration information that may be used by the operating system or a particular application.

Data is stored in the Registry in different formats. The use of different formats allows maximum flexibility for applications and programs. Windows XP supports the following data types:

- *Binary*—This data is either a 1 or a 0.
- *DWORD*—Binary, hex, or decimal formats are allowed.
- *String*—This is the text-string format.
- *Multiple String*—This is a text-string format that contains multiple human-readable values separated by NULL characters.
- *Expandable String*—This is an expandable text-string format containing a variable that is replaced by an application when used (%systemroot%\File.exe).

The HKEY_LOCAL_MACHINE key contains the value entries that control the local computer. These configuration items include information about hardware devices, applications, device drivers, kernel services, and physical settings. These data are used to establish the configuration of the hardware and operating system environment.

The HKEY_LOCAL MACHINE key has several important subkeys. The subkeys are the following:

- The HKEY_LOCAL_MACHINE\HARDWARE subkey contains information regarding physical devices on the PC. It includes device driver settings, configuration data, mappings, IRQ information, and other information that allows the operating system to properly interact with attached hardware.

- The subkey HKEY_LOCAL_MACHINE\SAM is a security-related hive. It contains the Security Accounts Manager (SAM) database, which includes information regarding the local user and group accounts stored on the PC, as well as group membership information for the user accounts.

- The subkey HKEY_LOCAL_MACHINE\SECURITY container holds the local security policy. This policy defines settings for the local PC, including password policy settings, user rights, audit policy information, and other information that controls the user's experience on the local computer.

- The subkey HKEY_LOCAL_MACHINE\SOFTWARE key contains data about all the installed software on a computer, including which file extensions should be mapped to the application.

- The subkey HKEY_LOCAL_MACHINE\SYSTEM contains information regarding booting Windows XP. This is required information, because it contains startup parameters, device driver loading information, and service credentials for background services.

The SYSTEM subkey is of particular note. This subkey has four additional subkeys, labeled as ControlSets keys. These keys are named and numbered (ControlSet001, ControlSet002, etc.) and contain four subkeys. The four subkeys are the following:

- *Control*—This container holds information used for controlling system startup, boot parameters, and the computer name.

- *Enum*—This container holds information regarding required device drivers and their configuration.

- *Hardware Profiles*—This container holds data specific to the hardware profile currently in use.

- *Services*—This container holds information about drivers, services, file systems, applications, and other required hardware components necessary to load all installed and active services during bootup.

There are four other major keys and one legacy key in the Registry. The five remaining keys are:

- The HKEY_CLASSES_ROOT key contains data regarding application associations and mapped file extensions, as well as COM object data. The contents of this key are copied from the HKEY_LOCAL_MACHINE\SOFTWARE\Classes subkey.

- The HKEY_CURRENT_CONFIG key holds data regarding the current hardware profile. This key is just a link to the HKEY_LOCAL_MACHINE\ SYSTEM\CurrentControlSet\HardwareProfiles\Current subkey.

- The HKEY_CURRENT_USER key contains information for the current user. This key is created upon logon by copying the appropriate subkey from the HKEY_USERS key.

- The HKEY_USERS key contains profiles for all users who have ever logged onto this system and the default user profile.

- HKEY_DYN_DATA exists on machines with Windows 95 or Windows 98 applications that use older versions of Plug and Play.

To edit or view the Registry, you can use regedit.exe, a graphical tool, or reg.exe, a command-line tool. Regedit grants the ability to search the Registry and to view and manipulate the registry keys. However, because the Registry is such a sensitive and critical data store, you should always exercise extreme caution when making changes in the Registry.

Static images of the Registry reside in %systemroot%\system32\config and in the %systemroot%\repair folder. When editing a particular key, the Registry allows you to export a key, which acts as a quick backup should an error be made or if the original settings need to be restored.

Errors in the Registry incurred during the current logon session can be fixed if the user uses the Last Known Good Configuration, which is a backup registry key. During startup, this choice can be selected to undo the errors made during the previous session. This option is only available only if a user has not actually logged on since the errors were made.

When working with the Registry, great care should be taken. Errors made during registry editing can result in an inoperable operating system and might require a reinstall or restoration from backup.

Additional registry-editing tools are included in the Microsoft Resource Kit. This kit is a separate purchase, but it includes useful tools such as regdump.exe, regfind.exe, compreg.exe, and others that an administrator may find valuable.

CHAPTER 13 SUMMARY

The six stages of the Windows XP boot phase are as follows:

1. *Power-on self test (POST)*—The POST is the first step in the boot sequence for any computer with an operating system. The POST determines the amount of real memory that exists and whether all necessary hardware components, such as a keyboard, are present.

2. *Initial startup*—The initial startup sequence involves numerous files and initialization procedures.

3. *Boot loader*—The boot loader is the collection of files on the system partition that is used to initiate loading of the operating system. The boot loader displays a boot menu if more than one OS is present or if an advanced boot option is needed.

4. *Selecting the operating system*—Ntldr reads the Boot.ini file and displays the operating system selections it contains. The screen that appears at this point is usually called the boot loader screen or the boot selection menu, and it represents the point at which users can select the operating system they want to load (or which form of Windows XP graphics operation they want to use).

5. *Detecting hardware*—Ntdetect.com is executed by the boot loader and is used to collect a list of hardware currently installed in the computer. Ntdetect checks the computer ID, bus/adapter type, video, keyboard, communication ports, parallel ports, disks, and mouse or pointing devices.

6. *Selecting a configuration*—After hardware is detected, the system needs to select a system configuration, otherwise known as a hardware profile. If only a single hardware profile is defined, this is the one that is used.

To assist in troubleshooting problems during the loading of the operating system, several advanced startup options are available. To effectively resolve a variety of problems, including Registry modifications and failed driver installs, you should be familiar with the following:

- *Safe Mode*—Windows XP boots with only required files and device drivers. No networking components are loaded.

- *Safe Mode with Networking*—Windows XP boots with only required files and device drivers, and networking components are loaded.

- *Safe Mode with Command Prompt*—Windows XP boots with only required files and device drivers; however, a command-line interface is loaded instead of a GUI.

- *Enable Boot Logging*—This option can enable or disable logging of the boot process. Information is written to a log file, which is located at %systemroot% \Ntbtlog.txt.

- *Enable VGA Mode*—Windows XP loads normally. However, only a basic VGA video display driver is loaded.

- *Last Known Good Configuration*—Windows XP boots using the Last Known Good Configuration, which is indicated by the last successful user logon. The driver and system settings in the registry from the last successful logon are restored.

- *Directory Services Restore Mode*—This is an option on domain controllers, and it permits the restoration of Active Directory objects.

- *Debugging Mode*—Windows boots normally. However, debugging information is sent via a serial cable to another computer. Information regarding using this option is available on the Microsoft Windows XP Professional Resource Kit.

The Boot.ini file is used by Windows XP when the system first loads. It identifies the location of operating system files. The Boot.ini file is divided into two main sections:

- The [boot loader] section of the Boot.ini file includes two items: timeout and default. The timeout setting determines the time the system waits for a user selection to continue booting the operating system. The default setting indicates the operating system that will be loaded by default if the user does not make an alternate choice. The default setting in Boot.ini lists the path to the default operating system.

- The [operating systems] section of Boot.ini lists the available operating systems. This section indicates the ARC path to the root of each operating system so that the proper files can be loaded.

The path to an operating system is in a format known as an ARC path. The format of the various parameters is as follows:

- *scsi(n) or multi(n)*—One of these is present, and it indicates the type of device where the OS files are loaded. The scsi parameter indicates that a SCSI drive is being used and that the onboard BIOS is disabled. The multi-parameter covers other hard drives and a SCSI drive with an enabled built-in BIOS.

- *disk(n)*—This identifies the SCSI bus number to use.

- *rdisk(n)*—This identifies the SCSI LUN number or selects hard disks attached to the adapter that contains the operating system.

- *partition(n)*—This selects the disk partition containing the operating system files.

- *\path*—This indicates the directory on the partition where the operating system files are found.

Modification of the Boot.ini file can be done manually, but preferably is done through Control Panel. The System applet allows modification of the timeout and default values in the Boot.ini file. If you want to rename an operating system choice that is shown on bootup, however, a text editor, such as Notepad, is required. This allows you to rename multiple instances of a single operating system to make bootup selection easier.

Windows XP goes through several steps in the load phase. These steps begin with loading the XP kernel. It is then initialized, preparing it for the rest of the startup phase. Services load and run in the background. XP then starts up, and users are then able to log on.

The boot process is an important link in running Windows XP. Your familiarity with its components can aid you in resolving problems and working efficiently in a Windows XP environment.

CHAPTER **14** SUMMARY

Disaster recovery is the process of getting a system back up and running after it has suffered damage or a loss to critical hardware, software, or data. Minimizing the loss and the time until the system is fully recovered can be critical. To achieve these goals, it is important for the system administrator to be familiar with all the options available in Windows XP.

IntelliMirror is one Windows XP feature that helps ensure availability of user data and computer configuration information. It has three key components:

- *User data management*—Backing up data
- *User settings management*—The recovery of a PC's configuration
- *Software installation and maintenance*—The installation and repair of installed applications

The data backup and data management component manages documents and data for a user. If a machine crashes, the user can still access data. If a user's data is corrupted on one machine, it can be restored using a copy of the data from the network. These options can be set up through folder direction, using a group policy, or through manual settings by the user.

PC configuration recovery is also important and is managed through IntelliMirror. A variety of settings are stored, including language settings, desktop schemes, and custom dictionaries. These can be stored on the network, and they are essentially a roaming profile—a group of settings that follows the user regardless of which PC they log onto on the domain.

The application installation and repair feature fixes essential application and system components that may be damaged or removed by an end user. The software installation and maintenance feature of IntelliMirror can rebuild the machine with the same applications that were previously installed. The Windows Installer service can reinstall and repair applications seamlessly.

To back up data, Windows XP includes the Microsoft Backup utility. Unlike older versions, this tool has excellent features, including the ability to schedule backups and to back up to just about any type of media, from tape drives and Zip drives to network drives and CD-R media. This gives end users a wealth of options when planning backup and restore strategies for their data. The backup data allows a complete system backup, including the System State data, which contains operating system components such as boot files and the Registry.

You should be familiar with these different backup options:

- *Copy backup*—This option backs up all the selected files. However, the archive bit is not cleared.
- *Normal (or full) backup*—This option backs up all selected files and clears the archive bit.
- *Daily backup*—This option backs up all files that have been modified on the day of the backup. It does not clear the archive bit.

- *Differential backup*—This backup option backs up all selected files that have been created or modified since the last full or incremental backup was performed. The archive bit is not cleared.

- *Incremental backup*—This option backs up the selected files that have been created or modified since the last normal or incremental backup.

The Automated System Recovery feature restores system files in the event of a system failure. This doesn't protect personal data stored on the computer. It protects files essential to the boot process. The system must be started with the original system CD or boot disks.

Windows XP provides additional features. An excellent feature is device driver rollback. If a new driver is installed and fails to operate properly, device driver rollback allows the user to go back to a prior driver known to be good. You can access the driver options through Device Manager by going to the properties for the device that is causing the error.

Windows File Protection (WFP) protects end users from accidentally deleting important files. Files such as .sys, .dll, .exe, .ocs, and system critical True Type font files are restored if they are accidentally deleted. WFP protects these files by constantly monitoring for their deletion or modification. If a protected file is deleted or modified, WFP restores the file back to a known good copy that matches its database of files.

To keep systems patched and secure, automatic updates and Windows Update can be utilized. Automatic updates can be run manually or scheduled. Windows Update checks the Microsoft Web site for updates for the Windows XP operating system. In addition, Windows Update is a Microsoft Web site that uses an ActiveX control to examine the operating system for missing patches and updates. After scanning, the user is presented a list of options for installation, and can elect to install some, all, or none of the suggested updates.

The Desktop Cleanup Wizard cleans unused items from the desktop. This is scheduled to occur automatically. It is designed to make management of the desktop easier.

Hibernate and standby options are also available. Each allows the system to resume where it left off. Hibernate, however, restores the system even when the battery is drained. Standby requires battery power, and data is lost if the battery is fully drained.

Other options for restoration include safe mode, system restore, the emergency repair process, the Recovery console, and remote OS installation. System restore keeps restore points, allowing a user to revert to a specific point in time. The emergency repair process attempts to restore system files that may have become corrupt. The Recovery console gives administrators a command-line interface from which to work, manage services, and copy files. Remote OS installation allows administrators to remotely install an operating system over the network. Each of these is useful under particular circumstances to restore a system to functionality or to tweak the operating system if, for instance, a service is running and is not allowing the system to start normally. By fully utilizing all of these tools, the majority of errors and problems encountered by users can be avoided or resolved. When disaster strikes, a prepared and knowledgeable administrator can make the best of a bad situation. However, a lack of familiarity with disaster recovery procedures can be costly.

CHAPTER 15 SUMMARY

The most important aspect of troubleshooting any computer is information. Although information gathering may appear to be a tedious process, it plays a vital role in building the foundation to troubleshoot quickly and efficiently.

While gathering information, it is helpful to focus your energy in the following areas: system hardware and software configurations; previous troubleshooting documentation; maintenance records; and configuration information. The collected information needs to be stored in a computer information file (CIF). Creating a CIF takes time, patience, and attention to detail. However, the time invested dramatically increases the efficiency of the troubleshooting process.

As important as it is to create a CIF, it is equally important to store a CIF in a secure and protected area. Ensure the CIF is updated on a regular basis and that you maintain an electronic form as well as a printed form of the CIF.

While troubleshooting, remember to follow common sense guidelines. Some specific guidelines are as follows: be familiar with the system's hardware and software; isolate the problem; investigate common points of failure; and try the easy, quick fixes first. These are just some of the guidelines; the rest are detailed in the main part of the chapter.

Windows XP has built-in tools designed to help the troubleshooting process. The tools are Event Viewer and Computer Management. They can save countless hours while troubleshooting.

Event Viewer records system messages regarding the failure and/or success of various key occurrences. These messages are stored in log files that are easily viewed for routine monitoring.

Windows XP Professional automatically creates the following logs: System log; Security log; Application log; Directory Service; DNS service; and File Replication Service. Each log records a different type of event that can be used as a clue during troubleshooting.

The Computer Management tools are grouped together in one console that is separated into three sections. Those sections are System Tools, Storage, and Services and Applications. Each section contains key tools that are essential for regular management and troubleshooting.

The first grouping of tools in the Computer Management console is called System Tools. These tools include Event Viewer, Shared Folders, Local Users and Groups, Performance Logs and Alerts, and Device Manager. The second grouping of tools is called Storage, and includes Removable Storage, Disk Defragmenter, and Disk Management. The last grouping in the Computer Management console is the Services and Applications grouping, and includes the Services, WMI Control, and Indexing Service tools.

Installing Windows XP does not always run as smoothly as planned. Therefore, it is important to understand the different variables that may affect the installation. Media errors are physical problems with the installation disk. In some cases, communication with the domain controllers can signify mistyped names or possible network failures. A stop message error or "blue screen" may hint of a problem with an incompatible or corrupted driver. Hardware can also create many problems, so ensure the hardware used is on the Microsoft hardware compatibility list (HCL). If a service fails because of a dependency, then you can check Event Viewer to see what that service depends on.

Common-sense troubleshooting is also useful for printer problems. The best way to troubleshoot printers is through systematic elimination of common problems:

1. First, check the physical components of the printer.

2. Next, make sure the printer is online.

3. Then, make sure that the print server is booted.

4. If you are still experiencing problems, ensure that the logical printers are installed on both the client side and server side.

5. Also, check the print queue for stalled jobs. You may have to stop and restart the spooler service.

Microsoft has included troubleshooting wizards to help you troubleshoot problems with common devices. These troubleshooters are a great place to start when diagnosing the problems. As your troubleshooting experience grows, you will rely less and less on these wizards.

Troubleshooting Remote Access Service (RAS) should always start with the physical connection. After that component has been checked, you need to ensure that your client settings for speed, protocol, and security match the settings that are configured on the server to which the client is trying to connect. Inspecting the Device.log and Modemlog.txt files can also give you useful information.

As with RAS troubleshooting, you should always check the physical connection when troubleshooting network settings. You might need to inspect your NIC drivers and verify that the settings are correct. You also will want to see if any other clients are experiencing the same type of problems. As a last-ditch effort, you can attempt to reboot the system and see if that fixes the problem.

When troubleshooting disk problems, use the Computer Management console. The Disk Management tool is under the Storage grouping and can give you a lot of information about the disks connected to the system. If users are having problems connecting to resources, it may be a permission problem. In such a case, you should log on with an account that has administrative permissions so that you can view and alter permissions as needed.

The Master Boot Record (MBR) is an area on the hard drive that determines the boot process. If the MBR becomes corrupt and must be repaired, you need to boot Windows XP from either the boot floppies or CD and access the Recovery Console. If an application fails while in Windows XP, then Dr. Watson automatically starts and tries to debug the application. To configure Dr. Watson problems, run drwtsn32.exe from the Run command.

Microsoft occasionally releases service packs to fix existing problems, to introduce new features, and to patch errors. Service packs include multiple hot fixes that can also be installed individually. Hot fixes are released before service packs and should be installed only if you are experiencing the problems that are defined by the hot fix.

C

Practice Exam

70-270 Installing, Configuring, and Administering Microsoft Windows XP Professional

Name:_____

Date:_____

1. You need to install Windows XP on a computer running Windows 2000 Professional. What command can be used to generate a compatibility report on the computer's hardware and software?

    a. E:\I386\INSTALL /checkupgrade

    b. E:\I386\WINNT /checkupgrade

    c. E:\I386\WINNT32 /checkupgradeonly

    d. E:\I386\WINNT32 /compat

2. Which file system is supported by Windows XP? (Choose all that apply.)

    a. NTFS

    b. FAT

    c. FAT32

    d. HPFS

3. Which of the following file systems does not support partitions larger than 2 GB?

    a. FAT

    b. FAT32

    c. NTFS

    d. none of the above

4. Which of the following operating systems does not have an upgrade path to Windows XP? (Choose all that apply.)

    a. Windows 95

    b. Windows 98

    c. Windows NT 4 Service Pack 4

    d. Windows 2000 Professional

5. Before performing an installation of Windows XP, you must uncompress all drives that have been compressed using which utility? (Choose all that apply.)

    a. NTFS compression

    b. DoubleSpace

    c. DriveSpace

    d. all of the above

6. Using the User State Migration tool, which folder is *not* transferred by default?

    a. My Documents

    b. My Pictures

    c. Desktop

    d. Favorites

    e. Documents and Settings

7. Which tool is used to create an answer file for an unattended installation?
    a. SYSPREP
    b. Setup Manager
    c. WINNT32
    d. RIS

8. You want to create an unattend file to install Windows XP from the installation CD. To do so, you must save the file as _____ .
    a. WINNT.INF
    b. WINNT.SIF
    c. UNATTTEND.TXT
    d. UNATTEND.INI

9. What is the name of the installation folder into which Windows XP is installed by default when performing an unattended installation?
    a. Windows
    b. Winnt
    c. Winnt32
    d. Windows XP

10. You want to install Windows XP on multiple computers using Remote Installation Services (RIS). What component is required for RIS? (Choose all that apply.)
    a. a DNS server
    b. Active Directory
    c. WINS
    d. a DHCP server

11. You want to use a disk-imaging tool to install Windows XP on 10 identical workstations. Which tool is used to prepare a Windows XP installation for disk imaging?
    a. Setup Manager
    b. DISKIMG
    c. DISKPREP
    d. SYSPREP

12. You are installing Windows XP on 20 new workstations using an unattended installation with UDF files. However, the unattended file specifies an organization name of ABC Company, while the UDF file specifies an organization name of XYZ Company. Which value is assigned to the computer?
    a. ABC Company
    b. XYZ Company
    c. The user is prompted to select an organization name.
    d. Neither is used, and the setting is left blank.

13. Windows XP supports Plug and Play (PnP) devices. Which device is automatically detected by Windows XP when the device is plugged in and does not require the computer to be turned off? (Choose all that apply.)
    a. USB
    b. PCI
    c. IEEE 1394
    d. SCSI
    e. ISA

14. **Which local Windows XP group has the required permissions to install a PnP device? (Choose all that apply.)**
    a. Power Users
    b. Users
    c. Administrators
    d. all of the above

15. **You want to use multiple monitors on your Windows XP computer, but you are not sure that the computer supports it. What type of video adapter supports multiple monitors? (Choose all that apply.)**
    a. PCI
    b. ISA
    c. EISA
    d. AGP

16. **You have just installed a second video adapter and monitor on your Windows XP computer. How do you determine which monitor is now the primary monitor?**
    a. Pop-up windows display on the primary monitor.
    b. The primary monitor is always on the left.
    c. The primary monitor is always on the right.
    d. The primary monitor is identified by a different background.

17. **Which of the following statements regarding driver signing is correct?**
    a. Driver signing indicates the driver has been tested by the manufacturer.
    b. Driver signing indicates the driver has been tested and certified for all Microsoft operating systems.
    c. Driver signing is used to ensure the driver has not been modified.
    d. all of the above

18. **You have used the file signature verification tool to identify all unsigned files on your Windows XP computer, and you have saved the results to a log file for future use. What is the default name of the log file that is created?**
    a. SIGNED.TXT
    b. UNSIGNED.TXT
    c. FILESIG.TXT
    d. SIGVERIF.TXT

19. **Driver signing information for a driver is stored in which type of file?**
    a. .drv
    b. .cat
    c. .sig
    d. .ver

20. You are experiencing problems with the network card driver that you updated on your Windows XP computer. You want to roll back the drivers to restore the previous driver. Which folder contains that previous driver?

    a. %SYSTEMROOT%\SYSTEM32\REINSTALLBACKUPS

    b. %SYSTEMROOT%\SYSTEM32\DRIVERS\BACKUPS

    c. %SYSTEMROOT%\SYSTEM32\BACKUPS\DRIVERS

    d. %SYSTEMROOT%\SYSTEM32\DRIVERS\ROLLBACK

21. You have added an extra hard drive to your Windows XP Professional computer. You want to combine the free space on the new hard drive with some free space available on the other hard drive to create a single logical partition. What type of volume should you create?

    a. simple volume

    b. striped volume

    c. spanned volume

    d. dynamic volume

22. Which of the following volumes is fault tolerant in Windows XP?

    a. simple volume

    b. striped volume

    c. spanned volume

    d. all of the above

    e. none of the above

23. You want to be able to install Windows XP Professional and another operating system on the same computer using a dynamic disk. Which of the following operating systems supports dual booting dynamic disks with Windows XP Professional? (Choose all that apply.)

    a. Windows 95

    b. Windows 98

    c. Windows NT

    d. Windows 2000 Professional

    e. none of the above

24. The power supply in your Windows XP workstation needs to be replaced. You want to be able to move the dynamic disk to another computer so that you can print some important documents. What operating systems support importing dynamic disks? (Choose all that apply.)

    a. Windows 98

    b. Windows NT

    c. Windows 2000 Professional

    d. none of the above

25. Which of the following types of dynamic volumes *cannot* be extended? (Choose all that apply.)

    a. system volumes

    b. boot volumes

    c. FAT32 volumes

    d. OEM partitions

26. Which of the following volumes *cannot* be deleted using Computer Management? (Choose all that apply.)
    a. boot volume
    b. system volume
    c. spanned volume
    d. volume containing a page file
    e. striped volume

27. You have added a second hard drive to your Windows XP Professional computer. You would like to create a mount point to the new hard drive. What file system must be used on this new hard drive?
    a. FAT
    b. FAT32
    c. NTFS
    d. any of the above

28. You are running out of hard drive space on your Windows XP Professional computer. You would like to compress a folder to save space, but the option to compress the folder is not available. What must you do to compress the folder?
    a. Reformat the partition as NTFS.
    b. Install Windows XP Service Pack 1.
    c. Convert the partition to NTFS.
    d. Upgrade the disk to a dynamic disk.

29. What is the default file share permission that is available in Windows XP? (Choose all that apply.)
    a. Read
    b. Write
    c. Modify
    d. Change
    e. Full Control
    f. List

30. You need to convert drive E: from FAT to NTFS on your Windows XP workstation. What is the correct command to do so?
    a. CONVERT E: /NTFS
    b. FORMAT E: /NTFS
    c. CONVERT E: /FS:NTFS
    d. You cannot convert from FAT to NTFS.

31. What happens when you move a compressed file from a folder on an NTFS volume to another folder on an NTFS volume on the same computer?
    a. The file retains its compression.
    b. The file inherits the compression attribute of the target folder.
    c. The user is prompted to select a compression attribute.
    d. The file is always uncompressed when moved.

32. Which of the following statements regarding compression is *false*?
    a. Compression is available only on NTFS partitions or volumes.
    b. Compression is available only on dynamic disks.
    c. Some files compress better than others.
    d. Both folders and files can be compressed.

33. You would like to give other users access to the printer attached to your Windows XP Professional computer. However, you do not want the users to delete other users' print jobs. What permission should you assign to the printer?
    a. Manage Printer
    b. Manage Documents
    c. Print
    d. Full Control

34. What *cannot* be encrypted using EFS? (Choose all that apply.)
    a. local files
    b. network files
    c. shared folders
    d. data transmitted over the network
    e. offline folders

35. A client needs to type in both Spanish and English on her Windows XP Professional computer. How can this be accomplished?
    a. Install a Spanish keyboard.
    b. Install a Spanish version of Windows XP in a dual boot configuration.
    c. Change the Regional and Language Options settings to the appropriate country.
    d. Install the appropriate second language in Regional and Language Options.

36. A user is trying to locate files she created in the My Documents folder. What is the location of this folder?
    a. C:\My Documents
    b. C:\Documents and Settings*Username*\My Documents
    c. C:\Documents and Settings\My Documents
    d. C:\Windows\ Documents and Settings*Username*\My Documents

37. You have been experiencing intermittent hardware crashes on a Windows XP computer. What utility is used to view the contents of the Memory.dmp file? (Choose all that apply.)
    a. Notepad.txt
    b. Dumpchk
    c. Dumpexam
    d. Dumpview

38. You need to configure a Windows XP Professional computer to share its Internet connection using ICS. What IP address range does ICS assign for the internal network?
    a. 10.0.0.0
    b. 172.16.0.0
    c. 172.32.0.0
    d. 192.168.0.0

39. You are setting up Windows XP to support incoming remote connections. Which LAN protocol is supported by Windows XP for remote access? (Choose all that apply.)

    a. TCP/IP

    b. NWLink

    c. NetBEUI

    d. AppleTalk

40. Which remote access protocol is used by Windows XP to connect to a Windows 3.1 remote access server?

    a. SLIP

    b. PPP

    c. L2TP

    d. RAS

    e. PPTP

41. A user needs to connect to her Windows XP Professional computer at the office from her Windows XP computer at home. She requires full access to the computer's hard drives and applications. What solution should you implement?

    a. Use Remote Desktop to connect to the work computer.

    b. Configure the work computer as a VPN server.

    c. Configure a VPN tunnel from the office firewall to the home computer.

    d. Install a third-party application.

42. Which of the following statements regarding standby mode is true? (Choose all that apply.)

    a. Standby mode is designed to be used for extended periods.

    b. Standby mode operates the system in a low-power state.

    c. Standby mode saves all data in memory.

    d. Standby mode shuts down the computer.

43. Which partition on the hard drive stores the data in RAM when hibernation is enabled?

    a. the boot partition

    b. the system partition

    c. the partition specified by user

    d. any partition with free space equal to the amount of RAM

44. The master boot record (MBR) on a computer is corrupt and now Windows XP does not start. What can be done to repair the MBR?

    a. Restore the MBR from a backup.

    b. Boot into safe mode and copy the MBR from another Windows XP system.

    c. Boot into the Recovery Console and repair the MBR.

    d. Reformat the hard drive.

45. You need to install some operating system upgrades on a Windows XP computer. You would like to be able to roll back the upgrades in case they conflict with a custom written application on the computer. What should you do before performing the upgrade?

    a. Back up the C:\WINDOWS folder.

    b. Create a restore point.

    c. Create an Emergency Restore Disk.

    d. Back up the System State.

46. **Which key is used to access safe mode in Windows XP?**
    a. F1
    b. F2
    c. F5
    d. F6
    e. F8

47. **You have created a local user named User1 on your Windows XP Professional computer. You have configured User1 as a limited user account. Which of the following tasks can a user of a limited limited user account perform? (Choose all that apply.)**
    a. Change his or her own password.
    b. Change the display options.
    c. Install new software.
    d. Change the picture associated with the account.
    e. Access all files on the local hard drive.

48. **A member of the Power Users group is given what type of user account?**
    a. Limited
    b. Standard
    c. Computer Administrator
    d. Local Administrator

49. **An application has stopped responding on your Windows XP computer. What utility can be used to shut down the application?**
    a. Computer Management
    b. Performance Monitor
    c. Task Manager
    d. Event Viewer

50. **By default, how large is the default page file on a Windows XP computer?**
    a. equal to the size of RAM
    b. 1.5 times the size of RAM
    c. twice the size of RAM
    d. RAM plus 12 MB

Glossary

access control list (ACL) — A list of security identifiers that are contained by a resource object. Only those processes with the appropriate access token can activate the services of that object.

access token — Objects containing the security identifier of an active process. These tokens determine the security context of the process.

account lockout policy — Defines the conditions that result in a user account being locked out.

activating Windows — A new Microsoft requirement to prevent software piracy by registering installations of Windows XP with the signature of its supporting hardware.

active (marked active) — The status of a primary partition that indicates to the computer's BIOS that it hosts the necessary files to boot an operating system.

Active Directory — A centralized resource and security management, administration, and control mechanism used to support and maintain a Windows XP domain. The Active Directory is hosted by domain controllers.

active partition — The partition the computer uses to boot.

Address Resolution Protocol (ARP) — The IP protocol used to resolve numeric IP addresses into their MAC layer physical address equivalents.

administrator — The Windows XP account designed to perform a full array of management functions. This is the most powerful account possible within the Windows XP environment.

Advanced RISC Computing (ARC) pathname — Naming convention used in the Boot.ini file to define the particular hard disk and partition where Windows XP operating system files reside.

alert — A watchdog that informs you when a counter crosses a defined threshold. An alert is an automated attendant looking for high or low values, and can consist of one or more counter/instance-based alert definitions.

answer file — A text file, also called a response file, that contains a set of instructions for installing Windows XP.

applet — A tool or utility found in the Control Panel that typically has a single focused purpose or function.

Application log — Records application events, alerts, and system messages.

application programming interface (API) — A set of software routines referenced by an application to access underlying application services.

architecture — The layout of operating system components and their relationships.

audit policy — Defines the events that are recorded in the Security log of the Event Viewer.

auditing — The process of tracking events by recording selected types of events in the Security log.

authentication — The process of validating a user's credentials to allow access to certain resources.

author mode — The condition of a console that allows users to add and remove snap-ins, create new windows, view the entire console tree, and save new versions of the console.

backup type — A backup configuration that determines how often data is backed up and how old and new files are handled. The types of backups are copy, daily, differential, incremental, and normal.

backup utility — The tool built in to Windows XP that enables users to back up and restore their data and system configurations in case of a hardware or software failure.

base priority — The lowest priority that a thread may be assigned, based on the priority assigned to its process.

baseline — A definition of what a normal load looks like on a computer system; it provides a point of comparison against which you can measure future system behavior.

basic storage — The drive division method that employs partitions.

bindery — The database used by versions of NetWare before 4.0 to store network resource configuration information.

binding — The process of developing a stack by linking together network services and protocols. The binding facility allows users to define exactly how network services operate for optimal network performance.

BIOS (basic input/output system) — A special PC ROM chip that contains sufficient program code to let a computer perform a POST routine, to check its hardware components, and to operate basic input and output routines for keyboard or mouse input, and screen output.

boot loader — The software that shows all operating systems currently available and, through a menu, permits the user to choose which one should be booted.

boot partition — The partition that hosts the main Windows XP system files and is the initial default location for the paging file. The boot partition can be the same partition as the system partition or it can be any other partition (or logical drive in an extended partition) on any drive hosted by the computer.

boot phase — Any of a number of stages in the Windows XP boot process, starting with the POST, through initial startup activities, to activation of a boot loader program, to selection of the operating system (or version) to boot, to hardware detection (Ntdetect), to selecting a configuration.

boot process — The process of bringing up a completely functional computer, starting from initial power-up (or reboot) through the boot phases and load phases involved in starting the hardware, finding a boot loader, and then loading and initializing an operating system.

boot selection menu — The list of bootable operating systems (or versions) that Boot.ini provides for display at the end of the Windows XP boot phase.

boot.ini — The text file that creates the Windows XP boot loader's menu.

bottleneck — A system resource or device that limits a system's performance. Ideally, the user should be the bottleneck on a system, not any hardware or software component.

bound application — An application capable of running in a virtual DOS machine.

certificate — An electronic identity verification mechanism. Certificates are assigned to a client or server by a Certificate Authority. When communications begin, each side of the transmission can decide to either trust the other party based on their certificate and continue the communications or not to trust and terminate communications.

characterization data file — The file responsible for rendering the GDI commands into DDI commands that can be sent to the printer. Each graphics driver renders a different printer language.

child process — A process spawned within the context of some Windows XP environment subsystems (Win32, OS/2, or POSIX) that inherits operating characteristics from its parent subsystem and access characteristics from the permissions associated with the account that requested it to be launched.

clean installation — The installation method in which an OS is installed without regard for pre-existing operating systems. In other words, all settings and configurations are set to the OS defaults.

client — A computer used to access network resources.

client application — An application or service that creates print jobs for output, which can be either end-user-originated or created by a print server itself (See also *print client*).

Client Service for NetWare (CSNW) — Service included with Windows XP Professional that provides easy connection to NetWare servers.

cluster — A group of one or more sectors into a single nondivisible unit.

Common Internet File System (CIFS) — An enhanced version of SMB used for file and print services.

complementary metal-oxide semiconductor (CMOS) — A special, battery-powered chip that can store not only the software necessary to conduct the POST, but also the basic, nonvolatile configuration information that POST uses to check the RAM installed in a system, the number and type of hard drives, the type of keyboard and mouse, and so forth.

Computer Information File (CIF) — A detailed collection of all information related to the hardware and software products that your computer (and even your entire network) comprises.

connecting to a printer — The negotiation of a connection to a shared printer through the Browser service from a client or service across the network to the machine where the shared printer resides.

connection-oriented — A class of network transport protocols that includes guaranteed delivery, explicit acknowledgement of data receipt, and a variety of data integrity checks to ensure reliable transmission and reception of data across a network. Although reliable, connection-oriented protocols can be slow because of the overhead and extra communication.

connectionless — A class of network transport protocols that makes only a "best-effort" attempt at delivery, and that includes no explicit mechanisms to guarantee delivery or data integrity. Because such protocols need not be particularly reliable, they are often much faster and require less overhead than connection-oriented protocols.

console — The collection of snap-ins and extensions saved as an .msc file loaded into the MMC that offers administrative controls.

context — The collection of Registry values and runtime environment variables in which a process or thread is currently running.

context switch — The act of unloading the context information for one process and replacing it with the information for another, when the new process comes to the foreground.

Control Panel — The collection of tools and utilities (called applets) within Windows, where most system- and hardware-level installation and configuration take place.

control set — A special set of Registry values that describes a startup configuration of a computer running Windows XP that is saved each time a Windows machine is shut down (as the current configuration) and each time a user successfully logs on for the first time after bootup (known as the Last Known Good Configuration).

cooperative multitasking — A computing environment in which the individual application maintains control over the duration that its threads use operating time on the CPU.

copy backup — A method of backing up all selected files without marking them as being backed up.

counter (or performance counter) — A named aspect or activity that the Performance tool uses to measure or monitor some aspect of a registered system or application object.

Counter log — A log that records measurements on selected counters at regular, defined intervals. Counter logs allow you to define exactly which counters are recorded (based on computer, object, counter, and instance).

creating a printer — Setting up a printer for local use.

critical section — In operating system terminology, this refers to a section of code that can be accessed only by a single thread at any one time, to prevent uncertain results from occurring when multiple threads attempt to change or access values included in that code at the same time.

daily backup — A method of backing up only the selected files that have been created or modified on the day that the backup is being performed. They are not marked as being backed up.

Data Link Control (DLC) — A network transport protocol that allows connectivity to mainframes, printers, and servers running Remote Program Load software.

data type — The format in which print jobs are sent to the spooler. Some data types are ready for printing (RAW) and some require further preparation (EMF). Also refers to the setting on a Registry value entry that defines the data format of the stored information.

defragmentation — The process of reorganizing files so that they are stored contiguously and no gaps are left between files.

demand paging — The act of requesting free pages of memory from RAM for an active application.

device — A physical component, either internal or external to the computer, that is used to perform a specific function. Devices include hard drives, video cards, network interface cards, printers, etc.

Device Driver Interface (DDI) — A specific code component that handles the translation of generic print commands into device-specific equivalents, immediately prior to delivery of a spool file to a print device.

differential backup — A method of backing up selected files that have been created or modified since the last full backup. They are not marked as being backed up.

direct-attached printer — A print device attached directly to a computer, usually through a parallel port. See also *network interface printer*.

disabled — The state of a user account, which is retained on the system but cannot be used to logon.

disk bottleneck — A system bottleneck caused by a limitation in a computer's disk subsystem, such as a slow drive or controller, or a heavier load than the system can handle.

Disk Management — The MMC snap-in used to manage drives.

disk quota — A feature in Windows that allows you to limit the amount of disk space that can be consumed by a user.

Distributed File System (DFS) — Combines shared resources from various locations throughout a network into a single hierarchical system.

DMA (Direct Memory Access) — A channel used by a hardware device to access memory directly, i.e., bypassing the CPU. Windows XP supports eight DMA channels, numbered 0 to 7.

domain — A collection of computers with centrally managed security and activities.

domain controller (DC) — A computer that maintains the domain's Active Directory, which stores all information and relationships about users, groups, policies, computers, and resources. It also authenticates domain logons and maintains the security policies and the account database for a domain.

domain model — The networking setup in which there is centralized administrative and security control. One or more servers are dedicated to the task of controlling the domain by providing access and authentication for shared domain resources to member computers.

Domain Name Service (DNS) — TCP/IP service that is used to resolve names to IP addresses.

domain security — The control of user accounts, group memberships, and resource access for all members of a network instead of for only a single computer.

domain user account — A user account that can be used throughout a domain.

DOS operating environment — A general term used to describe the reasonably thorough DOS emulation capabilities provided in a Windows XP virtual DOS machine (VDM).

DOS prompt — The common name for the command-line window available from DOS and Windows.

Dr. Watson — An application error debugger. This diagnostic tool detects application failures and logs diagnostic details.

drive letter — One of two methods of accessing formatted volumes under Windows XP. A drive letter can be assigned to a partition or volume or a drive configuration of multiple components.

driver — A software element that is used by an operating system to control a device. Drivers are usually device-specific.

dual-boot system — A computer that is configured to use two operating systems.

Dynamic Data Exchange (DDE) — A method of interprocess communication within the Windows operating system.

Dynamic Host Configuration Protocol (DHCP) — An IP-based address management service that permits clients to obtain IP addresses from a DHCP server. This allows network administrators to control and manage IP addresses centrally, rather than on a per-machine basis.

dynamic link library (DLL) — A collection of virtual procedure calls, also called procedure stubs, that provide a well-defined way for applications to call on services or server processes within the Win32 environment. DLLs have been a consistent aspect of Windows since Windows 2.0.

dynamic storage — The drive division method that employs volumes. It is a new standard supported only by Windows XP and Windows 2000.

Encrypted File System (EFS) — A security feature of NTFS under Windows XP that allows files, folders, or entire drives to be encrypted. Once encrypted, only the user account that enabled the encryption has the proper private key to decrypt and access the secured objects.

enhanced metafile (EMF) — Device-independent spool data used to reduce the amount of time spent processing a print job. Once it's queued, EMF data requires additional processing to prepare it for the printer.

environment subsystem — A mini-operating system running within Windows XP that provides an interface between applications and the kernel. Windows XP has three environment subsystems: Win32, OS/2, and POSIX, but only Win32 is required for Windows XP to function.

event — Any significant occurrence in the system or in an application that requires users to be notified or a log entry to be recorded. Types of events include audits, driver failures, user logon, process launching, system shutdown, etc.

Event Viewer — A system utility that displays one of three event logs: System, Security, and Application, wherein logged or audited events appear. The Event Viewer is often the first stop when monitoring a system's performance or seeking evidence of problems, because it is where all unusual or extraordinary system activities and events are recorded.

Executive Services — A set of kernel-mode functions that control security, system I/O, memory management, and other low-level services.

extended partition — A type of partition on a basic disk that can be divided into logical drives. Only a single extended partition can exist on a physical disk. When present, only three primary partitions can exist.

FAT (File Allocation Table) or **FAT16** — The file system used in versions of MS-DOS. Supported in Windows XP in its VFAT form, which adds long filenames and 4 GB file and volume sizes.

FAT32 — The 32-bit enhanced version of FAT introduced by Windows 95 OSR2 that expands the file and volume size of FAT to 32 GB. FAT32 is supported by Windows XP.

FDISK — A DOS utility used to partition a hard disk. The DOS FDISK tool can see and manipulate only primary NTFS partitions; it cannot even view logical drives in an extended partition formatted with NTFS.

file system — The method used to arrange, read, and write files on disk. Windows XP supports the NTFS, FAT, and FAT32 file systems.

File Transfer Protocol (FTP) — The protocol and service that provides TCP/IP-based file transfer to and from remote hosts and confers the ability to navigate and operate within remote file systems.

flush — Forcing the memory-resident copy of the Registry to be written to files stored on the hard drive. A flush occurs at shutdown, when forced by an application, or just after a Registry alteration.

folder redirection — A component of IntelliMirror technologies that uses group policies to place specified user folders on a share on the network.

format — Rewriting the track and sector information on a disk, it removes all data previously on the disk.

fragmentation — The division of a file into two or more parts, where each part is stored in a different location on the hard drive. As the level of fragmentation on a drive increases, the longer it takes for read and write operations to occur.

frame type — One of four available packet structures supported by IPX/SPX and NWLink. The four frame types supported are Ethernet 802.2, Ethernet 802.3, Ethernet II, and Ethernet SNAP.

gateway — A computer that serves as a router, a format translator, or a security filter for an entire network.

global group — A group that exists throughout a domain. A global group can be created only on a Windows Server system.

Graphical Device Interface (GDI) — The portion of the Windows XP operating system responsible for the first step of preparing all graphical output, whether to be sent to a monitor or to the printer.

groups — A named collections of users.

guest account — One of the least privileged user accounts built into Windows XP.

handle — A programming term that indicates an internal identifier for some kind of system resource, object, or other component that must be accessed by name (or through a pointer). In Task Manager, the number of handles appears on the Performance tab in the Totals pane. A sudden increase in the number of handles, threads, or processes can indicate that an ill-behaved application is running on a system.

hardware abstraction layer (HAL) — One of the few components of the Windows XP architecture that is written in hardware-dependent code. It is designed to protect hardware resources.

Hardware Compatibility List (HCL) — Microsoft's updated list of supported hardware for Windows XP.

hardware profile — A collection of custom device settings used on computers with changing physical components.

hive — A discrete body of Registry keys, subkeys, and values stored in a file.

HKEY_CLASSES_ROOT — This Registry key contains the value entries that control the relationships between file extensions (and therefore file format types) and applications. This key also supports the data used in object linking and embedding (OLE), COM object data, and file-class association data. This key actually points to another Registry key named HKEY_LOCAL_ MACHINE\Software\Classes and provides multiple points of access to make itself easily accessible to the operating system itself and to applications that need access to the compatibility information already mentioned.

HKEY_CURRENT_CONFIG — This Registry key contains the value entries that control the currently active hardware profile; its contents are rebuilt each time the system is booted. This key is derived from data stored in the HKEY_LOCAL_ MACHINE\System\CurrentControlSet\Hard wareProfiles\Current subkey. HKEY_CURRENT_ CONFIG exists to provide backward-compatibility with Windows 95/98 applications.

HKEY_CURRENT_USER — This Registry key contains the value entries that define the user environment for the currently logged-on user. This key is built each time a user logs on to the system. The data in this key are derived from the HKEY_USERS key and the Ntuser.dat and Ntuser.man files of a user's profile.

HKEY_LOCAL_MACHINE — This Registry key contains the value entries that control the local computer. This includes hardware devices, device drivers, and various operating system components. The data stored in this key are not dependent on a logged-on user or the applications or processes in use.

HKEY_USERS — This Registry key contains the value entries that define the user environments for all users who have ever logged on to this computer. As a new user logs on to this system, a new subkey is added for that user and is built either from the default profile stored in this key or from the roaming user profile.

hosts — A static file placed on members of a network to provide a resolution mechanism between host names and IP addresses.

hot fix — Similar to a service pack, except that a hot fix addresses only one problem, or a small number of problems, and may not be fully tested.

identification — The process of establishing a valid account identity on a Windows XP machine by supplying a correct and working domain name (if necessary) and account name.

imported user account — A local account created by duplicating the name and password of an existing domain account. An imported account can be used only when the Windows XP Professional system is able to communicate with the domain of the original account.

incremental backup — A method of backing up selected files that have been created or modified since the last normal or incremental backup. These files are marked as being backed up.

input locale — A combination language and keyboard layout used to define how data is entered into a computer.

input message queue — A queue for each process maintained by the Win32 subsystem that contains the messages sent to the process from the user, directing its threads to do something.

instance — A selection of a specific object when more than one is present on the monitored system; for example, multiple CPUs or hard drives.

Integrated Services Digital Network (ISDN) — A direct, digital dial-up PSTN Data Link-layer connection that operates at 64 KB per channel over regular twisted-pair cable between a subscriber site and a PSTN central office.

IntelliMirror — A set of features within Windows XP that utilizes policies, folder redirection, and the Windows Installer Service (WIS) for backing up and restoring users' data, personalized settings, and applications.

Internet Control Message Protocol (ICMP) — The protocol in the TCP/IP suite that handles communication between devices about network traffic, quality of service, and requests for specific acknowledgments (such as those used in the PING utility).

Internet Printing Protocol (IPP) — A new Windows XP protocol that adds Web support to the print subsystem. IPP allows remote users to submit print jobs for printing, view printer queues, and download print drivers.

Internet Protocol (IP) — The protocol that handles routing and addressing information for the TCP/IP protocol suite, IP provides a simple connectionless transmission that relies on higher layer protocols to establish reliability.

Internetwork Packet Exchange (IPX) — The protocol developed by Novell for its NetWare product. IPX is a routable, connection-oriented protocol similar to TCP/IP but much easier to manage and with lower communication overhead.

Internetwork Packet Exchange/Sequenced Packet Exchange (IPX/SPX) — The name of the two primary protocols developed by Novell for its NetWare network operating system. IPX/SPX is derived from the XNS protocol stack and leans heavily on XNS architecture and functionality. See also *IPX* and *SPX*.

interprocess communication (IPC) — The mechanism that defines a way for internal Windows processes to exchange information.

IPSec (IP Security) — An encrypted communication mechanism for TCP/IP to create protected communication sessions. IPSec is a suite of cryptography-based protection services and security protocols.

I/O port — The section of memory used by the hardware to communicate with the operating system. When an IRQ is used, the system checks the I/O port memory area for additional information about what function is needed by the device. The I/O port is represented by a hexadecimal number.

IRQ (interrupt request) — The interrupt request level that is used to halt CPU operation in favor of the device. Windows supports 16 interrupts, namely IRQ 0 to 15.

Kerberos version 5 — An authentication encryption protocol employed by Windows XP to protect logon credentials.

kernel — The core of the Microsoft Windows XP operating system. It is designed to facilitate all activity within the Executive Services.

kernel mode — Systems running in kernel mode are operating within a shared memory space and with access to hardware. Windows XP Executive Services operates in kernel mode.

key — A top-level division of the Registry. There are five keys in a Windows XP Registry. A key can contain subkeys.

language monitor — The part of the print monitor that sets up bidirectional messaging between the printer and the computer initiating the print job.

Last Known Good Configuration (LKGC) — The control set for Windows XP that is automatically saved by the system in a special set of Registry keys the first time a user logs on successfully to a system immediately after it has booted up. This information provides a safe fallback to use when booting the system the next time, if changes made to the Registry in the interim cause problems with booting (or if changes have been introduced that a user does not want to retain on that system).

Layer Two Tunneling Protocol (L2TP) — A VPN protocol developed by Cisco Systems, Inc. to improve security over Internet links by integrating with IPSec.

lmhosts — A file used in Microsoft networks to provide NetBIOS name-to-address resolution.

load phase — The Windows XP load phase begins when the kernel assumes control of the machine, and consists of the following five steps: (1) loading the kernel, (2) initializing the kernel, (3) loading services, (4) starting the Windows XP system, and (5) logging on. All five steps must be completed successfully for a complete load to occur.

Local Computer Policy — A Windows XP security control feature used to define and regulate security-related features and functions.

local groups — A group that exists only on the computer where it was created. A local group can have users and global groups as members.

local procedure call (LPC) — A technique to permit processes to exchange data in the Windows XP runtime environment. LPCs define a rigorous interface to let client programs request services, and to let server programs respond to such requests.

Local Security Policy — The centralized control mechanism that governs password, account lockout, audit, user rights, security options, public key, and IP Security.

local user account — A user account that exists on a single computer.

locked out — The state of a user account that is disabled due to logon attempts that have repeatedly failed.

logon authentication — The requirement to provide a name and password to gain access to the computer.

long file names (LFNs) — Filenames up to 256 characters in length, supported by all file systems under Windows XP.

mailslots — A connectionless version of named pipes; mailslots offer no delivery guarantees, nor do they acknowledge successful receipt of data.

mandatory profile — A user profile that does not retain changes once the user logs out. Mandatory profiles are used to maintain a common desktop environment for users.

Master Boot Record (MBR) — The partition table for a disk, and the code that permits that partition table to be read. A functioning MBR is required to boot a hard disk.

memory bottleneck — A system bottleneck caused by a lack of available physical or virtual memory that results in system slowdown or (in extreme cases) an outright system crash.

Microsoft Management Console (MMC) — The standardized interface into which consoles, snap-ins, and extensions are loaded to perform administrative tasks.

mirrored volume — A drive configuration of a single volume is duplicated onto another volume on a different hard drive. Provides fault tolerance. In Windows NT, a mirror on a drive hosted by a different drive controller was called duplexing, but this distinction is no longer used in Windows XP (Windows .NET Server only).

mismatched document — A document with incompatible printer and page settings (that is, the page settings are impossible to produce given the existing printer settings).

mode — A programming and operational separation of components, functions, and services.

modem (Modulator/Demodulator) — A Data-link layer device used to create an analog signal suitable for transmission over telephone lines from a digital data stream. Modern modems also include a command set to negotiate connections and data rates with remote modems and to set their default behavior.

mount point or mounted volume — A new drive-access technique that maps a volume or partition to an empty directory on an NTFS volume or partition.

MS-DOS — One of the most popular character-based operating systems for personal computers. Many DOS concepts are still in use by modern operating systems.

multi-boot system — A computer that hosts two or more operating systems that can be booted by selecting one from a boot menu or boot manager during each bootup.

multiprocessing — The ability to distribute threads among multiple CPUs on the same system.

Multi-Provider Router (MPR) — A file system service that can designate the proper redirector to handle a resource request that does not use UNC naming. The MPR lets applications written to older Microsoft specifications behave as if they used UNC naming. The MPR is able to recognize those UNCs that correspond to defined drive mappings receive copies of the domain security database or Active Directory.

multitasking — Sharing processor time between threads. Multitasking may be preemptive (the operating system may bump one thread if another one really needs access to the processor), or cooperative (one thread retains control of the processor until its turn to use it is over). Windows XP uses preemptive multitasking except in the context of the WOW operating environment, because Windows 3.x applications expect cooperative multitasking.

multithreaded process — A process with more than one thread running at a time.

multithreading — The ability of an operating system and hardware to execute multiple pieces of code (or threads) from a single application simultaneously.

Multiple Universal Naming Convention Provider (MUP) — A Windows XP software component that allows two or more UNC providers (for example, Microsoft networks and NetWare networks) to exist simultaneously. The MUP determines which UNC provider will handle a particular UNC request and forwards the request to that provider.

multiple-user system — An operating system that maintains separate and distinct user accounts for each person.

named pipes — Provides support for a connection-oriented message-passing service for clients and servers.

naming convention — A standardized regular method of creating names for objects, users, computers, groups, etc.

NDS tree — The hierarchical representation of the Novell Directory Services database on NetWare 4.0 and higher networks.

NetBIOS Extended User Interface (NetBEUI) — A simple transport program developed to support NetBIOS installations. NetBEUI is not routable, so it is not appropriate for larger networks.

NetBIOS Gateway — A service provided by remote access that allows NetBIOS requests to be forwarded independently of the transport protocol. For example, NetBEUI can be sent over the network through NWLink.

NetBIOS over TCP/IP (NBT) — A network protocol in the TCP/IP stack that provides NetBIOS naming services.

NetWare Core Protocol (NCP) — The protocol used by CSNW to make file and print services requests of NetWare servers.

network adapter (NIC) — Another name for network card; the piece of hardware that enables communication between the computer and the network.

network authentication — The act of connecting to or accessing resources from some other member of the domain network. Network authentication is used to prove that you are a valid member of the domain, that your user account is properly authenticated, and that you have access permissions to perform the requested action.

Network Basic Input/Output System (NetBIOS) — A client/server interprocess communication service developed by IBM in 1985. NetBIOS presents a relatively primitive mechanism for communication in client/server applications, but allows an easy implementation across various Microsoft Windows computers.

network bottleneck — A system bottleneck caused by excessive traffic on the network medium to which a computer is attached, or when the computer itself generates excessive amounts of such traffic.

Network Driver Interface Specification (NDIS) — Microsoft specification that defines parameters for loading more than one protocol on a network adapter.

Network Dynamic Data Exchange (NetDDE) — An interprocess communication mechanism developed by Microsoft to support the distribution of DDE applications over a network.

network interface printer — A print device attached directly to the network medium, usually by means of a built-in network interface integrated within the printer, but sometimes by means of a parallel-attached network printer interface.

network number — The specific network identifier used by IPX for internal and network communication.

new installation — See *clean installation*.

New Technology File System (NTFS) — The high-performance file system supported by Windows XP that offers file-level security, encryption, compression, auditing, and more. Theoretically supports volumes up to 16 exabytes, but Microsoft recommends volumes not exceed 2 terabytes.

normal (or full) backup — A method of backing up all selected files and marking them as being backed up.

Novell Directory Services (NDS) — The hierarchical database used by NetWare 4.0 and higher servers to store network resource object configuration information.

NTFS (New Technology File System) — The preferred file system of Windows XP. Supports file-level security, encryption, compression, auditing, and more. Supports volumes up to 2 TB.

ntldr — The Windows XP loader program that manages the boot and load phases of Windows XP on a PC.

NTLM (NT LAN Manager) authentication — The authentication mechanism used on Windows NT that is retained by Windows XP for backward compatibility.

NWLink — Microsoft's implementation of Novell's IPX/SPX protocol, used for Microsoft Networking or for facilitating connectivity with Novell networks.

object — Everything within the Windows XP operating environment is an object. Objects include files, folders, shares, printers, processes, etc. See also *performance object*.

Open Datalink Interface (ODI) — Novell's specification for network device communication.

operating system (OS) — Software designed to work directly with hardware to provide a computing environment within which production and entertainment software can execute, and which creates a user interface.

package — The name of the collection of installer files, transforms, and other code components that support automated deployment of Windows programs. This term may also be applied to the .msi files associated with the Microsoft Installer facility used to drive automated installations through the Microsoft Installer itself.

Packet Internet Groper (PING) — An IP-based utility that can be used to check network connectivity or to verify whether a specific host elsewhere on the network can be reached.

page — An individual unit of memory that the Virtual Memory Manager manipulates (moves from RAM to paging file and vice versa).

parent process — The Windows XP environment subsystem that creates a runtime process, and imbues that child process with characteristics associated with that parent's interfaces, capabilities, and runtime requirements.

partition — A space set aside on a disk and assigned a drive letter. A partition can take up all or part of the space on a disk.

partition boot sector — The partition that contains the information the file system uses to access the volume, including a physical description of the disk, the name and version of the operating system files, the bootstrap code, and an instruction that allows the Master Boot Record to find all this information.

password — A unique string of characters that must be provided before a logon or an access is authorized. Passwords are a security measure used to restrict initial access to Windows XP resources.

password policy — Defines the restrictions on passwords.

PC Cards — The modern name of the PCMCIA technology. PC Cards are credit card–sized devices typically used to expand the functionality of notebook or portable computers.

PCMCIA — The older name for the technology now called PC Cards. PCMCIA stands for Personal Computer Memory Card International Association.

peer-to-peer — A type of networking in which each computer can be a client to other computers and act as a server as well.

performance object — A component of the Windows XP Professional system environment; objects range from devices to services to processes.

Plug and Play (PnP) — A technology that allows an operating system to inspect and identify a device, install the correct driver, and enable the device, all without user interaction. Plug and Play simplifies the adding and removing of hardware and can often offer on-the-fly reconfiguration of devices without rebooting.

Point-to-Point Protocol (PPP) — A Network layer transport that provides connectivity over serial or modem lines. PPP can negotiate any transport protocol used by both systems involved in the link and can automatically assign IP, DNS, and gateway addresses when used with TCP/IP.

Point-to-Point Tunneling Protocol (PPTP) — Protocol used to connect to corporate networks through the Internet or an ISP.

port — Any physical communication channel to which a modem, direct cable, or other device can be connected to enable a link between two computers.

port monitor — The part of the print monitor that transmits the print job to the print device through the specified port. Port monitors are actually unaware of print devices as such, but only know that something is on the other end of the port.

power-on self test (POST) — The system check performed by all computers when they are turned on.

PPP MultiLink — A capability of remote access to aggregate multiple data streams into one network connection for the purpose of using more than one modem or ISDN channel in a single connection.

preemptive multitasking — A computing environment in which the operating system maintains control over the duration of operating time any thread (a single process of an application) is granted on the CPU.

primary partition — A type of partition on a basic disk that can be marked active. Up to four primary partitions can exist on a physical disk.

print client — A network client machine that transmits print jobs across the network to a printer for spooling and delivery to a designated print device or printer pool.

print device — In everyday language, a piece of equipment that provides output service—in other words, a printer. However, in Microsoft terminology, a printer is a logical service that accepts print jobs and delivers them to some print device for output when that device is ready. Therefore, in Microsoft terminology, a print device is any piece of equipment that can produce output, so this term would also describe a plotter, a fax machine, or a slide printer, as well as a text-oriented output device, such as an HP LaserJet.

print job — The contents of a completely or partially interpreted data file that contains text and control characters that will ultimately be delivered to a print device to be printed, or otherwise rendered in some tangible form.

print processor — Software that works with the printer driver to despool files and make any necessary changes to the data to format it for use with a particular printer. The print processor itself is a PostScript program that understands the format of a document image file and how to print the file to a specific PostScript printer or class of printers.

print provider — The server-side software that sends the print job to the proper server in the format that it requires. Windows XP supports both Windows network print providers and NetWare print providers.

print resolution — A measurement of the number of dots per inch (dpi) that describes the output capabilities of a print device; most laser printers usually produce output at 300 or 600 dpi. In gen-eral, the larger the dpi rating for a device, the higher quality its output will be (but high-resolution devices cost more than low-resolution ones).

print router — The software component in the Windows XP print subsystem that directs print jobs from one print server to another, or from a client to a remote printer.

print server — A computer that links print devices to the network and shares those devices with client computers on the network.

print spooler — A collection of Windows XP DLLs used to acquire, process, catalog, and dispense print jobs to print devices. The spooler acts like a holding tank; it manages an area on disk called the spool file on a print server, where pending print jobs are stored until they've been output. "Despooling" is the process of reading and interpreting what's in a spool file for delivery to a print device.

print server services — A collection of named software components on a print server that handles incoming print jobs and forwards them to a print spooler for post-processing and delivery to a print device. These components include support for special job handling that can enable a variety of client computers to send print jobs to a print server for processing.

printer (logical printer) — In Microsoft terminology, a printer is not a physical device, but rather a named system object that communicates between the operating system and some print device. The printer handles the printing process for Windows XP from the time a print command is issued, until a print job has been successfully output. The settings established for a printer in the Add Printer Wizard in the Printers and Faxes applet (Start | Printers and Faxes) indicate which print device (or devices, in the case of a printer pool) handle print output, and also provide controls over how print jobs are handled (banner page, special post-processing, and so forth).

printer driver — Special-purpose software components that manage communications between the I/O Manager and a specific print device. Ultimately, printer drivers make it possible for Windows XP to despool print jobs, and send them to a print device for output services. Modern printer drivers also allow the printer to communicate with Windows XP, and to inform it about print job status, error conditions (out of paper, paper jam, and so forth), and print job problems.

printer graphics driver — The part of the printer driver that renders GDI commands into device driver interface commands that may be sent to the printer.

printer interface driver — The part of the printer driver that provides an interface to the printer settings.

printer job language — A specialized language that provides printer control at the print-job level and enables users to change printer default levels such as number of copies, color, printer languages, and so on.

printer pool — A collection of two or more identically configured print devices to which one or more Windows XP printers direct their print jobs. Basically, a printer pool permits two or more printers to act in concert to handle high-volume printing needs.

printer priority — The setting that helps to determine which printer in a pool will get a given print job. The printer with the higher priority is more likely to get the print job.

process — The primary unit of execution in the Windows XP operating system environment. A process may contain one or more execution threads, all associated with a named user account, SID, and access token. Processes essentially define the container within which individual applications and commands execute under Windows XP.

processor bottleneck — A system bottleneck that occurs when demands for CPU cycles from currently active processes and the operating system cannot be met, usually indicated by high utilization levels or processor queue lengths greater than or equal to two.

product activation — A mechanism by which a product fails, if not registered within a specified time period. To be activated, a product must be registered with a correlated product key and hardware signature.

profile — See *user profile*.

public key policy — A security control of Windows XP where recovery agents for EFS and domain-wide and trusted certificate authorities are defined and configured. These policies can be enforced on a user by user basis.

Public Switched Telephone Networks (PSTN) — A global network of interconnected digital and analog communication links originally designed to support voice communication between any two points in the world, but quickly adapted to handle digital data traffic.

PXE (Pre-boot Execution) — A standard environment in PC98-compliant computers and network computers that can be used for a remote OS installation.

queue (print queue) — A series of files stored in sequential order waiting for delivery from a spool file to a print device.

RAID-5 volume (Redundant Array of Inexpensive Disks) — A drive configuration of three or more parts (up to 32) of one or more drives or three or more entire drives (up to 32). Data is written to all drives in equal amounts to spread the workload, and parity information is added to the written data to allow for drive failure recovery. Fault tolerance is provided. If one partition or drive fails in the set, the other members can re-create the missing data on the fly. After the failed member is replaced or repaired, the data on that drive can be rebuilt and restored. This is also known as disk striping with parity (Windows Server products only).

RAW — Device-dependent spool data that is fully ready to be printed when rendered.

real mode — A DOS term that describes a mode of operation for x86 CPUs, wherein they can address only 1 MB of memory, broken into 16 64-KB segments, where the lower ten segments are available to applications (640 KB), and the upper six segments are available to the operating system or to special application drivers—or, for Windows XP, to a VDM.

Recovery Console — A command-line interface that provides administrative tools useful for recovering a system that is not booting correctly.

Reg — A special command-line utility that users, programs, or the operating system can use to access, inspect, create, or modify Registry keys.

REG_BINARY — A Registry value entry data type that stores data in binary format.

REG_DWORD — A Registry value entry data type that stores data in binary, hex, or decimal format.

REG_EXPAND_SZ — A Registry value entry data type that stores data in expandable text-string format containing a variable that is replaced by an application when used (for example, *%Systemroot%\File.exe*).

Regedit — The 16-bit Registry editor. Regedit offers global searching and combines all of the keys into a single display. It can be used to perform searches, add new subkeys and value entries, alter the data in value entries, and import and export keys and subkeys.

Registry — The hierarchical database of system configuration data essential to the health and operation of a Windows system.

REG_MULTI_SZ — A Registry value entry data type that stores data in text-string format containing multiple human-readable values separated by null characters.

REG_SZ — A Registry value entry data type that stores data in text-string format.

Remote Access Service (remote access) — The service in Windows XP that allows users to log into the system remotely over phone lines.

remote execution (rexec) — The IP-based utility that permits a user on one machine to execute a program on another machine elsewhere on the network.

Remote Installation Preparation (RIPrep) — An installation used with remote OS installation whereby an administrator can take an entire image of one Windows XP Professional machine and install it onto other workstations. That image can include the OS as well as installed applications and configuration settings.

Remote Installation Services (RIS) — An optional service in Windows Server that works with various other services to enable remote installations, including a remote operating system installation.

remote OS installation — A component of Remote Installation Services (RIS) that can install Windows XP Professional on remote-boot-enabled PCs across a network.

remote shell (rsh) — The IP-based utility that permits a user on one machine to enter a shell command on another machine on the network.

removable storage device — Any type of floppy, cartridge, or drive that can be either removed between reboots or as a hot swappable device.

rendering — Graphically creating a print job.

Reverse Address Resolution Protocol (RARP) — The IP protocol used to map from a physical MAC-layer address to a logical IP address.

Scheduled Tasks — The Windows XP component used to automate the execution or launch of programs and batch files based on time and system conditions.

sector — The smallest division (512 bytes) of a drive's surface.

Secure Socket Layer/Transport Layer Security (SSL/TLS) — A mechanism used primarily over HTTP communications to create an encrypted session link through the exchange of certificates and public encryption keys.

Security Accounts Manager (SAM) — The database of user accounts, group memberships, and security-related settings.

security ID (SID) — A unique number that identifies a logged-on user to the security system. SIDs can identify one user or a group of users.

Security log — Records security-related events.

security options — Defines and controls various security features, functions, and controls of the Windows XP environment.

Sequenced Packet Exchange (SPX) — A connection-oriented protocol used in the NetWare environment when guaranteed delivery is required.

serial — A method of communication that transfers data across a medium one bit at a time, usually adding start and stop bits to ensure reliable delivery.

Serial Line Internet Protocol (SLIP) — An implementation of the IP protocol over serial lines. SLIP has been made obsolete by PPP.

server — The networked computer that responds to client requests for network resources.

service — A software element used by the operating system to perform a function. Services include offering resources over the network, accessing resources over the network, print spooling, etc.

service pack — A collection of code replacements, patches, error corrections, new applications, version improvements, or service-specific configuration settings from Microsoft that corrects, replaces, or hides the deficiencies of the original product, preceding service packs, or hot fixes.

setup boot disks (or floppies) — The disks used by Windows XP to initiate the installation process on computer systems that do not have an existing OS, do not have a CD-ROM that supports bootable CDs, or do not have network access to a Windows XP distribution file share. These disks can be created by running the MAKEBOOT file from the BOOTDISK directory on the distribution CD.

Setup Manager — The Windows XP tool that provides you with a GUI for creating an answer file.

share — A resource that can be accessed over the network.

shell — The default user process that is launched when a valid account name and password combination is authenticated by the WinLogon process for Windows XP. The Windows XP default shell is Windows Explorer. The default shell process manages the desktop, Start menu, taskbar, and other interface controls. The shell process defines a logged on user's runtime environment from this point forward, and supplies all spawned processes or commands with its access token to define their access permissions until that account logs out.

Simple Mail Transport Protocol (SMTP) — The IP-based messaging protocol and service that supports most Internet e-mail.

Simple Network Management Protocol (SNMP) — The IP-based network management protocol and service that makes it possible for management applications to poll network devices and permits devices to report on error or alert conditions to such applications.

simple volume — A drive configuration of all or part of a single drive. Does not provide any fault tolerance. NTFS volumes can be extended; FAT and FAT32 volumes cannot be extended.

snap-in — A component that adds control mechanisms to a console for a specific service or object, thereby extending the functionality of that console (as with snap-ins for the MMC).

spanned volume — A drive configuration of two or more parts (up to 32) of one or more drives or two or more entire drives. The elements of the spanned volume do not have to be equal in size. Data is written to the first drive in the volume until it is full, then it continues with the next drive. It is also called an extended volume. It does not provide fault tolerance. If one partition or drive in the set fails, all data is lost. Spanned volumes cannot be part of a striped volume or a mirrored volume. NTFS spanned volumes can be extended; FAT and FAT32 spanned volumes cannot be extended. The system partition/volume and boot partition/volume cannot be extended. Volume sets can be reduced in size only by breaking the set and creating a new set. The act of breaking the set destroys all data stored on the volume.

spooling — One of the print spooler functions, this is the act of writing the contents of a print job to a file on disk so they are not lost if the print server shuts down before the job is completed.

striped volume — A drive configuration of two or more parts (up to 32) of one or more drives or two or more entire drives (up to 32). Data is written to all drives in equal amounts (in 64 KB units) to spread the workload and improve performance. Each part or drive must be roughly equal in size. Does not provide any fault tolerance. If one partition or drive in the set fails, all data is lost. Striped volumes cannot be mirrored or extended.

subkey — A division of a Registry key, such as HKEY_ LOCAL_MACHINE. A subkey can contain other subkeys and value entries.

subnet — A portion of a network that might or might not be a physically separate network. A subnet shares a network address with other parts of the network but is distinguished by a subnet number.

subnet mask — The number used to define which part of a computer's IP address denotes the host and which part denotes the network.

subsystem — An operating environment that emulates another operating system (such as DOS) to provide support for applications created for that environment.

synchronization object — Any of a special class of objects within the Windows XP environment that are used to synchronize and control access to shared objects and critical sections of code.

SYSPREP — The Windows XP utility used to clone a system.

SYSDIFF — The Windows XP utility used to take a snapshot of a basic installation and, after changes have been made, record the changes and apply them to another installation.

System log — Records information and alerts about Windows XP Professional internal processes.

System Monitor — The utility that tracks registered system or application objects, where each such object has one or more counters that can be tracked for information about system behavior.

system partition — The active partition where the boot files required to display the boot menu and initiate the booting of Windows XP are stored.

System State data — A collection of system-specific data that can be backed up and restored using the Windows XP Backup utility.

Telnet — The TCP/IP-based terminal emulation protocol used on IP-based networks. Telnet permits clients on one machine to attach to and operate on another machine on the network as if the other machines were terminals locally attached to a remote host.

thread — In the Windows XP Professional run-time environment, a thread is the minimum unit of system execution and corresponds roughly to a task within an application, the Windows XP kernel, or within some other major system component. Any task that can execute in the background can be considered a thread (for example, run-time spell checking or grammar checking in newer versions of Microsoft Word). It's important to recognize that applications must be written to take advantage of threading (just as the operating system itself is).

Trace log — A log that records data only when certain events occur. Trace logs record nonconfigurable data from a designated provider when an event occurs.

transaction log — A file created by Windows XP to record Registry changes. These files, with a .log extension, are used to verify that changes to the Registry are made successfully.

transform — A specific type of Microsoft Installer file that usually ends in .mst and defines changes or customization to an existing Microsoft Installer package, and to the .msi file in which the base installer instructions reside. Because most vendors (and Microsoft) define .msi files for their programs and systems, it's often easier to customize an existing .msi file with an .mst transform, rather than defining a new installer package from scratch.

Transmission Control Protocol/Internet Protocol (TCP/IP) — A suite of Internet protocols upon which the global Internet is based. TCP/IP is the default protocol for Windows XP.

Transmission Control Protocol (TCP) — The reliable, connection-oriented IP-based transport protocol that supports many of the most important IP services, including HTTP, SMTP, and FTP.

Trivial File Transport Protocol (TFTP) — A lightweight alternative to FTP, TFTP uses UDP to provide only simple get-and-put capabilities for file transfer on IP-based networks.

unattended installation — A Windows XP installation that uses a script and does not require user interaction.

uniqueness database file (UDF) — A text file that contains a partial set of instructions for installing Windows XP. It is used to supplement an answer file when only minor changes are needed that don't require a new answer file.

Universal Naming Convention (UNC) — A multivendor, multiplatform convention for identifying shared resources on a network.

upgrade — The installation method in which data and configuration settings from the previous operating systems remain intact. The level or amount of retained data varies based on the existing operating system's type.

user account — A named security element used by a computer system to identify individuals and to record activity, control access, and retain settings. This entity contains all of the information that defines a user to the Windows XP environment.

User Datagram Protocol (UDP) — A lightweight, connectionless transport protocol used as an alternative to TCP in IP-based environments to supply faster, lower overhead access, primarily (but not exclusively) to local resources.

User mode — The condition of a console that prevents adding or removing snap-ins or re-saving the console file. Systems running in User Mode operate in virtual private memory areas for each process, so each process is then protected from all others. User-Mode processes may not manipulate hardware, but must request kernel-mode services to do this manipulation for them.

user profile — A collection of user-specific settings that retain the state of the desktop, Start menu, color scheme, and other environmental aspects across logons.

user rights assignment — Defines which groups or users can perform the specific privileged action.

User Rights Policy — Defines which groups or users can perform the specific privileged action.

value — The actual data stored by a value entry.

value entry — A named Registry variable that stores a specific value or data string. A Registry value entry's name is typically a multiword phrase without spaces and with title capitalization.

virtual device driver (VDD) — A device driver virtual DOS machines (VDMs) use to provide an interface between the application, which expects to interact with a 16-bit device driver, and the 32-bit device drivers that Windows XP provides.

virtual DOS machine (VDM) — A Win32 application that emulates a DOS environment for use by DOS and Win16 applications.

virtual memory — A Windows XP kernel service that stores memory pages that are not currently in use by the system in a paging file. This frees memory for other uses. Virtual memory also hides the swapping of memory from applications and higher-level services.

Virtual Memory Manager (VMM) — The part of the operating system that handles process priority and scheduling, providing the ability to preempt executing processes and schedule new processes.

volume — With basic storage, it is a collection of two to 32 partitions into a single logical structure. With dynamic storage, it is any division of a physical drive or collection of divisions into a drive configuration.

wide area network (WAN) — A geographically dispersed network of networks connected by routers and communications links. The Internet is the largest WAN.

Win16 — The collection of components, interfaces, and capabilities that permits Win16 applications to run within a VDM within the Win32 subsystem on Windows XP.

Win16-on-Win32 (WOW) VDM — The formal name for the collection of components, interfaces, and capabilities that permits the Win32 subsystem to provide native support for well-behaved 16-bit Windows applications.

Win16 operating environment — The collection of components, interfaces, and capabilities that permits Win16 applications to run within a VDM within the Win32 subsystem on Windows XP.

Win32 — The main 32-bit subsystem used by Win32 applications and other application subsystems.

Win32 subsystem — An operating environment that supports 32-bit Windows applications and that is required to run Windows XP.

Windows Installer Service (WIS) — A Windows XP component that manages the installation and removal of applications by applying a set of centrally defined setup rules during the installation process.

Windows Internet Name Service (WINS) — Service that provides NetBIOS-name-to-IP-address resolution.

WinLogon — The Windows XP process used to control user authentication and manage the logon process. WinLogon produces the logon dialog box where user name, password, and domain are selected; it also controls automated logon, warning text, the display of the shutdown button, and the display of the last user to log onto the system.

WINNT — The 16-bit Windows XP installation program.

WINNT32 — The 32-bit Windows XP installation program.

Wizard — A tool or utility that has an interactive step-by-step guide to walk you through a complex or detailed configuration process.

workgroup — A networking scheme in which resources, administration, and security are distributed throughout the network.

workgroup model — The networking setup in which users are managed jointly through the use of workgroups to which users are assigned.

X.25 — A standard that defines packet-switching networks.

Index